COLORADO
6TH EDITION

459816

Where to Stay and Eat
for All Budgets

Must-See Sights
and Local Secrets

Ratings You Can Trust

Fodor's Travel Publications   New York, Toronto, London, Sydney, Auckland
www.fodors.com

MAY 0 5 2004

FODOR'S COLORADO
Editor: Mary Beth Bohman

Editorial Production: David Downing
Editorial Contributors: Lori Cumpston, Jad Davenport, Bob Ehlert, Lois Friedland, Satu Hummasti, Christina Knight, Steve Knopper, Jeanne McGovern, Eric Peterson, Gregory Robl, Mark Sullivan, Kyle Wagner, Claire Walter
Maps: David Lindroth *cartographer;* Bob Blake and Rebecca Baer, *map editors*
Design: Fabrizio La Rocca, *creative director;* Guido Caroti, *art director;* Melanie Marin, *senior picture editor*
Production/Manufacturing: Robert B. Shields
Cover Photo (Vail): Ken Redding/Corbis

Sixth Edition

ISBN 1–4000–1320–8

ISSN 0276–9018

SPECIAL SALES
This book is available for special discounts for bulk purchases for sales promotions or premiums. Special editions, including personalized covers, excerpts of existing books, and corporate imprints, can be created in large quantities for special needs. For more information, write to Special Markets/Premium Sales, 1745 Broadway, MD 6-2, New York, New York 10019, or e-mail specialmarkets@randomhouse.com. Inquiries from Canada should be directed to your local bookseller or sent to Random House of Canada, Ltd., Marketing Department, 2775 Matheson Boulevard East, Mississauga, Ontario L4W 4P7. Inquiries from the United Kingdom should be sent to Fodor's Travel Publications, 20 Vauxhall Bridge Road, London SW1V 2SA, England.

AN IMPORTANT TIP & AN INVITATION
Although all prices, opening times, and other details in this book are based on information supplied to us at press time, changes occur all the time in the travel world, and Fodor's cannot accept responsibility for facts that become outdated or for inadvertent errors or omissions. So **always confirm information when it matters,** especially if you're making a detour to visit a specific place. Your experiences—positive and negative—matter to us. If we have missed or misstated something, **please write to us.** We follow up on all suggestions. Contact the Colorado editor at editors@fodors.com or c/o Fodor's at 1745 Broadway, New York, New York 10019.

PRINTED IN THE UNITED STATES OF AMERICA

10 9 8 7 6 5 4 3 2 1

DESTINATION
COLORADO

Colorado is a state of stunning contrasts. The Rockies create a mountainous spine that's larger than Switzerland, with 52 eternally snow-capped summits towering higher than 14,000 feet. Yet its eastern third is a sea of hypnotically waving grasslands, and its southwest, a vibrant multihue desert, carved with pink and mauve canyons, vaulting cinnamon spires, and gnarled red-rock monoliths. Its mighty rivers, the Colorado, Arkansas, and Gunnison, etch deep yawning chasms every bit as impressive as the shimmering blue-tinged glaciers and jagged peaks of the San Juan, Sangre de Cristo, and Front Ranges. Add to this glittering sapphire lakes and jade forests, and you have an outdoor paradise second to none. Though most people associate the state with skiing, residents have a saying, "We came for the winters, but we stayed for the summers." Whichever the season you choose for your visit, you too will likely find it difficult to leave Colorado behind. Have a wonderful trip!

Karen Cure

Karen Cure, Editorial Director

CONTENTS

Index

Maps

CloseUps

ABOUT THIS BOOK

There's no doubt that the best source for travel advice is a like-minded friend who's just been where you're headed. But with or without that friend, you'll have a better trip with a Fodor's guide in hand. Once you've learned to find your way around its pages, you'll be in great shape to find your way around your destination.

SELECTION

Our goal is to cover the best properties, sights, and activities in their category, as well as the most interesting communities to visit. We make a point of including local food-lovers' hot spots as well as neighborhood options, and we avoid all that's touristy unless it's really worth your time. You can go on the assumption that everything you read about in this book is recommended wholeheartedly by our writers and editors. Flip to On the Road with Fodor's to learn more about who they are. It goes without saying that no property mentioned in the book has paid to be included.

RATINGS

Orange stars ★ denote sights and properties that our editors and writers consider the very best in the area covered by the entire book. These, the best of the best, are listed in the Fodor's Choice section in the front of the book. Black stars ★ highlight the sights and properties we deem Highly Recommended, the don't-miss sights within any region. Fodor's Choice and Highly Recommended options in each region are usually listed on the title page of the chapter covering that region. Use the index to find complete descriptions. In cities, sights pinpointed with numbered map bullets ❶ in the margins tend to be more important than those without bullets.

SPECIAL SPOTS

Pleasures & Pastimes focuses on types of experiences that reveal the spirit of the destination. Watch for Off the Beaten Path sights. Some are out of the way, some are quirky, and all are worth your while. If the munchies hit while you're exploring, look for Need a Break? suggestions.

TIME IT RIGHT

Wondering when to go? Check On the Calendar up front and chapters' Timing sections for weather and crowd overviews and best days and times to visit.

SEE IT ALL

Use Fodor's exclusive Great Itineraries as a model for your trip. (For a good overview of the entire destination, follow those that begin the book, or mix regional itineraries from several chapters.) In cities, Good Walks guide you to important sights in each neighborhood; ▶ indicates the starting points of walks and itineraries in the text and on the map.

BUDGET WELL

Hotel and restaurant price categories from ¢ to $$$$ are defined in the opening pages of each chapter—expect to find a balanced selection for every budget. For attractions, we always give standard adult admission fees; reductions are usually available for children, students, and senior citizens. Look in Discounts & Deals in Smart Travel Tips for information on destination-wide ticket schemes. Want to pay with plastic? AE, D, DC, MC, V following restaurant and hotel listings indicate whether American Express, Discover, Diner's Club, MasterCard, or Visa are accepted.

BASIC INFO

Smart Travel Tips lists travel essentials for the entire area covered by the book; city- and region-specific basics end each chapter. To find the best way to get around, see the transportation section; see individual modes of travel ("By Car," "By Train") for details. We assume you'll check Web sites or call for particulars.

ON THE MAPS | Maps throughout the book show you what's where and help you find your way around. Black and orange numbered bullets ❶ ❶ in the text correlate to bullets on maps.

BACKGROUND | In general, we give background information within the chapters in the course of explaining sights as well as in CloseUp boxes.

FIND IT FAST | Within the book, chapters are arranged in a roughly counter-clockwise direction starting with Denver. Chapters are divided into small regions, within which towns are covered in logical geographical order; attractive routes and interesting places between towns are flagged as En Route. Heads at the top of each page help you find what you need within a chapter.

DON'T FORGET | Restaurants are open for lunch and dinner daily unless we state otherwise; we mention dress only when there's a specific requirement and reservations only when they're essential or not accepted—it's always best to book ahead. Hotels have private baths, phone, TVs, and air-conditioning and operate on the European Plan (a.k.a. EP, meaning without meals). We always list facilities but not whether you'll be charged extra to use them, so when pricing accommodations, find out what's included.

SYMBOLS

Many Listings

★ Fodor's Choice
★ Highly recommended
✉ Physical address
✛ Directions
🕮 Mailing address
☎ Telephone
🖷 Fax
🌐 On the Web
✍ E-mail
🎟 Admission fee
🕐 Open/closed times
▶ Start of walk/itinerary
▭ Credit cards

Outdoors

⛳ Golf
⛺ Camping

Hotels & Restaurants

🏨 Hotel
🛏 Number of rooms
♿ Facilities
🍴 Meal plans
✕ Restaurant
♨ Reservations
🏛 Dress code
🚭 Smoking
🍷 BYOB
✕🏨 Hotel with restaurant that warrants a visit

Other

☺ Family-friendly
🛈 Contact information
⇨ See also
✉ Branch address
☞ Take note

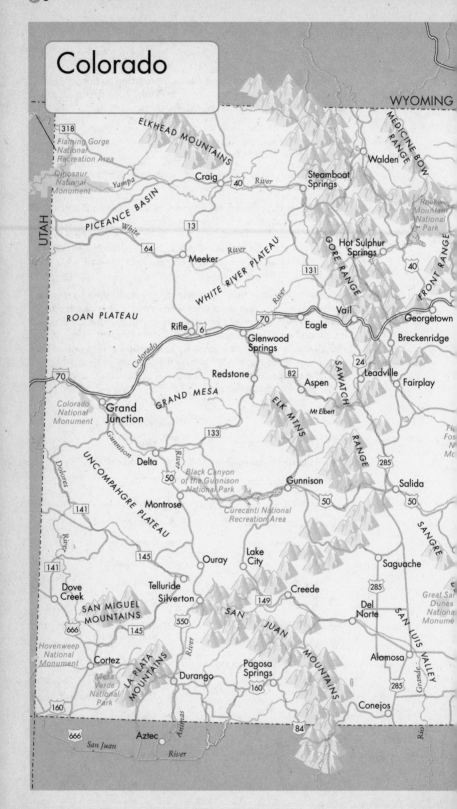

Colorado

WYOMING

UTAH

318

Flaming Gorge National Recreation Area

Dinosaur National Monument

ELKHEAD MOUNTAINS

Craig

40

River

Yampa

Steamboat Springs

Walden

MEDICINE BOW RANGE

Rocky Mountain National Park

PICEANCE BASIN

13

White

Meeker

River

WHITE RIVER PLATEAU

64

Hot Sulphur Springs

131

GORE RANGE

FRONT RANGE

40

River

ROAN PLATEAU

Rifle

6

Vail

Eagle

70

Georgetown

Breckenridge

Glenwood Springs

Colorado

70

Redstone

82

Aspen

24

Leadville

Fairplay

GRAND MESA

Mt Elbert

SAWATCH RANGE

Colorado National Monument

Grand Junction

ELK MTNS

133

Gunnison

Delta

50

Black Canyon of the Gunnison National Park

Gunnison

285

Salida

50

50

UNCOMPAHGRE PLATEAU

Dolores

141

River

Montrose

Curecanti National Recreation Area

SANGRE

145

Ouray

Lake City

Saguache

285

141

River

Dove Creek

Telluride

Silverton

SAN MIGUEL MOUNTAINS

666

145

550

Creede

149

SAN

JUAN

Del Norte

Great Sand Dunes National Monument

SAN LUIS VALLEY

Hovenweep National Monument

Cortez

LA PLATA MOUNTAINS

Durango

Pagosa Springs

160

MOUNTAINS

Alamosa

285

160

Mesa Verde National Park

River

Conejos

84

Rio Grande

666

Aztec

San Juan

River

Antimas

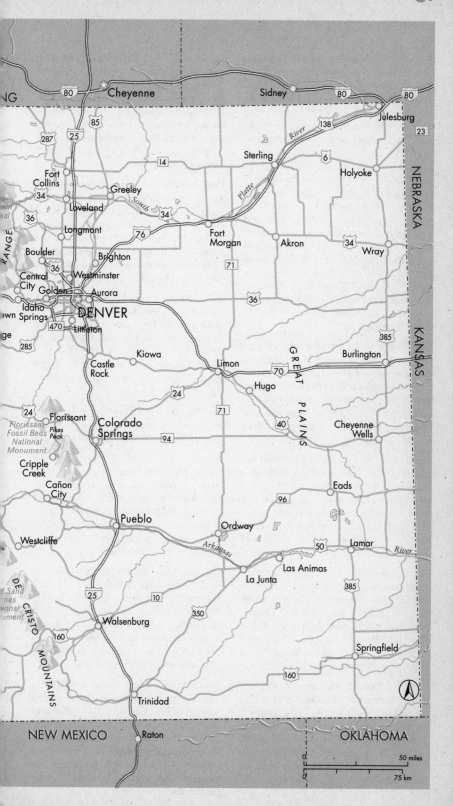

ON THE ROAD WITH FODOR'S

A trip takes you out of yourself. Concerns of life at home completely disappear, driven away by more immediate thoughts—about, say, what marvels will beguile the next day, or where you'll have dinner. That's where Fodor's comes in. We make sure that you know all your options, so that you don't miss something that's around the next bend just because you didn't know it was there. Because the best memories of your trip might well have nothing to do with what you came to Colorado to see, we guide you to sights large and small all over the region. You might set out to ski the Back Bowls at Aspen or to climb Pikes Peak, but back at home you find yourself unable to forget the views from Trail Ridge Road in Rocky Mountain National Park. With Fodor's at your side, serendipitous discoveries are never far away.

Our success in showing you every corner of the Centennial State is a credit to our extraordinary writers. Although there's no substitute for travel advice from a good friend who knows your style, our contributors are the next best thing—the kind of people you would poll for travel advice if you knew them.

Colorado native and Grand Junction resident Lori Cumpston spent a decade as a broadcast journalist before turning her talents to print. She worked as a newspaper humor columnist and a features writer. Her work has appeared in the *Washington Times,* the *Denver Post,* the *Rocky Mountain News,* and other publications.

Denver resident Jad Davenport spent 10 years as a war photographer before becoming a travel writer, and he now writes for such publications as *Travel & Leisure, National Geographic Adventure Magazine, Ski Magazine,* and the *Washington Post.* Raised in Colorado, he enjoys ice climbing and white-water kayaking.

Bob Ehlert brought a lifetime of writing and editing experience when he moved to Colorado Springs in 1999. In "The Springs," he is features editor for the *Gazette* newspaper. His work has also appeared in *Better Homes & Gardens,* the Minneapolis *Star-Tribune,* the *Philadelphia Inquirer,* and Norfolk's the *Virginian-Pilot.*

Lois Friedland is a Colorado-based journalist and editor who specializes in travel, skiing, and golf. She edits two annual travel publications. Her background includes authorship of travel- and ski-guide books, and stints as editor of a weekly newsletter about the winter sports industry's business side and as western editor of *Ski Magazine.*

From his home in northwest Denver, Steve Knopper writes regularly for *Rolling Stone* and the *Rocky Mountain News* and has contributed to *Esquire* and the *Chicago Tribune.* He wrote *The Complete Idiot's Guide to Starting a Band* with longtime Colorado rock manager Mark Bliesener. Amazingly, he doesn't ski.

Jeanne McGovern left Southern California for the Colorado Rockies more than 15 years ago; she has called Aspen home for the past 11 years. Formerly the executive director of the Aspen Writers' Foundation, McGovern now writes for the *Aspen Times, Sojourner* magazine, and other publications.

Eric Peterson is a Denver-based freelance writer who covers travel, business, and music for local and national publications.

Gregory Robl has lived on Colorado's Front Range for more than 30 years. A passionate traveler, he is always happy to return home to go cycling, hiking, and camping. His publications include a handbook about German-American genealogy and a series of newspaper articles about the fall of the Berlin Wall.

Kyle Wagner has been writing about restaurants and food in Denver for more than a decade, first for the alternative weekly *Westword* and now for the *Denver Post.* Her work also has appeared in the *Rocky Mountain News* and *Sunset* magazine. She lives in Denver with her two daughters, who prefer sushi to McDonald's.

Boulder-based Claire Walter contributes regularly to *Sunset* and *Ski Press.* Recent books include *Culinary Colorado* and *Snowshoeing Colorado.* She has been honored by the Society of American Travel Writers, the North American SnowSports Journalists Association, Colorado Ski Country USA, and the Colorado Center for the Book.

The heart of the Rocky Mountains from both an elevation perspective and a population point of view, Colorado has cities with more than 100,000 people—Denver, Colorado Springs, Fort Collins, and Pueblo among them—and vast swaths of nearly pristine wilderness. Beyond the cosmopolitan cultural scenes in places like Boulder and Aspen, there are more than 50 mountains with summits above 14,000 feet, not to mention three national parks, three national monuments, and acre after acre of national forest.

1 Denver

Colorado's capital and largest city, Denver has 2.5 million residents in its metropolitan area and continues to grow by leaps and bounds. The lively downtown area has a baseball stadium, amusement park, historic neighborhoods, and a vast parks system. Denver claims several top-flight cultural facilities, including the Denver Art Museum, the Denver Museum of Nature and Science, and the Denver Performing Arts Complex. The true beauty of Denver, however, is the combination of urban pleasures and pastimes with easy access to innumerable recreational options in the great outdoors.

2 North Central Colorado

At the foot of the Rocky Mountains, the college town of Boulder (home to the University of Colorado) balances a bohemian philosophy with a largely high-tech economy. Among the attractions are a great park and an urban trail system and free tours of the Celestial Seasonings tea plant and various microbreweries. North of Boulder is Fort Collins, another lively college town (Colorado State University was founded here in 1879) with a roadside gem in the Swetsville Zoo.

The wildlands and alpine tundra of Rocky Mountain National Park are just 45 mi northwest of Boulder. Inhabited by black bear, elk, and bighorn sheep, the park is an outdoors nut's dream, with miles and miles of trails to hike, scads of 14,000-foot peaks to climb, and mountain streams and lakes to fish. Estes Park, which abuts the park's eastern entrance, has motels, campgrounds, and cabin complexes on the banks of the Big Thompson and Fall rivers. Considerably less developed than Estes Park, Grand Lake is Rocky Mountain National Park's western gateway. This dinky resort town is on the shores of Colorado's largest natural lake.

3 I–70 & the High Rockies

Undeniably one of the country's most scenic interstates, Interstate 70 cuts through the heart of Colorado's high country, skirting some of the best-known winter playgrounds in the world. En route from Denver, the highway ascends into the foothills through the onetime mining hub of Idaho Springs and on to another historic mining gem in Georgetown before cruising through the Eisenhower Tunnel in the midst of serious ski country.

Summit County encompasses the highly-regarded ski-resort towns of Keystone, Breckenridge, and Copper Mountain. The next stop is the so-called Vail Valley, home to Vail, the world's largest single-mountain ski resort, and a string of towns and resorts.

Further from the highway, glitzy Aspen in the Roaring Fork Valley is also a serious skiing draw and well-known as the winter playland of the rich and famous. Historic Leadville is a bit worse for the wear, but provides an unfiltered glimpse into the mining economy that drove development here in the late 19th century. Even farther west (but closer to

I–70) is Glenwood Springs, full of Victorian charm and centered on a massive pool fed by mineral hot springs. In the state's northwest corner is Steamboat Springs, another ski resort that blends the luxury of Vail and Aspen with a dollop of cowboy charm.

4 Southwest Colorado

With a landscape that transitions from evergreen-clad fourteeners (14,000-foot peaks) to red desert speckled with impressive sandstone formations, Colorado's southwest quadrant is removed from the hustle and bustle of the Front Range and the I–70 corridor. It's one of the most beautiful spots in the state, home to a pair of national parks (Mesa Verde and Black Canyon of the Gunnison) and a soon-to-be national park (Great Sand Dunes National Monument).

The cities and towns here are smaller than those on the Front Range and full of charm. Durango has a delightful historic downtown and a lively nightlife. Also in town is the depot for the Durango and Silverton Narrow Gauge Railroad, which winds through spectacular scenery on its eight-hour round trips to artsy Silverton, a onetime mining town. Nestled in an idyllic box-canyon rife with trails and waterfalls, Telluride is a bit more bohemian and eccentric than resorts like Aspen and Vail, but it is one of the largest historic districts in the country and, come winter, a paradise for skiers. Further east, Crested Butte has a bevy of Victorian architecture.

5 South Central Colorado

Colorado Springs was Colorado's first resort town, luring Easterners in the 1870s and 1880s to its mineral springs, which were alleged to possess restorative powers. The base of the stately, looming Pikes Peak is just a few miles west of downtown. Downtown Colorado Springs has a number of museums and a variety of clubs and restaurants; the U.S. Air Force Academy, 10 mi north, is another draw.

Beyond Colorado Springs' city limits, outdoor recreation, especially in the river-rafting department, is excellent in south central Colorado. To the southwest, Cañon City is one white-water hub (and also the closest city to the 1,000-foot-deep Royal Gorge); farther north, Buena Vista and Salida are two more. Other attractions west of Colorado Springs include the casinos in historic Cripple Creek and Florrisant Fossil Beds National Monument. To the south, you can take in the world's largest mural in Pueblo or explore the Corazon de Trinidad (historic downtown Trinidad), just shy of the New Mexico state line.

6 Northwest Colorado

Little traveled in comparison with other regions in the state, northwest Colorado is a bastion of pristine wilderness and unusual geology. The major city is Grand Junction, known to locals as G. J. The city sits on the doorstep of some of the best recreational country in the state, where the forested mountain ecosystem transitions into an arid desert. Just east of Grand Junction via I–70, Palisade is Colorado's fruit and wine capital. Both communities are an easy drive from Grand Mesa, the world's largest flattop mountain (about 10,000 feet tall).

Other outdoors-oriented destinations in northwest Colorado include Colorado National Monument, where the road climbs to the top of a plateau in an area full of twisty canyons and impressive geological features; and Dinosaur National Monument, an archaeological hotbed and the site of one of the most breathtaking loop drives in the West.

Denver & Environs

3 days. The great thing about a visit to Denver: You can spend the first day in a bustling cosmopolitan city and be out in the mountains the next morning, with not another soul in sight.

DENVER 1 day. Downtown Denver is perfect for a daylong walking tour, with the Colorado State Capitol, the Denver Art Museum, and the Colorado History Museum conveniently positioned within a stone's throw of Civic Center Park. Have lunch at the art museum's café or on the 16th Street Mall downtown. After dinner, take in a play at the Denver Performing Arts Complex, attend a concert at a downtown venue, or catch a baseball game at Coors Field. If you still have the energy, check out the bustling nightlife in LoDo (lower downtown).

ROCKY MOUNTAIN NATIONAL PARK 1 day. From Denver, drive north through Boulder to the lively resort town of Estes Park. Have lunch, and then enter the park. Take a short hike on the park's eastern side before driving through the stunning alpine scenery of Trail Ridge Road. Double back to Estes Park for dinner and Boulder for the nightlife. Spend the evening of the second day in the hip, colorful town of Boulder.

THE NORTHERN FRONT RANGE 1 day. Head out to Golden, home of the Coors Brewery; Central City, where you can try your hand at gambling or just tour this gold-mining town returned to its glory days; and Georgetown, a charming old silver-mining town with a well-preserved downtown. From here, it's just an hour's drive back to Denver.

Highlights of the High Rockies

7 days. You could spend a lifetime exploring the Colorado Rockies and not see everything. Spend a week learning the basics—and planning for your next trip.

BRECKENRIDGE, VAIL, & ASPEN 2 days. Start in Breckenridge—considered by some to be Colorado's prettiest town. No trip to Colorado would be complete without a visit to Vail, so stop there for lunch. Your afternoon destination is Aspen—in summer, you can head south through Leadville and over Independence Pass; in winter, when the pass is closed, drive west to Glenwood Springs and south to Aspen. Both are scenic drives with interesting towns along the way; the Glenwood Springs route takes about an hour longer. Spend the night and the next full day in Aspen: skiing in the winter, visiting the nearby Maroon Bells Wilderness in summer, window-shopping year-round.

REDSTONE & CRESTED BUTTE 1 day. When you can tear yourself away from Aspen's chic charms, head north past Carbondale and south to Redstone. In summer, if you have a four-wheel-drive vehicle, you could cut through Keebler Pass to the funky mountain town of Crested Butte (you can even hike from Aspen to Crested Butte in a day, through the vibrant wildflower meadows of the Maroon Bells Wilderness). In winter, it's a four-hour drive.

TELLURIDE 1 day. Continue from Crested Butte on to Montrose and Ridgway and into Telluride, a perfectly preserved National Historic District in a stunning box canyon. Telluride deserves a full day—and night—of exploration in winter or summer. The gondola up to Mountain Village runs year-round late into the night and is a must-do.

DURANGO & MESA VERDE 3 days. Take your time driving the San Juan Skyway—perhaps the most scenic drive in a state known for breathtaking scenery—doubling back through Ridgway and driving south to Ouray for lunch before bedding down for the night in Durango. On the next day, ride the Durango and Silverton Narrow Gauge Railroad into the delightful old mining town of Silverton and back to Durango again in restored 1880s railcars. Have dinner in Durango. On the final day, drive to Mesa Verde National Park for a look at haunting Native American cliff dwellings. Spend the night in Ouray and soak in the hot springs before heading home.

Winter Snow-Sports Adventure

5 days. With more ski resorts than any other state, Colorado sees a tourism peak in winter. But the snow-sports only begin with skiing; snowmobiling, snowshoeing, and ice fishing are all popular cold-weather pastimes in the high country.

VAIL **2 days.** For the first two days of your vacation, stay in or around Vail and use it as a central base for downhill skiing. A Vail ski pass is good at a number of other resorts also owned by Vail Resorts, including Breckenridge and Arapahoe Basin. With runs for every skill level, Vail's vast terrain—not to mention its wealth of lodging and dining options—make it the best place to start hitting the slopes. On the first night, dine in Vail, or drive over to Beaver Creek for a romantic dinner at an even more exclusive resort. Day two should be reserved for skiing more of Vail, especially the legendary Back Bowls, or visiting one of her sister resorts.

GRAND LAKE **1 day.** Grand Lake is the self-proclaimed snowmobiling capital of Colorado. To get there from the Vail area, drive east on I–70 and north on U.S. 40 over Berthoud Pass—which can be treacherous in heavy snow, but rarely closes—and pass through Winter Park, Fraser, and Granby en route to Grand Lake. Set out on a pre-arranged guided snowmobiling trip on trails through the surrounding Arapaho National Forest, and enjoy dinner and a night's sleep in the tiny town afterwards.

WINTER PARK **1 day.** From Grand Lake, it's an easy drive back to Winter Park on U.S. 40, where you can get in another day of skiing at one of three interconnected mountains, or go cross-country skiing or snowshoeing in the backcountry or on the groomed trails at Devil's Thumb. Cap off the day with some snow tubing at the lit and lift-served hill in Fraser or a sleigh-ride dinner in Winter Park.

GLENWOOD SPRINGS **1 day.** Go back over Berthoud Pass and west through Vail on I–70 to the historic resort town of Glenwood Springs, named for the hot mineral springs that feed a large pool in the middle of town. A relaxing soak, a good meal, and a good night's sleep in a Victorian hotel make for a nice topper to four days of winter sports. Or you can sneak in a few more runs at Sunlight Mountain Resort, the local ski mountain.

Summer Outdoors Excursion

5 days. With 50 more 14,000-foot-tall peaks (54) than the rest of the lower 48 combined, Colorado is an unparalleled place for an adrenaline-charging excursion in the backcountry, where hikers, bikers, climbers, and anglers almost always find what they're looking for.

ROCKY MOUNTAIN NATIONAL PARK AREA **3 days.** Pick up a picnic lunch (and more supplies if you are planning to camp) in Estes Park at the east entrance, and then drive to one of the many trailheads snaking out of Moraine Park or the Bear Lake area. Take a day hike up Flattop Mountain or to Fern Falls, or pick another hike that suits your ability. Then either set up camp (it's best to nab a campsite at the in-park campgrounds early in the day) or return to Estes Park for a night indoors. On the second day, ascend above timberline on Trail Ridge Road to the alpine tundra and explore this unique ecosystem before descending to the Kawuneeche Valley on the park's western edge. If you have time, take another hike, and then grab a campsite at Timber Creek Campground, or drive into Grand Lake for a motel room or rental cabin. Spend day three exploring Grand Lake (or one of three reservoirs in the area). Rent a boat to fish or just cruise around the idyllic waters. Spend the night in Grand Lake, or drive south to Granby, Winter Park, or Georgetown to get a jump on day four.

LEADVILLE 1 day. Drive to historic Leadville, southwest of Georgetown, as a home base for a day of hiking. Try to climb one of the many fourteeners in the area (Mount Sherman is the easiest for a neophyte) or go on a less strenuous day hike right outside of town. Spend the night in Leadville, or head south to Buena Vista.

BUENA VISTA 1 day. Go on a full-day white-water-rafting trip on the Arkansas River with one of many licensed outfitters. If paddling is not your idea of fun, spend the day hiking in the Collegiate Peaks Wilderness Area. Spend the night at Mount Princeton Hot Springs Resort and enjoy a nice soak to ease any lingering aches and pains.

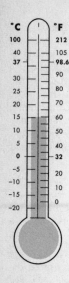

°C | | °F
100 — 212
40 — 105
37 — 98.6
30 — 90
25 — 80
20 — 70
15 — 60
10 — 50
5 — 40
0 — 32
-5 — 20
-10 — 10
-15 — 0
-20

The Colorado you experience will depend upon the season of your visit. Summer is a busy time. Hotels in tourist destinations book up early, especially in July and August, and hikers crowd the backcountry from June through Labor Day. Ski resorts buzz from December to early April, especially around Christmas and Presidents' Day. Many of the big resorts are becoming popular summer destinations as well.

If you don't mind capricious weather, spring and fall are opportune seasons to visit. Rates drop and crowds are nonexistent. Spring's pleasures are somewhat limited, since snow usually blocks the high country—and mountain-pass roads—well into June. But spring is a good time for fishing, rafting on rivers swollen with snowmelt, birding, and wildlife-viewing. In fall, aspens splash the mountainsides with gold, and wildlife come down to lower elevations. The fish are spawning, and the angling is excellent.

Climate

Summer in the Rocky Mountains begins in late June or early July. Days are warm, with highs often in the 80s, whereas nighttime temperatures fall to the 40s and 50s. Afternoon thunderstorms are common over the higher peaks. Fall begins in September, often with a week of unsettled weather around mid-month, followed by four to six gorgeous weeks of Indian summer—frosty nights and warm days. Winter creeps in during November, and deep snows arrive by December. Temperatures usually hover near freezing by day, thanks to the surprisingly warm mountain sun, dropping considerably overnight, occasionally as low as -60°F. Winter tapers off in March, though snow lingers into April on valley bottoms and into July on mountain passes.

At lower elevations (Denver, the eastern plains, and the southwestern corner of the state), summertime highs above 100°F are not uncommon, and the winters are still cold, with highs in the 20s and 30s at the height of winter. The entire state sees snowy winters, even on the plains—where some of the most powerful blizzards hit. Colorado has a reputation for extreme weather, to be sure, but that cuts two ways: no condition ever lasts for long.

Forecasts **Weather Channel Connection** ⊕ www.weather.com.

ASPEN, CO

Jan.	33F	1C	May	64F	18C	Sept.	71F	22C
	6	–14		32	0		35	2
Feb.	37F	3C	June	73F	23C	Oct.	60F	16C
	8	–13		37	3		28	– 2
Mar.	42F	6C	July	80F	27C	Nov.	44F	7C
	15	– 9		44	7		15	– 9
Apr.	53F	12C	Aug.	78F	26C	Dec.	37F	3C
	24	– 4		42	6		8	–13

ON THE CALENDAR

Hundreds of festivals and events are held annually in Colorado. Here are some of the better known—and better attended. If you plan to visit during one of them, book well in advance.

WINTER

Dec.

Christmas celebrations blanket most Rockies towns. For the holidays, many ski areas mount torchlight parades, with large groups of torch-bearing ski instructors tracing patterns down the mountainside. Contact resorts for details.

Denver hosts the World's Largest Christmas Lighting Display (☎ 303/892–1112), with 40,000 floodlights washing civic buildings in reds, greens, blues, and yellows.

Silverton searches for a yule log at its Yule Log Celebration (☎ 970/387–5522 or 800/752–4494). Georgetown hosts the Christmas Market (☎ 800/472–8230), a Christmas fair with sleigh rides through town.

The Vail Festival of Lights (☎ 970/479–1394) promotes a range of attractions, including Dickensian carolers, brilliant lighting displays, and Christmas ice-skating spectaculars.

Jan.

Denver's two-week National Western Stock Show and Rodeo (☎ 303/297–1166), the world's largest livestock show, is one of the month's big events.

Ski celebrations such as the Steamboat Springs Annual Cowboy Downhill (☎ 970/879–6111), the Aspen Winterskol (☎ 970/925–1940), and Breckenridge's Ullr Fest (☎ 970/453–6018) keep ski areas lively with races, torchlight skiing, and other events.

Feb.

Steamboat Springs hosts the oldest annual Winter Carnival (☎ 970/879–0880) west of the Mississippi.

Summit County is home to the Skijoring World Championships (☎ 970/668–2051).

The Ice Fishing Contest (☎ 970/723–4600) in Walden consists of fishing on four lakes for the eight largest fish. Leadville puts on an Ice Fishing Derby (☎ 970/486–8363).

SPRING

Mar.

More than 70 tribes convene for the Denver Powwow (☎ 303/892–1112 or 800/393–8559), with Native American dancers, artisans, and musicians.

Charity and celebrity events rope them in at many ski areas, including the Special Olympics Colorado (☎ 303/592–1361) winter events at Copper Mountain. Jimmie Heuga's Ski Express for MS (☎ 970/926–1290 or 800/367–3101), named for the bronze medalist in the 1964 Olympics slalom race, is a national series of races that raises money to fight Multiple Sclerosis. The charity event in Vail, the American Ski Classic (☎ 970/949–1999), is hosted by former president Gerald Ford.

Apr.	The ski towns of Aspen, Breckenridge, and Copper Mountain put on events to celebrate spring. A Taste of Vail (☎ 970/926–1494) showcases that area's superlative restaurants.
	The mountain bike racing event during the Fruita Fat Tire Festival (☎ 970/858–3894) lets riders loose on the world-famous Kokopelli Trail and the majestic Bookcliffs.
May	The Kinetic Conveyance Race (☎ 303/444–5226 ⊕ www.kbco.com) draws crowds to the Boulder Reservoir to see whose kinetic contraption can slip over the land and slog through the water to win the race and the $1,000 booty.
	Top international runners, along with 45,000 ordinary citizens, race 10 km through the streets of town during Memorial Day's Bolder Boulder (☎ 303/444–7223 ⊕ www.bolderboulder.com). Square dancers, belly dancers, and string quartets provide sideline entertainment for about 100,000 spectators.
	Don't forget to register your rubber duck for the Great Rubber Duck Race if you go to the Boulder Creek Festival (☎ 303/449–3825, 303/413–7216 for duck race ⊕ www.bouldercreekfestival. com) on Memorial Day weekend. The outdoor festival along Boulder Creek downtown offers art and crafts for sale, food, and live entertainment.
	In Fruita, Mike the Headless Chicken Festival (☎ 970/858–3894) throws together a microbrew festival, a chicken dance marathon, a 5-km race, and other kinds of fun and food.
SUMMER	
June	The season of music festivals and cultural events gets into swing with Telluride's weekend-long Bluegrass Festival (☎ 800/624–2422), the Aspen Music Festival (☎970/925–3254), Jazz Aspen (☎970/920–4996) in Snowmass, and Breckenridge's Genuine Jazz (☎ 970/453–6018). Grand Junction's Country Jam (☎ 800/530–3020) brings four days of country music and camp-outs during the third or fourth weekend of June.
	The Food-Wine Classic (☎ 970/925–1940) in Aspen is an epicurean extravaganza. Fort Collins's Annual Colorado Brewers' Festival (☎ 970/484–6500) comes to Old Town to show off the fermented products of 45 Colorado brewers. Glenwood Springs puts on Strawberry Days (☎ 970/945–6589).
	The Silly Home Built River Raft Race (☎ 719/456–0453), held in Las Animas on the Arkansas River, keeps spectators guessing which improbable floating devices will reach the finish line.
	Steamboat's Annual Cowboy Roundup Days (☎ 970/879–0880) combines rodeo events, a country-music festival, chili cook-off, a Cowboy Poetry gathering, and more.
	Crested Butte's Fat Tire Festival (☎ 970/349–6817), held the third week in June, is an outstanding mountain biking event with guided tours, clinics, and a competitive cross-country race.

	Boulder's Colorado Shakespeare Festival (☎ 303/492–0554), one of the three most popular Bard fests in the country, stages comedies and tragedies under the stars from mid-June through mid-August.
July	Arts events galore run throughout July, including Winter Park's Jazz and American Music Festivals (☎ 970/726–4118), and Vail's Bravo! Colorado Music Festival (☎ 970/827–5700). The Cherry Creek Arts Festival (☎ 303/355–2787 ⊕ www.cherryarts.org) is a juried outdoor event held in Denver in early July.
	There are guided walks and a host of seminars on identification, photography, and cooking at Crested Buttes's Wildflower Festival (☎ 970/349–6438 or 800/545–4505).
Aug.	Rodeos are typical late-summer fare; witness the Pikes Peak or Bust Rodeo (☎719/635–7506, 800/368–4748 outside the state), Colorado's largest rodeo, in Colorado Springs.
	Country fairs are also big business, especially Pueblo's star-studded state fair (☎ 800/876–4567).
	The Wild Mushroom Festival (☎ 970/728–4431 or 800/525–3455) sponsors seminars on cooking and medicinal uses and forays into the woods around Telluride. Visitors from as far away as the East Coast and Alaska join the corn-eating contest and the cook-off of the Olathe Sweet Corn Festival (☎ 877/858–6006 ⊕ www.olathesweetcornfest.com). Olathe lies between Grand Junction and Montrose on Highway 50.
	Vail hosts the International Festival of Dance (☎ 970/949–1999 or 970/476–2918), set amid the wildflowers in the outdoor Ford Amphitheater.
	Denver's Festival of Mountain and Plain: A Taste of Colorado (☎ 303/295–6330) showcases the city's restaurants over Labor Day weekend.
	A top music festival is Telluride's Jazz Celebration (☎ 970/728–7009).
AUTUMN	
Sept.	Major film festivals (☎ 970/925–6882, 970/453–6200, or 603/643–1255) take place in Aspen, Breckenridge, and Telluride.
	Estes Park's annual Longs Peak Scottish/Irish Highland Festival (☎ 970/586–6308 or 800/903–7837 ⊕ www.scotfest.com, www.irishscotfest.com) draws more than 60,000 visitors the weekend after Labor Day. Events include parades; clan and living history exhibits; seminars on Gaelic language; athletic, pipe band, and jousting competitions; folk concerts; and the *Ceilidh*—the Celtic New Year bash. Musical performances by well-known outfits such as the Royal Ulster Constabulary Pipe Band, the Royal Canadian Artillery Band, and the U.S. Air Force Honor Drill Team are usual highlights.

	A bike tour of vineyards, grape stomping, wine tasting, entertainment, food from area chefs, and more are part of the annual Colorado Mountain Wine Festival (☎ 800/764–3667) in Palisade.
Oct.	Oktoberfests and harvest celebrations dominate October, most notably Carbondale's Potato Days (☎ 970/963–1890), and the Cedaredge Applefest (☎ 800/436–3041).
	The Great American Beer Festival (☎ 303/447–0816) in Denver is the country's largest beer fest, offering samples of more than 1,000 brews.
Nov.	Look for Creede's Chocolate Festival (☎ 719/658–2374 or 800/327–2102), which puts chocolates of every size, shape, and description in every corner of the town.

Bicycling

Mountain biking has a huge following in Colorado and is more popular than touring on paved roads. Crested Butte vies with Moab, Utah, as the mountain-biking center of the Rockies; a storied trip over the demanding Pearl Pass in the 1970s is supposedly the origin of the mountain-biking craze. As for road cycling, the San Juan Mountains loop is as beautiful a ride as there is in the country. Valley roads tend to be clear of snow by mid- to late April; roads and trails at higher elevations may not be clear until several months later and may be snow-covered again by early October.

Colorado Cuisine: Beyond the Three Bs

In 1944, a Denver drive-in owner named Louis Ballast grilled a slice of cheese on top of a hamburger and became famous for patenting his invention, the cheeseburger. It has been suggested that Rocky Mountain cuisine consists of the three Bs: beef, buffalo, and burritos. Although these items certainly will appear on menus throughout the region, they are no longer the final word in Colorado.

Colorado is prime territory for game and fish. Antelope, elk, venison, and grouse are no strangers to the Rockies palate. Rainbow trout, salmon, and bass pulled from someone's favorite (and maybe secret) fishing spot find their way onto almost every menu. Rocky Mountain oysters (fried bull testicles) are famous—some would say infamous—for their size and taste. Be on the lookout for Colorado's sugar-sweet Rocky Ford cantaloupe, as well as tree-ripened apples, peaches, and pears from roadside stands.

As for beverages, Colorado has more microbreweries than any other state, and some of the local brews, such as Crested Butte's Fat Tire Ale, are available from regular beer outlets. Some parts of Colorado also possess excellent vineyards, and local wines are typically featured on restaurant menus.

Denver chefs serve this local bounty in unique combinations in their innovative contemporary restaurants. Denver is also the spot for cheap ethnic eats.

Dude Ranches

Dude ranches fall roughly into two categories: working ranches and guest ranches. Colorado has ranches on both ends of the spectrum. Working ranches, where guests participate in such activities as round ups and cattle movements, sometimes require experienced horsemanship. Guest ranches offer a wide range of activities in addition to horseback riding and only rarely request experienced riders. The slate of possible activities can vary widely from ranch to ranch. At most establishments, guests will be given some taste of the working-ranch experience with demonstrations of rodeo skills and the like. Fishing tends to be given second priority, and after that, anything goes. At a typical dude ranch, guests stay in log cabins and are served meals family-style in a lodge or ranch house.

Fishing

Trout, whether they be cutthroat, brown, rainbow, Mackinaw, brook, or lake, are the prime game fish in Colorado. This isn't exactly trophy fish country, but what the fish lack in size, they make up for in volume. Fishing licenses range in term from daily to annual and are available in many convenience stores and sporting goods shops. Tackle shops are a good place to feel out a region's most effective lures. Hire a knowledgeable guide or sign on with an outfitter for the best experience.

Hiking

There are thousands of miles of hiking trails in Colorado. The national parks have particularly well-marked and well-maintained trails, and admittance to all trails is free. In fact, hiking is sometimes the only way to get close to highlights on protected land. Hiking in the south is usually best in spring, when water is plentiful and before the heat of summer sets in. Primarily for safety reasons, overnight hikers are usually expected to register with park or forest rangers. Also keep in mind that run-ins with bears and mountain lions have become increasingly common, especially in northern Colorado.

Horse-Pack Trips

Horse-pack trips are great ways to visit the Colorado backcountry, since horses can travel distances and carry supplies that would be impossible for hikers. Although horsemanship isn't required for most trips, it is helpful, and even an experienced rider can expect to be a little sore for the first few days. June through August is the peak period for horse-packing trips; before signing up with an outfitter, inquire about the skills they expect.

National Parks

Colorado has a power trio of national parks, and each offers a completely different experience of the state, from some of its highest heights to some of its lowest depths. Rocky Mountain National Park has 355 mi of hiking trails and sweeping vistas of high-country lakes, meadows, pine forests, alpine tundra, and snow-dusted peaks. Long's Peak, the highest point in the park, is a surprisingly accessible hike for those in good shape. Mesa Verde National Park safeguards the 1,400-year-old cliff dwellings of the Ancestral Puebloans. Black Canyon of the Gunnison National Park is a vivid testament to the powers of erosion. The park contains the deepest 14 mi of the 48-mi-long canyon. Hiking trails along the canyon's rims have heart-stopping views of the chasm, which reaches depths of 2,700 feet and is a mere 40 feet wide in some spots.

Rock Climbing & Mountaineering

Climbing in its various forms—mountaineering, rock climbing, ice climbing—is a year-round sport in Colorado. Many fourteeners, such as Long's Peak in Rocky Mountain National Park, are a relatively easy (although long) ascent for the well conditioned and well prepared, but there are also dozens of highly technical climbs, such as the spires of El Dorado Canyon. In many areas, especially in the National Parks, climbing permits are required, primarily for safety reasons.

Generally speaking, the Colorado Rockies do not call for great expeditionary preparation. The range is very accessible and the climbs, by alpine standards, relatively short. There are few major climbs in Colorado that can't be accomplished in a day or two.

Shopping

Colorado somehow manages to combine a reverence for nature with a fascination for ski-resort glitz and a love of megamalls and discount outlet shopping centers.

Remarkable crafts, particularly Native American works, can be found throughout the state. The southwestern corner is generally thought to be the best place for Western and Native American arts and crafts, especially basketry, weaving, and beadwork. Cowboy hats, saddles, and other high-quality Western gear are also good purchases.

In Denver, the trendy warehouse galleries in the LoDo district stock weavings, pottery, jewelry, kachinas, and paintings. If antiquing is your thing, head for the dusty shops of South Broadway. Not surprisingly in a town this full of nature-lovers, Denver is also a great place to stock up on outdoors gear.

Skiing & Snowboarding

When the white gold falls in the Colorado High Country like manna from heaven, sun-screen smeared tourists cheer, locals call in sick, college students play hooky and the freeways clog with cars bristling with skis and snowboards. If you find yourself seduced as you catch air off the Continental Divide at Loveland or enchanted as you glide through spacious tree glades on "The Shadows" in Steamboat, you're not alone. Each year, more than 11 million skiers and snowboarders flock to the state for gravity-defying winter fun that lasts from mid-October through July 4.

The first recorded skiers in Colorado were several miners who, in 1859, strapped on 12-foot-long Norwegian skis to escape from a snowbound camp near present-day Breckenridge. Recreational skiing, however, didn't really get started until veterans of the U.S. Army's 10th Mountain Division, who trained at Camp Hale (near present-day Leadville) returned from World War II and began carving rough ski runs.

Today the state has 26 ski resorts, including seven of the 10 most popular in North America—Aspen, Breckenridge, Copper Mountain, Keystone, Steamboat, Vail, and Winter Park. With this many resorts, your options are endless. Feel like a small resort close to Denver with short lift lines and challenging terrain? Try Loveland or Arapahoe Basin, best-kept secrets with locals. Want to enjoy an extended vacation in a luxury resort? Check out the endless terrain and modern villages at Vail or Copper. Looking for resorts with character and fun après ski scenes? Aspen and Telluride, former mining towns tucked into spectacular valleys, have this in spades.

FODOR'S CHOICE

The sights, restaurants, hotels, and other travel experiences on these pages are our editors' top picks—our Fodor's Choices. They're the best of their type in the area covered by the book—not to be missed and always worth your time. In the destination chapters that follow, you will find all the details.

LODGING

$$$$	**The Broadmoor Hotel,** Colorado Springs. The Broadmoor reigns, simply, as king of Colorado hotels. Its service, attention to detail, and almost royal splendor—lakeside in the shadow of the Front Range—allow it to pamper its subjects like no other.
$$$$	**Ski Tip Lodge,** Keystone. After a long, hard day on the slopes, the cozy quilts and four–poster beds in this log cabin inn, Colorado's first ski lodge, are especially appealing.
$$$–$$$$	**Hotel Boulderado,** Boulder. Teddy Roosevelt loved to eat here. One of Colorado's classic hotels, Hotel Boulderado still has early-20th-century charm and great restaurants.
$$$–$$$$	**Stanley Hotel,** Estes Park. This 1909 white palace evokes the grand style of Estes Park in its early years as a resort. The elegant ballroom takes in views of the town and the high Rockies.
$$–$$$$	**The Cliff House,** Manitou Springs. What was once a stagecoach stop is now a small luxury hotel. The Cliff House combines Rocky Mountain Victorian architecture with such modern amenities as steam showers and even heated toilet seats.
$–$$$$	**The B&Bs on North Main Street,** Breckenridge. At this three-in-one B&B, you have your choice of Victorian inn; rustic, romantic cottage; or modern, riverside lodge. Decisions, decisions.
$–$$$$	**Strater Hotel,** Durango. Crystal chandeliers, beveled glass windows, and velvet curtains set the Old West scene in the painstakingly-restored Diamond Belle Saloon.
$–$$	**Ice Palace Inn Bed & Breakfast,** Leadville. Spend the night on a downy featherbed at this 1900 Victorian bed-and-breakfast, and you'll dream of a lost age when Horace Tabor romanced Colorado's very own Evita—the beautiful and ultimately tragic Baby Doe Taylor.
$–$$	**Sod Buster Inn Bed and Breakfast,** Greeley. One of the best urban B&Bs in the state blends the modern and historic in a unique octagonal building that feels Victorian—but was built in 1997.
$–$$	**Spruce Lodge Resort,** Grand Mesa. Tucked in the Grand Mesa National Forest, the resort has a luxurious VIP suite that kindles romance with a fireplace, built-in stereo system, liquor bar, and French doors that open onto a deck.

RESTAURANTS

$$$–$$$$	**The Fort,** Denver. The early West has been alive and well for 40 years at this reproduction of Old Bent's Fort in La Junta, Colorado, and that atmosphere combines with the skilled cooking of a veteran chef

and the best bison and beef available for an authentic Western experience.

$-$$ **The Boulder Dushanbe Teahouse,** Boulder. Tajik artisans traveled to Boulder to build the teahouse, a gift from Dushanbe, Boulder's sister city in Tajikistan. Excellent dishes from many world cuisines and more than 80 types of tea are served.

BUDGET RESTAURANTS

¢ **Jack 'n' Grill,** Denver. The city prides itself on superior green chile and a strong Hispanic community, and the family-run Jack 'n' Grill brings the two together in a way that highlights local flavors and local folks.

¢ **Slice O' Life Bakery,** Palisade. It's hard to put a price tag on just plain yummy, but this local favorite does just that with its melt-in-your-mouth pastries, sweet rolls, muffins, and fruitcakes concocted from secret family recipes handed down through the generations.

AFTER HOURS

The Colorado Avalanche, Denver. The Broncos' Super Bowl rings and the Rockies' record notwithstanding, the Colorado Avalanche is the most consistently exciting team in Denver. And the Pepsi Center, while cavernous for concerts and Nuggets basketball games, is perfect for the rowdiness and octopus-tossing of hockey.

Colorado Shakespeare Festival, Boulder. The Bard's comedies and tragedies are staged under the summer stars from late June to mid-August.

Red Rocks Amphitheatre, Morrison. In addition to its history of hosting acts like the Beatles and U2, Red Rocks is a beautiful old park with breathtaking views of both the rocks themselves and the city of Denver in the distance.

DRIVES

Mt. Evans Scenic and Historic Byway, Idaho Springs. You'll be sharing the road with curly-horned bighorn sheep and shaggy mountain goats which inhabit the alpine tundra on this 14,000-foot-high peak.

Palisade's Wine Country. Spin your wheels, either by car or bike, through Colorado's version of Napa Valley. You'll learn about everything from winemaking to grape complexity and growing conditions while sampling highly regarded Colorado wines.

Red Mountain Pass, Ouray. The Million Dollar Highway clings to the cliffs overhanging the Uncompaghre River far below this most spectacular stretch of the San Juan Skyway.

Trail Ridge Road, Rocky Mountain National Park. The road climbs more than 4300 feet and curves past spectacular viewpoints for 48 mi between Estes Park and Grand Lake.

NATURE

Yankee Boy Basin, Ouray. You'll need a four-wheel drive vehicle to get here, but the views of this vast alpine basin carpeted with wild-flowers are worth the trip.

Black Canyon of the Gunnison National Park, Montrose. Standing at the bottom of this narrow, 2,000-ft-deep chasm, it almost seems as if the rim is closing above your head.

Colorado Canyons National Conservation Area, Grand Junction. Nearly 123,000 acres of dramatic red-rock canyons, rugged plateaus, and remote trails beckon outdoor enthusiasts who prefer hiking, horseback riding, and mountain biking to being stuck in a big city-traffic jam.

Collegiate Peaks Wilderness Area, Buena Vista. The imposing beauty here is not just a roadside attraction—the surrounding wilderness area is a mecca for outdoors types of all stripes.

North Cheyenne Cañon Park, Colorado Springs. This city park encompasses more than 1,600 acres, replete with hummingbirds, waterfalls, a climbing wall, and moderate hikes.

Royal Gorge, Cañon City. Whether you view it from the white water below, descend on the incline railroad, or see it from the aerial tram or bridge, the 1,053-foot deep gorge is undeniably a natural wonder.

RAFTING

Arkansas River, Buena Vista. This is the second-most commercially rafted river in the United States for a reason: white water doesn't get much better than this.

Dinosaur National Monument. A raft trip on the Green River through Ladore Canyon tests the moxie of the daring. Described by some as one of the most beautiful stretches of river anywhere, the Green River goes on a wet and wild ride through several challenging rapids appropriately named Hell's Half Mile, Disaster Falls, and S.O.B.

SKI AREAS

Aspen Highlands, Aspen. Not for the faint of heart, the hike to the upper reaches of the Highland Bowl pays major dividends for those in the know. Nowhere else will you find controlled terrain with such awesome views, pristine powder, gnarly steeps, and generally outrageous extreme skiing.

Back Bowls, Vail. On powder days, the Back Bowls can offer intermediate and expert skiers a small slice of heaven.

Loveland Ski Area, Georgetown. It might seem small compared to the megaresorts nearby, but this favorite of locals offers some of the steepest and most challenging terrain in an uncrowded setting right on the spine of the Continental Divide.

URBAN CULTURE

Larimer Square, Denver. The heart of LoDo is a collection of restaurants and bars, new and old, from venerable Josephina's to new-kid Tumayo, lit up and comforting for partiers and wanderers alike.

Tattered Cover, Denver. Although gigantic bookstore chains continue to take over the rest of the world, the Tattered Cover (in Cherry Creek and LoDo) holds the line with a huge selection, comfy chairs, knowledgeable clerks, and decent prices.

VIEWS

Durango & Silverton Narrow Gauge Railroad, Durango. Steam back in time to the Old West. These coal-fired locomotives carried an estimated $300 million in precious metals on this track through the stunning canyons and remote forests.

Mesa Verde National Park, Cortez. Rugged canyon walls shelter an ancient city of Ancestral Puebloan cliff dwellings, perfectly preserved.

Town of Telluride. Tucked away at the headwaters of the San Miguel River, gorgeous Telluride nestles beneath the looming San Juan Mountains.

SMART TRAVEL TIPS

Finding out about your destination before you leave home means you won't squander time organizing everyday minutiae once you've arrived. The organizations in this section can provide information to supplement this guide; contact them for up-to-the-minute details, and consult the A to Z sections that end each chapter for facts on the various topics as they relate to Colorado's many regions. Happy landings!

AIR TRAVEL

BIKES IN FLIGHT

Most airlines accommodate bikes as luggage, provided they are dismantled and boxed. For bike boxes, often free at bike shops, you'll pay about $15 (at least $100 for bike bags) from airlines. International travelers can sometimes substitute a bike for a piece of checked luggage at no charge; otherwise, the cost is about $100. Domestic and Canadian airlines charge $80–$160.

BOOKING

When you book, **look for nonstop flights** and **remember that "direct" flights stop at least once.** Try to avoid connecting flights, which require a change of plane. Two airlines may operate a connecting flight jointly, so ask whether the same airline operates every segment of the trip; you may find that the carrier you prefer flies only part of the way. To find more booking tips and to check prices and make on-line flight reservations, log on to www.fodors.com.

CARRIERS

🛪 Major Airlines **Air Canada** ☎ 888/247-2262 ⊕ www.aircanada.com. **American Airlines** ☎ 800/433-7300 ⊕ www.aa.com. **British Airways** ☎ 800/247-9297 ⊕ www.ba.com. **Continental** ☎ 800/525-0280 ⊕ www.continental.com. **Delta** ☎ 800/221-1212 ⊕ www.delta.com. **Northwest** ☎ 800/225-2525 ⊕ www.nwa.com. **TWA** ☎ 800/433-7300. **United Airlines** ☎ 800/241-6522 ⊕ www.united.com. **US Airways** ☎ 800/428-4322 ⊕ www.usair.com.

🛪 Smaller Airlines **AirTran Airways** ☎ 800/247-8726 ⊕ www.airtran.com. **America West** ☎ 800/235-9292 ⊕ www.americawest.com. **ATA** ☎ 800/435-9282 ⊕ www.ata.com. **Frontier** ☎ 800/432-1359 ⊕ www.frontierairlines.com. **Horizon Air** ☎ 800/547-9308 ⊕ www.horizonair.com. **Mesa Airlines** ☎ 800/637-2247 ⊕ www.mesa-air.com. **Midwest Express** ☎ 800/452-2022 ⊕ www.2.midwestexpress.com. **Southwest** ☎ 800/435-9792 ⊕ www.iflyswa.com.

CHECK-IN & BOARDING

Always **ask your carrier about its check-in policy.** Plan to arrive at the airport about 2 hours before your scheduled departure time for domestic flights and 2½ to 3 hours before international flights. You may need to arrive earlier if you're flying from one of the busier airports or during peak air-traffic times.

If you're traveling during snow season, allow extra time for the drive to the airport. If you'll be checking skis, arrive even earlier.

To avoid delays at airport-security checkpoints, try not to wear any metal. Jewelry, belt and other buckles, steel-toe shoes, barrettes, and underwire bras are among the items that can set off detectors.

Assuming that not everyone with a ticket will show up, airlines routinely overbook planes. When everyone does, airlines ask for volunteers to give up their seats. In return, these volunteers usually get a several-hundred-dollar flight voucher, which can be used toward the purchase of another ticket, and are rebooked on the next flight out. If there are not enough volunteers, the airline must choose who will be denied boarding. The first to get bumped are passengers who checked in late and those flying on discounted tickets, so **get to the gate and check in as early as possible,** especially during peak periods.

Always **bring a government-issued photo I.D. to the airport;** even when it's not required, a passport is best.

CUTTING COSTS

The least expensive airfares to Colorado are priced for round-trip travel and must usually be purchased in advance. Airlines generally allow you to change your return date for a fee; most low-fare tickets, however, are nonrefundable. It's smart to **call a number of airlines and check the Internet;** when you are quoted a good price, **book it on the spot**—the same fare may not be available the next day, or even the next hour. Always **check different routings** and look into using alternate airports. Also, price off-peak flights, which may be significantly less expensive than others. Travel agents, especially low-fare specialists (⇨ Discounts & Deals), can be helpful.

Consolidators are another good source. They buy tickets for scheduled flights at reduced rates from the airlines, then sell them at prices that beat the best fare available directly from the airlines. Sometimes you can even get your money back if you need to return the ticket. Carefully read the fine print detailing penalties for changes and cancellations, purchase the ticket with a credit card, and **confirm your consolidator reservation with the airline.**

7 Consolidators AirlineConsolidator.com ☎ 888/468-5385 ⊕ www.airlineconsolidator.com; for international tickets. **Best Fares** ☎ 800/576-8255 ⊕ www.bestfares.com; $59.90 annual membership. **Cheap Tickets** ☎ 800/377-1000 or 888/922-8849 ⊕ www.cheaptickets.com. **Expedia** ☎ 800/397-3342 or 404/728-8787 ⊕ www.expedia.com. **Hotwire** ☎ 866/468-9473 or 920/330-9418 ⊕ www.hotwire.com. **Now Voyager Travel** ⊠ 45 W 21st St., 5th fl., New York, NY 10010 ☎ 212/459-1616 🖶 212/243-2711 ⊕ www.nowvoyagertravel.com. **Onetravel.com** ⊕ www.onetravel.com. **Orbitz** ☎ 888/656-4546 ⊕ www.orbitz.com. **Priceline. com** ⊕ www.priceline.com. **Travelocity** ☎ 888/709-5983, 877/282-2925 in Canada, 0870/876-3876 in the U.K. ⊕ www.travelocity.com.

ENJOYING THE FLIGHT

State your seat preference when purchasing your ticket, and then repeat it when you confirm and when you check in. For more legroom, you can request one of the few emergency-aisle seats at check-in, if you are capable of lifting at least 50 pounds—a Federal Aviation Administration (FAA) requirement of passengers in these seats. Seats behind a bulkhead also offer more legroom, but they don't have under-seat storage. Don't sit in the row in front of the emergency aisle or in front of a bulkhead, where seats may not recline.

Ask the airline whether a snack or meal is served on the flight. If you have dietary concerns, **request special meals when booking.** These can be vegetarian, low-cholesterol, or kosher, for example. It's a good idea to pack some healthful snacks and a small (plastic) bottle of water in your carry-on bag. On long flights try to maintain a normal routine, to help fight jet lag. At night, **get some sleep.** By day, **eat light meals, drink water** (not alcohol), and **move around the cabin** to stretch your legs. For additional jet-lag tips consult *Fodor's FYI: Travel Fit & Healthy* (available at bookstores everywhere).

Smoking is prohibited on all domestic flights within the United States.

FLYING TIMES

It takes about two hours to fly to Denver from Los Angeles, Chicago, or Dallas. From New York, the flight is about 3½ hours. London to Denver is about 12 hours, including a layover. From Sydney, flying to Denver will consume more than 20 hours, including one or two layovers.

HOW TO COMPLAIN

If your baggage goes astray or your flight goes awry, complain right away. Most carriers require that you **file a claim immediately.** The Aviation Consumer Protection Division of the Department of Transportation publishes *Fly-Rights*, which discusses airlines and consumer issues and is available on-line.

☷ Airline Complaints Aviation Consumer Protection Division ⌧ U.S. Department of Transportation, C-75, Room 4107, 400 7th St. NW, Washington, DC 20590 ☎ 202/366-2220 ⊕ www.dot.gov/airconsumer. **Federal Aviation Administration Consumer Hotline** ⌧ for inquiries: FAA, 800 Independence Ave. SW, Room 810, Washington, DC 20591 ☎ 800/322-7873 ⊕ www.faa.gov.

RECONFIRMING

Check the status of your flight before you leave for the airport. You can do this on your carrier's Web site, by linking to a flight-status checker (many Web booking services offer these), or by calling your carrier or travel agent.

AIRPORTS

The major air gateway to the Colorado Rockies is Denver International Airport (DIA); flights to smaller, resort-town airports generally connect through it. Colorado Springs Airport (COS) is also sizeable. During ski season, some of the major resort towns have increased service, and direct flights may be available.

☷ Denver International Airport ☎ 303/342-2000, 800/247-2336, 800/688-1333 TTY ⊕ www.flydenver.com. **Colorado Springs Airport** ☎ 719/550-1900 ⊕ www.flycos.com.

BIKE TRAVEL

Pedaling through Colorado is popular, especially in the Rocky Mountains. Many bikers travel from town to town (or between backcountry huts or campsites) during summer. Most streets in the larger cities have bike lanes, and Denver, Boulder, and Colorado Springs are especially bike-friendly. Cities and tourism organizations often offer free bike maps.

☷ Bike Maps National Geographic/Trails Illustrated ☎ 800/962-1643. **Off-Road Publications** ☎ 888/477-3374.

BUS TRAVEL

Greyhound Lines has regular intercity routes throughout the region, with connections from Denver to Grand Junction. Smaller bus companies provide intrastate and local service.

☷ Bus Information Colorado Mountain Express ☎ 800/525-6363. **Greyhound Lines** ☎ 800/231-2222. **RTD** ⌧ Denver ☎ 800/366-7433 or 303/299-6000. **Springs Transit Management** ⌧ Colorado Springs ☎ 719/385-7433.

BUSINESS HOURS

Most retail stores are open daily from 9 AM or 9:30 AM until 6 PM or 7 PM in downtown locations and until 9 or 10 in suburban shopping malls and in resort towns during high season. Downtown stores sometimes stay open later Thursday night. Normal banking hours are weekdays 9–5; some branches are also open on Saturday morning.

CAMERAS & PHOTOGRAPHY

Photographers love the Rockies—and with good reason. The scenery is America's best, and every season offers a multitude of breathtaking images. When you're at Native American sites, be sure to ask if taking pictures is appropriate. The *Kodak Guide to Shooting Great Travel Pictures* (available at bookstores everywhere) is loaded with tips.

☷ Photo Help Kodak Information Center ☎ 800/242-2424 ⊕ www.kodak.com.

EQUIPMENT PRECAUTIONS

Don't pack film and equipment in checked luggage, where it is much more susceptible to damage. X-ray machines used to view checked luggage are extremely powerful and therefore are likely to ruin your film. Try to **ask for hand inspection of film,** which becomes clouded after repeated exposure to airport X-ray machines, and **keep videotapes and computer disks away from metal detectors.** Always **keep film, tape, and computer disks out of the sun.** Carry an extra supply of batteries, and **be prepared to turn on your camera, camcorder, or laptop** to prove to airport-security personnel that the device is real.

CAR RENTAL

Rates in most major cities run about $35 a day and $175 a week for an economy car with air-conditioning, an automatic transmission, and unlimited mileage. This does not include tax on car rentals, which is 12.95% in Denver. Keep in mind if you are venturing into the Rockies that you will need a little oomph in your engine to get over the passes. If you plan to explore any back roads, an SUV is the best bet because it will have higher clearance. Unless you plan to do a lot of mountain exploring, a four-wheel drive is usually needed only in winter.

⚑ Major Agencies **Alamo** ☎ 800/327-9633 ⊕ www.alamo.com. **Avis** ☎ 800/331-1212, 800/879-2847 or 800/272-5871 in Canada, 0870/606-0100 in the U.K., 02/9353-9000 in Australia, 09/526-2847 in New Zealand ⊕ www.avis.com. **Budget** ☎ 800/527-0700, 0870/156-5656 in the U.K. ⊕ www.budget.com. **Dollar** ☎ 800/800-4000, 0124/622-0111 in the U.K., where it's affiliated with Sixt, 02/9223-1444 in Australia ⊕ www.dollar.com. **Hertz** ☎ 800/654-3131, 800/263-0600 in Canada, 0870/844-8844 in the U.K., 02/9669-2444 in Australia, 09/256-8690 in New Zealand ⊕ www.hertz.com. **National Car Rental** ☎ 800/227-7368, 0870/600-6666 in the U.K. ⊕ www.nationalcar.com.

CUTTING COSTS

For a good deal, **book through a travel agent who will shop around.** Also, **price local car-rental companies**—whose prices may be lower still, although their service and maintenance may not be as good as those of major rental agencies—and **research rates on the Internet.** Remember to ask about required deposits, cancellation penalties, and drop-off charges if you're planning to pick up the car in one city and leave it in another. If you're traveling during a holiday period, also make sure that a confirmed reservation guarantees you a car. In Denver, the rental agencies at the airport are considerably more expensive than their downtown counterparts.

INSURANCE

When driving a rented car you are generally responsible for any damage to or loss of the vehicle. You also may be liable for any property damage or personal injury that you may cause while driving. Before you rent, see what coverage you already have under the terms of your personal auto-insurance policy and credit cards.

For about $10 to $25 a day, rental companies sell protection, known as a collision- or loss-damage waiver (CDW or LDW), that eliminates your liability for damage to the car; it's always optional and should never be automatically added to your bill. In most states you don't need a CDW if you have personal auto insurance or other liability insurance. However, **make sure you have enough coverage to pay for the car.** If you do not have auto insurance or an umbrella policy that covers damage to third parties, purchasing liability insurance and a CDW or LDW is highly recommended.

REQUIREMENTS & RESTRICTIONS

To rent a car in Colorado, you must be at least 25 years old and have a valid driver's license; most companies also require a major credit card. Child seats are compulsory for children under five and cost $5 to $10 a day.

SURCHARGES

Before you pick up a car in one city and leave it in another, **ask about drop-off charges or one-way service fees,** which can be substantial. Note, too, that some rental agencies charge extra if you return the car before the time specified in your contract. To avoid a hefty refueling fee, **fill the tank just before you turn in the car,** but be aware that gas stations near the rental outlet may overcharge. It's almost never a deal to buy the tank of gas that's in the car when you rent it; the understanding is that you'll return it empty, but some fuel usually remains. You'll pay extra for child seats ($5–$10 a day) and usually for additional drivers (about $7 per day).

CAR TRAVEL

Colorado has the most mountainous terrain of the American Rockies and the scenery makes driving far from a tedious means to an end.

Before setting out on any driving trip, it's important to **make sure your vehicle is in top condition.** It is best to have a complete tune-up. At the least, you should check the following: lights, including brake lights, backup lights, and emergency lights; tires, including the spare; oil; engine coolant;

windshield-washer fluid; windshield-wiper blades; and brakes. For emergencies, take along flares or reflector triangles, jumper cables, an empty gas can, a fire extinguisher, a flashlight, a plastic tarp, blankets, water, and coins or a calling card for phone calls (cell phones don't always work in high mountain areas).

GASOLINE

In major cities throughout Colorado, gas prices are roughly similar to the rest of the continental United States; in rural and resort towns, prices are considerably higher. Although gas stations are plentiful in many areas, you can drive more than 100 mi on back roads without finding gas.

ROAD CONDITIONS

Colorado offers some of the most spectacular vistas and challenging driving in the world. Roads range from multilane blacktop to barely graveled backcountry trails; from twisting switchbacks considerably marked with guardrails to primitive campgrounds with a lane so narrow that you must back up to the edge of a steep cliff to make a turn. Scenic routes and lookout points are clearly marked, enabling you to slow down and pull over to take in the views.

One of the more unpleasant sights along the highway are roadkills—animals struck by vehicles. Deer, elk, and even bears may try to get to the other side of a road just as you come along, so **watch out for wildlife on the highways.** Exercise caution, not only to save an animal's life, but also to avoid extensive damage to your car.

◪ Road Condition Information **Colorado** ☎ 303/639-1111 statewide.

RULES OF THE ROAD

You'll find highways and national parks crowded in summer, and almost deserted (and occasionally impassable) in winter. Follow the posted speed limit, drive defensively, and **make sure your gas tank is full.** The law requires that drivers and front-seat passengers **wear seat belts.**

Always **strap children under age 4 or under 40 pounds into approved child-safety seats.** You may turn right at a red light after stopping if there is no sign stating otherwise and no oncoming traffic. When in doubt, wait for the green.

SPEED LIMITS

The speed limit on U.S. interstates is 75 mph in rural areas and 65 mph in urban zones.

WINTER DRIVING

Modern highways make mountain driving safe and generally trouble-free even in cold weather. Although winter driving can occasionally present real challenges, road maintenance is good and plowing is prompt. However, in mountain areas, tire chains, studs, or snow tires are essential. If you're planning to drive into high elevations, be sure to **check the weather forecast and call for road conditions** beforehand. Even main highways can close. Be prepared for stormy weather: **carry an emergency kit** containing warm clothes, a flashlight, some food and water, and blankets. It's also good to carry a cell phone, but be aware that the mountains can disrupt service. If you do get stalled by deep snow, **do not leave your car.** Wait for help, running the engine only if needed, and remember that assistance is never far away. Winter weather isn't confined to winter months in the high country (it's been known to snow on July 4th), so be prepared year-round.

CHILDREN IN COLORADO

Colorado is tailor-made for family vacations, offering dude ranches; historic railroads; mining towns; rafting; and many outdoor activities. Visitor centers and lodgings are often good at recommending places to spend time with children. The guides issued by the tourism office of Colorado have sections geared toward children.

For general advice about traveling with children, consult *Fodor's FYI: Travel with Your Baby* (available in bookstores everywhere).

◪ Local Information **Colorado Parent Magazine** ✉ 3801 E. Florida Ave., Suite 640, Denver, CO 80210 ☎ 303/320-1000.

FLYING

If your children are two or older, **ask about children's airfares.** As a general rule, infants under two not occupying a seat fly at greatly reduced fares or even for free. But if you want to guarantee a seat for an infant, you have to pay full fare. Consider flying during off-peak days and times; most airlines will grant an infant a seat without a ticket if there are available seats. Experts agree that it's a good idea to use safety seats aloft for children weighing less than 40 pounds. Airlines set their own policies: if you use a safety seat, U.S. carriers usually require that the child be ticketed, even if he or she is young enough to ride free, because the seats must be strapped into regular seats. And even if you pay the full adult fare for the seat, it may be worth it, especially on longer trips. Do **check your airline's policy about using safety seats during takeoff and landing.** Safety seats are not allowed everywhere in the plane, so get your seat assignments as early as possible.

When reserving, **request children's meals or a freestanding bassinet** (not available at all airlines) if you need them. But note that bulkhead seats, where you must sit to use the bassinet, may lack an overhead bin or storage space on the floor.

LODGING

Most hotels in Colorado allow children under a certain age to stay in their parents' room at no extra charge, but others charge for them as extra adults; be sure to **find out the cutoff age for children's discounts.**

Although most dude ranches are ideal for children of all ages, be sure you know not only the activities a ranch offers but also which are emphasized before booking your vacation. A few ranches may have age restrictions excluding very young children.

SIGHTS & ATTRACTIONS

Places that are especially appealing to children are indicated by a rubber-duckie icon (🐥) in the margin.

SPORTS & THE OUTDOORS

Altitude can be even more taxing on small lungs than on adult lungs, so **be conservative** when evaluating what level of activity your child will enjoy.

Some trip organizers arrange backpacking outings for families with small children, especially for family groups of eight or more. Short half-day or full-day bike trips with plenty of flat riding are possible at many Rocky Mountain resorts. Among the better resorts for this sort of activity are Aspen and Steamboat Springs. Winter Park resort has good instructional programs.

It is not advisable to take children under seven on extended rafting trips, except those specifically geared toward young children. Before taking an extended trip, you might want to test the waters with a half-day or one-day excursion. Trips aboard larger, motorized rafts are probably safest. Outfitters designate some trips as "adults only," with the cutoff usually being 16 years old.

CONSUMER PROTECTION

Whether you're shopping for gifts or purchasing travel services, **pay with a major credit card** whenever possible, so you can cancel payment or get reimbursed if there's a problem (and you can provide documentation). If you're doing business with a company for the first time, **contact your local Better Business Bureau and the attorney general's offices** in your state and (for U.S. businesses) the company's home state as well. Find out if any complaints have been filed in the past. Finally, if you're buying a package or tour, always **consider travel insurance** that includes default coverage (⇨ Insurance).

🔳 BBBs **Council of Better Business Bureaus** ✉ 4200 Wilson Blvd., Suite 800, Arlington, VA 22203 ☎ 703/276-0100 📠 703/525-8277 🌐 www.bbb.org.

CUSTOMS & DUTIES

IN AUSTRALIA

Australian residents who are 18 or older may bring home A$400 worth of souvenirs and gifts (including jewelry), 250 cigarettes or 250 grams of cigars or other tobacco products, and 1,125 ml of alcohol (including wine, beer, and spirits). Residents under 18 may bring back A$200 worth of goods. Members of the same family traveling together may pool their allowances. Prohibited items include meat products. Seeds, plants, and fruits must be declared upon arrival.

🔳 **Australian Customs Service** 🏛 Regional Director, Box 8, Sydney, NSW 2001 ☎ 02/9213-2000 or 1300/363263, 02/9364-7222 or 1800/803-006 quarantine-inquiry line 📠 02/9213-4043 🌐 www.customs.gov.au.

IN CANADA

Canadian residents who have been out of Canada for at least seven days may bring in C$750 worth of goods duty-free. If you've been away fewer than seven days but more than 48 hours, the duty-free allowance drops to C$200. If your trip lasts 24 to 48 hours, the allowance is C$50. You may not pool allowances with family members. Goods claimed under the C$750 exemption may follow you by mail; those claimed under the lesser exemptions must accompany you. Alcohol and tobacco products may be included in the seven-day and 48-hour exemptions but not in the 24-hour exemption. If you meet the age requirements of the province or territory through which you reenter Canada, you may bring in, duty-free, 1.5 liters of wine *or* 1.14 liters (40 imperial ounces) of liquor *or* 24 12-ounce cans or bottles of beer or ale. Also, if you meet the local age requirement for tobacco products, you may bring in, duty-free, 200 cigarettes and 50 cigars. Check with the Canada Customs and Revenue Agency or the Department of Agriculture for policies regarding meat products, seeds, plants, and fruits.

You may send an unlimited number of gifts (only one gift per recipient, however) worth up to C$60 each duty-free to Canada. Label the package UNSOLICITED GIFT—VALUE UNDER $60. Alcohol and tobacco are excluded.

🔼 **Canada Customs and Revenue Agency** ✉ 2265 St. Laurent Blvd., Ottawa, Ontario K1G 4K3 ☎ 800/461-9999, 204/983-3500, 506/636-5064 ⊕ www.ccra.gc.ca.

IN NEW ZEALAND

All homeward-bound residents may bring back NZ$700 worth of souvenirs and gifts; passengers may not pool their allowances, and children can claim only the concession on goods intended for their own use. For those 17 or older, the duty-free allowance also includes 4.5 liters of wine or beer; one 1,125-ml bottle of spirits; and either 200 cigarettes, 250 grams of tobacco, 50 cigars, *or* a combination of the three up to 250 grams. Meat products, seeds, plants, and fruits must be declared upon arrival to the Agricultural Services Department.

🔼 **New Zealand Customs** ✉ Head office: The Customhouse, 17–21 Whitmore St., Box 2218, Wellington ☎ 09/300-5399 or 0800/428-786 ⊕ www.customs.govt.nz.

IN THE U.K.

From countries outside the European Union, including the United States, you may bring home, duty-free, 200 cigarettes or 50 cigars; 1 liter of spirits or 2 liters of fortified or sparkling wine or liqueurs; 2 liters of still table wine; 60 ml of perfume; 250 ml of toilet water; plus £145 worth of other goods, including gifts and souvenirs. Prohibited items include meat products, seeds, plants, and fruits.

🔼 **HM Customs and Excise** ✉ Portcullis House, 21 Cowbridge Rd. E, Cardiff CF11 9SS ☎ 0845/010-9000 or 0208/929-0152, 0208/929-6731 or 0208/910-3602 complaints ⊕ www.hmce.gov.uk.

DISABILITIES & ACCESSIBILITY

Colorado is home to countless recreational opportunities for travelers with disabilities. Most ski areas offer adaptive ski programs. Winter Park is home to the National Sports Center for the Disabled, which offers year-round activities.

The majority of U.S. Forest Service campgrounds have wheelchair-accessible sites. Many resort towns have created opportunities for all types of visitors (on Independence Pass, for example, there's a short trail with sights marked in Braille). Access Tours leads nine-day trips for people who use wheelchairs or walk slowly, and can customize trips for groups of four or more.

Relay Colorado allows a person with a TTY machine to call someone without a TTY machine (and vice-versa) by relaying a message on the customer's behalf.

🔼 Local Resources **Access Tours** ☎ 800/929-4811. **Denver Commission for People with Disabilities** ☎ 303/913-8480. **National Sports Center for the Disabled** ☎ 970/726-1540. **Relay Colorado** ☎ 800/659-3656, 800/659-2656 TDD. **Rocky Mountain National Park** ☎ 970/586-1206 accessibility coordinator, Dana Leavitt. **Wilderness on Wheels** ☎ 303/403-1110 ⊕ wildernessonwheels.org.

LODGING

Despite the Americans with Disabilities Act, the definition of accessibility seems to differ from hotel to hotel. Some properties may be accessible by ADA standards for people with mobility problems but not for people with hearing or vision impairments, for example.

If you have mobility problems, ask for the lowest floor on which accessible services are offered. If you have a hearing impairment, check whether the hotel has devices to alert you visually to the ring of the telephone, a knock at the door, and a fire/emergency alarm. Some hotels provide these devices without charge. Discuss your needs with hotel personnel if this equipment isn't available, so that a staff member can personally alert you in the event of an emergency.

If you're bringing a guide dog, get authorization ahead of time and write down the name of the person with whom you spoke.

RESERVATIONS

When discussing accessibility with an operator or reservations agent, **ask hard questions.** Are there any stairs, inside *or* out? Are there grab bars next to the toilet *and* in the shower/tub? How wide is the doorway to the room? To the bathroom? For the most extensive facilities meeting the latest legal specifications, **opt for newer accommodations.** If you reserve through a toll-free number, consider also calling the hotel's local number to confirm the information from the central reservations office. Get confirmation in writing when you can.

SIGHTS & ATTRACTIONS

Most of Colorado's top sights and attractions are wheelchair-accessible in some way shape or form, but it can be hard to negotiate the terrain at such places as Pikes Peak, the Garden of the Gods, and Rocky Mountain National Park. But even in those areas, there are generally paved areas to facilities and overlooks that are wheelchair-friendly.

TRANSPORTATION

🛈 Complaints **Aviation Consumer Protection Division** (⇨ Air Travel) for airline-related problems. **Departmental Office of Civil Rights** ⊠ for general inquiries, U.S. Department of Transportation, S-30, 400 7th St. SW, Room 10215, Washington, DC 20590 ☎ 202/366-4648 🖶 202/366-9371 ⊕ www.dot.gov/ost/docr/index.htm. **Disability Rights Section** ⊠ NYAV, U.S. Department of Justice, Civil Rights Division, 950 Pennsylvania Ave. NW, Washington, DC 20530 ☎ ADA information line 202/514-0301, 800/514-0301, 202/514-0383 TTY, 800/514-0383 TTY ⊕ www.ada.gov. **U.S. Department of Transportation Hotline** ☎ for disability-related air-travel problems, 800/778-4838 or 800/455-9880 TTY.

TRAVEL AGENCIES

In the United States, the Americans with Disabilities Act requires that travel firms serve the needs of all travelers. Some agencies specialize in working with people with disabilities. **🛈** Travelers with Mobility Problems **Access Adventures** ⊠ 206 Chestnut Ridge Rd., Scottsville, NY 14624 ☎ 585/889-9096 ✉ dltravel@prodigy.net, run by a former physical-rehabilitation counselor. **Accessible Vans of America** ⊠ 9 Spielman Rd., Fairfield, NJ 07004 ☎ 877/282-8267, 973/808-9709 reservations 🖶 973/808-9713 ⊕ www.accessiblevans.com. **CareVacations** ⊠ No. 5, 5110-50 Ave., Leduc, Alberta, Canada, T9E 6V4 ☎ 780/986-6404 or 877/478-7827 🖶 780/986-8332 ⊕ www.carevacations.com, for group tours and cruise vacations. **Flying Wheels Travel** ⊠ 143 W. Bridge St., Box 382, Owatonna, MN 55060 ☎ 507/451-5005 🖶 507/451-1685 ⊕ www.flyingwheelstravel.com.

DISCOUNTS & DEALS

Be a smart shopper and **compare all your options** before making decisions. A plane ticket bought with a promotional coupon from travel clubs, coupon books, and direct-mail offers or purchased on the Internet may not be cheaper than the least expensive fare from a discount ticket agency. And always keep in mind that what you get is just as important as what you save.

DISCOUNT RESERVATIONS

To save money, **look into discount reservations services** with Web sites and toll-free numbers, which use their buying power to get a better price on hotels, airline tickets (⇨ Air Travel), even car rentals. When booking a room, always **call the hotel's local toll-free number** (if one is available) rather than the central reservations number—you'll often get a better price. Always ask about special packages or corporate rates.

🛈 Airline Tickets **Air 4 Less** ☎ 800/AIR4LESS; low-fare specialist.

🛈 Hotel Rooms **Accommodations Express** ☎ 800/444-7666 or 800/277-1064 ⊕ www.accommodationsexpress.com. **Quikbook** ☎ 800/789-9887 ⊕ www.quikbook.com. **RMC Travel** ☎ 800/245-5738 ⊕ www.rmcwebtravel.com. **Turbotrip.com** ☎ 800/473-7829 ⊕ www.turbotrip.com.

PACKAGE DEALS

Don't confuse packages and guided tours. When you buy a package, you travel on your own, just as though you had planned the trip yourself. Fly/drive packages, which combine airfare and car rental, are often a good deal. In cities, ask the local visitors bureau about hotel packages that include tickets to major museum exhibits or other special events.

EATING & DRINKING

Dining in Colorado is generally casual. Dinner hours are typically from 6 PM to 10 PM, but many small-town and rural eateries close by 9 PM. Aside from Mexican cuisine, authentic ethnic food is hard to find outside of the big cities.

The restaurants we list are the cream of the crop in each price category. Properties indicated by an ✕☐ are lodging establishments whose restaurant warrants a special trip.

RESERVATIONS & DRESS

Reservations are always a good idea; we mention them only when they're essential or not accepted. Book as far ahead as you can, and reconfirm as soon as you arrive. (Large parties should always call ahead to check the reservations policy.) We mention dress only when men are required to wear a jacket or a jacket and tie—which is almost never in the Rockies.

SPECIALTIES

Although you can find all types of cuisine in Colorado's major cities and resort towns, don't forget to try native dishes like trout, elk, and buffalo (the latter two have less fat than beef and are just as tasty). Organic fruits and vegetables are also readily available. When in doubt, go for a steak, forever a Rocky Mountain mainstay.

Rocky Mountain Oysters, simply put, are cow testicles (although they've been known to come from bulls, pigs, and even turkeys). They're generally served fried, although you can get 'em lots of different ways. You can find them all over the state, including at Coors Field in downtown Denver, but they're most often served at down-home eateries, county fairs, and the like.

WINE, BEER & SPIRITS

You'll find renowned breweries throughout Colorado, including, of course, the nation's third-largest brewer: Coors. There are dozens of microbreweries in Denver, Colorado Springs, Boulder, and the resort towns. The Colorado Brewers' Festival

takes place every June in Fort Collins. Although the region is not known for its wines, the wineries in the Grand Junction area have been highly touted recently.

ECOTOURISM

Although neither the Bureau of Land Management (BLM) nor the National Park Service has designated any parts of Colorado as endangered ecosystems, many areas are open only to hikers; vehicles, mountain bikes, and horses are banned. It is wise to respect these closures, as well as the old adage—**leave only footprints, take only pictures.** Recycling is taken seriously throughout the Rockies and you will find yourself very unpopular if you litter or fail to recycle your cans and bottles.

All archaeological artifacts, including rock etchings and paintings, are protected by federal law and must be left untouched and undisturbed.

For organized trips in the great outdoors, *see* Sports & the Outdoors.

🛂 **U.S. Bureau of Land Management** ☎ 303/239-3600. **National Park Service** ☎ 800/436-7275.

GAY & LESBIAN TRAVEL

Most resort towns are gay-friendly. Events of note are Gay Ski Week, held in Aspen every January; Boulder's Gay and Lesbian Film Festival in November; and June PrideFest parades in most larger cities. For details about the gay and lesbian scene, consult *Fodor's Gay Guide to the USA* (available in bookstores everywhere).

🛂 Gay- and Lesbian-Friendly Travel Agencies **Different Roads Travel** ✉ 8383 Wilshire Blvd., Suite 520, Beverly Hills, CA 90211 ☎ 323/651-5557 or 800/429-8747 (Ext. 14 for both) 🖷 323/651-3678 ✍ lgernert@tzell.com. **Kennedy Travel** ✉ 130 W. 42nd St., Suite 401, New York, NY 10036 ☎ 212/840-8659 or 800/237-7433 🖷 212/730-2269 ⊕ www.kennedytravel.com. **Now, Voyager** ✉ 4406 18th St., San Francisco, CA 94114 ☎ 415/626-1169 or 800/255-6951 🖷 415/626-8626 ⊕ www.nowvoyager.com. **Skylink Travel and Tour** ✉ 1455 N. Dutton Ave., Suite A, Santa Rosa, CA 95401 ☎ 707/546-9888 or 800/225-5759 🖷 707/636-0951; serving lesbian travelers.

GUIDEBOOKS

Plan well and you won't be sorry. Guidebooks are excellent tools—and you can take them with you.

For hikers, a good guidebook for the region you plan to explore—no matter how well marked the trails are—can be extremely helpful. Most hikers' guidebooks provide fairly detailed trail descriptions, including length and elevation gains and recommended side trips.

🔝 **Hiking Guidebooks** **Adventurous Traveler On-line Bookstore** 🌐 adventuroustraveler.com. **Falcon Books** ☎ 800/725-8303. **The Mountaineers** ✉ 300 3rd Ave. W, Seattle, WA 98119 ☎ 206/284-6310. **Sierra Club Books** ✉ 85 2nd St., 4th fl., San Francisco, CA 94105 ☎ 415/977-5500.

HOLIDAYS

Major national holidays are New Year's Day (Jan. 1); Martin Luther King Day (3rd Mon. in Jan.); Presidents' Day (3rd Mon. in Feb.); Memorial Day (last Mon. in May); Independence Day (July 4); Labor Day (1st Mon. in Sept.); Columbus Day (2nd Mon. in Oct.); Thanksgiving Day (4th Thurs. in Nov.); Christmas Eve and Christmas Day (Dec. 24 and 25); and New Year's Eve (Dec. 31).

INSURANCE

The most useful travel-insurance plan is a comprehensive policy that includes coverage for trip cancellation and interruption, default, trip delay, and medical expenses (with a waiver for preexisting conditions).

Without insurance you'll lose all or most of your money if you cancel your trip, regardless of the reason. Default insurance covers you if your tour operator, airline, or cruise line goes out of business. Trip-delay covers expenses that arise because of bad weather or mechanical delays. Study the fine print when comparing policies.

U.K. residents can buy a travel-insurance policy valid for most vacations taken during the year in which it's purchased (but check preexisting-condition coverage).

Always **buy travel policies directly from the insurance company**; if you buy them from a cruise line, airline, or tour operator that goes out of business you probably won't be covered for the agency or operator's default, a major risk. Before making any purchase, **review your existing health and home-owner's policies** to find what they cover away from home.

🔝 **Travel Insurers** In the U.S.: **Access America** ✉ 6600 W. Broad St., Richmond, VA 23230 ☎ 800/284-8300 🖨 804/673-1491 or 800/346-9265

🌐 www.accessamerica.com. **Travel Guard International** ✉ 1145 Clark St., Stevens Point, WI 54481 ☎ 715/345-0505 or 800/826-1300 🖨 800/955-8785 🌐 www.travelguard.com.

FOR INTERNATIONAL TRAVELERS

For information on customs restrictions, *see* Customs & Duties.

CAR RENTAL

When picking up a rental car, non-U.S. residents need a reservation voucher for any prepaid reservations that were made in the traveler's home country, a passport, a driver's license, and a travel policy that covers each driver.

CAR TRAVEL

Gasoline costs between $1.35 and $1.60 a gallon. Stations are plentiful. Most stay open late (24 hours a day along large highways and in big cities), except in rural areas, where Sunday hours are limited and where you may drive long stretches without a refueling opportunity. Highways are well paved. Interstate highways—limited-access, multilane highways whose numbers are prefixed by "I–"—are the fastest routes. Interstates with three-digit numbers encircle urban areas, which may have other limited-access expressways, freeways, and parkways as well. Tolls may be levied on limited-access highways. So-called U.S. highways and state highways are not necessarily limited-access but may have several lanes.

Along larger highways, roadside stops with rest rooms, fast-food restaurants, and sundries stores are well spaced. State police and tow trucks patrol major highways and lend assistance. If your car breaks down on an interstate, pull onto the shoulder and wait for help, or have your passengers wait while you walk to an emergency phone. If you carry a cell phone, dial *55, noting your location on the small green roadside mileage markers.

Driving in the United States is on the right. Do **obey speed limits** posted along roads and highways. Watch for lower limits in small towns and on back roads. Colorado requires front-seat passengers to wear seat belts. On weekdays between 6 and 10 AM and again between 4 and 7 PM **expect heavy traffic.** To encourage carpooling, some freeways have special lanes for so-called high-occupancy vehicles (HOV)—cars carrying more than one passenger.

Bookstores, gas stations, convenience stores, and rest stops sell maps (about $3) and multiregion road atlases (about $10).

CURRENCY

The dollar is the basic unit of U.S. currency. It has 100 cents. Coins include the copper penny (1¢); the silvery nickel (5¢), dime (10¢), quarter (25¢), and half-dollar (50¢); and the golden $1 coin, replacing a now-rare silver dollar. Bills are denominated $1, $5, $10, $20, $50, and $100, all green (except the new $20 bills) and identical in size; designs vary. The exchange rate at press time was US$.72 per Australian dollar, US$1.68 per British pound, US$.76 per Canadian dollar, and US$1.17 per Euro.

ELECTRICITY

The U.S. standard is AC, 110 volts/60 cycles. Plugs have two flat pins set parallel to each other.

EMERGENCIES

For police, fire, or ambulance, **dial 911** (0 in rural areas).

INSURANCE

Britons and Australians need extra medical coverage when traveling overseas.

⬛ Insurance Information In the U.K.: **Association of British Insurers** ✉ 51 Gresham St., London EC2V 7HQ ☎ 020/7600-3333 🖷 020/7696-8999 ⊕ www.abi.org.uk. In Australia: **Insurance Council of Australia** ✉ Insurance Enquiries and Complaints, Level 3, 56 Pitt St., Sydney, NSW 2000 ☎ 1300/363683 or 02/9251-4456 🖷 02/9251-4453 ⊕ www.iecltd.com.au. In Canada: **RBC Insurance** ✉ 6880 Financial Dr., Mississauga, Ontario L5N 7Y5 ☎ 800/565-3129 🖷 905/813-4704 ⊕ www.rbcinsurance.com. In New Zealand: **Insurance Council of New Zealand** ✉ Level 7, 111–115 Customhouse Quay, Box 474, Wellington ☎ 04/472-5230 🖷 04/473-3011 ⊕ www.icnz.org.nz.

MAIL & SHIPPING

You can buy stamps and aerograms and send letters and parcels in post offices. Stamp-dispensing machines can occasionally be found in airports, bus and train stations, office buildings, drugstores, and the like. You can also deposit mail in the stout, dark blue, steel bins at strategic locations everywhere and in the mail chutes of large buildings; pickup schedules are posted.

For mail sent within the United States, you need a 37¢ stamp for first-class letters weighing up to 1 ounce (23¢ for each additional ounce) and 23¢ for postcards. You pay 80¢ for 1-ounce airmail letters and 70¢ for airmail postcards to most other countries; to Canada and Mexico, you need a 60¢ stamp for a 1-ounce letter and 50¢ for a postcard. An aerogram—a single sheet of lightweight blue paper that folds into its own envelope, stamped for overseas airmail—costs 70¢.

To receive mail on the road, have it sent c/o General Delivery at your destination's main post office (use the correct five-digit ZIP code). You must pick up mail in person within 30 days and show a driver's license or passport.

PASSPORTS & VISAS

When traveling internationally, **carry your passport** even if you don't need one (it's always the best form of I.D.) and **make two photocopies of the data page** (one for someone at home and another for you, carried separately from your passport). If you lose your passport, promptly call the nearest embassy or consulate and the local police.

Visitor visas aren't necessary for Canadian or European Union citizens, or for citizens of Australia who are staying fewer than 90 days.

⬛ Australian Citizens **Passports Australia** ☎ 131-232 ⊕ www.passports.gov.au. **United States Consulate General** ✉ MLC Centre, Level 59, 19–29 Martin Pl., Sydney, NSW 2000 ☎ 02/9373-9200, 1902/941-641 fee-based visa-inquiry line ⊕ usembassy-australia.state.gov/sydney.

⬛ Canadian Citizens **Passport Office** ✉ to mail in applications: 200 Promenade du Portage, Hull, Québec J8X 4B7 ☎ 819/994-3500 or 800/567-6868 ⊕ www.ppt.gc.ca.

⬛ New Zealand Citizens **New Zealand Passports Office** ✉ For applications and information, Level 3, Boulcott House, 47 Boulcott St., Wellington ☎ 0800/22-5050 or 04/474-8100 ⊕ www.passports.govt.nz. **Embassy of the United States** ✉ 29 Fitzherbert Terr., Thorndon, Wellington ☎ 04/462-6000 ⊕ usembassy.org.nz. **U.S. Consulate General** ✉ Citibank Bldg., 3rd fl., 23 Customs St. E, Auckland ☎ 09/303-2724 ⊕ usembassy.org.nz.

⬛ U.K. Citizens **U.K. Passport Service** ☎ 0870/521-0410 ⊕ www.passport.gov.uk. **American Consulate General** ✉ Queen's House, 14 Queen St.,

Belfast, Northern Ireland BT1 6EQ ☎ 028/9032-8239 🖷 028/9024-8482 ⊕ www.usembassy.org.uk. **American Embassy** ✉ for visa and immigration information (enclose an SASE), Consular Information Unit, 24 Grosvenor Sq., London W1 1AE ✉ to submit an application via mail, Visa Branch, 5 Upper Grosvenor St., London W1A 2JB ☎ 09068/200-290 recorded visa information or 09055/444-546 operator service, both with per-minute charges, 0207/499-9000 main switchboard ⊕ www.usembassy.org.uk.

TELEPHONES

All U.S. telephone numbers consist of a three-digit area code and a seven-digit local number. Within many local calling areas, you dial only the seven-digit number. Within some area codes, you must dial "1" first for calls outside the local area. To call between area-code regions, dial "1" then all 10 digits; the same goes for calls to numbers prefixed by "800," "888," "866," and "877"—all toll free. For calls to numbers preceded by "900" you must pay—usually dearly.

For international calls, dial "011" followed by the country code and the local number. For help, dial "0" and ask for an overseas operator. The country code is 61 for Australia, 64 for New Zealand, 44 for the United Kingdom. Calling Canada is the same as calling within the United States. Most local phone books list country codes and U.S. area codes. The country code for the United States is 1.

For operator assistance, dial "0." To obtain someone's phone number within another area code, call directory assistance at (area code) 555-1212. For local numbers, dial 411 (free at public phones). To have the person you're calling foot the bill, phone collect; dial "0" instead of "1" before the 10-digit number.

At pay phones, instructions often are posted. Usually you insert coins in a slot (usually 25¢–50¢ for local calls) and wait for a steady tone before dialing. When you call long-distance, the operator tells you how much to insert; prepaid phone cards, widely available in various denominations, are easier. Call the number on the back, punch in the card's personal identification number when prompted, then dial your number.

LODGING

Accommodations in Colorado vary from the very posh ski resorts in Vail and Aspen to basic chain hotels and independent motels. Dude and guest ranches often require a one-week stay, and the cost is all-inclusive. Bed-and-breakfasts can be found throughout the state.

The lodgings we list are the cream of the crop in each price category. We always list the facilities that are available—but we don't specify whether they cost extra: When pricing accommodations, always ask what's included and what costs extra. Assume that hotels operate on the European Plan (EP, with no meals) unless we specify that they use either the Continental Plan (CP, with a Continental breakfast), Breakfast Plan (BP, with a full breakfast), or the Modified American Plan (MAP, with breakfast and dinner) or are all-inclusive (including all meals and most activities). Properties indicated by an ✕🖃 are lodging establishments whose restaurant warrants a special trip.

Properties are assigned price categories based on the range between their least and most expensive standard double rooms at high season (excluding holidays). Lodging taxes vary throughout the state.

🄵 General Information **Colorado Hotel and Lodging Association** ✉ 999 18th St., Suite 1240, Denver, CO 80202 ☎ 303/297-8335 ⊕ www.coloradolodging.com.

APARTMENT & VILLA RENTALS

If you want a home base that's roomy enough for a family and comes with cooking facilities, **consider a furnished rental.** These can save you money, especially if you're traveling with a group. Home-exchange directories sometimes list rentals as well as exchanges.

Rental accommodations are quite popular in Colorado's ski resorts and mountain towns. Condominiums and luxurious vacation homes dominate the Vail Valley and other ski-oriented areas, but there are scads of cabins in smaller, summer-oriented towns in the Rockies and the Western Slope.

🄵 International Agents **Hideaways International** ✉ 767 Islington St., Portsmouth, NH 03802 ☎ 603/430-4433 or 800/843-4433 🖷 603/430-4444 ⊕ www.hideaways.com, membership $129.

⊞ Local Agents **Colorado Mountain Cabins & Vacation Home Rentals** ⊠ 122 S. 16th St., Colorado Springs, CO 80904 ☎ 719/636–5147 or 866/425–4974 ⊕ www.coloradomountaincabins.com. **Colorado Central Reservations** ⊠ 100-788 Harbourside Dr., North Vancouver, British Columbia V7P 3R7 ☎ 888/256-8957 ⊕ colorado.rezrez.com.

⊞ Rental Listings **Colorado Directory** ⊠ 5101 Pennsylvania Ave., Boulder, CO 80303 ☎ 303/499–9343 or 888/222-4641 ⊕ www.coloradodirectory.com.

BED & BREAKFASTS

Charm is the long suit of these establishments, which generally occupy a restored older building with some historical or architectural significance. They're generally small, with fewer than 20 rooms. Breakfast is usually included in the rates. Bed and Breakfast Innkeepers of Colorado prints a free annual directory of its members.

⊞ Bed and Breakfast Innkeepers of Colorado ⊠ P.O. Box 38416, Colorado Springs, CO 80937 ☎ 800/265–7696 ⊕ www.innsofcolorado.org.

CAMPING

Camping is invigorating and inexpensive. Colorado is full of state and national parks and forests with sites that range from rustic (pit toilets and cold running water), to campgrounds with hot showers, paved trailer pads that can accommodate even jumbo RVs, and full hook-ups. Fees vary, from $6 to $10 a night for tents and up to $21 for RVs, but are usually waived once the water is turned off for the winter.

Sometimes site reservations are accepted (early birds reserve up to a year in advance); more often, they're not. Campers who prefer a more remote setting may camp in the backcountry; it's free, but you might need a permit, available from park visitor centers and ranger stations. If you're visiting in summer, **plan well ahead.**

The facilities and amenities at privately operated campgrounds are usually more extensive (swimming pools are common), reservations are more widely accepted, and nightly fees are higher: $7 and up for tents, $23 for RVs.

⊞ Colorado State Parks ⊕ www.coloradoparks. org. *The National Parks: Camping Guide* ⊠ Superintendent of Documents, U.S. Government Printing Office, Washington, DC 20402 ☎ 800/365-2267; $3.50.

GUEST RANCHES

If the thought of sitting around a campfire after a hard day on the range is your idea of a vacation, consider playing dude on a guest ranch. Wilderness-rimmed working ranches accept guests and encourage them to pitch in with chores and other ranch activities; you even may be able to participate in a cattle roundup. Luxurious resorts on the fringes of small cities offer swimming pools, tennis courts, and a lively roster of horse-related activities such as breakfast rides, moonlight rides, and all-day trail rides. Rafting, fishing, tubing, and other activities are usually available at both types of ranches. In winter, cross-country skiing and snowshoeing keep you busy. Lodgings can run the gamut from charmingly rustic cabins to the kind of deluxe quarters you expect at a first-class hotel. Meals may be gourmet or plain but hearty. Many ranches offer packages and children's and off-season rates. *See* Dude Ranches *in* Sports & the Outdoors.

⊞ Colorado Dude/Guest Ranch Association ⊕ Box 2120, Granby, CO 80446 ☎ 970/887-3128. **Old West Dude Ranch Vacations** ⊠ c/o American Wilderness Experience, 10055 Westmoor Dr., #215, Westminster, CO 80021 ☎ 800/444-3833.

HOME EXCHANGES

If you would like to exchange your home for someone else's, **join a home-exchange organization,** which will send you its updated listings of available exchanges for a year and will include your own listing in at least one of them. It's up to you to make specific arrangements.

⊞ Exchange Clubs **HomeLink International** ⊕ Box 47747, Tampa, FL 33647 ☎ 813/975-9825 or 800/638-3841 ⊕ 813/910-8144 ⊕ www.homelink. org; $110 yearly for a listing, on-line access, and catalog; $40 without catalog. **Intervac U.S.** ⊠ 30 Corte San Fernando, Tiburon, CA 94920 ☎ 800/756-4663 ⊕ 415/435-7440 ⊕ www.intervacus.com; $105 yearly for a listing, on-line access, and a catalog; $50 without catalog.

HOSTELS

Hostelling through Colorado is an inexpensive way to see the vast mountains, especially since many hostels are in resort towns and near national parks. Colorado has 10 hostels in such prime locations as Crested Butte, Breckenridge, and Glenwood Springs.

No matter what your age, you can **save on lodging costs by staying at hostels.** In some 4,500 locations in more than 70 countries around the world, Hostelling International (HI), the umbrella group for a number of national youth-hostel associations, offers single-sex, dorm-style beds and, at many hostels, rooms for couples and family accommodations. Membership in any HI national hostel association, open to travelers of all ages, allows you to stay in HI-affiliated hostels at member rates; one-year membership is about $28 for adults (C$35 for a two-year minimum membership in Canada, £13.50 in the U.K., A$52 in Australia, and NZ$40 in New Zealand); hostels charge $10–$30 per night. Members have priority if the hostel is full; they're also eligible for discounts around the world, even on rail and bus travel in some countries.

HI is also an especially helpful organization for road cyclists.

🏢 Organizations **Hostelling International–USA** ✉ 8401 Colesville Rd., Suite 600, Silver Spring, MD 20910 ☎ 301/495-1240 📠 301/495-6697 ⊕ www.hiayh.org. **Hostelling International–Canada** ✉ 400-205 Catherine St., Ottawa, Ontario K2P 1C3 ☎ 613/237-7884 or 800/663-5777 📠 613/237-7868 ⊕ www.hihostels.ca. **YHA England and Wales** ✉ Trevelyan House, Dimple Rd., Matlock, Derbyshire DE4 3YH ☎ 0870/870-8808 📠 0870/770-6127 ⊕ www.yha.org.uk. **YHA Australia** ✉ 422 Kent St., Sydney, NSW 2001 ☎ 02/9261-1111 📠 02/9261-1969 ⊕ www.yha.com.au. **YHA New Zealand** ✉ Level 3, 193 Cashel St., Box 436, Christchurch ☎ 03/379-9970 or 0800/278-299 📠 03/365-4476 ⊕ www.yha.org.nz.

HOTELS

Most hotels in Denver and Colorado Springs cater to business travelers, with such facilities as restaurants, cocktail lounges, swimming pools, exercise equipment, and meeting rooms. Room rates usually reflect the range of amenities offered. Most cities also have inexpensive hotels that are clean and comfortable but have fewer facilities. A new accommodations trend is the all-suite hotel, which gives you more room for the money; examples include Courtyard by Marriott and Embassy Suites. In resort towns, hotels are decidedly more deluxe, with every imaginable amenity in every imaginable price range; rural areas generally offer simple, sometimes rustic accommodations.

Many properties offer special weekend rates, sometimes up to 50% off regular prices. However, these deals are usually not extended during summer months, when hotels are normally full. The same discounts are often available at resort town hotels.

All hotels listed have private baths unless otherwise noted.

📞 Toll-Free Numbers **Best Western** ☎ 800/528-1234 ⊕ www.bestwestern.com. **Choice** ☎ 800/424-6423 ⊕ www.choicehotels.com. **Comfort Inn** ☎ 800/424-6423 ⊕ www.choicehotels.com. **Days Inn** ☎ 800/325-2525 ⊕ www.daysinn.com. **Doubletree Hotels** ☎ 800/222-8733 ⊕ www.doubletree.com. **Embassy Suites** ☎ 800/362-2779 ⊕ www.embassysuites.com. **Fairfield Inn** ☎ 800/228-2800 ⊕ www.marriott.com. **Hilton** ☎ 800/445-8667 ⊕ www.hilton.com. **Holiday Inn** ☎ 800/465-4329 ⊕ www.sixcontinentshotels.com. **Howard Johnson** ☎ 800/446-4656 ⊕ www.hojo.com. **Hyatt Hotels & Resorts** ☎ 800/233-1234 ⊕ www.hyatt.com. **La Quinta** ☎ 800/531-5900 ⊕ www.laquinta.com. **Marriott** ☎ 800/228-9290 ⊕ www.marriott.com. **Quality Inn** ☎ 800/424-6423 ⊕ www.choicehotels.com. **Radisson** ☎ 800/333-3333 ⊕ www.radisson.com. **Ramada** ☎ 800/228-2828, 800/854-7854 international reservations ⊕ www.ramada.com or www.ramadahotels.com. **Ritz-Carlton** ☎ 800/241-3333 ⊕ www.ritzcarlton.com. **Sheraton** ☎ 800/325-3535 ⊕ www.starwood.com/sheraton. **Sleep Inn** ☎ 800/424-6423 ⊕ www.choicehotels.com. **Westin Hotels & Resorts** ☎ 800/228-3000 ⊕ www.starwood.com/westin. **Wyndham Hotels & Resorts** ☎ 800/822-4200 ⊕ www.wyndham.com.

MOTELS

The once-familiar roadside motel is fast disappearing from the American landscape. In its place are chain-run motor inns at highway intersections and in rural areas off the beaten path. Some of these establishments offer basic facilities; others provide restaurants, swimming pools, and other amenities.

🏢 Motel Chains **Motel 6** ☎ 800/466-8356. **Quality Inn** ☎ 800/228-5151. **Rodeway Inns** ☎ 800/228-2000. **Shilo Inn** ☎ 800/222-2244. **Super 8 Motels** ☎ 800/800-8000. **Travelodge** ☎ 800/578-7878.

RESORTS

Ski towns throughout Colorado are home to dozens of resorts in all price ranges; the activities lacking at any individual property can usually be found in the town itself—in summer as well as winter. Off the slopes, there are both wonderful rustic and luxurious resorts, particularly in out-of-the-way spots near Rocky Mountain National Park and other alpine areas.

MEDIA

NEWSPAPERS & MAGAZINES

The state's largest daily newspapers are the *Denver Post,* the *Rocky Mountain News* (also Denver), and the *Colorado Springs Gazette.* Denver's free alternative weekly, *Westword,* is also widely read for its investigative journalism and entertainment content, and such monthly and semi-monthly titles as *5280* (Denver), *Mountain Gazette* (Frisco), and *Modern Drunkard* (Denver) are worth a read.

RADIO & TELEVISION

Although Colorado lacks purely local TV stations, most cities have network affiliates. In Denver, **ABC** is on channel 7, **CBS** is on channel 4, **FOX** is on channel 31 (or 13 on cable), and **NBC** is on channel 9. The state's largest radio station is **ABC,** at 850 AM. **National Public Radio** is on 1340 AM and 90.1 FM in Denver.

MONEY MATTERS

First-class hotel rooms in Denver cost from $75 to $175 a night, although some "value" rooms go for $40–$60, and, as elsewhere in the United States, rooms in budget chain motels go for around $40 nightly. Weekend packages, offered by most city hotels, cut prices up to 50% at the top establishments (but may not be available in winter or summer). As a rule, costs outside cities are lower, except in the deluxe resorts. In cities and rural areas, a cup of coffee costs between 50¢ and $1, the price for a hamburger runs between $3 and $5, and a beer at a bar generally is between $1.50 and $3; expect to pay double in resort towns like Aspen and Vail. Prices throughout this guide are given for adults. Substantially reduced fees are almost always available for children, students, and senior citizens. For information on taxes, *see* Taxes.

CREDIT CARDS

🔲 Reporting Lost Cards **American Express** ☎ 800/441-0519. **Diners Club** ☎ 800/234-6377. **Discover** ☎ 800/347-2683. **MasterCard** ☎ 800/622-7747. **Visa** ☎ 800/847-2911.

NATIONAL PARKS

Look into discount passes to save money on park entrance fees. For $50, the National Parks Pass admits you (and any passengers in your private vehicle) to all national parks, monuments, and recreation areas, as well as other sites run by the National Park Service, for a year. (In parks that charge per person, the pass admits you, your spouse and children, and your parents, when you arrive together.) Camping and parking are extra. The $15 Golden Eagle Pass, a hologram you affix to your National Parks Pass, functions as an upgrade, granting entry to all sites run by the NPS, the U.S. Fish and Wildlife Service, the U.S. Forest Service, and the Bureau of Land Management. The upgrade, which expires with the parks pass, is sold by most national-park, Fish-and-Wildlife, and BLM fee stations. A percentage of the proceeds from pass sales funds National Parks projects.

Both the Golden Age Passport ($10), for U.S. citizens or permanent residents who are 62 and older, and the Golden Access Passport (free), for those with disabilities, entitle holders (and any passengers in their private vehicles) to lifetime free entry to all national parks, plus 50% off fees for the use of many park facilities and services. (The discount doesn't always apply to companions.) To obtain them, you must show proof of age and of U.S. citizenship or permanent residency—such as a U.S. passport, driver's license, or birth certificate—and, if requesting Golden Access, proof of disability. The Golden Age and Golden Access passes are available only at NPS-run sites that charge an entrance fee. The National Parks Pass is also available by mail and via the Internet.

🔲 **National Park Foundation** ✉ 11 Dupont Circle NW, 6th fl., Washington, DC 20036 ☎ 202/238-4200 ⊕ www.nationalparks.org. **National Park Service** ✉ National Park Service/Department of the Interior, 1849 C St. NW, Washington, DC 20240 ☎ 202/208-6843 ⊕ www.nps.gov. **National Parks Conservation Association** ✉ 1300 19th St. NW, Suite 300, Washington, DC 20036 ☎ 202/223-6722 ⊕ www.npca.org.

🔲 Passes by Mail and On-Line **National Park Foundation** ⊕ www.nationalparks.org. **National Parks Pass** ✍ Box 34108, Washington, DC 20043 ☎ 888/467-2757 ⊕ www.nationalparks.org; check or money order payable to the National Park Service must include $3.95 for shipping and handling; or call for passes.

PACKING

For the most part, informality reigns in the Centennial State; jeans, sport shirts, and T-shirts fit in almost everywhere, for both men and women. The few restaurants and performing-arts events where dressier outfits are required, usually in resorts and larger cities, are the exception.

If you plan to spend much time outdoors, and certainly if you go in winter, **choose clothing appropriate for cold and wet weather.** Cotton clothing, including denim—although fine on warm, dry days—can be uncomfortable when it gets wet and when the weather's cold. A better choice is clothing made of wool or any of a number of new synthetics that provide warmth without bulk and maintain their insulating properties when wet.

In summer, you'll probably want to wear shorts during the day. Because early morning and night can be cold, and high passes windy, pack a sweater and a light jacket, and perhaps a wool cap and gloves. Try layering—a T-shirt under another shirt under a jacket—and peel off layers as you go. For walks and hikes, you'll need sturdy footwear. Boots should have thick soles and plenty of ankle support; if your shoes are new and you plan to do a lot of hiking, break them in at home. Bring a day pack for short hikes, along with a canteen or water bottle, and don't forget rain gear, a hat, sunscreen, and insect repellent.

In winter, prepare for subzero temperatures with good boots, warm socks and liners, long johns, a well-insulated jacket, and a warm hat and mittens. Dress in layers so you can add or remove clothes as the temperature fluctuates.

If you attend dances and other events at Native American reservations, dress conservatively—skirts or long pants for women, long pants for men—or you may be asked to leave.

When traveling to mountain areas, remember that sunglasses and a sun hat are essential at high altitudes; the thinner atmosphere requires sunscreen with a greater SPF than you might need at lower elevations.

In your carry-on luggage, **pack an extra pair of eyeglasses or contact lenses and enough of any medication** you take to last a few days longer than the entire trip. In luggage to be checked, **never pack prescription drugs, valuables, or undeveloped film.** And don't forget to carry with you the addresses of offices that handle refunds of lost traveler's checks. Check *Fodor's How to Pack* (available at on-line retailers and bookstores everywhere) for more tips.

To avoid customs and security delays, carry medications in their original packaging. Don't pack any sharp objects in your carry-on luggage, including knives of any size or material, scissors, and corkscrews, or anything else that might arouse suspicion.

To avoid having your checked luggage chosen for hand inspection, don't cram bags full. The U.S. Transportation Security Administration suggests packing shoes on top and placing personal items you don't want touched in clear plastic bags.

CHECKING LUGGAGE

You're allowed to carry aboard one bag and one personal article, such as a purse or laptop computer. Make sure what you carry on fits under your seat or in the overhead bin. Get to the gate early, so you can board as soon as possible, before the overhead bins fill up.

Baggage allowances vary by carrier, destination, and ticket class. On international flights, you're usually allowed to check two bags weighing up to 70 pounds (32 kilograms) each, although a few airlines allow checked bags of up to 88 pounds (40 kilograms) in first class. Some international carriers don't allow more than 66 pounds (30 kilograms) per bag in business class and 44 pounds (20 kilograms) in economy. On domestic flights, the limit may be 50 pounds (23 kilograms) per bag. Most airlines won't accept bags that weigh more than 100 pounds (45 kilograms) on domestic or international flights. Check baggage restrictions with your carrier before you pack.

Airline liability for baggage is limited to $2,500 per person on flights within the United States. On international flights it amounts to $9.07 per pound or $20 per kilogram for checked baggage (roughly $640 per 70-pound bag) and $400 per passenger for unchecked baggage. You can buy additional coverage at check-in for about $10 per $1,000 of coverage, but it often excludes a rather extensive list of items, shown on your airline ticket.

Before departure, **itemize your bags' contents** and their worth, and label the bags with your name, address, and phone number. (If you use your home address, cover it so potential thieves can't see it readily.) Include a label inside each bag and **pack a copy of your itinerary.** At check-in, **make sure each bag is correctly tagged** with the destination airport's three-letter code. Because some checked bags will be opened for hand inspection, the U.S. Transportation Security Administration (TSA) recommends that you leave luggage unlocked or use the plastic locks offered at check-in. TSA screeners place an inspection notice inside searched bags, which are re-sealed with a special lock.

If your bag has been searched and contents are missing or damaged, file a claim with the TSA Consumer Response Center as soon as possible. If your bags arrive damaged or fail to arrive at all, file a written report with the airline before leaving the airport.

🔢 Complaints **U.S. Transportation Security Administration Consumer Response Center** ☎ 866/289-9673 ⊕ www.tsa.gov.

SAFETY

Regardless of the outdoor activity or your level of skill, safety must come first. Remember: **know your limits!**

Many trails are at high altitudes, where oxygen is scarce. They're also frequently desolate. Hikers and bikers should **carry emergency supplies** in their backpacks. Proper equipment includes a flashlight, a compass, waterproof matches, a first-aid kit, a knife, and a light plastic tarp for shelter. Backcountry skiers should add a repair kit, a blanket, an avalanche beacon, and a lightweight shovel to their lists. Always **bring extra food and a canteen of water** as dehydration is a common occurrence at high altitudes. **Never drink from streams or lakes,** unless you boil the water first or purify it with tablets. Giardia, an intestinal parasite, may be present.

Always **check the condition of roads and trails, and get the latest weather reports** before setting out. In summer, take precautions against heat stroke or exhaustion by resting frequently in shaded areas; in winter, take precautions against hypothermia by layering clothing. Ultimately, proper planning, common sense, and good physical conditioning are the strongest guards against the elements.

ALTITUDE

You may feel dizzy and weak and find yourself breathing heavily—signs that the thin mountain air isn't giving you your accustomed dose of oxygen. Take it easy and **rest often for a few days until you're acclimatized.** Throughout your stay, drink plenty of water and watch your alcohol consumption. If you experience severe headaches and nausea, see a doctor. It is easy—especially in a state where highways climb to 12,000 feet and higher—to go too high too fast. The remedy for altitude-related discomfort is to go down quickly, into heavier air. Other altitude-related problems include dehydration and overexposure to the sun due to the thin air.

FLASH FLOODS

Flash floods can strike at any time and any place with little or no warning. The danger in mountainous terrain is heightened when distant rains are channeled into gullies and ravines, turning a quiet streamside campsite or wash into a rampaging torrent in seconds; similarly, desert terrain can become dangerous when heavy rains fall on land that is unable to absorb the water and thus floods quickly. Check weather reports before heading into the backcountry and be prepared to head for higher ground if the weather turns severe.

WILD ANIMALS

One of the most wonderful parts of the Rockies is the abundant wildlife. And although a herd of grazing elk or a bighorn sheep high on a hillside is most certainly a Kodak moment, an encounter with a bear or mountain lion is not. To avoid such an unpleasant situation while hiking, **make plenty of noise, keep dogs on a leash and small children between adults.** While camping, be sure to store all food, utensils, and clothing with food odors far away from your tent, preferably high in a tree (also far from your tent). If you do come across a bear or big cat, **do not run.** For bears, back away quietly; for lions, make yourself look as big as possible. In either case, be prepared to fend off the animal with loud noises, rocks, sticks, etc. And, like the saying goes, do not feed the bears—or any wild animals, whether they're dangerous or not.

When in any park, **give all animals their space.** If you want to take a photograph, use a long lens rather than a long sneak to approach closely. This is particularly important for winter visitors. Approaching an animal can cause stress and affect its ability to survive the sometimes brutal climate. In all cases remember that the animals have the right-of-way; this is their home, you are the visitor.

SENIOR-CITIZEN TRAVEL

To qualify for age-related discounts, **mention your senior-citizen status up front** when booking hotel reservations (not when checking out) and before you're seated in restaurants (not when paying the bill). Be sure to have identification on hand. When renting a car, ask about promotional car-rental discounts, which can be cheaper than senior-citizen rates. Also, many attractions offer lower admission prices for seniors.
▪ Educational Programs **Elderhostel** ⊠ 11 Ave. de Lafayette, Boston, MA 02111-1746 ☎ 877/426-8056, 978/323-4141 international callers, 877/426-2167 TTY ♿ 877/426-2166 ⊕ www.elderhostel.org.

SHOPPING

Although there are plenty of modern shopping malls across Colorado, especially in metro Denver, a trip through the state is an opportunity to buy authentic memorabilia and clothing—choose from cowboy boots, cowboy hats, bolero ties, and the like. It's also a great place to find Native American crafts. Small artisan colonies often neighbor ritzy resorts. These enclaves of creative souls produce some of the finest handcrafted wares anywhere; look for galleries and boutiques that showcase locals' work.

KEY DESTINATIONS

For Western goods such as saddles and cowboy hats, Durango can't be beat. Manitou Springs (just west of Colorado Springs) has an amazing array of galleries and artists' studios. The Pearl Street Mall in Boulder is loaded with bookstores and interesting independent retailers and boutiques. Aspen is the place for the latest in Western fashion and art. For everything else, Denver has it all, especially downtown and in and around the Cherry Creek Mall and the Park Meadows area (on the southern side of the metro area).

SMART SOUVENIRS

A great Colorado souvenir is anything carved from native aspen wood, such as a vase or a picture frame. You can't beat a photograph or poster of Rocky Mountain National Park, available throughout the park and shops in the gateway town of Estes Park. Beer-lovers should seek out a six-pack or souvenir from a microbrewery.

SPORTS & THE OUTDOORS

The Colorado Rockies is one of America's greatest playgrounds, and many area residents make exercise a high priority. Within an hour of leaving their homes and offices, Rockies jocks can do their thing in the midst of exquisite scenery—not boxed in at a gym watching wall-mounted televisions.

ADVENTURE TRIP OUTFITTERS

Many trip organizers specialize in one type of activity; however, a few companies guide a variety of active trips. (In some cases, these larger companies also act as a clearinghouse or agent for smaller outfitters.) Be sure to sign on with a reliable outfitter; getting stuck with a shoddy operator can be disappointing, uncomfortable, and even dangerous. Some sports—white-water rafting and mountaineering, for example—have organizations that license or certify guides, and you should be sure that the guide you're with is properly accredited.
▪ Outfitter Listings **America Outdoors** ⊘ Box 10847, Knoxville, TN 37939 ☎ 865/558-3595 ⊕ www.americaoutdoors.org. **Colorado Outfitters Association** ⊘ Box 1949, Rifle, CO 81650 ☎ 970/876-0543 ⊕ www.coloradooutfitters.org.
▪ Outfitters **Sierra Club Outings** ⊠ 85 2nd St., San Francisco, CA 94105 ☎ 415/977-5500 ⊕ www.sierraclub.org. **The World Outdoors** ⊠ 2840 Wilderness Pl. F, Boulder, CO 80301 ☎ 303/413-0938 or 800/488-8483 ⊕ www.theworldoutdoors.com.

BIKING

High, rugged country puts a premium on fitness. Even if you can ride 40 mi at home without breaking a sweat, you might find yourself struggling terribly on steep climbs and in elevations exceeding 10,000 feet. If you have an extended tour in mind, **acclimate yourself to the altitude and terrain** by arriving a couple of days early. Pretrip conditioning is likely to make your trip more enjoyable.

On tours where the elevation may vary 4,000 feet or more, the climate can change dramatically. Although the valleys may be scorching, high-mountain passes may still be lined with snow in summer. Pack clothing accordingly. (Bicycle racers often stuff newspaper inside their jerseys when descending from high passes to shield themselves from the chill.) Although you shouldn't have much problem renting a bike (trip organizers can usually arrange rentals), it's a good idea to bring your own pair of sturdy, stiff-bottom cycling shoes to make riding easier, and your own helmet. Some experienced riders bring not only their own shoes but their pedals if they use an interlocking shoe-and-pedal system. If you bring your own bike, be prepared to spend as much as $160 in special luggage handling. Summer and early fall are the best times to plan a trip; at other times, snow and ice may still obstruct high-terrain roads and trails.

Guided bike trips generally range in price between $80 and $150 per day, depending on lodging and meals. The Adventure Cycling Association is perhaps the best general source of information on biking in the Rockies, and can provide detailed maps and information on trip organizers. They also guide trips stretching along the Continental Divide. Hostelling-International (HI; ⇨ Lodging) is also a good connection for cycling tours. When you're in a ski resort town, check if lifts service mountain bikes. Remember that biking is not permitted in National Wilderness areas.

For serious road riders, especially would-be racers, the Carpenter/Phinney Bike Camps are conducted in Summit County and near Boulder by 1984 Olympic road champion Connie Carpenter and her husband, Davis Phinney, also an Olympic medalist and professional racer. One-week sessions focus on riding technique, training methods, and bicycle maintenance. 🏛 **Adventure Cycling Association** 🖃 Box 8308, Missoula, MT 59807 ☎ 406/721-1776 or 800/755-2453 ⊕ www.adventurecycling.org. **Carpenter/ Phinney Bike Camps** ☎ 303/442-2371 ⊕ www. bikecamp.com. **Colorado Plateau Mountain Bike Trail Association** ✉ Box 4602, Grand Junction 81502 ☎ 970/249-8055 ⊕ www.copmoba.com. **Timberline Adventures** ✉ 7975 E. Harvard, Suite J, Denver, CO 80231 ☎ 303/759-3804 or 800/417-2453 ⊕ www.timbertours.com.

DUDE RANCHES

Most dude ranches don't require previous experience with horses, although a few working ranches reserve weeks in spring and fall—when the chore of moving cattle is more intensive than in summer—for experienced riders. No special equipment is necessary, although if you plan to do much fishing, you're best off bringing your own tackle (some ranches have tackle to loan or rent). Be sure to **check with the ranch for a list of items you might be expected to bring.** If you plan to do much riding, a couple of pairs of sturdy pants, boots, a wide-brimmed hat to shield you from the sun, and outerwear that protects from rain and cold should be packed. Expect to spend at least $125 per day. Depending on the activities you engage in and the nature of your accommodations, the price can exceed $250 a day. *See* Guest Ranches *in* Lodging, as well.

FISHING

Field and Stream magazine is a leading source of information on fishing travel, technique, and equipment. For lists of guides to various rivers and lakes, contact the Colorado Tourism Office.

Fishing licenses, available at tackle shops and a variety of stores, are required in all Rocky Mountain states. The fishing season is year-round, though seasons for particular species vary. A few streams are considered "private," in that they are stocked by a local club; other rivers are fly-fishing or catch-and-release only, so be sure you **know the rules before making your first cast.** Tribal fishing licences are necessary on reservation land.

Rocky Mountain water can be cold, especially at higher elevations and in spring and fall (and winter, of course). You'd do well to **bring waterproof waders** or buy them when you arrive in the region. Outfitters and some tackle shops rent equipment, but you're best off bringing your own gear. Lures are another story, though: whether you plan to fish with flies or other lures, local tackle shops can usually give you a pretty good idea of what works best in a particular region, and you can buy accordingly.

In the mid-1990s, whirling disease—a parasitic infection that afflicts trout—began to reduce fish populations in some Rocky Mountain streams dramatically.

Efforts to curb the spread of the disease have met with some success, but some waters are still suffering from a diminished fish population.

A guide will cost about $250 per day and can be shared by two anglers if they are fishing from a boat, and possibly by three if they are wading. Lunch will probably be included and flies might be, although there may be an extra $15–$20 charge for these.

Orvis Fly Fishing Schools runs one of the most respected fishing instructional programs in the country and endorses other instructional programs. Summertime 2½-day programs take place in Evergreen, about 30 mi west of Denver.
🔲 Information and Licenses **Colorado Division of Wildlife** ✉ 6060 Broadway, Denver, CO 80216 ☎ 303/297-1192 ⊕ www.wildlife.state.co.us.
🔲 Instruction **Orvis Fly Fishing Schools** ☎ 800/239-2074 Ext. 784 ⊕ www.orvis.com. **Telluride Outside** ✉ 1982 W. Rte. 145, Box 685, Telluride, CO 81435 ☎ 970/728-3895 or 800/831-6230 ⊕ www.tellurideoutside.com.

GROUP TRIPS

Group sizes for organized trips vary considerably, depending on the organizer and the activity. Often, if you are planning a trip with a large group, trip organizers or outfitters will offer discounts of 10% and more, and are willing to customize trips. For example, if you're with a group interested in photography or in wildlife, trip organizers have been known to get professional photographers or naturalists to join the group. Recreating as a group gives you leverage with the organizer, and you should use it.

One way to travel with a group is to join an organization before going. Conservation-minded travelers might want to contact the Sierra Club, a nonprofit organization, which offers both vacation and work trips. Hiking trails tend to be maintained by volunteers (this is more often done by local hiking clubs). Park or forest rangers are the best resource for information about groups involved in this sort of work.

Individuals or groups wanting to test their mettle can learn wilderness skills through "outdoor schools."
🔲 **Boulder Outdoor Survival School** 🗍 Box 1590, Boulder, CO 80305 ☎ 303/444-9779 or 800/335-7404 ⊕ www.boss-inc.com. **Sierra Club** ✉ 85 2nd St., San Francisco, CA 94105 ☎ 415/977-5500 ⊕ www.sierraclub.org.

HIKING

Backpacker magazine (Rodale Press) is the leading national magazine that focuses on hiking and backpacking. Organized-trip costs can be as little as $30 a day. *See* Guidebooks for guidebook sources.
🔲 **American Hiking Society** 🗍 Box 20160, Washington, DC 20041 ☎ 301/565-6704 ⊕ www.americanhiking.org.

KAYAKING

The streams and rivers of the Rockies tend to be better suited to kayaking than canoeing. Steep mountains and narrow canyons usually mean fast-flowing water in which the maneuverability of kayaks is a great asset. A means of transport for less experienced paddlers is the inflatable kayak (it's easier to navigate and it bounces off the rocks). The best rivers for kayaking are in southern Colorado. Dvorak Expeditions (⇨ Rafting) leads trips on the rivers of southwestern Colorado and conducts clinics, including certification courses, for kayakers of all abilities.

To minimize environmental impact and ensure a sense of wilderness privacy (riverside campgrounds are often limited to one party per night), a reservation policy is used for many rivers of the West. Often, the reserved times—many of the *prime* times—are prebooked by licensed outfitters, limiting your possibilities if you're planning a self-guided trip. For those rivers with restricted-use policies, it's best to reserve through a guide company several months or more in advance. Also, try to be flexible about when and where to go; you might find that the time you want to go is unavailable, or you may find yourself closed out altogether from your river of choice. If you insist on running a specific river at a specific time, your best bet is to sign on with a guided trip (which will cost at least $100 a day).

Outfitters provide life jackets and, if necessary, paddles and helmets; they often throw in waterproof containers for cameras, clothing, and sleeping bags. Bring bug repellent as well as a good hat, sunblock, and warm clothing for overnight trips. The sun on a river can be intense, but once it disappears behind canyon walls, the temperature can drop 30°F or more. The best footwear is either water-resistant sandals or old sneakers.

MAPS

If you plan to go where trails might not be well marked or maintained, you'll need maps and a compass. Topographical maps are sold in well-equipped outdoor stores (REI and Eastern Mountain Sports, for example). Maps in several scales are available from the U.S. Geological Survey (USGS). Request a free index and catalog, from which you can order the maps you need. Many local camping, fishing, and hunting stores carry USGS and other detailed maps of their surrounding region. The U.S. Forest Service and the BLM also publish useful maps.

🚩 **Maps U.S. Geological Survey** ✉ Distribution Center, Box 25286, Federal Center, Denver, CO 80225 ☎ 303/202-4700 or 888/275-8747.

PACK TRIPS & HORSEBACK RIDING

Horsemanship is not a prerequisite for most trips, but it is helpful. If you aren't an experienced rider (and even if you are), you can expect to experience some saddle discomfort for the first day or two. If you're unsure of how much of this sort of thing you can put up with, sign up for a shorter trip (one to three days) before taking on an adventure of a week or longer. Another option is to spend a few days at a dude or guest ranch to get used to life in the saddle, then try a shorter, overnight pack trip organized by the ranch.

Clothing requirements are minimal. A sturdy pair of pants, a wide-brim sun hat, and outerwear to protect against rain are about the only necessities. Ask your outfitter for a list of items you'll need. You might be limited in the gear (extra clothing) or luxuries (alcoholic beverages) an outfitter will let you bring along. Trip costs typically range between $120 and $180 per day.

Pack trips tend to be organized by local outfitters or ranches rather than national organizations. Local chambers of commerce can usually provide lists of outfitters who work in a particular area.

🚩 **Outfitters Rocky Mountain Outdoor Center** ✉ 10281 Hwy. 50, Howard, CO 81233 ☎ 800/255-5784 🖷 719/942-3215 ⊕ www.americanadventure.com.

RAFTING

Unless you're an expert, **pick a recognized outfitter** if you're going into white water. Even then, you should be a good swimmer and in solid general health. Different companies are licensed to run different rivers, although there may be several companies working the same river. Some organizers combine river rafting with other activities, such as pack trips, mountain-bike excursions, extended hikes, fishing.

"Raft" can mean any of a number of things: an inflated raft in which passengers do the paddling; an inflated raft or wooden dory in which a licensed professional does the work; a motorized raft on which some oar work might be required. Be sure you know what kind of raft you'll be riding—or paddling—before booking a trip. Day trips typically run between $30 and $60 per person. Expect to pay between $80 and $120 per day for multiday trips.

🚩 **Outfitter Listings Colorado River Outfitters Association (CROA)** ✉ c/o Johnson Communications, 730 Burbank St., Broomfield, CO 80020 ☎ 303/280-2554 ⊕ www.croa.org. **River Travel Center** 🖑 Box 6, Point Arena, CA 95468 ☎ 800/882-7238 ⊕ www.rivers.com.

🚩 **Outfitters Wilderness Aware Rafting** ✉ Box 1550WS, Buena Vista, CO 81211 ☎ 800/462-7238 or 719/395-2112 ⊕ www.inaraft.com. **Dvorak Expeditions** ✉ 17921 U.S. 285, Nathrop, CO 81236 ☎ 800/824-3795 ⊕ www.dvorakexpeditons.com. **Rio Expeditions** ✉ 8249 Webster St., Arvada, CO 80003 ☎ 800/291-2080 ⊕ www.echotrips.com. **OARS** 🖑 Box 67, Angels Camp, CA 95222 ☎ 800/346-6277 ⊕ www.oars.com.

ROCK CLIMBING & MOUNTAINEERING

Before you sign on with any trip, be sure to clarify to the trip organizer your climbing skills, experience, and physical condition. Climbing tends to be a team sport, and overestimating your capabilities can endanger not only you but other team members. A fair self-assessment of your abilities also helps a guide choose an appropriate climbing route; routes (not unlike ski trails) are rated according to their difficulty. The way to a summit may be relatively easy or brutally challenging, depending on the route selected. You may want to get some instruction at a climbing wall before a trip to the Rockies.

Guide services usually rent such technical gear as helmets, pitons, ropes, and axes; be sure to ask what equipment and supplies you'll need to bring along. (Outfitters usually rent equipment on a per-item, per-day basis.) Some mountaineering stores rent climbing equipment. As for clothing, temperatures can fluctuate dramatically at higher elevations. Bringing several thin layers of clothing, including a sturdy, waterproof/breathable outer shell, is the best strategy for dealing with weather variations.

Organized-trip costs can vary considerably, depending on group size, length of climb, instruction rendered, and equipment supplied. Count on spending at least $80 a day. However, the cost of a small-group multiday instructional climb can push $200 a day. The American Alpine Institute leads trips around the world, ranging from training climbs to expeditionary first ascents. It is one of the most respected climbing organizations in the country.
⚡ Instructional Programs and Outfitters **American Alpine Institute** ⊠ 1515 12th St., N-4, Bellingham, WA 98225 ☎ 360/671-1505 ⊕ www.aai.cc. **Colorado Mountain School** ⌖ 341 Maraine Ave., Estes Park, CO 80517 ☎ 970/586-5758 or 888/267-7783 📠 970/586-5798 ⊕ www.cmschool.com. **Fantasy Ridge Alpinism** ⊠ Nugget Bldg., Suite 204, Box 1679, Telluride, CO 81435 ☎ 970/728-3546.

TOUR COMPANIES

Off the Beaten Path customizes trips within the Rockies that combine outdoor activities and learning experiences. Many trips cross the Montana-Wyoming border, but there are itineraries for Colorado as well. Timberline Adventures lead hiking and biking tours in the bigger national parks such as Glacier, Yellowstone, Zion, and Rocky Mountain National Park.
⚡ **Off the Beaten Path** ⊠ 7 E. Beall St., Bozeman, MT 59715 ☎ 800/445-2995 📠 406/587-4147 ⊕ www.offthebeatenpath.com. **Timberline Adventures** ⊠ 7975 E. Harvard, Suite J, Denver, CO 80231 ☎ 303/759-3804 or 800/417-2453 ⊕ www.timbertours.com.

TAXES

State sales tax is 2.9% in Colorado. Some areas have local sales and lodging taxes, which can be significant—in Denver, they total 13% on hotel rooms.

TIME

All of Colorado is in the Mountain Time Zone. Mountain time is two hours earlier than Eastern time and one hour later than Pacific time. The time in Colorado is one hour earlier than Chicago, seven hours earlier than London, and 17 hours earlier than Sydney.

TIPPING

It is customary to tip 15% at restaurants; in resort towns, 20% is increasingly the norm. For coat checks and bellman, $1 per coat or bag is the minimum. Taxi drivers expect 10% to 15%. In resort towns, ski technicians, sandwich makers, coffee baristas, and the like also appreciate tips.

TOURS & PACKAGES

Because everything is prearranged on a prepackaged tour or independent vacation, you spend less time planning—and often get it all at a good price.

BOOKING WITH AN AGENT

Travel agents are excellent resources. But it's a good idea to collect brochures from several agencies, as some agents' suggestions may be influenced by relationships with tour and package firms that reward them for volume sales. If you have a special interest, **find an agent with expertise in that area**; the American Society of Travel Agents (ASTA; ⇨ Travel Agencies) has a database of specialists worldwide.

Make sure your travel agent knows the accommodations and other services of the place being recommended. Ask about the hotel's location, room size, beds, and whether it has a pool, room service, or programs for children, if you care about these. Has your agent been there in person or sent others whom you can contact?

Do some homework on your own, too: local tourism boards can provide information about lesser-known and small-niche operators, some of which may sell only direct.

BUYER BEWARE

Each year consumers are stranded or lose their money when tour operators—even large ones with excellent reputations—go out of business. So **check out the operator.**

Ask several travel agents about its reputation, and try to **book with a company that has a consumer-protection program.** (Look for information in the company's brochure.) In the United States, members of the National Tour Association and the United States Tour Operators Association are required to set aside funds to cover payments and travel arrangements in the event that the company defaults. It's also a good idea to choose a company that participates in the American Society of Travel Agents' Tour Operator Program; ASTA will act as mediator in any disputes between you and your tour operator.

Remember that the more your package or tour includes, the better you can predict the ultimate cost of your vacation. Make sure you know exactly what is covered, and **beware of hidden costs.** Are taxes, tips, and transfers included? Entertainment and excursions? These can add up.

Tour-Operator Recommendations American Society of Travel Agents (⇨ Travel Agencies). **National Tour Association (NTA)** ✉ 546 E. Main St., Lexington, KY 40508 ☎ 859/226-4444 or 800/682-8886 🖷 859/226-4404 ⊕ www.ntaonline.com. **United States Tour Operators Association (USTOA)** ✉ 275 Madison Ave., Suite 2014, New York, NY 10016 ☎ 212/599-6599 or 800/468-7862 🖷 212/599-6744 ⊕ www.ustoa.com.

TRAIN TRAVEL

Amtrak connects 21 stations in Colorado to both coasts and all major American cities, with trains that run through Denver, Colorado Springs, Pueblo, and Grand Junction. The Ski Train runs between Denver's Union Station and Winter Park during ski season and summer.

Amtrak ☎ 800/872-7245 ⊕ www.amtrak.com. **Ski Train** ☎ 303/296-4754 ⊕ www.skitrain.com.

TRAVEL AGENCIES

A good travel agent puts your needs first. Look for an agency that has been in business at least five years, emphasizes customer service, and has someone on staff who specializes in your destination. In addition, **make sure the agency belongs to a professional trade organization.** The American Society of Travel Agents (ASTA)—the largest and most influential in the field with more than 20,000 members in some 140 countries—maintains and enforces a strict code of ethics and will step in to help mediate any agent-client disputes involving ASTA members if necessary. ASTA (whose motto is "Without a travel agent, you're on your own") also maintains a Web site that includes a directory of agents. (If a travel agency is also acting as your tour operator, *see* Buyer Beware *in* Tours and Packages.)

Local Agent Referrals American Society of Travel Agents (ASTA) ✉ 1101 King St., Suite 200, Alexandria, VA 22314 ☎ 703/739-2782 or 800/965-2782 24-hr hot line 🖷 703/739-3268 ⊕ www.astanet.com. **Association of British Travel Agents** ✉ 68-71 Newman St., London W1T 3AH ☎ 020/7637-2444 🖷 020/7637-0713 ⊕ www.abtanet.com. **Association of Canadian Travel Agents** ✉ 130 Albert St., Suite 1705, Ottawa, Ontario K1P 5G4 ☎ 613/237-3657 🖷 613/237-7052 ⊕ www.acta.ca. **Australian Federation of Travel Agents** ✉ Level 3, 309 Pitt St., Sydney, NSW 2000 ☎ 02/9264-3299 🖷 02/9264-1085 ⊕ www.afta.com.au. **Travel Agents' Association of New Zealand** ✉ Level 5, Tourism and Travel House, 79 Boulcott St., Box 1888, Wellington 6001 ☎ 04/499-0104 🖷 04/499-0786 ⊕ www.taanz.org.nz.

VISITOR INFORMATION

Tourist Information Colorado Tourism Office ✉ 1625 Broadway, #1700, Denver, CO 80202 ☎ 800/265-6723 ⊕ www.colorado.com. **Government Advisories Consular Affairs Bureau of Canada** ☎ 800/267-6788 or 613/944-6788 ⊕ www.voyage.gc.ca. **U.K. Foreign and Commonwealth Office** ✉ Travel Advice Unit, Consular Division, Old Admiralty Building, London SW1A 2PA ☎ 020/7008-0232 or 020/7008-0233 ⊕ www.fco.gov.uk/travel. **Australian Department of Foreign Affairs and Trade** ☎ 02/6261-1299 Consular Travel Advice Faxback Service ⊕ www.dfat.gov.au. **New Zealand Ministry of Foreign Affairs and Trade** ☎ 04/439-8000 ⊕ www.mft.govt.nz.

DENVER

FODOR'S CHOICE

Colorado Avalanche Ice Hockey Team

The Fort, *Morrison*

Jack 'n' Grill, *North Denver*

Larimer Square, *LoDo*

Red Rocks Amphitheatre, *Morrison*

Sod Buster Inn, *Greeley*

The Tattered Cover, *Cherry Creek & LoDo*

HIGHLY RECOMMENDED

SIGHTS   16th Street Mall, *LoDo*

Downtown Aquarium, *Jefferson Park*

Children's Museum of Denver, *Jefferson Park*

City Park

Denver Art Museum, *Civic Center*

Denver Botanic Gardens, *City Park*

Denver Museum of Nature and Science, *City Park*

Denver Performing Arts Complex, *LoDo*

Independence Stampede, *Greeley*

Kit Carson County Carousel, *Burlington*

The LoDo Neighborhood, *Downtown*

Six Flags Elitch Gardens, *Auraria*

SHOPPING   REI flagship store, *Jefferson Park*

Many other great hotels and restaurants enliven the Denver area.
For other favorites, look for the black stars as you read this chapter.

By Steve
Knopper, Eric
Peterson & Kyle
Wagner

YOU CAN TELL FROM ITS SKYLINE ALONE that Denver is a major metropolis, with a major league–baseball stadium at the center of downtown and parking-meter rates that rival even Chicago and New York. But look to the west to see where Denver distinguishes itself. You'll be driving along Interstate 70, for example, contemplating the industrial warehouses on the way back from Denver International Airport (DIA), and suddenly the Rocky Mountains, snow-peaked and breathtakingly huge, appear in the distance. This combination of urban sprawl and proximity to nature is what gives the city character. People spend their weeks commuting to LoDo, the business district and historic downtown, and their weekends reveling in the multitude of skiing, camping, hiking, biking, and fishing areas surrounding the city limits.

Throughout the 1960s and 1970s, when the city mushroomed on a huge surge of oil and energy revenues, Denver worked on the transition from Old West "cowtown" to a comfortable, modern place to live. The city demolished its large downtown "Skid Row" area, for example, and paved the way for developments such as the Tabor Center, the Auraria multicollege campus, and the surrounding suburbs. In the early '90s mayors Federico Peña and Wellington Webb championed massive DIA to replace the rickety Stapleton. Then the city lured major-league baseball, in the form of the purple-and-black Colorado Rockies, and built Coors Field in the heart of downtown. Around the stadium, planners developed LoDo, a business-and-shopping area including hip nightclubs, Larimer Square boutiques, and various bike and walking paths. The city's current mayor, John Hickenlooper, emerged from the LoDo district, having built his signature bar, the Wynkoop Brewery, into a downtown anchor.

In the last decade Denver developed into a telecommunications hub, attracting an influx of young, well-educated professionals lured by Colorado's outdoor mystique and encouraged by the megalopolis's business prospects. For a while in the '90s, it looked like economic diversity would free Denver from its historical boom-and-bust cycle, allowing the city to settle into a period of prosperity and optimism. Even the two-time Super Bowl champions Denver Broncos briefly gave the city an unparalleled sense of civic pride. Then came legendary quarterback John Elway's retirement and a failed experiment by the name of Brian Griese. The dot-com bust had a particularly cutting impact on Denver and its suburbs, and the city faces multimillion-dollar budget deficits for the first time in years, plus a statewide drought that has brought the future of city lawns and golf courses into question.

Many Denverites are unabashed nature lovers who can also enjoy the outdoors within the city limits, walking along the park-lined river paths downtown. (Perhaps as a result of their active lifestyle, Denverites are the "thinnest" city residents in the United States, with only 20% of the adult population overweight.) For Denverites, preserving the environment and the city's rich mining and ranching heritage are of equally vital importance to the quality of life. LoDo buzzes with jazz clubs, restaurants, and art galleries housed in carefully restored century-old buildings. The culturally diverse populace avidly supports the Denver Art Museum, the Denver Museum of Nature and Science, the Colorado History Museum, and the Museo de las Americas. The Denver Performing Arts Complex is the nation's second-largest theatrical venue, bested in capacity only by New York's Lincoln Center. An excellent public transportation system, including a popular, growing light rail and 400 mi of bike paths, makes getting around easy.

Those who don't know Denver may be in for a few big surprises. Although one of its monikers is the "Mile High City," another is "Queen City of

Numbers in the text correspond to numbers in the margin and on Downtown Denver and the Greater Denver Area maps.

If you have

3 days

Stay at the hotel 🏨 **Brown Palace** ⑩, a regal downtown fixture where you might spot a celebrity in the quiet, tea-serving lobby. On the first day, wander through **LoDo** ⑭, **Larimer Square** ⑬ and the **16th Street Mall,** where shopping and dining, both high-end and affordable, is plentiful. You won't need a car for any of this, especially if you ride the Cultural Connection Trolley, which loops around to various attractions. At night, during baseball season, take in a Rockies game at **Coors Field**; during football and hockey seasons, try for Broncos or Avalanche tickets. (If seats aren't available, the hapless-but-soon-to-improve Nuggets are your fall-back option.) If you have kids or are just death-defyingly inclined, play a day at **Six Flags Elitch Gardens** ⑰, bordering LoDo. On the third day, expand your exploration of downtown Denver by heading to the **Capitol Hill** area, where you can stop at the **Denver Art Museum** ⑤, the **Colorado History Museum** ③, and the **U.S. Mint** ⑦. Save 45 minutes for a quirky book-and-record shopping strip on Colfax Avenue. At night, the **Denver Performing Arts Complex** is bound to have something to pique your interest.

If you have

5 days

Follow the three-day itinerary and on your fourth day, drive out to **Black Hawk** and 🏨 **Central City,** the Old West mountain towns with low-stakes gambling. Despite more buffets and greed than the towns ever had in the old gold-mining days, the quaintness survives. Stay in Central City and catch a show at the **Central City Opera House.**

If you still have any money left after $5-per-hand blackjack, return to Denver by way of the City Park neighborhood. In addition to the sprawling, pond-filled park, attractions include the space-obsessed **Denver Museum of Nature and Science** ㉒ and the **Denver Zoo** ㉑. Or, rent transportation at the Bicycle Doctor and spend the last day on the **South Platte River Valley Path,** a set of concrete walks surrounding a creek that spills into the South Platte River. The river path takes you to a soothing spot behind the REI flagship store and leads to various relaxing parks to the east and Invesco Field at Mile High to the west.

1

---

the Plains." Denver is flat, with the Rocky Mountains as a backdrop; this combination keeps the climate delightfully mild. Denverites do not spend their winters digging out of fierce snowstorms and skiing out their front doors, though snow may arrive early and leave late. They take advantage of a comfortable climate (more than 300 days of sunshine a year), historic city blocks, a cultural center, and sky's-the-limit outdoor adventures just minutes from downtown. All of these factors make this appealing city more than just a layover between home and the Rockies.

EXPLORING DENVER

For many out-of-state travelers, Denver is a gateway city, a transitional stop before heading into the nearby Rocky Mountains. Often, visitors will simply fly into DIA, rent a car, ask for directions to I–70 and head west into the mountains. But it's worth scheduling an extra few days, or even a few hours, to delve into the city itself. LoDo is a far better party district than any of the sparse ski-bar areas in Vail or Brecken-ridge, for example, and the downtown museums and outdoor paths are hidden treasures (unless you happen to live here). The city is a fairly easy place to maneuver, with prominent hotels such as the Brown Palace, ex-cellent shopping at Cherry Creek and Larimer Square, sporting events ranging from the fabulous Avalanche to the hapless Nuggets, and plenty of (expensive) parking.

Getting Your Bearings

Unlike Chicago or Los Angeles, Denver defies easy weather predictions. Although its blizzards are infamous, snowstorms are often followed by beautiful spring weather just a day or two later. Ski resorts are packed from roughly October to April, and Denver itself often bears the traf-fic. Summers are festival-happy, with a rock-concert slate at nearby Red Rocks Amphitheatre and big names at the tent-covered Universal Lend-ing Pavilion (also known as CityLights), in the parking lot outside the Pepsi Center downtown. Perhaps the best time to visit, though, is spring and fall, when the heat isn't so hot, the snow isn't so plentiful, and crowds are relatively thin. Ski resorts are still as scenic, and less expensive.

Downtown

Denver's downtown is an intriguing mix of well-preserved monuments from the state's frontier past and modern high-tech marvels. You'll often catch the reflection of an elegant Victorian building in the mir-rored glass of a skyscraper. Hundreds of millions of dollars have been poured into the city in the past decade, in such projects as the Coors Field, the downtown home of Denver's baseball Rockies; the relocation of Six Flags Elitch Gardens—the first amusement park in the country to relocate into a downtown urban area; and an expansion of the light-rail system, which now runs from downtown into the southern suburbs. Lower Downtown, or LoDo, is a Victorian warehouse district revital-ized by the ballpark, loft condominiums, and numerous brewpubs, nightclubs, and restaurants, which are particularly abuzz during the sum-mer baseball season.

Numbers in the text correspond to numbers in the margin and on the Downtown Denver map.

a good tour

Denver presents its official face to the world at the **Civic Center** ❶ ▶, a three-block-long park that runs from Bannock Street to Broadway south of Colfax Avenue and north of 14th Avenue. To the east, lawns, gar-dens, and a Greek amphitheater form a serene backdrop for the **State Capitol** ❷. Southeast of the Civic Center on Broadway is the vibrant **Col-orado History Museum** ❸. Walk west one block on 13th Avenue to reach the **Denver Public Library's Central Library** ❹, and cross over Acoma Plaza (or take the underground walkway) to the **Denver Art Museum** ❺. The **Byers-Evans House Museum** ❻, a snapshot of Denver's Victorian be-ginnings, is just south of here on Bannock Street. Head back to 14th Avenue and turn left to reach the **U.S. Mint** ❼, the source of all those coins stamped with a *D*. From the mint, continue north on Cherokee Street to Tremont Place and the **Denver Firefighters Museum** ❽. A block away on 14th Street is the **Trianon Museum and Art Gallery** ❾.

Continue on Tremont Place to the Denver Pavilions, an open-air shop-ping and entertainment complex. Farther up the street is the historic **Brown Palace** ❿ hotel. Walk or catch a free shuttle up the pedestrian-only **16th Street Mall.** As you head north you'll see the **Daniels and**

Mile High Menus

As befits a multiethnic crossroads, Denver lays out a dizzying range of eateries. Head for LoDo, 32nd Avenue in the Highland District, or south of the city for the more inventive kitchens. Try Federal Street for cheap ethnic eats—especially Mexican and Vietnamese—and expect more authentic takes on classic Italian, French, and Asian cuisines than the city has ever boasted before. Throughout Denver, trendy restaurants' menus defy the descriptions of New American or fusion, and instead pull from international ingredients that can be paired with indigenous regional products in unique ways. Dozens of nationally recognized chefs are gaining the attention of food magazines and winning culinary competitions. In keeping with the nationwide trend, Denver's high-end hotel restaurants have upped the ante on quality that independent eateries are meeting and raising in return.

Denver Rocks

Colorado's moments of pop-music history have been spectacular. Many happened at Red Rocks Amphitheatre, where the Beatles performed in 1964 and U2's Bono made his famous "this song is not a rebel song—this song is 'Sunday Bloody Sunday' " speech in 1983. The Denver–Boulder area was a huge hub for country-rock in the '70s, and members of the Eagles, Poco, Firefall, and others made their homes here, at least briefly. Some of the most famous spots have closed, but rock fans can tour the hallowed ground—the Rainbow Music Hall, host of R.E.M., Miles Davis, and Bob Dylan shows (now a Walgreen's at Monaco and Evans); Ebbet's Field, where Steve Martin and Lynyrd Skynyrd made early-career appearances in the '70s, at 15th and Curtis; and the original Auditorium Theatre, where Led Zeppelin performed its first U.S. show in 1968, at 14th and Curtis. The local scene remains strong, with the Samples, Big Head Todd and the Monsters, Leftover Salmon, String Cheese Incident, Apples In Stereo, and Dressy Bessy building audiences in recent years. Check the *Westword* for listings for shows.

Fisher Tower ⑪. Just past it is the festive **Tabor Center** ⑫ mall. Across 16th Street from Tabor Center is Writer Square, whose shops line the entrance to classy **Larimer Square** ⑬. **LoDo** ⑭, the hip arts district, is northwest of Larimer Square.

TIMING   Downtown is remarkably compact and can be toured on foot in an hour or less, but a car is recommended for exploring outside of downtown proper. The Denver Art Museum merits at least two to three hours and the Colorado History Museum can be covered in an hour or two. Once you've done the museum rounds, save some time for browsing and people watching along the 16th Street Mall and Larimer Square. LoDo is a 30-block-square area that takes several hours to meander through.

What to See

❿ **Brown Palace.** The grande dame of Denver hotels was built in 1892 and is still considered the city's most prestigious address. Famous guests have included Dwight D. Eisenhower, Winston Churchill, the Spice Girls, and Shaquille O'Neal. Even if you can't afford a room, the Brown Palace lobby is a great place to sit on comfortable old couches, drink tea, and listen to piano standards (or harp, during afternoon tea). Reputedly this

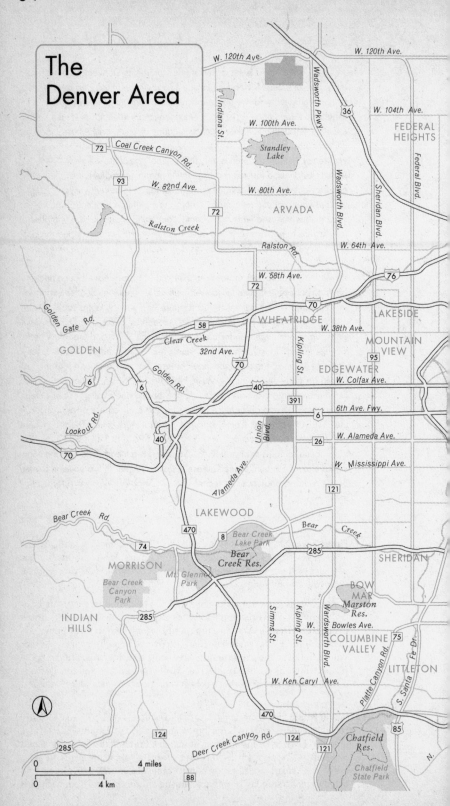

The Denver Area

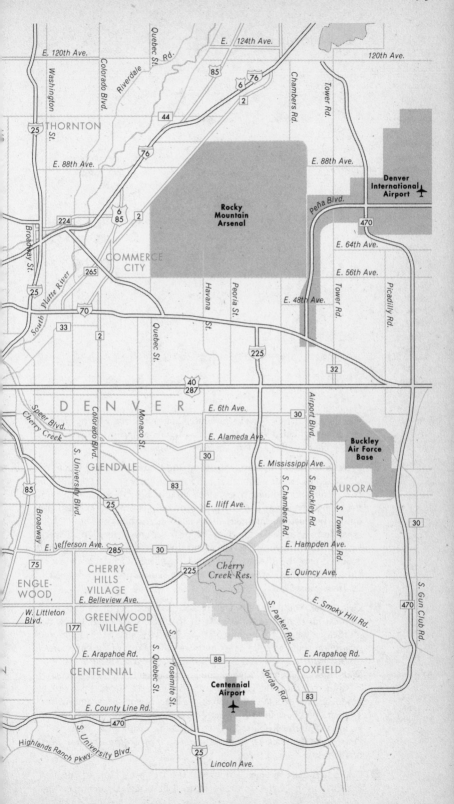

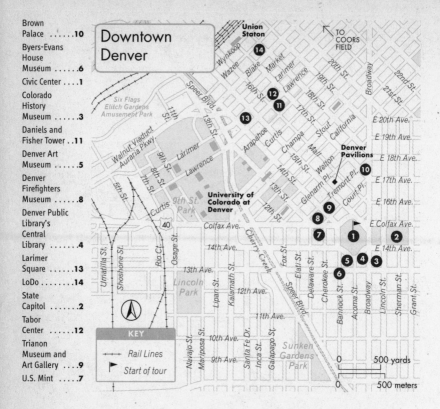

Downtown
Denver

KEY

↤ Rail Lines

▶ Start of tour

was the first atrium hotel in the United States; its ornate lobby and nine stories are crowned by a Tiffany stained-glass window. ✉ *321 17th St., LoDo* ☎ *303/297–3111* ⊕ *www.brownpalace.com.*

⑥ Byers-Evans House Museum. Sprawling and detailed, red and black, this elaborate Victorian went up in 1883 as the home of *Rocky Mountain News* publisher William Byers. (He sold it in 1889 to William Evans of the Denver Tramway Company.) Restored to its pre–World War I condition, the historic landmark has occasional exhibitions and regular tours. Its main appeal is the glimpse it provides into Denver's past, specifically 1912 through 1924. The furnishings are those the Evans family acquired over the 80-some years they lived here. ✉ *1310 Bannock St., Civic Center* ☎ *303/620–4933* ⊕ *www.coloradohistory.org* ✆ *$3* ◷ *Tues.–Sun. 11–3.*

▶ ❶ Civic Center. You'll find a peaceful respite in this three-block park in the cultural heart of downtown, site of the State Capitol. A Greek amphitheater, which was built in 1919 and underwent a $1.3-million renovation in summer 2003, is set in the middle of one of the city's largest flower gardens. Two of the park's statues, *Bronco Buster* and *On the War Trail,* depicting a cowboy and an Indian on horseback, were commissioned in the '20s. Festivals such as Cinco de Mayo, Taste of Colorado, and the People's Fair keep things lively here in spring and summer. The park was born in 1906, when Mayor Robert Speer asked New York architect Charles Robinson to expand on his vision of a "Paris on the Platte." ✉ *Bannock St. to Broadway south of Colfax Ave. and north of 14th Ave., Civic Center.*

❸ Colorado History Museum. The state's frontier past is vibrantly depicted in this flagship of the Colorado Historical Society. Changing exhibits highlight eras from the days before white settlers arrived to the boom periods of mining. General exhibit themes include the growth of historic preservation and black cowboys in the American West. Permanent displays include Conestoga wagons, great old touring cars, and an extraordinary time line called "The Colorado Chronicle 1800–1950," which covers the state's history in amazing detail. The mixed media display stretches 112 feet, 6 inches, and dedicates 9 inches to each year. It's crammed with artifacts from rifles to land-grant surveys and old daguerreotypes. The museum is easy to spot by its huge, colorful mural of native Americans, miners, and red rocks. The large brick area outside the front door, complete with grassy strip, is a great place to relax if you're walking through downtown. ☒ *1300 Broadway, Civic Center* ☏ *303/866–3682* ⊕ *www.coloradohistory.org* ☒ *$5* ⊙ *Mon.–Sat. 10–4:30, Sun. noon–4:30.*

⓫ **Daniels and Fisher Tower.** This 330-foot-high, 20-floor structure emulates the campanile of St. Mark's Cathedral in Venice, and it was the tallest building west of the Mississippi when it was built in 1909. William Cooke Daniels originally commissioned the tower to stand adjacent to his five-story department store. In the '70s, when the city razed the department store during an urban-renewal project, preservationists saved and renovated the tower. It reopened in 1981 as an office building. Today, it's the city's most convenient clock tower and is particularly striking—the clock is 16 feet high—when viewed in concert with the fountains in the adjacent Skyline Park. ☒ *16th and Arapahoe Sts., LoDo.*

★ ☾ ❺ **Denver Art Museum.** Uniquely displayed holdings in Asian, pre-Columbian, Spanish Colonial, and Native American art are the hallmarks of this model of museum design, which also has extensive special exhibits. Among the museum's regular holdings: John DeAndrea's sexy, soothing, life-size polyvinyl painting *Linda* (1983), Claude Monet's dreamy flowerscape *Le Bassin des Nympheas* (1904), and Charles Deas' red-cowboy-on-horseback *Long Jakes, The Rocky Mountain Man* (1844). The works are thoughtfully lit, but dazzling mountain views sometime steal your attention away. For children there's the imaginative hands-on exhibits and video corners. The Adventures in Art Center offers hands-on art classes and exploration for children and adults. To the east of the museum is a concrete outdoor plaza—you'll know it by the huge, orange metal sculpture—that leads to the Denver Public Library next door. Standing a block or so east of the museum, check out the curvy, lumpy skyline of the art museum and library. The museum is scheduled to undergo a $90.5-million, 146,000-square-foot expansion to the south of the current building, to be completed in 2006. ☒ *100 W. 14th Ave. Pkwy., Civic Center* ☏ *720/865–5000* ⊕ *www.denverartmuseum.org* ☒ *$6, free Sat. for Colorado residents* ⊙ *Tues.–Sat. 10–5, Wed. until 9, Sun. noon–5.*

> **need a break?** The Denver Art Museum's restaurant, **Palettes** (☒ 100 W. 14th Ave. Pkwy. ☏ 303/629–0889) and its café spin-off, **Palettes Express,** is the product of another kind of artist. Chef Kevin Taylor, a local fixture who also runs bistro jou jou and Restaurant Kevin Taylor, fills the menu with colorful, usually healthful dishes like fruit-stuffed pork and flash-fried calimari. The Express has outdoor tables in the plaza between the museum and the Denver Public Library.

☾ ❽ **Denver Firefighters Museum.** Denver's first firehouse was built in 1909 and now serves as a museum where original items of the trade are on view, including uniforms, nets, fire carts and trucks, bells, and switchboards. Artifacts and photos document the progression of firefighting machinery, from horses and carriages in the early 1900s to the flashy red-and-white trucks of today. The museum rents out its second floor for weddings and parties; climbing in and out of the fire trucks for hours at a time while eating cake is particularly exciting for kids. ✉ *1326 Tremont Pl., LoDo* ☎ *303/892–1436* ⊕ *www.denverfirefightersmuseum. org* ⏲ *$4* ⏱ *Mon.–Sat. 10–2.*

❹ **Denver Public Library's Central Library.** Originally built in the mid-'50s, the Central Library underwent a massive, Michael Graves–designed renovation in 1995. It's a sprawling complex with round towers and tall, oblong windows, and various sculptures decorate the expansive lawn (including a giant horse on a chair). The map and manuscript rooms, Gates Western History Reading Room (with amazing views of the mountains), and three-story atrium Schlessman Hall merit a visit. The library houses a world-renowned collection of books, photographs, and newspapers that chronicle the American West, as well as original paintings by Remington, Russell, Audubon, and Bierstadt. The children's library is notable for its captivating design and its unique, child-friendly multimedia computer catalog. The library is the cornerstone of the Civic Center Cultural Complex, intended to be a center for Western Americana, with shared exhibits and collections with the Denver Art Museum and Colorado History Museum. ✉ *10 W. 14th Ave. Pkwy., Civic Center* ☎ *720/865–1111* ⊕ *www.denver.lib.co.us* ⏱ *Mon. and Tues. 10–9, Thurs.–Sat. 10–5:30, Sun. 1–5.*

off the beaten path

FORNEY TRANSPORTATION MUSEUM – Uprooted in 1999 from its Platte River Valley location, this museum is a trivia-laden gem. It reopened in 2001 outside of the downtown loop (north on Brighton Boulevard, adjacent to the Denver Coliseum on the south side of I–70) with a much-improved layout and most of the same exhibits. Inside a converted warehouse are an 1898 Renault coupe, Teddy Roosevelt's tour car, Amelia Earhart's immaculately maintained "Goldbug," and a Big Boy steam locomotive, among many other former vehicles of the country's railroads and highways. Other exhibits consist of antique bicycles, cable cars, experimental carplanes, and even the "Zabeast," a 1975 Pontiac entirely covered in bumper stickers. Anyone who grew up on model cars or Lionel trains will wander this eccentric museum in a happy daze. ✉ *4303 Brighton Blvd., Globeville* ☎ *303/297–1113* ⊕ *www.forneymuseum.com* ⏲ *$7* ⏱ *Mon.–Sat. 9–5.*

❸ **Larimer Square.** Larimer Square is on the oldest street in the city, immortalized by Jack Kerouac in his seminal book, *On the Road*. It was saved from the wrecker's ball by a determined preservationist in the 1960s, when the city went demolition-crazy in its eagerness to present a more youthful image. Much has changed since Kerouac's wanderings, as Larimer Square's rough edges have been cleaned up in favor of upscale retail and chic restaurants. The Square has become a serious late-night party district thanks to spillover from the expanded LoDo neighborhood and Rockies fans flowing out from the baseball stadium. Shops line the arched redbrick courtyards of **Writer Square,** Denver's most charming shopping district. Specialty shops, such as Overland Sheepskin and Tewksbury & Co., do business here in some of the city's oldest retail buildings. Note that area parking meters are the most expensive in the city. ✉ *Larimer and 15th Sts., LoDo* ☎ *303/685–8143* ⊕ *www. larimersquare.com.*

FodorśChoice
★

★ ❹ **LoDo.** The historic lower downtown area is home to art galleries, nightclubs, and restaurants ranging from Denver's most upscale to its most down-home. This part of town was once the city's thriving retail center, then it fell into disuse and slid into slums. Since the early 1990s, LoDo has metamorphosed into the city's cultural center, thanks to its resident avant-garde artists, retailers, and loft dwellers who have taken over the old warehouses and redbricks. The handsome **Coors Field** (✉ Blake and 20th Sts., LoDo), home of baseball's Colorado Rockies, has further galvanized the area. Its old-fashioned brick and grillwork facade, ornamented with 41 blue, green, and white terra-cotta columbines (the state flower), was designed to blend in with the surrounding Victorian warehouses. As with cuddly Wrigley Field, on the north side of Chicago, Coors Field has engendered a nightlife scene of sports bars, restaurants, and dance clubs. ✉ *From Larimer St. to the South Platte River, between 14th and 22nd Sts., LoDo* ⊕ *www.lodo.org.*

off the beaten path

MUSEO DE LAS AMÉRICAS – The region's first museum dedicated to the achievements of Latinos in the Americas has a permanent collection as well as rotating exhibits that cover everything from Hispanics in the state legislature to Latin American women artists in the 20th century. Among the permanent pieces are the oil painting *Virgin of Solitude* (circa 1730) and a Mayan polychrome jar (circa 650–950), in addition to contemporary works. ✉ *861 Santa Fe Dr., Lincoln Park* ☎ *303/571–4401* ⊕ *www.museo.org* ☞ *$4* ⊙ *Tues.–Sat. 10–5.*

★ **16th Street Mall.** Outdoor cafés, historic buildings, and tempting shops line this pedestrians-only 12-block thoroughfare, shaded by red-oak and locust trees. The Mall's businesses run the entire socioeconomic range. There are high-class joints like Bravo Ristorante, in the Adam's Mark hotel, where the waitstaff sings showtunes; decent tavern food at the Paramount Cafe, around the corner from the Paramount Theatre; and plenty of fast-food chains. Although some Denverites swear by the high-falutin Cherry Cheek Shopping District, the 16th Street Mall covers every retail area and is a more affordable, diverse experience. You can find Denver's best people watching here, with more than 1,000 chairs set out along its length so you can take in the sights. The rose-and-gray granite mall is scrubbed clean every day. Catch one of the free shuttle buses that run the length of downtown. Pay attention when you're wandering across the street, as the walking area and bus lanes are the same color and hard to distinguish. ✉ *LoDo.*

❷ **State Capitol.** Built in 1886, the capitol was constructed mostly of materials indigenous to Colorado, including marble, granite, and rose onyx. Especially inspiring is the gold-leaf dome, a reminder of the state's mining heritage. You can normally climb to the dome's interior balcony for a panoramic view of the Rockies, but the dome is closed indefinitely for rotunda repairs. You can get to the 18th step, which is exactly 1 mi high (above sea level). The legislature sessions are generally January through May, and visitors are welcome to sit in third-floor viewing galleries above the House and Senate chambers. ✉ *200 E. Colfax Ave., Capitol Hill* ☎ *303/866–2604* ☞ *Free* ⊙ *Bldg.; weekdays, 7–5:30. Tours Sept.–May, weekdays 9–2:30; June–Aug., weekdays 9–3:30.*

⓬ **Tabor Center.** This festive shopping mall has about 55 stores (mostly chains such as Casual Corner and Petite Sophisticate) and attractions, including fast-food eateries, strolling troubadours, jugglers and fire-eaters, and splashing fountains. ESPN Zone, a sports-theme restaurant, exemplifies the recent Tabor Center trend of super-popular eateries and only mildly popular shopping. A concierge desk at the Lawrence Street entrance is staffed with friendly people who offer free walking tours around the city. During random times of the year, horse-drawn carriages out front wait to give rides around downtown. ⊠ *Larimer and Lawrence Sts. on 16th St., LoDo* ☎ *303/572–6868.*

⑨ Trianon Museum and Art Gallery. This tranquil museum houses a collection of 18th- and 19th-century European furnishings and objets d'art dating from the 16th century onward. Guided tours are offered on the hour. ⊠ *335 14th St., LoDo* ☎ *303/623–0739* 🖃 *$1* ⊘ *Mon.–Sat. 10–4.*

⑦ U.S. Mint. Free tours of this facility give a glimpse of the coin-making process, as presses spit out thousands of coins a minute. There are also several exhibits on the history of money and a restored version of Denver's original mint, prior to numerous expansions. More than 14 billion coins are minted yearly, and the nation's second-largest hoard of gold is stashed away here. To arrange a visit, contact your U.S. congressperson's office (the U.S. Mint Web site provides a link with contact information and foreigners can pick any representative to contact); school groups can call 303/405–4759. The gift shop, which sells many different kinds of authentic coins and currency, is in the Tremont Center, across Colfax Avenue from the Mint. ⊠ *W. Colfax Ave. and Cherokee St., Civic Center* ☎ *303/405–4761* ⊕ *www.usmint.gov* 🖃 *Free* ⊘ *Gift shop, weekdays 9–3:30* ☞ *Tours by appointment only; 2-week advance notice is required.*

Platte River Valley

Less than a mile west of downtown is the booming Platte River Valley. Once the cluttered heart of Denver's railroad system, it's now overflowing with attractions. The imposing glass facade of the NFL Broncos' new Invesco Field at Mile High, the stately Pepsi Center sports arena, the Downtown Aquarium, and the flagship REI outdoors store are but four more crowd pleasers to add to the growing list in Denver. The South Platte River Valley concrete path, which extends several miles from downtown to the east and west, snakes along the water through many out-of-the-way parks and trails. Also, after much construction, the 15th Street bridge is particularly cyclist- and pedestrian-friendly, connecting LoDo with growing northwest Denver in a seamless way. The sights in this area are so popular that the city plans to complete a light rail system that will connect the attractions with downtown by the end of the decade.

a good tour

Leave Interstate 25 at Exit 211 (23rd Avenue). Take the first right east of the interstate (Children's Museum Drive) to get to the **Children's Museum of Denver** ⑮ ▶, which has its own parking lot. Get back on 23rd Avenue, where you'll see the **Downtown Aquarium** ⑯ and the sporting goods store REI down the street. To reach **Six Flags Elitch Gardens** ⑰, get back on Interstate 25 going south, exit on Speer Boulevard south, and take a right at the sign for the park.

TIMING The Platte River Valley can be a destination for an entire day if you're interested in riding the roller coasters at Six Flags, and touring the aquarium and the Children's Museum require about two hours each. You'll have to tour the area by car.

Numbers in the text correspond to numbers in the margin and on the Greater Denver map.

What to See

★ ✋ ▶ ⑮ **Children's Museum of Denver.** This is one of the finest museums of its kind in North America, offering constantly changing hands-on exhibits that engage children in discovery. The Maze-eum is a walk-through musical maze. Children can build a car on an assembly line and send it careen-

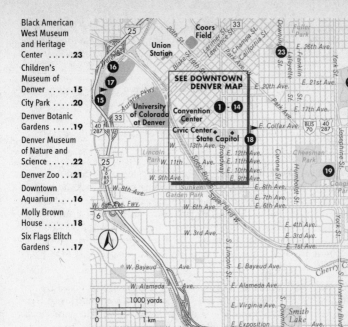

ing down a test ramp at the Inventions display. At Arts á la carte, kids paint, dance, sing, and otherwise develop their creative talents. One of the biggest attractions is the Center for the Young Child, a 3,700-square-foot playscape aimed at newborns through four-year-olds and their caregivers. (Don't worry, the museum contains "wash this toy" buckets to keep slobbered artifacts from infecting other children.) A trolley ($2) clatters and clangs the 2 mi down the South Platte River from the museum to the REI flagship store, which has some interactive fun for the kids, too. The trolley also connects to the Downtown Aquarium. ✉ 2121 Children's Museum Dr., off Exit 211 of I–25, Jefferson Park ☎ 303/433–7444 ⊕ www.cmdenver.org ✉ $6; free the 1st Fri. of every month ۝ Weekdays 9–4, weekends 10–5.

★ ⑯ **Downtown Aquarium.** On the north side of the Platte River across from Six Flags Elitch Gardens, the tentatively named Downtown Aquarium, formerly Colorado's Ocean Journey, is the only million-gallon aquarium between Chicago and the West Coast. It has four sections that show water and aquatic life in all its forms, from the seas to the river's headwaters in the Colorado mountains. The mountain-to-ocean journeys of two great rivers—the Colorado River and Indonesia's Kampar River—are depicted by a pair of multisensory exhibits in the 106,500-square-foot aquarium. Other major displays include Depths of the Pacific, Sea Otter Cove, and a rotating seasonal exhibit. Whether the aquarium will stick around in its present form is open to question, however, as the aquarium sunk into multimillion-dollar debt and had to declare bankruptcy. Houston-based Landry's Restaurants, Inc., bought the facility in early 2003 and announced plans to open several seafood restaurants on the premises, including one with video screens playing clips from *Jaws.* Several months after the purchase, Landry's had yet to make many major changes at the aquarium, however. ⊠ *700 Water St., off Exit 211 of I–25, Jefferson Park* ☎ *303/561–4450* ⊕ *www.oceanjourney.org* ⊠ *$14.95* ⊙ *June–Aug., daily 10–6; Sept.–May, daily 10–5.*

need a break? Down the street from the REI store, along the bicycle path on 15th Street, **My Brother's Bar** (⊠ 2376 15th St. ☎ 303/455–9991) is a homey neighborhood tavern that serves many different microbrews, burgers—buffalo and beef—and sandwiches of all kinds. The bar name isn't on the facade, so you might wander by once or twice before figuring out where it is.

Platte River Greenway. Just behind the REI flagship store, this serene park is at the center of the South Platte River Valley path. Its rocks and rapids are especially attractive in summer for kayakers, bicyclists, and hikers. Several newly built sidewalks extend down the Platte River to the east (toward the suburbs) and west (toward Invesco Field at Mile High). A pathway in yet another direction leads to LoDo. From the park, it's about a 20-minute walk to the 16th Street Mall and Coors Field. ⊠ *1416 Platte St., Jefferson Park.*

★ ☙ ⑰ **Six Flags Elitch Gardens.** This elaborate and thrilling park was a Denver family tradition long before its 1995 relocation from northwest Denver to its current home on the outskirts of downtown. The park's highlights include hair-raising roller coasters and thrill rides such as the corkscrewing Flying Coaster, the loop-de-looping Boomerang, the freefalling Tower of Doom, and the bouncing Turbobungy. For younger kids and squeamish parents, the park has plenty of gentler, Bugs Bunny–hosted attractions. Twister II is an update of the classic, wooden Mister Twister, from the original Elitch Gardens, and a 100-foot-high Ferris wheel that provides sensational views of downtown. A 10-acre water-adventure park is included in the standard entry fee. ⊠ *I–25 and Speer Blvd., Auraria* ☎ *303/595–4386* ⊕ *www.sixflags.com/elitchgardens* ⊠ *$35.99 unlimited-ride pass* ⊙ *June–Labor Day, daily; Apr. and May, Sept. and Oct., Fri.–Sun.; hrs vary so call ahead.*

East of Downtown

The area east of downtown is home to two of the city's finest parks, as well as some grand old residential neighborhoods.

a good tour You'll need transportation on this tour, as it covers an area more spread out than downtown. If you don't have a car, Denver has an excellent bus system. Head east from the Civic Center on 14th Avenue to the flamboyant **Molly Brown House** ⑱ ☞. Continue east on 14th Street and south on York Street for a peaceful interlude at the **Denver Botanic Gardens** ⑲. Denver's most impressive public space is **City Park** ⑳ reached by heading north on York Street. Go east on 23rd Avenue for the main entrance to the **Denver Zoo** ㉑. From here it's a short walk across the park (or a drive, on Colorado Boulevard south), to the **Denver Museum of Nature and Science** ㉒. Finish up your day with a stop at the **Black American West Museum and Heritage Center** ㉓ by getting back on York Street north and going west on 31st Avenue.

TIMING You'll want to set aside a full day to do these sights justice. If you have children or are an animal lover, you could easily spend half a day in City Park, exploring the Denver Zoo and the Denver Museum of Nature and Science. Garden enthusiasts could spend half a day in the Denver Botanic Gardens in summer, when the many theme gardens are in full bloom; in the off-season, the conservatory is still a good respite for an hour. There are often evening hours and musical performances in the Denver Botanic

Gardens in summer, and the Denver Museum of Natural History stays open late on Friday night. The Molly Brown House and the Black American West Museum and Heritage Center are worthy of at least an hour each. In the off-season (October through April), both are closed Monday and have shortened hours on Sunday.

Numbers in the text correspond to numbers in the margin and on the Greater Denver Area map.

What to See

㉓ Black American West Museum and Heritage Center. The revealing documents here depict the vast contributions that African Americans made to opening up the West. Nearly a third of the cowboys and many pioneer teachers and doctors were African Americans. One floor is devoted to black cowboys; another to military troops such as the Buffalo Soldiers. Changing exhibits focus on topics such as the history of black churches in the West. ⊠ *3091 California St., Five Points* ☎ *303/292–2566* 🖭 *$6* ⊙ *June–Aug., daily 10–5; Sept.–May, Wed.–Fri. 10–2, weekends 10–5.*

★ ⑳ **City Park.** Acquired by the city in 1881, Denver's largest public space (370 acres) contains rose gardens, lakes, a golf course, tennis courts, a huge, community-built children's playground, and several small lakes. A shuttle runs between two of the city's most popular attractions: the Denver Zoo and the Denver Museum of Natural and Science, both located on the premises. ⊠ *City Park.*

★ ⑲ **Denver Botanic Gardens.** The horticultural displays in thoughtfully laid-out theme gardens—more than 15,000 plant species from Australia, South Africa, and the Himalayas, and especially the western United States—are at their peak in summer, but the tropical conservatory alone is worth a visit in the off-season. Spring brings a brilliant display of wildflowers to the world-renowned rock alpine garden. Tea ceremonies take place some summer weekends in the tranquil Japanese garden, and artists such as folk-rocker Richard Thompson, country chanteuse k.d. lang, and bluegrassy jazzman Bela Fleck have performed as part of the summer concert series. ⊠ *1005 York St., City Park* ☎ *720/865–3500* ⊕ *www.botanicgardens.org* 🖭 *$6.50* ⊙ *Daily 9–5, selected evening hrs in summer.*

★ ⟲ ㉒ **Denver Museum of Nature and Science.** With one of the city's best views of the Rocky Mountains, this recently renovated facility is one of the country's largest, holding a rich combination of traditional collections—dinosaur remains, animal dioramas, a mineralogy display, an Egyptology wing—and intriguing hands-on exhibits. In the Hall of Life, you can test your health and fitness on various contraptions and receive a personalized health profile. Another permanent exhibit, Prehistoric Journey, covers the seven stages of Earth's development, with each "envirorama" representing the sights and sounds of a specific area of North America or Australia at a particular time. Explore Colorado allows you to take a scenic trip through the state, with an experienced naturalist describing the regional wildlife and forests along the way. The massive complex also includes an IMAX movie theater and the Gates Planetarium. The planetarium's Space Odyssey exhibit simulates a trip to Mars and thoroughly annotates the stars in the night sky. Although it's not part of any exhibit, the impressively refurbished eating-and-relaxation area (toward the rear) has a full-window panoramic mountain view as a backdrop. ⊠ *2001 Colorado Blvd., City Park* ☎ *303/322–7009 or 800/925–2250* ⊕ *www.dmns.org* 🖭 *Museum $9, IMAX $8; $13 for a joint museum–IMAX pass* ⊙ *Daily 9–5; open until 7 on Tues. Memorial Day–Labor Day.*

An old-fashioned greasy-spoon diner that specializes in huge
pancakes and spicy huevos rancheros, **Pete's Kitchen** (✉ 1962 E.
Colfax Ave. ☎ 303/321–3139) is just a few minutes by car from the
Denver Museum of Nature and Science. It's often packed,
particularly on Sunday morning, so prepare to fight for parking, wait
for a table, and resign yourself to a seat at the counter.

Denver Zoo. A bright peacock greets you at the door of the nation's fourth-
most-visited zoo, whose best-known exhibit showcases man-eating Ko-
modo dragons in a lush re-creation of a cavernous riverbank. The
Conservation Carousel ($1) rotates in the center of the 80-acre zoo, with
hand-crafted endangered species as mounts. Also of note is the 7-acre
Primate Panorama, which houses 31 species of primates in state-of-the-
art environments that simulate the animals' natural habitats. Other
highlights include a nursery for baby animals; seal shows; the world's
only painting rhinoceros, Mshindi; the electric Safari Shuttle, which snakes
through the property as guests are treated to a lesson on the zoo's inhabitants; and the usual lions, tigers, bears, giraffes, monkeys, and one
extremely hairy elephant. The exhibits are spaced far apart along sprawling concrete paths, so build in enough time to visit everything. ✉ *E. 23rd
Ave. between York St. and Colorado Blvd., City Park* ☎ *303/376–
4800* ⊕ *www.denverzoo.org* ✉ *$10 Oct.–Mar., $11 Apr.–Sept.*
⊘ *Oct.–Mar., daily 10–5; Apr.–Sept., daily 9–6.*

Molly Brown House. This Victorian confection, on Pennsylvania Street
between East 13th and 14th avenues, not far from the capitol, celebrates
the life and times of the scandalous, "unsinkable" Molly Brown. The
heroine of the *Titanic* courageously saved several lives and continued
to provide assistance to survivors back on terra firma. Costumed guides
and period furnishings in the museum, including flamboyant gilt-edge
wallpaper, lace curtains, tile fireplaces, and tapestries, evoke bygone days.
The museum collects and displays artifacts that belonged to Brown, as
well as period items dating to 1894–1912, when the Browns lived in
the house. A bit of trivia: Margaret Tobin Brown was known as Maggie, not Molly, during her lifetime. Meredith Willson, the composer-lyri-
cist of the musical, *The Unsinkable Molly Brown,* based on Brown's life,
thought Molly was easier to sing. Tours run every half hour. ✉ *1340
Pennsylvania St., Capitol Hill* ☎ *303/832–4092* ⊕ *www.mollybrown.
org* ✉ *$6.50* ⊘ *June–Aug., Mon.–Sat. 10–3:30, Sun. noon–3:30;
Sept.–May, Tues.–Sat. 10–3:30, Sun. noon–3:30.*

WHERE TO EAT

By Kyle
Wagner

WHAT IT COSTS				
	$$$$	$$$	$$	$	¢
AT DINNER	over $25	$19–$25	$13–$18	$8–$12	under $8

Prices are for a main course at dinner, excluding sales tax of 3.5%–8%.

American

$–$$ ✕ **Wynkoop Brewing Co.** This trendy yet unpretentious local institution
was Denver's first brewpub and now its owner, John Hickenlooper, is
Denver's mayor. Try the terrific shepherd's pie or charbroiled elk medallions with brandy peppercorns. Wash it down with one of the Wynkoop's
trademark microbrews—try either the exemplary Railyard Ale or the
spicy chili beer. Then check out the gallery, pool hall, and cabaret for a

full night of entertainment. ✉ *1634 18th St., LoDo* ☎ *303/297–2700* 🍴 *AE, D, DC, MC, V.*

¢–$$ ✗ **Rocky Mountain Diner.** In the heart of the downtown business district, you can come in and sample all-American fill-ups of cowboy steak, pan-charred rib eye served with crisp onions, or the very popular buffalo meat loaf. Don't miss the real mashed potatoes, gravy, and all the fixings. ✉ *800 18th St., Downtown* ☎ *303/293–8383* 🍴 *AE, D, DC, MC, V.*

¢–$ ✗ **CityGrille.** Politicians and construction workers rub shoulders while chowing down on the great hamburgers and green chile served at City-Grille, which sits across the street from the State Capitol. The eatery has won numerous local awards and national attention for both the burger, a half-pounder of ground sirloin, and the chili, a gringo stew of pork, jalapeños, and tomatoes that's spicy and addictive. In addition, the three-martini lunch lives on in this power-packed spot. ✉ *321 E. Colfax Ave., Capitol Hill* ☎ *303/861–0726* 🍴 *AE, DC, MC, V.*

¢–$ ✗ **My Brother's Bar.** Drop by one of Denver's oldest bars to listen to classical music while slurping down a giant, juicy burger that comes with a plastic tub full of condiments. Laid-back and filled with locals, the inside dining room competes with the fence-lined back patio for popularity, and the beer list is invitingly large. This is one of Denver's most beloved late-nighters, too, serving food until 1:30 AM. ✉ *2376 15th St., Downtown* ☎ *303/455–9991* 🍽 *Reservations not accepted* 🍴 *MC, V* ⊗ *Closed Sun.*

¢–$ ✗ **Sam's No. 3.** Three sons of a Greek immigrant have reprised their father's all-American diner in this updated version. Sam Armatas opened his first eatery in Denver in 1927, and the sons use the same recipes Pop did, from the famous red and green chiles to the overloaded Coney Island–style hot dogs and the creamy rice pudding. The room is a combination of retro diner and a fancy Denny's, and the bar is crowded with theatergoers and hipsters after dark. Good luck choosing your meal: the menu is 10 pages long, with Greek and Mexican favorites as well as diner classics. The chunky mashed potatoes rule, and breakfast comes fast. ✉ *1500 Curtis St., Downtown* ☎ *303/534–1927* 🍴 *AE, D, DC, MC, V.*

¢–$ ✗ **Spicy Pickle Sub Shop.** A spicy pickle does indeed come with every order at this hopping deli, which makes giant subs and panini, all filled with Boar's Head meats and house-made spreads. The breads are baked locally, and the side salads are good quality. ✉ *988 Lincoln St., Downtown* ☎ *303/860–0730* 🍽 *Reservations not accepted* 🍴 *AE, MC, V.*

¢ ✗ **Hotcakes.** This jumping Capitol Hill spot is a breakfast and lunch hangout. Weekend brunch draws crowds of bicyclists and newspaper readers in search of the croissant French toast, "health nut" pancakes, colossal omelets, and scrumptious skillets. ✉ *1400 E. 18th Ave., Capitol Hill* ☎ *303/830–1909* 🍴 *D, MC, V* ⊗ *No dinner.*

Barbecue

¢ ✗ **Brother's BBQ.** Two brothers from England traveled the southern United States to make it their business to know everything there is to know about barbecue, and they decided to share the information with Denver. The result is some of the best 'cue in town, from St. Louis–style ribs to beef brisket, pulled pork, and chicken. The sauces are a mishmash of their favorites, including a vinegary one and a sweet one, and the baked beans use their smoked meats for extra flavor. Get the family pack: one pound of meat, four buns, two sides and the sauces, all for $16. Eat in at one of the metal tables amid license plates and knickknacks from the boys' travels, or get it packed up nicely to go. ✉ *568 N. Washington St., Central Denver* ☎ *720/570–4227* 🍽 *Reservations not accepted* 🍴 *MC, V.*

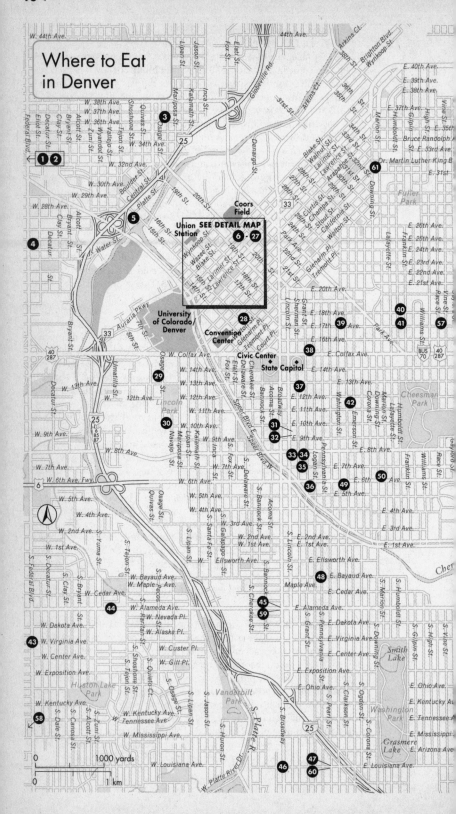

Where to Eat in Denver

SNACKING IN HIGHLANDS

ONCE A BOOMING AREA *where gold-miners and immigrants landed en route from the Rocky Mountains to the city,* northwestern Denver's Highlands neighborhood went bad after the '80s oil bust, but has since come back as a bohemian mix of Hispanic families and laid-back, home-buying yuppies. The neighborhood's heart is the 32nd Avenue–Lowell Boulevard intersection, which has a wine store, flower shop, cheese shop, several quirky shopping opportunities, and more than a dozen restaurants. The area sandwich-and-ice-cream specialist is **Heidi's Brooklyn Deli** (✉ *3130 Lowell Blvd., Highlands* ☎ *303/477–2605),* anchoring the main intersection. Behind its pastel-colored storefront **Bang!** (✉ *3472 W. 32nd Ave., Highlands* ☎ *303/455–1117)* serves upscale fish and steak dishes. The New

Mexican café **Julia Blackbird's** (✉ *3617 W. 32nd Ave., Highlands* ☎ *303/433–2688)* has spicy salsa and strawberry lemonade to die for. Across the street from the bank is the tony **Highlands Garden Cafe** (✉ *3927 W. 32nd Ave., Highlands* ☎ *303/458–5920),* a cozy (if pricey) first-date spot.

Brazilian

$$–$$$ ✕ **Café Brazil.** Worth the trip to the Highlands neighborhood, this always-packed spot is the place for shrimp and scallops sautéed with fresh herbs, coconut milk, and hot chiles; *feijoda completa*, the Brazilian national dish of black-bean stew and smoked meats, accompanied with fried bananas; or grilled chicken breast in a sauce of palm oil, red chile, shallots, and coconut milk. This not-quite hole-in-the-wall is favored by locals in the know. ✉ *3611 Navajo St., Highlands* ☎ *303/480–1877* ⌖ *Reservations essential* ▭ *No credit cards* ⊘ *Closed Sun. and Mon. No lunch.*

Chinese

$–$$$$ ✕ **Little Ollie's.** Black dominates the glossy interior of the swank Ollie's, which has a large outdoor patio and exceptionally well-crafted Chinese food. The whole steamed sea bass in black-bean sauce is one of the favorite items on the menu, along with mu shu pork and crispy duck. The lunch specials make it popular mid-day, and the wine list is unusually well chosen for a Chinese restaurant. Reservations are taken for parties of six or more. ✉ *2364 E. 3rd Ave., Cherry Creek North* ☎ *303/316–8888* ▭ *AE, MC, V.*

$–$$ ✕ **Imperial Chinese.** Papier-mâché lions greet you at the entrance of this sleek Szechuan stunner, probably the best Chinese restaurant in a 500-mi radius. Seafood is the specialty. Try the steamed sea bass in ginger or the spicy, fried Dungeness crab. ✉ *431 S. Broadway, Central Denver* ☎ *303/698–2800* ▭ *AE, DC, MC, V* ⊘ *No lunch Sun.*

¢–$$ ✕ **King's Land Seafood Restaurant.** Like a Chinese eatery in New York or San Francisco, King's Land does dim sum to perfection, serving it daily during the week for lunch and during their crazy, jam-packed weekends. Choose from dozens of little tidbits along with soup and desserts, or go with the regular menu, also available at night, which includes a delectable duck, and seafood specialties. The dining room is huge and always noisy, and the staff doesn't speak much English. Just close your eyes and point. ⊠ *2200 W. Alameda Ave., West Denver* ☎ *303/975–2399* ⚹ *Reservations essential* ⊟ *AE, MC, V.*

Contemporary

$$$$ ✕ **Clair de Lune.** Local favorite chef Sean Kelly has opened a tiny, exclusive restaurant that caters to foodies. There are only six tables, so call as far ahead as possible. It's worth it to squeeze into the quaint, blue space that feels like the moment just before the moon comes up. Kelly cooks a different menu nightly based on local availability and his own whims. What's always on the menu is a plateau de fruits de mer, which includes well-chilled shellfish and a vegetarian option, and his salads are superb symphonies of flavor. The wine list is well chosen and fairly priced, and the staff aims to please. Kelly makes the innovative desserts, too. ⊠ *1313 E. 6th Ave., Central Denver* ☎ *303/831–1992* ⚹ *Reservations essential* ⊟ *No credit cards* ⊗ *Closed Sun. and Mon. No lunch.*

$$$$ ✕ **Restaurant Kevin Taylor.** Elegant doesn't begin to describe the green-and-gold space that is this regal restaurant in the Hotel Teatro. Exclusive upholstery, flatware, and dishes add to the upscale attitude, as does the formal service style and a pricey but top-shelf wine list. The contemporary menu has an updated French bent, with such classics as *pot au feu* (literally "pot on fire," it's meat and vegetables slowly cooked in water) sharing space with roasted red deer fillets and squash blossoms stuffed with *Boursin* (a triple-cream cheese with herbs and garlic). The tasting menu, geared to theatergoers heading to the Denver Center for Performing Arts complex a mere block away, offers a rare chance to try a variety of chef Taylor's eclectic creations, and the stone-lined wine cellar makes for intimate private dining. ⊠ *1106 14th St., Downtown* ☎ *303/820–2600* ⚹ *Reservations essential* ⊟ *AE, DC, MC, V* ⊗ *Closed Sun. No lunch.*

★ $$$–$$$$ ✕ **Adega Restaurant + Wine Bar.** The best indication that Denver can dish it out just like the big cities, cosmopolitan Adega is styled with sleek lines, complementing textures, and a vast wine room that sits at the edge of the dining areas like a giant shrine. The food is cutting-edge, too, since chef Bryan Moscatello, a *Food & Wine* magazine Best New Chefs–award winner, has a suave way with sumptuous ingredients such as foie gras, duck confit, and exotic seafoods. The bar menu of retro comfort foods is fun, too. ⊠ *1700 Wynkoop St., LoDo* ☎ *303/534–2222* ⚹ *Reservations essential* ⊟ *AE, DC, MC, V* ⊗ *Closed Sun. No lunch.*

$$$–$$$$ ✕ **Flow Lounge and Restaurant.** One of the newest additions to Denver's burgeoning roster of hotel restaurants, Flow sits in the boutique-style Luna Hotel in the heart of bustling LoDo. Wall-enclosed waterfalls, curtain-secluded dining spaces, and a late-night bar crowd make Flow one of the hippest spots, too, especially considering the 20-item, snack-oriented bar menu. There's a drink price for every budget, the service is as hip as the clientele, and chef Duy Pham's menu makes good use of the most upscale ingredients to be had. Get anything with foie gras or escargots. ⊠ *1612 Wazee St., LoDo* ☎ *303/572–3300* ⚹ *Reservations essential* ⊟ *AE, D, DC, MC, V* ⊗ *Closed Sun. No lunch.*

$$$–$$$$ ✕ **Highland's Garden Café.** Chef–owner Pat Perry follows the philosophy of Alice Waters and her infamous Chez Panisse: use what's fresh that day. The result is an ever-changing menu that takes advantage of Colorado's unique produce and meats, and Perry puts them together in interesting and refreshing ways. And as the name implies, the outdoor patio is surrounded by elaborate gardens, and the inside dining rooms, which occupy two Victorian houses, are painted with trompe l'oeil

views into gardens, as well. ⊠ *3927 W. 32nd Ave., Highlands* ☏ *303/458–5920* ⚑ *Reservations essential* ☰ *AE, D, DC, MC, V* ☻ *Closed Sun. and Mon. Lunch Fri. only.*

$$$–$$$$ ✕ **Mizuna.** Chef–owner Frank Bonanno knows how to transform butter and cream into comforting masterpieces at this cozy, charming eatery that sports warm colors and intimate seating. His menu is reminiscent of California's French Laundry, with quirky dishes such as "liver and onions" bringing foie gras and a sweet-onion tart, and his Italian heritage has given him the ability to work wonders with red sauce. Be sure to try the griddlecakes for dessert, and expect to be served by the most professional staff in town. ⊠ *225 E. 7th Ave., Central Denver* ☏ *303/832–4778* ⚑ *Reservations essential* ☰ *AE, DC, MC, V* ☻ *Closed Sun. and Mon. No lunch.*

$$$–$$$$ ✕ **Potager.** The menu changes monthly at the industrial-designed Potager, whose name, which means "kitchen garden," refers to the herb-rimmed back patio. Exposed ducts and a high ceiling give the dining room a trendy feel, and the floor-to-ceiling front windows allow the hip to be seen and the twinkling lights outside and in to be reflected for a warm glow. Dishes always include some kind of risotto of the day, along with several fish dishes and the ever-popular goat cheese souffle. The wine list is all over the map but well priced, and the servers are among the most savvy in town. ⊠ *1109 Ogden St., Central Denver* ☏ *303/832–5788* ⚑ *Reservations not accepted* ☰ *AE, MC, V* ☻ *Closed Sun. and Mon. No lunch.*

$$–$$$$ ✕ **1515 Restaurant.** Owner Gene Tang seems to be one of the hardest working men in the restaurant business, judging by the personal attention he gives the tables in his two-story place. Walking past the first-floor bar gives diners the feeling of being someplace important, as locals hang out and keep their eyes on the door. Once upstairs, though, it's all business, with efficient servers bringing a succession of world-beat fare that's highly structural and eminently flavorful. Braised lamb shank shares space on the menu comfortably with sake-glazed ahi, and trendy foams can be found alongside textbook crab cakes. The menu also offers a few vegetarian options, meat lovers can try Kobe beef, and the wine list is a wonder—affordable and daring. Lunch is a low-priced alternative. ⊠ *1515 Market St., LoDo* ☏ *303/571–0011* ⚑ *Reservations essential* ☰ *AE, D, DC, MC, V* ☻ *Closed Sun. No lunch Sat.*

$$–$$$$ ✕ **The Fourth Story.** At the top of the Tattered Cover Book Store, the librarylike dining room holds the extra appeal of the many books that line the shelves, all available for perusing while you dine. The menu offers combinations of local ingredients and international foods such as cornmeal-crusted halibut with coriander broth and roasted duck with smoked figs and blood-orange jus. The tea selection is tops, and the staff knows its stuff. Added bonus: this is one of Denver's few rooms with a view that includes a peek at the mountains. ⊠ *2955 E. 1st Ave., Cherry Creek North* ☏ *303/322–1824* ⚑ *Reservations essential* ☰ *AE, D, DC, MC, V* ☻ *No dinner Sun.*

$$–$$$$ ✕ **Mel's Bar and Grill.** Taking its moniker from proprietor Mel Masters, this cheery Cherry Creek bistro is a perennial favorite of local and national critics. Italian and French traditions are injected with the occasional Asian spin, and the seasonal menu can always be counted on for its delectable mussels *La Cagouille*, award-winning Caesar salad, and exceptional grilled-salmon and beef-tenderloin dinners. The atmosphere is gracious and unpretentious, with a jazz combo performing nightly. The bar here doubles as a laid-back neighborhood hangout and serves up some of Denver's best (and biggest) burgers. ⊠ *235 Fillmore St., Cherry Creek North* ☏ *303/333–3979* ⚑ *Reservations essential* ☰ *AE, D, DC, MC, V* ☻ *No lunch Sun.*

$$-$$$$ ✕ **Strings.** This light, airy restaurant with its wide-open kitchen resembles an artist's loft. It's a preferred hangout for Denver's movers and shakers as well as for visiting celebs, whose autographs on head shots, napkins, and program notes hang on the walls. The specialties include seafood dishes and pasta, and the desserts are amazingly intricate and well crafted. ✉ *1700 Humboldt St., Central Denver* ☎ *303/831–7310* ⌂ *Reservations essential* ▤ *AE, D, DC, MC, V* ⊘ *No lunch Sun.*

$$-$$$$ ✕ **Vesta Dipping Grill.** The building and space have won national architectural awards, and it's easy to see why. The sensual swirls of fabric and copper throughout the room make diners feel as though they're inside a giant work of art, and the clever, secluded banquettes are among the most sought-after seats in town. The menu is clever, too, and the competent grill masters in the kitchen put out expertly cooked meats, fish, and vegetables, all of which can be paired with some of the three dozen dipping sauces that get their inspiration from chutneys, salsas, mother sauces, and barbecue. The wine list is as cool as the clientele. ✉ *1822 Blake St., LoDo* ☎ *303/296–1970* ⌂ *Reservations essential* ▤ *AE, D, DC, MC, V* ⊘ *No lunch.*

$$-$$$ ✕ **bistro jou jou.** The less expensive little sister of the upscale Kevin Taylor restaurant in the Hotel Teatro, the mustard-colored jou jou is 1930s funky, more casual, and focused on lighter fare served at breakfast, lunch, and dinner. Comfort food such as mashed potatoes and macaroni and cheese come as sides to roasted pork and grilled tuna, and the breakfast options pull from all over the world. Brunch is served on weekends, and the theater crowd loves the one-block proximity to the Denver Center for Performing Arts complex. A great wooden bar invites customers to linger. ✉ *1106 14th St., Downtown* ☎ *303/228–0770* ⌂ *Reservations essential* ▤ *AE, DC, MC, V.*

$–$$ ✕ **Dazzle Supper Club.** If it's martinis and jazz you're after, come to this art-deco space that allows for a groovy bar scene on one side and groovy dining on the other. The menu is as retro as the atmosphere, with an emphasis on comfort foods with a twist (check out the gourmet macaroni and cheese), and live music most nights makes for a laid-back feel. The cocktail roster, printed inside old jazz albums, is one of the most intricate around. ✉ *930 Lincoln St., Central Denver* ☎ *303/839–5100* ▤ *AE, DC, MC, V* ⊘ *No lunch.*

¢–$ ✕ **WaterCourse Foods.** In a town known for its beef, WaterCourse stands out as one of a handful of eateries devoted to the vegetarian. This casual, low-key place offers three meals a day, most of which are based on fruits, vegetables, whole grains, and meatlike soy substitutes. There are vegan and macrobiotic dishes available, along with items for those who eat cheese and eggs. The Reuben is amazing. ✉ *206 E. 13th Ave., Capitol Hill* ☎ *303/832–7313* ▤ *MC, V* ⊘ *Closed Mon.*

French

$$$–$$$$ ✕ **Tante Louise.** This longtime Denver favorite, just 15 minutes from downtown by car, resembles an intimate French country home. Fireplaces, candlelight, and classical music attract a decidedly mature crowd. About one-third of the seasonally changing menu is French, one-third is new American, and one-third features low-fat dishes. The service is among the best in town, and the staff loves its job. ✉ *4900 E. Colfax Ave., East Denver* ☎ *303/355–4488* ▤ *AE, D, DC, MC, V* ⊘ *Closed Sun. No lunch.*

$$-$$$$ ✕ **Aix.** The foods of Provence are showcased in a small, whimsically chic eatery that is part urban-hipster and part auberge. Dishes include a Napoleon made from crab and zucchini, a French-olive-stuffed quail and herb-lacquered salmon, and the clam-risotto appetizer is to die for. The room can get noisy once it's full, but the black-clad staff tries hard and the wine list is decidedly French. The Sunday brunch is a hit; the menu

changes weekly. ✉ *719 E. 17th Ave., Central Denver* ☎ *303/831–1296* ▭ *AE, D, DC, MC, V* ⊗ *Closed Mon. No dinner Sun. No lunch.*

$–$$ ✕ **Le Central.** This homey bistro serves excellent mussel dishes and provincial French specialties, including beef *Bourguignonne* (braised in red wine and garnished with mushrooms and onions), salmon *en croûte* (wrapped in pastry and baked), and steak au poivre. A real find, you can depend on Le Central for fabulous food, great service, and a surprisingly low tab. ✉ *112 E. 8th Ave., Central Denver* ☎ *303/863–8094* ▭ *AE, D, DC, MC, V.*

German

$–$$$ ✕ **Cafe Berlin.** The white walls are covered with German frescos, and tables with white linens set the tone for a serious time at this family-run restaurant. No fake beer-house stuff here: the potato pancakes taste like your German grandma made them, and the liver pâté and home-made German bread are as authentic as it gets. The kitchen attempts to lighten up heavy items such as dumplings, spaetzle, and wiener schnitzel, and the sweet-and-sour cabbage is amazing. Finish off with an apple strudel, and check out the German-beer roster. ✉ *2005 E. 17th Ave., Central Denver* ☎ *303/377–5896* ▭ *D, MC, V* ⊗ *No lunch weekends.*

Indian

$$–$$$ ✕ **India House.** Diners get to see their food being prepared in the tandoori in this beautiful renovation of the longtime Denver Indian eatery Delhi Darbar. The spicing is gentle and the preparations skillful on the lengthy, well-chosen menu, which includes vegetarian options. A local favorite is the *shahi sabz,* vegetables in a nut-strewn cream sauce, and the housemade ice creams are delicious. The market-price lobster dishes are special, too. ✉ *1514 Blake St., LoDo* ☎ *303/595–0680* ▭ *AE, D, DC, MC, V.*

$–$$ ✕ **Little India.** The all-you-can-eat lunch buffet for $6.50, which spreads out dozens of well-prepared Indian dishes, is the big draw for Denverites at this casually elegant restaurant between downtown and Cherry Creek. Little India's menu has nearly 100 items, but it specializes in curries, *vindaloos,* and *biryanis,* all of which are expertly spiced. Be sure to try one of the many specialty *naans* (tandoori-baked flatbread). The sweet mango *lassi,* a yogurt drink, is delightfully rich. ✉ *330 E. 6th Ave., Central Denver* ☎ *303/871–9777* ▭ *MC, V.*

Italian

$$$–$$$$ ✕ **Barolo Grill.** This restaurant looks like a chichi farmhouse, as if Martha Stewart went gaga over an Italian count. Dried flowers in brass urns, hand-painted porcelain, and straw baskets are everywhere. The food isn't pretentious in the least, however. It's more like Santa Monica meets San Stefano—bold, yet classic, healthful, yet flavorful. Choose from duckling stewed in red wine, fresh pastas, and gnocchi, all well made and fairly priced. ✉ *3030 E. 6th Ave., Central Denver* ☎ *303/393–1040* ⌕ *Reservations essential* ▭ *AE, D, DC, MC, V* ⊗ *Closed Sun. and Mon. No lunch.*

$$–$$$$ ✕ **Campo de Fiori.** As bright and airy as the marketplace this Italian eatery is named for, Campo serves up fresh, regional fare that makes it one of the busiest spots in town. Some come for the spacious, see-and-be-seen bar scene, some for the simple but flavorful fare, but all are treated well by the experienced staff. The food includes fried calamari, bruschetta, and grilled fresh vegetables as starters, and the entrées are a mix of pastas and grilled meats. The room is filled with tile-topped tables and surrounded by wall murals evocative of the Italian countryside. ✉ *300 Fillmore St., Cherry Creek North* ☎ *303/377–7887* ⌕ *Reservations essential* ▭ *AE, DC, MC, V.*

$–$$$$ ✕ **Carmine's on Penn.** It's hard to pick out this house from the ones that surround it in this cozy neighborhood, but the steady crowds streaming in and out of its art-lined dining rooms are a sure sign. They come for the family-style servings, double and triple portions for the same price many places charge for one, and the food is outstanding, to boot. Tomatoes, garlic, basil, and good-quality olive oil make up the basis of many of the meals, and the sauces are superb: puttanesca, bolognese, *boscaiolo* (a rich mushroom sauce). The menu is written out on chalkboards on the walls, and there's a private back room for big groups. ✉ *92 S. Pennsylvania St., Washington Park* ☎ *303/777–6443* ⌕ *Reservations essential* ▭ *AE, D, DC, MC, V* ⊗ *Closed Mon. No lunch.*

★ **$$–$$$**   ✕ **Panzano.** The dining room is filled with fresh flowers and sided by windows that let in the natural light, and that makes this space within the Hotel Monaco cheerful and bright. Three meals a day are served, but it's lunch and dinner that focus on true Italian, cooked by talented chef Jennifer Jasinski, who is making a national splash as a smart interpreter of the cuisine. Everything on the menu is multilayered, such as white asparagus salad with basil aioli, watercress, and endive; or risotto made with caramelized acorn squash and foie gras mousse. The breads are baked in-house, and the superior service and accommodating atmosphere make for a pleasant dining experience. The large, roomy bar is available for dining, too. ✉ *909 17th St., Central Denver* ☎ *303/296–3525* ⌕ *Reservations essential* ▭ *AE, D, DC, MC, V.*

$–$$$ ✕ **Luca d'Italia.** The restaurant's steel-gray, orange-and-red contemporary decor belies the fact that it's one of the most authentic Italian restaurants in the city. Chef–owner Frank Bonanno calls upon his Italian grandmother to re-create small-town Italy through wild boar with pappardelle, duck-liver-stuffed ravioli and house-cured capocollo and homemade cheeses, and his tiramisu and dairy-free chocolate sorbet have to be tasted to be believed. Service is as impeccable as at Bonanno's other restaurant, Mizuna, and the wine list is agreeably priced and heavy on interesting Italians. ✉ *711 Grant St., Central Denver* ☎ *303/832–4778* ⌕ *Reservations essential* ▭ *AE, D, DC, MC, V* ⊗ *Closed Sun. and Mon. No lunch.*

¢–$$ ✕ **Anthony's Pizza.** The closest Denver gets to a New York slice, this two-story spot has a standing counter as well as a sit-down dining area upstairs. Fold each triangle in half, tilt it to let it drip, and inhale. ✉ *1550 California St., Downtown* ☎ *303/573–6236* ▭ *MC, V* ⊗ *Closed Sun.*

¢–$$ ✕ **Pasquini's Pizzeria.** Come to this informal, popular spot to indulge in fresh, homemade pastas, pizzas, and calzones. Individual pizzas are the house specialty. Don't miss the bakery's fresh Italian breads. ✉ *1310 S. Broadway, Central Denver* ☎ *303/744–0917* ▭ *AE, D, DC, MC, V* ⊗ *No dinner Sun.*

Japanese

★ **$–$$$$**   ✕ **Sushi Den.** With a sister restaurant in Japan and owners who import sushi-grade seafood to the United States, it's easy to see why Denverites count on this chic sushi bar to provide the best quality available. Novices and sushi experts alike will find that the sushi chefs here can meet their every request, and the cooked dishes are just as well prepared (don't miss the steamed fish baskets). There's almost always a wait to get in (sometimes for two hours) and parking can be a hassle, but this is the place to be for serious sushi-heads. Check out the tony crowd and feast your eyes on the luxurious fabrics and well-designed furniture. Although the entrée prices aren't overly high, the sushi itself commands top dollar. ✉ *1487 S. Pearl St., Central Denver* ☎ *303/777–0826* ⌕ *Reservations not accepted* ▭ *MC, V* ⊗ *No lunch weekends.*

$$–$$$ ✕ **Domo.** Domo's owners pride themselves on fresh flavors and the pains-taking preparation of Japanese country foods, as well as one of the largest sake selections in town. Everything is prepared to order, and it's worth the wait: this is where you'll find some of Denver's best seafood, curry dishes, and vegetarian fare. The house specialty is *wankosushi*—three to five servings of sushi accompanied by rice, soup, and six of Domo's tantalizing side dishes. The restaurant also houses a cultural-education center, a museum, and a Japanese garden. ✉ *1365 Osage St., Central Denver* ☎ *303/595–3666* ▭ *MC, V* ☉ *Closed Sun.–Wed.*

¢–$$$ ✕ **Sonoda's.** In the below-street-level dining room and sushi bar, the blue colors, aquariums, and colorful fish hanging everywhere make you feel as though *you're* inside a fish tank. Instead, you're just getting to take advantage of the wares of some savvy sushi chefs, who match pace with a kitchen that puts out great grilled fish, teriyaki, and tempura, too. The meals all come with sides of salad, vegetables, and rice, and the sake selection is competitive. The staff is eager to turn first-timers on to entry-level sushi, and the sushi chefs themselves are unusually friendly. ✉ *1620 Market St., Downtown* ☎ *303/337–3800* ▭ *MC, V* ☉ *No lunch Sun.*

Mexican

$$–$$$ ✕ **LoLa.** Tableside guacamole, more than 90 tequilas, superior margaritas and a clever, glass-lined bar area are just a few of the reasons the lovely LoLa has become a locals hangout. The food is modern Mexican, with fresh seafood in *escabeche* (marinated, poached fish), *ceviche* (lime-cooked fish), and salads, as well as smoked rib eye and chicken *frito* (fried chicken). The candlelit dining room is comfy and relaxing, and a Mexican-style brunch is served Sunday. ✉ *1469 S. Pearl St., Central Denver* ☎ *720/570–8686* ⚱ *Reservations not accepted* ▭ *AE, DC, MC, V.*

$$–$$$ ✕ **Tamayo.** Chef–owner Richard Sandoval brought his popular concept of modern, upscale Mexican from New York to Denver, and it's just as welcome here. The food is classic Mexican with a twist, such as seafood tacos, *huitlacoche* (edible fungus) soup, elaborate moles, and chocolate tamales for dessert. The tequila flights are a favorite at the large, inviting bar, which is highlighted by a mural made of semiprecious stones (made by artist and restaurant namesake Rufino Tamayo). In season, the outdoor patio offers a rare view of the mountains, and the interior is filled with screens made from blonde wood and Spanish art. ✉ *1400 Larimer St., Larimer Square* ☎ *720/946–1433* ⚱ *Reservations essential* ▭ *AE, MC, V* ☉ *No lunch weekends.*

$–$$ ✕ **Lime.** A basement-level hidden gem, Lime is green and white, gently lighted, and always happening. The made-to-order deep-fried tortilla chips arrive at the table when you do, and the salsas are zippy and well crafted. Imbibers are treated to a half-shot in a lime shell, and the Mighty Margarita is the only way to go from there. Shrimp stuffed with jalapeños and cream cheese (called scorpions), the tamales, and chiles rellenos are all winners, and the bar is a fun place for late-night snacking. ✉ *1424 Larimer St., Larimer Square* ☎ *303/893–5463* ▭ *AE, MC, V* ☉ *Closed Sun. No lunch.*

¢–$$ ✕ **Blue Bonnet Cafe and Lounge.** Its location out of the tourist loop, in a fairly seedy neighborhood southeast of downtown, doesn't stop the crowds (mostly tourists) from lining up early for this restaurant. The early Western, Naugahyde decor and fantastic jukebox set up an upbeat mood for killer margaritas and some of the best burritos and green chile in town. ✉ *457 S. Broadway, Central Denver* ☎ *303/778–0147* ⚱ *Reservations not accepted* ▭ *MC, V.*

$ ✕ **Jack 'n' Grill.** The friendly family that runs this small, pepper-decorated place moved to Denver from New Mexico, and they brought their love of chiles with them. The green chile is fire-breathing spicy, and the red is a smoky, complex brew. The best item, though, is the plate of *vaquero* tacos, chicken or beef, slathered with a sticky-sweet barbecue sauce and served on buttery tortillas. Lunch is always packed, so arrive early. There's no liquor license. ☒ *2424 Federal Blvd., North Denver* ☎ *303/964–9544* ⌔ *Reservations not accepted* ▭ *MC, V* ☉ *Closed Sun. and Mon.*

¢ ✕ **Tosh's Hacienda.** At the northernmost light-rail stop, Tosh's rewards arrivals with hearty and healthy Mexican fare in a festive atrium bedecked in tile and Southwestern art. Specialties include stuffed *sopaipillas* (puffy, deep-fried pockets), spinach enchiladas, and a whole host of seafood offerings. Kids can order off the children's menu. The service is brisk and attentive at this fiftysomething eatery, and the margaritas spiced with prickly pear cactus are decidedly different. ☒ *3090 Downing St., Central Denver* ☎ *303/295–1861* ⌔ *Reservations not accepted* ▭ *MC, V.*

Seafood

$$–$$$$ ✕ **Del Mar Crab House.** Ahoy, mateys, to the most nautically themed eatery in landlocked Denver. Even better, some of the freshest fish is found here, all served in the most austere manner possible to allow the natural flavors to shine. The below-street-level restaurant has a seafood market in addition to its daily roster of fresh options, including lobster, crab, shrimp, and oysters, and the low-price happy hour is a locals' favorite. There are steaks for the landlubbers, as well, and the clam chowder and crab bisque are smart starters. ☒ *1453 Larimer St., Larimer Square* ☎ *303/825–4747* ▭ *AE, D, DC, MC, V.*

$–$$$ ✕ **Jax Fish House.** A popular oyster bar serves as the foyer to the ever-busy Jax, whose brick-lined back dining room packs in the crowds, especially when there's a ball game at Coors Field three blocks away. A dozen different types of oysters are freshly shucked each day, and they can be paired with one of the house-made, fruit-infused vodkas or chile-fired shooters. The main courses make use of fresh catches such as ahi, scallops, snapper, and shrimp, and although there are a couple of meat dishes, only the truly fish-phobic should go there. The sides are fun, too: beignets, succotash, frittatas. The Oreo pie for dessert is a must-have. ☒ *1539 17th St., LoDo* ☎ *303/292–5767* ⌔ *Reservations essential* ▭ *AE, DC, MC, V.*

Southwestern

$–$$ ✕ **Julia Blackbird's.** Julia Blackbird herself cooks the food at this colorfully decorated eatery that specializes in cooking from northern New Mexico. The tiny, narrow space feels like Blackbird's home, and her staff is as welcoming as if it were theirs, too. Baked goods are made from blue corn, stews of hominy and beans abound, and the chiles are stuffed with goat cheese and smothered in a thick, chile-spiked sauce. Forget about beer to wash it down with—there's no liquor license. ☒ *3617 W. 32nd Ave., Highlands* ☎ *303/433–2688* ⌔ *Reservations not accepted* ▭ *MC, V* ☉ *Closed Mon. No dinner Sun.*

Steak–Western

$$$–$$$$ ✕ **The Fort.** This adobe structure, complete with flickering luminarias
FodorśChoice and a piñon bonfire in the courtyard, is a perfect reproduction of Bent's
★ Fort, a Colorado fur-trade center. Buffalo meat and game are the specialties; the elk with huckleberry sauce and tequila-marinated quail are especially good. Intrepid eaters might try the buffalo bone-marrow appetizer, jalapeños stuffed with peanut butter, or Rocky Mountain oysters. Costumed characters from the fur trade wander the restaurant, playing the mandolin and telling tall tales. ☒ *U.S. 285 and Rte. 8, Morrison* ☎ *303/697–4771* ▭ *AE, D, DC, MC, V* ☉ *No lunch.*

$$$–$$$$ ╳ **Morton's of Chicago.** The Denver outpost of this nationally revered steak house is as swank and overwhelming as the rest, with dark woods, white linens, and the signature steak knives at each place setting. Diners are greeted by expert staff wielding the cuts of the day and their accompaniments, and once choices are made the experience is almost always seamless. The steaks themselves are superb, prime and well aged, grilled to specifications and unadorned. Be forewarned that all sides cost extra, and they are big enough to feed two or three. The extensive wine list is pricey, and the delicious desserts are enormous (check out the souffle for two, which must be ordered at the start of the meal). ⊠ *1710 Wynkoop St., LoDo* ☎ *303/825–3353* ⌂ *Reservations essential* ▭ *AE, DC, MC, V* ✆ *No lunch.*

$$$–$$$$ ╳ **Palm Restaurant.** This Denver outpost of the longtime New York steak house serves meat, seafood, pork chops, and other American dishes à la carte. The walls are bedecked with caricatures of local celebrities, and there's a chance you might see one in person—the restaurant is a favorite of local politicians, executives, and athletes, and with good reason: the steaks and the portions are both superlative. ⊠ *1672 Lawrence St., Downtown* ☎ *303/825–7256* ▭ *AE, D, DC, MC, V* ✆ *No lunch weekends.*

$$–$$$$ ╳ **Buckhorn Exchange.** If hunting makes you queasy, don't enter this Denver landmark, a shrine to taxidermy where 500 pairs of eyes stare down at you from the walls. The handsome men's-club decor—with pressed-tin ceilings, burgundy walls, red-checker tablecloths, rodeo photos, shotguns, and those trophies—probably looks the same as it did when the Buckhorn first opened in 1893. Rumor has it Buffalo Bill was to the Buckhorn what Norm Peterson was to *Cheers*. The dry-aged, prime-grade Colorado steaks are huge, juicy, and magnificent, as is the game. For an appetizer, try the smoked buffalo sausage or navy bean soup. ⊠ *1000 Osage St., Central Denver* ☎ *303/534–9505* ▭ *AE, D, DC, MC, V* ✆ *No lunch weekends.*

$$–$$$$ ╳ **Denver ChopHouse & Brewery.** This is the best of the many LoDo brewpubs and restaurants surrounding the Coors Field ballpark. Housed in the old Union Pacific Railroad warehouse, the restaurant has a clubby atmosphere, with dark-wood paneling and exposed brick. The food is basic American, and there's plenty of it: steaks, seafood, and chicken served with hot corn bread and honey butter, and "bottomless" salads tossed at the table. ⊠ *1735 19th St., LoDo* ☎ *303/296–0800* ▭ *AE, DC, MC, V.*

$$–$$$$ ╳ **Keg Steakhouse.** Right across from Coors Field, the Canada-based Keg is in a prime position to be packed throughout the baseball season. But it's full year-round for other reasons: the choice-grade beef, encrusted with a signature blend of salty spices, is grilled the way you request. The best cut is the "baseball," a 12-ounce hunk of fillet, and unlike the big-boy steak houses, the sides here actually come with the meat. Ladies are usually more comfortable here than at the "men's club" steak chains, and the room dominated by a giant painting of Colorado's Maroon Bells offers a combination of relaxed but elegant dining. The kids' menu is reasonably priced. ⊠ *1890 Wynkoop St., LoDo* ☎ *303/296–0023* ⌂ *Reservations essential* ▭ *AE, D, DC, MC, V* ✆ *No lunch weekends.*

$$–$$$$ ╳ **Sullivan's Steakhouse.** Sullivan's bills itself as a more affordable steak house, and although technically that's true, it's easy to spend just as much here as at any other top-tier steak joint. Still, it's worth it, because the hand-carved, aged Black Angus beef is of high quality, well grilled, and accompanied by stellar sides such as grill-greasy onion rings and chunky mashed potatoes. The wood-lined bar room is filled with high tables and makes for a fun gathering place, especially when there's live jazz. The overall feel is that of a 1940s club. ⊠ *1745 Wazee St., LoDo*

☎ *303/295–2664* ⚠ *Reservations essential* 🍽 *AE, D, DC, MC, V* ⊘ *No lunch weekends.*

Swiss

$$–$$$$ ╳ **La Fondue.** Each table has its own stove setup that allows diners to cook the foods they choose, and the choices are what makes the experience so special. Sit in an elegant, warmly colored space that manages to be casual and classy at the same time, all the while simmering seafood, beef, and chicken to your liking in one of the flavored broths. You can then dip the foods into a variety of seasoned sauces while savvy servers keep an eye on the proceedings. Don't be alarmed by the seemingly high prices: all of the fondue meals are for two, and include a starter of cheese as well as salads and dessert, the latter of which involves decadent chocolate. ⊠ *1040 15th St., Downtown* ☎ *303/534–0404* ⚠ *Reservations essential* 🍽 *AE, D, DC, MC, V* ⊘ *No lunch.*

Vietnamese

★ **$–$$** ╳ **New Saigon.** Picked as Denver's best Vietnamese by every local publication for more than a decade, New Saigon is always crowded with folks trying to get at their crispy egg rolls, shrimp-filled spring rolls, and cheap but hefty noodle bowls. With nearly 200 dishes on the menu, this vast, avocado-color eatery has everything Vietnamese covered, including 30-some vegetarian dishes and 10 with succulent frogs legs. Service can be spotty and not much English is spoken, but the staff goes overboard trying to help and never steers anyone wrong. It's best to go at off times to ensure a seat. ⊠ *630 S. Federal Blvd., West Denver* ☎ *303/936–4954* ⚠ *Reservations not accepted* 🍽 *MC, V.*

WHERE TO STAY

By Kyle Wagner

Denver has lodging choices ranging from the stately Brown Palace to the commonplace YMCA, with options such as bed-and-breakfasts and business hotels in between. Unless you're planning a quick escape to the mountains, consider staying in or around downtown, where most of the city's attractions are within walking distance. Most of the hotels cater to business travelers, with accordingly lower rates on weekends (many establishments slash their rates in half on Friday and Saturday).

WHAT IT COSTS				
$$$$	**$$$**	**$$**	**$**	**¢**
FOR 2 PEOPLE over $200	$151–$200	$111–$150	$70–$110	under $70

Prices are for two people in a standard double room in high season, excluding service charges and 5.4%–9.8% tax.

★ **$$$$** ▦ **Brown Palace.** This grande dame of Colorado lodging has hosted public figures from President Eisenhower to the Beatles since it first opened its doors in 1892. The details are exquisite: a dramatic nine-story lobby is topped with a glorious stained-glass ceiling, and the Victorian rooms have sophisticated wainscoting and art deco fixtures. The hotel pays equal attention to modern necessities, such as high-speed Web access, business services, and cordless telephones. The Palace Arms, its formal restaurant, has won numerous awards, including several from *Wine Spectator* magazine. The Churchill cigar bar sells rare cigars and single-malt scotches. ⊠ *321 17th St., Downtown, 80202* ☎ *303/297–3111 or 800/321–2599* 🖷 *303/312–5900* ⊕ *www.brownpalace.com* 🛏 *230 rooms, 25 suites* ♨ *4 restaurants, room service, in-room data ports, in-room fax, some refrigerators, cable TV, some in-room VCRs, gym, hair salon,*

2 bars, shops, laundry service, concierge, business services, parking (fee), no-smoking rooms ▤ *AE, D, DC, MC, V.*

★ **$$$$** ▦ **Hotel Teatro.** Black-and-white photographs, costumes, and scenery from plays that were staged in the Denver Performing Arts Complex across the street are displayed in the several grand public areas of this hotel. The earth-tone rooms are sleek, simple, and stylish, featuring the latest in technology; spacious bathrooms have separate tubs and showers have top-of-the-line amenities. The ninth-floor rooms have balconies. There are two highly regarded restaurants here: a casual bistro, jou jou, and the contemporary and elegant Restaurant Kevin Taylor. ✉ *1100 14th St., Downtown, 80202* ☎ *303/228–1100 or 888/727–1200* 🖷 *303/ 228–1101* ⊕ *www.hotelteatro.com* ⤺ *111 rooms, 8 suites* ⚿ *2 restaurants, in-room data ports, in-room fax, cable TV, gym, bar, laundry service, concierge, business services, parking (fee), no-smoking rooms* ▤ *AE, D, DC, MC, V.*

$$$$ ▦ **Westin Tabor Center.** This sleek, luxurious high-rise opens right onto the 16th Street Mall and all the downtown action. Rooms are oversize and done in grays and taupes, with white duvets, piles of cushy pillows, and contemporary prints on the walls. The fourth-floor pool has one of the best views of the Rockies in all of downtown. The hotel buys blocks of tickets for weekend shows at the Denver Performing Arts Complex for guests' exclusive use. The Palm, a branch of the Manhattan-based steak house, is a favorite eating and drinking spot for local luminaries. ✉ *1672 Lawrence St., Downtown, 80202* ☎ *303/572–9100 or 800/ 937–8461* 🖷 *303/572–7288* ⊕ *www.westin.com* ⤺ *430 rooms* ⚿ *2 restaurants, room service, in-room data ports, cable TV, pool, health club, racquetball, 2 bars, laundry service, concierge, business services, parking (fee), no-smoking rooms* ▤ *AE, D, DC, MC, V.*

★ **$$$–$$$$** ▦ **Hotel Monaco.** Celebrities and business travelers check into this hip property with modern perks and art deco–meets–classic-French style. The unabashedly colorful guest rooms feature original art, custom headboards, glass-front armoires, and CD players. The service is similarly a cut above: room service is available 24 hours, pets are welcome, and guests without pets are given the complimentary company of a goldfish. The hotel's mascot, a Jack Russell terrier named Lily Sopris is one of Denver's best-known canines. ✉ *1717 Champa St., Downtown, 80202* ☎ *303/296–1717 or 800/397–5380* 🖷 *303/296–1818* ⊕ *www. monaco-denver.com* ⤺ *157 rooms, 32 suites* ⚿ *Restaurant, room service, in-room data ports, in-room fax, some in-room hot tubs, minibars, cable TV, gym, hair salon, health club, spa, bar, laundry service, concierge, business services, parking (fee), some pets allowed, no-smoking rooms* ▤ *AE, D, DC, MC, V.*

★ **$$$–$$$$** ▦ **Luna Hotel.** One of Denver's newest hotels, the boutique-style Luna is in the heart of LoDo and in the middle of the city's bustling nightlife. Romantic and urban-chic guest rooms are furnished in sleek, dark woods and velvety fabrics, and each contains a French press coffee maker, a minibar full of juices and water rather than alcohol, flat-screen televisions, and a DVD library. For a fee, you can access wireless Internet. With only 21 guest quarters, Luna can focus on pampering; room service delivers complimentary crepes each morning (from Velocity, the creperie on the lobby level), and a personal concierge is available to guests day and night. Flow, an upscale, fusion restaurant with a snazzy bar and private-dining areas, is one of the best restaurants in town. ✉ *1612 Wazee St., LoDo, 80202* ☎ *303/572–3300 or 866/724–5862* 🖷 *303/ 623–0773* ⊕ *www.thelunahotel.com* ⤺ *19 rooms, 2 suites* ⚿ *2 restaurants, room service, in-room data ports, minibars, cable TV, bar, laundry service, concierge, Internet, business services, parking (fee); no smoking* ▤ *AE, D, DC, MC, V.*

$$–$$$$ 🏨 **Embassy Suites Hotel & Athletic Club Denver Downtown.** With half of the rooms classified as suites, the hotel's appeal for business travelers and families is high (kids will love that the pool is open all year and it's a quick walk to Coors Field). Cheery, brightly colored rooms have extra-large desks, as well as wet bars, microwaves, and refrigerators. Forgo breakfast in your room for the complimentary cooked-to-order dishes in the comfy Foothills Lounge. The Club Deli/Starbucks makes smoothies, and there's a manager's reception each evening in an area with a view of LoDo. ✉ *1881 Curtis St., LoDo, 80202* ☎ *303/297–8888 or 800/733–3366* 🖷 *303/298–1103* ⊕ *www.esdendt.com* ⇨ *360 rooms, 355 suites* ♧ *3 restaurants, room service, in-room data ports, kitchenettes, microwaves, cable TV, pool, hot tub, gym, bar, dry cleaning, laundry service, concierge, Internet, business services, parking (fee), no-smoking rooms* ▤ *AE, D, DC, MC, V* ⋈ *BP.*

$–$$$$ 🏨 **Adam's Mark.** The city's largest hotel for conventions is composed of two distinct structures: a former Radisson designed by I. M. Pei and the onetime May D&F Department Store across the street. The glittering glass hotel—among the 25 largest in the country—includes more than 1,000 rooms and 130,000 square feet of meeting space. The location, at one end of the 16th Street Mall, is ideal. ✉ *1550 Court Pl., Downtown, 80202* ☎ *303/893–3333 or 800/444–2326* 🖷 *303/626–2543* ⊕ *www.adamsmark.com/denver* ⇨ *1,225 rooms, 100 suites* ♧ *3 restaurants, room service, in-room data ports, cable TV, pool, gym, hair salon, health club, sauna, steam room, 3 bars, dry cleaning, laundry service, concierge, business services, convention center, parking (fee), no-smoking rooms* ▤ *AE, D, DC, MC, V.*

$–$$$$ 🏨 **Denver Marriott City Center.** The newly renovated Denver Marriott touts half of its rooms as being geared toward the business traveler. The hotel is a three-block walk to the Denver Convention Complex and it offers 25,000 square feet of meeting space of its own. Rooms are small but classy, with a strong "executive" feel (many stripes, much leather). The cozy, fall-color Great Divide Lounge and the savvy American fare at Allies American Grille please all guests, whether they're on an expense account or not. ✉ *1701 California St., Downtown, 80202* ☎ *303/297–1300 or 800/228–9290* 🖷 *303/298–7474* ⊕ *www.denvermarriott.com* ⇨ *613 rooms, 14 suites* ♧ *Restaurant, room service, in-room data ports, cable TV, indoor pool, hot tub, sauna, gym, bar, dry cleaning, laundry service, concierge, Internet, business services, parking (fee), no-smoking rooms* ▤ *AE, D, DC, MC, V.*

$–$$$$ 🏨 **Hyatt Regency.** The Hyatt is close to Larimer Square, the theaters, the 16th Street Mall, and the Colorado Convention Center. A stone fireplace makes for an inviting lobby and the roomy quarters are done in beige-and-violet tones with black accents. The Colorado-theme eatery 1876 (named for the year of statehood) is decorated in wrought iron and cherrywood and serves contemporary Front Range favorites. The fitness center is one of the most well-rounded of any hotel's in town. ✉ *1750 Welton St., Downtown, 80202* ☎ *303/295–1234 or 800/233–1234* 🖷 *303/292–2472* ⊕ *www.denver.regency.hyatt.com* ⇨ *526 rooms, 30 suites* ♧ *Restaurant, room service, minibars, cable TV, pool, hot tub, gym, laundry service, concierge, business services, parking (fee and free), no-smoking rooms* ▤ *AE, D, DC, MC, V.*

$–$$$$ 🏨 **Loews Denver Hotel.** The 12-story steel-and-black-glass facade conceals the unexpected and delightful Italian baroque motif within. Spacious rooms are done in earth tones and blond wood, and have such lovely touches as fresh flowers, fruit baskets, and Renaissance-style portraits. The formal Tuscany restaurant serves sumptuous Italian cuisine. Guests may use a nearby health club, and a Continental breakfast is included on Sunday. The only drawback of this property is its location: halfway between downtown and the Denver Tech Center, with little in the immediate vicinity. ✉ *4150 E. Mississippi Ave., Southeast Denver, 80222* ☎ *303/782–9300 or 800/345–9172* 🖷 *303/758–6542* ⊕ *www.loewshotels.com* ⇨ *183 rooms, 19 suites* ♿ *Restaurant, room service, in-room data ports, in-room fax, minibars, cable TV, health club, bar, laundry service, concierge, business services, free parking, no-smoking rooms* ▤ *AE, D, DC, MC, V.*

$–$$$$ 🏨 **Warwick Hotel.** This stylish business hotel ideally located on the edge of downtown, underwent a monumental $20 million renovation that was completed in 2001. The stylish, oversize rooms and suites are some of the nicest in town, with brass and mahogany furnishings and the latest in high-tech perks. All rooms contain wet bars and private terraces with exceptional city views. A restaurant, Randolph's, serves contemporary American cuisine three meals daily. ✉ *1776 Grant St., Downtown, 80203* ☎ *303/861–2000 or 800/525–2888* 🖷 *303/839–8504* ⊕ *www.warwickhotels.com* ⇨ *220 rooms, 20 suites* ♿ *Restaurant, room service, in-room data ports, in-room safes, minibars, cable TV, pool, health club, 2 bars, concierge, business services, parking (fee), no-smoking rooms* ▤ *AE, D, DC, MC, V.*

★ $$–$$$ 🏨 **Oxford Hotel.** During the Victorian era this hotel was an elegant fixture on the Denver landscape, and civilized touches still include complimentary shoe shines, afternoon sherry, and morning coffee. Rooms are furnished with French- and English-period antiques and the Cruise Room bar re-creates an art deco ocean liner. Although the Oxford is a notch down from the Brown Palace in most respects, it's also less expensive and is home to McCormick's Fish and Oyster House, Denver's premier seafood restaurant. Several art galleries are nearby. ✉ *1600 17th St., LoDo, 80202* ☎ *303/628–5400 or 800/228–5838* 🖷 *303/628–5413* ⊕ *www.theoxfordhotel.com* ⇨ *80 rooms* ♿ *Restaurant, room service, in-room data ports, minibars, cable TV, some in-room VCRs, gym, hair salon, health club, hot tub, spa, 2 bars, business services, parking (fee), no-smoking rooms* ▤ *AE, D, DC, MC, V.*

$–$$$ 🏨 **Adagio Bed & Breakfast.** The music room of this 1892 Victorian mansion has a grand piano and rooms are named after composers. The theme continues with breakfast, served adagio—or at your leisure. Guest rooms have lace-trim linens, period furniture, and different color schemes and special amenities, such as the pink Brahms room with a two-person jetted tub, or the Holst room, with its lapis walls and four-poster bed. The Copland Suite has a living room, working gas fireplace with original mantel, and a whirlpool bath. The Adagio is close to Cheesman Park and Denver Botanic Gardens, as well as minutes from downtown or Cherry Creek. This B&B also stands out because of its business-friendly options, such as in-room data ports and telephones, along with cable television. The hired chef is restaurant-quality, and you can choose a full-meal plan for an additional cost. ✉ *1430 Race St., Capitol Hill, 80206* ☎ *303/370–6911 or 800/533–3241* ⊕ *www.adagiobb.com* ⇨ *6 rooms, 1 suite* ♿ *Dining room, in-room data ports, cable TV, business services; no smoking* ▤ *AE, MC, V* ❙◎❙ *BP, MAP.*

$–$$$ 🏨 **Burnsley.** This 16-story, Bauhaus-style tower is a haven for executives seeking peace and quiet close to downtown. The tastefully appointed suites have balconies and full kitchens. Marble foyers and old-fashioned riding prints decorate the rooms. Many suites have a sofa bed, making this a good bet for families. The swooningly romantic restaurant is a perfect place to pop the question. ✉ *1000 Grant St., Downtown, 80203* ☎ *303/830–1000 or 800/231–3915* 🖷 *303/830–7676* ⊕ *www.burnsley. com* ⇨ *80 suites* ♿ *Restaurant, room service, kitchenettes, microwaves, in-room data ports, cable TV, pool, bar, laundry service, concierge,* *business services, some pets allowed (fee), no-smoking rooms* ▤ *AE, D, DC, MC, V.*

$–$$$ 🖫 **Capitol Hill Mansion Bed & Breakfast Inn.** The dramatic turret and intense rust color of this Richardson Romanesque Victorian mansion built in 1891 is enough to draw you in. Inside are eight elegantly appointed rooms done in varying themes, such as Rocky Mountain, Victorian, and Colonial. The Gold Banner suite is cheerfully yellow, with a separate sitting room and gas-log fireplace, and it, along with several other rooms, has a view of the Rockies. Breakfast and afternoon refreshments are included, along with samplings of Colorado wines. ✉ *1207 Pennsylvania St., Capitol Hill, 80203* ☎ *303/839–5221 or 800/839–9329* 🖷 *303/839–9046* ⊕ *www.capitolhillmansion.com* ⟿ *8 rooms, 3 suites* ♻ *Dining room; no smoking* ▤ *AE, D, DC, MC, V* ⊖ *BP.*

$–$$$ 🖫 **Courtyard by Marriott.** This stunningly renovated historic building (it used to be Joslins Department Store) sits right on the 16th Street Mall, which means everything downtown is but a few blocks or a free Mall shuttle away. The lobbies and public spaces are modern Western in theme, and the cream-color, sparsely decorated rooms offer high-speed Internet access and city and mountain views. The Rialto Cafe, a New American–style eatery, is one of Denver's better hotel restaurants and its patio on the Mall provides an eyeful of Denverites. There's also a Starbucks on site. ✉ *934 16th St., Downtown, 80202* ☎ *303/571–1114 or 888/249–1810* 🖷 *303/571–1141* ⊕ *www.marriott.com* ⟿ *177 rooms, 15 suites* ♻ *Restaurant, room service, in-room data ports, cable TV, indoor pool, hot tub, gym, bar, dry cleaning, laundry service, concierge, Internet, business services, parking (fee), no-smoking rooms* ▤ *AE, D, DC, MC, V.*

$–$$$ 🖫 **The Gregory Inn LoDo.** Decorated to resemble an old English Inn, the Gregory in the historic Curtis Park neighborhood captures old-world charm through the use of mossy colors and exquisite linens and accents. All of the rooms, each with its own luxurious atmosphere, have private baths, and many have small sitting rooms. There's also a sumptuous Carriage House, which contains a full kitchen, washer and dryer, and dining and living areas. Breakfast is served each morning in the dimly lit, soothing Gathering Room. ✉ *2500 Arapahoe St., LoDo, 80205* ☎ *303/295–6570 or 800/925–6570* 🖷 *303/296–2151* ⊕ *www.gregoryinn.com* ⟿ *8 rooms, 1 suite* ♻ *Dining room, in-room data ports, some cable TV, business services; no children under 12, no smoking* ▤ *AE, D, DC, MC, V* ⊖ *BP.*

★ $–$$$ 🖫 **Magnolia Hotel.** The Denver outpost of a Texas-based chain, the Magnolia has spacious, elegant rooms with sophisticated furnishings (some with fireplaces) and warm colors, all built within the confines of the 1906 former American Bank Building. Breakfast is included, as is an evening guest reception, drink coupons for the jazzy, retro-hip Harry's Bar, and late-night cookies and milk. One block off the 16th Street Mall, the Magnolia is well situated for downtown and LoDo conveniences. ✉ *818 17th St., Downtown, 80202* ☎ *303/607–9000 or 888/915–1110* 🖷 *303/607–0101* ⊕ *www.themagnoliahotel.com* ⟿ *246 rooms, 119 suites* ♻ *Room service, in-room data ports, cable TV, gym, steam room, bar, dry cleaning, laundry service, concierge, business services, parking (fee), no-smoking rooms* ▤ *AE, D, DC, MC, V* ⊖ *BP.*

$–$$$ 🖫 **Queen Anne Inn.** North of downtown in the regentrified Clements historic district (some of the neighboring blocks have yet to be reclaimed), this inn made up of adjacent Victorians is a delightful, romantic getaway for B&B mavens. Both houses have handsome oak wainscoting and balustrades, 10-foot vaulted ceilings, numerous bay or stained-glass windows, and such period furnishings as brass and canopy beds, cherry and pine armoires, and oak rocking chairs. The best accommodations are the four "gallery suites" dedicated to Audubon, Rockwell, Calder, and Remington. A full breakfast and afternoon tastings of Colorado wines are offered daily. ✉ *2147 Tremont Pl., Central Denver, 80205* ☎ *303/296–6666 or 800/432–4667* 🖶 *303/296–2151* ⊕ *www.queenannebnb. com* ⇨ *10 rooms, 4 suites* ⚹ *Dining room, in-room data ports, some in-room hot tubs, some cable TV, business services, no smoking* ▭ *AE, D, DC, MC, V* |◉| *BP.*

¢–$$$ ▦ **Executive Tower Hotel.** The rooms are stark and austere, with white walls and a simple blue and rose decor, and given that the Denver Performing Arts Complex is right across the street, they're a real value. The lobby-level restaurant, Jenny's, sits under a real tree and serves up straightforward American cuisine. The outdoor tennis court and indoor racquetball courts afford a way to work it off. ✉ *1405 Curtis St., Downtown, 80202* ☎ *303/571–0300 or 800/525–6651* 🖶 *303/825–4301* ⊕ *www.exectowerhotel.com* ⇨ *307 rooms, 2 suites* ⚹ *Restaurant, room service, in-room data ports, cable TV, tennis court, pool, gym, sauna, steam room, racquetball, bar, dry cleaning, laundry service, concierge, parking (fee), no-smoking rooms* ▭ *AE, D, DC, MC, V.*

¢–$$$ ▦ **Four Points by Sheraton Denver/Cherry Creek.** Mountain views, proximity to Cherry Creek shopping, and a complimentary shuttle service to anywhere within a 5-mi radius count among this Sheraton outpost's advantages. Rooms are forest green and brown, with modern art and oversized chairs. Not only is the outdoor pool area nicely landscaped, but the pool itself is heated. The Boulevard Bistro serves American classics, and guests receive a daily pass to Bally's Total Fitness Center next door. ✉ *600 S. Colorado Blvd., Glendale, 80246* ☎ *303/757–3341* 🖶 *303/756–6670* ⇨ *210 rooms* ⚹ *Restaurant, room service, in-room data ports, cable TV, pool, gym, hair salon, bar, dry cleaning, laundry service, business services, free parking, some pets allowed, no-smoking rooms* ▭ *AE, D, DC, MC, V.*

$–$$ ▦ **Holiday Chalet B&B.** Stained-glass windows and homey accents throughout make this 1896 Victorian brownstone exceptionally charming. It's also conveniently situated in Capitol Hill, the neighborhood immediately east of downtown. Many of the rooms have overstuffed Victorian armchairs and such historic touches as furniture once owned by Baby Doe Tabor. Some units have tile fireplaces, others have small sitting rooms. Each room has a full kitchen, a holdover from the building's days as an apartment building, and full breakfast is included. Across a serene courtyard, the Oak & Berries Tea Room serves a light lunch with tea Thursday through Sunday. ✉ *1820 E. Colfax Ave., Capitol Hill, 80218* ☎ *303/321–9975 or 800/626–4497* 🖶 *303/377–6556* ⊕ *www.bbonline. com/co/holiday* ⇨ *10 rooms* ⚹ *Dining room, in-room data ports, kitchenettes, some microwaves, cable TV, in-room VCRs, library, some pets allowed; no smoking* ▭ *AE, D, DC, MC, V* |◉| *BP.*

$–$$ ▦ **Holiday Inn Select Denver/Cherry Creek.** The Cherry Creek shopping district is 4 mi away and the major museums and the zoo a five-minute drive from this bustling hotel, which provides coveted mountain views from many of its rooms. The entrance is impressive, with stone-supported pillars and Southwestern effects, whereas the rooms are decorated in browns, oranges, and golds, with velvety upholstery and leather chairs. The full-service, wood-dominated Front Range Grill is a contemporary American eatery, and Selections Espresso and More is a great stop for morning coffee and house-baked pastries. At night, Olives Martini Bar brings in Denverites, as well. ✉ *455 S. Colorado Blvd., Cherry Creek, 80246* ☎ *303/388–5561 or 888/388–6129* 🖶 *303/388–0059* ⊕ *www. cherrycreekhoteldenver.com* ⇨ *281 rooms, 9 suites* ⚹ *Restaurant, coffee shop, room service, in-room data ports, cable TV, indoor pool, gym, hair salon, bar, dry cleaning, laundry service, concierge, business services, free parking, no-smoking rooms* ▭ *AE, D, DC, MC, V.*

$–$$ ⊡ **Merritt House.** This beautiful, well-run, antiques-filled 1889 Queen Anne Victorian B&B serves a full breakfast with a different selection of made-to-order items each day. Originally designed by Brown Palace architect Frank Edbrooke, the inn's rooms are replete with interesting interior angles, original hardwood floors, and an assortment of antiques and reproductions. Large bay windows with window seats frame the third-story room's four-poster bed and vaulted ceiling. Five of the rooms have double whirlpool baths. Locals put their guests up at this find only 10 blocks from downtown. ⊠ *941 E. 17th Ave., Capitol Hill, 80218* ☎ *303/861–5230 or 877/861–5230* ⊕ *www.merritthouse.com* ⇋ *10 rooms* ⊟ *AE, D, DC, MC, V* ⊠ *BP.*

$–$$ ⊡ **Red Lion Hotel.** A stone's throw from Invesco Field at Mile High, the Red Lion provides free parking and complimentary shuttles to downtown (which is half a mile away). Guests and locals alike hang out at the Skybox Grill and Sports Bar on the 14th floor, which has a panoramic view of the Denver skyline and surrounding attractions. Rooms are done in red, white, and warm-yellow colors, with plenty of space to maneuver and an oversize desk. ⊠ *1975 Bryant St., Downtown, 80203* ☎ *303/433–8331 or 800/388–5381* ⊞ *303/455–7061* ⊕ *www.redliondenverdowntown. com* ⇋ *171 rooms* ⌂ *Restaurant, room service, in-room data ports, cable TV, pool, gym, bar, laundry service, concierge, business services, free parking, no-smoking rooms* ⊟ *AE, D, DC, MC, V.*

¢–$$ ⊡ **Comfort Inn–Downtown.** The advantages of this popular chain hotel are its reasonable rates and its location in the heart of downtown. It even shares some amenities, such as the fitness center and parking, with the esteemed Brown Palace hotel across the street. Rooms are somewhat cramped, but the corner ones on the upper floors have wraparound windows with panoramic views. A complimentary deluxe Continental breakfast is included in the rate. ⊠ *401 17th St., Downtown, 80202* ☎ *303/ 296–0400 or 800/237–1431* ⊞ *303/297–0774* ⊕ *www.choicehotels. com* ⇋ *231 rooms, 19 suites* ⌂ *Restaurant, room service, in-room data ports, cable TV, some in-room VCRs, laundry service, business services, parking (fee), no-smoking rooms* ⊟ *AE, D, DC, MC, V* ⊠ *CP.*

¢–$ ⊡ **La Quinta Inn Downtown.** This tidy, reasonably priced chain hotel is less than a mile north of central downtown. The rooms are simple, with white walls and mint carpeting. The unusual-shaped pool is under cover from the sun on one half. ⊠ *3500 Park Ave. W, North Denver, 80216* ☎ *303/458–1222 or 866/725–1661* ⊞ *303/433–2246* ⊕ *www.laquinta. com* ⇋ *106 rooms, 2 suites* ⌂ *Cable TV, pool, laundry service, free parking* ⊟ *AE, D, DC, MC, V.*

★ **¢–$** ⊡ **Ramada Limited Capitol Hill.** As the name suggests, this Ramada is within walking distance of the State Capitol, as well as just nine blocks east of downtown and the 16th Street Mall. A Southwestern feel pervades the leather-couch-dominated Western-style lobby and lounge area. Rooms have dark carpeting and red and rose colors. The Senor Sol restaurant continues the Southwestern motif and serves foods from both sides of the border. ⊠ *1150 E. Colfax Ave., Capitol Hill, 80217* ☎ *303/831– 7700 or 800/272–6232* ⊞ *303/894–9193* ⊕ *www.ramada.com* ⇋ *152 rooms, 8 suites* ⌂ *Restaurant, room service, in-room data ports, in-room safes, cable TV, pool, gym, bar, laundry service, business services, free parking, no-smoking rooms* ⊟ *AE, D, DC, MC, V.*

SPORTS & THE OUTDOORS

Denver is a city that can consistently, enthusiastically support three professional sports teams. Unfortunately, it has four (not counting soccer)—the Colorado Rockies, Colorado Avalanche, Denver Broncos, and Denver Nuggets. In recent years, the Nuggets have been the odd team out, as the Rockies, Avalanche, and Broncos have all reached or won championships in their respective sports. But the Nuggets may be about to catch up, given a nucleus of new, young players.

What's great about Denverites is that most aren't just spectators. After a game, they go out and do stuff—hiking, bicycling, kayaking, and, yes, playing the team sports themselves. The city, with its super-cheap recreation-center fees, encourages a fit lifestyle.

Auto Racing

Bandimere Speedway (✉ 3051 S. Rooney Rd., Morrison ☎ 303/697–6001) features NHRA Championship Drag Racing from April through October.

Baseball

The Colorado Rockies, Denver's National League baseball team, plays April–October in **Coors Field** (✉ 2001 Blake St., LoDo ☎ 303/292–0200 or 800/388–7625). Because of high altitude and thin air, the park is among the hardest in the Major Leagues for pitchers—and the Rockies have had a tough time preserving young arms. But for an exhibition team, they've been surprisingly competitive over the past decade.

Basketball

The Denver Nuggets of the National Basketball Association have been the ugly duckling in Denver's professional-sports scene for years. However, they have raised expectations lately with several top-draft picks and exciting young players. The Nuggets play at the **Pepsi Center** (✉ 1000 Chopper Circle, Auraria ☎ 303/405–8555). The 19,000-seat arena, which opened in 1999, is also the primary spot in town for large musical acts such as Bruce Springsteen and Christina Aguilera.

Bicycling & Jogging

The **Denver Parks Department** (☎ 720/913–0696) has suggestions for biking and jogging paths throughout the metropolitan area's 250 parks, including the popular Cherry Creek and Chatfield Reservoir State Recreation areas. With more than 400 mi of off-road paths in and around the city, cyclists can move easily between urban and rural settings. Just south of downtown, the **Bicycle Doctor** (✉ 860 Broadway, Golden Triangle ☎ 303/831–7228) repairs and rents street and mountain bikes for $10 to $40 a day.

The well-kept **Cherry Creek Bike Path** (✉ Cherry Creek, LoDo) runs from Cherry Creek Shopping Center to Larimer Square downtown alongside the peaceful creek of its name. The scenic **Highline Canal** (✉ Auraria, Cherry Creek, LoDo) has 70 mi of mostly dirt paths through the metro area running an almost completely level grade. **Platte River Greenway** (✉ Auraria, Cherry Creek, LoDo) is a 20-mi-long path for in-line skating, bicycling, and jogging that runs alongside Cherry Creek and the Platte River. Much of it runs through downtown Denver. There are 12 mi of paved paths along the expensively renovated **South Platte River** (✉ Platte River Valley, LoDo) heading into downtown. West of the city, paved paths wind through **Matthews-Winters Park** (✉ South of I–70 on CO 26, Golden) near both Golden and Morrison. It's dotted with plaintive pioneer graves amid the sun-bleached grasses, thistle, and columbine. The **Deer Creek Canyon** (✉ Littleton) trail system is popular with mountain bikers, running through forested foothills southwest of Denver near the intersection of C–470 and Wadsworth Avenue.

Fitness Clubs

Denver has more fitness clubs per capita than any other American city. Get your free, out-of-town visitor pass at **Bally's Total Fitness** (✉ 720 S.

CloseUp

STAKING OUT THE STOCK SHOW

DURING THE NATIONAL WESTERN STOCK SHOW, *held in mid-January at the* **Denver Coliseum** *(✉ 4655 Humboldt St., east of I–25 on I–70, Elyria ☎ 303/297–1166 Ext. 810 ⊕ www.nationalwestern.com), thousands of repressed cowpokes retrieve their string ties and worn boots and indulge in two weeks of hootin', hollerin', and celebratin' the beef industry.*

Whether you're a professional rancher or bull rider, or just plan to show up for the people watching, the Stock Show is a rich, colorful glimpse of Western culture. The pros arrive to make industry connections, show off their livestock, and perhaps land a few sales. The entertainment involves nightly rodeo events, presentations of prized cattle (some going for thousands of dollars), and "Mutton Bustin." The latter is one of those rowdy rodeo concepts that usually has no place in a genteel

metropolis like Denver: kids, 6 years and younger, don huge hockey-goalie helmets and hold for dear life onto the backs of bucking baby sheep.

At the trade show you can buy hats and boots, of course, but also yards of beef jerky and quirky gift items like caps from the Universal Semen Sales company. Just be sure to call first and ask for directions; although parking is plentiful, the Coliseum, usually home of straightforward sporting and entertainment events, becomes a labyrinth of lots and shuttles.

Colorado Blvd., Englewood ☎ 303/782–9424), which has a wide array of exercise equipment, including stationary bikes and weight machines. The state-of-the-art **Colorado Athletic Club** (✉ 1630 Welton St., LoDo ☎ 303/623–2100) is a 40,000-square-foot, full-service facility offering more than 60 aerobics and yoga classes weekly. The club has cardio-vascular and fitness equipment; weight training; racquetball and basketball courts; and a running track, among other features. Complimentary day passes are available to guests of many major hotels. On the expensive side, **Athletic Club at Denver Place** (✉ 1849 Curtis St., LoDo ☎ 303/294–9494) rivals Colorado Athletic Club in terms of weight-training and fitness equipment, but it's slightly more ensconced in downtown culture—the basketball court is in a second-floor bridge that overlooks LoDo. The City of Denver operates 29 **Recreation Centers** (☎ 720/913–0696), many of which have indoor pools, weight rooms, basketball courts, and other amenities. A nonresident day pass is $5.

Football

The National Football League's Denver Broncos play September–December at the $400-million **Invesco Field at Mile High** (✉ 1701 Bryant St., Exit 210B off I–25, Sun Valley ☎ 720/258–3000). Broncos owner Pat Bowlen footed the $1-million for the seven larger-than-life bronze horses running up the hill next to the stadium's south entrance. Every game has sold out for 30 years, so tickets are not easy to come by, despite the Broncos' tepid success in the post-John Elway world.

Golf

Six courses are operated by the City of Denver and are open to the public. Greens fees for all range from $17 to $24. For same-day tee times, you can call the starters at an individual course, but for advance reservations golfers must call the **main reservation system** (☎ 303/784–4000) up to three days in advance. **City Park** (✉ E. 25th Ave. and York St., City Park ☎ 303/295–4420) is a fairly plain course near downtown with a few good skyline views. The 69-par **Evergreen** (✉29614 Upper Bear Creek, Evergreen ☎ 303/674–4128) is made of undulating fairways in a mountainous, forested setting. **Kennedy** (✉ 10500 E. Hampden Ave., Hampden ☎ 303/751–0311) is a popular spot with three 9-hole courses as well as a par-3 course. Fairly flat **Overland Park** (✉ S. Santa Fe Dr. and Jewell Ave., Overland ☎ 303/698–4975) has quite a few bunkers. Donald Ross–designed **Wellshire** (✉ 3333 S. Colorado Blvd., Bonnie Brae ☎ 303/692–5636) with small, subtly breaking greens and tree-lined fairways. **Willis Case** (✉ W. 50th Ave. and Vrain St., Highland ☎ 303/458–4877) is hilly and wide open.

Arrowhead Golf Club (✉ 10850 W. Sundown Trail, Littleton ☎ 303/973–9614), 45 minutes from downtown in Roxborough State Park, was designed by Robert Trent Jones and is set impressively among red sandstone spires. **The Ridge at Castle Pines** (✉ 1414 Castle Pines Pkwy., Castle Rock ☎ 303/688–0100) is an 18-hole Tom Weiskopf–designed course with great mountain views and dramatic elevation changes. It's ranked among the nation's top 100 public courses.

Hiking

Mt. Falcon Park looks down on Denver and across at Red Rocks. It's amazingly tranquil, laced with meadows and streams, and shaded by conifers. The trails are very well marked. ✉ *Off Rte. 8, Morrison exit, or U.S. 285, Parmalee exit, Aurora.*

Fodor'sChoice ★ Fifteen miles southwest of Denver, **Red Rocks Park and Amphitheatre** is a breathtaking, 70-million-year-old wonderland of vaulting oxblood-and-cinnamon-color sandstone spires. The outdoor music stage is set in a natural 9,000-seat amphitheater (with perfect acoustics, as only nature could have designed) that has awed the likes of Leopold Stokowski and the Beatles. Tickets to concerts are available through Ticketmaster, but hiking in this metro Denver park is free. The Red Rocks Visitor Center, opened before the 2003 concert season after a multimillion-dollar renovation, is at the top of the amphitheater, built underground. ✉ *Off U.S. 285 or I–70, Morrison.*

Roxborough State Park has an easy 2-mi loop trail through rugged rock formations, offering beautiful vistas and a unique look at metro Denver and the plains. This trail is wheelchair accessible. ✉ *I–25 south to Santa Fe exit, take Santa Fe Blvd., south to Titan Rd. Turn right, and follow signs, Littleton.*

Hockey

Fodor'sChoice ★ The Colorado Avalanche of the National Hockey League are wildly popular in Denver, winning the Stanley Cup in 1996 and beating the New Jersey Devils for an encore in 2001. Although they've been relatively disappointing since, and legendary goalie Patrick Roy retired after the 2003 season, the still-exciting team plays at the **Pepsi Center** (✉ 1000 Chopper Pl., Auraria ☎ 303/405–8555), a 19,000-seat arena.

Horse Racing

Horse racing takes place June through August at **Arapahoe Park** (✉26000 E. Quincy Ave., Aurora ☎ 303/690–2400).

Tennis

The city has 28 parks with tennis courts. For information call the **Denver Parks Department** (☎ 720/913–0696).

Chatfield and Cherry Creek marinas rent sailboats, powerboats, and Jet Skis (April–October at Cherry Creek and Memorial Day–Labor Day at Chatfield). **Chatfield Marina** (⊠ Chatfield State Park, Littleton ☎ 303/791–5555) is on the fringes of the Rocky Mountains 15 mi south of downtown and attracts wakeboarders, waterskiers, and tubers. Southeast of Denver, the **Cherry Creek Marina** (⊠ Cherry Creek State Park, Aurora ☎ 303/779–6144) serves the 850-acre reservoir of the same name, a sailing hot spot.

NIGHTLIFE & THE ARTS

Friday's *Denver Post* and *Rocky Mountain News* both publish calendars of the week's events, as does the slightly alternative *Westword,* which is free and published on Wednesday. Downtown and LoDo are where most Denverites make the nightlife scene. Downtown features more mainstream entertainment, whereas LoDo is home to fun, funky rock clubs and small theaters. Remember that Denver's altitude can intensify your reaction to alcohol.

The ubiquitous **TicketMaster** (☎ 303/830–8497) is Denver's prime agency, selling tickets to almost all concerts, sporting events, and plays that take place in the Denver area. On the theatrical side of the spectrum, the **Ticket Bus** (☎ No phone), on the 16th Street Mall at Curtis Street, sells tickets from 10 until 6 weekdays, and half-price tickets on the day of the performance.

The Arts

★ The **Denver Performing Arts Complex** is a huge, impressively high-tech group of theaters connected by a soaring glass archway to a futuristic symphony hall. The complex hosts more events than any other performing arts center in the world. Run by the 30-year-old Denver Center for the Performing Arts, the complex's anchors are the round, relaxing Temple Hoyne Buell Theatre, built in 1991, and the more impressive, ornate Auditorium Theatre, built in 1908. Both host large events, from classical orchestras to comedian Jerry Seinfeld to country singer Lyle Lovett. Some of the other five theaters include the small Garner Galleria Theatre, where the comedy *I Love You, You're Perfect, Now Change* has packed the house for several years running, and the mid-size Space Theatre. Both the ballet and opera have their seasons here. But even if you're not seeing a show, the central plaza and its many cafés and poster displays is an entertaining and centrally located place to meet. Guided tours for groups of five or more are available by appointment only. ⊠ *Box office, 14th and Curtis Sts., LoDo* ☎ *303/893–4000* ⊕ *www.denvercenter.org.*

Fiddler's Green (⊠ 6350 Greenwood Plaza Blvd., Greenwood Village ☎ 303/220–7000) hosts larger outdoor concerts in summer. Although many compare this nondescript amphitheater unfavorably to Red Rocks, regular concertgoers may find the small details, such as parking and individual seating, more comfortable.

Downtown, the **Paramount Theatre** (⊠ 1631 Glenarm Pl., LoDo ☎ 303/623–0106) is the venue for many large-scale rock concerts. Designed by renowned local architect Temple H. Buell in the art-deco style in 1930, the lovingly maintained Paramount is both an elegant place to see shows and a rowdy, beer-serving party location for rock fans.

Fodor'sChoice ★ The exquisite 9,000-seat **Red Rocks Amphitheatre** (✉ Morrison, off U.S. 285 or I–70 ☎ 303/640–2637), amid majestic geological formations in nearby Morrison, is renowned for its natural acoustics. Although Red Rocks is one of the best places in the country to hear live music, be sure to leave extra time when visiting—parking is sparse, crowds are thick, paths are long and extremely uphill, and seating is usually general admission. In 2003, after a two-year renovation, the park unveiled its underground visitor center, located at the top of the amphitheater.

In summer, the tent-covered **Universal Lending Pavilion** (✉ 1700 7th St., Auraria ☎ 303/405–6080), in the parking lot between the Pepsi Center and Six Flags Elitch Gardens, sponsors outdoor concerts. Rocker Elvis Costello and Godfather of Soul James Brown have been prominent guests. It's also known as CityLights.

Symphony, Opera & Dance

The **Colorado Symphony Orchestra** performs at Boettcher Concert Hall (✉ 13th and Curtis Sts., LoDo ☎ 303/640–2862). **Opera Colorado** (☎ 303/778–1500) has a spring season, often with internationally renowned artists, at the Denver Performing Arts Complex. The **Colorado Ballet** (☎ 303/837–8888) specializes in the classics; performances are staged at the Denver Performing Arts Complex.

Theater

The **Bug Theatre Company** (✉ 3654 Navajo St., Highland ☎ 303/477–9984) produces primarily cutting-edge, original works in Denver's Highlands neighborhood. **Denver Center Attractions** (✉ 14th and Curtis Sts., at DPCA's Temple Buell and Auditorium theaters, LoDo ☎ 303/893–4100) brings Broadway road companies to town. The **Denver Center Theater Company** (✉ 14th and Curtis Sts., LoDo ☎ 303/893–4100) presents high-caliber repertory theater, including new works by promising playwrights, at the Bonfils Theatre Complex (part of the Denver Performing Arts Complex). **El Centro Su Teatro** (✉ 4725 High St., Elyria ☎ 303/296–0219) is a Latino-Chicano company that puts on mostly original works and a variety of festivals during its May to September season. **Hunger Artists Ensemble Theater** (✉ Denver Civic Theater, 721 Santa Fe Dr., Civic Center ☎ 303/893–5438) presents dramas, comedies, and adaptations of works from the likes of Shakespeare, James Joyce, and Tom Stoppard.

Nightlife

Bars & Brewpubs

Known for its Royal Red shrimp, big burgers, and even bigger breakfasts, the **Bear Creek Tavern** (✉ 25940 Hwy. 74, Kittredge ☎ 303/674–9929) is a plain-spoken fixture favored by bikers and locals. The views near Ofallon Park are spectacular.

The Denver ChopHouse & Brewery (✉ 1735 19th St., LoDo ☎ 303/296–0800) is a high-end microbrewery on the site of the old Union Pacific Railroad headhouse—with the train paraphernalia to prove it. It's a bit expensive for a brewpub, but if you hang out after Broncos games you might encounter local sports celebrities celebrating or commiserating.

Mynt Lounge (✉ 1424 Market St., LoDo ☎ 303/825–6968) is relatively new to LoDo, but has already established a chichi reputation with its fruity martinis (try the Strawberry Banana) and Miami-style pastel colors.

Rock Bottom Brewery (✉ 1001 16th St., LoDo ☎ 303/534–7616) is a perennial favorite, thanks to its rotating special brews and reasonably priced pub grub.

The **Wynkoop Brewing Co.** (✉ 1634 18th St., LoDo ☎ 303/297–2700) is more famous in recent years for its owner—Denver Mayor John Hickenlooper—than for its brews, food, or ambience. But it remains one of the city's best-known bars, a relaxing, slightly upscale, two-story joint filled with halfway-decent bar food, the usual pool tables, and games and beers of all types. It has anchored LoDo since it was a pre-Coors Field warehouse district.

Cabaret

Downstairs in the Wynkoop Brewpub, the **Impulse Theater** (✉ 1634 18th St., LoDo ☎ 303/297–2111) hosts everything from top-name jazz acts to up-and-coming stand-up comedians to cabaret numbers.

Comedy Clubs

Three area improv groups make their home at **Bovine Metropolis Theater** (✉ 1527 Champa St., LoDo ☎ 303/758–4722), which also stages satirical productions. Denver comics have honed their skills at **Comedy Works** (✉ 1226 15th St., LoDo ☎ 303/595–3637) for 20 years. Well-known performers often drop by.

Country Music Clubs

The **Grizzly Rose** (✉ 5450 N. Valley Hwy., I–25 at Exit 215, Globeville ☎ 303/295–1330) has miles of dance floor, national bands, and gives two-step dancing lessons—and sells plenty of Western wear, from cowboy boots to spurs. This club boomed in the early '90s, when Garth Brooks and Billy Ray Cyrus were huge, and has more recently settled into its solidly popular incarnation. Classic-rock bands are big, in addition to country acts big and small. The suburban **Stampede Grill & Dance Emporium** (✉ 2430 S. Havana St., Aurora ☎ 303/337–6909) is another cavernous boot-scooting spot, with dance lessons and a restaurant.

Dance Clubs

The Castle (✉ 83 E. 120th Ave., Thornton ☎ 303/607–7570), located in a suburban hotel-chain conference room, is one of several local dance clubs jumping on the Miami theme (salsa nights, cumbia DJs, and the like). **Deadbeat Club** (✉ 4040 E. Evans Ave., Virginia Village ☎ 303/758–6853), a cavernous building with three dance floors, is where the cool college crowd goes to get carded. The **Funky Buddha Lounge** (✉ 776 Lincoln St., Capitol Hill ☎ 303/832–5075) distinguishes itself with the Ginger Bar, an upstairs outdoors dance area with live DJs six nights a week. The venerable dance club **Rock Island** (✉ Wazee and 15th Sts., LoDo ☎ 303/572–7625) caters to the young and hip.

Dinner Theater

The **Country Dinner Playhouse** (✉ 6875 S. Clinton St., Greenwood Village ☎ 303/799–1410) serves a meal before the performance, which is usually a Broadway-style show.

Gay Bars

Charlie's (✉ 900 E. Colfax Ave., Capitol Hill ☎ 303/839–8890) offers country-western atmosphere and music.

Jazz Clubs

Brendan's Pub (✉ 2009 Larimer St., LoDo ☎ 303/308–9933) attracts local and national blues talents. **El Chapultepec** (✉ 1962 Market St., LoDo ☎ 303/295–9126) is a cramped, fluorescent-lit, bargain-basement Mexican dive. Still, the limos parked outside hint at its enduring popularity: this is where Ol' Blue Eyes used to pop in, and where visiting musicians, including the Marsalis brothers, continue to jam after hours. Hidden in the back of a parking lot, the hipster favorite **Herb's Hideout** (✉ 2057 Larimer St., LoDo ☎ 303/299–9555) is a gloriously nostalgic bar with dim lighting and checkerboard floors. Taking the stage are smooth jazz and blues acts, and the occasional DJ. LoDo's slickly contemporary **Sambuca Jazz Café** (✉ 1320 15th St., LoDo ☎ 303/629–5299) serves up live jazz and Mediterranean cuisine on a nightly basis.

Rock Clubs

Of Denver's numerous smoky hangouts, the most popular is the regally restored **Bluebird Theater** (✉ 3317 E. Colfax Ave., Capitol Hill ☎ 303/322–2308), which showcases local and national acts, emphasizing rock, hip-hop, ambient, and the occasional evening of cinema. **Cricket on the Hill** (✉ 1209 E. 13th Ave., Capitol Hill ☎ 303/830–9020) is a somewhat seedy Denver institution, presenting a mix of rock, blues, acoustic, and alternative music. The **Fillmore Auditorium** (✉ 1510 Clarkson St., Capitol Hill ☎ 303/837–1482), Denver's classic San Francisco concert hall spin-off, looks dumpy on the outside but is elegant and impressive inside. Before catching a big-name act such as Coldplay, LL Cool J, or No Doubt, scan the walls for beautiful color photographs of past club performers.

The **Gothic Theatre** (✉ 3263 S. Broadway, Englewood ☎ 303/380–2333) came to age in the early '90s, with a steady stream of soon-to-be-famous alternative-rock acts such as Nirvana and the Red Hot Chili Peppers. It has since reinvented itself as a community venue for theater, music, and charity events. Down-home **Herman's Hideaway** (✉ 1578 S. Broadway, Overland ☎ 303/777–5840) showcases mostly local rock, with a smattering of reggae and blues thrown in. The **Lions Lair** (✉ 2022 E. Colfax Ave., Capitol Hill ☎ 303/320–9200) is a beautiful dive where punk-rock bands and occasional name acts (like British rocker Graham Parker) perform on a tiny stage just above a huge, square, central bar. The **Mercury Café** (✉ 2199 California St., Five Points ☎ 303/294–9281) triples as a health-food restaurant (sublime tofu fettuccine), fringe theater, and rock club specializing in acoustic sets, progressive, and newer wave music. The **Ogden Theatre** (✉ 935 E. Colfax Ave., Capitol Hill ☎ 303/830–2525) is a classic old theater that specializes in alternative-rock acts such as the Breeders and the Flaming Lips.

SHOPPING

Denver may be the best place in the country for shopping for recreational gear. Sporting-goods stores hold legendary ski sales around Labor Day. The city's selection of books and Western fashion is also noteworthy.

Malls & Shopping Districts

The **Denver Pavilions** (✉ 16th St. Mall between Tremont and Welton Sts., LoDo ☎ 303/260–6000 ⊕ www.denverpavilions.com) is downtown Denver's newest shopping and entertainment complex, a three-story, open-air structure that houses national stores like Barnes & Noble, NikeTown, Ann Taylor, Talbot's, and a Virgin Records Megastore. There are also several restaurants, including Denver's Hard Rock Cafe, and a 15-screen movie theater, the UA Denver Pavilions. Most of the restaurants and theaters are national chains, so don't expect distinctive local flavor, but it's a practical complement to Larimer Square a few blocks away. When attending a movie here, build in extra minutes to locate sparse downtown parking and maneuver the various steps and escalators leading to the box office.

Historic **Larimer Square** (✉ 14th and Larimer Sts., LoDo) houses distinctive shops and restaurants. Some of the square's retail highlights are the Vespa scooter dealership; Earthzone, a gallery of art fashioned from fossils and minerals; and John Atencio Designer Jewelry. **Tabor Center**

(✉ 16th St. Mall, LoDo) is a light-filled atrium whose 20 specialty shops and restaurants include the ESPN Zone theme restaurant and Sunglass Hut. Others, such as the Best of Denver store, showcase uniquely Coloradan merchandise and souvenirs. **Writer Square** (✉ 1512 Larimer St., LoDo) has Tiny Town—a doll-size village inhabited by Michael Garman's inimitable figurines—as well as shops and restaurants.

In a pleasant, predominantly residential neighborhood 2 mi from downtown, the **Cherry Creek** shopping district has retail blocks and an enclosed mall. At Milwaukee Street, the granite-and-glass behemoth **Cherry Creek Shopping Mall** (✉ 3000 E. 1st Ave., Cherry Creek ☎ 303/388–3900) holds some of the nation's top retailers. Its 160 stores include Abercrombie & Fitch, Eddie Bauer, Banana Republic, Burberry's, Tiffany & Co., Lord & Taylor, Louis Vuitton, Neiman Marcus, Polo–Ralph Lauren, and Saks Fifth Avenue. Just north of the Cherry Creek Shopping Mall is the district **Cherry Creek North** (✉ between 1st and 3rd Aves. from University Blvd. to Steele St., Cherry Creek ☎ 303/394–2904), an open-air development of tree-lined streets and shady plazas, with art galleries, specialty shops, and fashionable restaurants.

The upscale **Park Meadows** (✉ I–25, 5 mi south of Denver at County Line Rd., Littleton) is a mall designed to resemble a ski resort, with a 120-foot-high log-beam ceiling anchored by two massive stone fireplaces. In addition to Colorado's first Nordstrom, the center includes more than 100 specialty shops. On snowy days, "ambassadors" scrape your windshield while free hot chocolate is served inside.

Between Denver and Colorado Springs, **Prime Outlets at Castle Rock** (✉ Exit 184 off I–25, Castle Rock) offers 25%–75% savings on everything from appliances to apparel at its more than 50 outlets.

Specialty Shops

Antiques Dealers

South Broadway between 1st Avenue and Evans Street, as well as the side streets off this main drag, is chockablock with dusty antiques stores, where patient browsing could net some amazing bargains.

Antique Mall of Lakewood. More than 80 dealer showrooms make for one-stop shopping. ✉ 9635 W. Colfax Ave., Lakewood ☎ 303/238–4914.

Bookstores

FodorsChoice ★ **The Tattered Cover.** A must for all bibliophiles, the Tattered Cover may be the best bookstore in the United States, not only for the near-endless selection of volumes (more than 400,000 on four stories at the Cherry Creek location and 300,000 in LoDo) and helpful, knowledgeable staff, but also for the incomparably refined atmosphere. Treat yourself to the overstuffed armchairs, reading nooks, and afternoon readings and lectures. ✉ 1st Ave. at Milwaukee St., Cherry Creek ☎ 303/322–7727 ✉ 1628 16th St., LoDo ☎ 303/436–1070.

Craft & Art Galleries

LoDo has the trendiest galleries, many in splendidly and stylishly restored Victorian warehouses.

African Gems. Formerly a South African–art dealer, this Cherry Creek store now deals exclusively in gems and, if the owner's plans work out, diamonds. The art is still on the walls. ✉ Josephine St. and 3rd Ave., Cherry Creek ☎ 303/595–0965.

Camera Obscura Gallery. One of the oldest and best photography galleries between the east and west coasts carries images both contemporary and vintage. ✉ 1309 Bannock St., Capitol Hill ☎ 303/623–4059.

David Cook–Fine American Art. David Cook specializes in historic Native American art and regional paintings, particularly Santa Fe modernists. ✉ *1637 Wazee St., LoDo* ☎ *303/623–8181.*

Mudhead Gallery. This gallery sells museum-quality Southwestern art, with an especially fine selection of Santa Clara and San Ildefonso pottery, and Hopi kachinas. ✉ *555 17th St., across from the Hyatt, LoDo* ☎ *303/293–0007* ✉ *321 17th St., in the Brown Palace, LoDo* ☎ *303/293–9977.*

Native American Trading Company. The collection of weavings, pottery, jewelry, and regional paintings is outstanding. ✉ *213 W. 13th Ave., Golden Triangle* ☎ *303/534–0771.*

Old Santa Fe Pottery. The 20 rooms are crammed with Mexican masks, pottery, rustic Mexican furniture—and there's even a chip dip and salsa room. ✉ *2485 S. Santa Fe Dr., Overland* ☎ *303/871–9434.*

Pismo. Cherry Creek has its share of chic galleries, including Pismo, which showcases exquisite handblown-glass art. ✉ *235 Fillmore St., Cherry Creek* ☎ *303/333–2879.*

Department Stores

Foley's. Nine department stores throughout metropolitan Denver offer good values; their main store is in the Cherry Creek Shopping Mall. ✉ *15 S. Steele St., Cherry Creek* ☎ *303/333–8555.*

Sporting Goods

Gart Brothers Sports Castle. At this huge, multistory shrine to Colorado's love of the outdoors, entire floors are given over to a single sport. There are many other branches throughout Denver. ✉ *1000 Broadway, Civic Center* ☎ *303/861–1122.*

★ **REI.** Denver's REI flagship store, one of three such shops in the country, is yet another testament to the city's adventurous spirit. Located in a historic building, the store's 94,000 square feet are packed with all stripes of outdoors gear and some special extras: a climbing wall, a mountain-bike track, a white-water chute, and a "cold room" for gauging the protection offered by coats and sleeping bags. There's also a Starbucks inside. Behind the store is the Platte River Greenway, a park path and water area that's accessible to dogs, kids, and kayakers. ✉ *1416 Platte St., Jefferson Park* ☎ *303/756–3100.*

Western Paraphernalia

Cry Baby Ranch. This rambunctious assortment of 1940s and '50s cowboy kitsch is at Larimer Square. ✉ *1422 Larimer St., LoDo* ☎ *303/623–3979.*

SIDE TRIPS WEST OF DENVER

Less than a half-hour's drive from Denver is Golden, which is also a good jumping-off point for the gambling towns of Central City and Black Hawk.

Golden

15 mi west of Denver via I–70 or U.S. 6 (West 6th Ave.).

Golden was once the territorial capital of Colorado. City residents have smarted ever since losing that distinction to Denver by "dubious" vote in 1867, but in 1994, then-Governor Roy Romer restored "ceremonial" territorial-capital status to Golden. Today, the city is one of Colorado's fastest-growing, boosted by the high-tech industry as well as longtime employers Coors Brewery and Colorado School of Mines.

a good
tour

Start at the **Coors Brewery** and take the free tour and tasting. Then walk west on **12th Street,** a National Historic District that includes **Clear Creek History Park.** Go south on Arapahoe one block to the Armory, and then continue on Arapahoe into the **Colorado School of Mines.** From here you'll need a car; take 10th Street east out of town about 2 mi to the **Colorado Railroad Museum.** If there are children in the group, get on Interstate 70 west to Colfax Avenue west (U.S. 40) to the rides of **Heritage Square.** Otherwise, get off on 6th Avenue west (U.S. 6) to 19th Street to the **Buffalo Bill Grave and Museum.** (From Heritage Square, take Heritage Road [Route 93] north to U.S. 6 west.)

TIMING   Golden is a 25-minute drive from Denver, and you can see downtown and the Colorado School of Mines in an hour or two. The Coors Brewery tour takes about an hour. To drive to and visit the Colorado Railroad Museum and Buffalo Bill Grave and museum will take one to two hours.

What to See

Buffalo Bill Grave and Museum. Contrary to popular belief, Bill Cody—Pony Express rider, cavalry scout, and tireless promoter of the West—never expressed a burning desire to be buried here: the *Denver Post* bought the corpse from Bill's sister, and bribed her to concoct a teary story about his dying wish. Apparently, rival towns were so outraged that the National Guard had to be called in to protect the grave from robbers. Adjacent to the grave is a small museum with art and artifacts detailing Cody's life and times, as well as a run-of-the-mill souvenir shop. The drive up **Lookout Mountain** to the burial site offers a sensational panoramic view of Denver that alone is worth the price of admission. You can also hike up Lariat Look, a winding trail that leads to Buffalo Bill's Grave, starting at 19th Avenue in west Golden. The trail leads to other trailheads branching out from the Jefferson County Nature Center at the peak. Two-thirds of the way up, find the Stapleton Trail that takes you up Lookout Mountain. ⊠ *Rte. 5 off I–70 Exit 256, or 19th Ave. out of Golden* ☎ *303/526–0747* ⊕ *www.buffalobill.org* ✉ *$3* ☉ *May–Oct., daily 9–5; Nov.–Apr., Tues.–Sun. 9–4.*

Clear Creek History Park. This park in the National Historic District interprets the Golden area circa 1843–1900 via restored structures and reproductions, including a tepee, prospector's camp, schoolhouse, and cabins. ⊠ *11th and Arapahoe Sts.* ☎ *303/278–3557* ✉ *$3; $4 for park and Astor House* ☉ *June–Aug., Tues.–Sat. 10–4:30; Sept., Sat. 10–4:30; Oct.–Apr., by appointment only, 2 wks notice required for tours; Apr.–mid-May, Sat. 10–4:30.*

Colorado Railroad Museum. Just outside Golden is this must-visit for any choo-choo lover. More than 50 vintage locomotives and cars are displayed outside. Inside the replica-1880 masonry depot are historical photos and puffing Billy (nickname for steam trains) memorabilia, along with an astounding model train set that steams through a miniature, scale version of Golden. New for 2001 was a roundhouse where visitors can witness a train's restoration in progress. ⊠ *17155 W. 44th Ave.* ☎ *303/279–4591* ⊕ *www.crrm.org* ✉ *$7* ☉ *Daily 9–5.*

Colorado School of Mines. The nation's largest and foremost school of mineral engineering has a lovely campus containing an outstanding **geology museum** with minerals, gemstones, and fossils from around the world and a reproduction of a gold mine. Guided tours are available Tuesday through Thursday when student volunteers are available. Also on campus is the prominent **U.S.G.S. National Earthquake Information Center** (⊠ 1711 Illinois St. ☎ 303/273–8500), which is responsible for pinpointing seismic activity all over the country. Tours are by appointment Tuesday through Thursday, from 9–11 and 1–3. ⊠ *1310 Maple St.* ☎ *303/273–3815* ⊕ *www.mines.edu* ✉ *Free* ☉ *Geology museum Mon.–Sat. 9–4, Sun. 10–4; closed Sun. May–Aug.*

Coors Brewery. Thousands of beer lovers make the pilgrimage to this venerable brewery each year. One of the world's largest, it was founded in 1873 by Adolph Coors, a 21-year-old German stowaway. The free tour lasts a half hour and explains not only the brewing process, but also how "Rocky Mountain mineral water" is packaged and distributed locally. Informal tastings are held at the end of the tour for those 21 and over; souvenirs are available at the gift shop. ⊠ *13th and Ford Sts.* ☎ *303/277–2337* ⊕ *www.coors.com* ✉ *Free* ☉ *Mon.–Sat. 10–4* ☞ *Children under 18 must be accompanied by an adult.*

ↂ **Heritage Square.** This re-creation of an 1880s frontier town has an opera house, a narrow-gauge railway train ride, a Ferris wheel, a water slide, a bungee-jumping tower, specialty shops, and a music hall that stages original comedies and musicals as well as traditional melodramas. A vaudeville-style review ends each evening's entertainment. ⊠ *U.S. 40 and Rte. 93* ☎ *303/279–2789* ✉ *Entrance to park is free; admission varies per ride* ☉ *Shops Memorial Day–Labor Day, Mon.–Sat. 10–8, Sun. noon–8; Labor Day–Memorial Day, Mon.–Sat. 10–6, Sun. noon–6; rides June–Sept., daily, hrs vary* ☉ *Rides closed Mar.–May, Sept., and Oct.*

12th Street. This National Historic District has a row of handsome 1860s brick buildings. Among the monuments is the **Astor House** (⊠ Corner of 12th and Arapahoe Sts. ☎ 303/278–3557 ✉ $3 ☉ Tues.–Sat. 10–4:30, Sun. noon–4), a museum with period furnishings. Colorado's first **National Guard Armory** (⊠ Corner of 13th and Arapahoe Sts.) was built in 1913 and is the largest cobblestone building in America.

Central City & Black Hawk

18 mi from Golden via U.S. 6 west and Rte. 119 north.

When limited-stakes gambling was introduced in 1991 to the beautifully preserved old mining towns of Central City and Black Hawk, howls of protest were drowned out by cheers from struggling townspeople. Fortunately, strict zoning laws were legislated to protect the towns' architectural integrity, and by and large the laws have successfully handled the steady stream of tour buses. Gaming here is restricted to blackjack, poker, and slots, and the maximum bet is $5.

There are nearly 40 casinos in Black Hawk and Central City. All are in historic buildings dating to the 1860s—from jails to mansions—and their plush interiors have been lavishly decorated to re-create the Old West era—a period when this town was known as the "Richest Square Mile on Earth." They all serve meals and offer some entertainment. The most popular are Bullwhackers and Harrah's Glory Hole. Although no longer a casino, the Teller House is one of the most historic buildings in either town. Note that when gambling first began in the Colorado mountains, Central City was the place to go; the trend has since flip-flopped, with Central City dropping and Black Hawk skyrocketing in recent years. Many casinos offer B-level musical entertainment—singer Pat Boone was one of the recent star attractions—for something to do when you've lost at the tables. Buffets and hotel deals are prevalent, too, but this is no Las Vegas.

a good tour

Both towns can be explored on foot. Starting in Central City, park in one of the pay lots in town and begin at the west end of town, at the **Thomas House Museum.** Walk a block down Eureka Street to the **Central City Opera House** and **Teller House.** Take a detour on Main Street to browse the shops and casinos, and then head back down Eureka Street. Just before the Central Palace casino, you'll see a set of steep stairs; take them directly up to the **Gilpin County Historical Society Museum.** Go back down the stairs and walk the downhill mile to Black Hawk, to the **Mountain City Historic Park** on Gregory Street. If you don't feel like walking back uphill to Central City, catch a free shuttle in front of the Bull Durham or Eureka casinos.

TIMING   Both towns are about a 45-minute drive from Denver. Bus transportation is also available from Denver and Golden through most of the casinos and the Opera House. You can cover Central City and Black Hawk's main attractions in a few hours. If you're the gaming type, set aside extra time to try your luck. Although the casinos are open year-round, the museums are open only in summer.

What to See

Central City Opera House. Opera has been staged here almost every year since opening night in 1878. Lillian Gish has acted, Beverly Sills has sung, and many other greats have performed in the Opera House. Because there's no central heating, performances are held in summer only. ⊠ *200 Eureka St., Central City* ☎ *303/582–5283 tours, 303/292–6700 Denver box office* ⊕ *www.centralcityopera.org* ☜ *Tours $5* ☉ *Tours Memorial Day–Labor Day, daily 11–4; Apr. and May, Sept. and Oct., weekends 11–4.*

Gilpin County Historical Society Museum. Photos and reproductions, as well as vintage pieces from different periods of Gilpin County history, paint a richly detailed portrait of life in a typical rowdy mining community. ⊠ *228 E. High St., Central City* ☎ *303/582–5283* ⊕ *www.coloradomuseums.org/gilpin.htm* ☜ *$3; $5 in conjunction with admission to the Thomas House Museum* ☉ *June–Sept., daily 11–4; Oct.–May, by appointment only.*

Mountain City Historic Park. Apart from the casinos, this city block is the prime attraction in Black Hawk, consisting of a dozen historic homes and commercial structures from the town's heyday. It's a nice stroll that offers a glimpse of intermingling Victorian and Gothic architectural styles. ⊠ *Gregory St., Black Hawk* ☎ *303/582–5221* ☜ *Free* ☉ *Daily.*

Teller House. Built in 1872 by Senator Henry Teller, the first U.S. Secretary of the Interior from Colorado, this edifice was once one of the West's ritziest hotels. The floor of the famous Face Bar is adorned with the portrait of a mystery woman named Madeline, painted in 1936 by Herndon Davis. Some say it was created as a lark, others bet it was done for the price of a drink. Although it recently operated as a restaurant, today it serves somewhat generic box lunches only during the six-week summer opera season. Tours are available. ⊠ *120 Eureka St., Central City* ☎ *303/582–5283* ☐ *AE, D, MC, V* ☉ *June–Aug., weekdays 11–4; Apr., May, Sept., and Oct., weekends 11–4.*

Thomas House Museum. This 1874 house is an example of Victorian mountain elegance. It depicts the life of a middle-class turn-of-the-20th-century family through family photos and heirlooms such as period quilts and feather hats. ⊠ *209 Eureka St., Central City* ☎ *303/582–5283* ⊕ *www.coloradomuseums.org/thomasho.htm* ☜ *$3; $5 in conjunction with admission to the Gilpin County Historical Society Museum* ☉ *June–Sept., Fri.–Mon. 11–4; Oct.–May, by appointment only.*

Where to Stay & Eat

Virtually every casino has a restaurant with the usual mediocre $4.99 daily specials and all-you-can-eat buffets. The only eatery outside a casino is Central City's Teller House, which is open in accordance with opera season.

$$–$$$$ ✕ **White Buffalo Grille.** Regarded as the best casino restaurant in the area, the White Buffalo serves up steaks and seafood with Southwestern panache. The steaks are mesquite-broiled and served with poblano bordelaise and shallot jam; another good bet is the chile-glazed swordfish with kiwi-pineapple salsa. The atmosphere is upscale and the views from the all-glass enclosure on a bridge above Richmond Street are divine. ✉ *Lodge Casino, 240 Main St., Black Hawk* ☎ *303/582–1771* ▭ *AE, D, DC, MC, V* ☉ *Closed Mon. No lunch.*

$–$$ 🏨 **Golden Rose Victorian Hotel.** On the second floor of a historic bank building (1875), this establishment is a departure from the standard casino accommodations. Each room is named after a luminary from Central City's mining era: the Madam Lou Bunch Room is decorated a bit more aggressively than your typical historic inn—with red wallpaper and a "kissing couch"—but the accommodations are otherwise mellow, equipped with antiques, reproductions, and details down to period wallpaper. The hotel entrance is off Eureka Street. ✉ *101 Main St., Central City, 80427* ☎ *303/582–3737* ⤷ *5 rooms* ⏚ *Coffee shop* ▭ *AE, MC, V.*

THE EASTERN PLAINS

Although the Rocky Mountains are the state's enduring symbol, one-third of Colorado is prairie land—vast stretches of hypnotically rolling corn and wheat fields, Russian thistle, and tall grasses coppered by the sun. This is middle America, where families have been ranching and farming the same plot of land for generations; where county fairs, livestock shows, and high-school football games are the main forms of entertainment; where the Corn and Bible belts stoically tighten a notch in times of adversity. Off the interstate highway, the two-lane byways give a sense of the slower pace of life in this region's communities.

If you want to get in touch with America's roots, here is a good place to begin. The small one-horse towns such as Heartstrong and Last Chance—names redolent of the heartland—tell an old story, that of the first pioneers who struggled across the continent in search of a better life. The Pony Express and Overland trails cut right through northeast Colorado (James Michener set his epic historical novel *Centennial* in this territory), where even today you'll find weathered trading posts, lone buttes that guided the weary homesteaders westward, and down-home friendly people who take enormous pride in their land and their heritage.

Greeley

55 mi northeast of Denver via U.S. 85, 53 mi west of Fort Morgan.

Surrounded by a seemingly endless sea of farmland, Greeley is first and foremost an agricultural and ranching hub, with more than half its modern economy related to the beef industry. But it hasn't always been that way—the city began in 1869 as an experimental Utopian colony guided by onetime *New York Tribune* agriculture editor Nathan Meeker and named after his boss, Horace Greeley. With nearly 80,000 residents, modern Greeley is as all-American as it gets, with a historic downtown anchored by stockyards, the 11,000-student University of Northern Colorado, and annual events that run the gamut from rodeos to art exhibitions.

Comprised of 32 relocated and restored structures dating from 1850 to World War II, **Centennial Village** tells the story of Greeley's past through beet field shanties, Victorian homes, and onetime places of business. Guided tours are offered several times daily (on no particular schedule), but you are welcome to wander around on your own as well. ⊠ *1475 A St.* ☎ *970/350–9220* ⊕ *www.greeleymuseums.com* ⊠ *$5* ⊙ *Mid-Apr.–mid-Oct., Tues.–Sat., 10–4. Closed mid-Oct.–mid-Apr.*

★ First held in the 1800s to honor local potato farmers, the big annual event in town is the **Greeley Independence Stampede,** attracting nearly a half million people in recent years. Professional rodeo events are the big draw, but there are also country and classic-rock concerts, parades, art shows, fireworks, and a demolition derby. ⊠ *600 N. 14th Ave.* ☎ *800/ 982–2855 or 970/356–2855* ⊕ *www.greeleystampede.org* ⊠ *Admission varies by event* ⊙ *Late June–early July, daily.*

The spot to delve into the engaging story of Greeley founder Nathan Meeker is the **Meeker Home Museum,** his home from 1870 until his death at the hands of angry Utes in 1879. Guided tours of the Victorian abode reveal his story and many others via six restored and furnished rooms, with about a third of the contents being holdovers from the Meeker clan. ⊠ *1324 9th Ave.* ☎ *970/350–9220* ⊕ *www.greeleymuseums.com* ⊠ *Free; donations accepted* ⊙ *Mid-Apr.–mid-June and Sept.–mid-Oct., Tues.–Sat. 10–4; June–Aug., Tues.–Fri. 1–5.*

The only Atlas E nuclear-missile silo now open for public tours, **Missile Site Park** just west of Greeley city limits is a holdover from the Cold War. Manned from 1960 to 1965, the silo is now a museum owned by the city, with guided one-hour tours available with advance reservations. The park also has rest rooms, a playground, and campsites. ⊠ *10611 Spur 257* ☎ *970/356–4000 Ext. 4833* ⊠ *Free* ⊙ *May–early Oct., daily, 7–4.*

Sports & the Outdoors

GOLF Lined with grassy mounds, the 18-hole **Boomerang Links** (⊠ 7304 W. 4th St. ☎ 970/351–8934) is an excellent municipal facility with a lighted driving range, pro shop, and restaurant. Greens fees for 18 holes are $24 weekdays and $30 weekends. Another city-owned facility, **Highland Hills** (⊠ 2200 Clubhouse Dr. ☎ 970/330–7327) is a stunning 18-hole course with rolling hills and fairways bordered by lusher than expected trees. On-site are chipping and putting greens, a driving range, a pro shop (lessons available), and a grill. Greens fees for 18 holes are $18 weekdays and $30 weekends.

HIKING & **Island Grove Regional Park** (⊠ D St. and 14th Ave. ☎ 970/350–9392)
RUNNING is the hub of Greeley's recreational activities, with ball fields, sports venues, a pool, and jogging trails. A planned expansion of the **Poudre Trail** (⊹ along the Cache La Poudre River from W. 71st Ave. to the town of Windsor ☎ 970/350–9783) will eventually connect Island Grove Regional Park with the Weld/Larimer county line. The trail, 8 mi long at this writing, attracts those on foot (and rollerblades and bikes). The best plains hiking in the area is to be found in **Pawnee National Grassland** (⊠ 50 miles northeast of Greeley ☎ 970/353–5004) on the Pawnee Buttes Trail, a 1.5-mi trail to stark, rocky cliffs that are a habitat for hawks and falcons. The trail is closed from March through June to protect the nesting birds.

Where to Stay & Eat

$$–$$$$ ✕ **Potato Brumbaugh's.** Named for a character in James Michener's epic *Centennial*, Potato Brumbaugh's is the place to go for an upscale meal in Greeley. The bar area is clad with hundreds of framed photos of reg-

ulars, who keep coming back for the prime rib, steaks, seafood, and lighter dishes. ⊠ *2400 17th St. (in Cottonwood Square shopping center)* ☎ *970/356–6340* ⊟ *AE, D, DC, MC, V* ⊘ *No lunch on weekends.*

♨ **$–$$**   ✕ **Coyote's Southwestern Grill.** All of the tried-and-true standbys—burritos, enchiladas, tacos, and the like—are here, but Coyote's goes the extra mile by adding a few contemporary twists, such as the tequila shrimp scampi or the Ranchero cream pasta. The house specialties are blue-corn enchiladas and the Coyote burrito, jammed with chicken or beef and smothered in spicy green chile. The dining room has exposed ceilings and modern Southwestern art and ironwork; there's also an outdoor patio. A kid's menu (and crayons) are available. ⊠ *5250 W. 9th St. Dr.* ☎ *970/336–1725* ⊟ *AE, D, MC, V.*

¢   ✕ **Canterbury Tea Room.** A stately 1898 Victorian in the historic Monroe neighborhood houses this lunchtime spot. Impressionistic prints and chandeliers adorn the tearoom, where patrons enjoy imported teas. British specialties, such as shepherd's pie and a beef stew made with Guiness Stout, share the menu with sandwiches and salads. The desserts are baked fresh daily. ⊠ *1229 10th Ave.* ☎ *970/356–1811* ⊟ *AE, MC, V* ⊘ *No dinner.*

¢   ✕ **State Armory.** This local favorite resides in a 1921 brick terra-cotta building that served as a National Guard Armory until 1959. Today it's a beer-and-burger joint, decorated with everything from antique stained glass windows to rusty license plates and from macrame to burlap bags. The menu is dominated by the Armory's "world famous" burgers, with a smattering of other sandwiches and kids' plates. After dark, State Armory becomes a bustling nightclub. ⊠ *614 8th Ave.* ☎ *970/352–7424* ⊟ *MC, V.*

★ **$$–$$$**   🏠 **Greeley Guest House.** A thoroughly modern B&B on the western outskirts of town, the Greeley Guest House combines the best aspects of a full-service hotel with the intimacy of a small inn. Attractive, contemporary-meets-rustic rooms are packed with such perks as complimentary snacks and soda and high-speed Internet access. Immaculately groomed lawns and gardens with seating surround the inn. ⊠ *5401 West 9th St.,* ☎ *800/314–3684 or 970/353–9373* ⊕ *www.greeleyguesthouse.com* ⇆ *19 rooms* ⚬ *In-room data ports, in-room hot tubs, kitchens, microwaves, refrigerators, cable TV, business services, meeting rooms; no smoking* ⊟ *AE, MC, V* ⋮⊙⋮ *BP.*

$–$$ 🏠 **Sod Buster Inn Bed and Breakfast.** The 1997 Sod Buster was built a
Fodor'sChoice   century after most of its neighbors, but this urban inn blends seamlessly
★   into the historic Monroe District. The three-story octogonal structure is warm and inviting, surrounded by a wraparound porch and capped by a rooster weathervane. Up a spiral staircase on the second floor, the rooms are named after local historic luminaries and decorated with an eye for rustic elegance; many have clawfoot tubs and canopy beds. ⊠ *1221 9th Ave., 80631* ☎ *888/300–1221 or 970/392–1221* 🖷 *970/ 392–1222* ⊕ *www.sodbusterinn.com* ⇆ *10 rooms* ⚬ *Cable TV; no TV in some rooms, no smoking* ⊟ *AE, DC, MC, V* ⋮⊙⋮ *BP.*

$ 🏠 **Best Western Regency Hotel.** The most complete hotel in downtown Greeley, the Best Western Regency offers reliably clean rooms with a king bed or two queens. Two spa suites have in-room hot tubs, and deluxe rooms have fridges and microwave ovens. New owners renovated the property in 2003, giving the hotel a fresh, new feel. ⊠ *701 8th St., 80631* ☎ *970/353–8444 Ext. 478* 🖷 *970/353–4269* ⊕ *www.bestwestern. com/regencyhotel* ⇆ *148 rooms, 4 suites* ⚬ *Restaurant, in-room data ports, some in-room hot tubs, some refrigerators, some microwaves, cable TV, indoor pool, bar, nightclub, laundry service, business services, meeting rooms, some pets allowed (fee), no-smoking rooms* ⊟ *AE, D, DC, MC, V* ⋮⊙⋮ *CP.*

CAMPING   ⚠ **Greeley RV Park & Campground.** Surrounded by farmland and tall,
¢   shady trees, this is Greeley's largest and best campground. ✉ *501 E.*
27th St., 80631 ☎ *800/572–2130 or 970/353–6476* ⊕ *www.*
greeleyrvpark.com 🛏 *97 full hook-ups* ♨ *Flush toilets, full hook-ups,*
dump station, drinking water, laundry facilities, showers, grills, electricity,
public telephone, general store ⊟ *MC, V.*

¢   ⚠ **Missile Site Park.** At the defunct Atlas E missile silo west of Greeley,
there is a bare-bones campground with a playground and a smattering
of open space. The views of the Rockies are inspiring, but the thought
of nukes once sitting underground here is a tad unsettling. ✉ *10611 Spur*
257, 80634 ☎ *970/381–7451* 🛏 *20 sites* ♨ *Flush toilets, dump sta-*
tion, drinking water, grills ⊟ *No credit cards.* ☉ *Open May–Oct.*

Nightlife & the Arts

THE ARTS   Scholars act out the parts of historic celebrities such as Babe Ruth and
Will Rogers at the **High Plains Chautauqua** (✛ Aims Community College
and other Greeley locations ☎ 800/449–3866 or 970/352–3567). This
celebration of bygone traveling tent shows takes place in early August.
The annual **University of Northern Colorado/Greeley Jazz Festival** (✉ Union
Colony Civic Center, 701 10th Ave. ☎ 970/356–5000) offers three
days of jazz concerts, clinics, and other events in late April. Primarily
student and junior ensembles play, but guest artists also appear. The oldest summer-stock theatre west of the Mississippi, the **University of North-**
ern Colorado Little Theatre of the Rockies (✛ at various venues on the
University of Northern Colorado campus ☎ 970/351–2200) stages
four plays annually from May to July. Recent productions included Neil
Simon's *The Gingerbread Lady* and *Oliver!*

NIGHTLIFE   Country music lovers and line-dancers flock to **Cactus Canyon** (✉ in the
Greeley Mall at U.S. 34 and 23rd Ave. ☎ 970/351–8178), which hosts
modern dance-music nights as well. The margaritas are so potent at **Rio**
Grande (✉ 825 9th St. ☎ 970/304–9292) that the staff places a three-
marg limit on patrons. The festive bar and Mexican restaurant attracts
a bustling, diverse crowd. Beyond its legendary burgers, the **State Ar-**
mory (✉ 614 8th Ave. ☎ 970/352–2474) is a heck of a beer joint, featuring dance music, rock-bottom drink specials, and theme nights.

Fort Morgan

68 mi from Denver via I–76 east.

Fort Morgan, the seat of Morgan County, is a major agricultural center for corn, wheat, and sugar beets, the big cash crops in these parts.
But its true claim to fame is as bandleader Glenn Miller's birthplace.

Displays at the **Fort Morgan Museum** describe the town's 1864 origins as
a military fort constructed to protect gold miners. Other exhibits include
Glenn Miller memorabilia; artifacts from the Koehler Site, an excavated
landfill nearby that revealed a prehistoric campsite; and classic Americana such as a 1920s soda fountain from an old drugstore. On your way
out, pick up a downtown walking-tour brochure describing the handsome buildings that line Main Street. ✉ *414 Main St.* ☎ *970/867–*
6331 ⊕ *www.ftmorganmus.org* 🎟 *Free* ☉ *Weekdays 10–5, Sat. 11–5.*
Also open 6–8 PM Tues.–Thurs.

Sports & the Outdoors

BICYCLING   Every September, the 200-mi **Pedal the Prairie** biking event (✉ 100 En-
sign St. ☎ 800/354–8660 or 970/687–6707) takes riders on a three-day
jaunt around Colorado's eastern plains, starting and finishing in Fort
Morgan.

Where to Stay & Eat

$–$$$ ✕ **Country Steak-Out.** Fort Morgan's first steak house—a combination between a diner and a barn—looks as if it hasn't changed since the Dust Bowl era. After a long day of following behind pickup trucks with bumper stickers that admonish you to "Eat beef," you might as well succumb to the succulent steaks served here. There are also numerous chicken dishes and a lunch buffet Tuesday through Friday afternoons. ✉ *19592 E. 8th Ave.* ☎ *970/867–7887* ▤ *AE, D, MC, V* ☉ *Closed Mon. No dinner Sun.*

$ ▦ **Best Western Park Terrace.** Clean, pleasant rooms with cable TV are what you'll find in this comfortable chain motel. Bikes are available for guest use. ✉ *725 Main St., 80701* ☎ *970/867–8256 or 888/593–5793* 🖶 *970/867–8256* ⊕ *www.bestwestern.com* ⤴ *24 rooms* ♨ *Restaurant, cable TV, pool, hot tub, bicycles, no-smoking rooms* ▤ *AE, D, DC, MC, V.*

Sterling

46 mi from Fort Morgan via I–76 east.

Peaceful, prosperous Sterling is a town of graceful whitewashed houses with porch swings and shady trees that fringe neighborhood streets. Sterling bills itself as "The City of Living Trees," a tribute to local artist Brad Rhea, who has chiseled living trees into fanciful works of art: towering giraffes, festive clowns, golfers (at the country club), and minutemen (at the National Armory). Several downtown buildings, listed on the National Register of Historic Places, are examples of turn-of-the-20th-century pioneer architecture; among them is Logan County Courthouse.

The **Overland Trail Museum,** a reproduction of an old fort carved out of rock, lays out homesteading life, with painstaking re-creations of a typical blacksmith shop and schoolhouse, as well as exhibits of Plains Natives and pioneer clothing and utensils. Displays in a separate building detail the history of the Rural Electric Administration. ✉ *Jct. of U.S. 6 and I–76* ☎ *970/522–3895* ▱ *$2* ☉ *Nov.–Mar., Tues.–Sat. 10–4; Apr.–Oct., Mon.–Sat. 9–5, Sun. 1–5; holidays 10–5.*

off the beaten path

FT. SEDGWICK AND DEPOT MUSEUMS – Mark Twain once called Julesburg "the wickedest city in the West," though today it's hard to picture the sleepy town as Sodom and Gomorrah rolled into one. Julesburg, 54 mi northeast of Sterling on Interstate 76, was the proud site of the only Pony Express station in Colorado, duly celebrated at the summer-only Depot Museum, with assorted paraphernalia, from mail patches to saddles. The year-round Fort Sedgwick Museum focuses on the area's broader history, from its Native past to its later military importance. ✉ *114 E. 1st St., Julesburg* ☎ *970/474–2061* ▱ *$1* ☉ *June–Sept., Mon.–Sat. 9:30–4:30, Sun. 1–4:30; Oct.–May (Fort Sedgwick Museum only) weekdays 9:30–4:30.*

Sports & the Outdoors

FISHING & BOATING   Anglers seeking catfish, trout, walleye, and muskie head for the 3,000–acre **North Sterling Reservoir** (✉ 24005 CR 330 ☎ no phone), just north of Sterling. Both motorboats and human-powered vessels are allowed on the reservoir, which is surrounded by bluffs and has a campground.

Where to Stay & Eat

☙ **¢–$** ✕ **Shake, Rattle & Roll.** If you're in the mood for hearty portions with a side helping of nostalgia, this neon-bedecked re-creation of a '50s-style diner will oblige you. The walls are plastered with records, concert posters, and other memorabilia; the steaks and the milkshakes lure the locals time and time again. ✉ *1107 W. Main St.* ☎ *970/526–1700* 🖃 *AE, D, DC, MC, V.*

★ **$–$$** 🏨 **Old Library Inn.** A historic Carnegie library that first opened in 1918, this grand structure has been converted into a B&B. All named for former librarians, the unique rooms are not strictly Victorian. A wedding dress reflects silver light in the Lulu Boone Room, and antique Mission decor blends with contemporary amenities (including a whirlpool) in the Bertha Rogers Room. ✉ *210 S. 4th St., 80751* ☎ *970/522–3800* ⊕ *www.oldlibraryinn.com* ↝ *3 rooms* ⚘ *In-room hot tub, library; no smoking* 🖃 *MC, V* ⦿ *BP.*

$ 🏨 **Best Western Sundowner.** This property is a notch above the usual chain motel. It is adjacent to a park and has many shady lawns on-site. The pool has a small island in the middle, favored by sunbathers. The spacious, tasteful rooms are colorful and bright. Continental breakfast is included in the room rate. ✉ *125 Overland Trail St., 80751* ☎☎ *970/522–6265 or 800/528–1234* ⊕ *www.bestwestern.com* ↝ *30 rooms* ⚘ *Pool, gym, hot tub, laundry facilities, no-smoking rooms* 🖃 *AE, D, DC, MC, V* ⦿ *CP.*

Limon

78 mi from Denver via I–70 east.

A ferocious twister leveled Limon in 1990, but its residents banded together and today there are few apparent signs of the devastation. The town's past is displayed at the **Limon Heritage Museum,** offering collections of saddles and arrowheads, five restored railroad cars (including a restored 1914 railroad diner and a Union Railroad caboose), and changing photo and graphics exhibits, all housed in the original Union Pacific and Rock Island railroad depot and a newly constructed modern exhibition hall. ✉ *891 1st St.* ☎ *719/775–8605* ▢ *Free; donations accepted* ⊙ *June–Aug., Mon.–Sat. 1–8.*

en route   Aside from providing splendid vistas of the plains (and even six states on the clearest of days), the intriguing **Genoa Tower Museum** houses an eclectic collection of Native American artifacts, fossils, weird tools, and Elvis Presley memorabilia. Owner Jerry Chubbock says, "If it ain't here, it don't exist." The Ripleyesque display of animal monstrosities seems to support his boast. ✉ *Exit 371, off I–70 (follow signs from exit), about 10 mi east of Limon* ☎ *719/763–2309* ▢ *$1* ⊙ *Daily 8–8; call ahead.*

Burlington

73 mi from Limon via I–70 east.

Folks in Burlington, 12 mi from the Kansas border, take their history seriously. Exhibit A is **Old Town,** a lovingly authentic re-creation of a 1900s Old West village, with more than 20 restored turn-of-the-20th-century buildings complete with antique frontier memorabilia. Daily cancans take place throughout the summer in the Longhorn Saloon, a happily cheesy reproduction of an Old West watering hole. It's a hoot and a half. ✉ *I–70 Exit 437* ☎ *719/346–7382 or 800/288–1334* ▢ *$6* ⊙ *Mon.–Sat. 9–5; Sun. noon–5.*

★ ۞ Designated one of Colorado's 13 National Historic Landmarks, the **Kit Carson County Carousel** is a fully restored and operational carousel hand carved by the Philadelphia Toboggan Company in 1905. It's one of fewer than 170 carousels to retain its original paint. Forty-six exquisitely detailed creatures bob and weave to the jaunty accompaniment of a 1909

Wurlitzer Monster Military Band Organ. Among the residents here are richly caparisoned camels, fiercely toothsome tigers, and gamboling goats. ⊠ *Burlington Fairgrounds, 15th St. at Colorado Ave.* ☎ *719/346–8070* ☜ *25¢* ☉ *Memorial Day–Labor Day, daily 1–8.*

Sports & the Outdoors

FISHING & **Bonny State Reservoir** (✛ 18 miles north of Burlington on U.S. 385
BOATING ☎ 719/354–7306) is the best place near the Colorado–Kansas border to beat the summer heat, with opportunities for fishing, swimming, camping, boating, and other water sports.

Where to Stay & Eat

$ ✕ **Shanghai City.** Burlington is heavy on fast food and chains, but this Chinese restaurant at the Burlington Inn motel is a safe—albeit unexpected—bet for lunch or dinner. The menu is fairly typical for an American Chinese restaurant: Egg rolls, kung pao, and Szechuan specialties are all present and accounted for. ⊠ *450 S. Lincoln St.* ☎ *719/346–5555 Ext. 3* ▱ *MC, V.*

★ $$$–$$$$ 🏨 **Claremont Inn.** Twenty miles west of Burlington in Stratton, this lavish B & B is quite the departure from the plains' standard roadside motels. The three-story, Palladian-style Claremont blends romance, country charm, and classic elegance in its uniquely-decorated guest rooms. The public areas are striking, from the high ceilings of the ornate Great Hall to the cozy environs of the Claremont Theatre, where guests can take in a movie. ⊠ *800 Claremont Dr. (I–70 Exit 419), Stratton 80836* ☎ *719/348–5125 or 888/291–8910* ➭ *8 rooms* ☖ *Restaurant, cable TV, pool, hot tub, business services; no smoking* ▱ *AE, D, DC, MC, V* ⊠ *BP.*

¢ 🏨 **Chaparral Budget Host.** This serviceable motor lodge near Old Town offers the usual amenities, such as cable TV. ⊠ *405 S. Lincoln St. (I–70, Exit 437), 80807* ☎ *719/346–5361 or 800/456–6206* ➭ *39 rooms* ☖ *Cable TV, pool, hot tub* ▱ *AE, D, DC, MC, V.*

Shopping

For the best (and hokiest) selection of souvenirs, head for the **Old Town Emporium** (⊠ I–70 Exit 437 ☎ 719/346–7382). Western-themed toys and frontier-themed trinkets predominate.

DENVER A TO Z

AIRPORTS & TRANSFERS

DIA is 15 mi northeast of downtown. It's served by most major domestic carriers and many international ones, including Air Canada, American, America West, Continental, Delta, Frontier, Mesa, Northwest, Sun Country, TWA, United, and USAirways. Arrive at the airport with plenty of time before your flight, preferably two hours; DIA's check-in and security-check lines are particularly long.

Between the airport and downtown, Super Shuttle makes door-to-door trips. The region's public bus service, Regional Transportation District (RTD) runs SkyRide to and from DIA; the trip takes 50 minutes, and the fare is $8 each way. There's a transportation center in the airport just outside baggage claim. A taxi ride costs $43–$55 to downtown.

🛈 **Denver International Airport** ☎ 800/247-2336 ⊕ www.flydenver.com.
🛈 Taxis & Shuttles **Regional Transportation District** ☎ 303/299-6000 for route and schedule information ⊕ www.rtd-denver.com. **Super Shuttle** ☎ 303/370-1300.

BUS TRAVEL TO & FROM DENVER
🛈 **Greyhound Lines** ⊠ 1055 19th St., LoDo ☎ 800/231-2222.

BUS TRAVEL WITHIN DENVER

The region's public bus service, RTD, is comprehensive, with routes throughout the metropolitan area. The service also links Denver to outlying towns such as Boulder, Longmont, and Nederland. You can buy bus tokens at grocery stores or pay with exact change on the bus. Fares vary according to time and zone. Within the city limits, buses cost $1.15. You can also buy a Cultural Connection Trolley ticket for $16 at several convenient outlets throughout downtown, from the trolley driver, or from most hotel concierges. The trolley operates daily, every half hour 9–6, linking 18 prime attractions from the Brown Palace Hotel downtown to the Molly Brown House in Capitol Hill. Tickets are good for the entire day.

🚌 **Cultural Connection Trolley** ☎ 303/289-2841. **RTD Light Rail** ☎ 303/299-6000 or 800/366-7433 ⊕ www.rtd-denver.com.

CAR RENTAL

Rental car companies include Advantage, Alamo, Avis, Budget, Dollar, Enterprise, Hertz, and National. All have airport and downtown representatives.

CAR TRAVEL

Reaching Denver by car is fairly easy, except during rush hour when the interstates (and downtown) get congested. Interstate highways 70 and 25 intersect near downtown; an entrance to I-70 is just outside the airport.

When you're looking for an address within Denver, make sure you know whether it's a street or avenue. Speer Boulevard runs alongside Cherry Creek from northwest to southeast through downtown; numbered streets run parallel to Speer and most are one-way. Colfax Avenue (U.S. 287) runs east–west through downtown; numbered avenues run parallel to Colfax. Broadway runs north–south. Other main thoroughfares include Colorado Boulevard (north–south) and Alameda Avenue (east–west). Try to avoid driving in the area during rush hour, when traffic gets heavy. Interstates 25 and 225 are particularly slow-going given the long-term Transportation Expansion Project (T-REX), which will eventually add a light-rail system along the highways, plus bicycle lanes and other improvements.

PARKING Finding an open meter has become increasingly difficult in downtown Denver, especially during peak times such as Rockies games and weekend nights. Additionally, most meters have two-hour limits until 10 PM. Mayor John Hickenlooper made high parking-meter costs—at 25 cents for 10 minutes, more expensive than New York City and Chicago in some downtown areas—a central issue in his successful 2003 campaign. So expect some changes, perhaps for the better. However, there's no shortage of pay lots ($5 to $25 per day).

EMERGENCIES

Concentra Medical Center is a full medical clinic. HealthOne and Health Advisors offer a free referral service. Rose Medical Center refers patients to doctors from 8 to 5:30 and is open 24 hours for emergencies. Exempla St. Joseph Hospital is open 24 hours. Walgreens and King Soopers pharmacies are both open around the clock.

🦷 Dentists **American Dental Referral** ☎ 888/657-6453. **Dental Referral Service** ☎ 800/428-8773.

🏥 Hospitals **Concentra Medical Centers** ✉ 1860 Larimer St., Suite 100, LoDo ☎ 303/296-2273. **Exempla St. Joseph Hospital** ✉ 1835 Franklin St., Capitol Hill ☎ 303/837-7111. **Health Advisors** ☎ 303/777-6877. **HealthOne** ☎ 877/432-5846. **Rose Medical Center** ✉ 4567 E. 9th Ave., Hale ☎ 303/320-2121.

24-Hour Pharmacies **King Soopers** ⊠ 3100 S. Sheridan Blvd., Bear Valley ☎ 303/937-4404. **Walgreens** ⊠ 2000 E. Colfax Ave., City Park ☎ 303/331-0917.

MEDIA

NEWSPAPERS & MAGAZINES
The *Denver Post* and the *Rocky Mountain News*, now under a joint operating agreement, are Denver's two daily newspapers. *Westword* is an alternative, liberal-leaning weekly that's published every Wednesday, focusing on local politics, media, and entertainment. The bimonthly *5280 Magazine* is a light lifestyle/arts/entertainment publication.

SAFETY

Although Denver is a generally peaceful city, the crime rate has increased slightly in recent years as the population has boomed. (And the economic downturn has only made the rates jump even further; as of early 2003, police are warning of increases in murders and gang activity.) There are a few shadier areas on the outskirts of downtown, but violent crimes are few and far between. As always, paying attention to your surroundings is your best defense.

TAXIS

Cabs are available by phone and at the airport and can generally be hailed outside major hotels, for $1.60 minimum, $1.60 per mi. However, at peak times—during major events and at 2 AM when the bars close—taxis are very hard to come by.

Taxi Companies **Freedom Cab** ☎ 303/292-8900. **Metro Taxi** ☎ 303/333-3333. **Yellow Cab** ☎ 303/777-7777.

TOURS

BUS TOURS
Gray Line of Denver's Cultural Connection Trolley is designed to take you from attraction to attraction, but riders can remain on the trolley for the full two-hour ride. Actually Quite Nice Brew Tours' 23-seat Brewmobile hauls beer aficionados to the best microbreweries in Metro Denver, which it touts as the "Napa Valley of Brewing."

Fees & Schedules **Actually Quite Nice Brew Tours** ☎ 303/431-1440. **Gray Line of Denver** ☎ 303/289-2841.

WALKING TOURS
Gunslingers, Ghosts and Gold conducts humorous and trivia-filled walking tours of downtown ($15) that focus on both the historic and the supernatural and cover a few miles in two hours. Lower Downtown District, Inc., offers guided tours of historic Denver. Self-guided walking-tour brochures are available from the Denver Metro Convention and Visitors Bureau.

Fees & Schedules **Gunslingers, Ghosts and Gold** ☎ 303/860-8687. **Lower Downtown District, Inc.** ☎ 303/628-5428.

TRAIN TRAVEL

Union Station, a comfortable old building in the heart of downtown, filled with vending machines and video games if you just can't find them anywhere else, has Amtrak service. RTD's Light Rail service's original 5⅓-mi track links southwest and northeast Denver to downtown. RTD recently extended the tracks down to the city's southern suburbs; the peak fare is $1.15 within the city limits.

RTD Light Rail ☎ 303/299-6000 ⊕ www.rtd-denver.com. **Union Station** ⊠ 17th Ave. at Wynkoop St., LoDo ☎ 303/534-2812.

TRANSPORTATION AROUND DENVER

In downtown Denver, free shuttle-bus service operates about every 10 minutes until 1 AM, running the length of the 16th Street Mall (which bisects downtown) and stopping at two-block intervals. If you plan to spend much time outside downtown, a car is advised, although Denver has one of the best city bus systems in the country and taxis are available.

VISITOR INFORMATION

The Denver Metro Convention and Visitors Bureau, open weekdays 9–5 and Saturday 9–2, is downtown above the Wolf Camera store on California Street. It provides information and free maps, magazines, and brochures, as does an information center at the Tabor Center (same hours).
🏢 **Denver Metro Convention and Visitors Bureau** ✉ 918 16th St., LoDo, Denver 80202 ☎ 303/892–1112 or 800/393–8559 🖷 303/892–1636 ⊕ www.denver.org.

NORTH CENTRAL COLORADO

2

FODOR'S CHOICE

Boulder Dushanbe Teahouse, *Boulder*

Colorado Shakespeare Festival, *Boulder*

Hotel Boulderado, *Boulder*

Trail Ridge Road, *Rocky Mountain National Park*

Stanley Hotel, *Estes Park*

HIGHLY RECOMMENDED

RESTAURANTS Canino's, *Fort Collins*

Flagstaff House, *Boulder*

Lyons Soda Fountain, *Lyons*

Sweet Basilico Café, *Estes Park*

HOTELS Aspen Lodge at Estes Park Ranch, *Estes Park*

C Lazy U Guest Ranch, *Granby*

Edwards House B&B, *Fort Collins*

Gold Lake Mountain Resort & Spa, *Ward*

Rapids Lodge, *Grand Lake*

SIGHTS Boulder Bookstore, *Boulder*

Chautauqua Park, *Boulder*

Flagstaff Mountain, *Boulder*

Peak-to-Peak Highway, *Nederland to Estes Park*

OUTDOORS Bear Lake Nature Trail, *Rocky Mountain National Park*

Bolder Boulder 10–K

Chautauqua Trail/Mesa Trail, *Boulder*

Eldorado Canyon State Park, *Boulder*

Golf at the Grand Elk Ranch & Club, *Granby*

Hiking in Nederland

Hiking & Mountain Biking in Lyons

Long Peak, *Rocky Mountain National Park*

St. Peter's Fly Shop, *Fort Collins*

By Gregory
Robl

NORTH CENTRAL COLORADO BECAME PART OF THE UNITED STATES in 1803 through the Louisiana Purchase—hence towns with names like La Porte, Platteville, La Salle, and Lafayette, as well as the river named Cache la Poudre. Coal mines between Boulder and Broomfield attracted settlers and many Italian immigrants in the late 1800s and early 1900s, but the region grew mostly on agriculture and ranching. In Grand County, where ranching is still a livelihood for many, guest ranches and golf courses provide an indulgent retreat from the hectic pace of the Front Range cities. Waterskiing, sailing, canoeing, ice-fishing, and snowmobiling have made Grand Lake village and Colorado's "Great Lakes" a destination for even vacationing Coloradans. Out-of-state leisure travelers first came in the early 20th century to benefit from both the curative qualities of the dry air and the waters of spas like Eldorado Springs and Hot Sulphur Springs. Reminders of a grand style of touring exist in resort towns such as Estes Park and Grand Lake, the gateways to one of the state's most heralded attractions, Rocky Mountain National Park.

Singer John Denver brought renewed international interest to the area with his ballad *Rocky Mountain High* back in 1972. The wilderness of Rocky Mountain National Park spans three ecosystems and is home to 900 species of plants, 250 species of birds, and 25 species of mammals—including elk, deer, moose, bobcats, and even black bears.

Exploring North Central Colorado

Fort Collins and Boulder are the two most prominent and characteristic cities of the region. Between these two energetic university towns, you'll find the sprawling cities of Loveland and Longmont and a few former coal mining towns with homey, small town character like Marshall, Louisville, Lafayette, and Erie. To the west are the proud, independent mountain hamlets of Lyons, Nederland, Ward, and Jamestown. Beyond the high peaks are broad valleys dotted with unpretentious ranching communities like Granby and Kremmling, and right in the middle of it all is the area's crown jewel, Rocky Mountain National Park, and its resorts, Grand Lake and Estes Park. Despite their proximity, each town in the region has its own milieu—a distinct character and a unique history—as though hundreds of miles separated them. Throughout the region are never-ending vistas of green pastures and fields of grain, snow capped granite peaks, pine- and aspen-forested valleys, raging rivers and meandering streams, deep canyons, and manicured greenbelts—all shared by wildlife and humans.

About the Restaurants

Thanks to the influx of people from around the world, and their willingness and means to pay for quality food, diners here have curious and educated palates. Restaurants in north central Colorado run the gamut from simple diners with tasty, homey basics to elegant, world-class restaurants with wine lists numbering hundreds of wines. Increasingly, eateries are featuring organic ingredients and many serve exclusively organic meals. Even places catering to college students know that their existence depends on good meals made and priced honestly. Some restaurants take reservations, but many, particularly in the middle range, seat on a first-come, first-served basis. Popular establishments fill fast, especially on weekends. The mitigating consolation is that there is doubtless another satisfying restaurant nearby.

About the Hotels

North central Colorado is full of franchise motels and hotels, often at the access points to cities. There are equally as many independent

Numbers in the text correspond to numbers in the margin and on the North Central Colorado map.

If you have
3 days

Start in ▣ **Boulder** ❶–⓫ by cycling the Boulder Creek Path or the Marshall Mesa, or hiking near the Flatirons after a breakfast at the Chautauqua Dining Hall. After lunch you can poke around the town or antique in **Niwot.** ⑬. On day two, head toward ▣ **Estes Park** ㉓, but first take in the scenery along the Peak-to-Peak Highway, diverting long enough for a light lunch in Gold Hill or an old-fashioned ice-cream soda in **Lyons** ⑭. Hike near Bear Lake or to Fern Lake in **Rocky Mountain National Park** ㉔ and work up an appetite for dinner in one of Estes Park's fine restaurants. On day three, drive up Fall River Road—keeping a sharp eye out for wildlife—to Rocky Mountain National Park's Alpine Visitors Center. Linger there for the views and to learn about the alpine ecosystem before driving back along Trail Ridge Road, with its many scenic viewpoints. After lunch, peruse the shops and galleries along Elkhorn Avenue, learn to kayak on Lake Estes, or visit the Trail Ridge Winery near Loveland.

If you have
5 days

Follow the three-day itinerary, replacing the drive up Fall River Road on day three with a guided horseback ride or rock-climbing lesson in the national park. Try the Sweet Basilico for lunch, and follow the afternoon itinerary. On day four take your time along Trail Ridge Road and at the Alpine Visitors Center before descending the hairpin curves to ▣ **Grand Lake** ㉕ for lunch. Hike along the Colorado River to Lulu City or trot around Monarch Lake. There's time to stroll the boardwalk before dinner. On day five you can play 18 holes near ▣ **Granby** ㉖ at the Sol Vista or Grand Elk Ranch clubs; sail, canoe, or boat on Shadow Mountain Reservoir; cycle up to Willow Creek Pass; or mountain-bike in the Arapahoe National Recreation Area. The spa at **Hot Sulphur Springs** ㉗ will revive you before a hearty dinner. Don't miss the rodeo in Granby if it's the season.

If you have
7 days

Follow the five-day itinerary but replace days four and five with the following itinerary. On day four, drive to ▣ **Fort Collins** ⑮–㉒; hike or mountain-bike in Horsetooth Mountain Park, or cycle along the Poudre River in town. In the afternoon, tour a brewery or take the kids to the Swetsville Zoo. Learn about raptors at the Environmental Learning Center or take in some history at the Avery House and the Fort Collins Museum. Relax over a leisurely Italian dinner at Canino's before checking out the vibrant music scene. On day five, let the guides from St. Peter's Fly Shop take you on a float trip for trout, or get an adrenaline rush on an A-1 whitewater raft trip on the Cache la Poudre River. Later in the afternoon you can get your land legs back by wandering the galleries and shops in Old Town Square before an elegant dinner at Nico's Catacombs or a zesty Mexican meal at Rio Grande. Spend your last two days and nights in ▣ **Granby** ㉖, following the five-day itinerary.

2

innkeepers who either offer simple rooms with the basics or grand palaces with a level of service you might expect in New York, Paris, or London—each with its own Western-style flair. Bed-and-breakfasts and small inns range from old-fashioned fluffy places to modern, sleek buildings with an understated lodge feel. Guest ranches and spas are eternal favorite places to escape and be pampered in between having fun outdoors.

	WHAT IT COSTS				
	$$$$	**$$$**	**$$**	**$**	**¢**
RESTAURANTS	over $25	$19–$25	$13–$18	$8–$12	under $8
HOTELS	over $200	$151–$200	$111–$150	$70–$110	under $70

Restaurant prices are for a main course at dinner, excluding sales tax of 6.75%–8%. Hotel prices are for two people in a standard double room in high season, excluding service charges and 5.4%–9.8% tax.

Timing

Visiting the Front Range is pleasurable during any season. The propensity of sunny days makes outdoor activities possible nearly every day. Wintertime in the urban corridor can be mild, but the mountainous regions are cold and snowy. Snowfall along the Front Range is highest in spring, particularly March, making for excellent skiing, but poor car travel. Spring is capricious—75 °F one day and a blizzard the next—and June can be hot or cool and rainy. July typically ushers in high summer, which can last through September, although most 90-plus–degree days occur in July and early August. In the higher mountains, summer temperatures are generally 15–20 degrees cooler than in the urban corridor. Afternoon summer thunderstorms can last 30 minutes or all evening. Fall has crisp sunny days and cool nights, some cold enough for frost in non-urban areas.

Art and music festivals start up in May and continue through September. With them comes an increase in tourist traffic. Spring and summer are the best times to watch for wildlife or fish.

BOULDER

25 mi northwest of Denver via U.S. 36

No place in Colorado better epitomizes the state's outdoor mania than Boulder, where sunny weather keeps locals busy through all seasons. There are nearly as many bikes as cars in this uncommonly beautiful and beautifully uncommon city embroidered with 30,000 acres of parks and greenbelts and laced with more than 200 mi of trails for hiking, walking, jogging, and biking. Boulder started taxing itself in 1967 in order to buy greenbelts and in 2000 had a referendum (failed) on the ballot to provide free public transportation for city residents. Even in winter, residents cycle to work and jog on the open-space paths. It's nearly a matter of civic pride to spend a lunch hour playing frisbee, in-line skating, hiking with the family dog, and even rock climbing on the Flatirons.

Personal styles in this vibrant and liberal city run the gamut from the latest trends out of Los Angeles and New York to the punkish look of neon blue hair and an armor of body piercings. Natty professorial togs are still common in this university town, as is the proverbial Boulder three-piece suit: a T-shirt, fleece vest, and shorts, completed by Birkenstock sandals. The city is home to the University of Colorado at Boulder, the Buddhist Naropa University, the Boulder College of Massage

North America's Highest Paved Road

Within Rocky Mountain National Park, Trail Ridge Road curves 48 mi and climbs more than 4300 feet in elevation. Between the gateways Estes Park and Grand Lake, take your take your time at myriad turnouts to gaze over verdant valleys—brushed with yellowing aspen in the fall—that slope between the glacier-etched granite peaks. The road takes you through three ecosystems: montane, subalpine, and arctic tundra. The *Trail Ridge Road Guide,* available at visitors centers, explains what you are seeing. The temperature lowers at each stop, and by the time you're at the Alpine Visitors Center, the warm, lush valleys are far below, and you'll find yourself in a chilly, windy meadow of low-lying plants and flowers more suited to the Arctic. The highest point on the road is at 12,183 feet in elevation, past the point where the road crosses the Continental Divide at Milner Pass—elevation 10,758 feet.

2

Fall-Foliage Drive

An afternoon drive through Boulder Canyon to Nederland and along the Peak-to-Peak Highway north from there is a rite of autumn. Fall comes early to the Rockies when the sky is deeper blue, the high mountains are white with fresh snow, the air is dry and cool, and stands of aspens distinguish themselves from the evergreen pine forests with golden leaves. A stop at Boulder Falls is de rigeur, and the route can take a couple directions after Nederland. You could continue on to Estes Park via Routes 72 and 7 for a relaxing dinner as the sun sets behind the peaks of Rocky Mountain National Park. Or, turn off just before Ward to the former mining town of Gold Hill for dinner at the Gold Hill Inn. Then wind down Sunshine Canyon as the lights of nighttime Boulder flicker before you.

A Hike at Chautauqua Park

In Boulder, hiking trails in all categories of difficulty take walkers to the base of the imposing Flatirons and to the tops of pine-covered Flagstaff and Green mountains. Even a short walk up the grassy slope between Chautauqua Park and the base of the mountain brings out hikers and their dogs to take in some sun. After an early-morning hike, the dining hall at Chautauqua Park fills with hungry people ready to tuck into a hearty breakfast. Afternoon walkers relax on the park's gently sloping lawn with a picnic from Wild Oats or Whole Foods and gaze up at the foothills stretching along the Front Range.

Therapy, the National Center for Atmospheric Research, the National Institute of Standards and Technology, and the nationally popular *E-Town* radio show.

Exploring

Downtown

① **Pearl Street** between 8th and 20th streets is the city's hub, an eclectic collection of classy boutiques, consignment shops, eccentric bookstores, art galleries, cafés, bars, and restaurants. A few national retailers have hung out their signs among the home-grown businesses along the four-block pedestrian mall, but beyond 11th Street to the west and 15th Street to the east, the milieu evokes the early days of the Pearl Street Mall.

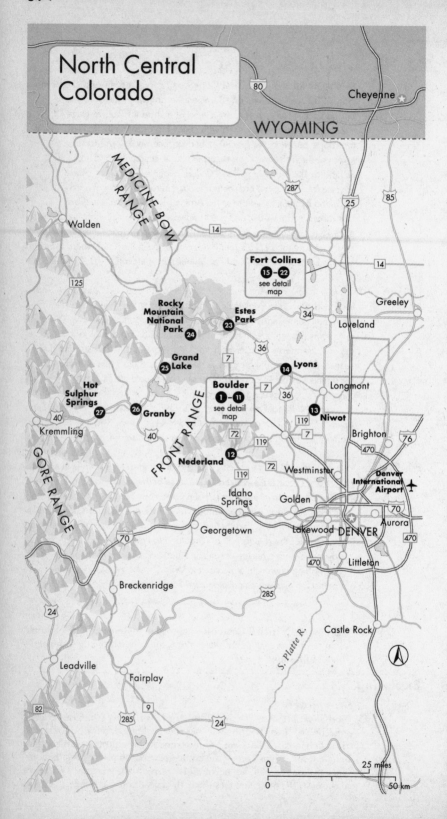

North Central Colorado

WYOMING

Cheyenne

MEDICINE BOW RANGE

Walden

287

80

25

85

14

14

Greeley

Fort Collins
15 – 22
see detail map

Rocky Mountain National Park

24

Estes Park

23

34

Loveland

125

Grand Lake

25

7

36

Boulder
1 – 11
see detail map

Lyons

14

Longmont

Hot Sulphur Springs

27

26

Granby

FRONT RANGE

7

36

119

13

Niwot

Brighton

76

40

Kremmling

40

72

119

7

GORE RANGE

Nederland

12

119

72

Westminster

470

Denver International Airport

Idaho Springs

Golden

70

70

Georgetown

Lakewood

DENVER

Aurora

470

Breckenridge

285

Littleton

470

24

Castle Rock

S. Platte R.

Leadville

Fairplay

82

285

9

24

0   25 miles

0   50 km

➋ The late-9th- and early-20th-century commercial structures of the **Downtown Boulder Historic District** once housed mercantile stores and saloons. The period architecture—including Queen Anne, Italianate, and Romanesque styles in stone or brick—has been preserved, but stores inside cater to modern tastes, with gourmet coffees and Tibetan prayer flags. The area is bounded by the south side of Spruce Street between 10th and 16th streets, Pearl Street between 9th and 16th streets, and the north side of Walnut Street between Broadway and 9th Street.

➌ Three blocks north of Pearl Street and west of Broadway is **Mapleton Historic District.** This neighborhood of turn-of-the-20th-century homes shaded by old maple and cottonwood trees is bounded roughly by Broadway, the alley between Pearl and Spruce streets, 4th Street, and the alley between Dewey Street and Concord Avenue.

Historic Boulder (✉ 646 Pearl St. ☎ 303/444–5192) sells brochures ($3) for seven self-guided walking tours, including the University of Colorado at Boulder, University Hill (known as "The Hill"), Chautauqua Park, the Mapleton Historic District, and the Downtown Boulder Historic District. The annual Tour of Homes (early May) and the Historic Homes for the Holidays (first weekend of December) tours are highly popular with locals. Be sure to reserve tickets for the holiday tour ($15).

➍ The **Boulder Museum of Contemporary Art** hosts local and national contemporary art exhibits and, on Thursday evenings, performance art, dance, experimental film, and poetry readings. ✉ *1750 13th St.* ☎ *303/443–2122* 🔳 *$4* 🕙 *Tues.–Sat. 10–6.*

University & Boulder

➎ South of downtown is the **University of Colorado at Boulder.** Red sandstone buildings with tile roofs (built in the "Rural Italian" architectural style that Charles Z. Klauder created in the early 1920s) outline the campus's green lawns and small ponds. The original campus began in 1875 with the construction of Old Main, which borders the **Norlin Quadrangle** (on the National Register of Historic Places), a broad lawn where students sun themselves or play a quick round of Frisbee between classes. The **CU Heritage Center** (✉ Old Main Bldg. on Norlin Quadrangle ☎ 303/492–6329 🔳 free 🕙 weekdays 10–4, Sat. 10–2 during the academic year) preserves the history of the university—including notable student pranks and a lunar sample on long-term loan from NASA. Also displayed are the personal memorabilia of alumni such as Marilyn Van Derbur, Robert Redford, and Glenn Miller. One room is devoted to CU's 17 astronauts, including Ellison Onizuka, who was killed aboard the *Challenger* space shuttle in 1986, and Kalpana Chawla, who died on the *Columbia* in 2003. The natural history collection at the **University of Colorado Museum** (✉ Henderson Bldg. ☎ 303/492–6892 🔳 free 🕙 weekdays 9–5, weekends 10–4) includes dinosaur relics and has permanent and changing exhibits. ✉ *University Memorial Center* ☎ *303/492–1411, 303/492–6301 to reserve a tour* ⊕ *www.colorado. edu* 🔳 *Free* 🕙 *Campus tours year-round, weekdays 9:30 and 1:30, Sat. 10:30* ☞ *Reservations essential.*

Star shows and laser shows set to classic compositions like *Peter and the Wolf* or the music of well-known rock bands entertain at the university's **Fiske Planetarium/Sommers-Bausch Observatory.** During the academic year, shows begin on Friday at 7:30 PM and 10 PM and on selected Tuesdays and Saturdays at 7:30 PM. Matinees take place during summer on Wednesday and Saturday at 2. The observatory is open Friday evening from 9 to 11, weather permitting. ✉ *Regent Dr.* ☎ *303/492–5001* ⊕ *www.colorado.edu/fiske* 🔳 *Shows $5; matinees $4; observa-*

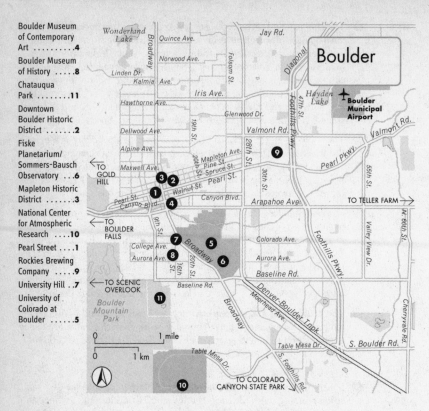

tory free ☾ *Year-round, days vary. Observatory, Fri. 9–11* ☾ *Closed on university holidays.*

❼ A favorite college student hangout is the bohemian neighborhood **University Hill** ("The Hill"; ✉ 13th St. between Pennsylvania St. and College Ave.), which is home to eateries, music and dance venues, record shops, bars, coffeehouses, and hip boutiques.

> **need a break?** The actor Robert Redford worked at **The Sink** (✉ 1165 13th St. ☎ 303/444–7465) during his student years. The restaurant has served great pizza, burgers, beer, and other student dietary staples since 1949.

❽ Housed in the 1889 Harbeck-Bergheim mansion, the **Boulder Museum of History** documents the history of Boulder and the surrounding region from 1858 to the present. If you're interested in the sartorial styles of the 19th century (whether rugged cowboy and miner duds or high-society finery), this museum will delight. It's home to one of Colorado's largest clothing collections, with items dating as far back as 1820. ✉ 1206 Euclid Ave. ☎ 303/449–3464 ⊕ www.boulderhistorymuseum. org ☑ $3 ☾ Tues.–Fri. 10–4, weekends noon–4.

❾ The scent of hops fills the air during free tours and ale and lager tastings at the **Rockies Brewing Company,** Colorado's first microbrewery. ✉ 2880 Wilderness Pl. ☎ 303/444–8448 ⊕ www.boulderbeer.com ☑ Free ☾ Tours weekdays 2 PM.

❿ Talking about the weather is *not* boring at the **National Center for Atmospheric Research,** where the hands-on exhibits, video presentation, and one-hour tour fires up kids' enthusiasm for what falls out of the sky.

I. M. Pei's famous buildings stand majestically on a mesa at the base of the mountains, where you can see mule deer and other wildlife. After browsing the field guides and science kits in the gift shop, follow the interpretive Walter Orr Roberts Nature and Weather Trail to learn about the mesa's weather, climate, plants, and wildlife. The .4-mi loop is wheelchair accessible. ✉ *1850 Table Mesa Dr., 80305, from southbound Broadway turn right on Table Mesa Dr.* ☎ *303/497–1174* ⊕ *www.ncar.ucar.edu* ✉ *Free* ☉ *Weekdays 8–5, weekends 9–4. Tour daily at noon.*

★ ⓫ For the prettiest views of town, follow Baseline Drive (west from Broadway) up to **Chautauqua Park** (✉ 900 W. Baseline Rd.), site of the Colorado Music Festival, and a favorite oasis of locals on weekends. Continue farther up Flagstaff Mountain to Panorama Point and Boulder Mountain Park, where people jog, bike, and climb.

> **off the beaten path**

CELESTIAL SEASONINGS – North America's largest herbal-tea producer (sealing eight million tea bags every 24 hours) offers free tours of its factory. Before the tour, you can sample from more than 60 varieties of tea and view the sewing machine used to sew the company's first 10,000 tea bags in 1969. The famous "Mint Room" will clear your tear ducts and sinuses. Teas, foodstuffs, teapots, and T-shirts are sold in the gift shop. The café, open weekdays, serves breakfast from 7:30 to 9:30 and lunch from 11 to 2:30. ✉ *4600 Sleepytime Dr., 8 mi northeast of downtown Boulder* ☎ *303/581– 1202* ⊕ *www.celestialseasonings.com* ✉ *Free* ☉ *Tours hourly; Mon.–Sat. 10–3, Sun. 11–3.*

The **Leanin' Tree Museum of Western Art** is one of the country's largest privately owned collections of post-1950 cowboy and Western art. More than 200 paintings of Western landscapes, wildlife, and the pioneers' ranch life, and 85 bronze sculptures by renowned, contemporary artists including Bill Hughes and Frank McCarthy, recall an era in the Boulder Valley before lattés and herbal tea. The superlative collection ranges from traditionalists in the Remington and Bierstadt manner to stylistic innovators of the Western genre. The museum is brought to you by folks who make humorous Western-theme greeting cards—one room is devoted to the paintings of the original greeting-card genius, Lloyd Mitchell. ✉ *6055 Longbow Dr.* ☎ *303/530–1442* ⊕ *www.leanintree. com* ✉ *Free* ☉ *Weekdays 8–4:30, Sat. 10–4.*

Sports & the Outdoors

The **City of Boulder Open Space & Mountain Parks** office (✉ 66 S. Cherryvale Rd. ☎ 303/441–3440 ⊕ www.ci.boulder.co.us/openspace) sells an excellent water- and tear-resistant map of hiking, cycling, and equestrian trails they administer and can give you information on the easy to moderate hiking in the area parks. Many trails are open to dogs, provided they are leashed. Be prepared for short thunderstorms during summer afternoons.

Boulder's admirable park system includes the trademark red sandstone **Flatirons.** These massive rock upthrusts, so named for their flat faces, are popular among rock climbers and hikers. You can see them from almost every vantage point in town.

★ Drive the hairpin switchbacks to the top of **Flagstaff Mountain** (✉ Flagstaff Rd. 💲 $3 per vehicle) for incredible views of Boulder and the Continental Divide. From the parking area walk out to the amphitheater to

THE GRAND DAYS OF THE SPA

Colorado's scenery has long attracted high-profile personalities like Teddy Roosevelt and Walt Whitman, but many early travelers were asthma, tuberculosis, and arthritis sufferers who came to the dry climate to convalesce. From the early to the mid-twentieth century, healing spas and resorts like Hot Sulphur Springs and Eldorado Springs sprang up in the mountains of North Central Colorado and were destinations for long-term visitors. The list of the rich or famous who visited is long: Robert Frost visited his daughter, Marjorie, in Boulder while she recuperated in the early 1930s, and Dwight and Mamie Eisenhower honeymooned at Eldorado Springs. The therapeutic tradition continues today. Refurbished hot springs and spas are regaining their popularity, and the National Jewish Medical and Research Center in Denver specializes in treatments for respiratory ailments.

look down into the crevasses of the foothills. A nighttime visit will afford you endless views of the glittering cities of the Front Range.

★ **Eldorado Canyon State Park,** with its awe-inspiring canyon of steep walls and pine forests, offers outdoor activities for everyone—even birdwatchers and artists. Kayakers get adrenaline rushes on the rapids of South Boulder Creek, while rock climbers scale the world–renowned, vertical, granite canyon walls. Picnickers can choose from 42 spots, and anglers' catches average 8 inches. Hikers have 12 mi of trails to wander. The **Streamside** (1 mi round-trip) and **Fowler** (1½ mi round-trip) interpretive trails are close to the creek. Portions are wheelchair-accessible. For the best views of the canyon and the Front Range plains, head up **Rattlesnake Gulch Trail.** The 3 mi (round-trip) switchback trail ends at an overlook where you can see the high Rockies of the Continental Divide. Snowshoeing is popular here in winter. Mountain bikers crank on Rattlesnake Gulch Trail and Fowler Trail. **Eldorado Canyon Trail** is open to horseback riding. ⊕ *Drive south on Broadway (Hwy. 93) 3 mi to Eldorado Canyon Dr. (Rte.170). The paved road ends at the village of Eldorado Springs. Drive through town to the park entrance* ☎ *303/ 494–3943* ⊕ *www.parks.state.co.us* ✉ *$6 per vehicle.*

★ Memorial Day brings the annual 10-km **Bolder Boulder** (☎ 303/444–7223 ⊕ www.bolderboulder.com), when top international runners, along with 45,000 other citizens, run the country's fourth-largest race. About 100,000 spectators line the route and fill CU's Folsom Stadium to cheer on the participants. Rock bands, jazz musicians, African drumming groups, "Elvis" crooners, belly dancers, and classical quartets spur on the runners. The race ends in Folsom Stadium for a ceremony that includes a flyover by U.S. Air Force fighter jets and skydivers who parachute onto the stadium field.

Bicycling

You can rent a mountain bike for four hours to three days at **Full Cycle** (✉ 1211 13th St. ☎ 303/440–7771). **University Bicycles** (✉ 839 Pearl St. ☎ 303/444–4196) rents bikes (helmet and map included) for four hours to one week.

The **Boulder Creek Path** winds through town for about 9 mi from the mouth of Fourmile Canyon west of Boulder to the intersection of Arapahoe Avenue and Cherryvale Road, connecting to over 200 mi of city and greenbelt trails and paths. For more strenuous mountain biking, head west out of town to **Walker Ranch** (✉ 8 mi west of town on Flagstaff Rd.); the 7½-mi loop has great views of the Indian Peaks. To get there take Baseline Road west; it becomes Flagstaff Road at the sharp curve before the steep incline. For less challenging cycling but a scenic 7.2-mi, two-hour ride nonetheless, the **Betasso Preserve Loop** is 4 mi west of Broadway on Canyon Boulevard in Boulder Canyon. Look for the trail-head turnout on the left. The **Foothills Trail**, accessed either off North 4th Street or from the intersection of Linden Street and Wonderland Hill Avenue, offers a somewhat technical 8-mi ride out to Boulder Reservoir. You'll have mountain views on the way back to Boulder. Add on an-other 6-mi jaunt to Lefthand Valley Reservoir by taking the Lefthand Trail from the north side of the Sage/Eagle Trail loop.

To test your quadriceps, take the **Switzerland Trail**, a 9 to 13-mi ride with a nice drop to the hamlet of Sunset, and a climb up to Gold Hill. ✛ *From Broadway drive west 5 mi on Canyon Boulevard/Hwy. 119 and turn right onto Sugarloaf Rd. After 5 mi turn right at Sugarloaf Mountain Rd. The parking area is 1 mi farther.*

If cycling on flatter, less rugged terrain with views of the mountains en-tices you more than cycling in them, a few trails will not disappoint. The Community Ditch portion of the **Marshall Mesa/Community Ditch Trail** is open to mountain bikers. The 8-mi round-trip ride takes you up through pine stands and over a plateau where you can look down on Boulder, with the Flatirons and the Rockies in full view. The trail con-tinues across Highway 93 almost to Eldorado Springs. (✛ Drive south on Broadway to Marshall Dr. and turn left. Parking and the trailhead are on the right.) The **East Boulder & Teller Farm Trails** trailhead is about 7 mi east of downtown Boulder on Arapahoe Avenue. If you include the Gunbarrel Farm spur, you'll see plenty of birds at the lakes and marshes along the 14-mi round-trip ride. (✛ Drive east on Arapahoe Ave., past 75th St. Watch for the trailhead sign on the left.)

Bird-Watching

Ornithologists have spotted kestrels, falcons, and the occasional bald eagle in the steep cliffs of **Eldorado Canyon State Park.** Owls, chickadees, nuthatches, and woodpeckers are at home in the pine forests along South Boulder Creek in the park.

Walden Ponds and **Sawhill Ponds,** formerly a gravel quarry, are now home to songbirds, waterfowl, and raptors. More than 3 mi of groomed paths encircle and connect the ponds and lead into wooded areas along Boulder Creek, where owls roost. April to May is when most birds mi-grate through the Front Range, although the ponds are home to plenty of year-round residents. ✛ *Drive north on 28th St. (U.S. Hwy. 36) and turn right at Valmont Rd. Drive east 4 mi and turn left at 75th St. The sign marking the ponds is about ½ mi farther ☉ Dawn to dusk.*

Fishing

Colorado fishing licences are available at local sporting goods stores and outfitters. Eldorado Canyon State Park ranger Craig Preston has pub-lished a pamphlet describing both fly and baited-hook fishing in the park. It's available at the visitors center.

If you want to hire a fly-fishing guide for the world-class waters of the Colorado and South Platte rivers, or one who will show you where the rare greenback cutthroat trout lives, **Kinsley Outfitters** (✉ 1155 13th St. ☎ 303/442–6204 or 800/442–7420 ⊕ www.kinsleyoutfitters.com), en-dorsed by Orvis, will arrange a personalized half- or full-day guided fish-ing trip that includes transportation, lunch and snacks, and gear.

Afternoon or day trips for groups are the specialty of **Front Range Anglers** (✉ 629B S. Broadway ☎ 303/494–1375 ⊕ www.frontrangeanglers. com). Fees include lunch, lessons, transportation, and gear. Private guides offer half-day and full-day (dawn to dusk) trips for one to three people to premier public and private fishing spots.

Whether you want to buy a few flies or set up a guided tour, **Rocky Mountain Anglers** (✉ 1904 Arapahoe Ave. ☎ 303/447–2400 ⊕ www. rockymtanglers.com) can get you ready. The guides have access to private ranches and know where to find secluded fishing holes on public lands. Fees include transportation, gear, and lunch.

Golf

Flatirons Golf Course (✉ 5706 Arapahoe Ave. ☎ 303/442–7851) is an 18-hole public course with views of the mountains. Local favorite **Indian Peaks Golf Course** (✉ 2300 Indian Peaks Trail, Lafayette, Baseline Rd. to Indian Peaks Trail, 10 mi east of Boulder ☎ 303/666–4706) is an 18-hole course with views of the Continental Divide, including some of the "fourteeners" (mountain peaks over 14,000 feet) not visible from Boulder.

Hiking

★ Chautauqua Park, Green Mountain, and Flagstaff Mountain each have easy to strenuous "circle hikes." Locals love the **Chautauqua Trail/ Mesa Trail** (✉ 900 W. Baseline Rd.) loop that leads southwest from the parking lot at Chautauqua Park to the Flatirons (1.6-mi round-trip, about 1 hour) with great views of the city. The 2-mi round–trip **Royal Arch** trail spurs off the loop and follows along the base of the Flatirons. The **McClintock/Enchanted Mesa** (✉ 900 W. Baseline Rd.) trail starts behind Chautauqua's amphitheater and gives you 2½ easy miles to watch the rock climbers on the Flatirons, spot wildflowers, and look out over the city.

Green Mountain rewards ambitious hikers with beautiful vistas of the Front Range and the Indian Peaks. To get there drive west on Baseline Road and turn left at the sharp curve. The **Gregory Canyon, Ranger, E. M. Greenman,** and **Saddle Rock** trails create a 5½-mi loop that takes three to four hours to hike. To get to Green Mountain's summit (8,144 feet), take the Gregory Canyon Trail to the Ranger Trail. At the intersection with Green Mountain West Ridge trail, turn left. Go on to the summit and and descend along the E. M. Greenman and Saddle Rock trails after taking in the view.

Flagstaff Mountain offers hikers a moderately difficult, hour-long walk to May's Point (1½ mi) for a look at the Indian Peaks. Drive west on Baseline Road to the sharp curve that is Flagstaff Road, and then turn right at Summit Road. The **Boy Scout Trail** starts at Sunrise Amphitheater.

Mt. Sanitas and **Sanitas Valley** trails get you into the mountains without having to go far out of Boulder. The 3½ mi loop starts on the right-hand side of Mapleton Avenue, just one mile west of Broadway.

Carry a picnic to the **Red Rocks** and relax with lunch and the views of Boulder (1½ mi round-trip, about one hour). From the intersection of Broadway and Mapleton, drive 1 mi west to the parking area. North Boulder Creek drops into Middle Boulder Creek at **Boulder Falls,** a spectacular place to take a break and admire the grand scenery. The walk to the 70-foot-high falls is less than ¼ mi round-trip. ✦ *Drive west from Broadway on Canyon Blvd. (Rte. 119) 8 ½ mi into Boulder Canyon. Watch for the sign marking the falls. Parking is on the left.*

For a relaxing amble through a riparian environment, take the **Boulder Creek Path,** which winds from west of Boulder through downtown and past the university to the eastern part of the city. Within the eastern city limits are ponds, gaggles of Canada geese, and prairie dog colonies. People-watching is half the fun: you'll see cyclists, joggers, and roller-blading dads and moms with their babies in jogging strollers. You'll have great views of the mountains as you walk back toward downtown. Walk west along the path from Broadway to Boulder Canyon and you'll see kayakers negotiating the boulders and inner-tubers cooling off in the summer heat.

In-line Skating

In-line skating on paved multiuse paths is a popular way to get around in Boulder. The **Boulder Creek Path** is the best place to start; from here you can take off on a spur and explore. **Play It Again Sports** (✉ 653 S. Broadway ☎ 303/499–2011) rents in-line skates for $10 per day.

Inner-Tubing

In July and August, when the daytime temperatures can reach the 90s, Boulderites take to tubing in Boulder Creek. The **Conoco** gas station (✉ 1201 Arapahoe Ave., at Broadway ☎ 303/442–6293) sells inner tubes ($12–$17) and Boulder Creek is less than a block away. The station is open from 7 AM until 9 PM weekdays, 8 AM to 9 PM Saturday, and 8 AM until 6 PM Sunday.

Kayaking & Canoeing

Kayakers run the slaloms in Clear Creek, Lefthand Canyon, and the South Platte, but Boulder Creek from within Boulder Canyon midway into the city is one of the locals' favorites. Water in the creek can create Class II–III rapids when summer conditions are right. If calmer waters suit your watercraft-handling style, you can take a canoe to or rent one at the **Boulder Reservoir** and paddle about while taking in great views of the Rockies. ✉ *6 mi northeast of downtown. Drive northeast on Rte. 119 and turn left at Jay Rd. Turn right immediately onto 51st St. and drive on to the sign that marks the entrance station* ☎ *303/441–3456* ✉ *$5.*

Rentals at **Boulder Outdoor Center** (✉ 2707 Spruce St. ☎ 303/444–8420 or 800/364–9376 ⊕ www.boc123.com) include all equipment and helmets and life preservers. The center also organizes group kayaking trips to rivers on the Front Range.

Snowshoeing

Winter sports in Colorado is not limited to skiing. You can strap on a pair of snowshoes and tramp along trails you would walk in summer. Snowshoers pack a lunch and a thermos of hot cocoa, soy chai, or tea and take in stunning views while getting a bit of exercise. Even in January, the Front Range has milder daytime temperatures and lots of sunny days. Don't forget the sunscreen—at this altitude, you can sunburn quickly in winter. Dressing in layers is advisable; in the forests, you'll be warm, but out in the open, the wind can be frigid.

For $10 per day you can rent snowshoes from **Boulder Outdoor Center** (✉ 2707 Spruce St. ☎ 303/444–8420 or 800/364–9376 ⊕ www.boc123. com).

Brainerd Lake has well-marked trails and gorgeous views of the snow-covered Indian Peaks and the Continental Divide. ✉ *5 mi west of Rte. 72 (Peak-to-Peak Hwy.) on Brainard Lake Rd. (Rte. 102) at Ward, drive west on Rte. 119 to Nederland and turn north at Rte. 72.*

On sunny winter days, snowshoers head to **Peaceful Valley Campground** for crisp pine-forest-scented air and plenty of powder. ⊕ *Drive 14 mi north from Boulder on U.S. Hwy. 36 to Lyons and turn left at Rte. 7. Continue 12 mi on Rte. 7, then 4 mi south on Rte. 72 (Peak-to-Peak Hwy.).*

Where to Stay & Eat

Boulderites are well-traveled and enjoy everything from a tangy pizza slice for lunch to tempura with sweet eel sauce or tandoori grilled meats and naan for dinner. The cuisines of the more than 300 restaurants here include ethnic surprises like Nepalese, Indian, Ethiopian, Caribbean, and Moroccan. Prices reflect the high quality, but most eateries are both reasonable and geared to the large student population. Smoking is banned in all Boulder workplaces, restaurants, and bars.

★ **$$$$** ✕ **Flagstaff House.** Sit on the enclosed patio at one of Colorado's finest restaurants and drink in the sublime views of Boulder from the side of Flagstaff Mountain. Chef Mark Monette has fresh fish flown in daily, grows some of the herbs for his cuisine, and is noted for his exquisite combinations of ingredients—some organic—and fanciful, playful presentations. The menu changes daily, but sample inspirations include ragout of porcini, trumpet royal, and shiitake mushrooms; buffalo filet mignon and foie gras Wellington; and Alaskan troll king salmon, grilled with shrimp brochette. The wine list is remarkably comprehensive. ⊠ *1138 Flagstaff Rd.* ☎ *303/442–4640* ⌂ *Reservations essential* ▭ *AE, D, DC, MC, V* ⊗ *No lunch.*

$$$$ ✕ **Gold Hill Inn.** This humble log cabin hardly looks like a bastion of haute cuisine, but the six-course, $26 prix-fixe dinner is something to rave about. Entrées may include broiled, stuffed trout; leg of lamb marinated for four days in buttermilk, juniper berries, and cloves; or paella. The inn also hosts occasional "murder mystery" nights using professional actors. ⊠ *401 Main St., Gold Hill, Sunshine Canyon, 10 mi from Boulder, take Mapleton Ave. west from Broadway. It becomes Sunshine Canyon Rd.* ☎ *303/443–6461* ▭ *No credit cards* ⊗ *Closed Nov.–Apr. and Mon. and Tues. No lunch.*

$$$$ ✕ **Mataam Fez.** Eat with your hands at this lavish Moroccan restaurant that looks as if it came straight from *The Arabian Nights*. The prix-fixe dinner ($29.95) includes five courses, with such fragrant dishes as lamb with honey and almonds, and hare with paprika couscous. ⊠ *2226 Pearl St.* ☎ *303/440–4167* ▭ *AE, D, DC, MC, V* ⊗ *No lunch.*

$$–$$$$ ✕ **Red Lion Inn.** A local institution for natives and travelers, this beautiful inn is just a few minutes up Boulder Canyon from town. For a feeling of the Alps, ask to be seated in the original dining room—with its fireplace, antlers, Austrian murals, and white napery. The stone walls and potbellied stove in the bar make it a cozy place to wait for a table. The Red Lion is revered for its excellent game: wild boar, quail, or fillet of buffalo. Start with wild game sausage, then try the elk or caribou steak. Or order a satisfying old-fashioned specialty, such as steak Diane, or one of the daily specials. ⊠ *Boulder Canyon Dr.* ☎ *303/442–9368* ⌂ *Reservations essential* ▭ *AE, D, MC, V* ⊗ *No lunch.*

$$–$$$$ ✕ **Sunflower.** Storefront-size windows allow plenty of light into the colorfully painted dining room where chef and owner Jon Pell serves savory meals based on fresh, organic ingredients, such as tempeh scallopini and a bamboo steamer. Entrées, like the New York strip steak and buffalo steak are exclusively organic and free-range. End your lunch or dinner with chocolate raspberry mousse, creamy and decadent without any dairy product, refined sugar, or eggs (Mr. Pell spent 16 years developing the dessert; he won't share the recipe). Brunch is served on weekends, from 10 to 3. ⊠ *1701 Pearl St.* ☎ *303/440–0220* ▭ *AE, MC, V.*

QUICK BITES

BOULDER OFFERS PLENTY of eateries with excellent food that is healthy, prepared to order, and inexpensive.

For breakfast try a crisp, light brioche or buttery croissant at **Breadworks** (✉ 2644 Broadway ☎ 303/444–5667). Lunch is a filling meat or vegetarian sandwich—made with one of their own artisan breads, a savory soup, and a saucer-sized cookie. The ginger snaps are spicy and rich. **Illegal Pete's** (✉ 1447 Pearl St. ☎ 303/440–3955 ✉ 1320 College Ave. ☎ 303/444–3055) serves hefty wrap-style burritos made to order with fresh ingredients and a choice of three salsas. If you're hankering for a delicious Philly-style steak-and-cheese sandwich or a New York–style deli sandwich, **Salvaggio's Italian Delicatessen** (✉ 2609 Pearl St. ☎ 303/938–1981 ✉ 1107 13th St. ☎ 303/448–1200 ✉ 1397 Pearl St. ☎ 303/545–6800) will make one to order with your choice of deli meats and cheeses. **Falafel King** (✉ 1314 Pearl St. ☎ 303/449–9321) has excellent pita pockets of hot and crispy falafel, spicy gyros, or marinated grilled chicken breast. Get an order of tabouli, hummus, or dolmas to round out lunch and finish it off with a piece of sweet and gooey baklava. The thin and crispy pizzas at **Abo's** (✉ 637 S. Broadway ☎ 303/494–1274 ✉ 2761 Iris Ave. ☎ 303/443–1921 ✉ 1911 Broadway ☎ 303/443–9113 ✉ 1110 13th St. ☎ 303/443–3199) will not disappoint. Get just a slice or two, or you can order a whole pizza for a family lunch in the park. **Whole Foods** (✉ 2905 Pearl St. ☎ 303/545–6611) has a sushi bar, a deli with ready-made sandwiches, panini, pizza, and a salad bar.

$$–$$$$ ✕ **Sushi Zanmai.** The restaurant section is a cool, sleek place to enjoy delectable seafood. But the action's really at the zany sushi bar, where the chefs periodically burst into song: "If You Knew Sushi" is a popular request. There's always karaoke here, although the official night is Saturday (10 to midnight). ✉ 1221 Spruce St. ☎ 303/440–0733 ⊟ AE, MC, V ⊘ No lunch weekends.

$–$$$ ✕ **Zolo Grill.** The inventive and superlative Southwestern cuisine here shows a masterful fusion of traditional Mexican and Native American dishes. Huge picture windows overlook an active shopping center and the Flatirons beyond. Blond-wood furnishings, striking abstract art, and a high-tech open kitchen complete the urbane decor. The bartender will craft your margarita with one of about 80 tequilas. There's a good wine and beer list, and some vintages are available by the glass. ✉ 2525 Arapahoe Ave. ☎ 303/449–0444 ⊟ AE, DC, MC, V.

¢–$$$ ✕ **Mediterranean Café.** After work, when all of Boulder shows up to enjoy tapas, "The Med" becomes a real scene (you may feel quite closed in, despite the restaurant's light and airy design). The decor is Portofino meets Santa Fe, with abstract art, terra-cotta floors, and brightly colored tile. The open kitchen turns out daily specials such as barbecued mahimahi and horseradish-crusted tuna—dishes complemented by an extensive, well-priced wine list. During happy hour, weekdays from 3 to 6:30, various tapas are just $2. ✉ 1002 Walnut St. ☎ 303/444–5335 ⊟ AE, D, DC, MC, V.

$–$$ ✕ **Boulder Dushanbe Teahouse.** Unique to Colorado, this teahouse is a gift from Boulder's sister city, Dushanbe, Tajikistan. Tajik artisans hand-crafted the building in a traditional style that includes ceramic Islamic art and a carved, painted ceiling. The menu presents a culinary cross section of the world; your meal could include such dishes as Persian lamb

Fodor'sChoice ★

kabob, Burmese coconut curry, and Amazonian poached halibut. The house-tea gingerbread is a favorite. Relax during high tea at 3 PM (reservations required) with one of more than 80 varieties of tea. Creekside patio tables have views of the park. Brunch is served on weekends. ✉ *1770 13th St.* ☎ *303/442–4993* ▭ *AE, D, MC, V.*

$–$$ ✕ **Da Gabi Cucina.** It's well worth the quest to find this jewel of a stylish restaurant in an out-of-the-way strip mall. Both the food and personal, knowledgeable service are exquisite. Tapas such as calamari fritti, mussels, and bruschetta are tasty starters. Try the *zuppa di pesce* (fish soup) with homemade linguini, the chicken marsala, or the gnocchi in Gorgonzola cream sauce. Whether you're looking for low light and romance or simply a nice place to meet a friend, you'll find it here. ✉ *3970 N. Broadway* ☎ *303/786–9004* ▭ *AE, DC, MC, V* ☉ *No lunch.*

¢–$ ✕ **Efrain's.** It's worth the drive for the savory *chile verde* (green chili) that Efrain cooks every day for the burritos. His family's homey café has simple, green-painted arbors and hand-painted tables. The porch is great for relaxing before dinner with a margarita, served in a pint-size mason jar. Efrain prepares low-fat, authentic entrées with fresh beef and succulent pulled chicken. The large-grain rice is light, and refried beans are creamy but not greasy. Finish your meal with a crisp, hot *sopapilla* (a light, fried pastry served hot with honey). Expect to wait for a table on a weekend night. ✉ *101 E. Cleveland St., Lafayette, drive 11 mi east on Baseline Rd. to Lafayette and turn right on Public Rd.* ☎ *303/666–7544* ▭ *AE, D, MC, V* ☉ *Closed Tues.*

¢ ✕ **Burnt Toast Restaurant.** This homey café in a 100-year-old, four-square house advertises "COLD COFFEE AND SURLY SERVICE," but the hearty breakfasts served until 2 PM and the bit of Turkish flair on the menu and in the presentation exceed what you might be led to expect. Omelettes are hot and fluffy, potatoes savory and crisp, and the buttery coffee cake is laced with spices and nuts. The cappuccinos are crafted carefully, with perfectly frothy caps. Have a light breakfast of home-baked pastries at the coffee bar, or eat in the sunny dining room, which houses an eclectic collection of antique wooden tables. Don't miss the black-and-white photographs of toasters in natural surroundings—they're almost epigrammatic. ✉ *1235 Pennsylvania Ave.* ☎ *303/440–5200* ▭ *AE, D, DC, MC, V* ☉ *No lunch or dinner.*

★ $$$$ ✕▨ **Gold Lake Mountain Resort & Spa.** There are no exercise machines or in-room phones and TVs at this casual, environmentally responsible resort, where you can dip into four lakeside hot pools. Come here to revive your body and soul with activities like canoeing, fly-fishing, snowshoeing, and hiking—and luxurious spa treatments (including an herbal remedy for altitude sickness). You'll slumber peacefully beneath a huge, goose-down comforter in a rustic, 1920s lakeside cabin with period antiques and slate and zinc bathrooms. Executive chef Eric Skokan of Alice's Restaurant ($$$$; reservations essential) has a gift for drawing savory and indulgent three- or seven-course spa meals out of whole, organic ingredients like seabass, figs, and pistachios. The restaurant mills its own flours and bakes all its pastries and breads. Ask the knowledgeable servers to pair wines with the courses of your dinner; they never miss. ✉ *3771 Gold Lake Rd., Ward 80481, 32 mi northwest of Boulder* ☎ *303/459–3544 or 800/450–3544* ☎ *303/459–3541* ⊕ *www.goldlake.com* ⇨ *18 cabins* ☼ *Restaurant, hot tub, sauna, spa, mountain bikes, hiking, horseback riding, cross-country skiing, ice-skating, bar; no room phones, no room TVs* ▭ *D, MC, V.*

$$$–$$$$ ▨ **Coburn House.** Designer-architect Scott Coburn succeeded in creating a tasteful lodging providing the business services of a hotel and the intimacy of an inn. The "no shoes" policy protects guests from the noise of hard soles on hardwood floors. Modern Western furnishings, such as hand-carved wood and iron beds, work desks, and pine armoires lend a warm elegance to the oversize rooms. An environmentally friendly hotel, the Coburn uses low-flush toilets, reduced-flow showerheads, and 100% cotton linens. The self-serve breakfast buffet is as light or filling as you like and features coffee cake, fruit, yogurt, juice, and coffee. ⊠ *2040 16th St., 80302* ☎ *303/545–5200 or 800/858–5811* ⊟ *303/440–6740* ⊕ *www.coburnhouse.com* ⤶ *12 rooms* ⟳ *In-room data ports, business services, meeting rooms; no smoking* ⊟ *AE, MC, V* ⎮⊚⎮ *CP* ⤳ *No children under 14.*

$$$–$$$$
Fodor'sChoice
★

🏨 **Hotel Boulderado.** The gracious lobby of this elegant 1909 beauty has a soaring stained-glass ceiling, and the mezzanine beckons with romantic nooks galore. When choosing a room, opt for the old building, with spacious quarters filled with period antiques and reproductions. The new wing is plush and comfortable but has less Victorian character. Mountain views and smoking rooms are available on request. The restaurant, Q's, serves stylish contemporary American cuisine. The Catacombs Blues Bar is always hopping and has live music three nights a week. Guests have access to the nearby health club, The Pulse. ⊠ *2115 13th St., 80302* ☎ *303/442–4344 or 800/433–4344* ⊟ *303/442–4378* ⊕ *www.boulderado.com* ⤶ *160 rooms* ⟳ *3 restaurants, in-room data ports, 2 bars, business services, meeting rooms, no-smoking rooms* ⊟ *AE, D, DC, MC, V.*

$$–$$$
🏨 **Briar Rose B&B.** Innkeeper Margaret Weisenbach makes guests feel completely at home at this appealing B&B. There are six rooms in the sturdy, 1890s brick main house and four in the adjacent carriage house. The individually decorated rooms abound in froufrou, such as floral carpeting and flowers stenciled above the headboards. All rooms have down comforters and private baths; the most expensive have wood-burning fireplaces. ⊠ *2151 Arapahoe Ave., 80302* ☎ *303/442–3007* ⤶ *10 rooms* ⊟ *AE, DC, MC, V* ⎮⊚⎮ *BP.*

$$–$$$
🏨 **Millennium Hotel Boulder.** This relatively large property has an unusual semicircular design, set amid immaculate gardens dotted with splashing fountains. Spacious rooms, some with mountain views, are done up in light woods and pastel colors. In keeping with Boulder's environmental concerns, the rooms have been designated as ecologically sound, with all trash recycled and water treated and recirculated. ⊠ *1345 28th St., 80302* ☎ *303/443–3850 or 800/545–6285* ⊟ *303/443–1480* ⊕ *www.millennium-hotels.com* ⤶ *269 rooms* ⟳ *Restaurant, in-room data ports, cable TV with movies, 15 tennis courts, indoor-outdoor pool, gym, hot tubs, bicycles, basketball, bar, playground, laundry service, business services, meeting rooms, car rental, travel services* ⊟ *AE, D, DC, MC, V.*

$–$$$
🏨 **Colorado Chautauqua Association.** The association was founded in 1898 as part of the Chautauqua movement and still fulfills its charge to provide a venue for recreation and cultural and educational enrichment. Guests enjoy lectures, concerts, and silent films accompanied by a pianist. The upgraded, fully furnished lodge rooms and cottages retain their unique historic charm and include linens and cooking utensils (in rooms with kitchens), but do not include daily housekeeping. The lawn is a terrific spot for a picnic on a sunny afternoon. ⊠ *900 Baseline Rd., 80302* ☎ *303/442–3282* ⊟ *303/449–0790* ⊕ *www.chautauqua.com* ⤶ *22 rooms, 60 cottages* ⟳ *Restaurant, 4 tennis courts, hiking, concert hall, playground, pets allowed; no room phones, no room TVs* ⊟ *MC, V.*

$–$$$
🏨 **Inn on Mapleton Hill.** Tall trees shade this impressive redbrick Victorian with forest green trim. The sunny, individually decorated guest rooms have hardwood or brass beds, rocking chairs and armoires, throw rugs, lace curtains, and hand-stenciled walls; two also have marble gas-burning fireplaces. The location, on a quiet residential street two blocks from the Pearl Street Mall, is ideal. Owners Judi and Ray Schultze are happy

to share their local expertise with you. Lasting friendships have been made over breakfasts of homemade granola, cinnamon French toast, and great coffee. ⊠ *1001 Spruce St., 80302* ☎ *303/449–6528* 🖷 *303/415–0470* ⊕ *www.innonmapletonhill.com* 🖙 *7 rooms* ⊟ *AE, MC, V* ⊙| *BP* 🖙 *No children under 12.*

$$ 🏨 **Pearl Street Inn.** The decor is reserved and refined at this B&B, favoring fresh flowers, light colors like sage, plush carpeting, watercolors of Colorado scenery, antiques, and brass or mahogany four-poster beds. Full breakfasts with crispy waffles and homemade granola are served in the dining alcove and garden courtyard with a fountain. Guests can enjoy an evening drink or a complimentary glass of wine at the mahogany, copper-top bar. ⊠ *1820 Pearl St., 80302* ☎ *303/444–5584 or 888/810–1302* 🖙 *8 rooms* ⚒ *Bar* ⊟ *AE, MC, V* ⊙| *BP.*

$$ 🏨 **Quality Inn & Suites Boulder Creek.** This independently owned inn, just a 10-minute walk from downtown Pearl Street and 5 minutes from Colorado University, provides the personal attention and services of a B&B, including a free hot-breakfast buffet. The caring staff has been known to scrape ice off guests' car windshields. The well-lighted, spacious rooms, with custom iron lamps and wood and leather furniture in rich earth tones, create a sophisticated yet comfortable feel. Rooms have kitchenettes with microwaves, refrigerators, and granite countertops. ⊠ *2020 Arapahoe Ave., 80302* ☎ *303/449–7550 or 888/449–7550* 🖷 *303/449–1082* ⊕ *www.qualityinnboulder.com* 🖙 *40 rooms, 6 suites* ⚒ *In-room data ports, kitchenettes, indoor pool, gym, hot tub, sauna, laundry service, business services* ⊟ *AE, D, MC, V* ⊙| *BP.*

$ 🏨 **Foot of the Mountain.** This series of connecting rooms is near the mouth of Boulder Canyon and the Boulder Creek Path. It seems far from Boulder's bustle, yet it's only a few minutes' walk from downtown. Each cozy cabin has either a mountain or stream view and is outfitted with TV, phone, heater, mini-refrigerator, and large bath—but no air-conditioning. Pets can board too, for an extra charge. ⊠ *200 Arapahoe Ave., 80302* ☎ *303/442–5688* 🖷 *303/442–5719* ⊕ *www.footofthemountainmotel.com* 🖙 *18 rooms* ⚒ *Refrigerators, pets allowed (fee); no a/c* ⊟ *AE, D, MC, V.*

CAMPING   △ **Pawnee Campground.** Within the Brainard Lake Recreation Area, ¢ campers here have access to the fishing and excellent hiking trails around the lake but don't have to pay the entrance fee. At an elevation of 10,350 feet you're high enough for views of the peaks of the Continental Divide, but low enough to be in spruce and fir forests. All sites accommodate RVs, tents, campers, and trailers. The maximum vehicle length is 45 feet. ⊠ *5 mi west of Rte. 72 (Peak-to-Peak Hwy.) on Brainard Lake Rd. (Rte. 102) at Ward* ☎ *303/541–2500* 🖷 *303/541–2515* ⊕ *www.fs.fed.us/arnf/districts/brd/camping/pawnee.htm* ⚒ *Pit toilets, drinking water, fire grates, picnic tables; no hook-ups, no showers* 🖙 *55 sites* 🖾 *$13* ⊙ *Mid-June–Sept.*

Nightlife & the Arts

Nightlife

BARS & LOUNGES   Business lunches and after-work gatherings take place at the **Corner Bar** (⊠ 2115 13th St. ☎ 303/442–4344) in the Hotel Boulderado. It's a contemporary American pub with outdoor seating. **The Foundry** (⊠ 1109 Walnut St. ☎ 303/447–1803) is where the hip of all ages hang out; in back is a cigar bar and smoking parlor, and above is a rooftop deck with its own bar. The main bar has 11 pool tables and a mezzanine overlooking all the action. The **Mediterranean Café** (⊠ 1002 Walnut St. ☎ 303/444–5335) is the place to see and be seen. Bartenders at **Rio Grande Mexican Restaurant** (⊠ 1101 Walnut St. ☎ 303/444–3690) make Boulder's best margaritas (no frilly variations—just classic margs). The **West End Tavern** (⊠ 926 Pearl St. ☎ 303/444–3535), with its rooftop deck, is a popular after-work hangout serving good pub grub.

BREWERIES   The microbrewery **Rockies Brewing Company** (⊠ 2880 Wilderness Pl. ☎ 303/444–8448) has a bar. Good beer and upscale pub fare are served at lunch and dinner at the **Walnut Brewery** (⊠ 1123 Walnut St. ☎ 303/447–1345).

MUSIC & DANCE   Bands and DJ's on Friday and Saturday draw the crowds to cut a rug
CLUBS   in Bentley's Lounge at **The Broker** (⊠ 555 30th St. ☎ 303/449–1752). Free salsa lessons are given Tuesday night. In the Hotel Boulderado, the **Catacombs Blues Bar** (⊠ 2115 13th St. ☎ 303/443–0486) presents local and national blues and rock talent Wednesday through Saturday. For blues jams, head here on Monday night. The art deco **Fox Theater** (⊠ 1135 13th St. ☎ 303/447–0095) movie palace hosts touring music talent as well as the occasional Disco Inferno night of dancing. There's live music, from reggae to samba, every night and dancing Wednesday through Sunday at the **Trilogy Wine Bar** (⊠ 2017 13th St. ☎ 303/473–9463). Rock acts like Flash Cadillac appear at **Tulagi** (⊠ 1129 13th St. ☎ 303/938–8090), also the venue for hip-hop dance nights on Saturday and karaoke on Tuesday.

The Arts

DINNER SHOW   Dine while you catch a popular Broadway musical at **Boulder's Dinner Theater** (⊠ 5501 Arapahoe Ave. ☎ 303/449–6000 or 888/634–6459 ⊕ www.theatreinboulder.com).

FESTIVALS   Between late June and early August the **Colorado Music Festival** (⊠ Chautauqua Park, 900 Baseline Rd. ☎ 303/440–7666 or 866/464–2626 📠 303/449–0071 ⊕ www.coloradomusicfest.org) brings classical music to Chautauqua Auditorium. Visiting artists have included the Santa Fe Guitar Quartet and the Takás Quartet, as well as plenty of international talent such as William Barton, a Didjeridu performer from Australia, and Lynn Harrell, who plays a 1673 Stradivarius. Evening meals are available in the dining hall, or pack a picnic and settle in on the Green to take in views of the mountains before the concert.

Fodor'sChoice   CU's Mary Rippon Outdoor Theater is the venue for the annual **Col-**
★   **orado Shakespeare Festival** (☎ 303/492–0554 ⊕ www.coloradoshakes. org), presenting the Bard's comedies and tragedies from early July to mid-August.

Early May finds Boulderites at the Boulder Reservoir for the annual **Kinetic Challenge** race. The competition requires each team to build a craft that can race over the land, slog through the mud, and not sink in the water. Teams are allowed to provide their own judges and bribe other judges. Speed is not necessarily the determining criterion—creativity and on-board sculpture count, too. ✣ *Drive northeast on Rte.119 and turn left at Jay Rd. Turn right immediately onto 51st St. and drive on to the sign that marks the entrance station* ⊕ *www.kbco.com/kinetics.*

The **Boulder Creek Festival** (☎ 303/449–3825 ⊕ www.bouldercreekevents. com/festival) lasts all Memorial Day weekend: you can feast at the pancake breakfast, browse the bazaar, learn about alternative healing, and see regional artistic talent at the art show and the artists' marketplace. Children have fun with dance, theater, and hands-on activities at the *Kids' Place.* Live music runs the gamut: Irish, Senegalese, John Philip Sousa, and jazz. Don't miss the *Great Rubber Duck Race* on Memorial Day afternoon. Buy a rubber duck for $5 and compete against hundreds of others in Boulder Creek.

The Boulder Philharmonic (⊠ University of Colorado, Macky Auditorium and Old Main Theatre ☎ 303/449–1343) presents its own concert season, as well as chamber music concerts, the Boulder Ballet Ensemble, and performances by visiting divas such as Kathleen Battle. The art deco **Boulder Theater** (⊠ 2032 14th St. ☎ 303/786–7030 ⊕ www.bouldertheater.com) is a venue for top touring bands and movies as well as for the radio show *E-Town* (⊕ www.etown.org). E-Town emcees Helen and Nick Forster host musical talent and discuss environmental and community issues. Concerts take place throughout the summer at Boulder's peaceful **Chautauqua Community Hall** (⊠ 900 Baseline Rd. ☎ 303/442–3282 ⊕ www.chautauqua.bouldernet.com/programs.html). Performers have included Branford Marsalis, Hot Rize, k.d. lang, and the Afro Celt Sound System.

At the University of Colorado, the superb **College of Music** (☎ 303/492–8008 ⊕ www.cuconcerts.org) presents concerts year-round, including chamber music by the internationally renowned Takás String Quartet. The **Department of Theater and Dance** (☎ 303/492–8181 ⊕ www.colorado.edu/TheatreDance) stages excellent student productions throughout the year.

Shopping

University Hill (or "The Hill"), centered around 13th Street between College Avenue and Pennsylvania Street, is a great place for hip duds, new and used CDs, and CU apparel. The metropolitan area's newest shopping center is **Flatiron Crossing** (⊠ U.S. 36 between Boulder and Denver ☎ 720/887–9900) in Broomfield. Shoppers can hit stores such as Nordstrom's, Coach, Borders, and Sharper Image, browse at a few locally-owned jewelers and galleries, and take a break in the food court or in one of the fine restaurants. Boulder's **Pearl Street Mall** (⊠ Pearl St. between 11th and 15th Sts.) is a shopping extravaganza, with upscale boutiques, art galleries, bookstores, shoe shops, and stores with home and garden furnishings. Street musicians and magicians, caricaturists, and buskers with love birds are magnets for locals and visitors.

Antiques Dealers

Boulder County's most beautiful collection of restored antique furniture is east of the city at **West's Antiques** (⊠ 409 S. Public Rd., Lafayette ☎ 303/666–7200). From Boulder drive east about 11 mi on Baseline Road and turn right on Public Road.

Bookstores

Boulder has one of the largest concentrations of used-book sellers in the United States. Most shops are on Pearl Street between 8th and 20th streets. Some specialize in titles such as computer books, works of the beat generation, or mysteries.

★ **Boulder Bookstore** (⊠ 1107 Pearl St. ☎ 303/447–2074) has thousands of new and used books in all genres, including a great selection of photography, history, and art books about Colorado. It also carries a few out-of-town and foreign newspapers and periodicals.

Mystery fans will find just the right thriller from the huge selection at **High Crimes** (⊠ 946 Pearl St. ☎ 303/443–8346).

Sip a robust latté from the in-house café at **Trident Booksellers** (⊠ 940 Pearl St. ☎ 303/443–3133) while browsing the eclectic collection of mostly used books—including foreign language, but also many new books at mark-down prices.

Boutiques

Alpaca Connection (⊠ 1326 Pearl St. ☎ 303/447–2047) offers Indian silks, Bolivian alpaca, and Ecuadorian merino-wool garments. **Chico's** (⊠ 1205 Pearl St. ☎ 303/449–3381) traffics in funky jewelry and natural fibers and fabrics from around the globe. **Fresh Produce** (⊠ 1218 Pearl St. ☎ 303/442–7507) is a Boulder-based company that makes brightly colored and whimsically designed cotton clothing for adults and children. **Jacque Michelle** (⊠ 2670 Broadway ☎ 303/786–7628) has fashionably casual yet unpretentious women's clothing. The store also sells fun greeting cards and cutting-edge gifts.

Children's Items

Boulder kids' favorite store to try–and buy–new toys is **Grandrabbit's Toy Shoppe** (⊠ 2525 Arapahoe Ave. ☎ 303/443–0780). **Little Mountain** (⊠ 1136 Spruce St. ☎ 303/443–1757) carries outdoor clothing for children, and rents child-carrier backpacks and all-terrain strollers.

Craft & Art Galleries

Art Source International (⊠ 1237 Pearl St. ☎ 303/444–4080) is Colorado's largest antique-print and -map dealer. **Artesanias** (⊠ 1468 Pearl St. ☎ 303/442–3777) sells Zapotec rugs, Mexican santos, decorative iron, and handcrafted furniture. **Boulder Arts & Crafts Cooperative** (⊠ 1421 Pearl St. ☎ 303/443–3683), owned by 45 artists, is popular for pottery and photography. The 150-odd Colorado artists represented create everything from hand-painted silk scarves and handwoven garments to glass art and furniture. **Hangouts** (⊠ 1328 Pearl St. ☎ 303/442–2533) carries Mayan- and Brazilian-design handmade hammocks. **McLaren Markowitz Gallery** (⊠ 1011 Pearl St. ☎ 303/449–6807) features fine jewelry, sculpture, paintings, and pottery—primarily with a Southwestern look. **The Middle Fish** (⊠ 1500 Pearl St. ☎ 303/443–0835) has quirky one-of-a-kind clocks crafted from a combination of metals, locally made jewelry, mosaic mirrors, and unusual gifts.

Food

Wild Oats (⊠ 1651 Broadway at Arapahoe Ave. ☎ 303/442–0909) is an organic supermarket, with everything from "cruelty-free" cosmetics and herbal and homeopathic remedies to glorious produce and picnic supplies. At the deli, the three-salad plate is a lunch bargain at $5.99—choose from the selection of healthy, fresh salads like salmon penne, curried turkey, and green lentil. The store has a self-serve salad bar, a juice bar, and a coffee bar, and also makes and sells sushi, pizza, panini, and baked goods.

From April through October the **Boulder Farmers' Market** (⊠ 13th St. between Canyon Blvd. and Arapahoe St.) sells baked goods, plants, and seasonal produce from 4 PM to 8 PM Wednesday, and Saturday from 8 AM until 2 PM.

Gift Stores

Two Hands Paperie (⊠ 803 Pearl St. ☎ 303/444–0124) carries elegant European stationery, handmade paper, and handcrafted, leather-bound journals. Try out an antique or new fountain pen, and select a well of emerald or havana ink to fill it. **Where the Buffalo Roam** (⊠ 1320 Pearl St. ☎ 303/938–1424) sells quirky T-shirts, CU and Colorado souvenirs, and tacky trinkets.

Home & Garden

The store to visit for the finest selection in crockery, cookware, table linen, and kitchen utensils (many from Europe), as well as gourmet food items and cookbooks, is **Peppercorn** (⊠ 1235 Pearl St. ☎ 303/449–5847 or 800/447–6905). Gardeners will find treasures at **The West End**

Gardener (⊠ 777 Pearl St. ☏ 303/938–0607), purveyors of vintage garden tools and accessories.

Outdoor Gear

McGuckin Hardware (⊠ Village Shopping Center, 2525 Arapahoe St. ☏ 303/443–1822) is a Boulder institution that stocks home appliances and gadgets, hardware, and a mind-boggling array of outdoor merchandise. The omniscient salespeople know where everything is. **Mountain Sports** (⊠ 2835 Pearl St. ☏ 303/442–8355 ⊠ 821 Pearl St. ☏ 303/443–6770) sells the gear to tackle those athletic pursuits that Boulderites revel in. **Boulder Army Store** (⊠ 1545 Pearl St. ☏ 303/442–7616) packs the racks and shelves tightly with genuine, name-brand, surplus outdoor clothing and camping gear marked a few dollars less than regular retail.

> **en route** Scenic Sunshine Canyon Road/Gold Hill Road links Boulder to the Peak-to-Peak Highway (Rte. 72) near Ward. Drive west from Broadway on Mapleton Avenue, which becomes Sunshine Canyon Road at the mouth of Sunshine Canyon and then Gold Hill Road farther up the canyon. This largely untraveled shortcut to Estes Park is only partially paved, but suitable for all vehicles. You'll wind through Sunshine Canyon up to the ridge with views of the Indian Peaks and the Continental Divide. The road drops down into the former mining town of Gold Hill. Stop at the **Gold Hill General Store** (⊠ 531 Main, Gold Hill ☏ 303/443–7724 ☉ Daily) for a tasty, made-to-order sandwich and a bowl of hearty homemade soup before driving the last few miles to the Peak-to-Peak Highway.

THE NORTHERN FRONT RANGE

Geographically, the Front Range comprises the mountains that slope down east from the Continental Divide to the foothills along the high plains. Demographically, it is the heavily-populated corridor between Cheyenne, Wyoming and Pueblo, Colorado. Locals say that, except for Denver, eastern Colorado begins on the east side of Interstate 25. The Front Range in north central Colorado is a blend of cities with historic downtowns, verdant buffers full of recreational opportunities, and just enough farms and ranches to remind you what some now toney suburban areas looked like as recently as 10 years ago.

Nederland

⑫ *16 mi west of Boulder via Canyon Blvd. (Rte. 119).*

A funky mountain hamlet at the top of Boulder Canyon and on the scenic Peak-to-Peak Highway, "Ned" embodies that small, mountain-town spirit in look and attitude: laid back, independent, and friendly. The downtown retains the character of its gold-mining days and has several good bars, cafés, and restaurants. Shops sell used books, antiques, organic groceries, and gemstones.

Sports & the Outdoors

HIKING Nederland is the gateway to skiing at Eldora Mountain Resort and high-
★ altitude hiking in the **Indian Peaks Wilderness**. Parking at trailheads in the wilderness area is limited, so plan to start out early in the day. Since there is no central access point to the area, contact the U.S. Forest Service **Boulder Ranger District Office** (⊠ 2140 Yarmouth Ave. ☏ 303/541–2500 or 303/541–2519 ⊕ www.fs.fed.us/arnf/districts/brd/indian-peaks) or its Web site for trail information and driving directions. Permits are not required for day visitors.

SKIING   With a 1,400-foot vertical drop (the longest run is 3 mi), **Eldora Mountain Resort** has 53 trails, 12 lifts, and 680 acres; 25 mi (40 km) of groomed Nordic track; and a 17-foot-tall half-pipe-terrain park for snowboarding. Tucked away in the mountains at 9,300 feet (summit elevation is 10,800 feet), Eldora's annual snowfall is more than 300 inches. The day lodge has a cafeteria-style restaurant. ☒ *5 mi west of Nederland off Hwy. 119* ☎ *303/440–8700* ⊕ *www.eldora.com* ☉ *Mid-Nov.–mid-Apr., daily 9–4; weekends and holidays 8:30–4* ☜ *$33.*

★   The **Peak-to-Peak Highway,** which winds from Central City through Nederland to Estes Park, is not the quickest route to the eastern gateway to Rocky Mountain National Park, but is certainly the most scenic. You'll pass through the old mining towns of Ward and Allenspark and enjoy spectacular mountain vistas and, in the fall, golden stands of aspen. Mt. Meeker and Long's Peak rise magnificently behind every bend in the road. The descent into Estes Park provides grand vistas of snow-covered alpine peaks and green valleys. ☒ *From Nederland drive north on Hwy. 72. Turn left at the intersection with Hwy. 7 and continue to Estes Park.*

Where to Stay & Eat

$$–$$$ ✕ **Black Forest Restaurant.** One of Colorado's premier wild-game and fowl restaurants is reminiscent of a southern German restaurant. The dining room has heavy wood furniture, a stone fireplace, and landscape paintings. Specialties are elk, goose, pheasant, and traditional German fare, all good and filling. The atrium has an indoor 20-foot waterfall and panoramic views of the snowcapped peaks of the Continental Divide. A smoking parlor and full bar are on the premises. ☒ *24 Big Springs Dr.* ☎ *303/279–2333 or 303/582–9971* ⊟ *AE, D, MC, V.*

$–$$ ✕ **Neapolitan's.** Meat-filled and vegetarian calzones are monstrous in size, and included in the price are a salad dripping with Gorgonzola and toasted rolls redolent of garlic. If you've got room for more after your meal, order the hot fudge sundae topped with homemade sauce that's made with Ghiradelli chocolate. The tiny, rustic restaurant is a favorite with locals and skiers. Enjoy your lunch on the patio in summer. ☒ *1 First St.* ☎ *303/258–7313* ⊟ *AE, D, MC, V* ☉ *No lunch weekdays.*

$–$$ ▣ **Best Western Lodge at Nederland.** Built in 1994 with rough-hewn timber, this lodge is ultramodern within. All rooms are no-smoking and spacious and have refrigerators, coffeemakers, and hair dryers; rooms upstairs have cathedral ceilings, and those downstairs have gas fireplaces. The enthusiastic staff will help to arrange any outdoor activity you desire—and the possibilities are just about endless. An excellent choice for those who want to be central, the property is within a half-hour's drive of Boulder, the Eldora ski area, and Central City. ☒ *55 Lakeview Dr., 80466* ☎ *303/258–9463 or 800/279–9463* ☐ *303/258–0413* ⊕ *www.nedlodge.com* ⇗ *23 rooms, 1 suite* ♻ *Refrigerators, cable TV, hot tub; no smoking* ⊟ *AE, D, DC, MC, V.*

CAMPING   The **Indian Peaks Wilderness** is open to backcountry camping between June 1st and September 15th and requires a permit from the **Boulder Ranger District Office** (☒ 2140 Yarmouth Ave., 80301 ☎ 303/541–2500 or 303/541–2519 ☐ 303/541–2515 ⊕ www.fs.fed.us/arnf/districts/brd/indian-peaks ☜ $5 for 1–14 days).

¢   ⚠ **Kelly–Dahl Campground.** At an elevation of 8,600 feet, this campground is 4 mi south of Nederland and close to limited-stakes gambling in Central City and Black Hawk. It's also near the Rollins Pass Railroad Grade and the Boulder Wagon Road, two rough, gravel historical roads with great scenery and heart-stopping precipices. All sites accommodate RVs, tents, campers, or trailers. The maximum vehicle length is 40 feet. ☒ 4 *mi south of Nederland on Rte. 119* ☎ *303/541–2500* ⊟ *303/541–2515* ⊕ *www.fs.fed.us/arnf/districts/brd/camping/kellydahl.htm* ⚲ *Drinking water, fire grates, picnic tables, playground; no hook-ups, no showers* ⟿ *46 sites* ⊟ *$13* ⊙ *Mid-May–mid-Oct.*

Nightlife & the Arts

Locals head to the **Acoustic Café** (⊠ 95 E. First St. ☎ 303/258–3209 ⊕ www.acousticcafe.net) Sunday afternoon for pick-up bluegrass jam sessions. Local bluegrass talent is scheduled during the week. Call for ticket information and pre-sales.

The Nederland Music & Arts Festival, a weekend of bluegrass, world beat, and jazz music known as the **NedFest** (☎ 303/415–5665 ⊕ www. nedfest.com), takes place the first weekend in August on the west shore of Barker Reservoir. A couple of thousand people come to relax in the sun, dance, or stroll by the art stands. Entrance ($28) is steep, but children under 10 are free.

Niwot

⑬ *10 mi northeast of downtown Boulder via the Diagonal Hwy. (Rte. 119) at Niwot Rd.*

Niwot is the Arapahoe Indian word for "left hand," and this is where Chief Niwot (born ca. 1820) and his tribe lived along the banks of Left Hand Creek until the early 1860s. European settlers arrived in the latter half of the 1800s to take up farming after gold mining in the mountains became less lucrative. The town's importance grew once the railroad came in the 1870s. Antiques aficionados have made Niwot their mecca in Boulder County. The historic district, full of brick buildings decorated with flower boxes, runs along 2nd Avenue and the cross streets Franklin and Murray. **The Eye Opener** (⊠ 136 2nd Ave. ☎ 303/ 652–8137) serves delicious coffee drinks, plus gourmet sandwiches and pastries. Authentic ingredients and fresh focaccia make for tasty panini at **Treppeda's** (⊠ 300 2nd Ave. ☎ 303/652–1607) Enjoy a crunchy cannoli or cookie and an espresso for dessert at the bar.

Where to Stay

$$–$$$ ⊞ **Niwot Inn.** A wood-trimmed, two-story, vaulted atrium gives the feel of a grand Colorado lodge, but with a more contemporary and understated elegance. Spacious, handsome rooms, all named for Colorado "fourteeners," have leather chairs, desks, and wrought-iron lamps. The inviting sitting room with a grand fireplace, hardwood floors with carpets, and leather couches is where the complimentary breakfast buffet is served. Colorado mountain scenery is rendered in photographs and chalk drawings found throughout the inn. ⊠ 342 2nd Ave. ⅅ Box 1044, 80544 ☎ 303/652–8452 ⊟ 303/652–4189 ⊕ www.niwotinn.com ⟿ 14 rooms ⚲ In-room data ports, Internet, meeting room ⊟ AE, DC, MC, V ⊙⏐ CP.

Nightlife & the Arts

Left Hand Grange Hall (⊠ 195 2nd Ave. ☎ 303/931–6101 ⊕ www. niwotacoustic.com) is one of the oldest continuously running granges in Colorado (traditionally, where community events take place). The excellent acoustics here make the perfect venue for the Niwot Acoustic Series, which hosts locally- and nationally-renowned folk and pop-folk artists from September to June.

Shopping

You'll find antiques dealers and a few notable shops in the Niwot historic district. Just ¼ mi east of old Niwot is Cottonwood Square, with a grocer, a gas station, a handful of gift shops, and a few eateries, including an Irish-style pub and a Mexican restaurant.

ANTIQUES DEALERS **Lockwood House Antiques** (⊠ 198 2nd Ave. ☎ 303/652–2963) specializes in furniture and beautiful Victorian building materials. The store has its own warehouse in Longmont. Call for hours and directions. For a good selection of antique housewares, collectibles, and furniture head to **Twiggs** (⊠ 165 2nd Ave. ☎ 303/652–9065). **Wise Buys Antiques** (⊠ 190 2nd Ave. 80544 ☎ 303/652–2888) restores fireplace mantels—some with mirrors—and usually has more than a hundred in stock.

GIFTS You'll find bright, colorful home furnishings and herb blends from Italy and France as well as locally made jewelry at **Casalta House of Mediterranean Style** (⊠ 124 2nd Ave. ☎ 303/652–2755). Owner Tisha Wood designs and makes table linens and clothes with fabrics she imports from France.

Lyons

⑭ *14 mi north of Boulder on U.S. 36.*

Lyons is the Front Range's ideal feng shui town according to resident Timothy Oakes, professor and expert in the geography of China—a quirky yet appropriate description for this peaceful, down-to-earth community just inside the red sandstone foothills at the confluence of the North St. Vrain and South St. Vrain creeks. The cafés, restaurants, and antiques stores serve more than just the small population of 1,600. Visitors also come for the recreation opportunities and top-notch music festivals.

Sports & the Outdoors

BIRD-WATCHING Ornithologists gather at **Bohn Park** at sunrise and sunset to spot some of the many species of songbirds that reside along St. Vrain Creek. Golden eagles have been sited in the red cliffs on the southwest side of town. ✦ *From northbound U.S. 36, turn left onto Park St. and then left onto 2nd St.*

HIKING & MOUNTAIN BIKING ★ **Hall Ranch** (⊠ ¾ mi west of Lyons on Hwy. 7; marked trailhead on right ☉ dawn–dusk) is open to hikers, mountain bikers, and equestrians. A 10½-mi loop provides mountain views and an interpretive display about the area's ecosystem and the roles that prairie dogs and raptors play in it. Start on the Bitterbrush trail and connect to the Nelson loop at 3½ mi, all the while crossing meadows and ascending and descending through stands of pine trees and rock outcroppings.

Rabbit Mountain, home to raptors, prairie dogs, coyotes, and an occasional prairie rattlesnake, has several trails that afford views of the high Rockies and the plains. The 5-mi **Eagle Wind Trail** loop has short spurs to viewpoints. From the parking area head out on the trail to the gravel road and then right onto the singletrack loop. The **Little Thompson Overlook Trail** forks off to the left before you come to the gravel road. Go left on the gravel road to reach **Indian Mesa Trail**, a gravel road that ends at private property but has views. ✦ *Drive 1 mi east on Rte. 66 from the intersection with U.S. 36 to 53rd St. Turn left and drive 3 mi to the parking lot ☉ Dawn–dusk.*

Where to Stay & Eat

$–$$ ✕**Gateway Café.** Locals head here to enjoy an upscale fusion of Japanese and Western cuisines in a casual atmosphere. Start with some vegetarian *gyozas* (dumplings) and move on to tempura or soft-shelled crabs with wasabi sauce. Grass-fed lamb chops and chokecherry braised buffalo short ribs are just two of the succulent meat dishes that are smoked and then grilled. The cozy dining room is filled with paintings, stained glass, and a huge wood-framed mirror. ✉ *432 Main St.* ☎ *303/823–5144* 🖃 *AE, MC, V* ⊘ *Closed Mon. and Tues. No lunch.*

★ ¢ ✗ **Lyons Soda Fountain.** This fountain has been satisfying cravings for thick, handmade malts and ice-cream sodas and treats since 1921. The tiny shop with the original marble backdrop and mirror also has espresso drinks and sandwiches on the menu. The hours are daily, 7–7. ✉ *400 Main St.* ☎ *303/823–5393* 🖃 *AE, DC, MC, V.*

CAMPING Three campgrounds west of Lyons are tucked away in quiet forests. Each has recreational opportunities and is an easy drive from Estes Park, Lyons, and Boulder. Peaceful Valley and Camp Dick campgrounds have recreational opportunities for hikers, mountain bikers, four-wheel-drive and off-road vehicle enthusiasts, and horseback riders. Although reservations can be made through the **National Recreation Reservation Service** (☎ 877/444–6777 🌐 www.reserveusa.com), half of the sites in these campgrounds are not reservable and are filled on a first-come, first-served basis. Weekends are popular, so if you don't have a reservation, the rangers recommend arriving before noon on Friday.

¢ 🏕 **Olive Ridge Campground.** Marvel at Long's Peak—14,255 feet tall—which towers above the quiet campground, at 8,400 feet, in Roosevelt National Forest. Hiking trails to the Rocky Mountain National Park's Wild Basin are easily accessed. Tents, campers, trailers, and RVs are welcome at all sites. The maximum vehicle length is 40 feet. ✉ *20 mi west of Lyons on Rte. 7 or 15 mi south of Estes Park on Rte. 7 (Peak-to-Peak Hwy.)* ☎ *303/541–2500* 🖶 *303/541–2515* 🌐 *www.fs.fed.us/arnf/ districts/brd/camping/olive-ridge.htm* ⚴ *Pit toilets, drinking water, fire grates, picnic tables, playground; no hook-ups, no showers* ⤳ *56 sites* 🏷 *$13* ⊘ *Mid-May–mid-Oct.*

¢ 🏕 **Peaceful Valley Campground.** Creekside in a forested valley at 8650 feet, this campground is small and welcomes RVs, trailers, tents, and campers at all sites. Maximum vehicle length is 55 feet. ✉ *12 mi west of Lyons on Rte. 7, then 4 mi south on Rte. 72 (Peak-to-Peak Hwy.)* ☎ *303/541–2500* 🖶 *303/541–2515* 🌐 *www.fs.fed.us/arnf/districts/ brd/camping/peaceful-valley.htm* ⚴ *Pit toilets, drinking water, fire grates, picnic tables, no hook-ups, no showers* ⤳ *17 sites* 🏷 *$13* ⊘ *Mid-May–mid-Oct.*

¢ 🏕 **Camp Dick Campground.** Sleep peacefully under the stars along Middle St. Vrain Creek. This forested valley at an elevation of 8,650 feet has plenty of trails, and all sites accommodate RVs, tents, trailers, and campers. Maximum vehicle length is 55 feet. ✉ *12 mi west of Lyons on Rte. 7, then 4 mi south on Rte. 72 (Peak-to-Peak Hwy). Drive through Peaceful Valley Campground and then 1 mi* ☎ *303/541–2500* 🖶 *303/541–2515* 🌐 *www.fs.fed.us/arnf/districts/brd/camping/campdick. htm* ⚴ *Pit toilets, drinking water, fire grates, picnic tables; no hook-ups, no showers* ⤳ *41 sites* 🏷 *$13* ⊘ *Mid-May–mid-Oct.*

Nightlife & the Arts

The many professional musicians and instrument makers who live in Lyons are behind its vibrant music scene. The summer outdoor music season kicks off with **Lyons Good Old Days** at the end of June, and goes into September with mid-week concerts in Sandstone Park (at 4th and Railroad avenues). Cafés and restaurants host bands regularly, and some residents even invite performers to use their living rooms as stages. For information about current events, check the Web site www. musicinlyons.com.

Planet Bluegrass (☎ 303/823–0848 or 800/624–2422 🌐 www.bluegrass. com) presents artists such as the Indigo Girls, Patty Griffin, and Warren Haynes at the four bluegrass festivals it holds in Lyons from July through September: *RockyGrass, Folks Festival, Kinfolk Festival,* and the *Festival of the Mabon.*

Fort Collins

50 mi from Estes Park via U.S. 34 east and I–25 north; 65 mi from Denver International Airport via Peña Blvd., E–470, and I–25.

The old neighborhoods of Fort Collins still have elm tree-lined streets thanks to agricultural scientists at Colorado State University (CSU), who were able to keep the vicious Dutch Elm disease at bay. The city was established to protect traders from the natives, while the former negotiated the treacherous Overland Trail. After the flood of 1864 swept away Camp Collins—a cavalry post near today's town of LaPorte—Colonel Will Collins established a new camp on 6,000 acres where Fort Collins stands today. The town grew on two industries: education (CSU was founded here in 1879) and agriculture (rich crops of alfalfa and sugar beets). With six microbreweries crafting ales, lagers, and stouts, the city has the most microbreweries per capita in the state.

The Fort Collins Convention & Visitors Bureau has designated a historic walking tour of more than 20 buildings, including the original uni-

15 versity structures and the stately sandstone **Avery House,** named for Franklin Avery, who planned the old town's broad streets when he surveyed the city in 1873. ✉ *328 W. Mountain Ave.* ☎ *970/221–0533* 🎫 *Free* 🕑 *Wed. and Sun. 1–3.*

16 **Old Town Square** (✉ Mountain and College Aves.), a National Historic District, is a pedestrian zone with sculptures and fountains. Restored buildings house shops, cafés, galleries, and bars. During summer musicians and theater groups entertain Tuesday at noon and Thursday evenings.

17 The **Fort Collins Museum** has an 1860s cabin from the original military camp and a 1905 vintage schoolhouse on its grounds. The collection contains artifacts representing Fort Collins history, from Native Americans through fur trappers to CSU professor Donald Sutherland, held hostage by terrorists in Beirut during the 1980s. ✉ *200 Matthews St.* ☎ *970/221–6738* ⊕ *www.fcgov.com/museum* 🎫 *Free* 🕑 *Tues.–Sat. 10–5, Sun. noon–5.*

18 CSU's **Environmental Learning Center** is a 1.2-mi trail loop within a 200-acre nature preserve. The raptor cages and the walk through wetland animal habitat are an excellent educational family activity, and fun for anyone curious about animal habitats. Staff conduct special walks like the full-moon hike, Saturday picnics with naturalists, and sunrise bird-watching strolls. The learning center loop is 1 mi east of the Timberline and Drake Road intersection, on Drake Road. ✉ *Information Center, 3745 E. Prospect Rd.* ☎ *970/491–1661* ⊕ *www.cnr.colostate. edu/elc* 🎫 *Free* 🕑 *Information center mid-May–Aug., daily 10–5, Sept.–Apr., weekends 10–5. Learning Center year-round, daily dawn–dusk.*

19 **Swetsville Zoo** is the unique creation of an insomniac dairy farmer, who stayed up nights fashioning more than 150 dinosaurs, birds, insects, and other fantastic creatures from old farm equipment. ✉ *4801 E. Harmony Rd., ¼ mi east of I–25* ☎ *970/484–9509* 🎫 *Free* 🕑 *Daily dawn–dusk.*

20 Take a guided tour or guide yourself through the **New Belgium Brewing Company** and sample the tasty brews. Call to book for Friday and Saturday. ✉ *500 Linden St.* ☎ *970/221–0524* ⊕ *www.newbelgium.com* 🎫 *Free* 🕑 *Tours weekdays, noon, 2, and 4; Sat., hourly from 11–4.*

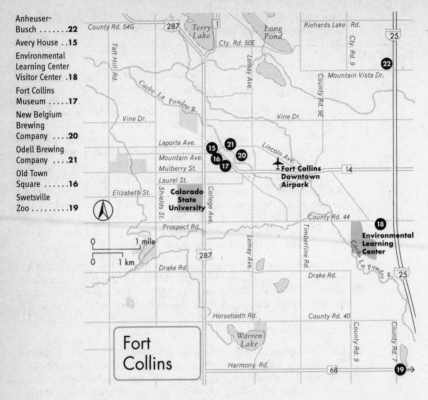

㉑ Dating to 1989, the **Odell Brewing Company** was one of the first microbreweries to open shop in town—out of a pickup truck bed. ✉ *800 E.
Lincoln Ave.* ☎ 970/498–9070 ✐ *Free* ☉ *Tours weekdays, 10, 11, and
3; Sat., 1, 2, and 3.*

㉒ Learn lots of facts about the large-scale brewing process at **Anheuser-
Busch** during a free tour. Tours start every 45 minutes (every half-hour
on weekends) and last one hour and 20 minutes. ✉ *2351 Busch Dr.*
☎ 970/490–4691 ⊕ *www.budweisertours.com* ✐ *Free* ☉ *June–Aug.,
daily 9:30–5; Sept., daily 10–4; Oct.–May, Thurs.–Mon. 10–4.*

off the
beaten
path

⚠ **COLORADO STATE FOREST STATE PARK –** Rugged peaks, thick
forests, and burbling streams make up this 70,768-acre park. Here
you can fish for trout, boat the azure alpine lakes, ride horseback,
hike or bicycle 130 mi of trails, and explore a few four-wheel-drive
roads with views of the 12,000-foot Medicine Bow and Never
Summer mountain ranges. Outfitters in Walden, 21 mi west of the
park, arrange guided fly-fishing and horseback riding trips. **Never
Summer Nordic** (✉ Box 1983, Fort Collins 80522 ☎ 970/482–
9411) rents the yurts in state park to cross-country skiers for hut-to-
hut ski trips. ✉ *56750 Hwy. 14, Walden, drive 75 mi west on Rte.
14 from Ft. Collins or 53 mi north of Granby on U.S. 40 and Rte.
125 to Walden and 21 mi east on Rte. 14 to the park* ☎ 970/723–
8366 ⊕ *www.coloradoparks.org* ✐ *$5 a day per vehicle.*

Sports & the Outdoors

BICYCLING   Both paved-trail cycling and single-track mountain biking are within easy
access of town. The **Poudre River Trail** (17 mi round-trip) is an easy riparian jaunt within Fort Collins. ✛ *Trailheads at Lions Park on North*

Overland Trail and at the Environmental Learning Center on East Drake Rd.

The **Spring Creek Trail** (13 mi round-trip) is another easy spin through town. ✛ *Trailheads are at Southwest Community Park on South Overland Trail and at the Environmental Learning Center on East Drake Rd.*

For short, single-track rides, Pineridge and Maxwell trails do not disappoint and connect to other trails for longer adventures: head west on Drake Road to where it bends right and becomes South Overland Trail; turn left on County Road 42C and drive almost 1 mi to the posted fence opening.

Serious gearheads crank at **Horsetooth Mountain Park** on the southwest side of Horsetooth Reservoir. Several single tracks and Jeep trails provide any level of challenge. **Recycled Cycles** (✉ 4031 S. Mason St. ☏ 970/223–1969 ⊕ www.recycled-cycles.com) rents city bikes, mountain bikes, road bikes, kid trailers, and tandem cycles for $10 per day.

FISHING Horsetooth Reservoir, Red Feather Lakes, and Cache la Poudre River are locally renowned for excellent fishing. The knowledgeable chaps at
★ **St. Peter's Fly Shop** (✉ 202 Remington St. ☏ 970/498–8968 or 888/211–7250) arrange half-day to full-day guided or instructional wade and float trips in northern Colorado and southern Wyoming that can include permits for waters not open to the public. The staff gladly provides information on conditions to independent fishermen, too.

GOLF **Collindale Golf Course** (✉ 1441 E. Horsetooth St. ☏ 970/221–6651) is an 18-hole public golf course.

HIKING & Twenty-eight miles of trails in **Horsetooth Mountain Park** offer easy to dif-
HORSEBACK ficult hikes and rides, all with views of the mountains to the west and
RIDING the plains to the east. Purchase a permit at the park entrance. ✛ *Drive west on Harmony Rd. to Taft Hill Rd.; then take 38E to park entrance* ☏ *970/679–4570* ⊕ *www.co.larimer.co.us/parks.*

You'll see wildlife and plenty of wildflowers along the trails in **Lory State Park.** ✉ *708 Lodgepole Dr., Bellvue, drive north on U.S. 287 and take the Bellvue exit onto 23N. Turn left and drive almost 1½ mi and turn right onto 25G. The park entrance is 1½ mi farther.*

RAFTING & The Cache la Poudre River is famous for its rapids, and river trips fill
KAYAKING fast. It's wise to book with an outfitter at least two weeks in advance. The state-certified guides of **A-1 Wildwater** (✉ 317 Stover St., 80524 ☏ 970/224–3379 or 800/369–4165 ⊕ www.A1Wildwater.com) provide kayaking instruction and guided tours as well as daylong and half-day trips for groups. Multiday trips are available, too.

Where to Stay & Eat

Lodging in Fort Collins is mainly franchise hotels and inns. However, the city has a couple of enchanting B&Bs that are close to downtown and outdoor activities.

$$$–$$$$ ✕**Nico's Catacombs.** The chefs here excel in traditional Continental cuisine—including table-side cooking—with no trendy versions or fluffy variations on the classics. Diners savor the house specialties (Dover sole, bouillabaisse, Châteaubriand, and rack of lamb) in subterranean brick caverns outfitted with wood tables and dark upholstery—the appropriate old-world ambience for a restaurant that features more than 500 wines. Daily specials may be fresh sea bass, elk loin, or veal. Reservations are strongly recommended. Shorts are not allowed. ✉ *115 S. College Ave.* ☏ *970/482–6426* ▭ *AE, D, DC, MC, V* ⊘ *No lunch.*

★ $$ ✕ **Canino's.** Hearty Italian specialties are served in this historic, four-square house that still has a few stained-glass windows. Appetizers like bruschetta and entrées such as cioppino, pollo cacciatora, eggplant Parmigiana, and veal marsala are made in classic Italian style. The menu is rounded out with pizzas and pasta dishes like baked mostaccioli and spinach lasagna. Tables are set in wood-trimmed rooms that have hardwood floors with carpets. Homemade cheesecake, tiramisu, or gelato—paired with a robust espresso—finish dinner on a sweet note. ⊠ *613 S. College Ave.* ☎ *970/493–7205* ▭ *AE, D, DC, MC, V.*

¢–$$ ✕ **Rio Grande Mexican Restaurant.** One of the best Mexican restaurants in the area, the Rio Grande always satisfies with such old favorites as sopaipillas, burritos, and Mexican steak, as well as more fiery Tex-Mex fare. Mini-margaritas cost $3, and they're strong enough to impart a pleasant buzz. ⊠ *143 W. Mountain Ave.* ☎ *970/224–5428* ▭ *AE, MC, V.*

¢ ✕ **Starry Night.** Espresso drinkers sip their sustenance under the night-blue ceiling while reading, chatting, or mulling over the sunflowers and the mural *Starry Night over Fort Collins* inspired by van Gogh. Beyond breakfast, there's soups, salads, and sandwiches at lunch and dinnertime. ⊠ *112 S. College Ave.* ☎ *970/493–3039* ▭ *MC, V.*

★ $$–$$$ ▥ **Edwards House B&B.** This quiet Victorian inn with hardwood floors and light, birchwood trim is four blocks from downtown. Guests enjoy gourmet breakfasts that include espresso drinks and dishes such as gingerbread pancakes or eggs Florentine. The video library is well stocked for those who forego relaxing on the large front porch or reading in the parlor. Rooms exude an old-fashioned elegance without being fussy, and are appointed with sleigh or canopy beds, gas stoves, Jacuzzis or clawfoot tubs, writing desks, and slate fireplaces. ⊠ *402 W. Mountain Ave., 80521.* ☎ *970/493–9191 or 800/281–9190* ⊟ *970/484–0706* ⊕ *www.edwardshouse.com* ⤳ *8 rooms* ⌂ *Dining room, cable TV, in-room VCRs, video library, meeting room* ▭ *AE, D, MC, V* ⊙❙ *BP.*

¢–$ ▥ **Fort Collins Plaza Inn.** This locally owned establishment is unspectacular, but it's a better buy than the nearby franchise competitors. Rooms are simple and standard: beige walls, veneered furniture, and queen- or king-size beds. ⊠ *3709 E. Mulberry St., 80524* ☎ *970/493–7800 or 800/434–5548* ⊟ *970/493–1826* ⊕ *www.plaza-inn.com* ⤳ *135 rooms* ⌂ *Restaurant, cable TV, indoor-outdoor pool, hot tub, sauna, bar, dry cleaning* ▭ *AE, D, DC, MC, V* ⊙❙ *CP.*

CAMPING ⚠ **Colorado State Forest State Park.** Sharing this forest with you are
¢ deer, fox, kestrels, moose, chipmunks, and songbirds. During the winter you can snowshoe, snowmobile or cross-country ski the hut-to-hut system. The visitors center hosts kids programs, interpretive hikes, and educational programs. Outfitters in Walden, 21 mi west of the park, arrange guided fly-fishing and horseback riding trips. Simple day admission to the park is $5. Groceries, gas, and emergency services are available in Walden. ⊠ *56750 Hwy. 14, Walden, drive 75 mi west on Rte. 14 from Ft. Collins or 53 mi north of Granby on U.S. 40 and Rte. 125 to Walden and 21 mi east on Rte. 14 to the park* ☎ *303/470–1144 or 800/678–2267* ⊟ *970/723–8325* ⊕ *www.coloradoparks.org* ⌂ *Pit toilets, dump station, drinking water, fire grates, fire pits, picnic tables, ranger station* ⤳ *158 sites, 2 cabins, 5 yurts* ▨ *$12* ▭ *AE, D, MC, V* ⊙ *Year-round.*

¢ ⚠ **Roosevelt National Forest.** Campgrounds and backcountry camping abounds in the 800,000 acres of the forest. A total of 45 campgrounds with 1,074 sites (some with group sites for 15–75 persons) accommodate RVs, campers, tents, and trailers. Some campgrounds have electrical and/or water hook-ups and showers. Some have drinking water. Campgrounds are generally open between late May and the middle of October, but this depends on the weather. Backcountry camping requires permits. ⊠ *Canyon Lakes Ranger District Visitor Center, 1311 S. College, Fort Collins* ☎ *970/498–2770, 877/444–6777 for reservations* ☎ *970/ 498–2726* ⊕ *www.fs.fed.us/r2/arnf; www.reserveusa.com to book a site* ⅋ *Pit toilets, fire grates, picnic tables* ⟿ *1074 sites (some with electrical and/or water hook-ups)* ☜ *$7–$13* ☰ *AE, D, MC, V* ☉ *Late May–mid-Oct.*

Nightlife

BARS & LOUNGES The sports bar **C, B & Potts** (⊠ 1415 W. Elizabeth St. ☎ 970/221–1139) is known for its burgers and international selection of beers. The establishment has both its own brewery and a pool hall with six tables and a full bar. A place to hang (usually with the college crowd) is **Coopersmith's Pub & Brewery** (⊠ 5 Old Town Sq. ☎ 970/498–0483). Coopersmith's own pool hall just outside the front door at 7 Old Town Square has 12 tables and serves pizza. College students line the bar at **Lucky Joe's Sidewalk Saloon** (⊠ 25 Old Town Sq. ☎ 970/493–2213).

ROCK CLUBS **Lindens Brewing Co.** (⊠ 214 Linden St. ☎ 970/482–9291) has live music Wednesday through Saturday. Past acts include Wide Spread Panic and Bo Diddley. The kitchen serves creole specialties and pub fare. **Mishawaka Inn** (⊠ 13714 Poudre Canyon, 25 mi north of Fort Collins on Rte. 14 ☎ 970/482–4420), an outdoor amphitheater on the banks of the Poudre River, corrals touring bands on the weekends.

Shopping

Old Town Square (⊠ College and Mountain Aves. and Jefferson St.) and adjacent Linden Street have historic buildings that house galleries, bookshops, cafés, brewpubs, shops, and a martini bar. The shopkeepers at the **Children's Mercantile Company** (⊠ 111 N. College Ave. ☎ 970/ 484–9946 or 888/326–8465) enjoy playing with the toys as much as the young customers do. The shop carries books, CDs, imported toys like Lego and Rokenbok, and classics like marbles, dolls, and stuffed animals. Western furniture is handcrafted and signed at **Mountain Woods Furniture** (⊠ 11 Old Town Sq. ☎ 970/416–0701). Throws, pillows, blankets, and other accessories—all handmade by artisans—complement the aspen and pine lodge-style pieces. Shipping is available. **Trimble Court Artisans** (⊠ 118 Trimble Ct. ☎ 970/221–0051), a co-op with more than 40 members, sells paintings, jewelry, clothing, weavings, stained glass, and pottery.

ROCKY MOUNTAIN NATIONAL PARK REGION

This wilderness of more than 265,000 acres of forested valleys, wildlife habitat, rushing rivers, shimmering lakes, and high alpine meadows, all tucked between soaring granite peaks, was established as a national park in 1915. The park's two resort towns are Grand Lake and Estes Park.

Estes Park

❷❸ *22 mi from Lyons via U.S. 36 northwest; 40 mi from Nederland via Rte. 72 and Rte. 7 (the Peak-to-Peak Hwy.).*

The scenery on the U.S. 36 approach to Estes Park gives little hint of the grandeur to come. If ever there was a classic picture-postcard Rockies view, Estes Park has it. Even the McDonald's has glorious views and a facade that complements its surroundings, thanks to strict zoning laws requiring that businesses present a rustic exterior. The town itself is very family-oriented, albeit somewhat kitschy: many of the small hotels lining the roads are mom-and-pop outfits that have been passed down through several generations.

As a resort town, Estes attracted the attention of genius entrepreneur F. O. Stanley, inventor of the Stanley Steamer automobile and several photographic processes. In 1905, having been told by his doctors he would soon die of tuberculosis, he constructed the regal **Stanley Hotel** on a promontory overlooking the town. Stanley went on to live another 30-odd years, an extension that he attributed to the area's fresh air. The hotel soon became one of the most glamorous resorts in the Rockies, a reputation it holds to this day. The hotel was the inspiration for Stephen King's horror novel, *The Shining,* part of which he wrote while staying here.

Archaeological evidence displayed at the **Estes Park Area Historical Museum** makes an eloquent case that Native Americans used the area as a summer resort. The museum also has an assortment of pioneer artifacts and changing exhibits. ⊠ *200 4th St.* ☎ *970/586–6256* ⊠ *$2.50* ⊙ *May–Oct., Mon.–Sat. 10–5, Sun. 1–5; Nov.–Apr., Fri.–Sat. 10–5, Sun. 1–5.*

The **MacGregor Ranch Museum,** on the National Register of Historic Places, offers views of the Twin Owls and Long's Peak (towering more than 14,000 feet). Although the ranch was homesteaded in 1873, the present house was built in 1896; it provides a well-preserved record of typical ranch life. ⊠ *MacGregor Ave., off U.S. 34* ☎ *970/586–3749* ⊠ *Free* ⊙ *June–Aug., Tues.–Fri. 10–4.*

off the beaten path

TRAIL RIDGE WINERY – Colorado may not show up on oenologists' maps like California or France do, but grapes once grew wild in the state, and today they are cultivated for wines. This inconspicuous winery produces a spicy gewurztraminer, buttery chardonnays, oakey merlots, creamy rieslings, and smooth cabernet sauvignons, all with grapes from Colorado's famous fruit growing regions near Grand Junction. ⊠ *4113 W. Eisenhower Blvd. (U.S. 34), Loveland, drive east on U.S. 34 from Estes Park. The winery is on the left side of U.S. 34 before the city. Watch for the sign on the left as you leave the canyon* ☎ *970/635–0949* ⊕ *www.TrailRidgeWinery.com* ⊙ *Daily 10–5.*

Sports & the Outdoors

Rocky Mountain National Park, 5 mi from Estes Park, is ideal for snowshoeing, cross-country skiing, photographing wildlife, rock climbing, hiking, and fishing.

FISHING   The **Big Thompson River,** east of Estes Park along U.S. 34, is popular for its good stock of rainbow and brown trout. **Rocky Mountain Adventures** (☎ 970/586–6191 or 800/858–6808) offers guided fly- and float-fishing trips on the Cache la Poudre River.

GOLF   **Estes Park Golf Club** (⊠ 1080 S. St. Vrain St. ☎ 970/586–8146) is one of the oldest and prettiest 18-hole courses in the state. The grazing elk seldom allow golfers to play through.

HORSEBACK   **Sombrero Ranch** (☎ 970/586–4577) leads trail rides through the Estes
RIDING   Park region, including Rocky Mountain National Park.

RAFTING &   Whitewater rafting trips fill up fast, so it's a good idea to book with an
KAYAKING   outfitter a couple of weeks in advance. **Rapid Transit Rafting** (☎ 970/586–8852 or 800/367–8523) arranges guided rafting trips on the Colorado and Cache la Poudre rivers.

Rocky Mountain Adventures (☎ 970/586–6191 or 800/858–6808 ⊕ www. shoprma.com) provides half- and full-day kayaking-instruction trips on Lake Estes. All gear is included.

Where to Stay & Eat

$$–$$$$ ✕ **Nicky's Cattleman Restaurant.** Elegant wood beams, oak paneling, maroon carpeting and upholstery, and a huge picture window fronting the mountains and Fall River make this one of the most sophisticated restaurants in town. The steak house ages and cuts its own meat, and specialties include sensational sirloin prepared Greek style with onions, peppers, and feta, and prime rib broiled in rock salt. Nicky's also offers motor-lodge rooms, cabins, and condominiums. ⊠ *1350 U.S. 34* ☎ *970/586–5376* ⊟ *AE, D, DC, MC, V.*

$–$$$$ ✕ **Dunraven Inn.** The more than 12,000 one-dollar bills wallpapering the bar are guests' specially autographed tips for owner Dale Hatcher. In a canyon just outside town, this casual and popular restaurant serves dependably good Italian cuisine, steaks, and fresh fish. The dining room has an old English ceiling, tartan carpet, and dark wood paneling embellished with many copies of Da Vinci's *Mona Lisa,* all nicely visible in the low light. A dress code bans cut-off shorts and tank tops. ⊠ *2470 Hwy. 66* ☎ *970/586–6409* ⊟ *AE, D, MC, V* ☉ *No lunch.*

★ $–$$ ✕ **Sweet Basilico Café.** This tiny, homey place is a local favorite for basic Italian classics like lasagna, manicotti, and eggplant Parmesan. Sandwiches made with homemade focaccia are delicious, and the minestrone satisfies wonderfully. Reservations are strongly recommended. ⊠ *401 E. Elkhorn Ave.* ☎ *970/586–3899* ⊟ *AE, D, MC, V.*

¢–$$ ✕ **Ed's Cantina.** Huge burritos and tasty burgers are reliable choices at this popular hangout. Lighthearted antiques adorn the walls. ⊠ *362 E. Elkhorn Ave.* ☎ *970/586–2919* ⊟ *AE, D, MC, V.*

¢–$$ ✕ **Estes Park Brewery.** Beer chili is the specialty here. The menu otherwise includes the usual pizza, burgers, sandwiches, and chicken or steak dinners. ⊠ *470 Prospect Village Dr.* ☎ *970/586–5421* ⊟ *AE, D, MC, V.*

★ $$$–$$$$ ▦ **Aspen Lodge at Estes Park Ranch Resort and Conference Center.** The main building is the largest log structure in Colorado, with cathedral ceilings, antler chandeliers, and a vaulted stone fireplace. Rustic lodge rooms (variously decorated with Native American weavings and original art) have balconies and thrilling mountain views. There are also 23 nicely appointed cabins with gingerbread trim. Rides are offered to a 2,000-acre working ranch, and you can two-step or square dance in the homey lounge after an excellent dinner. The full breakfast buffet is included. The many outdoor activities available include snowshoeing and ice hockey on the lake. ⊠ *6120 Rte. 7, 80517* ☎ *970/586–8133 or 800/332–6867* ⊕ *www. estesvalleyresorts.com* ⇨ *52 rooms, 23 cabins* ♿ *Restaurant, 2 tennis courts, pool, gym, hot tub, sauna, fishing, basketball, horseback riding, racquetball, cross-country skiing, ice-skating, bar, children's programs, laundry service, convention center* ⊟ *AE, D, DC, MC, V* ⇨ *3-night minimum* ᵀⓄᴵ *BP.*

$$$–$$$$ ▦ **Stanley Hotel.** Perched regally on a hill commanding the town, the
Fodor's Choice Stanley is one of Colorado's great old hotels. The sunny rooms, deco-
★ rated with antiques and period reproductions, are not as sumptuous as they once were. Still, there is an incomparable air of history to this 1909 hotel, along with all the modern conveniences. The MacGregor Room is the classiest ballroom in town. Outdoor seating by the waterfall is available at the restaurant, The Cascade. ⊠ *333 Wonderview Ave., 80517* ☎ *970/586–3371 or 800/976–1377* 🖷 *970/586–3673* ⊕ *www.stanleyhotel.com* ⇨ *138 rooms* ♿ *Restaurant, coffee shop, pool, bar, video game room, meeting room, travel services* ⊟ *AE, D, DC, MC, V.*

$$–$$$$ ⬚ **Estes Park Center/YMCA of the Rockies.** This 890-acre, family-friendly property has a wealth of attractive and clean lodging options among its four lodges and many cabins. A couple can rent a simple, rustic pine cabin, and an extended family (up to 10 people) has plenty of space in the newer cabins, which have modern kitchen appliances and televisions. Lodge rooms can be outfitted with queen beds or bunk beds for the kids. The Barclay Reunion Lodge can house up to 72 people in 17 rooms. A meal plan is available for the all-you-can-eat buffet. ✉ *2515 Tunnel Rd., 80511* ☎ *970/586–3341 or 303/443–4743* 🖷 *303/449–6781* ⊕ *www. ymcarockies.org* ⇆ *688 rooms, 220 cabins* ⬧ *Restaurant, miniature golf, tennis, indoor pool, gym, basketball, roller-skating rink, recreation room, playground, meeting room* ▤ *MC, V* ⫯◯⫯ *MAP.*

$$–$$$$ ⬚ **Lake Shore Lodge.** This open, lodge-style building is the only hotel on Lake Estes and a 1-mi bike and walking path provides easy access to town. Rooms have either lake or mountain views and are generously appointed with amenities, replica brass light fixtures, blond-wood furniture, and an easy chair or couch. A suite comes with a fireplace, Jacuzzi, kitchenette, and balcony that overlooks the lake. An upstairs lounge is a quiet place to read the paper after the full breakfast buffet. ✉ *1700 Big Thompson Ave., 80517* ☎ *970/577–6400 or 800/332–6867* ⊕ *www.estesvalleyresorts.com* ⇆ *54 rooms, 6 suites* ⬧ *Restaurant, in-room data ports, indoor pool, gym, hot tub, sauna, bar, lounge, recreation room, meeting rooms* ▤ *AE, D, MC, V* ⫯◯⫯ *BP.*

$$–$$$$ ⬚ **Taharaa Mountain Lodge.** Every room at this luxury B&B accesses the wraparound deck and its views of the high Rockies and Estes Valley. Rooms are decorated with individual themes, from Ute Indian to Southwestern, and all have a fireplace. Enjoy happy hour in the Great Room. The full breakfast hints at the owners' Southern heritage. ✉ *3110 S. St. Vrain St., 80517, 4 mi south of Estes Park* ☎ *970/577–0098 or 800/ 597–0098* 🖷 *970/577–0819* ⊕ *www.taharaa.com* ⇆ *12* ⬧ *In-room data ports, pool, gym, sauna, some hot tubs* ▤ *AE, D, MC, V* ⟳ *2-night minimum* ⫯◯⫯ *BP.*

$–$$$ ⬚ **Boulder Brook.** Luxury suites at this secluded spot on the river are tucked in the pines, yet close to town. All have a full kitchen or kitchenette, private deck, gas fireplace, and jetted tub. ✉ *1900 Fall River Rd., 80517* ☎ *970/586–0910 or 800/239–0910* ⊕ *www.boulderbrook.com* ⇆ *16 suites* ⬧ *Kitchenettes, cable TV, in-room VCRs* ▤ *AE, D, MC, V.*

$–$$$ ⬚ **Lake Estes Inn & Suites.** All the well-maintained rooms are decorated in burgundy and forest green with light, sand-color walls and dark-stain or blond-wood furniture. Family units have two sleeping rooms and sleep up to eight. The newer chalet suites have sitting rooms with fireplaces, oak cabinets, Jacuzzis, and kitchens. Ask for a unit with a lake view. ✉ *1650 Big Thompson Ave., Hwy. 34, 80517* ☎ *970/586–3386* ⊕ *www. estesvalleyresorts.com* ⇆ *58 rooms* ⬧ *Refrigerators, pool, hot tub, sauna, playground, laundry facilities* ▤ *AE, D, DC, MC, V* ⫯◯⫯ *CP.*

CAMPING   ⚠ **Roosevelt National Forest.** Both developed and backcountry camping
¢   abounds in the 800,000 acres of the forest. Forty-five campgrounds with 1074 sites (some with group sites for 15–75 persons) accommodate RVs, campers, tents, or trailers. Some campgrounds have electrical and/or water hook-ups and showers. Some have drinking water. Campgrounds open and close for the season depending on the weather, but are generally open between late May and the middle of October. Backcountry camping requires permits. ✉ *Canyon Lakes Ranger District Visitor Center, 1311 S. College, Fort Collins 80524* ☎ *970/498–2770* 🖷 *970/498–2726* ⊕ *www.fs.fed.us/r2/arnf* ⬧ *Pit toilets, fire grates, picnic tables* ⇆ *1,074 sites (some with electrical and/or water hook-ups)* ▨ *$7–$13* ⬧ *www. reserveusa.com, 877/444–6777* ▤ *AE, D, MC, V* ☉ *Late May–mid-Oct.*

Cabin & Condo Rentals

Range Property Management (⌂ Box 316, Estes Park 80517 ☎ 970/586–7626 or 888/433–5211 🖷 970/577–8881 ⊕ www.rangeprop.com) rents properties in the Estes Park area.

Nightlife & the Arts

NIGHTLIFE
The locals' favorite after-work hangout is **J. R. Chapins Lounge** (✉ Holiday Inn, 101 S. St. Vrain St. ☎ 970/586–2332). Blues and rock bands play at **Lonigans** (✉ 110 W. Elkhorn Ave. ☎ 970/586–4346) on weekends. The venerable **Wheel Bar** (✉ 132 E. Elkhorn Ave. ☎ 970/586–9381) is among the choice watering holes.

FESTIVALS
A traditional tattoo kicks off the **Longs Peak Scottish/Irish Highland Festival** (☎ 970/586–6308 or 800/903–7837 ⊕ www.scotfest.com), a three-day fair of athletic competitions (Highland games), Celtic music, dancing, a parade, and seminars on Scottish genealogy. The festival takes place the weekend after Labor Day.

Shopping

Although shopping in Estes Park includes many run-of-the-mill trinket, T-shirt, and souvenir shops typical of resort towns, the number of proper galleries is increasing as Estes Park becomes a more upscale resort.

CRAFT & ART
GALLERIES
The cooperative **Earthwood Artisans** (✉ 145 E. Elkhorn Ave. ☎ 970/586–2151) features the work of stained-glass artists, photographers, jewelers, sculptors, and potters. **Glassworks** (✉ 323 Elkhorn Ave. ☎ 970/586–8619) offers glassblowing demonstrations and sells a rainbow of glass creations. **Michael Ricker Pewter** (✉ 2050 Big Thompson, 2 mi east of town on U.S. 34 ☎ 970/586–2030) gives free tours of its production area and museum, where you can see the world's largest pewter sculpture. **Spectrum** (✉ No. 8 Park Theatre Mall, Elkhorn Ave. ☎ 970/586–2497) sells fine arts and crafts exclusively by Colorado studio artists, including spectacular nature photography, hand-thrown and signed pottery, and hand-turned wood crafts made from mesquite, aspen, or cedar.

GIFTS
The Christmas Shoppe (✉ Park Theatre Mall, Elkhorn Ave. ☎ 970/586–2882) delights children of all ages with every conceivable Noel-related ornament, doll, curio, and knickknacks from around the world.

WESTERN
PARAPHERNALIA
Rustic Mountain Charm (✉ 116, 165, and 344 E. Elkhorn Ave. ☎ 970/586–0512) has local foodstuffs and home accessories with the lodge look, including furniture, quilts, baskets, and throws; one location is exclusively for clothing. Permeated by the pungent aroma of leather, **Stage Western Family Clothing** (✉ 104 Moraine Ave. ☎ 970/586–3430) carries imaginative cowboy hats, boots, and belts.

Rocky Mountain National Park

㉔ *5 mi from Estes Park via U.S. 36 or U.S. 34; 55 mi from Fort Collins via I–25 south and U.S. 34 west.*

A savage clawing of the earth by volcanic uplifts and receding glaciers has resulted in a majestic landscape of three distinct ecosystems in this national park: verdant mountain valleys towering with proud ponderosa pines and Douglas firs; higher and colder subalpine mountains with wind-whipped trees (krummholz) that grow at right angles; and harsh, unforgiving alpine tundra with dollhouse-size versions of familiar plants and wildflowers. The park teems with wildlife, from beaver to bighorn sheep.

Fodor'sChoice ★ **Trail Ridge Road** (U.S. 34—the world's highest continuous paved highway) runs 48 mi across the park and accesses several hikes along its meandering way, through terrain filigreed with silvery streams and turquoise lakes. The views around each bend—of moraines and glaciers, and craggy hills framing emerald meadows carpeted with columbine and Indian paintbrush—are truly awesome: nature's workshop on an epic scale. **Many Parks Curve** affords views of the crest of the Continental Divide and of the **Alluvial Fan,** a huge gash a vicious flood created after an earthen dam broke in 1982. Erosion occurred immediately, rather than over the millions of years that nature usually requires. Trail Ridge Road is open only from June to mid-October. A loop up 11-mi-long, one-way Old Fall River Road to the **Alpine Visitor Center** (11,796-foot elevation) and back down along Trail Ridge Road is a scenic alternative to driving Trail Ridge Road twice. Start at **West Horseshoe Park,** which has the park's largest concentrations of sheep and elk, and head up the paved and gravel Old Fall River Road, passing **Chasm Falls.** Early visitors to the park traveled Old Fall River Road before Trail Ridge Road was built.

Fairly close to the park's entrance through Estes Park is the **Moraine Park Museum,** where lectures, slide shows, and displays explain the park's geology and botany. ⊠ *Bear Lake Rd., off U.S. 36* ☜ *Free* ☼ *May–Sept., daily 9–5.*

Twisting, 9-mi-long **Bear Lake Road** winds past shimmering waterfalls perpetually shrouded with rainbows. The drive offers superlative views of Long's Peak (14,255-foot summit) and the glaciers surrounding Bear Lake. Two free shuttle bus routes operate along Bear Lake Road from mid-June to mid-October. The first runs from near the Fern Lake Trail Head to the Moraine Park Museum and on to Glacier Basin Campground. The second runs from the campground to the Bear Lake Trailhead.

The park has five visitor centers: **Beaver Meadows** (⊠ Park Headquarters, U.S. 36, southwest of Estes Park); **Alpine** (⊠ Trail Ridge Rd., at Fall River Pass); **Lily Lake** (⊠ Rte. 7, south of Estes Park); **Fall River** (⊠ U.S. 34, west of Estes Park); and **Kawuneeche** (⊠ U.S. 34, near Grand Lake). All offer maps, brochures, newsletters, and comprehensive information on the park and its facilities. Check for ranger-led nature programs and for children, activities offered by the Junior Ranger program. ⊠ *Rocky Mountain National Park, Estes Park 80517* ☏ *970/586–1206* ⊕ *www.nps.gov* ☜ *$15 per vehicle for 1- to 7-day pass* ☼ *Year-round.*

Sports & the Outdoors

BICYCLING Mountain biking is not allowed on trails within the park, but you can ride **Trail Ridge Road** for 23 mi from the park entrance at Beaver Meadows to the Alpine Visitors Center. You're rewarded with the fast ride back down. For a more level ride, **Bear Lake Road** has views and less climb.

FISHING With a Colorado license, you can fish in most lakes and streams. Inquire with a ranger. **Estes Angler** arranges guided half- and full-day fly-fishing trips—including horseback and overnight backpacking excursions into the park's quieter regions. ⊠ *338 W. Riverside Dr., Estes Park* ☏ *970/586–2110 or 800/586–2110* ⊕ *www.estesangler.com.*

HIKING There are 78 peaks in the park that rise above 12,000 feet, several of which require no technical skills to reach the summit. Even the summit of Long's Peak, the highest point in the park at 14,255 feet, has a walkable route leading to it. The ease of access to trails makes the park relatively crowded in summer; as many as 800 hikers and climbers have registered to ascend Long's Peak on a single day. The elevation can steal

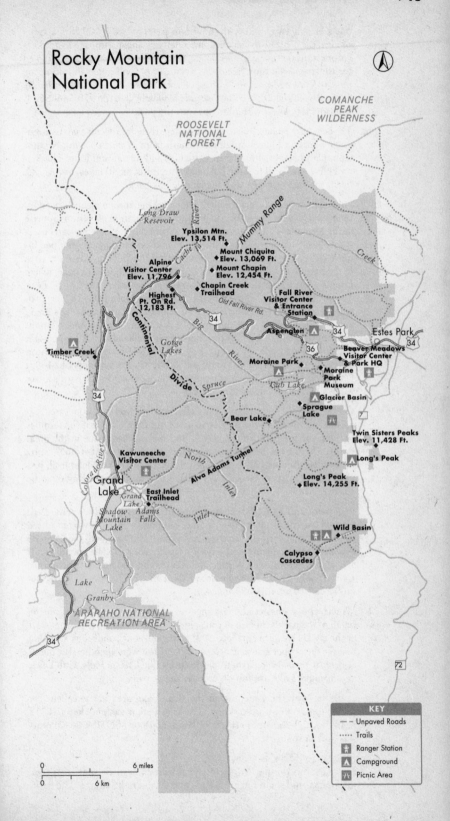

Rocky Mountain National Park

COMANCHE PEAK WILDERNESS

ROOSEVELT NATIONAL FOREST

Long Draw Reservoir

Mummy Range

Cache la River

Ypsilon Mtn.
Elev. 13,514 Ft.

Mount Chiquita
Elev. 13,069 Ft.

Alpine
Visitor Center
Elev. 11,796

Mount Chapin
Elev. 12,454 Ft.

Highest
Pt. On Rd.
12,183 Ft.

Chapin Creek
Trailhead

Old Fall River Rd.

Fall River
Visitor Center
& Entrance
Station

Creek

Continental

Gorge Lakes

34

Aspenglen

34

Estes Park

34

36

Beaver Meadows
Visitor Center
& Park HQ

Timber Creek

Big River

Divide

Spruce

Moraine Park

Moraine
Park
Museum

Club Lake

34

Glacier Basin

Sprague
Lake

Bear Lake

Twin Sisters Peaks
Elev. 11,428 Ft.

Long's Peak

7

Kawuneeche
Visitor Center

North

Alva Adams Tunnel

Inlet

Long's Peak
Elev. 14,255 Ft.

Colorado River

Grand
Lake

East Inlet
Trailhead

Grand
Lake

Inlet

Shadow
Mountain
Lake

Adams
Falls

Wild Basin

Calypso
Cascades

Lake Granby

ARAPAHO NATIONAL RECREATION AREA

34

72

KEY

— · — Unpaved Roads

.... Trails

Ranger Station

Campground

Picnic Area

0 ____ 6 miles

0 ____ 6 km

one's breath away, but with mountain bases above 9,000 feet, ascents of even the 14,000-footers become relatively short climbs. Most hikers ignore trails on the park's west side, leaving the footpaths less trafficked for those seeking more solitude in nature. A good guide to hiking the park is *Rocky Mountain National Park: Classic Hikes and Climbs,* by Gerry Roach (Fulcrum). The **Colorado Mountain Club** (☎ 970/586–6623) sponsors day and overnight trips into the park.

★ The **Bear Lake Nature Trail** is a point of departure for several easy-to-strenuous walks and hikes ranging in length from .6 mi to 8½ mi. A jaunt from **Cub Lake** is of moderate difficulty and just 2.3 mi long. The 8½-mi **Fern Lake Trail** to Bear Lake has waterfalls, small lakes, and views. From the lake you can take the shuttle bus back.

Hikers with the stamina for challenging hiking at high altitude head up
★ **Long's Peak,** 8 mi one-way and an 4,855-foot gain in elevation. Sunrise at the **Keyhole** is a treat, and the views from the top are singularly awesome. Nontechnical access is limited to mid-July to early September. Inquire with a ranger about conditions before starting out. An alternative to the summit of Long's is the 4-mi (one-way) walk to **Chasm Lake,** where Long's is the dramatic backdrop. Go left at the fork in the Long's Peak Trail. A walk to the summits of the **Twin Sisters Peaks** (11,428 feet) provides a strenuous but shorter (3.7-mi one-way) hike than Long's Peak, and has great views of both Long's Peak and the Front Range. A popular but tough hike starts at the **Chapin Pass Trailhead** about 7 mi up Old Fall River Road. It's 3½ mi one-way and a 2,874-foot gain in elevation to the summit of **Ypsilon Mountain;** you'll bag the summits of Mount Chapin and Mount Chiquita on the way. Gaze out across the park's lower valleys before hiking back to the car.

On the west side of the park, the **Colorado River Trail** is a moderate, 3.7-mi one-way walk to the ghost town of **Lulu City,** excellent for families looking for the bighorn sheep, elk, and moose that reside in the area. Part of the trail is the former stagecoach route that went from Granby to Walden. Adams Falls are quickly accessed by the **East Inlet Trail,** just .3 mi one-way from Grand Lake village or 2 mi from the Kawuneeche Visitor Center.

ROCK CLIMBING   Beginners and experts will find enough climbing to fill weeks. **Petit Grepon** and the **Diamond** (the east face of Long's Peak) are two renowned classic climbs. Learn climbing and rappelling technique with the **Colorado Mountain School** during half-day or two-day courses. The friendly staff also arranges introductory trips, full-day climbs, and longer expeditions. Call to book. ⊠ *351 Moraine Ave., Estes Park* ☎ *970/586–5758 or 888/ 267–7783* ⊕ *www.cmschool.com.*

SNOWSHOEING &   Winter offers cross-country skiing and easy to strenuous snowshoeing
NORDIC SKIING   on all of the park's 347 mi of trails, including ski-touring trails that start at the park's western entrance. Ask a ranger about conditions and plan to have the proper gear with you as though you were spending the night. Shorter trips of 1½ to 3 mi to destinations like **Chasm Falls, Cub Lake,** and **Sprague Lake** are fun on a crisp, sunny winter day.

Trails in **Moraine Park** and in the **Bear Lake** area are excellent for snowshoeing and nordic skiing. The **Estes Park Mountain Shop** (⊠ 358 E. Elkhorn Ave., Estes Park ☎ 970/586–6548 or 800/504–6642) rents skis and snowshoes.

Where to Stay & Eat

There are no dining or lodging establishments in the park, so seek sustenance and shelter in Estes Park and Grand Lake village. The park, however, is rich with scenic picnic areas. All have tables and pit or flush toilets.

¢ ✕ **Trail Ridge Store Snack Bar.** At the Alpine Visitor Center on Trail Ridge Road you can get snacks and a quick meal of sandwiches, burgers, and soup. ✉ *Trail Ridge Rd.* ☎ *970/586–3097* ⊟ *AE, D, MC, V* ⊘ *Closed mid-Oct–May.*

CAMPING Five top-notch campgrounds in the park accommodate tents, trailers, and RVs (only two accept reservations; the others fill up on a first come, first serve basis). Backcountry camping requires advance reservations or a day-of-trip permit, so contact **Backcountry Permits, Rocky Mountain National Park** (✉ Beaver Meadows Visitor Center, U.S. 36 southwest of Estes Park ☎ 970/586–1242 ⊘ 7–7) before starting out.

¢ ⛺ **Aspenglen Campground.** Near the Park's east entrance, close to Estes Park, is this forested and quiet campground. The sites fill on a first-come, first-serve basis. All sites accommodate RVs, tents, trailers, or campers. Drive past Fall River Visitor Center on U.S. 34 and turn left at the campground road. Firewood and ice are for sale. ⚐ *Flush toilets, drinking water, fire grates, public telephone* ⇗ *54 sites* ⊞ *$18* ⚐ *Reservations not accepted* ⊟ *No credit cards* ⊘ *Mid-May–late Sept.*

¢ ⛺ **Glacier Basin Campground.** Here you'll be in the shade of lodgepole pines on the banks of Glacier Creek and have access to a network of many popular trails. Rangers come here for campfire programs. All sites accommodate RVs, tents, trailers, or campers. Firewood and ice are for sale here. ⊕ *Drive 5 mi south from U.S. 36 along Bear Lake Rd.* ☎ *800/365–2267* ⊕ *www.reservations.nps.gov* ⚐ *Flush toilets, dump station, drinking water, fire grates, public telephone* ⇗ *150 sites* ⊞ *$18; $35–$65 for group sites* ⚐ *Reservations essential* ⊟ *D, MC, V* ⊘ *June–mid-Sept.*

¢ ⛺ **Long's Peak Campground.** Hikers going up Long's Peak can stay at this tent-only campground. It's also near other trailheads, including Twin Sisters. Sites are filled on a first-come, first-serve basis and are limited to six people. Ice and firewood are sold in summer. ✉ *9 mi south of Estes Park on Rte. 7* ⚐ *Flush toilets, pit toilets, drinking water (mid–May to mid–Sept.), fire grates, ranger station* ⇗ *26 tent sites* ⊞ *$18 per site* ⚐ *Reservations not accepted* ⊟ *No credit cards* ⊘ *Year-round.*

¢ ⛺ **Moraine Park Campground.** This popular campground with ranger-led campfire programs is near hiking trails as well as the activities in Estes Park. The views are of Moraine Park and the peaks beyond. You'll hear the elk bugling if you camp here during September or October. Sites accommodate RVs, tents, trailers, and campers, but are limited to six people (except at group sites). ✉ *Drive south on Bear Lake Road from U.S. 36 ¾ mi to campground entrance* ☎ *800/365–2267* ⊕ *www.reservations.nps.gov* ⚐ *Flush toilets, pit toilets, dump station, drinking water (mid–May to mid–Sept.), fire grates, public telephone* ⇗ *247 sites* ⊞ *$18; $25–$50 for group sites* ⚐ *Reservations essential from mid–May–mid–Sept.* ⊟ *D, MC, V* ⊘ *Year-round.*

¢ ⛺ **Timber Creek Campground.** Anglers love this spot on the Colorado River, 10 mi from Grand Lake village. The campground fills on a first-come, first-serve basis and is near the recreation opportunities in Grand County. In the evening you can sit in on ranger-led campfire programs. All sites accommodate RVs, tents, trailers, or campers and are limited to six people. Firewood is sold here. ✉ *Trail Ridge Rd. 12 mi west of the Alpine Visitor Center or 10 mi north of Grand Lake village* ⚐ *Flush toilets, pit toilets, dump station, drinking water (mid–May to mid–Sept.), fire grates, public telephone* ⇗ *100 sites* ⊞ *$18* ⚐ *Reservations not accepted* ⊟ *No credit cards* ⊘ *Year-round.*

GRAND COUNTY

Grand County is the high country and rolling ranchlands at once. Vistas of the Rockies to the east and south and of the Gore Range to the west seem out of place for these grasslands that the early French explorers named Middle Park. By the time the Moffat Railroad came to Grand County in 1905, ranchers were already living on the flat, open meadows.

Although Grand County is ranching country, the word "range" today evokes more the excellent golf courses instead of the plain where a cowboy herds cattle. The town of Granby has two golf courses, and Grand County hosts several annual tournaments. Summer brings droves of anglers and cyclists, and large-game hunters replace them in the late fall. The area west of Grand Lake along U.S. 40 is marked by a number of small towns with top-class resorts and guest ranches. The entire area is a paradise for golfers, anglers, cyclists, hikers, and winter sports enthusiasts.

Grand Lake

㉕ *54 mi from Estes Park via U.S. 34 (Trail Ridge Rd.—closed in winter); 109 mi from Denver via U.S. 40 and 34.*

Grand Lake village is doubly blessed by its surroundings. It is the western gateway to Rocky Mountain National Park and also sits on the shores of the state's largest natural lake, the highest-altitude yacht anchorage in America. According to Ute legend, the fine mists that shroud the lake at dawn are the risen spirits of women and children whose raft capsized as they were fleeing a marauding party of Cheyennes and Arapahoes. Grand Lake feeds into two much larger man-made reservoirs, Lake Granby and Shadow Mountain Lake, forming the "Great Lakes of Colorado." Even with its wooden boardwalks, Old West–style storefronts, and usual assortment of souvenir shops and motels, the town seems less spoiled than many other resort communities.

en route Even if you're not traveling on to Steamboat Springs or Glenwood Springs, the 69-mi (one-way) **Colorado River Headwaters Scenic & Historic Byway** between Grand Lake and State Bridge is worth a side trip. The route takes you along the Colorado River, past the hot springs, ranches, and reservoirs, through wide spaces with views of mountains, along deep canyons, and through a seemingly incongruous sage-covered desert. Follow U.S. 34 west out of Grand Lake to U.S. 40. Drive west to Kremmling, and turn south on Route 9. Watch for the sign that marks the Trough Road, and turn right. This gravel road snakes along the precipices of Gore Canyon and has turnouts where you can get a good look at the roaring Colorado River in the bottom of the canyon. Continue to the intersection with Route 1 and turn left to go on to State Bridge. From State Bridge you can take Route 131 north to Steamboat Springs, or south to Interstate 70 to Glenwood Springs. This route is not suitable for large RVs.

Sports & the Outdoors

With views of snowy peaks and verdant mountains from any vantage point, Grand Lake village is favored by Coloradans for sailing, canoeing, waterskiing, and fishing on Shadow Mountain Reservoir, Grand Lake, and Lake Granby. During winter, it is *the* snowmobiling capital and ice-fishing destination. No matter what your favorite outdoor activity—even lounging lakeside with a book—Grand Lake is the perfect choice.

Grand Lake Sports (✉ 900 Grand Ave. ☎ 970/627–8124 ⊕ www. grandspiritsports.com) is an all-purpose outfitter that rents snowshoes, bikes, kayaks, canoes, and accessories like kid trailers for bicycles. When they're not at work, staff members are out hiking and biking the region, and therefore give excellent advice about fun outdoor experiences for thrill-seeking adventurers as well as families.

BICYCLING Car traffic can be heavy on U.S. 34, whose shoulders are broad south of Grand Lake village, but are narrow in spots to the north of it. About 170 mi of easy to strenuous mountain-biking trails lace the **Arapahoe National Forest** west of Grand Lake. ⊕ *Drive south on U.S. 34 to County Rd. 4 and turn right. Gates mark the trailheads a few miles in.*

Clutches of road cyclists buzz through Grand Lake on their way up the steep switchbacks of **Trail Ridge Road** (U.S. 34) to **Rock Cut** in Rocky Mountain National Park. The 28-mi route climbs 3100 feet from Grand Lake. The route from Grand Lake south to U.S. 40 west and then north on Route 125 to **Willow Creek Pass** is over rolling terrain and climbs 1770 feet to the summit through quiet aspen and pine forests. You'll encounter little traffic, and moose and deer are often just off the road.

BIRD-WATCHING The islands in Shadow Mountain Reservoir and Lake Granby are wildlife refuges. The best way to get close to the osprey that nest on the islands as well as other migrating birds is by canoe or foot trail. Be sure to take binoculars, since you are not permitted to land on the islands. **East Shore Trail** and **Knight Ridge Trail** will take you along the shores of Shadow Mountain Reservoir and Lake Granby for spotting opportunities. ⊕ *Access trails either from Grand Lake village between Grand Lake and Shadow Mountain Reservoir, or from the Green Ridge Campground at the south end of Shadow Mountain Reservoir.*

BOATING & There's plenty of water to share here. Anglers enjoy plentiful catches of
FISHING trout, mackinaw, and kokanee salmon; recreational sailors and waterskiers ply acres of water; and paddlers still get to canoe in peace. Ice fishers will not want to miss the big contest held the first weekend in February on Lake Granby. Contestants must catch five different species of fish, and winners collect from the booty of $20,000 in cash and prizes. **Beacon Landing** rents 20-, 24-, and 29-foot pontoon boats and fishing equipment, including ice augers and ice rods. ✉ *1 mi off Hwy. 34 on County Rd. 64, drive south 5 mi on U.S. 34 to County Rd. 64 and turn left* ☎ *970/627–3671.*

Call the **Trail Ridge Marina** (✉ Shadow Mountain Lake, 4 mi south of Grand Lake on U.S. 34 ☎ 970/627–3586) for information on renting pontoon boats by the hour.

GOLF **Grand Lake Golf Course** is an 18-hole course 8,420 feet above sea level. ✉ *County Rd. 48, drive north on U.S. 34 about ½ mi and turn left at the sign* ☎ *970/627–8008.*

HIKING Arapahoe National Recreation Area and Rocky Mountain National Park have trails ranging from easy to strenuous. Some trails into Rocky Mountain National Park start at the edge of Grand Lake village. If you hike in the backcountry, be sure you're outfitted for adverse weather. At the southeast end of Lake Granby, the **Indian Peaks Wilderness Area** is great for hiking. You can access the wilderness area by driving south from Grand Lake village on U.S. 34 to County Road 6. Follow the lakeshore road about 10 mi to the parking area. The Forest Service's

Sulphur Ranger District administers the wilderness and has information on trails and regulations. ✉ *9 Ten Mile Drive, Granby* ⌂ *Box 10, Granby 90446* ☏ *970/887–4100* ⊕ *www.fs.fed.us/arnf/districts/srd/index.htm* ⊙ *Weekdays 8–4:30.*

The **East Inlet Loop** from the end of the Grand Lake village boardwalk takes you on an easy ½-mi walk to scenic **Adams Falls,** just beyond the end of Grand Lake. The area around **Monarch Lake** is popular with families for the selection of trails and the views of the Indian Peaks and the Continental Divide. Trails range in distance from 1.5 to 10.8 mi one-way. The loop around Monarch Lake is 3.8 mi. ✛ *Drive south on U.S. 34 to County Rd. 6 and follow the road 10 mi to the trailhead.*

HORSEBACK RIDING For scenic and relaxing early morning breakfast rides, guided fishing trips to remote streams and lakes, winter sleigh rides, guided rides into the wilderness or Rocky Mountain National Park, or private camping trips, the **Sombrero Ranch** (☏ 970/627–3514 ⊕ www.sombrero.com) will make all the arrangements. The ranch is at the west end of Grand Lake village.

NORDIC SKIING & SNOWSHOEING When crystalline snow glitters under the clear blue sky, it's time to strap on skis or snowshoes and traverse the hiking trails in Rocky Mountain National Park, the Arapahoe National Recreation Area, and the Indian Peaks Wilderness Area. The **Grand Lake Recreation District** (☏ 970/627–8872) has 18 mi (29 km) of cross-country ski trails with vistas of the Never Summer Range and the Continental Divide. **Never Summer Mountain Products** (✉ 919 Grand Ave. ☏ 970/627–3642) rents cross-country skis and snowshoes.

SNOWMOBILING Many consider Grand Lake to be Colorado's snowmobiling capital, with more than 300 mi of trails (150 mi groomed), many winding through virgin forest. There are several rental and guide companies in the area. **Grand Lake Motor Sports** (✉ 10438 Hwy. 34 ☏ 970/627–3806). **Grand Lake Snowmobile Rental** (✉ 143 County Road 48 ☏ 970/627–8502 or 800/355–2733). **On The Trail** (✉ 902 Grand Ave. ☏ 970/627–8866 or 888/627–2429). **Spirit Lake Rentals** (✉ 829 Grand Ave. ☏ 970/627–9288).

Where to Stay & Eat

$–$$ ✗ **Mountain Inn.** Fine family-style meals are served in this rustic, vertical-log restaurant. Á-la-carte selections are also available. The food ranges from Rocky Mountain oysters to flavorful prime rib, beer-batter shrimp, and salmon and trout specialties. The real standouts are the fried chicken and chicken-fried steak, cooked in cast-iron skillets for homemade flavor. ✉ *612 Grand Ave.* ☏ *970/627–3385* ▭ *D, MC, V.*

¢–$$ ✗ **Sagebrush BBQ & Grill.** Barbecue ribs, chicken, and catfish draws local and out-of-town attention to this homey café. Meals can be sized appropriately for larger or smaller appetites. Comforting sides such as baked beans, corn bread, cole slaw, and potatoes top off the large plates. ✉ *1101 Grand Ave.* ☏ *970/627–1404* ▭ *AE, D, DC, MC, V.*

★ $ ✗▥ **Rapids Lodge.** This handsome lodgepole-pine structure is one of the oldest hotels in the area. The seven lodge rooms—each with ceiling fan—are frilly, with dust ruffle quilts, floral wallpaper and fabrics, and such mismatched furnishings as old plush chartreuse armchairs, claw-foot tubs, and carved-hardwood beds. Condos, all with kitchenettes, are modern, but with less fussy furnishings. The delightful restaurant ($$–$$$; reservations advised) is Grand Lake's most romantic for fine dining, with stained glass, timber beams, and views of the roaring Tonahatu River. The specialty is Rapids Tournedo—an eight-ounce filet mignon. The chefs excel with fish, elk, seafood, and steak, too. ✉ *209 Rapids La., 80447* ☏ *970/627–3707* 🖶 *970/627–8573* ⊕ *www.rapidslodge.com* ⇗ 7 *rooms, 32 suites and condos* ⚭ *Restaurant, some kitchenettes, cable TV, bar* ⊟ *AE, MC, V* ⊘ *Closed Apr. and Nov.*

$–$$ 🏨 **Western Riviera.** This friendly motel books up far in advance, thanks to its low prices, affable owners, and comfortable accommodations. Even the cheapest units—although small—are pleasant, done in mauve and earth tones. All rooms face the lake. ✉ *419 Garfield Ave., 80447* ☎ *970/627–3580* 🖷 *970/627–3320* ⊕ *www.westernriv.com* ↩ *15 rooms* ⚭ *Cable TV, hot tub* ⊟ *MC, V.*

¢–$$ 🏨 **Mountain Lakes Lodge.** The scent of the pine forest welcomes you to the Mawhorters' charming and comfortable log cabins that accommodate two to six people. David built the furniture himself, and Karen whimsically decorated the cabins with animal and sports themes—down to the curtains and drawer pulls. The Little Log House has three bedrooms and can house seven people. Some cabins have private decks and gas stoves. All have fully equipped kitchenettes, with microwaves, coffee makers, and toasters. Dogs are enthusiastically welcomed. ✉ *10480 U.S. 34* 🕭 *Box 160, 80447* ☎ *970/627–8448* ⊕ *www.mountainlakeslodge. com* ↩ *10 cabins, 1 house* ⚭ *Kitchenettes, cable TV, fishing, playground; no a/c, no room phones* ⊟ *MC, V.*

$ 🏨 **Best Value Inn Bighorn Lodge.** This downtown motel has a rustic look, which helps it blend in with its surroundings. Rooms are spotless and come with ceiling fans and soundproof walls. ✉ *613 Grand Ave., 80447* ☎ *970/627–8101* ↩ *20 rooms* ⚭ *Cable TV, hot tub* ⊟ *AE, D, DC, MC, V.*

$ 🏨 **Grand Lake Lodge.** This retreat built of lodgepole pine in 1921 calls itself "Colorado's favorite front porch," thanks to its stupendous views of Grand and Shadow Mountain lakes. The restaurant offers the same gorgeous vistas, in addition to fish and wild game specialties. Cabins are cozy, clean, and comfortably but simply furnished—no TVs or phones. The resort abuts Rocky Mountain National Park and has foot-trail access to the park. Stables are available. 🕭 *Box 569, 80447* ✛ *Off U.S. 34, 1 mi north of Grand Lake* ☎ *970/627–3967* 🖷 *970/627– 9495* ⊕ *www.grandlakelodge.com* ↩ *56 cabin units* ⚭ *Restaurant, pool, hot tub, horseback riding, bar; no room phones, no room TVs* ⊟ *AE, D, MC, V* ⊘ *Closed mid-Sept.–May.*

CAMPING ⚠ **Arapahoe National Recreation Area.** Five lakeside campgrounds—
¢ Stillwater, Cutthroat Bay, Green Ridge, Arapahoe Bay, and Willow Creek—keep you close to recreational activities. ✉ *South of Grand Lake on Willow Creek Reservoir, Lake Granby, or Shadow Mountain Reservoir* ☎ *970/887–0056 or 877/444–6777* ⊕ *www.reserveusa.com* ⚭ *Flush toilets, pit toilets, dump station, drinking water, fire grates, picnic tables, public telephone, ranger station* ↩ *21 partial hook-ups (water and electricity) at Stillwater, 272 multiuse sites, 29 tent sites, 4 group sites* 🖾 *$5 vehicle entrance fee, partial hook-ups $21, tent sites $16* ⚭ *Reservations essential mid-May–early Sept.* ⊟ *AE, D, MC, V* ⊘ *Mid-May–Sept.*

Cabin & Condo Rentals

RE/MAX Resorts of Grand County (🕭 Box 39, Grand Lake 80447 ☎ 970/ 627–1131 or 877/982–2155 ⊕ www.grandlakerentalproperties.com) arranges rentals around Grand Lake.

Nightlife & the Arts

The hands-down local favorite is the **Stagecoach Inn** (✉ 920 Grand Ave., on the Boardwalk ☎ 970/627–8079), as much for its cheap booze and good eats as for the live entertainment on weekends.

The professional **Rocky Mountain Repertory Theatre** (☎ 970/627–3421 ⊕ www.rkymtnhi.com/rkymtnrep) stages performances of popular productions like *Fiddler on the Roof* and *The Last Five Years* in an old log building in the village.

Shopping

Shopping in Grand Lake tends toward the usual panoply of resort-town souvenir shops, although a handful stand out. **Grand Lake Art Gallery** (⊠ 1117 Grand Ave. ☎ 970/627–3104) purveys superlative weavings, pottery, stained glass, gourds, and landscapes, primarily by regional artists. **Humphrey's Cabin Fever** (⊠ 1100 Grand Ave. ☎ 970/627–8939), the log building with the green roof, sells upscale cabin collectibles, rustic home furnishings, clothes, bedding, and ceramics in all price ranges. For outdoor gear and clothing, head for **Never Summer Mountain Products** (⊠ 919 Grand Ave. ☎ 970/627–3642), which also rents cross-country skis and snowshoes.

Granby

26 *20 mi from Grand Lake via U.S. 34 south*

After Granby Hillyer platted Granby in 1913, the county became one of the largest lettuce-producing regions in the United States—using the railroad as transport—until a blight infected the soil. Today, Granby (elevation 7935 feet) is still the town that serves the working ranches in Grand County, and you'll see plenty of cowboys, especially if you go to one of the weekly rodeos in Granby in summer. The town is 15 minutes from Rocky Mountain National Park and 15 minutes from the ski resorts Winter Park and Mary Jane and the mountain biking trails of the Fraser Valley.

Sports & the Outdoors

The *National Geographic Trails Illustrated Map* No. 503 (Winter Park/Grand Lake) has excellent coverage of hiking and biking trails in the area with information about regulations.

The **Greater Granby Area Chamber of Commerce** (⊠ 81 W. Jasper ☎ 970/887–2311) has a free *Grand County Trail Map* that shows trails for hiking, biking, horseback riding, snowmobiling, and snowshoeing as well as information about regulations.

Watch cowboys demonstrate their rodeo skills at the **Flying Heels Rodeo Arena** (☎ 970/887–2311) in Granby every Saturday night in June. The rodeo finale and fireworks show is on the Saturday nearest the Fourth of July holiday. Contact the Greater Granby Chamber of Commerce for information.

BIRD-WATCHING The reservoir at **Windy Gap Wildlife Viewing Area** is on the waterfowl migration route for geese, pelicans, swans, eagles, and osprey. The park has information kiosks, viewing scopes, viewing blinds, a picnic area, and a nature trail that's also wheelchair accessible. ⊠ *2 mi west of Granby on U.S. 40 where it meets Rte. 125* ☎ *970/725–6200* ☉ *May–Sept., daily dawn to dusk.*

FISHING Although Shadow Mountain Reservoir, Lake Granby, and Grand Lake yield big catches, including kokanee salmon and mackinaws, serious fly fishers head to the rivers and streams of Grand County for relaxing solitude with excellent fishing in riparian areas. Angling on the **Fraser River** begins downstream from Tabernash and is not appropriate for families or dogs. At **Willow Creek** you'll bag plenty of rainbow trout and brookies. The **Colorado River** between Shadow Mountain Dam and Lake Granby and downstream from Hot Sulphur Springs is open to anglers. The **Sulphur Ranger District** of the U.S. Forest Service provides fishing information and regulations. ⊠ *9 Ten Mile Dr., Granby*

80446 ☎ 970/887–4100 ⊕ *www.fs.fed.us/arnf/districts/srd/index.htm*
🕐 *Weekdays 8–4:30.*

GOLF The scenery and wildlife viewing opportunities at Grand County's four
golf courses make good excuses for being distracted during a critical putt
or drive. You can expect secluded greens, expansive vistas, and a deer
or grouse interrupting the game at these world-class courses.

★ Craig Stadler designed the challenging par-71 course at **Grand Elk Ranch
& Club.** Greens fees include a cart and use of the locker room. ⊠ *1310
10 Mile Dr., drive south on U.S. 40 to 10 Mile Dr. and turn right*
☎ *970/887–9122 or 877/389–9333* ⊕ *www.grandelk.com.*

The **Sol Vista Golf Club** is tucked back in a valley at the end of a gravel
road, entirely within the mountains and meadows, and has roomy practice facilities as well as a large deck at the clubhouse. ⊹ *Drive 2 mi south
on U.S. 40 from Granby to the Inn at Silver Creek. Turn left and drive
past the lodge to the gravel road marked by the sign. Follow road about
3 mi into the valley* ☎ *970/887–2709 or 800/405–7669* ⊕ *www.
solvistagolf.com.*

HIKING There is plenty of mountain hiking around Grand Lake and in Rocky
Mountain National Park. Arapahoe National Forest and the Indian Peaks
Wilderness Area are accessible east from Tabernash or from the south
side of Lake Granby.

MOUNTAIN Indian Peaks Wilderness Area is not open to mountain biking, but there
BIKING are moderate and difficult trails in the Arapahoe National Forest. Grand
County has several hundred miles of easy to expert-level bike trails, many
of which are former railroad rights-of-way and logging roads. The **Doe
Creek Trail, Strawberry Trail**, and **West Strawberry Trail** (ending at Strawberry Lake) network is a good workout of steep uphill climbs (and descents) with deadfall and plenty of forest scenery. ⊹ *From Tabernash
take County Rd. 84 (Meadow Creek Rd.) to the gate at the trailhead.*

Where to Stay & Eat

Dining establishments in Granby cater effectively to both ranchers and
tourists. There are not many eateries in town, but you'll find bakeries
and cafés, robust coffee and espresso drinks, and a handful of restaurants that serve dependably good, filling meals. Granby has a few motels, but the lodgings listed here are generally north and west of town.

$–$$ ✕ **Longbranch Restaurant.** This popular Western-style coffee shop has a
warming fireplace, rustic wood interior, and wagon-wheel chandeliers.
The menu spans German, Mexican, Continental, and American cuisine,
and not surprisingly, the quality is uneven. Stick to what the German
owners do best—goulash, schnitzel, sausages, and sauerbraten, and
heavenly homemade spaetzle. The bar serves many domestic and foreign beers as well as a few microbrews. ⊠ *185 E. Agate Ave. (U.S. 40)*
☎ *970/887–2209* ☰ *MC, V.*

$–$$ ✕ **Silver Spur Steakhouse and Saloon.** When locals can't decide what
they're craving, they come here for Mexican dishes made with succulent pulled chicken or ground beef; crispy fish and chips; and daily specials like fried chicken and beef and vegetable soup. It's a comfortable,
roomy setting with uncluttered neo-Western decor. Friday and Saturday
feature Alaskan King Crab, lobster tails, and prime rib. A well-stocked
sports bar in back always has a game on. ⊠ *15 E. Agate (U.S. 40)* ☎ *970/
887–1411* ☰ *AE, D, DC, MC, V.*

★ $$$$ ▥ **C Lazy U Guest Ranch.** This deluxe guest ranch attracts an international clientele, including both Hollywood royalty and the real thing.
You enjoy your own personal horse, luxurious Western-style accom-

modations (with humidifiers), fine meals, live entertainment, and any outdoor activity you can dream up—it's the ultimate in hedonism without ostentation. The instructors are top-notch, the ratio of guests to staff is nearly one to one, and the children's programs are unbeatable. The minimum stay is a week in summer and two nights in winter. All meals are included. ⌖ *Box 379, Granby 80446* ☎ *970/887–3344* ≜ *970/887– 3917* ⊕ *www.clazyu.com* ⇄ *19 rooms, 20 cabins* ♨ *Restaurant, 2 tennis courts, pool, gym, hot tub, sauna, fishing, horseback riding, racquetball, cross-country skiing, bar, children's programs* ▤ *No credit cards* ☉ *Late May–mid-Oct. and mid-Dec.–mid-Jan.* ⊘| *FAP.*

Hot Sulphur Springs

㉗ *10 mi from Grandby via U.S. 40.*

The county seat, Hot Sulphur Springs (population 512), is a faded resort town whose hot springs were once the destination for trains packed with people, including plenty of Hollywood types in the 1950s.

Soak or get a pampering spa treatment at the newly renovated **Hot Sulphur Springs Resort & Spa,** which has 22 pools. ⊠ *U.S. 40* ☎ *970/725– 3306 or 800/510–6235* ⊕ *www.hotsulphursprings.com* ✎ *$15.50* ☉ *Daily 8 AM–10 PM.*

The old Hot Sulphur School is now the **Grand County Museum.** Artifacts depict Grand County history, including the original settlers 9,000 years ago, the role of pioneer women, and the archaeology of Windy Gap. Photographs show life in the early European settlements, and the original county courthouse and jail are on the site. ⊠ *U.S. 40* ☎ *970/725– 3939* ✎ *$3* ☉ *Call for hrs.*

Kremmling, 17 mi farther west, is known as a sportsman's paradise for its year-round recreation, including mountain biking, river rafting, hunting, fishing, and cross-country skiing.

Where to Stay & Eat

¢ ✕▥ **Riverside Hotel.** Colorado is full of fun and funky finds, such as this 1903 hotel that you enter through a jungle of plants. The lobby, dominated by a magnificent fieldstone fireplace with cluttered mantel, leads into a grand old mirrored bar and a cozy dining room ($$) with a huge potbellied stove, a piano, landscape paintings, and views of the Colorado River. Steaks are simple but well prepared, and fish is fresh as can be. The guest rooms are filled with iron or oak beds, floral quilts, heavy oak dressers or armoires, and washbasins or sinks. Corner rooms are the sunniest and most spacious. ⊠ *509 Grand Ave., Hot Sulphur Springs 80451* ☎ *970/725–3589* ⇄ *17 rooms with shared baths* ♨ *Restaurant, bar* ▤ *No credit cards.*

$$$$ ▥ **Latigo Ranch.** Considerably more down-to-earth than many other Colorado guest ranches, Latigo has a caring staff that does everything it can to give you an authentic ranch experience. Accommodations are in comfortable, carpeted, one- to three-bedroom contemporary log cabins, fitted with wood-burning stoves. Although providing fewer amenities than comparable properties, the ranch offers views of the Indian Peaks range, complete seclusion (17 mi—and 30 minutes on heart-stopping roads—to the nearest town), and superb cross-country trails. Owner Jim Yost was an anthropologist, and Randy George, a chemical engineer, now engineers the "nouvelle ranch cuisine." Remember to bring your own beer, as the Latigo doesn't have an alcohol license. ⊠ *County Rd. 1911, Box 237, Kremmling 80459* ☎ *970/724–9008 or 800/227–9655* ⊕ *www.latigotrails.com* ⇄ *10 cabins* ♨ *Dining room, pool, hot tub, fishing, horseback riding, cross-country skiing, tobogganing, recreation*

room, laundry facilities ▭ *No credit cards* ⊙ *Closed Apr.–May and mid-Oct.–mid-Dec.* ⎟◯⎟ *FAP.*

NORTH CENTRAL COLORADO A TO Z

To research prices, get advice from other travelers, and book travel arrangements, visit www.fodors.com.

AIRPORTS & TRANSFERS
Commercial passenger carriers serve north central Colorado through Denver International Airport (DIA), 23 mi northeast of downtown Denver. Granby, Fort Collins, and Boulder have municipal airports but no commercial service.

DIA's Ground Transportation Information Center assists visitors with car rentals, door-to-door shuttles, public transportation, wheelchair services, charter buses, and limousine services. Boulder is approximately 45 mi (45 minutes–1 hour) from DIA; Granby approximately 110 mi (a little more than 2 hours); Fort Collins approximately 80 mi (1.25–1.5 hours); and Estes Park approximately 80 mi (about 2 hours).

Estes Park Shuttle serves Estes Park and Rocky Mountain National Park from Denver, DIA, and Boulder. Super Shuttle serves Boulder, and Shamrock Airport Shuttle serves Fort Collins. Home James serves Granby, Grand Lake, and the guest ranches.

▪ **Airport & Shuttle Information Denver International Airport** ⊠ 8500 Peña Blvd., Denver ☎ 303/342-2000 ⊕ www.flydenver.com. **Estes Park Shuttle** ☎ 970/586-5151. **Ground Transportation Information Center** ☎ 800/247-2336 or 303/342-4059. **Super Shuttle** ☎ 303/227-0000 Boulder. **Home James** ☎ 970/726-5060 or 800/359-7536. **Shamrock Airport Shuttle** ☎ 970/482-0505.

BUS TRAVEL
Greyhound Lines serves most of the major towns in the region. The expansive network of the Regional Transportation District (RTD) includes service from Denver and Denver International Airport to and within Boulder, Lyons, Niwot, Nederland, and the Eldora Ski Resort. Transfort serves Fort Collins's main thoroughfares.

▪ **Greyhound Lines** ☎ 800/229-9424 ⊕ www.greyhound.com. **Regional Transportation District (RTD)** ☎ 303/299-6000 or 800/366-7433 ⊕ www.rtd-Denver.com. **Transfort** ☎ 970/221-6620 ⊕ fcgov.com/transfort.

CAR RENTAL
Several car rental agencies have offices in Boulder and Fort Collins.

▪ **Boulder Contacts Avis** ☎ 303/499-1136 or 800/831-2847 ⊕ www.avis.com. **Budget** ☎ 303/341-2277 or 800/527-7000 ⊕ www.budget.com. **Enterprise** ☎ 303/449-9466 or 800/736-8222 ⊕ www.enterprise.com. **Hertz** ☎ 303/413-8023 or 800/654-3131 ⊕ www.hertz.com.

▪ **Fort Collins Contacts Avis** ☎ 970/229-9115 or 800/831-2847 ⊕ www.avis.com. **Enterprise** ☎ 970/224-2592 or 800/736-8222 ⊕ www.enterprise.com.

CAR TRAVEL
Interstate 25, the most direct route from Denver to Fort Collins, is the north–south artery that connects the cities in the urban corridor along the Front Range. From Denver, U.S. 36 runs through Boulder, Lyons, and Estes Park to Rocky Mountain National Park. The direct route from Denver to Grand County is Interstate 70 west to U.S. 40 (Empire exit) and to U.S. 34. If you are driving directly to Fort Collins or Estes Park and Rocky Mountain National Park from Denver International Airport, the E-470 tollway connects DIA's Peña Boulevard to Interstate 25. Expect extensive road construction along the northern Front Range; arte-

rial routes, state highways, and city streets are being rebuilt to accommodate increasing traffic in the urban corridor. Bicyclists are common except on arteries; state law gives them the same rights and holds them to the same obligations as any other vehicle. U.S. 36 between Boulder and Estes Park is heavily traveled, especially on summer weekends, and public parking in Estes Park fills up fast. Colorado routes 119, 72, and 7 have much less traffic.

Gasoline and service are available in all larger towns and cities in the region. Although CDOT plows roads efficiently, a winter snowstorm can slow traffic with wet, slushy, or icy conditions. A cell phone is recommended, since some mountain roads have long, uninhabited stretches. 🚗 **AAA Colorado** ☎ 303/753-8800. **CDOT Road Information** ☎ 303/639-1111 or 877/315-7623 ⊕ www.dot.state.co.us, www.cotrip.org. **Colorado State Patrol** ☎ 303/239-4500 Ext. *277 (cellular). **Rocky Mountain National Park Road Information** ☎ 970/586-1333.

EMERGENCIES
🚑 Ambulance or Police **Emergencies** ☎ 911.

🚑 24-Hour Medical Care **Boulder Community Hospital** ✉ 1100 Balsam Ave., Boulder ☎ 303/440-2273 ⊕ www.bch.org. **Estes Park Medical Center** ✉ 555 Prospect Ave., Estes Park ☎ 970/586-2317 ⊕ www.epmedcenter.com. **Poudre Valley Hospital** ✉ 1024 S. Lemay Ave., Fort Collins ☎ 970/495-7000 ⊕ www.pvhs.org. **Granby Medical Center** ✉ 480 E. Agate (U.S. 40), Granby ☎ 970/887-2117 ⊕ www.summitmedctr.org.

LODGING
CAMPING Campgrounds in the region are developed, scenic, and quiet, particularly within Rocky Mountain National Park, the Arapahoe National Recreation Area, and the Roosevelt National Forest. There are private campgrounds throughout the area, and both the National Forest Service and Rocky Mountain National Park administer many campgrounds as well as backcountry camping, which requires permits.
🏕 **National Recreation Reservation Service** ☎ 877/444-6777 ⊕ www.reserveusa.com. **Rocky Mountain National Park** ☎ 800/365-2267 ⊕ www.reservations.nps.gov.

MEDIA
NEWSPAPERS & In Boulder, the *Daily Camera* covers news and events. The paper's Friday
MAGAZINES section has listings of exhibits, concerts, and restaurants. The *Colorado Daily* also covers local entertainment. In Grand County, *Ski-Hi News* and *Friday's Daily Tribune* report news as well as events of interest to visitors. Grand County's *Trails* is a seasonal publication tailored to tourists. The *Coloradoan* is the Fort Collins news daily with entertainment listings. Rocky Mountain National Park publishes *High Country Headlines*. The *Trail Gazette* in Estes Park includes an entertainment section every Friday.

TELEVISION & The main national networks and local evening and nightly news shows
RADIO are carried on Denver channels, 2, 4, 7, and 9 in north central Colorado, including Grand County. Channels 6 and 12 are public broadcasting stations. Greeley's KUNC (FM 91.5) broadcasts National Public Radio's syndicated news and entertainment programs across the northern Front Range and also has the best local news coverage, plus a Friday entertainment segment. Denver's wittiest morning show is on KIMN (FM 100.3). For classical music, tune to KVOD (FM 90.1). In Grand County, AM 930 covers local news and events.

SPORTS & THE OUTDOORS
FISHING You'll need a license to fish.
🎣 The **Colorado Division of Wildlife** ✉ 6060 Broadway, Denver 80216 ☎ 303/297-1192 ⊕ www.wildlife.state.co.us.

TAXIS
🚖 **Boulder Yellow Cab** ☎ 303/442-2277. **Shamrock Taxi** ✉ Fort Collins ☎ 970/482-0505.

TRAIN TRAVEL
Amtrak provides all passenger rail service to and within north central Colorado. The Chicago–San Francisco *California Zephyr* stops in downtown Denver, in Winter Park/Fraser, and in Granby, once each day in both directions.
🚂 **Amtrak** ☎ 800/872-7245, 303/534-2812 in Denver ⊕ www.amtrak.com.

VISITOR INFORMATION
🏛 **Boulder Convention & Visitors Bureau** ✉ 2440 Pearl St., Boulder 80302 ☎ 303/442-2911 or 800/444-0447 🖨 303/938-2098 ⊕ www.bouldercoloradousa.com. **Lyons Chamber of Commerce** 🖉 Box 426, Lyons 80540 ☎ 303/823-5215. **Estes Park Area Chamber of Commerce** ✉ 500 Big Thompson Ave., Estes Park 80517 ☎ 970/586-4431 or 800/443-7837 🖨 970/586-2816 ⊕ www.estesparkresort.com. **Fort Collins Area Convention & Visitors Bureau** ✉ 3745 E. Prospect Rd. #200, Fort Collins 80525 ☎ 970/491-3388 or 800/274-3678 🖨 970/491-3389 ⊕ www.ftcollins.com. **Granby Chamber of Commerce** ✉ 81 W. Jasper Ave. 🖉 Box 35, Granby 80446 ☎ 970/887-2311 or 800/325-1661 🖨 970/887-3895 ⊕ www.granbychamber.com. **Grand Lake Chamber of Commerce** 🖉 Box 57, Grand Lake 80447 ☎ 970/627-3372 or 800/531-1019 🖨 970/627-8007 ⊕ www.grandlakechamber.com. **Nederland Area Chamber of Commerce** 🖉 Box 85, Nederland 80466 ☎ 303/258-3936 or 800/221-0044 ⊕ www.nederlandchamber.org.

I-70 & THE HIGH ROCKIES

FODOR'S CHOICE

B&Bs on North Main Street, *Breckenridge*

Ice Palace Inn, *Leadville*

Loveland Ski Area, *Georgetown*

Mt. Evans Scenic and Historic Drive, *Idaho Springs*

Ski Tip Lodge, *Keystone*

Skiing Aspen Highlands, *Aspen*

Skiing the Back Bowls, *Vail*

HIGHLY RECOMMENDED

SIGHTS   international Pack Burro Race, *Leadville*

Phoenix Gold Mine, *Idaho Springs*

St. Mary's Glacier, *Idaho Springs*

OUTDOORS   Boating on Lake Dillon, *Dillon/Silverthorne*

Golf at Keystone River Course, *Keystone*

Horseback Riding in Steamboat Springs

Mountain Biking in Winter Park

Whitewater Rafting in Breckenridge

Many other great hotels and restaurants enliven this area. For other favorites, look for the black stars as you read the chapter.

Jad Davenport,
Lois Friedland
& Jeanne
McDonald

FEARLESSLY SLICING THROUGH THE CONTINENTAL DIVIDE, Interstate 70 passes through or near many of Colorado's most fabled resorts and towns: Aspen, Vail, Breckenridge, Steamboat, Keystone, Snowmass, Copper Mountain, Beaver Creek, Winter Park. True powder hounds intone those names like a mantra to appease the snow gods, speaking in hushed tones of the gnarly mogul runs and wide-open bowls on top of the world. Here is the image that lingers when most people think of Colorado: a snowglobe come to life, with picture-postcard mining towns and faux-Tyrolean villages framed by cobalt skies and ice-capped peaks. To those in the know, Colorado is just as breathtaking the rest of the year, when meadows are woven with larkspur and columbine, the maroon mountains flecked with the jade of juniper and the white of aspen.

Like most of Colorado, the High Rockies blend old and new. It is old mining towns like Leadville, whose muddy streets still ring with lusty laughter from bars and saloons. Here flamboyant millionaires built grandiose monuments to themselves before dying penniless. The region is also modern resorts such as Vail, whose founding just over three decades ago involved monumental risks (and monumental egos). The High Rockies is fur trappers and fur-clad models, rustlers and Rastafarians, heads of cattle and heads of state. One thing links all the players together: a love of the wide-open spaces. Here, those spaces are as vast as the sky.

Most visitors on their way to the magnificent ski resorts along I–70 whiz through the Eisenhower Tunnel and cross the Continental Divide without paying much attention to the extraordinary engineering achievements that facilitate their journey. The highway and the tunnel are tributes to human ingenuity and endurance: before their completion in the 1970s, crossing the High Rockies evoked the long, arduous treks of the pioneers.

Exploring the High Rockies

West of Denver, I–70 takes you through a series of ecosystems that mimic with altitude what typically comes with latitude. The vanilla-scented ponderosa pines in the foothills melt into stands of spruce and lodgepole pines as the road begins to rise. These taper out around 11,200 feet when you reach that magical threshold known as the timberline, where alpine tundra takes over. In terms of climate, in 40 mi you have effectively driven from Denver to Nome, Alaska.

About the Restaurants

It's easy to work up an appetite in the High Rockies, whether you are skiing tree glades in the morning or hiking through alpine meadows in the afternoon. Part of your planning for any trip into the mountains involves what to do for lunch, as there aren't many options in out-of-the-way destinations. Your best bet is to hit a deli in downtown Denver before you leave or stop at a side street sandwich shop in one of the towns along the way. Dining is casual in this part of the state. You won't find the wide variety of cuisines you would in Denver, but crackling fireplaces and tree-lined vistas will more than make up for it. Although most menus feature meat, vegetarian options are becoming more common, especially in the resort towns. Before you tackle the winding road back to your hotel, remember that at this altitude, every alcoholic drink has the impact of two at sea level.

About the Hotels

From rustic cabins made of lodgepole pines to lavish resorts that look as if they were built by Swiss or Austrian architects (and some were), you can find a little bit of everything in the High Rockies. Bed-and-breakfasts are a popular option, especially in small towns. Resorts naturally feature more upscale accommodations, either in the form of all-inclusive hotels or self-catered condominiums. When booking through a central reservation office, as is the practice for most resorts, remember to have the staff spell out exactly what is included. Some condos don't include maid service, linen changes, or other services that are taken for granted at standard hotels. Keep in mind that the best deals usually involve ski packages.

WHAT IT COSTS				
	$$$$	$$$	$$	$	¢
RESTAURANTS	over $25	$19–$25	$13–$18	$8–$12	under $8
HOTELS	over $200	$151–$200	$111–$150	$70–$110	under $70

Restaurant prices are for a main course at dinner, excluding sales tax of 6.75%–8%. Hotel prices are for two people in a standard double room in high season, excluding service charges and 5.4%–9.8% tax.

Timing

You can't go wrong when it comes to picking a season to visit the High Rockies, partly because the weather changes so frequently. Where else can you lounge around in shorts in the middle of February or carve some turns through the snow in the middle of July?

Although summer and winter are the most popular times to enjoy the High Rockies, many are put off by the traffic snarls that can double the time required for trips up and down I–70. Spring and fall, when far fewer people venture in this direction, are much calmer. In the off-season the mountains take on completely different moods. If you don't expect the brilliant foliage of New England, you won't be disappointed by the fiery shimmer of the aspens in the fall. This usually begins in late September, about the same time snow starts sticking to the highest peaks. And nothing beats spring skiing, when you can meander down a snow-covered trail in the blazing sun. Wear sunblock or you'll get the infamous "raccoon eyes."

Keep in mind when planning a trip to the High Rockies that you should never underestimate the weather. Summer heat combined with high altitudes can leave you dehydrated. Make sure to drink plenty of water. Blizzards can occur at any time of the year, and lightning is a very real peril during summer.

THE CENTRAL FRONT RANGE

Idaho Springs

❶ *33 mi west of Denver via I–70; 13 mi west of Denver via U.S. 6.*

Colorado prospectors struck their first major vein of gold here on January 7, 1859. That year, local mines dispatched half of all the gold used by the U.S. Mint—ore worth a whopping $2 million. Today the quaint town recalls its mining days, especially along downtown's **Miner Street,** where pastel Victorians will transport you back to a century giddy with all that glitters.

During gold-rush days, the **Argo Gold Mill** processed more than $100 million worth of the precious metal. To transport the ore, workers dug through solid rock to construct a 22,000-foot-long tunnel. When completed in 1910, the Argo Tunnel was the longest in the world. During tours of the facility, guides explain how this monumental engineering feat was accomplished. ✉ *2350 Riverside Dr.* ☎ *303/567–2421* ⊕ *www.historicargotours.com* 💲 *$10* ⊘ *May–Sept., daily 9–6, weather permitting.*

Numbers in the text correspond to numbers in the margin and on the High Rockies map.

If you have 3 days

Three days is a perfect amount of time for getting a taste of the High Rockies. Rent a car, pick up a sandwich at a Denver deli, and put the city in your rearview mirror. Within 10 minutes of leaving Denver, the foothills will close in around you and you'll be on your way to the historic town of ▣ **Idaho Springs** ❶ to explore a working mine, try your hand at gold panning, and grab a slice of pizza and beer at one of the local pubs.

Wake up early the next day and make your way up beautiful Fall River Road to the trailhead for St. Mary's Glacier. With a lunch packed, you're ready for a ¾-mi hike through the pine forests to the base of a massive snowfield. Build a snowman in July, picnic beside a gurgling stream, and watch the summer snowboarders shred the melting ice. Feeling adventurous? Tackle 13,000-foot-tall James Peak, 3 mi beyond the glacier. Speed through the Eisenhower Tunnel en route to the highest town in North America. Spend the night in ▣ **Leadville** ❿ at one of the many historic inns and restored Victorians.

On your final day, head back down I–70 and hop on the Mt. Evans Scenic and Historic Byway for a winding drive to the top of this 14,000-foot-high peak. Spectacular views east of the plains and west of the endless mountains will greet you on the summit. Dress warmly: it might be 100°F down in Denver, but it could be snowing on top of the peak.

If you have 5 days

Follow the three-day itinerary, but start off by catching the ski train from Denver to ▣ **Winter Park** ❷. This all-day excursion lends a distinctly European flavor to a day of fun in the snow. For the complete experience, spend a night in Winter Park and take advantage of the local bars and restaurants. If snow is lacking, Winter Park has great mountain-bike trails and hiking.

If you have 7 days

With a full week to explore, drive west on I–70 to **Georgetown** ❸, a town that gives you a taste of rough-and-tumble life on the frontier. The town that grew rich on silver is well worth a look. From there, head to **Breckenridge** ❼, considered by many to be the prettiest town in the High Rockies. No trip to Colorado is complete without a visit to ▣ **Vail** ⓫ so head here to bunk down for the night. Your destination the next morning is ▣ **Aspen** ⓱— in summer you can head south through Leadville and over Independence Pass, while in winter you should drive west to Glenwood Springs and then veer south. Both are scenic drives with plenty to catch the eye along the way. Plan to spend a few nights in this capital of glitz and glamour. On day five head north to ▣ **Steamboat Springs** ⓮, which has more than enough to keep you here for a couple of days. Savor a soak in the thermal springs, window shop downtown art galleries, and sample some of the High Rockies' better restaurants. On your last morning, head back to Denver.

★ Just outside town is the **Phoenix Gold Mine,** still operating today. A seasoned miner leads visitors underground, where they can wield 19th-century excavating tools or pan for gold. Whatever riches you find are yours to keep. ⊠ *Off Trail Creek Rd.* ☎ *303/567–0422* ☜ *$10; $5 for gold-panning only* ☉ *Daily 10–6, weather permitting.*

Idaho Springs presently prospers from the hot springs at **Indian Springs Resort.** Around the springs, known to the Ute natives as the "healing waters of the Great Spirit," are geothermal caves that were used by several tribes as a neutral meeting site. The hot springs and a mineral-water swimming pool are the primary draws for the resort, but the scenery is equally fantastic. ⊠ *302 Soda Creek Rd.* ☎ *303/989–6666* ⊕ *www. indianspringsresort.com* ☜ *$17* ☉ *Daily 7:30 AM–10:30 PM.*

Within sight of Indian Springs Resort is a 600-foot waterfall, Bridal Veil Falls. The imposing **Charlie Tayler Water Wheel**—the largest in the state—was constructed in the 1890s by a miner who attributed his strong constitution to the fact that he never shaved, took baths, or kissed women. ⊠ *South of Idaho Springs on I–70.*

★ A vision of alpine splendor is **St. Mary's Glacier.** From the exit, it is a beautiful 10-mi drive up a forested hanging valley to the glacier trailhead. The glacier, technically a large snowfield compacted in a mountain saddle at timberline, is thought to be the southernmost glacier in the United States. During drought years it all but vanishes, whereas a wet winter creates a wonderful Ice Age playground throughout the following summer. Ninety percent of visitors are content to make the steep ¾-mi hike up to the base of the glacier and admire the snowfield and sparkling sapphire lake. But with a bit more effort, the intrepid can hike up the rocky right-hand side of the snowfield to a plateau less than a mile above for sweeping views of the Continental Divide. For those equipped for a summit attempt, 13,294-foot-high James Peak beckons farther west on the Continental Divide, 2 mi distant. Because of its proximity to Denver, St. Mary's Glacier is a popular weekend getaway for summer hikers, snowboarders and skiers. Although it is on Forest Service land, there are no facilities or parking. Recently, private homeowners tired of vacationers parking along their property petitioned the Forest Service and the Colorado Department of Transportation to remove the St. Mary's Glacier sign on I–70, replacing it with the functional Fall River Road/Alice sign. Parking is still a challenge on weekends, but you risk a ticket if you ignore the "no parking" signs. ✛ *I–70 Exit 238, west of Idaho Springs.*

★ The incomparable **Mt. Evans Scenic and Historic Byway**—the highest paved road in the United States—leads to the summit of 14,264-foot-high Mt. Evans. This is one of only two 14,000-foot peaks in the United States that you can drive up (the other is her southern sister, Pikes Peak). The pass winds past several placid lakes and through stands of towering Douglas firs and bristlecone pines. This is one of the best places in the state to catch a glimpse of shaggy white mountain goats and regal bighorn sheep. Small herds of the nimble creatures stroll from car to car looking for handouts. Feeding them is prohibited, however. Keep your eyes peeled for other animals, including deer, elk and feather-footed ptarmigans. From Idaho Springs, State Road 103 leads south 15 mi to the entrance to the road. ⊠ *State Rd. 3* ☎ *303/567–3000* ⊕ *www. mtevans.com* ☜ *$10* ☉ *Memorial Day–late Sept.*

Built in the 1870s to transfer ore to Central City, the **Oh-My-God Road** climbs nearly 2,000 feet above Idaho Springs. After traveling along a series of hairpin curves you arrive at the summit, where you are treated

Get Above the Clouds

To really experience the High Rockies, you need to park your car, lace up your boots, and hit the trail. The I–70 corridor leads to a number of excellent trailheads, including St. Mary's Glacier and Guanella Pass. Most trails are well marked in wooded areas, but fade away once you cross timberline. At that point, keep your eyes peeled for small piles of stones called "cairns" that signal the way. It's essential that you let someone know where you are going and when you plan to be back. In summer it's best to start hikes early in the day, since violent thunderstorms are practically guaranteed every afternoon. Several of Colorado's "Fourteeners"—peaks over 14,000-feet—provide easy access to those in search than-aired thrills. Try scaling Mt. Evans, Mt. Bierdstadt, and the twin peaks of Grays and Torreys.

Go Back in Time

With so much natural beauty spreading across the horizon, it's easy to overlook the incredible human history behind the state. But look closely. Hillsides are cratered with old mines, dirt roads lead to abandoned villages, and towns are slowly restoring their treasured Victorians. Some of the best places to get a true sense of how Colorado was transformed from an untamed territory to a celebrity escape are Georgetown and Leadville. Both have historic railroads that let you ride the rails that brought prosperity to the region.

to sweeping views of Mt. Evans. The dusty road is often busy with mining traffic, so keep your windows up and your eyes open. ✛ *Hwy. 279.*

Where to Stay & Eat

$–$$ ✕ **Beau Jo's Pizza.** This always-hopping pizzeria is the area's original après-ski destination. A stop here is mandatory—as is a taste of the roasted garlic-cream pizza sauce served on Beau Jo's famous olive oil and honey pizza crust. Wash it all down with a signature Mineshaft Ale. ⊠ *1517 Miner St.* ☎ *303/567–4376* ▭ *AE, D, MC, V.*

$–$$ ✕ **Buffalo Bar & Restaurant.** No surprise as to the specialties here: burgers, fajitas, chili, and steak sandwiches, all made with heart-healthy bison meat. A Western theme dominates the dining room, where the walls are jam-packed with frontier memorabilia. The ornate bar dates from 1886. Stop by in the evening for great live music. ⊠ *1617 Miner St.* ☎ *303/567–2729* ▭ *AE, D, DC, MC, V.*

$–$$ ✕ **Tommyknocker Brewery & Pub.** Harking back to gold-rush days, this cozy bar has a large fireplace that is a great place to warm up after a visit to the High Country. The suds have a distinctly local flavor and sport names like Lost Dutchman Gold Ale and Pick Axe Pale Ale. In addition to fare such as buffalo burritos, the brewery also has plenty of vegetarian options. ⊠ *1401 Miner St.* ☎ *303/567–2688* ▭ *AE, D, MC, V.*

Winter Park

❷ *36 mi from Idaho Springs or 67 mi from Denver, via I–70 west and U.S. 40 north.*

Denverites have come to think of Winter Park as their own personal ski area—and understandably so, as it's owned by the City of Denver. Its proximity (it's a 1½-hour drive from the capital) makes it a favorite of

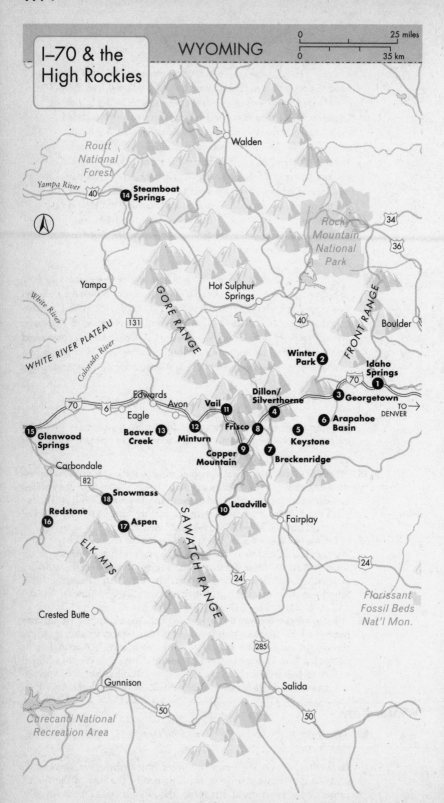

I–70 & the High Rockies

WYOMING

0 — 25 miles
0 — 35 km

Routt National Forest

Yampa River

40 **14** Steamboat Springs

Rocky Mountain National Park

34

36

Yampa

White River

131

WHITE RIVER PLATEAU

Colorado River

GORE RANGE

Hot Sulphur Springs

Walden

40

FRONT RANGE

Boulder

Winter Park **2**

Idaho Springs **1**

70

3 Georgetown

TO → DENVER

Edwards

70 6

Avon

Eagle

15 Glenwood Springs

Beaver Creek **13**

Minturn **12**

Vail **11**

Frisco

8

Dillon/ Silverthorne

4

6 Arapahoe Basin

5

Keystone

9

7

Breckenridge

Copper Mountain

Carbondale

82

Snowmass **18**

Redstone **16**

17 Aspen

ELK MTS

SAWATCH RANGE

10 Leadville

Fairplay

24

Florissant Fossil Beds Nat'l Mon.

Crested Butte

24

285

Gunnison

50

Salida

50

Curecanti National Recreation Area

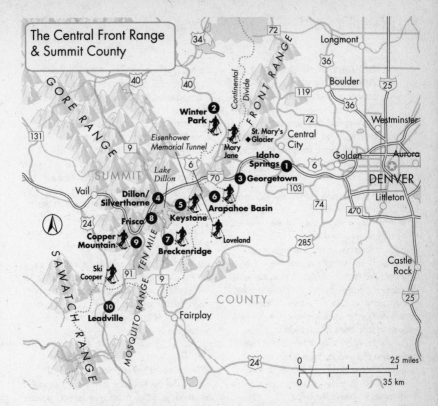

The Central Front Range & Summit County

daytrippers, but Winter Park has also become a destination in its own right. Packed all winter with locals who know the skiing is the most affordable in the area, it's equally popular in summer with hikers and bikers. Winter Park has had few tourist attractions beside its natural beauty. Change is on the horizon, though, as development at Winter Park—anchored by the Zephyr Mountain Lodge, a slope-side village comprised of condominiums, restaurants, bars, and shops—comes to fruition.

Winter Park is really three interconnected ski areas: Winter Park, flanked by Mary Jane and Vasquez Ridge. Head to Vasquez Ridge for splendid intermediate cruising; Mary Jane for some of the steepest, most thrilling bumps in Colorado; and Winter Park for a pleasing blend of both. You have room to spread out, but it's easy to lose your skiing buddies. And once that happens, it's difficult to find them again.

Downhill Skiing & Snowboarding

The skiing at Winter Park and Vasquez Ridge leans heavily toward extremely wide, nicely groomed intermediate trails. It's terrific skiing for families, groups, and schussboomers who enjoy speeding past the ski patrol. On busy weekends, Vasquez Ridge is the best place for escaping crowds, partly because this area is a bit more difficult to find. For experts *really* trying to escape crowds, the chutes and headwalls of Vasquez Cirque are the place to be.

Mary Jane is 2,610 vertical feet of unrelenting moguls, with just a couple of groomed runs. The Timberline Lift behind Mary Jane provides access to above-the-tree-line skiing at Parsenn Bowl. The pitch is moderate, making the bowl a terrific place for intermediate skiers to try powder and crud-snow skiing.

CloseUp

HITTING THE SLOPES

ALTHOUGH DOWNHILL SKIING HAS LONG BEEN the classic winter activity, snowboarding—once the bastion of teenage shredders in baggy pants—is fast catching up as a mainstream sport. Telemarking and cross-country skiing still have loyal followings, though they tend to prefer the wide open backcountry to the more populated resorts.

While it snows somewhere in the Colorado high country every month—and resorts can open their lifts as early as October and close as late as July 4—the traditional ski season usually runs from December until early April. Christmas through New Year's Day and the month of March tend to be the busiest periods for most ski areas. The slower months of January and February often yield good package deals, as do the early and late ends of the season. Cross-country skiers can take advantage of low avalanche danger in the autumn and spring for some back country exploration. Colorado has one of the highest avalanche death rates in North America, so backcountry skiing should only be undertaken by people with avalanche training and the correct gear (avalanche beacon, shovel, and probe poles).

Equipment Rental
Rental equipment is available at all ski areas and at ski shops around resorts or in nearby towns. It's often more expensive to rent at the resort where you'll be skiing, but then it's easier to go back to the shop if something doesn't fit. Experienced skiers can "demo" (try out) premium equipment to get a feel for new technology before upgrading.

Lessons
In the United States, the Professional Ski Instructors of America (PSIA) has devised a progressive teaching system that is used at most ski schools. This allows skiers to take lessons at different ski areas. Classes range in length from hour-long skill clinics to half or full-day workshops. Deals can be had for first-time and beginner skiers and snowboarders who attend morning clinics and then try out their new skills on beginner and intermediate slopes for the remainder of the day.

Most ski schools follow the PSIA teaching approach for children, and many also incorporate SKIwee, another standardized teaching technique. Classes for children are arranged by ability and age group; often the ski instructor chaperons a meal during the teaching session. Children's ski instruction has come a long way in the last 10 years; instructors specially trained in teaching children, and equipment designed for little bodies mean that most children can now begin to ski successfully as young as three or four. Helmets are often de rigueur.

The Winter Park National Sports Center for the Disabled, the largest such center in the world, specializes in teaching skiers with disabilities and has welcomed over 50,000 new aficionados to the winter recreational world.

Lift Tickets
With some lift ticket prices just shy of $100, the best advice is to shop around. Single-day, adult, holiday-weekend passes cost the most, but better bargains can be had through off-site purchase locations (check newspaper Sunday sections and local supermarkets, such as King-Sooper's and Safe Way), multiple-day passes, and season passes. You can always call a particular resort's central reservations line to ask where discount lift tickets can be purchased. With a little leg work, you should never have to pay full price.

Lodging
Most ski areas offer several kinds of accommodations—lodges, condominiums, hotels, motels, inns, bed-and-breakfasts. For longer vacations, request the resort area's accommodations brochure, since a package rate may offer the best deal. Combinations can include rooms, meals, lift tickets, gear rental and even ski lessons.

Trail Rating
Ski areas mark and rate trails and slopes–Easier (green circle), Intermediate (blue square), Advanced (black diamond), and Expert (double black diamond).

— Jad Davenport

FACILITIES 3,060-foot vertical drop; 2,762 skiable acres; 9% beginner, 34% intermediate, 57% advanced; 8 high-speed quad chairs, 3 triple chairs, 7 double chairs.

LESSONS & For adult skiers and snowboarders, the **Winter Park Ski and Snowboard**
PROGRAMS **School** (✉ Balcony House ☎ 970/726–1564) has half-day lessons starting at $49. Daylong children's programs, which include lunch, start at $106. Winter Park is home to the **National Sports Center for the Disabled** (✉ Box 1290, 80482 ☎ 303/316–1540), one of the country's best program for skiers with disabilities.

LIFT TICKETS $54. Savings of up to 25% on multi-day tickets.

RENTALS Winter Park Resort has rental packages starting at $22 at **West Portal Boots and Boards** (✉ West Portal Station ☎ 970/726–1665). **Slopeside Gear and Sport** (✉ Zephyr Mountain Lodge ☎ 970/726–1665) rents skiing and snowboarding gear. Rental equipment is also available from several shops downtown.

Nordic Skiing

BACKCOUNTRY South of Winter Park, **Berthoud Pass** (✉ Hwy. 40 ☎ 800/754–2378
SKIING ⊕ www.berthoudpass.com) is a hard place to define. As a ski area, it has been opened and closed so often that there's no guarantee that the lifts will be running. Even when they are, only a portion of the trails are reachable. Skiers and snowboarders must hike to the best terrain, returning to the base via shuttle buses from pickup points along the highway. Whatever the means of going up and down, Berthoud is well worth a visit for experienced, well-conditioned skiers and riders.

TRACK SKIING About 7 mi northwest of Winter Park, **Devil's Thumb Ranch** grooms more than 65 mi of cross-country trails. Some skiing is along fairly level tree-lined trails, some with more ups and downs and wide-open views. The ranch has rentals, lessons, and backcountry tours. ✉ *3530 County Rd. 83, Tabernash 80478* ☎ *970/726–5632 or 800/933–4339* ⊕ *www. devilsthumbranch.com* 🎟 *Trail fee $16.*

Snow Mountain Ranch, 12 mi northwest of Winter Park, has a 62-mi trail system that includes almost 2 mi lit for night skiing. The ranch is a YMCA facility (with discounts for members) and has such added bonuses as a sauna and an indoor pool. Lessons, rentals, and on-site lodging are available. ✉ *1101 County Rd. 53, Granby 80446* ☎ *970/887–2152* ⊕ *www. ymcarockies.org* 🎟 *Trail fee $3.*

Other Sports & the Outdoors

BICYCLING Winter Park is one of the leading mountain-biking destinations in the
★ Rockies, with some 50 mi of trails crisscrossing the main part of the resort and hundreds of miles more off the beaten path. **Slopeside Gear and Sport** (✉ Zephyr Mountain Lodge ☎ 970/726–1665) gives tips about the best trails and rents bikes every day in summer.

FISHING The **Sulphur Ranger District** (✉ 9 Tenmile Dr., Granby ☎ 970/887–4100) provides information about fishing in Winter Park and the surrounding region.

GOLF With three courses, **Pole Creek Golf Club** (✉ County Rd. 51 ☎ 970/887–9195) has fantastic views of the mountains. Designed by Denis Griffiths, the 27-hole course is consistently ranked among the top public courses by *Golf Digest*.

You might share a tee with an elk at **Grand Elk Golf Course** (✉ 1321 Tenmile Dr. ☎ 877/389–9333). This 18-hole course, designed by PGA great Craig Stadler, may remind well-heeled enthusiasts of traditional heathland greens in Britain.

Lush wetlands create natural obstacles at the 18-hole **SolVista** golf course (✉ 63331 Hwy. 40 ☎ 888/283–7458). The front nine run along the Fraser River.

HORSEBACK RIDING   For leisurely horseback riding tours of the Fraser Valley, your best bet is the stable at **Grand Adventures** (✉ Hwy. 40 ☎ 970/726–9247). Kids love the nightly hayrides.

SNOWMOBILING   Rentals and guided tours are available from **Trailblazer Snowmobile Tours** (✉ County Rd. 50 ☎ 970/726–8452 or 800/669–0134). Rates range from $40 per hour to $165 for a full-day tour.

SNOW TUBING   Two lifts, groomed trails, and a warming hut at **Fraser Snow Tubing Hill** (✉ County Rd. 72 ☎ 970/726–5954) make your tubing most enjoyable. And the hill is lit at night, no less. The rate is $14 per hour.

Where to Stay & Eat

$$$$ ✕ **Dining Room at Sunspot.** Reached via gondola, this log-and-stone structure is a real stunner. Douglas fir beams and Southwestern rugs on the walls add to the rustic charm. The real draw is the view, but be sure to arrive early enough to catch a glimpse of it. The five-course prix-fixe menu includes game and fish paired with side dishes such as wild rice and potatoes roasted in olive oil and herbs. ✉ *Top of Zephyr Express Lift* ☎ *970/726–1446* ⚓ *Reservations essential* ▤ *AE, D, DC, MC, V* ⊘ *No dinner Sat. Nov.–Mar.*

$$–$$$ ✕ **Deno's Mountain Bistro.** A sizable selection of beers from around the world helps make this casual establishment the liveliest spot in town. But what sets it apart is a wine list that's comprehensive and fairly priced—a rarity in low-key Winter Park. The cellar full of fine vintages is a labor of love for Deno, the powerhouse behind the restaurant. The menu he's put together is just as imaginative, with everything from double-cut pork chops to grilled trout to the best burgers in town. Everything is expertly prepared and served by friendly staffers who really know their stuff. ✉ *78911 U.S. 40* ☎ *970/726–5332* ▤ *AE, D, MC, V.*

$–$$ ✕ **Last Waltz.** A crackling fireplace lends a homey feeling to this family restaurant. The huge menu jumps from seafood to south-of-the-border favorites. The Tex-Mex dishes are best: zesty *calientitas* (deep-fried jalapeños filled with cream cheese and served with salsa) and home-roasted *chiles rellenos* (stuffed hot peppers) are especially noteworthy. Breakfast and brunch will power you for those mogul runs. ✉ *78336 U.S. 40* ☎ *970/726–4877* ⚓ *Reservations not accepted* ▤ *AE, D, DC, MC, V.*

★ $–$$$ ✕▥ **Gasthaus Eichler.** Antler chandeliers cast a cheery glow as Strauss waltzes lilt softly in the background at this quaint little guest house. Here you'll find Winter Park's most romantic dining spot ($$–$$$), where fondues bubble and veal and other meats are grilled to perfection. The cozy guest rooms charm you with their lace curtains, wooden armoires, and beds piled high with down comforters. If you can't do without modern amenities, there are also cable TVs and hot tubs. The rates are quite economical when you consider that they include breakfast and dinner. ✉ *78786 U.S. 40, 80482* ☎ *970/726–5133 or 800/543–3899* ⊕ *www. gasthauseichler.com* �){*15 rooms* ⚒ *Restaurant, cable TV, in-room hot tubs* ▤ *AE, MC, V* ⦿ *MAP.*

$ ✕▥ **Peck House.** A 45-minute drive from Winter Park, this red-roofed inn is Colorado's oldest continually operating hostelry. The barnlike structure was built in 1860 as a boardinghouse for wealthy mine investors. The dining room ($$–$$$) is crammed with period antiques, including tinted lithographs and etched-glass shades for the gas lamps that once hung in the state capitol. Game is the house specialty: expertly prepared quail and venison (perfect with the hearty cabernet sauce) are among the standouts. A Sunday brunch is offered in July and August. The charming rooms (with hot tubs) are awash in Victorian splendor. The inn is on U.S. 40, 2 mi north of I–70. ⊠ *Box 428, Empire 80438* ☏ *303/569–9870* 🖷 *303/569–2743* ⊕ *www.thepeckhouse.com* ⟳ *11 rooms, 10 with bath* ⚹ *Restaurant, in-room hot tubs; no room phones, no room TVs* ▤ *AE, D, DC, MC, V* ⦿l *CP.*

$$–$$$$ ⬚ **Iron Horse Resort.** On the banks of the Fraser River, this was the first ski-in/ski-out facility in Winter Park. Guests who return year after year keep the condominium complex among the most popular lodgings in the area. The studios are perfect for couples, and the one- and two-bedroom apartments are often booked by families. Most apartments have have full kitchens and balconies with views of a grove of aspens. ⦂l *Iron Horse Dr., Box 1286, 80482* ☏ *970/726–8851 or 800/621–8190* 🖷 *970/726–2321* ⊕ *www.ironhorse–resort.com* ⟳ *113 rooms* ⚹ *Restaurant, pool, health club, 4 hot tubs, steam room, ski shop, bar, business services, meeting rooms* ▤ *AE, D, DC, MC, V.*

$–$$$$ ⬚ **Zephyr Mountain Lodge.** The only ski-in/ski-out lodging in Winter Park Village, Zephyr Mountain Lodge is steps away from the express lift. The lobby has a fireplace that makes it a great spot to relax after a day on the slopes. The rooms, decorated in vivid greens and purples, have great views of the nearby mountains. ⊠ *201 Zephyr Way, 80482* ☏ *800/729–5813* 🖷 *970/726–5993* ⊕ *www.zmlwp.com* ⟳ *175 rooms* ⚹ *Restaurant, coffee shop, gym, 2 hot tubs, ski shop, laundry service* ▤ *AE, D, DC, MC, V.*

$$–$$$ ⬚ **Anna Leah B&B.** You'll feel like you're visiting a good friend's home when you check into this B&B, thanks to congenial owner Patricia Handel. She will bend over backwards to accommodate almost any request. The inn is just beyond the town of Fraser, about 5 mi from Winter Park. With balconies overlooking the Arapahoe National Forest and the Continental Divide, it has a wonderfully serene atmosphere. A full breakfast and evening desserts are included in the price. ⊠ *1001 County Rd. 8, Fraser 80442* ☏ *970/726–4414* 🖷 *970/726–5033* ⊕ *www.annaleah.com* ⟳ *5 rooms* ⚹ *Dining room, hot tub* ▤ *No credit cards* ⦿l *BP.*

$$–$$$ ⬚ **Vintage Hotel.** This is the most pet-friendly place in town. One of Winter Park's top resorts, the Vintage is in the middle of it all. Spacious, comfortable rooms look out onto the mountains. Configurations range from standard hotel rooms (some with kitchenettes and fireplaces) to one- and two-bedroom suites. ⊠ *100 Winter Park Dr., 80482* ☏ *970/726–8801 or 800/472–7017* 🖷 *970/726–9250* ⊕ *www.vintagehotel.com* ⟳ *118 rooms* ⚹ *Restaurant, kitchenettes (some), pool, gym, hot tub, sauna, bar* ▤ *AE, D, DC, MC, V.*

$$–$$$ ⬚ **Wild Horse Inn.** Tucked into the woods on the way to Devil's Thumb Ranch, this rustic retreat is a bit off the beaten path. Your reward, however, is complete relaxation. The rooms, many with beamed ceilings and four-poster beds, have private balconies overlooking the forest. Best of all, after an exhausting day of skiing you can book an hour with the on-site massage therapist. ⊠ *1536 County Rd. 83, 80482* ☏ *970/726–0456* ⊕ *www.wildhorseinncolorado.com* ⟳ *7 rooms* ⚹ *Breakfast room, hot tub, sauna* ▤ *AE, D, DC, MC, V.*

$–$$$ ⬚ **Sundowner Motel.** With its sharply peaked roof, the Sundowner is probably the most charming motel on the strip. It's also a great bargain, considering the free shuttle to the ski area. The rooms, many recently renovated, are decorated in earthy tones. ⊠ *78869 U.S. 40, 80482* ☏ *970/726–9451 or 970/726–5452* 🖷 *970/726–5452* ⊕ *www.thesundownermotel.com* ⟳ *38 rooms* ⚹ *Indoor pool, hot tub* ▤ *AE, D, DC, MC, V.*

¢–$ 🏠 **Woodspur Lodge.** This log-cabin lodge sits on the edge of the Arapahoe National Forest, about 1½ mi from Winter Park. The decor in the A-frame structure is more rustic than posh, with furnishings hewn from locally grown lodgepole pines. Rooms are small, so the emphasis is on mingling in the common areas. All-you-can-eat breakfasts and dinners are included in the room rate, and are served in a dining area with a giant fireplace and a soaring ceiling. ✉ *111 Van Anderson Dr., 80482* ☎ *970/726–8417 or 800/626–6562* 🖷 *970/726–8553* ⊕ *www.woodspur. com* ↩ *32 rooms* ⚒ *Dining room, 2 outdoor hot tubs, sauna, recreation room* ⊟ *D, MC, V* |○| *FAP.*

CONDOMINIUMS   **Destinations West** handles the nicest accommodations in the valley, ranging from top-end homes to luxurious condos. ⊘ *Box 3478, 80482* ☎ *800/ 545–9378* 🖷 *970/726–4534* ⊕ *www.toski.com/destinations.*

Nightlife

For a bit of local color, head down the road a ways to Fraser and the **Crooked Creek Saloon** (✉ 401 Zerex St. ☎ 970/726–9250). The motto here is "Eat till it hurts, drink till it feels better." Locals show up for the cheap beer during happy hour. The under-30 crowd hangs out at the **Pub** (✉ 78260 Hwy. 40 ☎ 970/726–4929), grooving to local bands. **Marvin's Hideaway** (✉ 78259 Hwy. 40 ☎ 970/726–7660) caters to a slightly older crowd with a fine selection of Colorado wines served in Reidel stemware. The pace here is the relaxing tempo of live jazz.

If you've never done your laundry while sipping a brew, don't miss **Buckets** (✉ 78415 Hwy. 40 ☎ 970/726–3026), a combination bar and coin laundry conveniently located in the basement of the Winter Park Movie Theater. This friendly place seems to attract just as many tourists as locals.

Shopping

Cooper Creek Square (✉ 47 Cooper Creek Way ☎ 970/726–8891) is filled with inexpensive souvenir shops and fine jewelers, upscale eateries and local cafés, plus live entertainment all summer in the courtyard.

Georgetown

❸   *50 mi from Denver via I–70 west; 41 mi from Winter Park via U.S. 40 south and I–70 west.*

Georgetown rode the crest of the silver boom during the second half of the 19th century. Most of the impeccably maintained brick buildings that make up the town's historic district date from that period. Fortunately, Georgetown hasn't been tarted up, so it provides a true sense of what gracious living meant in those rough-and-tumble times. Located just west of where I–70 and U.S. 40 intersect, Georgetown is close enough to attract daytrippers from Denver, but its quiet charms warrant more than a hurried visit.

Dating from 1867, **Hamill House** once was the home of silver magnate William Arthur Hamill. The Gothic revival beauty displays most of its original wall coverings and furnishings. Don't miss the gleaming white structure's unique curved-glass conservatory. ✉ *3rd and Argentine Sts.* ☎ *303/569–2840* ⊕ *www.historicgeorgetown.org* ✎ *$5* ⊙ *June–Sept., daily 10–4; Oct.–Dec., Tues.–Sun. 10–4; Jan.–May, by appointment.*

The elaborate **Hotel de Paris,** built almost single-handedly by Frenchman Louis Dupuy in 1878, was one of the Old West's preeminent hostelries. Now a museum, the hotel depicts how luxuriously the rich were accommodated: Tiffany fixtures, lace curtains, and hand-carved furniture re-create an era of opulence. ⊠ *409 6th St.* ☏ *303/569–2311* 🖼 *$4* ⊙ *June–Sept., daily 10–4:30; Oct.–Jan., weekends 10–4:30.*

Hop on the **Georgetown Loop Railroad,** a 1920s narrow-gauge steam train that connects Georgetown with the equally historic community of Silver Plume. The 6-mi round-trip excursion takes about 70 minutes and winds through vast stands of pine and fir before crossing the 95-foot-high Devil's Gate Bridge, where the track actually loops back over itself as it gains elevation. In Silver Plume, you can tour the Lebanon Silver Mill and Mine. ⊠ *100 Loop Dr.* ☏ *303/569–2403 or 800/691–4386* ⊕ *www.gtownloop.com* 🖼 *$15.50* ⊙ *June–Sept., daily 9:20–4.*

South of Georgetown, the **Guanella Pass Scenic Byway** treats you to marvelous views of the Mt. Evans Wilderness Area. Make sure to park at Georgetown Lake, where you can catch a glimpse of the state's largest herd of rare bighorn sheep. ⊠ *Rte. 381.*

Sports & the Outdoors

DOWNHILL SKIING

FodorsChoice ★

Loveland Ski Area is considered small potatoes, but only because of its proximity to the monster resorts of Summit County. Actually, Loveland, the closest ski area to Denver, has a respectable 1,365 acres serviced by 11 lifts. It's split between Loveland Valley, a good place for beginners, and Loveland Basin, a good bet for everyone else. Loveland Basin has excellent glade and open-bowl skiing and snowboarding, especially on the 2,410-foot vertical drop. Best of all, it opens early and usually stays open later than any other ski area except Arapahoe Basin. ⊠ *I–70 Exit 216, 12 mi west of Georgetown* ☏ *303/569–3203* ⊕ *www.skiloveland. com* ⊙ *Mid-Oct.–May, weekdays 9–4, weekends 8:30–4.*

Where to Stay & Eat

$–$$

✕ **Red Ram.** This Georgetown landmark has been serving up some of the region's tastiest meals since the 1950s. The secret is keeping the menu simple: burgers, ribs, and south-of-the-border favorites such as fajitas. Black-and-white photos of the town's heyday bedeck the walls. Stop by on weekends when there's live entertainment. ⊠ *606 6th St.* ☏ *303/ 569–2300* 🖃 *AE, D, MC, V.*

$$–$$$

🏨 **Alpine Hideaway.** Innkeeper Dawn Janov refers to her romantic retreat as a "memory maker," and she couldn't be more on target. The cozy rooms, all with hot tubs, fireplaces, and spectacular views, are furnished by theme—the Mountain Contemporary has a wrought-iron bed, the Scandinavian has down-filled comforters, and the Country Irish has pastel landscapes of Ireland adorning the walls. ✑ *Box 788, 80444* ☏ *303/569–2800 or 800/490–9011* ⊕ *www.alpinehideawaybb. com* 🛏 *3 rooms* ♨ *Hot tubs* 🖃 *MC, V.*

Shopping

Georgetown Antique Emporium (⊠ 501 Rose St. ☏ 303/569–2727) specializes in oak and brass antiques. The **Trading Post** (⊠ 510 6th St. ☏ 303/569–3375) carries Western paraphernalia, from pottery to jewelry to moccasins.

en route

As you travel west along I–70 you'll reach one of the world's engineering marvels, the 8,941-foot-long **Eisenhower Memorial Tunnel.** Most people who drive through take its presence for granted, but until the first lanes were opened in 1973, the only route west through the mountains was the perilous Loveland Pass, a heart-pounding roller-coaster ride. Snow, mud, and a steep grade proved the downfall of many an intrepid motorist. In truly inclement weather the eastern and western slopes were completely cut off from each other. Authorities first proposed the tunnel in 1937. Geologists warned about unstable rock; through more than three decades of construction, their direst predictions came true as rock walls crumbled, steel girders buckled, and gas pockets caused mysterious explosions. When the project was finally completed, more than 500,000 cubic yards of solid granite had been removed from Mt. Trelease. The original cost estimate was $1 million. By the time the second bore was completed in 1979, the tunnel's cost had skyrocketed to $340 million.

SUMMIT COUNTY

The top of the Rockies, Summit County is surrounded by dozens of breathtaking peaks. Here you'll find a string of superb resorts—Keystone, Breckenridge, and Copper Mountain—each with its own personality. With its eye-popping vistas, it's little wonder that Summit County attracts skiers and snowboarders from around the globe. So popular is this highest county in the state, thanks to its proximity to Denver, multitude of activities, and nearly unlimited variety of ski terrains, that it welcomes an immense flow of visitors, especially on weekends. Unfortunately, when you combine the traffic heading to Summit County and beyond (Vail is over the next pass from Frisco), the result is often terrible traffic snarls along woefully narrow I-70.

Dillon/Silverthorne

❹ *23 mi from Georgetown or 73 mi from Denver via I–70 west.*

Dillon can't seem to sit still. Founded in 1883 as a stagecoach stop and trading post for men working in the mines, Dillon has had to pack up and move three times since its conception. It was first relocated to be closer to the Utah and Northern Railroad, and then to take advantage of the nearby rivers. Finally, in 1955, bigwigs in Denver drew up plans to dam the Blue River so they could quench the capital's growing thirst. The reservoir would submerge Dillon under more than 150 feet of water. Once again the town was moved, this time to pine-blanketed hills mirrored in sapphire water. Residents agreed that no building in the new location would be higher than 30 feet so as not to obstruct the view of the reservoir—now gratefully called Lake Dillon.

Dillon's borders now blend with those of neighboring Silverthorne, where dozens of factory outlets are filled with locals and travelers vying for bargains. This is a resort region with all the comforts of home. Combined, the two towns have hotels, restaurants, and stores galore.

★ Located more than 9,000 feet above sea level, **Lake Dillon** is one of the most beautiful bodies of water in the region. The ice-blue reservoir, set between the towns of Dillon and Frisco, has 25 mi of shoreline. You can rent boats at the marinas in either town. If you're sailing, check to see if the locals are wearing wet suits that day, especially in early summer or fall.

Sports & the Outdoors

BICYCLING Summit County attracts cyclists with its 40 mi of paved bike paths and extensive network of backcountry trails. There are dozens of trailheads from which you can travel through gentle rolling terrain, up the sides of mountains, and along ridges for spectacular views. Starting in Dillon, you could bike around the reservoir to Frisco. From there you could ride the Blue River Pathway, largely along the river, to Breckenridge. Or you could ride through beautiful Tenmile Canyon all the way to Copper Mountain. If you're really fit, you could even continue your ride over Vail Pass and down into Vail Village. The **Summit County Chamber of Com-**

merce (⊠ 246 Rainbow Dr., Silverthorne ☎ 800/530–3099 ⊕ www.
experiencethesummit.com) has detailed information about bike trails in
the area. Ask for a free Summit County Bike Trail Guide that outlines,
with great detail, your options. Listings include distance, difficulty, and
elevation changes.

BOATING At **Dillon Marina** (⊠ Lake Dillon ☎ 970/468–5100 ⊕ www.dillonmarina.
com) you can rent a rowboat, a sailboat, or just about anything else that
floats. Reserve ahead in high season.

FISHING A favorite with locals, **Cutthrout Anglers** (⊠ 400 Blue River Pkwy., Silverthorne ☎ 888/876–8818 or 970/262–2878) is chockful of items for
avid fly fishermen. There's a one-day fly-fishing school for beginners and
float-trip adventures for those with a bit more experience.

HORSEBACK
RIDING
There's horseback riding in summer and sleigh rides in winter at **Bar T
Outfitters** (☎ 970/468–6916 ⊕ www.bar-t-outfitters.com). Get up at
the crack of dawn for the breakfast rides, which include a heaping help-
ing of bacon and eggs.

Where to Stay & Eat

Chain hotels line I–70 near the road to Dillon/Silverthorne. Here you'll
find the Sheraton, Days Inn, and Holiday Inn, among others. These are
generally more modestly priced than lodging in the towns. But before
assuming that one of these hotels is your best bet, compare the total price
of your trip, including lodging, lifts, and lessons. It may turn out that
a package at a resort is actually more affordable.

$$–$$$ ✕ **Historic Mint.** Built in 1862, this raucous eatery originally served as a
bar and brothel. The olden days are still evident in the bar's brass handles and hand-carved wood, as well as in the antiques and vintage photographs covering the walls of the dining area. Red meat reigns supreme,
although you will find chicken and fish on the menu. Either way, you
cook your own meal on lava rocks sizzling at 1,100°F. If you prefer to
leave the cooking to the chef, there's a prime rib special. A well-stocked
salad bar complements your entrée. ⊠ *347 Blue River Pkwy., Silverthorne* ☎ *970/468–5247* ⊕ *www.mintsteakhouse.com* ▭ *MC, V.*

★ **$–$$** ✕ **Dillon Dam Brewery.** Non-smokers gravitate to this smoke-free space,
and locals who light up find it worthwhile to refrain long enough to belly
up to the horseshoe-shaped bar. Sample the award-winning ales and lagers
while you munch on burgers, sandwiches, or pub grub. The menu is steps
above average bar food. Try barbecued pork or the grilled salmon marinated in ale, lime, cilantro, and chili peppers. Fresh Ruby Red rainbow
trout comes on a bed of cranberry-almond wild rice and is topped with
a honey-lime yogurt sauce. ⊠ *100 Dam Rd., Dillon* ☎ *970/262–7777*
▭ *AE, D, MC, V.*

★ ¢ ✕ **Blue Moon Bakery.** In addition to its excellent bagels, this stylish deli
in the Summit Plaza Shopping Center serves up tasty soups and pastas
and a good selection of cold cuts and cheeses. The morning menu features homemade granola, scones, muffins, turnovers, and one of the best
breakfast burritos in Summit County. You can eat in or take out, but
get there before it closes at 4 PM. ⊠ *253 Summit St., Silverthorne*
☎ *970/513–0513* ▭ *AE, D, DC, MC, V* ⊗ *No dinner.*

Nightlife

The bars and clubs in Dillon rock well after midnight, especially on winter nights when the towns are packed with skiers and snowboarders.
Across from the post office, **Pug Ryan's Steak House & Brewery** (⊠ 104
Village Pl., Dillon ☎ 970/486–2145) is a popular brew pub that attracts
villagers and vacationers. **The Tiki Bar** (⊠ Dillon Marina, Dillon ☎ 970/
262–6309) has the best sunset views in Summit County. Enjoy them from

the deck overlooking Lake Dillon while you sip your rumrunner and munch on peel-and-eat shrimp. **Wild Bill's Pizza Saloon** (✉ 119 La Bonte, Dillon ☎ 970/468–2006) serves up pizzas, grinders, and some of the area's best buffalo wings.

Shopping

Silverthorne Factory Stores (✉ I–70 Exit 20, Silverthorne ☎ 970/468–9440) is a sprawling complex with more than 50 discount outlets. Clusters of shops are color-coded for your shopping convenience. The Red Village has Tommy Hilfiger, Eddie Bauer, and other upscale clothing shops. If you need sneakers, the Blue Village is home to the Nike Factory Store. For dishes, head to the Mikasa Factory Outlet in the Green Village.

Keystone

⑤ *8 mi from Dillon via U.S. 6 east.*

One of the region's most laid-back destinations, Keystone is understandably popular with families. Its trails are spread across three adjoining peaks: Keystone Mountain, North Peak, and the Outback. Through the years, as the resort added more runs, it morphed from a beginner's paradise on Keystone Mountain to an early-season training stop for the national ski teams that practice on the tougher terrain on North Peak. Today it's a resort for all types of skiers and riders, whether they prefer gentle slopes, cruising, or high-adrenaline challenges—the latter since the addition of the Outback's steep bowls.

For the most part, the planners were sensitive to the environment, favoring colors and materials that blend inconspicuously with the natural surroundings. Lodging, shops, and restaurants are located in Lakeside Village, the older part of the resort, and in River Run, a newer area at the base of the gondola that has become the heart of Keystone. Everything at the resort is operated by Keystone, which makes planning a vacation here one-stop shopping. Keystone is quickly becoming a magnet in summer, with a small lake for water sports, mountain-biking and hiking trails, two golf courses that have been ranked highly by golf magazines, and a variety of outdoor concerts and events.

Downhill Skiing & Snowboarding

What you see from the base of the mountain is only a fraction of the terrain you can enjoy when you ski or snowboard at Keystone. There's plenty more to Keystone Mountain, and much of it is geared toward novice and intermediate skiers. The Schoolmarm Trail has 3½ mi of runs where you can practice turns. Keystone Mountain is easily reached from the base via high-speed chairs or the River Run gondola. You can ski or ride down the back side of Keystone Mountain to reach North Peak, a mix of groomed cruising trails and ungroomed bump runs.

If you prefer to bypass North Peak, the River Run gondola is a short walk from the Outpost gondola, which takes you to the Outpost Lodge (home to the Alpenglow Stube, which at 11,444 feet above sea level is advertised as the "highest gourmet restaurant in the country"). From here, it's an easy downhill run to the third mountain, appropriately named the Outback because of its wilderness setting. Some glades have trees thinned just enough for skiers and riders who are learning to explore gladed terrain; other sections are reserved for advanced skiers. Weather permitting, the resort also has snow cat tours that whisk you up to powder skiing on some of the state's steepest terrain.

Keystone has the largest lighted night-skiing operation in the state. Other after-dark activities include tubing and moonlight showshoe tours.

✉ *Hwy. 6* ☎ *800/239–1639 or 970/468–2316* ⊕ *www.keystoneresort. com* ☉ *Late Oct.–late Apr.*

FACILITIES
2,900-foot vertical drop; 1,861 skiable acres; 12% beginner, 34% intermediate, 54% advanced; 2 gondolas, 1 super six lift, 5 high-speed quad chairs, 1 quad chair, 1 triple chairs, 4 double chairs, 7 surface lifts and carpets.

LESSONS & PROGRAMS
Keystone has a variety of instructional programs, from half-day group lessons to specialty clinics, including mogul classes and women's seminars. Keystone runs an excellent children's program, with ski groups for kids from 2 months to 16 years of age. A notable special program is the Mahre Training Center, intensive three- and five-day clinics hosted by Phil or Steve Mahre, both Olympic medalists.

LIFT TICKETS
Few skiers pay the walk-up rate for a one-day lift ticket. A variety of season passes are available through Vail Resorts, which owns Keystone, Breckenridge, Vail, and Beaver Creek. Most vacationers purchase lift-and-lodging packages or multi-day lift passes at discounted rates online.

RENTALS
Rental packages (skis, boots, and poles, or snowboards and boots) start at around $21 per day for a basic package but increase quickly for high-performance gear. Cheaper ski and snowboard stores are found in Breckenridge, Dillon, Frisco, and Silverthorne.

CHILDCARE
Keystone has a variety of childcare choices. There are Children's Centers at the base of River Run and at the Mountain House. The minimum age is two months. A learn-to-ski program teaches the basics to kids from 3 to 14. The resort also has private classes for families.

Nordic Skiing

The **Keystone Cross-Country Center** (✉ River Course Clubhouse ☎ 970/496–4250), has 35 mi of trails available for track skiing, skate skiing, and snowshoeing. Lessons and rentals of cross-country skis and snowshoes are available.

Other Sports & the Outdoors

FISHING
Summit Guides (⌖ Lakeside Village at Keystone ☎ 970/468–8945) has full- and half-day fishing trips throughout Summit, Grand, and Eagle counties. This company also offers float trips on several rivers.

GOLF
With 36 challenging holes, Keystone has become popular with golfers as soon as the snow has melted. **Keystone Ranch Golf Course** (✉ 1239 Keystone Ranch Rd. ☎ 970/496–4250) is ranked among the top 50 resort courses in the U.S. by *Golf Digest.* The par-72 course, designed by Robert Trent Jones Jr., has a links-style front nine; the back nine has a traditional mountain-valley layout. Holes play past lodgepole pines, meander around sage meadows, and include some carries across water.

★ **The Keystone River Course** (✉ 115 River Course Rd. ☎ 970/496–4250) is a par-71 stunner designed by Michael Hurdzan and Dana Fry. The front nine runs around the Snake River, whereas the back nine threads through a stand of lodgepole pines. Dramatic elevation changes and a variety of bunkers and water hazards combine to test golfers of all levels. Add magnificent views of the Continental Divide and Lake Dillon and it's easy to see why it has become so popular.

ICE-SKATING
During winter, Keystone Lake freezes to become the country's largest outdoor **ice-skating rink** (✉ Lakeside Village ☎ 970/496–4386 or 800/354–4386). You can rent skates, sleds, or even hockey sticks for an impromptu game. Lessons in figure-skating and hockey are available. Weather permitting, skating runs from late November to early March.

Where to Stay & Eat

★ **$$$$** ✕ **Alpenglow Stube.** The competition has heated up in recent years, but Alpenglow Stube remains among the finest mountaintop restaurants in Colorado. The decor is warmly elegant, with exposed wood beams, a stone fireplace, and floral upholstery. At night, the gondola ride you take to get here is alone worth the cost of the meal. Dinner is a six-course extravaganza, starting with the signature pine-cone pâté, followed perhaps by rack of caribou in a sauce made from pear liqueur. Lunch is equally delectable, with particularly fine pasta specials. Remove your ski boots and put on the plush slippers reserved for diners. ⊠ *North Peak* ☎ *970/496–4386 or 800/354–4386* ⚇ *Reservations essential* ▱ *AE, D, DC, MC, V* ⊘ *No lunch mid-Apr.–mid-Nov.*

★ **$$$$** ✕ **Keystone Ranch.** This 1930s homestead was once part of a working cattle ranch, and cowboy memorabilia is strewn throughout, nicely blending with stylish throw rugs and Western crafts. The gorgeous and massive stone fireplace is a cozy backdrop for sipping an aperitif or after-dinner coffee. Chef David Welch's seasonal six-course menu emphasizes local ingredients, including farm-raised game and fresh fish. You're in luck if the menu includes elk with wild mushrooms in juniper sauce with quince relish or Gorgonzola flan. ⊠ *Keystone Ranch Golf Course* ☎ *970/496–4386 or 800/354–4386* ⚇ *Reservations essential* ▱ *AE, D, DC, MC, V* ⊘ *No lunch Oct.–May.*

$$$$ ✕ **Ski Tip Lodge.** In this ski lodge dating from the 1800s, almost every-
Fodor's Choice thing on the menu will melt in your mouth. The four-course, prix-fixe
★ dinner is a favorite in the area for its American cuisine with a Colorado twist. The main course may be a wood-grilled pork tenderloin or roast pheasant with game sausage, or seafood fricassee with coconut and lime. The delicious homemade bread and soup are a meal in themselves. Adjourn to the cozy lounge for the decadent desserts and special coffees. ⊠ *0764 Montezuma Rd., 1 mi off U.S. 6* ☎ *970/496–4386 or 800/354–4386* ▱ *AE, D, DC, MC, V.*

$$–$$$ ✕ **Kickapoo Tavern.** This rustic bar and grill in Jackpine Lodge features local microbrews on tap and big portions of home-style dishes such as chunky beef stew, hearty sandwiches, and burritos said to be "as big as a barn." The central location, pleasant outdoor patio, and TVs tuned to sporting events keep the place hopping both après ski and après night-ski. ⊠ *River Run Plaza* ☎ *970/496–4386 or 800/354–4386* ▱ *AE, MC, V.*

$ ✕ **Cala Inn.** A street sign noting the distance to Galway is the first clue that you've entered an Irish pub. It's a scruffy, smoky place where diners and drinkers sit around wood tables inhaling pub fries, bangers and mash, and steak and kidney pie. If you're brave enough, down a "Nessie" shot. ⊠ *40 Cove Blvd.* ☎ *970/468–1899* ▱ *MC, V.*

★ **$$$–$$$$** ▦ **Keystone Lodge.** The cinder-block structure gives no hint of the gracious, pampered living just inside the door. Rooms with king-size beds are on the small side, whereas rooms with two queen-size beds tend to be more generously proportioned. Many rooms have terraces overlooking the trees. All units are nicely appointed in rich mountain colors, with plenty of amenities. The lodge is next to the tiny lake in Keystone Village, and close to several restaurants and shops. Perhaps best of all, a short shuttle ride takes you directly to the slopes. ⌂ *Keystone Resort, Box 38, 80435* ☎ *970/496–4500 or 877/753–9786* ≜ *970/468–4343* ⊕ *www.keystone-lodge.com* ⬚ *152 rooms* ⚘ *3 restaurants, 2 tennis courts, outdoor pool, health club, 2 hot tubs, bar, children's programs, convention center* ▱ *AE, D, DC, MC, V.*

$$–$$$ ▦ **Ski Tip Lodge.** Opened as a stop along the stagecoach route back in
Fodor's Choice the 1880s, this property was turned into the state's first ski lodge in the
★ 1940s by skiing pioneers Max and Edna Dercum. The rooms in this charming log cabin have been given quaint names such as Edna's Eyrie.

They're all individually decorated with homespun furnishings and accessories, such as quilts and hand-knitted throw rugs. Some rooms have dramatic four-poster beds. In winter you can relax in the sitting room, in front of a wood-burning fireplace. In summer, retreat to the patio for a view of the surrounding mountains. A delicious breakfast is included in the room rate. ⌂ *Keystone Resort, Box 38, 80435* ☎ *970/496–4500 or 877/753–9786* 🖨 *970/468–4343* ⊕ *www.keystoneresort.com* ⤴ *11 rooms, 2 suites* ♨ *Restaurant, bar; no room phones, no room TVs* ⊟ *AE, D, DC, MC, V* ⍓*BP.*

CONDOMINIUMS **Keystone Resort Corporation** (☎ 970/496–4500 or 877/753–9786) operates most of the lodgings at the resort, which range from hotel-style rooms at Keystone Lodge and the Inn at Keystone to a wide range of apartments. The condos are located in Lakeside Village, River Run, and Ski Tip. Free shuttles ferry visitors to other parts of the resort.

Nightlife

Across from Mountain View Plaza, **The Goat** (⌧ Hwy. 6 ☎ 970/513–9344) has two bars filled with twenty- and thirtysomethings drinking whiskey and beer. There's live music most nights. Live music with rockabilly leanings makes the **Snake River Saloon** (⌧ 23074 U.S. 6 ☎ 970/468–2788) a good spot to stop for a beer. The fun-loving crowd is mostly under 35.

Shopping

Lakeside Village has a wide range of shops selling everything from chocolate to tchotchkes. **River Run**, at the base of the River Run gondola, has upscale shops selling designer ski clothing and contemporary silver jewelry.

Arapahoe Basin

❻ *6 mi from Keystone via U.S. 6 east.*

Arapahoe Basin was the first ski area to be built in Summit County. It has changed—but not a lot—since its construction in the 1940s, and most of A-Basin's dedicated skiers like it that way. It's America's highest ski area, with a base elevation of 10,780 feet and a summit of 13,050 feet. Many of the runs start above the timberline, ensuring breathtaking views (and the need for some extra breaths). Aficionados love the seemingly endless intermediate and expert terrain and the wide-open bowls that stay open into June (sometimes July). "Beachin' at the Basin" has long been one of the area's most popular summer activities. If you've got your heart set on slope-side accommodations or fine dining, look elsewhere: A-Basin has no rooms and serves only the most basic cafeteria food. You'll have to set up your base camp in nearby Keystone, Breckenridge, Frisco, Dillon, or Silverthorne and shuttle in for the day.

Downhill Skiing & Snowboarding

What makes Arapahoe delightful is also what makes it dreadful in bad weather: its elevation. Much of Arapahoe's skiing is above the tree line and when a storm moves in, you can't tell up from down.

If that sounds unpleasant, consider the other side of the coin: on sunny spring days, Arapahoe is a wonderful place because the treeless terrain surrounded by craggy peaks is reminiscent of the Alps. Intermediate-level skiers can have a great time here on the easier trails. But A-Basin is best known for its expert challenges: the East Wall, a steep face with great powder-skiing possibilities; Pallavicini, a wide tree-lined run; and the West Wall, from which skiers of varying degrees of bravado and sobriety like to launch themselves. After a long battle with the U.S. Forest Service, A-Basin won permission to install a snowmaking machine for certain trails. It wasn't needed during the 2002–03 season, which lasted until July. 🔅 *Box 8787, 80435* ☎ *970/468–0718* ⊕ *www. arapahoebasin.com* ⊘ *Mid-Nov.–mid-June or early July.*

FACILITIES 2,250-foot vertical drop; 490 skiable acres; 15% beginner, 45% intermediate, 20% advanced, 20% expert; 2 triple chairs, 3 double chairs.

LESSONS & Contact **Arapahoe Basin Central Reservations** (☎ 970/468–0718) for in-
PROGRAMS formation on regular classes and ski clinics.

LIFT TICKETS $30–$46, depending on the season. Multi-day tickets can save you as much as 20%.

RENTALS Rental packages (skis, boots, and poles) start at $20 per day. Ski stores in Breckenridge, Dillon, Frisco, and Silverthorne are even cheaper.

Breckenridge

❼ *22 mi from Keystone via U.S. 6 west, I–70 west, and Rte. 9 south.*

Breckenridge was founded in 1859, when gold was discovered in the surrounding hills. For the next several decades the town's fortunes rose and fell as its lodes of gold and silver were discovered and exhausted. Throughout the latter half of the 19th century and the early 20th century, Breckenridge was famous as a mining camp that "turned out more gold with less work than any camp in Colorado," according to the *Denver Post*. Dredging gold out of the rivers continued until World War II. Visitors today can still see evidence of the gold-dredging operations in the surrounding streams.

At 9,603 feet above sea level and surrounded by peaks that climb much higher, Breckenridge is the oldest continuously occupied town on the western slope. The town was originally dubbed Breckinridge, but the spelling was changed after its namesake, a former U.S. vice president, became a Confederate brigadier general in the Civil War. Due to an error by a cartographer, Breckenridge wasn't included on the official U.S. map until 1936, when the error was discovered by a member of the Breckenridge Women's Club.

Much of the town's architectural legacy from the mining era remains, so you'll find stores fit into authentic Victorian storefronts and restaurants and B&Bs tucked into Victorian homes. Surrounding the town's historic core, Breckenridge is packed with condos and hotels set in the woods and along the roads threading the mountainsides towards the base of the Peak 8.

Festivals run rampant here, and it's rare to show up when locals aren't celebrating. Among the best festivals are the annual Chevy Truck U.S. Snowboard Grand Prix and the International Snow Sculpture championships in January, the Spring Massive Festival in April, Genuine Jazz in Breckenridge in June, and the Toast of Breckenridge in August. In summer, the National Repertory Orchestra performs at the Riverwalk Center near the center of town.

Downtown Breckenridge has one of Colorado's largest historic districts, with about 250 buildings in the National Register of Historic Places. The district is roughly a compact 12 square blocks, bounded by Main, High, and Washington streets and Wellington Road. There are some 171 buildings with points of historical interest. Information about the district is available at the **Summit Historical Society** (⊠ 309 N. Main St. ☎ 970/ 453–9022 ⊕ www.summithistorical.org). It publishes walking tours that take you past many prominent structures, from simple log cabins to Victorians with lacy gingerbread trim, all lovingly restored.

Dating from 1875, the **Edwin Carter Museum** (✉ 111 Ridge St. ☎ 970/453–9022) is dedicated to the "log cabin naturalist" who helped to create Denver's Museum of Nature and Science. Look for realistic stuffed animals, including a large buffalo and a burro carrying a miner's pack.

A century ago, the **Washington Gold Mine** (✉469 Illinois Gulch Rd. ☎970/453–9022) was one of the area's largest producers of gold and silver. Five shafts burrowed deep underground. Tours include a visit to the mine and to a prospector's cabin. At **Lomax Placer Gulch** (✉ 301 Ski Hill Rd. ☎ 970/453–9022) you can learn how chemists determined the quality of the ore from nearby mines and discover the uses of tools such as sluices, riffles, and flumes. You can also pan for gold.

Since gold was discovered here in 1887, **The Country Boy Mine** (✉ 0542 French Gulch Rd. ☎ 970/453–4405 ⊕ www.countryboymine.com) has been one of the region's top producers. During tours of the facility you can belly up to the stove in the restored blacksmith shop. The mine has hay rides in summer and sleigh rides in winter.

Downhill Skiing & Snowboarding

With plenty of facilities for snowboarders, Breckenridge is popular with young people. There are several terrain parks and an area where you can learn to freeride. The resort's slopes are spread across four interconnected mountains in the Tenmile Range, named Peaks 7, 8, 9, and 10. Peak 7 and Peak 8 have above-the-timberline bowls and chutes. The lower reaches of Peak 7 have some of the country's prettiest intermediate-level terrain accessible by a lift. Peak 8 and Peak 9 have trails for all skill levels. Peak 10 has long trails with roller-coaster runs.

Owing to the town's proud heritage, many runs are named for the old mines, including Bonanza, Cashier, Gold King, and Wellington. During one week each January the town declares itself an "independent kingdom" during the wild revel called Ullr Fest, which honors the Norse god of snow. ☎ 970/453–5000 ⊕ *www.breckenridge.com* ☺ *Late Oct.–late May, daily 8:30–4.*

FACILITIES 3,398-foot vertical drop; 2,208 skiable acres; 13% beginner, 32% intermediate, 55% advanced; 2 high-speed six-person lifts, 6 high-speed quad chairs, 1 triple chair, 6 double chairs, 12 surface lifts.

LESSONS & PROGRAMS Contact the **Breckenridge Ski & Ride School** (☎ 888/576–2754) for information about lessons and specialty clinics. The Children's Ski and Ride School at Peak 8 has its own lift.

LIFT TICKETS Few skiers and riders pay the walk-up rate for a one-day lift ticket. Breckenridge skiers use a variety of season passes sold by Vail Resorts, which owns Breckenridge, Beaver Creek, Keystone, and Vail. Most vacationers purchase lift and lodging packages, or buy advance multi-day lift passes at discounted rates online.

RENTALS Rental packages (skis, boots, and poles; snowboards and boots) start at $20 per day. Prices vary, but not dramatically. If you can't find your brand of high performance equipment in the first store you try, you're sure to find it elsewhere.

CHILDCARE Breckenridge has a variety of childcare programs. All-day classes or half-day classes are available. Early drop-off is an option if you want to get to the slopes before everyone else. Classes meet at the Kids' Castle at Peak 8 and Beaver Run and the Village on Peak 9.

Nordic Skiing

BACKCOUNTRY SKIING They don't call this place Summit County for nothing—mountain passes above 10,000 feet allow for relatively easy access to high-country terrain and some of the area's best snow. But remember this word of caution: avalanche-related deaths are all too common in Summit County (more often involving snowmobilers than skiers). Don't judge an area solely on appearances, as slopes that look gentle may slide. Never head into the backcountry without checking weather conditions, without wearing appropriate clothing, or without carrying survival gear. For information on snow conditions and avalanche dangers, contact the **Dillon Ranger District Office of the White River National Forest** (☎ 970/468–5400).

One popular touring route is the trip to Boreas Pass, just south of Breckenridge. The 12-mi-long trail follows the route of a former railroad, with good views of distant peaks along the way. The **Summit County Huts Association** (✉ Box 2830, 80424 ☎ 970/453–9860 ⊕ www.summithuts.org) has four backcountry cabins where skiers can spend the night. If you're traveling farther afield, there are also cabins available through the **10th Mountain Division Hut Association** (☎ 970/925–5775 ⊕ www.huts.org).

TRACK SKIING The **Breckenridge Nordic Center** (☎ 970/457–7889) has 18½ mi of groomed tracks for classic and skate skiing, as well as ungroomed trails in the Golden Horseshoe. There's also 6 mi of marked snowshoe trails.

Other Sports & the Outdoors

Alpine Events (✉ 1516 Blue Ridge Rd. ☎ 970/262–0374) has a full range of summer and winter activities. In warm weather there are tours of the backcountry in all-terrain vehicles; cattle drives; and "saddle and paddle" days (combining horseback riding and rafting). In winter, there's snowmobiling, dogsledding, and sleigh rides.

FISHING **Blue River Anglers** (✉ 209 N. Main St. ☎ 970/968–2107), runs fly-fishing tours on the Blue, South Platte, and Williams Fork rivers, as well as various lakes and streams in the area. You can expect to catch 18- to 20-inch rainbow and brown trout.

Mountain Anglers (☎ 970/453–4665) organizes fishing trips, including float trips on the Colorado River, half-day trips on streams near Breckenridge, and all-day trips for rivers farther away.

FITNESS **Breckenridge Recreation Center** (✉ 800 Airport Rd. ☎ 970/453–1734) is a 62,000-square-foot facility with a fully equipped health club, two swimming pools, climbing walls, and indoor tennis and racquetball courts. Outdoor facilities include clay tennis courts, basketball courts, a skateboard park, and bike paths.

GOLF The 27-hole **Breckenridge Golf Club** (✉ 200 Clubhouse Dr. ☎ 970/453–9104) is the world's only municipally owned course designed by Jack Nicklaus. You may play any combination of the three sets: the Bear, the Beaver (with beaver ponds lining many of the fairways), or the Elk. The course resembles a nature reserve as it flows through mountainous terrain and fields full of wildflowers.

HORSEBACK RIDING For horseback riding, locals recommend **Breckenridge Stables** (⌂ Village Rd. ☎ 970/453–4438).

RAFTING **Breckenridge Whitewater Rafting** (✉ 842 N. Summit Blvd. Frisco ☎ 800/507–7703 or 970/668–1665 ⊕ www.breckenridgewhitewater.com) runs stretches of the Colorado, Arkansas, and Eagle rivers. The company also has guided fishing trips on the Colorado River and whitewater rafting through Gore Canyon.

Performance Tours Rafting (☎ 800/328–7238) leads expeditions on the Arkansas, Blue, and the upper Colorado rivers for newcomers looking for some action and experienced rafters ready for extremes. The company is based in Buena Vista, but will pick up groups in Breckenridge for all-day trips.

Whitewater Kayak Park (☎ 970/453–1734) is a playground for kayakers, with splash rocks, eddie pools, and S-curves. The park is open from April through August.

SNOWMOBILING **Good Times Adventures** (✉ 6061 Tiger Rd. Breckenridge ☎ 970/453–7604) runs snowmobile trips on more than 40 mi of groomed trails, through open meadows, and along the Continental Divide to 11,585-foot-high Georgia Pass.

Where to Stay & Eat

$$$–$$$$ ✕ **Pierre's Riverwalk Café.** A restaurant for all seasons, this little place lets you sit in the cozy upstairs dining room in winter or outside on the terrace when the weather is warmer. Chef Pierre Luc whips up innovative American and French cuisine in an open kitchen, then serves it with flair. The menu changes seasonally, but lobster crepes and escargots are usually among the appetizers, and roasted half duckling in ginger-orange-honey sauce and grilled loin of veal with pesto sauce are popular entrées. Ask your server to suggest something from the extensive wine list. ✉ 137 S. Main St. ☎ 970/453–0989 ▣ DC, MC, V ☉ Closed Mon.

★ $$–$$$ ✕ **Café Alpine.** With stained-glass windows set high on white walls, this intimate restaurant is one of the prettiest in town. The menu, which changes daily, focuses on foods found in the region. Entrées include such dishes as Asian-style seared jumbo sea scallops, creole-seasoned tenderloin medallions, and grilled ruby red trout. At the tapas bar (after 5 PM) you can sample specialties such as coriander- and-black-pepper–crusted tuna sashimi, garlic herb brie, and truffled white bean hummus. Café Alpine serves more than a dozen wines by the glass. It's a great place for lunch, when you can try one of the terrific soups, salads, or sandwiches. ✉ 106 E. Adams Ave. ☎ 970/453–8218 ▣ AE, D, MC, V.

$–$$ ✕ **Blue Moose.** Locals flock here for the hearty breakfasts of eggs, oatmeal, pancakes, and much more. At lunch, choose from one of the satisfying sandwiches, burritos, pastas, or salads. Neither the food nor the decor is fancy, but a meal here will hit the spot. ✉ 540 S. Main St. ☎ 970/453–4859 ▣ MC, V ☉ No dinner.

$–$$ ✕ **Downstairs at Eric's.** Loud, dark, and lots of fun, this place is video game central. Kids hang out in the arcade while their folks watch sports on the big-screen TVs. Pizzas are popular here—try them topped with veggies, seafood, or "garbage" (the management's colorful term for everything). The sandwiches are just as good. The Avalanche Burger is smothered with pizza sauce and mozzarella cheese, and the Philly Burger is topped with sautéed green peppers, onions, and melted Swiss cheese. It's good with chicken, too. ✉ 111 S. Main St. ☎ 970/453–1401 ▣ DC, MC, V.

$–$$ ✕ **Giampietro Pasta & Pizzeria.** The smell of freshly baked pizza will draw you to the door of this Italian eatery. Peek through the window and you'll see families huddled around tables covered with red checked tablecloths. There are lots of pastas on the menu, from classic baked ziti to tasty spaghetti with shrimp and pesto. Hungry diners gravitate toward the New York–style pizza with the works and the Sicilian-style deep-dish pizza. Feeling creative? Build your own calzone or pizza from the huge list of ingredients. A take-out menu is available. ✉ 100 N. Main St. ☎ 970/453–3838 ▣ MC, V.

$-$$ ✕ **Quandry Grille.** Overlooking pretty Maggie Pond, this barn-size place in Main Street Station serves up classic Western cuisine. Grab a seat at one of the rough-hewn wooden tables and enjoy a burger made with a half pound of beef or buffalo meat, chicken breast, or even black beans. Other choices range from burritos to bourbon chicken to trout fresh from the White River. ☒ *505 S. Main St.* ☏ *970/547–5969* ▭ *AE, DC, MC, V.*

$$$$ ▥ **Main Street Station.** One of the newer properties in Breckenridge, Main Street Station is a complex of four buildings. Grand Central, East, and West all have condos on the upper floors above retail outlets selling everything from ski gear to fresh flowers. The fourth building is a Hyatt Vacation Club with well-furnished studios and one- to four-bedroom condos. There are plenty of amenities, including 24-hour room service and grocery delivery. Continental breakfast in the comfortable Pioneer Club is part of the package. Many rooms overlook Maggie Pond, a popular gathering spot in the summer. The hustle and bustle of Main Street is just outside. ☒ *505 S. Main St., 80424* ☏ *888/832–7893* ☐ *970/547–5909* ⊕ *www.eastwestresorts.com* ⇆ *82 rooms* ⚭ *Restaurant, room service, pool, gym, hot tub, sauna, concierge* ▭ *AE, DC, MC, V* ⏃ *CP.*

$$$-$$$$ ▥ **Allaire Timbers Inn.** Nestled in a wooded area, this stone-and-timber log cabin has a living room dominated by a stone fireplace, as well as a reading loft and a sunroom with a green slate floor and hand-crafted log furniture. The main deck has a hot tub and spectacular views of the Tenmile Range. The cozy rooms have a rustic ambiance, with wood furniture and beds piled with handmade duvets. Two larger rooms (not quite accurately called suites) have king-size four-poster beds, two-person hot tubs, and river-rock fireplaces. A hearty breakfast is included, as are afternoon drinks. It's a 10-minute walk to Main Street. ☒ *9511 S. Main St., 80424* ☏ *970/453–7530 or 800/624–4904* ☐ *970/453–8699* ⊕ *www.allairetimbers.com* ⇆ *8 rooms, 2 suites* ⚭ *Outdoor hot tub* ▭ *AE, D, MC, V* ⏃ *BP.*

$$$-$$$$ ▥ **Lodge & Spa at Breckenridge.** Although it has the disadvantage of being on a mountainside beyond the downtown area, this lodging more than compensates with breathtaking views of the Tenmile Range from nearly every angle. There's regular shuttle service to the town and the ski area. The place resembles a cozy chalet, with rustic yet modern decor throughout. Well-lit, spacious rooms have plenty of amenities. Upgrade to a suite and you'll also have a fireplace and a kitchenette. The full-service spa and health club is a great place to relax after a morning of skiing. ☒ *112 Overlook Dr., 80424* ☏ *970/453–9300 or 800/736–1607* ☐ *970/453–0625* ⊕ *www.thelodgeatbreck.com* ⇆ *45 rooms, 1 house* ⚭ *Restaurant, cable TV, indoor pool, health club, 2 indoor hot tubs, 2 outdoor hot tubs, spa, meeting room* ▭ *AE, D, DC, MC, V* ⏃ *CP.*

$$-$$$$ ▥ **Hunter Placer Inn.** If you prefer a polished ambiance rather than the rustic style so prevalent in Breckenridge, consider this Bavarian-style lodge. It's a three-floor property in the woods, on the road heading up to Peak 8. The Southwest minisuite on the upper floor has a balcony with great views, but the smaller Country Cottage room is just as popular because of its private deck. A full breakfast is served on elegant Spode china. ☒ *275 Ski Hill Rd., 80424* ☏ *800/472–1430 or 970/453–7573* ☐ *970/453–2335* ⊕ *www.hunterplaceinn.com* ⇆ *3 suites, 5 rooms* ⚭ *Breakfast room* ▭ *AE, MC, V* ⏃ *CP.*

$$-$$$$ ▥ **Mountain Thunder Lodge.** Rising above the trees, this lodge constructed from rough-hewn timber brings to mind old-fashioned ski lodges. But the property, which opened in 2003, has modern amenities such as Internet access and a state-of-the-art gym. The condos all have fully furnished kitchens and snug living rooms where chairs are pulled up to rock fireplaces. The property is tucked into the woods on the road leading

up to Peak 8, but it's less than a five-minute walk from Main Street. The lodge has shuttle service to the slopes for guests. ⊠ *50 Mountain Thunder Dr., 80424* ☎ *888/989–1233* ⊕ *www.mtnthunderlodge.com* ➯ *71 rooms* ⚷ *Kitchens, refrigerators, pool, gym, hot tub* ⊟ *AE, D, DC, MC, V.*

$$–$$$$ 🏨 **Village at Breckenridge.** The word "village" puts it mildly, as this sprawling resort is spread over 14 acres of mountainous terrain. There's a wide variety of accommodations, from lodge-style rooms to three-bedroom condos, all ski-in/ski-out. The decor is just as varied, running from Southwestern chic to gleaming chrome-and-glass units. Studios and efficiencies all have kitchenettes. ⊡ *Box 8329, 80424* ☎ *970/453–2000 or 800/800–7829* ➚ *970/453–5116* ⊕ *www.villageatbreckenridge.com* ➯ *295 rooms* ⚷ *3 restaurants, some kitchenettes, indoor-outdoor pool, health club, 9 hot tubs, sauna, ice-skating, 3 ski shops, bar, theater, meeting rooms* ⊟ *AE, D, DC, MC, V.*

$–$$$$ 🏨 **B&Bs on North Main Street.** Innkeepers Fred Kinat and Diane Jaynes
Fodor'sChoice have lovingly restored three adjacent buildings on Main Street. An 1885
★ miner's cottage called the Williams House, once their home, now holds rooms reminiscent of the Victorian era. The Willoughby Cottage next door is a romantic retreat, complete with a gas-burning fireplace, hot tub, kitchenette, and rustic antique furnishings. A river runs past the modern, timber-frame Barn Above the River, which has five country-style rooms. These bedrooms have a deck or patio overlooking the river. One room has extra-long beds. ⊠ *303 N. Main St., 80424* ☎ *970/ 453–2975 or 800/795–2975* ➚ *970/453–5258* ⊕ *www.breckenridge-inn.com* ➯ *12 rooms* ⊟ *AE, DC, MC, V* ⏶⊘ *BP.*

$$–$$$ 🏨 **Great Divide Lodge.** Close to the ski areas and dozens of shops and restaurants, this lodge is in the middle of it all. Planned as a condominium, the complex has enormous studio and one-bedroom apartments, all of which have sophisticated Southwestern decor. There are thoughtful touches, such as plush robes in the baths and gourmet coffee for the coffeemakers. The one surprising omission is air-conditioning. ⊠ *550 Village Rd., 80424* ☎ *970/453–3150* ➚ *970/547–3012* ⊕ *www. greatdivelodge.com* ➯ *208 rooms* ⚷ *Restaurant, in-room data ports, minibars, indoor pool, cable TV, health club, hot tubs, ski shop, bar, business services, convention center, meeting rooms; no a/c* ⊟ *AE, D, DC, MC, V.*

CONDOMINIUMS Several companies handle condominiums in the area. **Breckenridge Accommodations** (⊡ Box 1931, 80424 ☎ 970/453–9140 or 800/872–8789 ⊕ www.breckenridgeaccommodations.com) has a selection ranging from snug studios to roomy houses. All are in downtown Breckenridge. **Breckenridge Central Lodging** (⊡ Box 709, 80424 ☎ 970/453–2160 or 800/858–5885 ⊕ www.skibcl.com) has more than 60 condo complexes in and around Breckenridge. **East West Resorts** (⊡ Box 2009, 80424 ☎ 800/525–2258 ⊕ www.eastwestresorts.com) manages Main Street Station and other complexes.

Nightlife

Breckenridge attracts an international clientele. The town has long been popular with a young, lively crowd that stays out until early morning.

BARS & LOUNGES **Breckenridge Brewery** (⊠ 600 S. Main St. ☎ 970/453–1550), serves eight microbrews, from Avalanche Amber Ale to Oatmeal Stout. It's a great après-ski spot. On the lower level of La Cima Mall, **Cecilia's** (⊠ 520 S. Main St. ☎ 970/453–2243) is a lounge with a mouthwatering array of martinis. Smokers head to the cigar parlor. **Downstairs at Eric's** (⊠ 111 S. Main St. ☎ 970/453–1401) is standing room only when there's a game. There are four big-screen TVs and 34 smaller ones scattered around the bar, so you don't have to worry about missing a touchdown. More than 120 brands of bottled beers make this a favorite of aficionados. With maroon velour wallpaper and lacy curtains, **Hearthstone** (⊠ 130 S. Ridge St. ☎ 970/453–1148) hints at its roots as a bordello. Skiers and locals scarf down the happy-hour specials, including jalapeño-stuffed shrimp.

MUSIC CLUBS **Tiffany's** (⊠ 20 Village Rd. ☎ 970/453–6000 Ext. 8732) is a lively après-ski destination. On weekends there's a DJ and dancing.

Shopping

Main Street, stretching the entire length of Breckenridge, has an abundance of shopping. There's everything from T-shirt shacks to high-end boutiques to art galleries. It's a good idea to spend an evening window-shopping before breaking out your wallet. In a quaint Victorian house, the **Bay Street Company** (⊠ 232 S. Main St. ☎ 970/453–6303) carries colorful hand-painted furniture and collectibles. At **Images of Nature** (⊠ 505 S. Main St. ☎ 970/547–2711), the walls are covered with outstanding photographs by photographer Thomas D. Mangelsen, who documents the great outdoors. Western paintings, Navajo weavings, and cowboy memorabilia are on display at the **Paint Horse Gallery** (⊠ 226 S. Main St. ☎ 970/453–6813). **Skilled Hands Gallery** (⊠ 110 S. Main St. ☎ 970/453–7818) looks like an arts-and-crafts show, with a large selection of souvenirs ranging from wood carvings to wind chimes.

Frisco

❽ *9 mi from Breckenridge via Rte. 9.*

Keep going past the hodgepodge of strip malls near the interstate and you'll find that low-key Frisco has a downtown district trimmed with restored B&Bs. The town is a low-cost-lodging alternative to pricier resorts in the surrounding communities.

Pretty **Frisco Historic Park** re-creates the boom days. Stroll through 10 buildings dating from the 1880s, including a fully outfitted one-room schoolhouse, a jail, and a log chapel. ⊠ *Main and 2nd Sts.* ☎ *970/668–3428* 🎟 *Free* ⊙ *Labor Day–Memorial Day, Tues.–Sat. 11–4; Memorial Day–Labor Day, Tues.–Sun. 11–4.*

Where to Stay & Eat

$$-$$$ ✕ **Silverheels at the Ore House.** At this longtime favorite, you can join the locals who gather around the bar for margaritas and tapas from 11 AM to 11 PM. The selection of tapas varies with the season, but may include such *bocadillos* (mouthfuls) as seared ahi tuna with ginger, brie with sweet chili relish, and sweet-hot chicken tequila sausages. Entrées range from a south-of-the-border combo that includes enchiladas and chilis rellenos to paella made with hot sausage. ⊠ *603 Main St.* ☎ *970/668–0345* ▤ *AE, DC, MC, V.*

$-$$ ✕ **Fiesta Jalisco.** With a sunny deck overlooking Tenmile Creek, this casual eatery serves up great margaritas and south-of-the-border specialties such as blackened fish tacos. The Taos tacos, with cheese, pinto beans, and roasted vegetables, are especially tasty. ⊠ *450 W. Main St.* ☎ *970/668–5043* ▤ *AE, DC, MC, V.*

$-$$ ✕ **Frisco's Bar & Grill.** There are no frills here, just juicy burgers, cheesy nachos, and spicy chicken wings, all served up to a boisterous crowd. The neon signs on the walls add a homey touch. ⊠ *720 Granite St.* ☎ *970/668–5051* ▤ *AE, D, MC, V.*

¢ ✕ **Log Cabin Café.** The is the best breakfast spot in Frisco, and arguably in the county. Basics such as eggs and bacon are most popular, but you can also chow down on biscuits and gravy with hashbrowns or *huevos* *rancheros* (Mexican-style scrambled eggs) with green chili. The Mountain Man, which includes an 8-ounce strip steak or two pork chops, is big enough for two. Amazingly, you can also get heart-healthy selections. Photographs depicting historic Frisco hang on the walls. ⌧ *121 Main St.* ☎ *970/668–3947* 🗏 *MC, V* ⊗ *No dinner.*

$$–$$$ 🖭 **Hotel Frisco.** After a day on the slopes, you can toast your toes by the river-rock fireplace in the lobby of this lodge. Among the historic buildings on Main Street, it's near all the best shops and restaurants. Easy access to Copper Mountain, Breckenridge, Keystone, and Vail make this a find in any season. ⌧ *308 Main St., 80443* ☎ *970/668–5009 or 800/ 262–1002* 🖷 *970/668–0695* ⊕ *www.hotelfrisco.com* ⇱ *12 rooms, 1 suite* ⌧ *In-room data ports, hot tub* 🗏 *AE, MC, V.*

Nightlife

Boisterous **Backcountry Brewery** (⌧ Main St. at Hwy. 9 ☎ 970/668–2337) is home to Great American Beer Festival gold medal–winner Telemark IPA and other homemade brews. The **Moose Jaw** (⌧ 208 Main St. ☎ 970/668–3931) is a locals' hangout. Pool tables beckon, and a plethora of old-time photographs, trophies, and newspaper articles makes the barn-wood walls all but invisible.

Shopping

Odds and ends fill the **Junk-Tique Antique Barn** (⌧ 313 Main St. ☎ 970/ 668–3040). Don't miss the locomotive dating from 1875.

Copper Mountain

❾ *7 mi from Frisco via I–70 south.*

Skiers who haven't driven past Copper Mountain within the last few years won't recognize the resort. Once little more than a series of strip malls strung along the highway, Copper Mountain is now thriving, courtesy of a $500 million facelift by its owner. The resort's heart is a pedestrian-only village, anchored by Burning Stones Plaza, which is prime people-watching turf. High-speed ski lifts march up the mountain on one side of the plaza, and the other three sides are flanked by condominiums with retail shops and restaurants on the ground floors. Lodgings extend westward toward Union Creek and eastward to Copper Station, where a six-pack high-speed lift ferries skiers uphill.

In winter, Burning Stones is filled with skiers on their way to and from the slopes and shoppers browsing for gifts to give to those left at home. In summer, people relax on condo balconies or restaurant patios as they listen to free concerts on the plaza or watch athletes inch up the 37-foot-high climbing wall. Kids can also learn to kayak or float in paddleboats.

Downhill Skiing & Snowboarding

Copper Mountain's slogan—"the place where the skiers ski and the boarders ride"—is more than accurate. The resort's 2,400 acres are spread across several peaks where the terrain is naturally separated into areas for beginners, intermediates, and expert skiers and snowboarders. The Union Creek area contains gentle, tree-lined trails for novices. The slopes above the Village at Copper and Copper Station are an invigorating blend of intermediate and advanced trails. Several steep moguled runs are clustered on the eastern side of the area, and have their own lift. At the top of the resort, and in the vast Copper Bowl, there's challenging above-tree-line skiing. Freeriders gravitate to the Super Pipe, the Terrain Park, and Hollywood Hits. Weather permitting, several days each week expert skiers can grab a free first-come/first-served snow cat ride up Tucker Mountain for an ungroomed, wilderness-style ski experience.

FACILITIES 2,601-foot vertical drop; 2,450 skiable acres; 21% easier, 25% more difficult, 36% advanced, 18% expert; 1 high-speed six-person chair, 4 high-speed quad chairs, 5 triple chairs, 5 double chairs, 4 surface lifts, 3 conveyor lifts.

LESSONS & PROGRAMS Copper Mountain's **Ski and Ride School** (☎ 970/968–2318) has a variety of classes for skiers and snowboarders, private lessons, and special sessions such as Level Busters (to help you make quantum leaps in skills), Bro Sessions (men only), and Sister Sessions (women only). Copper's Kids Sessions, divided into groups based on age and skill level, are designed to both teach and entertain. After-school sessions are available for those 3 to 15 years old, and there's Kids' Night Out, popular among parents who want an evening without the children.

LIFT TICKETS The price of lift tickets varies widely, as few visitors pay the walk-up rate. Vacationers usually purchase lift-and-lodging packages, which include discounted lift rates. Copper Mountain has last minute deals online at www.coppersavers.com. Many skiers and riders purchase passes which save 20% or more.

RENTALS Rental packages (skis, boots, and poles) for children start at $16 per day. For adults, packages start at $20 per day for sport ski packages and go as high as $32 per day for high-performance equipment. Snowboard rental packages (snowboard and boots) start at $20 for kids and $35 for adults. Helmet rentals begin at $10.

CHILDCARE Copper Mountain Resort has ski-school options for older kids, and childcare for youngsters. The smell of chocolate-chip cookies wafts from the Belly Button Bakery, day care for those two to four years old. Belly Button Babies accepts kids six weeks to two years old. Children's programs are based at the Schoolhouse in Union Creek.

Other Sports & the Outdoors

BICYCLING There are hundreds of miles of bike paths around the resort, leading up and down mountainsides and through high-country communities. During summer there are weekly group rides for early risers. **Team Managers** (✉ The Village at Copper ☎ 800/458–8386 ⊕ www.coppercolorado. com) has all the gear you need for cycling in the area.

For serious riders, especially would-be racers, the **Carpenter/Phinney Bike Camps** (☎ 303/442–2371 ⊕ www.bikecamp.com) are conducted in Summit County by Olympic medalists Connie Carpenter and Davis Phinney. Week-long sessions focus on riding technique, training methods, and bicycle maintenance.

GOLF Copper Mountain has reasonably priced golf and lodging packages for those interested in playing the two 18-hole courses. Right at the resort, **Copper Creek Golf Club** (✉ Wheeler Circle, Copper Mountain ☎ 970/968–3333), is a par-70, 6,053-yard course designed by Pete and Perry Dye. It flows up and down some of the ski trails at the base of the mountain and between condos and town homes in the resort's East Village.

About 15 minutes from Copper Mountain, **Raven Golf Club at Three Peaks** (✉ Silverthorne ☎ 970/262–3636) is an 18-hole beauty that has been called the best mountain course in Colorado. Each hole on this par-72, 7,413-yard course has dramatic views of the Gore Mountain Range.

Where to Stay & Eat

$$–$$$ ✕ **Endo's Adrenaline Café.** Enjoy rock music as you climb atop one of the high bar stools at this high energy establishment. Start with crunchy bruschetta, then move on to a grilled turkey melt or a half-pound burger.

This place is easy to find at the base of the American Eagle lift. ⊠ *The Village at Copper* ☎ 970/968–3070 ⊟ *AE, MC, V.*

$$–$$$ ✕ **Indian Motorcycle Café and Lounge.** There's excitement in the air, or maybe it's just the roar of the high-end motorcycles on display. You can't zoom away on one of bikes (although you can order one), but you can purchase souvenirs, ranging from T-shirts to leather jackets, in the gift shop. Relax on leather couches in the comfortable lounge and watch the big game on the big-screen TV, then dine on wood-fired pizza or sesame-crusted salmon in the dining room. ⊠ *Burning Stone Plaza* ☎ 970/968–2099 ⊟ *AE, MC, V.*

$$–$$$ ✕ **JJ's Rocky Mountain Tavern.** With a menu that changes depending on the season, this lively American bistro in East Village serves fresh and flavorful fare. Entrées include blackened salmon salad, pepper-grilled New York–strip steak, and pasta Genovese. Basics include tasty stone-oven pizzas and calzones. ⊠ *Copper Station* ☎ 970/968–2318 ⊟ *AE, D, DC, MC, V.*

$ ✕ **The Swivel.** When the snow's so good that you don't want to slow down, stop here for a quick bite at the base of the American Eagle lift. The proprietors are justifiably proud of the creative soups and salads—and the irresistibly gooey chocolate-chip cookies. ⊠ *The Village at Copper* ☎ 970/968–3070 ⊟ *AE, D, DC, MC, V* ⊘ *No dinner.*

$$–$$$$ ▥ **Copper Mountain Resort.** The resort runs the majority of lodging in the area, ranging from standard hotel rooms to spacious condos and town homes. No matter where you stay, you have use of the beautiful Copper Mountain Racquet & Athletic Club. The Village at Copper is the center of activity, as it's close to most of the shops and restaurants. The complex has studios and one- to four-bedroom units, many with fireplaces and balconies. East Village is not as centrally located, but provides easier access to the mountain's more challenging terrain. ⊠ *209 Tenmile Circle, 80443* ☎ 970/968–2882 *or* 800/458–8386 ⊟ 970/968–6227 ⊕ *www.coppercolorado.com* ⇥ *800 rooms* ⌂ *5 restaurants, 3 cafeterias, coffee shop, 18-hole golf course, 8 tennis courts, pool, health club, hot tub, sauna, hiking, horseback riding, racquetball, ice-skating, cross-country skiing, ski shop, playground, business services, meeting rooms* ⊟ *AE, D, DC, MC, V.*

Nightlife

Whether it's a warm afternoon in the winter or a cool evening in the summer, one of the best places to kick back is one of the tables spreading across Burning Stones Plaza. At the base of the American Eagle lift, **Endo's Adrenaline Café** (⊠ The Village at Copper ☎ 970/968–3070) is the place to be for après-ski cocktails. In the evenings there's live music and a raucous crowd. The East Village is home to **JJ's Rocky Mountain Tavern** (⊠ Copper Station ☎ 970/968–2318), the best place for a beer after a long day on the bumps. DJ Moe Dixon, a favorite with the locals, has people dancing on the tables when he spins on Wednesday and Thursday. **Pravda** (⊠ The Village at Copper ☎ 970/968–2222), a Russian-theme night spot, rocks all night long. Doormen are clad in KGB-style trench coats and fur hats, and bartenders aren't stingy with the vodka.

Shopping

Retail shops fill the ground floors of The Village at Copper, a pedestrian-only plaza. Visit the **Copper Clothing Company** (⊠ The Village at Copper ☎ 970/968–2318) for a fleece pullover to keep you warm on the slopes, a baseball cap to shade your face, and beer mugs and other remembrances of your trip—all with Copper Mountain logos, of course. **Giggleworks** (⊠ The Village at Copper ☎ 970/968–2318) is the place to buy gifts for the kids you left with grandma. There's a wide selection of interactive toys and games. Shop for ski and snowboard gear, book your ski lessons, and reserve rental equipment at **Mountain Adventure Center** (⊠ The Village at Copper ☎ 970/968–2318). A "paint your own pottery" store, **Ready, Paint, Fire** (⊠ The Village at Copper ☎ 970/968–2318) lets you make you own souvenirs. They'll even ship your purchases back home.

Leadville

⑩ *24 mi from Copper Mountain via Rte. 91 south; 31 mi from Vail via U.S. 24 south; 57 mi from Aspen via Rte. 82 east and Rte. 24 north (summer only).*

Sitting in the mountains at 10,430 feet, Leadville is America's highest incorporated town. In the middle of summer, the drive over Independence Pass is nothing short of spectacular. In the history of Colorado mining, perhaps no town looms larger than Leadville. Two of the state's most fascinating figures lived here: mining magnate Horace Tabor and his wife Elizabeth Doe McCourt, the central figures in John LaTouche's Pulitzer Prize–winning opera *The Ballad of Baby Doe*.

The larger-than-life Tabor amassed a fortune of $12 million, much of which he spent building monuments to himself and his "Baby Doe." His power peaked when his money helped him secure a U.S. Senate seat in 1883. He married his ambitious mistress, Baby Doe, after divorcing the faithful Augusta. The Tabors incurred the scorn of high society by throwing their money around in what was considered a vulgar fashion. In 1893, the repeal of the Sherman Act caused the price of silver to plummet, and Tabor was penniless. He died a pauper in 1899, admonishing Baby to "hang on to the Matchless," his most famous mine, which he was convinced would restore her fortunes. It never did. Baby Doe became a recluse, rarely venturing forth from her tiny unheated cabin beside the mine entrance. She froze to death in 1935.

The legacy of the Tabors can be found at several attractions in town. The **Tabor Home** is the modest dwelling where Horace lived with his first wife. The gray clapboard house is opened for groups of 10 or more, so call to arrange a tour. ⊠ *116 E. 5th St.* ☎ *719/486–2092* ☉ *Memorial Day–Labor Day, by appointment* 🎟 *$3.*

The three-story **Tabor Opera House** opened in 1879, when it was proclaimed the "largest and best west of the Mississippi." It hosted luminaries such as Harry Houdini, John Philip Sousa, and Oscar Wilde. ⊠ *308 Harrison St.* ☎ *719/486–8409* 🎟 *$4* ☉ *Memorial Day–Labor Day, Sun.–Fri. 9–5:30.*

The **Matchless Mine** and Baby Doe's squalid cabin are 1 mi east of downtown. Peer into the dark shaft, then pay a visit to the small museum with its tribute to the tragic love story of Horace and Baby Doe Tabor. ⊠ *E. 7th St.* ☎ *719/486–3900* ⊕ *www.matchlessmine.com* 🎟 *$5* ☉ *Memorial Day–Labor Day, daily 9–5; Labor Day–Memorial Day, Thurs.–Mon. 9–5.*

The **National Mining Hall of Fame and Museum** covers virtually every aspect of mining, from the discovery of precious ore to fashioning it into coins and other items. Dioramas in the beautiful brick building explain extraction processes. ⊠ *120 W. 9th St.* ☎ *719/486–1229* ⊕ *www. leadville.com* 🎟 *$6* ☉ *May–Oct., daily 9–5; Nov.–Apr., Mon.–Sat. 10–4.*

On a tree-lined street in downtown Leadville you'll find **The Healy House and Dexter Cabin,** an 1878 Greek revival house and an 1879 log cabin— two of Leadville's earliest residences. The lavishly decorated rooms of the clapboard house yield clues as to how the town's upper crust, such as the Tabors, lived and played. ✉ *912 Harrison St.* ☎ *719/486–0487* 💲 *$3.50* 🕐 *Memorial Day–Labor Day, daily 10–4:30.*

The **Heritage Museum** paints a vivid portrait of life in Leadville at the turn of the last century, with dioramas depicting life in the mines. There's also furniture, clothing, and toys from the Victorian era. ✉ *120 E. 9th St.* ☎ *719/486–1878* 💲 *$4* 🕐 *Memorial Day–late Oct., daily 10–4.*

Still chugging along is the **Leadville, Colorado & Southern Railroad Company,** which can take you on a breathtaking trip to the Continental Divide. The train leaves from Leadville's century-old depot and travels beside the Arkansas River to its headwaters at Freemont Pass. The return trip takes you down to French Gulch for views of Mt. Elbert, Colorado's highest peak. ✉ *326 E. 7th St.* ☎ *719/486–3936* 💲 *$24* 🕐 *Memorial Day–Labor Day, daily departures at 10 and 2.*

★ Eccentricity is still a Leadville trait, as witnessed by the **International Pack Burro Race.** The annual event, held the first weekend of August, takes man and beast over Mosquito Pass. The event is immortalized with thousands of T-shirts and bumper stickers that read, "Get Your Ass Over the Pass."

Sports & the Outdoors

CANOEING & KAYAKING There's no better way to see the high country than by exploring its lakes and streams. **Twin Lakes Canoe & Kayak** (✉ 6451 State Hwy. 82 ☎ 719/486–2710) supplies equipment to beginners who just want to stay cool and to experts wanting to run the rapids.

GOLF Play North America's highest 9-hole green—and watch your distance increase in the thin mountain air—at the **Mt. Massive Golf Course** (✉ 259 County Rd. 5 ☎ 719/486–2176). The greens fee is an affordable $10.

HORSEBACK RIDING If you're feeling like it's time to hit the trail, contact **George's Wild Wet Horseback Rides** (✉ 225 Harrison Ave. ☎ 719/486–0739). Rides can be tailored to all skill levels. **Mega Mountain Magic** (✉ 212 Augusta Dr. ☎ 719/486–4570) has a stable of horses ready for the trail.

SKIING Located 9 mi west of Leadville, **Ski Cooper** (✉ Rte. 24 ☎ 719/486–3684 ⊕ www.skicooper.com 🕐 Late-Nov.–early Apr., daily 9–4) has 385 skiable acres that are perfect for beginning or intermediate skiers. If you're up for a challenge, there are also 2,400 acres of pristine backcountry powder.

SNOWMOBILING Skiing extreme slopes isn't the only way to feel the blast of powder on your face. Fire up your own mechanical beast with **Alpine Snowmobiles** (✉ 4037 Hwy. 91 ☎ 719/486–9899). Snowmobiling fans often head to **2 Mile Hi Ski-Doo** (✉ 400 E. 6th St. ☎ 719/486–1183).

Where to Stay & Eat

$–$$ ✕ **The Grill.** Run by the Martinez family since 1965, this local favorite draws a standing-room-only crowd. The service is sometimes slow, but that leaves time for another of the marvelous margaritas. Tex-Mex dishes are the specialty here, including the hand-roasted green chilis. In summer you can retreat to the patio to toss horseshoes. ✉ *715 Elm St.* ☎ *719/486–9930* 🍴 *Reservations essential* 🚭 *MC, V.*

$–$$ 🏨 **Delaware Hotel.** This beautifully restored hotel is one of the best examples of high Victorian architecture in the area, so its no surprise it's listed in the National Register of Historic Places. The columned lobby is graced with brass fixtures, crystal chandeliers, and rich oak paneling. The comfortable rooms are individually decorated with graceful touches like lace curtains and antique heirloom quilts. There are also modern conveniences such as cable TV. A Continental breakfast is included in the rate. ⊠ *700 Harrison Ave., 80461* ☏ *719/486–1418 or 800/748–2004* 🖷 *719/486–2214* ⊕ *www.delawarehotel.com* 🖘 *36 rooms* ♨ *Cable TV, hot tub* ⊟ *AE, D, DC, MC, V* ⏧ *CP.*

$–$$ 🖭 **Ice Palace Inn Bed & Breakfast.** Named for a grandiose hotel that was
Fodor's Choice   built in 1895, the Ice Palace was built with lumber taken from the ice-
★   cold original (some 5,000 tons of ice sculptures adorned rooms).
Rooms in this lovingly restored Victorian are warmly decorated with
period antiques and luxurious featherbeds. Innkeepers Giles and Kami
Kolakowski are just as inviting. A full breakfast and afternoon tea are
included in the room rate. Don't forget your slippers; no shoes are allowed on the inn's plush carpets. ⊠ *813 Spruce St., 80461* ☏ *719/
486–8272 or 800/754–2840* 🖷 *719/486–0345* ⊕ *www.icepalaceinn.
com* 🖘 *5 rooms* ♨ *Dining room, no-smoking rooms* ⊟ *AE, D, DC,
MC, V* ⏧ *BP.*

VAIL VALLEY

Vail Valley, conjured up as a marketing term several years ago, has become a reality in most visitors' minds. Today, the valley starts where
the condos and timeshares appear as you're driving down from Vail Pass.
From this end of town, called East Vail, the valley stretches all the way
past Edwards, about 20 mi to the west. It encompasses Vail Village, Eagle-
Vail, Minturn, Avon, Beaver Creek, Arrowhead and Edwards, a string
of resorts straddling the highway and tucked into the mountains. The
vibe in these places varies dramatically, from Beaver Creek, where the
art-filled plazas are linked by escalators; to Edwards, a rapidly growing area where towering condo complexes house shops and restaurants
on the ground floor, to Vail Village, filled with styles of lodging, dining
and shopping appealing to a wide range of tastes. And there's no reason that you have to stay put in one place. It's common for those staying in one of town to ski, dine, or shop in the others, because it's so
easy to go from one to another.

In winter, this region is famous for the glittering resorts of Vail and Beaver
Creek. Between these two areas, skiers and snowboarders have almost
7,000 acres at their disposal. The variety of terrains is mind-boggling.
Beginners aren't limited to the bunny slopes near the lodges; they can
practice their turns on some of the higher peaks. At the end of the day
they can ski down one of the long, winding trails to the bottom or grab
a lift. Intermediates have more long, corduroy-groomed runs than they
could explore in a week. Advanced skiers and experts have a quiver full
of moguled runs, ranging from baby bumps for beginners to bus-size
bumps, some even iced down for national freestyle contests. Everyone
from intermediates to hotshots can explore the vast bowls.

If downhill skiing isn't your thing, you can explore the wilderness on
groomed cross-country trails that thread through tall pines, sometimes past
deer or elk which eye you cautiously. Meandering through the woods on
snowshoes is a great way to see this alpine wonderland. Riding a snowmobile along trails through icy meadows to the crest of the Continental
Divide ensures spectacular views. Tucked under blankets on a horse-
drawn sleigh, you're at the perfect angle to view the stars overhead.

In summer, these resorts are great bases from which you can explore
the high country by foot, horseback, raft, or bike. Lifts take you uphill
to dozens of trails leading around the peaks. Some trails are designated
for bikers, others for hikes. In addition, there are hundreds of miles of
trails weaving through the White River National Forest. Warm-weather
weekends are filled with an exciting range of cultural events, including

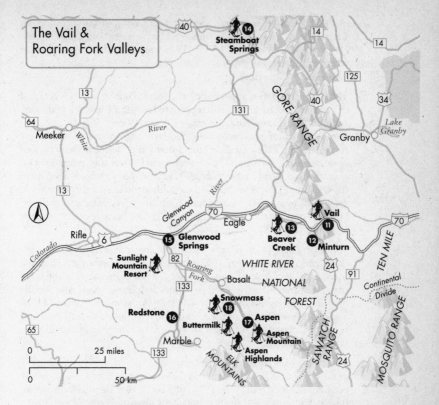

The Vail &
Roaring Fork Valleys

performances by groups such as the New York Philharmonic and the
Bolshoi Ballet.

Any time of year, you can get up early for a hot air balloon ride that
gives you a bird's-eye view of the mountains. In the afternoon you can
check into a spa to be pampered with a range of treatments ranging from
fabulous facials to relaxing massages. Or you can simply shop. In general, you'll find fairly inexpensive items in Edwards, high-end boutiques in Beaver Creek, and a little bit of everything in Vail.

Vail

⓫ *20 mi from Copper Mountain or 100 mi from Denver via I–70 west.*

Consistently ranked as one of North America's leading ski destinations,
Vail has a reputation few can match. The four-letter word means Val-
halla for skiers of all skill levels. Vail has plenty of open areas where
novices can learn the ropes. It can also be an ego-building mountain for
intermediate and advanced skiers who hit the slopes only a week or two
a season. Some areas, like Blue Sky Basin, make you feel like a pro.

Vail is one of the least likely success stories in skiing. Seen from the village, the mountain doesn't look at all imposing. There are no glower-
ing glaciers, no couloirs, and no chutes slashed from the rock. Even local
historians admit that the Gore Creek Valley in which Vail sits was an
impoverished backwater, too isolated to play a prominent or colorful
role in Colorado history, until the resort opened its gates in 1962.

In truth, the men who lent their names to the valley and resort deserve
more notoriety than notice. Sir St. George Gore was a wealthy, swag-
gering, drunken lout of a baronet who went on a three-year bacchanal

in the 1850s and butchered every herd of elk and buffalo in sight. Charles Vail, the otherwise obscure chief engineer of the Colorado Highway Department from 1930 to 1945 was—according to townspeople who dealt with him—an ornery cuss who was rumored to accept kickbacks from contractors.

Then two visionaries appeared on the scene: Pete Seibert, a veteran of the 10th Mountain Division that prepared for alpine warfare in the surrounding Gore and Sawatch ranges during World War II, and Earl Eaton, a uranium prospector who had grown up in and surveyed these ranges. In 1957 they ascended the mountain now known as Vail, and upon attaining the summit discovered what skiers and riders salivate over: the Back Bowls, more than 3,000 acres of open glades formed when the Ute Indians set "spite fires" to the timberland in retaliation for being driven out by ranchers and miners. After five years of bureaucratic red tape and near financial suicide, Seibert's dream became reality, and the resort known as Vail was created.

Vail wasn't much to look at in the early years—at the base of the mountain there were a handful of buildings vaguely resembling a Bavarian hamlet. Today's visitors only get a sense of that ambiance in the heart of the village, now surrounded by condo complexes, hotels, and upscale homes in a large village that sprawls for miles along both sides of I–70 and climbs up the sides of the mountains. It's informally sectioned into residential East Vail, upscale Vail Village, and more modest and utilitarian Lionshead.

The 1990s were an era of consolidation in the ski industry, and many of the major resorts were snapped up by companies that were, or shortly became, publicly traded. In 1996, in a move that surprised the ski industry, Vail purchased Breckenridge and Keystone resorts, then began selling stock as Vail Resorts. Since then, the company has purchased Heavenly in California, Snake River Lodge & Spa in Wyoming, and lodges at several other resorts. Among the positive aspects of this consolidation was the creation of flexible passes allowing skiers to use the lifts on nearly all the company's properties.

Vail, along with most savvy ski resorts, actively courts families through special packages, classes for youngsters, and activities geared to people of all ages. At Vail, kids can play in specially designed ski parks like Chaos Canyon and Fort Whippersnapper. After a day on the slopes, the whole family can get in on the action at Adventure Ridge, where activities range from snowmobile rides to laser tag.

In terms of size, Vail overwhelms nearly every other ski area in North America. There are 5,289 acres popular with skiers and riders of all skill levels. Areas are clearly linked by a well-placed network of lifts and trails. The Front Side is draped with long trails; the infamous Back Bowls beckon powder skiers. A few hours of adventure skiing in Blue Sky Basin is a must for intermediate to advanced skiers and riders.

Vail is equally attractive in summer and fall. The same slopes are popular with hikers and mountain bike fanatics, who can take their bikes to the top on a lift. The village hosts a wide variety of festivals, starting with the Teva Mountain Games, showcasing such sports as kayaking, rafting, and mountain biking. Then there's the Big Wheels, Brews and Chili Festival, the Vail Wine and Food Festival, and the Annual Vail Jazz Party, to name just a few. There are also free outdoor concerts by up-and-coming musicians, as well as concerts by some of the biggest names in the business.

Vail is only a few decades old, so there aren't many sights. But there are two places worth a visit. The **Betty Ford Alpine Gardens**, open daily from snowmelt (around Memorial Day) to snowfall (Labor Day or a bit later), are an oasis of forsythia, heather, and wild roses. These are the highest public botanical gardens in North America. ⊠ *Ford Park* ☎ *970/476–0103* ⊕ *www.bettyfordalpinegardens.org.*

The **Colorado Ski Museum/Ski Hall of Fame** traces the development of the sport throughout the world, with an emphasis on Colorado's contributions. On display are century-old skis and tows, early ski fashions, and an entire room devoted to the 10th Mountain Division, an Army division that trained nearby. ⊠ *231 S. Frontage Rd.* ☎ *970/476–1876* ⊕ *www.skimuseum.net* ⊡ *$1* ⊙ *Tues.–Sun. 10–5.*

Downhill Skiing & Snowboarding

Year after year, Vail logs more than a million "skier days" (the ski industry's measure of ticket sales), perpetuating its ranking as one of the top two or three most popular resorts in North America. From the top of China Bowl to the base of the Lionshead Gondola, the resort is more than 7 mi across. The vast acreage is roughly divided into three sections: the Front Side, the Back Bowls, and Blue Sky Basin.

Fodor'sChoice ★ Vail is perhaps best known for its legendary **Back Bowls,** more than 3,000 acres of wide open spaces that are sensational on sunny days. Standing in any one of them, it's difficult to get a visual perspective, as skiers on the far side resemble Lilliputians. These bowls stretch from the original Sun Up and Sun Down to Game Creek on one side and Teacup, China, Siberia, and Outer Mongolia bowls on the far side. The terrain ranges from wide, groomed swatches for intermediate skiers to seemingly endless bump fields to glades so tight that only an expert boarder can slither between the trees. When there's fresh powder, these bowls beckon to skiers intermediate and above. But after the fresh snow has been tracked up by skiers and pummeled by wind and sun, it may be wise for less-than-expert skiers to stay in the groomed sections of the bowls.

The Front Side of Vail Mountain delivers a markedly different experience. Here there's lots of wide-trail skiing, heavily skewed toward groomed intermediate runs, especially off the Northwood Express, Mountaintop Express, and Avanti Express lifts, as well as the slopes reachable via the Eagle Bahn gondola. Pockets of advanced and expert terrain are tucked in and around the blue-marked slopes. The upper parts of Riva Ridge (the Glade) and the top of Prima (the Cornice) are just a few of places you'll find skilled skiers. The best show in town is on Highline (you can see it while riding Chair 10), where the experts groove through the moguls and those with a bit less experience careen around the bumps. The other two extremely difficult double-black-diamond trails off this slow lift are the best cruisers on the mountain for skilled skiers.

It takes time to reach Blue Sky Basin, made up of three more bowls, but it's worth the effort. Tucked away in a secluded corner of Vail, this 645-acre area has been left in a wilder state, and the majority of the terrain is never groomed. Intermediate skiers will find a few open trails with spectacular views of rugged mountain peaks. For advanced and expert skiers, the real fun is playing in glades and terrain with names such as Heavy Metal, Skree Field, the Divide, and Champagne Glade. ☎ *800/404–3535* ⊕ *www.vail.com* ⊙ *Mid-Nov.–mid-Apr., daily 9–4.*

FACILITIES 3,450-foot vertical drop; 5,289 skiable acres; 18% beginner, 29% intermediate, 53% expert (the majority of this terrain is in the Back Bowls); 1 gondola, 14 high-speed quad chairs, 1 regular quad, 3 triple chairs, 5 double chairs, 10 surface lifts.

LESSONS & PROGRAMS — The **Vail and Beaver Creek Ski and Snowboard School** (☎ 970/476–3239) runs classes for skiers of all levels. The school at Vail has almost 1,000 instructors who teach in 30 languages. Afternoon-only group lessons are $65 to $80, depending on the season. All-day lessons are $75 to $100. Special workshops and clinics are offered throughout the year. Beginners take three-day courses that include equipment rental and lift passes. Workshops for women, teen sessions, and telemark courses are among the programs targeting specific groups.

LIFT TICKETS — Few skiers pay the walk-up rate for a one-day lift ticket. Colorado's Front Range skiers purchase a variety of season passes. Most vacationers purchase lift-and-lodging packages, or go online to buy multi-day lift passes at discounted rates. A lift ticket purchased at either Vail or Beaver Creek may also be used at Breckenridge, Keystone, and Arapahoe Basin.

RENTALS — **Vail Sports** (✉ 600 Lionshead Pl. ☎ 970/479–0600) is within steps of the lifts. The shop rents a wide range of ski gear, including high-end equipment. Prices for skis range from $17 to $45 a day. Book online and save up to 10% on daily rentals and up to 20% for rentals of five days or more. At Lionshead, **One Track Mind Snowboard Shop** (✉ 492 E. Lionshead Circle ☎ 970/476–1397) you can rent everything you need for snowboarding.

Nordic Skiing

BACKCOUNTRY SKIING — The 10th Mountain Division Hut and Trail System reaches far into the backcountry around Vail. One route continues all the way to Aspen. Maps and other information are available through the **10th Mountain Division Hut Association** (✉ 1280 Ute Ave., Aspen 81611 ☎ 970/925–5775 ⊕ www.huts.org). Hut reservations should be made at least a month in advance.

If you aren't familiar with the area's backcountry trails, hiring a guide is a good idea. In Vail, contact **Paragon Guides** (✐ Box 130, Vail 81618 ☎ 970/926–5299).

TRACK SKIING — The cross-country skiing at the **Vail Nordic Center** (✉ 1778 Vail Valley Circle ☎ 970/476–9090) is on a golf course. It's not the most beautiful route, but it's free.

Other Sports & the Outdoors

Activities Desk of Vail (☎ 970/476–9090) has the lowdown on events in the area.

BICYCLING — A popular summer destination for both road bikers and mountain bikers, Vail has a variety of paved bike paths (including one which leads up to Vail Pass), plus dozens of miles of dirt mountain bike trails. You can take bikes on lifts heading uphill, then head downhill on an array of routes. **Vail Bike Services** (✉ 450 E. Lionshead Circle ☎ 970/476–1233) is the place to get more information about the trails around Beaver Creek.

Each summer, riders from around the region participate in races sponsored by the **Beaver Creek & Vail Summer Adventure Ridge Mountain Challenge** (✉ 700 S. Frontage Rd. E ☎ 970/479–2280 ⊕ www.vailrec.com).

FITNESS — Deciding to get a massage or spa treatment is the easy part—deciding where to get it is a bigger problem, because there are many outstanding spas and health clubs in the area. The **Aria Spa & Health Club** (✉ 1300 Westhaven Dr. ☎ 970/476–7400) is one of the best places to be pampered. If you're up for a full-spa experience, ask about the Symphony for the Senses packages, spa days designed just for you. This huge facility in the Vail Cascade Resort & Spa also has racquetball, basketball, and tennis courts. In the Sonnenalp Resort, the lovely **Sonnenalp Spa** (✉ 20

Vail Rd. ☎ 970/476–5656) is a European-style facility where you can relax on one of the lounge chairs around a big fireplace as you sip juice from the nearby bar. **Vail Mountain Athletic Club** (✉ 352 E. Meadow Dr. ☎ 970/476–7960) is a full-service health club with such extras as an indoor climbing wall.

GOLF
Golfers who love to play mountain courses know that some of the best are in Vail Valley. These courses meander through the valleys dividing the area's soaring peaks. The region is home to more than a dozen courses, and there are another half-dozen within easy driving distance. It's all just a matter of where you are staying and how much you want to spend. Some courses are only open to members and to guests at certain lodges.

Guests at the Sonnenalp Resort get preferred tee times at the **Sonnenalp Golf Course** (✉ 1265 Berry Creek Dr., Edwards ☎ 907/477–5370), a Robert Cupp–Jay Morrish design that threads through an upscale neighborhood. There are some serious elevation changes. The area's cheapest course is at the **Vail Golf Club** (✉ 1778 Vail Valley Dr. ☎ 970/479–2260), a municipal course which rolls along between homes and condominiums in East Vail.

HIKING
Paragon Guides (✉ Box 130, 81618 ☎ 970/926–5299) offers backcountry adventures. In summer, there's rock climbing, mountain biking, and day and overnight llama treks in and around Vail Valley. In winter, the company runs daylong ski trips through the backcountry, and three- to six-day trips along the 10th Mountain Division Hut System.

HORSEBACK RIDING
One of the best ways to see Vail Valley is from the back of a horse. On scenic Sweetwater Lake, **A. J. Brink Outfitters** (✉ 3406 Sweetwater Rd., Sweetwater ☎ 970/524–9301) has day and overnight horseback excursions high in the Flat Tops Wilderness.

About 12 mi north of Vail, **Piney River Ranch** (✉ Piney Lake ☎ 970/476–3941) has pony rides for kids and guided one-hour horseback rides for adults.

NATURE CENTERS
Vail has several centers where locals and visitors can get more information about exploring the great outdoors. The **Vail Nature Center** (✉ 601 Vail Valley Dr. ☎ 970/479–2291) is located in an old homestead just across from the Betty Ford Alpine Gardens. You can sign up for half-day and full-day backcountry hikes, wildflower walks, morning birding expeditions, and evening beaver pond tours. During winter, backcountry snowshoe excursions and photography classes are available at the **Vail Nordic Center** (✉ 1778 Vail Valley Dr. ☎ 970/479–2264).

SNOWMOBILING
Adventure Ridge (✉ 600 Lionshead Circle ☎ 970/476–9090), at the top of Lionshead, leads twilight snowmobile excursions, as well as snowshoe, snow inner-tubing, and ice-skating trips.

Where to Stay & Eat

$$$$ ✕ **Game Creek Club.** Getting to this private club is certainly half the fun, as you must catch a gondola up the mountain, then hop on a snow cat to get across Game Creek Bowl. The Bavarian-style lodge is members-only for lunch, but open to the public for dinner all year and for an outstanding Sunday brunch during summer. Be prepared to linger over a multicourse prix-fixe meal as you enjoy spectacular views of the slopes and the mountains beyond. You might start with a house-cured gravlax and mesclun salad with toasted goat cheese, followed by grilled venison strip loin or a porcini-crusted dry-aged sirloin. ✉ *278 Hanson Ranch Rd.* ☎ *970/479–4280* ♤ *Reservations essential* ▭ *AE, D, DC, MC, V* ☺ *No lunch.*

★ $$$$ ✕ **Sweet Basil.** The decor may be understated—blond-wood chairs and buff-colored walls—but chef Bruce Yim's contemporary cuisine is anything but. He serves up American favorites with unmistakable Mediterranean and Asian influences. He uses the freshest ingredients available, so the menu changes several times each season. You might find grilled-crab dumplings, seared Hawaiian ahi, or grilled-beef tenderloin with foie-gras ravioli and wild mushroom and barley ragout. Pair these entrées with one of the hundreds of wines from the restaurant's award-winning cellar. Leave room for luscious desserts such as hot sticky toffee pudding cake or chocolate banana–cream tart. ⊠ *193 E. Gore Creek Dr.* ☎ *970/476–0125* ▭ *AE, MC, V.*

$$$–$$$$ ✕ **Larkspur.** An open kitchen bustling with activity is the backdrop at Larkspur, popular with a parka-clad crowd at lunch and well-dressed diners in the evening. Chef Thomas Salamunovich has a talent for blending cuisines, so the menu is filled with creative entrées such as pumpkin seed–crusted salmon with wild mushroom–potato ravioli and duck breast with foie gras and duck-confit stuffing. Leave room for decadent desserts such as warm chocolate spice cake and petite doughnuts with chocolate and espresso sabayon. ⊠ *Golden Peak Lodge* ☎ *970/479–8050* ⌲ *Reservations essential* ▭ *AE, MC, V.*

$$$–$$$$ ✕ **Terra Bistro.** With dark-wood furniture and walls hung with black-and-white photographs, this sleek, sophisticated space looks as if it belongs in a big city. Only the crackling fireplace reminds you that this is Vail. The menu focuses on contemporary American cuisine that throws in a few Asian, Mediterranean, and Southwestern influences. White bean and squash sauté and peppered beef tenderloin in a cabernet reduction are headliners. The herbed Yukon Gold potatoes are a satisfying side. The restaurant is in the Vail Mountain Lodge & Spa, so it's no surprise that organic produce and free-range meat and poultry are used whenever possible. ⊠ *352 E. Meadow Dr.* ☎ *970/476–6836* ▭ *AE, D, MC, V.*

$$–$$$$ ✕ **Chap's Grill & Chophouse.** This steak house in the Vail Cascade Resort earned its reputation by serving only the tenderest cuts of meat. Locals rave about the dry-aged beef ribeye and the Blackfoot buffalo ribeye. But Chap's is also a well-regarded seafood restaurant, which is why you'll find such tempting entrées as seared ahi and 1½-pound Nova Scotia lobsters. Savory soups, such as caramelized lobster and corn bisque, are good starters. Finish the meal with chocolate-lava cake—it has a molten-truffle center that melts in your mouth. ⊠ *Vail Cascade Resort, 1300 Westhaven Dr.* ☎ *970/479–7014* ▭ *AE, D, DC, MC, V.*

$$–$$$ ✕ **Alpenrose Restaurant & Patisserie.** It began as a bakery in 1976, so this restaurant's sugar-coated decor doesn't come as a surprise; it's as over-the-top as a wedding cake. Dusted with sugar and drowning in butter, the freshly made desserts are so good and so bad for you. The schnitzel and steak tartare are delicious at dinner, as are the seafood specials. ⊠ *100 E. Meadow Dr.* ☎ *970/476–3194* ▭ *AE, MC, V* ☉ *No lunch Tues.*

★ $$–$$$ ✕ **La Bottega.** This casual, small restaurant has a loyal following that appreciates the creative northern Italian fare. Customers especially love the lunch specials, which include creative pizzas from the stone ovens. In true bistro fashion, the specials are posted on a huge blackboard. Some people turn out for a glass of vino in the wine bar, which takes up one side of the establishment. The cellar is one of the best in town. ⊠ *100 East Meadow Dr.* ☎ *970/476–0280* ▭ *D, MC, V.*

$–$$$ ✕ **Blu's.** More of a bistro than a restaurant, this longtime favorite enjoys a great location in the heart of Vail Village. Its popularity is due to a fun, affordable menu. The food is fresh and zippy, from schnitzel to meat loaf to chicken-fried steak. It's constantly hopping at breakfast and lunch, when the prices are much cheaper than at dinner. ⊠ *193 E.*

Gore Creek Dr. ☎ 970/476–3113 ⚓ *Reservations not accepted* ▭ *AE, DC, MC, V.*

$–$$ ✕ **Bada Bing Gourmet Pizza Company.** This locally owned pizza place lets you pick up your order or have it delivered. You won't be able to refuse such special pies as the "Sleeps Wit Da Fishes" and the "Wise Guy." ⊠ *1000 Lionsridge Rd.* ☎ 970/477–2232 ▭ *AE, MC, V.*

$–$$ ✕ **Bart & Yeti's.** Grilled Portobello-mushroom sandwiches, spicy Southwestern green chili, and Irish stew are among the choices at this laid-back restaurant. Pictures of cowboys on horseback, wagon wheels, and other odds and ends line the rough log walls. If you want a full meal, entrées include favorites like barbecued baby-back ribs and crispy fried chicken. The deck is a popular gathering spot in warm weather. The place is in Lionshead, just north of the Eagle Bahn gondola. ⊠ *Lionshead* ☎ 970/476–2754 ▭ *AE, D, MC, V.*

$ ✕ **Pazzo's Pizzeria.** This hole-in-the-wall is right in the heart of Vail Village. It serves some of the best pizzas in the area, ready to eat in the dining room or take to one of the tables outside. Create your own masterpiece from a list of more than 20 ingredients, or opt for the cheesy lasagna, the chicken Parmigiana, or one of the chubby calzones. Ask about the happy-hour specials. There's a second branch of Pazzo's in Avon. ⊠ *122 East Meadow Dr.* ☎ 907/476–9026 ▭ *AE, MC, V* ⊠ *82 E. Beaver Creek Blvd., Avon* ☎ 970/949–9900 ▭ *AE, MC, V.*

$$$$ ▦ **Galatyn Lodge.** This luxury lodge in a quiet part of Vail Village maintains a low profile, which is just the approach its regulars prefer. A staff is on call 24 hours a day to see to your every need. There are a handful of four-bedroom apartments that can be partitioned off into smaller spaces. All of these apartments are spacious, luxuriously decorated, and have kitchens with all the latest gadgets. ⊠ *365 Vail Valley Dr., 81657* ☎ 970/479–2418 or 800/943–7322 🖷 970/479–0102 ⇲ *3 4-bedroom apartments* ⚲ *Pool; no smoking* ▭ *AE, MC, V.*

$$$$ ▦ **Lodge at Vail.** If what's important is "location, location, location," this ski-in/ski-out lodge has it all. The first facility to open in Vail, it has condos of many shapes and sizes. Some of the original rooms, decorated by their owners, have a homey feel. The newer wing has some lovely suites with more space and marble baths. The signature restaurant, the highly-rated Wildflower, serves creative American cuisine. Skiers can stoke up at the expansive breakfast and lunchtime buffets at Cucina Rustica, the hotel's other restaurant. It becomes a Tuscan grill at dinner. Mickey's piano bar has long been a favored après-ski spot. ⊠ *174 E. Gore Creek Dr., 81657* ☎ 970/476–5011 or 800/367–7625 🖷 970/476–7425 ⊕ *www.lodgeatvail.com* ⇲ *123 rooms, 44 1-, 2- and 3-bedroom condos* ⚲ *2 restaurants, pool, gym, hot tub, sauna, spa, ski shop, bar* ▭ *AE, D, DC, MC, V.*

★ **$$$$** ▦ **Sonnenalp Resort.** Both the truly luxurious accommodations and the matchless service make this European-style lodge an outstanding place to stay. The owners, members of the Fassler family, have been in the hotel business for generations. The rooms have a wide variety of configurations, including some that are perfect for families. Stucco walls and wood beams call to mind the lodges of Austria, and the heated marble floors in the large bathrooms add a touch of elegance. Some rooms have fireplaces. The superb restaurants include the Western saloon Bully Ranch (great barbecue) and Ludwig's (fine Continental fare). ⊠ *20 Vail Rd., 81657* ☎ 970/476–5656 or 800/654–8312 🖷 970/476–1639 ⊕ *www. sonnenalp.com* ⇲ *2 rooms, 90 suites* ⚲ *2 restaurants, in-room data ports, indoor pool, health club, 2 indoor hot tubs, 1 outdoor hot tub, spa, bar* ▭ *AE, D, DC, MC, V.*

$$$$ ▦ **Vail Cascade Resort & Spa.** Down-to-earth yet luxurious is the best way to describe this ski-in/ski-out hotel. Despite its size, it manages to maintain an intimate feel. Rooms reflect a "mountain eclectic" decor, with rich plaid and floral fabrics, wicker furniture, and wrought-iron lamps. The restaurant has garnered acclaim for its outstanding grilled foods and fine selection of wines. Guests have access to the adjoining Aria Spa & Club and the full-service health club with racquetball, squash, and basketball courts. The best deals at any time of year are the packages, which might include lift tickets in winter or sports massages in summer. ☒ *1300 Westhaven Dr., 81657* ☎ *970/476-7111* 🖷 *970/479-7020* ⊕ *www. vailcascade.com* 🛏 *292 rooms, 27 suites, 78 condominiums* ⚭ *Restaurant, tennis courts, pool, hair salon, health club, hot tubs, spa, 2 ski shops, bar, cinema, business services, meeting rooms* ▤ *AE, DC, MC, V.*

$$$-$$$$ ▦ **Sitzmark Lodge.** This cozy lodge buzzes with a dozen languages, thanks to the international guests who return year after year. Rooms, which range from moderate to large, have balconies that look out onto Vail Mountain or Gore Creek. Some have gas-burning fireplaces to keep things comfortable. The decor is a blend of light woods and cheerful floral fabrics. The staff is extremely friendly, encouraging guests to congregate in the sunny, split-level living room on winter afternoons for complimentary mulled wine. A Continental breakfast is served in winter. ☒ *183 Gore Creek Dr., 81657* ☎ *970/476-5001 or 888/476-5001* 🖷 *970/476-8702* ⊕ *www.sitzmarklodge.com* 🛏 *35 rooms* ⚭ *Restaurant, room service, in-room safes, in-room data ports, refrigerators, pool, hot tub, sauna* ▤ *D, MC, V.*

$$-$$$ ▦ **Gasthof Gramshammer.** Pepi Gramshammer, a former Austrian Olympic ski racer who runs some of the country's best intensive ski programs, operates this guest house. The charming rooms, all done up in pastels, are filled with original oil paintings and fluffy down comforters. Pepi's and Antlers, the property's two fine restaurants, have a European ambience, with stucco walls and wood-beam ceilings. In keeping with the theme, the waitresses are done up in dirndls. ☒ *231 E. Gore Creek Dr., 81657* ☎ *970/476-5626 or 800/610-7374* 🖷 *970/476-8816* ⊕ *www. pepis.com* 🛏 *38 rooms* ⚭ *2 restaurants, gym, 2 hot tubs, sauna, ski shop, bar* ▤ *AE, D, MC, V.*

★ $$ ▦ **Roost Lodge.** This small hotel brags about its economical rates. It's true to this promise, and then some. It also has comfortable rooms, many with charming touches such as four-poster beds. There's a sauna perfect for warming up after a day at the slopes and a heated pool to cool you off after hiking or biking. The helpful staff serves up a complimentary Continental breakfast during ski season. The hotel is on the access road next to I-70, but a free shuttle drops you at the base of the mountain. ☒ *1783 N. Frontage Rd. W, 81657* ☎ *970/476-5451 or 800/873-3065* 🖷 *970/476-9158* ⊕ *www.roostlodge.com* 🛏 *70 rooms, 2 suites* ⚭ *Pool, hot tub, sauna* ▤ *AE, DC, MC, V.*

CONDOMINIUMS   **Vail/Beaver Creek Reservations** (☎ 800/525-2257) is the place for one-stop shopping. You can buy lift tickets, arrange ski and snowboard lessons, get updates on events and activities, and book lodging at many of the hotels and condominium properties in the Vail Valley. **Vail Valley Chamber and Tourism** (☎ 800/824-5737) operates a central reservations service for properties in Vail, Avon, and Beaver Creek. It also gives out information on events and activities and reports on snow conditions.

Nightlife & the Arts

THE ARTS   Stretching from late June through early August, the annual **Bravo! Vail Valley Music Festival** (🖃 Box 2270, 81658 ☎ 877/812-5700 ⊕ www. vailmusicfestival.org) is a month-and-a-half-long celebration of music. Among the performers that are in residence for a few days or more than a week are the New York Philharmonic and the Dallas Symphony Orchestra. Chamber-music concerts, many performed by the ensemble-in-residence, are popular events. There's also music from an American composer-in-residence.

Held early in August, the annual **Vail International Dance Festival** (☎ 970/949–1999 ⊕ www.vvf.org/dance.cfm) hosts an unparalleled collection of ballet and modern dance groups from around the globe. The performers vary from year to year, but frequently include guest artists from the American Ballet Theatre, the Bolshoi Ballet, and other world-class companies. In recent years, visitors enjoyed Dance Cuba, performing the hottest steps from Havana, and "Steppin' Out with Ballroom's Best," choreographed by a three-time ballroom-dancing champion. Most of the performances are at Vail's Gerald R. Ford Amphitheater, an outdoor venue in Vilar Pavilion where some people sit in the seats, but many more recline on blankets on the surrounding lawn.

NIGHTLIFE Near the gondola in Lionshead, **Garfinkel's** (⊠ 536 W. Lionshead Mall ☎ 970/476–3789) has plenty of televisions where you can catch the game. It's open late, especially on weekends. In the Lodge at Vail, **Mickey's** (⊠ 174 E. Gore Creek Dr. ☎ 970/476–5011) attracts the après-ski crowd. A pianist plays soothing standards. **The Red Lion** (⊠ 304 Bridge St. ☎ 970/476–7676) is a tradition in Vail. It's standing-room only in the afternoons, and a bit mellower in the evening. Most nights there's guitar or piano music. **Sarah's** (⊠ 356 E. Hanson Ranch Rd. ☎ 970/476–5641) showcases Helmut Fricker, a Vail institution who plays accordion while yodeling up a storm. A young crowd scarfs down excellent late-night pizzas at **Vendetta's** (⊠ 291 Bridge St. ☎ 970/476–5070).

In the heart of Vail Village, **FuBar** (⊠ 333 Bridge St. ☎ 970/476–0360) is hopping all night. There are several theme rooms, including one with a 1950s-style jukebox that cranks out classic rock. Then there's the Red Room, a smoking lounge and a dance club with a disco ball and a floor with glow-in-the-dark stars. **Sanctuary** (⊠ 304 Bridge St. ☎ 970/479–0500) is a stylish club right above the Tap Room in Vail Village. The terrific sound system entices crowds onto the dance floor. The quieter lounge has a wood-burning fireplace where you can chat.

Shopping

Shopping options in the pedestrian-only streets of Vail Village include high-end boutiques, ski and snowboard shops, art-and-crafts galleries, and stores filled with T-shirts and other souvenirs.

BOUTIQUES For years, a golden bear (papa-, mama- or baby-size) on a chain has been a popular souvenir from this ski resort. **The Golden Bear** (⊠ 286 Bridge St. ☎ 970/476–4082) makes many versions of its namesake, as well as other popular items such as hammered golf necklaces and bracelets. You can also purchase ski clothing and accessories. Stocking everything from buffalo-hide coats to bowls filled with potpourri, **Gorsuch** (⊠ 263 Gore Creek Dr., ☎ 970/476–2294 ⊠ 70 Promenade, Beaver Creek ☎ 970/949–7115) is an odd combination of an upscale boutique and a sporting goods store. **Pepi's Sports** (⊠ 231 Bridge St. ☎ 970/476–5202) sells chic ski clothing and accessories from designers such as Bogner, Skea, Descente, and Spyder. Especially popular are women's clothing lines such as Trina Turk, Votre Nom, and DKNY City.

GALLERIES **Aboriginal Arts** (⊠ 5124 Grouse La. ☎ 970/476–7715) stocks handmade jewelry, wood carvings, and feather masks from around the South Pacific and the Americas. The **Clagget/Rey Gallery** (⊠ 100 E. Meadow Dr. ☎ 970/476–9350) is the place to purchase canvases and sculptures by well-known western artists. **Menzel** (⊠ 242 E. Meadow Dr. ☎ 970/476–6617) specializes in fanciful furniture and other items crafted from 200-year-old pine. The shop also sells beautiful glassware.

You'll be dazzled by hand-blown creations at the **Pismo Gallery** (⊠ 122 E. Meadow Dr. ☎ 970/476–2400). The outstanding collection of hand-blown glass ranges from perfume bottles to paperweights.

SPORTING GOODS Across from the Children's Fountain, **Gore Range Mountain Works** (⊠ Gore Creek Dr. ☎ 970/476–7625) carries mountaineering gear for hard-core climbers, as well as mountain fashions for everyone.

Minturn

⑫ *5 mi from Vail or 105 mi from Denver via I–70 west.*

The Vail Valley stretches far beyond the town of Vail. As you travel west along I–70, Exit 171 leads to this quaint community. Minturn began to thrive in 1987, when the Rio Grande Railway extended a narrow-gauge line into town to carry away the zinc, copper, silver, and lead extracted from nearby mines. The main street has an eclectic collection of antiques, curio, and other shops, plus popular restaurants tucked into the old buildings. You might begin a sojourn here by visiting **Minturn Cellars Winery** (⊠ 107 Williams St. ☎ 970/827–4065), a wine-tasting room, which features some of the finest local wines.

Sports & the Outdoors

SNOWMOBILING **Nova Guides** (⊠ 1923 Main St. Minturn ☎ 970/949–4232) has snowmobile rentals and guided tours.

Where to Stay & Eat

★ $$–$$$ ✕ **Minturn Country Club.** This homey hangout is one of those "you've gotta go" places people talk about after returning home. Steaks, prime rib, fish, and chicken are all delicious. You have only yourself to blame if you wanted your meat medium rare and it came out well done, as you cook your meal yourself. ⊠ *Main St., Minturn* ☎ *970/827–4114* ⌂ *Reservations not accepted* ☰ *MC, V* ⊘ *No lunch.*

$–$$ ✕ **The Saloon.** After a day on the slopes, reward yourself with margaritas made with real lime juice and baskets of tortilla chips served with homemade salsa. No wonder the place is always packed with locals. In a dining room that calls to mind the Old West, you can chow down on such specialties as *chiles rellenos* (stuffed peppers) and a steak and quail plate. There's even a children's menu. ⊠ *146 N. Main St.* ☎ *970/827–5954* ⌂ *Reservations not accepted* ☰ *AE, MC, V* ⊘ *No lunch.*

$–$$$ ▦ **Minturn Inn.** This three-story log home dates from 1915, making it one of the town's oldest residence. The owners, Tom and Cathy Sullivan, converted it into a charming inn with theme rooms. Business was brisk, so they added the neighboring Eagle Street Bed & Breakfast and the Grouse Creek Inn. These properties have two-person hot tubs, river rock fireplaces, and private decks or patios overlooking the Eagle River. Hearty breakfasts and afternoon wine and cheese are included. ⊠ *442 Main St., 81645* ☎ *970/827–9647 or 800/646–8876* 🖷 *970/827–5590* ⊕ *www.minturninn.com* ⇆ *18 rooms, 1 cabin* ⌂ *Breakfast room, hot tub* ☰ *AE, D, MC, V.*

Shopping

Two Elk Gallery (⊠ 102 Main St., ☎ 970/827–5307) showcases a dizzying array of home furnishings, including handcrafted items by local artisans ranging from antler chandeliers to leatherwork.

Beaver Creek

⑬ *12 mi from Vail or 110 mi from Denver via I–70 west.*

As with the majority of the area's resorts, the heart of Beaver Creek is a mountainside village. What sets Beaver Creek apart is that it is a se-

ries of cascading plazas connected by escalators. In this ultraposh en-
clave, even boot-wearing skiers and snowboard-hauling riders ride the
escalators from the hotels and shuttle stops on the lower levels. Opened
in 1980 as a smaller version of Vail, Beaver Creek has overshadowed
its older sibling. In fact, its nearest rival in the luxury market is Utah's
Deer Valley.

Locals know that Beaver Creek is the best place to ski on weekends when
Vail is too crowded, or anytime there's fresh powder. Beaver Creek is
just far enough from Denver that it doesn't get the flood of daytrippers
who flock to Vail and the other Front Range resorts. The slopes of Beaver
Creek Mountain are connected to those of even ritzier Bachelor Gulch.
These are close to Arrowhead, creating a village-to-village ski experience like those found in Europe.

Savvy travelers have learned that Beaver Creek is even more lovely in
summer, when diners can enjoy a meal on a spacious patio, mountain
bikers can hitch a ride uphill on the chairlift, and golfers can play on
the beautiful Beaver Creek Course or one the dozen others in the Vail
Valley. On special evenings you can attend concerts, get tickets to the
theater, or head to a performance at the Beaver Creek Vilar Center for
the Arts. In Beaver Creek you have easy access to all of the activities in
Vail Valley.

Beaver Creek speaks loudly and clearly to a settled and affluent crowd,
but visitors on a budget can also enjoy the resort's many attractions.
Just drive past the pricier lodgings in the village and opt instead for a
room in nearby Avon, Edwards, or even Vail.

Downhill Skiing & Snowboarding

Beaver Creek is a piece of nirvana, partly because of its system of trails
and partly because of its enviable location two hours from Denver. Although only a third the size of Vail, Beaver Creek is seldom crowded.
The skiable terrain extends from the runs down Beaver Creek to the slopes
around Bachelor Gulch to the network of trails at Arrowhead. You can
easily ski from one village to another.

Beaver Creek has a little of everything, from smoother slopes for beginners to difficult trails used for international competitions. Grouse
Mountain, in particular, is famed for its thigh-burning bump runs. Beginners have an entire peak, at the summit of Beaver Creek Mountain,
where they can learn to ski or practice on novice trails. (And newcomers can return to the village on one of the lifts if they are too tired to
take the long trail all the way to the bottom.) Intermediate-level skiers
have several long cruising trails on the lower half of Beaver Creek
Mountain and in Larkspur Bowl. Both locations also have black-dia-
mond trails, so groups of skiers and snowboarders of varying abilities
can ride uphill together. The Birds of Prey runs are aptly named, because
the steepness of the trails can be a surprise for skiers who mistakenly
think they are skilled enough to take on this challenging terrain.

The slopes of neighboring Bachelor Gulch are a mix of beginner and
intermediate trails. Here you can often find fresh powder hours after
it's gone elsewhere. Many of the open slopes weave past multimillion-
dollar homes where the cost of real estate is even higher than in Beaver
Creek. The Ritz-Carlton Bachelor Gulch, which sits at the base of the
lift, is one of the region's most beautiful hotels. A stop here is a must
for any architecture buff. Many skiers plan to arrive in time for a
hearty lunch at Remington's or an après-ski cocktail in the Buffalo Bar
or the Fly Fishing Library. There are shuttles handy to take you back
to Beaver Creek.

The third village in the area, Arrowhead, has the best and usually the least crowded intermediate terrain. Locals take advantage of sunny days by sitting on the spacious deck at the Broken Arrow Café. It's not much more than a shack, but the burgers can't be beat. Developed as a ski area for residents of the gated community of Arrowhead, Beaver Creek was linked to the nearby slopes via lifts when purchased by Vail Resorts. **Beaver Creek** ☎ 800/404–3533 ⊕ *www.beavercreek.com* ☉ *Late Nov.–mid-Apr., daily 9–4.*

FACILITIES 3,340-foot vertical drop; 1,625 skiable acres; 34% beginner, 39% intermediate, 27% advanced; 7 high-speed quad chairs, 3 triple chairs, 3 double chairs.

LESSONS & PROGRAMS The **Vail and Beaver Creek Ski and Snowboard School** (☎ 970/476–3239) runs classes at both resorts. At Beaver Creek there are about 600 instructors; lessons are offered in more than 20 languages. Afternoon-only group lessons are $65 to $80, depending upon the season. All-day lessons are $75 to $100. Special workshops and clinics are offered throughout the year. Beginners take three-day courses that include equipment rental and lift passes. Workshops for women, teen sessions, and telemark courses are among the programs targeting specific groups of skiers.

LIFT TICKETS Most vacationers purchase lift-and-lodging packages for Beaver Creek, or go online to www.snow.com and purchase multi-day lift passes at discounted rates. A lift ticket purchased at Beaver Creek may also be used at Vail, Breckenridge, Keystone, and Arapahoe Basin.

RENTALS **Beaver Creek Sports** (⊠ Beaver Creek Village ☎ 970/854–5400) rents ski equipment for $20 to $45, depending upon whether you choose regular or high-performance gear.

Nordic Skiing

TRACK SKIING The prettiest place for cross-country skiing is McCoy Park, with more than 19 mi of trails groomed for traditional cross-country skiing, skate-skiing, and snowshoeing, all laid out around a mountain peak. To reach McCoy Park, take the Strawberry Park chairlift—a plus because it gets you far enough from the village that you're in a pristine environment. The groomed tracks have a fair amount of ups and downs (or perhaps because the elevation rises to 9,840 feet, it just seems that way). Lessons, equipment rentals, and guided tours are available through **Beaver Creek Nordic Sports Center** (☎ 970/845–5313).

Other Sports & the Outdoors

The **Activities Desk of Vail** (☎ 970/476–9090) gives you the lowdown on many of the activities in the region, summer or winter.

BICYCLING Each summer, riders from around the region participate in races sponsored by the **Beaver Creek & Vail Summer Adventure Ridge Mountain Challenge** (⊠ 700 S. Frontage Rd. E, Vail ☎ 970/479–2280 ⊕ www.vailrec.com).

FITNESS Whether you're looking for a full-body massage or a workout on state-of-the-art equipment, it's easy to find in Beaver Creek. In the Park Hyatt Beaver Creek, the **Allegria Spa** (⊠ 136 E. Thomas Pl. ☎ 970/748–7500) has a full range of services, including a wonderful "barefoot" massage.

GOLF If you're serious about improving your game, check into the **Chuck Cook Golf Academy** (⊠ 376 Red Sky Rd., Wolcott ☎ 970/477–8350). Named one of the top 50 instructors by *Golf Digest,* Cook has coached U.S. Open champions Payne Stewart, Tom Kite and Corey Pavin. Cook uses high-tech tools at the academy's intense two- and three-day sessions. For example, he employs four cameras to record your swing so that he can analyze everything from your stance to your grip.

The first four holes of the **Beaver Creek Course** (⊠ 103 Offerson Rd. ☎ 970/845–5775) plummet downward through a narrow ravine. Then the course meanders through a curvaceous valley before climbing back uphill. Guests of the Park Hyatt at Beaver Creek get preferred tee times.

The **Cotton Ranch Golf Club** (⊠ 530 Cotton Ranch Dr., Gypsum ☎ 970/524–6200) designed by Pete Dye, climbs around a rocky mesa. There are plenty of blind holes and precipitous drop-offs, especially on the eighth hole.

At the Lodge & Spa at Cordillera, the **Course at Cordillera** (⊠ 2205 Cordillera Way, Edwards ☎ 970/926–5100) is actually three 18-hole courses and a 10-hole course. Hotel guests can play the Jack Nicklaus–designed Summit Course, which surrounds a peak like a string of pearls. Hale Irwin's Mountain Course runs through aspen groves, past lakes, and through meadows surrounded by luxury homes. The Valley Course is something of a misnomer, as it's chock-full of elevation changes and tee shots over vertigo-inspiring ravines. The Dave Pelz–designed 10-hole course lets you show off (or make you practice) your short-game skills.

A few miles west of Beaver Creek, the **Red Sky Golf Club** (⊠ 376 Red Sky Rd., Wolcott ☎ 970/477–8400) is a tony private club where members alternate with guests on two courses designed by Tom Fazio and Greg Norman. The Tom Fazio course's front nine are laid out on sagebrush-covered hills, but the back nine flows up and down a mountainside covered with groves of junipers and aspens. The Greg Norman Course sprawls through a broad valley. Some shots require carries across jagged ravines. Norman's signature bunkers abound, guarding slippery greens. In order to play at Red Sky Golf Club, you must be staying in the Lodge at Vail, the Pines Lodge in Beaver Creek, the Ritz-Carlton Bachelor Gulch, or other hotels owned by Vail Resorts.

HIKING The **Beaver Creek Hiking Center** (⊠ Beaver Creek Village ☎ 970/845–9090) arranges everything from easy walks to difficult hikes. If you're traveling with kids, ask about educational programs.

HORSEBACK **Beaver Creek Stable** (⊠ Box 2050, Eagle ☎ 970/845–9090) arranges
RIDING outings ranging from one-hour rides to all-day excursions. Many trips include a tasty picnic lunch. In the evenings there are hayrides and sunset rides.

Where to Stay & Eat

$$$$ ✕ **Beano's Cabin.** One of the memorable experiences during a trip to Beaver Creek is traveling in a sleigh to this former hunting lodge. (In summer, you can get here on horseback or even by shuttle van.) During the journey, your driver will undoubtedly fill you in on some local history. The pine-log cabin, warmed by a crackling fire, is an unbeatable location for a romantic meal. Choose from among the entrées that change with the seasons. Pair pan-seared buffalo carpaccio with wood-grilled venison, then top it all off with a bourbon pecan torte. ⊠ *Larkspur Bowl* ☎ *970/949–9090* ⌣ *Reservations essential* ▤ *AE, MC, V.*

$$$$ ✕ **Remington's.** In this stunning two-story space in the Ritz-Carlton, hammered wrought-iron chandeliers cast a flattering light on the diners—a mix of casually dressed skiers and hikers and business executives taking a meeting. Ski slopes rise just outside the wall of windows. Innovative regional cuisine is perhaps the best way to describe the entrées created by executive chef Stephan Schupbach, who hails from Switzerland. The menu changes often, but look for creatively prepared bison, salmon, steak, and Colorado trout. ⊠ *0130 Daybreak Ridge Rd., Avon* ☎ *970/748–6200* ⌣ *Reservations essential* ▤ *AE, MC, V.*

★ $$$$ ✕ **Splendido.** With elegant marble columns and custom-made Italian linens, this posh eatery is the height of opulence. Chef David Walford is a master of new American cuisine, and he borrows freely from many traditions. He is equally adept at turning out rack of lamb with rosemary as he is grilling up an elk loin with braised elk osso buco. Retire for a nightcap to the classically elegant piano bar, where Bob Finnie tickles the ivories. ⊠ *17 Chateau La.* ☎ *970/845–8808* ▤ *AE, D, DC, MC, V* ☉ *No lunch.*

$$$–$$$$ ✕ **Mirabelle.** Set in a restored farmhouse at the entrance to Beaver Creek, Mirabelle is one of the area's loveliest restaurants. Chef Daniel Joly serves superb Belgian–French cuisine. His preparations are a perfect blend of colors, flavors, and textures. The menu changes regularly, but if available try hot foie gras with caramelized golden apples, and roasted elk medallions in a red-wine sauce accompanied by poached baby pear, potato gnocchi, and rhubarb coulis. Depending on your point of view, the elaborate desserts are either heavenly or sinful. The extensive wine list has garnered notice from *Wine Spectator.* ⊠ *55 Village Rd.* ☎ *970/949– 7728* ▤ *AE, D, MC, V* ☉ *Closed Sun. No lunch.*

$$$–$$$$ ✕ **TraMonti Ristorante.** This breezy trattoria in The Charter at Beaver Creek showcases the vibrant cuisine of chef Curtis Cooper. He loves experimenting with bold juxtapositions of flavors and is most at home with creative pizzas, such as spicy shrimp with fennel, roasted peppers, basil, feta, and infused garlic oil. Try lobster ravioli in saffron cream sauce, spaghetti puttanesca, or the osso buco. ⊠ *120 Offerson Rd.* ☎ *970/ 949–5552* ▤ *AE, MC, V* ☉ *No lunch.*

$$$–$$$$ ✕ **Vue.** This bistro in the Park Hyatt Beaver Creek Resort & Spa got its name because diners are treated to a lovely view of the outdoor ice rink at Beaver Creek Village. In this intimate space, dinners for two are made even more intimate when diners share a plush banquette. European-trained executive chef Pascal Coudouy shows off his range with constantly changing menus. Look for starters such as lobster consommé and caviar, followed by pan-seared black bass or gingerbread-crusted rack of lamb. For a sample of his skills, try the six-course tasting menu. ⊠ *136 E. Thomas Pl., Beaver Creek* ☎ *970/949–1234* ⌕ *Reservations essential* ▤ *AE, MC, V* ☉ *Closed Sun. and Mon.*

★ $$–$$$ ✕ **Toscanini.** You have a ringside seat at the ice rink in the heart of Beaver Creek when you dine at this casual eatery. The menu is authentic Italian, starting with a variety of dipping oils for the fresh bread, then antipasti such as oven-roasted mushrooms topped with fontina and a balsamic reduction. Entrées include gourmet pizzas, such as the "Pizza Anatra" with duck confit, carmelized onions, grilled red radicchio, and Gorgonzola. Don't pass up the grilled Argentine ribeye steak with Colorado goat cheese, baby carrots, and demi-glace. ⊠ *Market Square* ☎ *970/845–5590* ▤ *AE, D, MC, V.*

$–$$$ ✕ **The Gashouse.** This longtime hangout set inside a 1930s-era log cabin has walls covered with hunting trophies. (If stuffed animal heads aren't your thing, think twice about eating here.) Locals swear by the steak, prime rib, and fresh salmon. Stop in for a brew and some buffalo wings and watch how some of the Vail Valley residents kick back. ⊠ *4 mi west of Beaver Creek on Rte. 6, Edwards* ☎ *970/926–3613* ▤ *AE, MC, V.*

$–$$ ✕ **Fiesta's.** The Marquez sisters, Debbie and Susan, use old family recipes brought to Colorado by their great-grandparents to create great Southwestern cuisine. Among the favorites are chicken enchiladas in a white jalapeño sauce and blue-corn enchiladas served Santa Fe–style with an egg on top. Handmade corn tamales are stuffed with pork and smothered in a classic New Mexican–chile sauce. The eatery in Edwards Plaza is brightly decorated with New Mexican–folk art and paintings. More than 20 tequilas keep the bar—and patrons—hopping. ⊠ *57 Edwards Access Rd., Edwards* ☎ *970/926–2121* ▤ *AE, D, MC, V.*

$-$$ ✕ **Gore Range Brewery.** After a morning on the slopes or an afternoon playing a few rounds of golf, locals gravitate here for a burger or spicy ribs and a locally brewed beer. In the Edwards Village Center, the place is a blend of high-tech styling and a laid-back aura. ⊠ *0105 Edwards Village Blvd., Edwards* ☎ *970/926–2739* ▭ *AE, MC, V.*

$-$$ ✕ **Narayan's.** When it's time for the lunch buffet, the locals who fill this no-frills restaurant in the Christy Lodge hop from table to table catching up on the latest news. For dinner, there's a full menu of culinary offerings from Nepal. Carefully prepared entrées include chicken *tikka*, made with fresh ginger, garlic, and a light tomato and onion sauce full of herbs and spices (it's also a delicious vegetarian dish when made with chickpeas). The stomach-filling soups are full of chunks of lamb or chicken. Curries and other Indian dishes round out the menu. ⊠ *47 E. Beaver Creek Blvd., Avon* ☎ *970/748–1404* ▭ *AE, D, MC, V.*

$$$$ ▦ **Beaver Creek Lodge.** A central atrium grabs all the attention at this European-style lodge. Rooms are generously proportioned—you'll probably get more space for your money here than at most other properties in the heart of the village. Rooms have kitchenettes (a few have full kitchens) and gas-burning fireplaces to keep out the chill. The Beaver Creek Chophouse is the perfect place to fuel up after a day on the slopes. ⊠ *26 Avondale La., 81620* ☎ *970/845–9800* ⎙ *970/845–8242* ⊕ *www.beavercreeklodge.net* ⤳ *72 suites* ⚲ *Restaurant, kitchenettes, indoor-outdoor pool, health club, hot tub, spa, ski shop, bar, meeting room* ▭ *AE, MC, V.*

★ $$$$ ▦ **The Charter at Beaver Creek.** With its elegantly angled blue-slate roof, this sprawling property is one of the area's handsomest accommodations. Wisps of smoke from the fireplaces found in many rooms rise above, giving the place a homey feel. There are plenty of choices for rooms, including one- to five-bedroom condominiums, many with balconies that let you gaze over the tops of the trees. The location is perfect—the ski-in/ski-out hotel is a short walk from the main plaza at Beaver Creek. Relax at the pool or indulge yourself with a facial at the spa. For dinner there's the casual Terrace Restaurant. ⊠ *120 Offerson Rd., 81620* ☎*970/949–6660 or 800/525–6660* ⎙*970/949–6709* ⊕*www.thecharter. com* ⤳ *65 rooms, 115 condominiums* ⚲ *2 restaurants, refrigerators, cable TV, in-room VCRs, 2 pools, 2 hot tubs, gym, spa, ski shop, business services, meeting rooms, convention center* ▭ *AE, MC, V.*

★ $$$$ ▦ **Lodge & Spa at Cordillera.** An aura of quiet luxury prevails at this mountaintop lodge, with a decor that calls to mind the finest alpine hotels. The rooms vary quite a bit in size; those in the newer wing tend to be larger. There are wood-burning fireplaces in some of the older rooms, whereas the newer rooms have gas fireplaces. You can luxuriate in the spa after a morning spent hiking or cross-country skiing, or swim in the indoor pool with a view of the mountains through the wall of windows. Don't miss a meal at Picasso, which for years has been one of the region's top restaurants. The lodge is in the gated community of Cordillera, 15 minutes from Beaver Creek. The lodge operates a shuttle to the lifts. ⊠ *2205 Cordillera Way* ⮹ *Box 1110, Edwards 81632* ☎ *970/926– 2200 or 800/877–3529* ⎙ *970/926–2486* ⊕ *www.cordillera-vail.com* ⤳ *56 rooms* ⚲ *4 restaurants, 3 18-hole golf courses, 1 10-hole short course, indoor and outdoor pools, health club, 2 hot tubs, spa, cross-country skiing, bar, business services, meeting rooms; no smoking* ▭ *AE, D, MC, V.*

$$$$ ▦ **Park Hyatt Beaver Creek Resort & Spa.** With a magnificent antler chandelier and towering windows opening out onto the mountain, the lobby of this hotel manages to be both cozy and grand. Rooms are designed with skiers in mind, so they have nice touches like heated towel racks. Perhaps the ultimate in pampering is stepping into your warmed and

waiting ski boots. Once the boots are off, enjoy a hot toddy by the outdoor fire pit. The on-site Allegria Spa and the nearby Beaver Creek Golf Club (with preferred tee times for guests) make this hotel popular with nonskiers. ✉ *136 E. Thomas Pl., 81620* ☎ *970/949–1234 or 800/ 233–1234* 🖷 *970/949–4164* ⊕ *www.beavercreek.hyatt.com* ➦ *275 rooms, 31 suites* ♨ *2 restaurants, deli, in-room data ports, 5 tennis courts, pool, health club, 8 hot tubs, spa, 2 bars, lounge, children's programs, business services, meeting rooms* 🖃 *AE, D, DC, MC, V.*

$$$$ 🏨 **Pines Lodge.** This ski-in/ski-out lodge is a winner, combining upscale accommodations with an unpretentious atmosphere. The aura of laid-back luxury comes from little extras such as afternoon tea by the fireplace in the lobby and a ski concierge who can arrange a complimentary guided tour or a free wax for your skis. Rooms vary in size, so ask for one at the end facing the mountain, which have an extra sofa for contemplating the views from the large windows. Many rooms have balconies overlooking the ski area. The Grouse Mountain Grill serves up superb new American cuisine in an unparalleled setting with huge picture windows. ✉ *141 Scott Hill Rd., 81620* ☎ *970/845–7909 or 800/ 367–7625* 🖷 *970/845–7809* ⊕ *www.rockresorts.com* ➦ *60 rooms, 12 suites* ♨ *Restaurant, in-room data ports, refrigerators, cable TV, in-room VCRs, pool, gym, hot tub, spa, bar, lobby lounge, laundry service* 🖃 *AE, D, MC, V.*

★ $$$$ 🏨 **The Ritz-Carlton Bachelor Gulch in Beaver Creek.** This log and timber building with elaborate stonework is, in a word, spectacular. The hotel's design is reminiscent of the grand old lodges in national parks like Yellowstone and Yosemite. The rooms—many with stone fireplaces—have a distinctly Western ambiance. For extra pampering stay on the club level, with its concierge service and never-ending supply of food and beverages in the private lounge. But no matter where you stay, you'll get the level of service Ritz regulars expect. The excellent restaurant serves regional cuisine. For cocktails and cigars there's the intimate Fly Fishing Library (worth a look just to see the fishing lures on the walls). ✉ *0130 Daybreak Ridge, Avon 81620* ☎ *970/748–6200* 🖷 *970/748–6300* ⊕ *www.riztcarlton.com* ➦ *208 rooms, 29 suites* ♨ *Restaurants, room service, in-room data ports, in-room safes, minibars, tennis courts, pool, health club, hot tubs, spa, bar, lounge, children's programs, business services, meeting rooms* 🖃 *AE, D, MC, V.*

CONDOMINIUMS **Vail/Beaver Creek Reservations** (☎ 800/525–2257) lets you book ahead at properties all over Vail Valley. You can also buy lift tickets, arrange ski lessons, and get updates on events and activities. **Vail Valley Chamber and Tourism** (☎ 800/824–5737) operates a central reservations service for properties in Vail, Avon, and Beaver Creek. It also gives out information on events and activities and reports on snow conditions in the winter.

Nightlife & the Arts

THE ARTS **Vilar Center for the Arts** (✉ 68 Avondale La. ☎ 970/949–8497) is an artwork in itself, with gold-color wood paneling and an etched-glass mural re-creating with bold strokes the mountains outside. Seating more than 500, the horseshoe-shape auditorium has great views from just about every seat. Throughout the year there's a stellar lineup of events, including concerts by orchestras and pop stars, great theater, and even a circus. In the surrounding plazas you'll find many art galleries. Just walking around Beaver Creek is a feast for the eyes, because sculptures are set almost everywhere you look.

NIGHTLIFE The boisterous **Coyote Café** (✉ 210 The Plaza ☎ 970/949–5001) is a kick-back-and-relax sort of place where locals hang out in the afternoon and evening. If you're into local brews or giant margaritas, head to the **Dusty Boot Saloon** (✉ St. James Place ☎ 970/748–1146). At the base of the mountain, **McCoy's Café** (✉ Village Hall ☎ 970/949–1234) draws crowds most afternoons in the winter months with live music. After attacking the moguls, unwind with a glass of wine or a single-malt scotch in the **Whiskey Elk** (✉ 136 E. Thomas Pl. ☎ 970/949–1234). You can relax on overstuffed sofas and chairs placed around the fire-place at this lounge in the Park Hyatt Beaver Creek. There's quieter music during après-ski hours and more raucous entertainment several evenings each week.

Shopping

Christopher & Co. (✉ Edwards Village Center, Edwards ☎ 970/926–8191) has vintage poster art dating from the 1890s to the 1950s. Depictions of American and European ski resorts are found among the more than 3,000 posters on display. You may not find the village's namesake crea-tures fashioned in precious metals, but **The Golden Bear** (✉ Village Hall ☎ 970/845–7881) has plenty of papa, mama, and baby bears. There's also eye-catching jewelry and other accessories.

Walk carefully around the **Pismo Gallery** (✉ Village Hall ☎ 970/949–0908), as there's an outstanding collection of hand-blown glass. Look for the frag-ile, colorful creations by Dale Chihuly. There are lampshades, perfume bottles, and other gorgeous items. Although the **Shaggy Ram** (✉ Edwards Village Center, Edwards ☎ 970/926–7377) sounds like it would stock mostly Western items, this shop is a large treasure trove of French and English antiques. Items range from fringed lamps to crystal decanters to elegant old desks. Look for the shop near the Gore Range Brewery.

STEAMBOAT

Steamboat got its name from French trappers who, after hearing the bub-bling and churning hot springs, mistakenly thought a steamboat was chugging up the Yampa River. The town is a place where Stetson hats are sold for shade and not for souvenirs, and the Victorian-era build-ings, most of them fronting the main drag of Lincoln Avenue, were built to be functional, not ornamental. It was founded in the 1800s as a ranch-ing and farming community, setting it apart from the mining towns of Breckenridge and Aspen. These early settlers were responsible for the advent of skiing in the area; they strapped wooden boards to their feet so they could get around town in winter.

Steamboat Springs

⑭ *86 mi from Beaver Creek via I–70 west and U.S. 131 north; 170 mi from Denver via I–70 west, Rte. 9 north, and U.S. 40 north.*

Steamboat Springs is aptly nicknamed Ski Town, U.S.A., since it has has sent more athletes to the Winter Olympics than any other ski town in the nation. The most famous alumnus is probably 1964 slalom silver medalist Billy Kidd, whose irrepressible grin and 10-gallon hat are in-stantly recognizable. When he's around, Kidd takes visitors for a run down the mountain and offers free pointers. The entrance to town is roughly marked by the amusingly garish 1950s neon sign from the Rab-bit Ears Motel, a newly designated historic landmark.

When sizing up the mountain, keep in mind that the part that's visible from below is only the tip of the iceberg—much more terrain lies con-cealed in back. Steamboat is famed for its eiderdown-soft snow; in fact, the term "champagne powder" was coined (and even copyrighted) here to describe the area's unique feathery drifts, the result of Steamboat's fortuitous position between the arid desert to the west and the moisture-magnet of the Continental Divide to the east, where storm fronts duke it out.

If you're looking for hellacious steeps and menacing couloirs, you won't find them in Steamboat, but you will discover what is perhaps the finest tree skiing in America. Beginning and intermediate skiers rave about the wide-open spaces of Sunshine Bowl and Storm Peak. Steamboat also earns high marks for its comprehensive children's programs and the Billy Kidd Center for Performance Skiing, where you can learn demanding disciplines such as powder, mogul, and tree skiing.

The ski resort of Steamboat Mountain Village, with its maze of upscale condos, boutiques, and nightclubs, is certainly attractive. It's a bit too spread out—and too new—to have developed much character. To its credit, though, this increasingly trendy destination has retained much of its down-home friendliness, providing the trappings while avoiding the trap of other resorts.

The **Tread of Pioneers Museum,** in a beautifully restored Queen Anne Victorian home, is an excellent spot to bone up on local history. It includes ski memorabilia dating to the turn of the 20th century, when Carl Howelsen opened Howelsen Hill, still the country's preeminent ski-jumping facility. ⊠ *8th and Oak Sts.* ☎ *970/879–2214* ◻ *$3* ◷ *Apr.–Oct., Tues.–Sat. 11–5; Nov.–Mar., Mon.–Sat. 11–5.*

There are more than 100 hot springs in the Steamboat Springs area. In the middle of town, **Steamboat Springs Health and Recreation Hot Springs** gets its waters from the all-natural Steamboat Hot Springs. The modern facility has a lap pool, relaxation pool, water slide, and health club. ⊠ *3rd St. and Lincoln Ave.* ☎ *970/879–1828* ◻ *$7* ◷ *Daily 7 AM–9:45 PM.*

About 7 mi west of town, the **Strawberry Park Natural Hot Springs** is a bit remote and rustic. If you're not sure of the way, go with a guide. After dark, clothing is optional. ⊠ *Strawberry Park Rd.* ☎ *970/879–0342* ◻ *$5 before 5 PM; $10 after 5 PM and on weekends* ◷ *Daily 10 AM–10:30 PM.*

In summer, Steamboat serves as the gateway to magnificent **Medicine Bow/Routt National Forest,** with a wealth of activities from hiking to mountain biking to fishing. Among the nearby attractions are the 283-foot **Fish Creek Falls** and the splendidly rugged **Mt. Zirkel Wilderness Area.** To the north, two sparkling man-made lakes, **Steamboat** and **Pearl,** are a draw for those into fishing and sailing. During winter, the area is just as popular. Snowshoers and backcountry skiers are permitted to use the west side of Rabbit Ears Pass, whereas snowmobilers are confined to the east side.

Downhill Skiing & Snowboarding

The **Steamboat Ski Area** is perhaps best known for its tree skiing and "cruising" terrain—the latter term referring to wide, groomed runs perfect for intermediate-level skiers. The abundance of cruising terrain has made Steamboat immensely popular with those who ski once or twice a year and who aren't looking to tax their abilities. Set on a predominantly western exposure—most ski areas sit on north-facing exposures—the resort benefits from intense sun, which contributes to the mellow atmosphere. In addition, one of the most extensive lift systems in the region allows skiers to take a lot of fast runs without having to spend much time waiting in line. The Storm Peak and Sundown high-speed quads, for example, each send you about 2,000 vertical feet in less than seven minutes. Do the math: a day of more than 60,000 vertical feet is entirely within the realm of possibility.

All this is not to suggest, however, that Steamboat is a piece of cake for more experienced skiers. The 950 acres of Morningside Park encompass advanced and intermediate terrain. Steamboat is renowned as a breeding ground for top mogul skiers, and for good reason. There are numerous mogul runs, but most are not particularly steep. The few with a vertical challenge, such as Chute One, are not especially long. If you're looking for challenging skiing at Steamboat, take on the trees. The ski area has done an admirable job of clearing many gladed areas of such nuisances as saplings, underbrush, and fallen timber, making Steamboat tree skiing much less hazardous than at other areas. The trees are also where advanced skiers—as well as, in some places, confident intermediates—can find the best of Steamboat's much ballyhooed powder. Statistically, Steamboat doesn't report significantly more snowfall than other Colorado resorts, but somehow snow piles up better than at the others. Ask well-traveled Colorado skiers, and they'll confirm that when it comes to consistently good, deep snow, Steamboat is hard to beat. ✉ *2305 Mt. Werner Circle* ☎ *970/879–6111* ⊕ *www.steamboat.com* ⊙ *Late-Nov.–mid-Apr., daily 9–4.*

The tiny **Howelsen Ski Area,** in the heart of Steamboat Springs, is the oldest ski area in Colorado. Howelsen, with 3 lifts, 15 trails, and a 440-foot vertical drop, is home of the Steamboat Springs Winter Sports Club. It's the largest ski-jumping complex in America, and a major Olympic training ground. ✉ *845 Howelsen Pkwy.* ☎ *970/879–8499* ⊙ *Dec.–Mar., Mon. 11–6, Tues.–Fri. 11–9, weekends 9–4:30.*

FACILITIES 3,668-foot vertical drop; 2,939 skiable acres; 14% beginner, 56% intermediate, 30% advanced; one 8-passenger gondola, 4 high-speed quad chairs, 1 quad chair, 6 triple chairs, 6 double chairs.

LESSONS & PROGRAMS Two-hour group lessons begin at $38; all-day lessons are $57. Clinics in moguls, powder, snowboarding, and "hyper-carving"—made possible by the relatively new shaped skis—are available. General information about the area's ski areas is available through the **Steamboat Ski and Resort Corporation** (☎ 970/879–6111 Ext. 531). Intensive two- and three-day training camps in racing and advanced skiing are offered through the **Billy Kidd Center for Performance Skiing** (☎ 970/879–6111 Ext. 543). Programs for kids from 6 months to 15 years of age are offered through the **Kids' Vacation Center** (☎ 970/879–6111 Ext. 218). Daycare is also available.

Snow cat skiing—where a vehicle delivers you to hard-to-reach slopes—has been called the poor man's version of helicopter skiing, although at $200 to $300 a day, it's not exactly skiing for the lunch-pail crowd. But snowcat users don't have to worry about landing and can get to places that would be inaccessible by helicopter. Buffalo Pass, northeast of Steamboat, is reputed to be one of the snowiest spots in Colorado, and that's why it's the base for **Steamboat Powder Cats** (☎ 970/879–5188 or 800/288–0543). There's a maximum of 24 skiers per group, so the open-meadow skiing is never crowded.

LIFT TICKETS $64. Savings of 5% or less on multiday tickets. Children 12 and under ski free when adults purchase a 5-day ski ticket.

RENTALS Equipment packages are available at the gondola base as well as at ski shops in town. Packages (skis, boots, and poles) average about $16 a day, less for multi-day rentals. Call **Steamboat Central Reservations** (☎ 970/879–4070 or 800/922–2722) for rental information.

Nordic Skiing

BACKCOUNTRY SKIING The most popular area for backcountry skiing around Steamboat Springs is Rabbit Ears Pass, southeast of town. It's the last pass you cross if you're driving from Denver to Steamboat. Much of the appeal is its easy access to high country trails from U.S. 40. There are plenty of routes you can take. Arrangements for backcountry tours can be made through **Steamboat Ski Touring Center** (⌂ Box 775401, 80477 ☎ 970/879–8180).

A popular backcountry spot is Seedhouse Road, about 25 mi north of Steamboat near the town of Clark. A marked network of trails across the rolling hills has good views of distant peaks. For maps and information on snow conditions, contact the **Hahn's Peak Ranger Office** (✉ 57 10th St., Box 771212, 80477 ☎ 970/879–1870).

Touring and telemarking rentals are available at various ski shops in the Steamboat area. One of the best is the **Ski Haus** (✉ 1457 Pine Grove Rd. ☎ 970/879–0385).

TRACK SKIING Laid out on and along the Sheraton Steamboat Golf Club, **Steamboat Ski Touring Center** has a relatively gentle 18½-mi trail network. A good option for a relaxed afternoon of skiing is to pick up some vittles at the Picnic Basket in the main building and enjoy a picnic along Fish Creek Trail, a 3-mi-long loop that winds through pine and aspen groves. Rental packages (skis, boots, and poles) are available. ⌂ *Box 775401, 80477* ☎ *970/879–8180* ▨ *Trail fee $10.*

Some guest ranches in the area groom their tracks. **Home Ranch** (⌂ Box 822, Clark 80428 ☎ 970/879–1780), 20 mi north of Steamboat, has 25 mi of trails. **Vista Verde Guest Ranch** (⌂ Box 465, 80477 ☎ 970/879–3858 or 800/526–7433) has a well-groomed network of tracks, as well as access to the adjacent national forest.

Other Sports & the Outdoors

Dogsledding, hot-air ballooning, and snowmobiling can be arranged by calling the activities department at **Steamboat Central Reservations** (☎ 970/879–4070 or 800/922–2722).

GOLF Expect to see plenty of wildlife at the **Sheraton Steamboat Golf Club** (✉ 2000 Clubhouse Dr. ☎ 970/879–1391). A bear was once spotted on the 18-hole championship course designed by the legendary Robert Trent Jones Jr.

HORSEBACK RIDING Because of the ranches surrounding the Yampa and Elk rivers, Steamboat is full of real cowboys as well as visitors trying to act the part. Horseback riding is one of the most popular pastimes here. Riding, instruction, and extended pack trips are offered at a number of ranches in the area, although some may require a minimum stay of a week. One facility that has the full gamut of activities, from hour-long tours to journeys lasting several days, is **Del's Triangle 3 Ranch** (⌂ Box 333, Clark 80428 ☎ 970/879–3495). It's about 20 mi north of Steamboat via Highway 129. **Sombrero Ranch** (✉ 835 River Rd. ☎ 970/879–2306) has one-hour guided tours perfect for novices. Every Friday and Saturday evening in summer, rodeos are held at the **Howelsen Rodeo Grounds** (✉ 5th St. and Howelsen Pkwy. ☎ 970/879–1818).

ICE DRIVING Here's one for anyone who's either been intimidated by snowy roads or gotten teenage thrills from executing donuts on icy shopping-mall parking lots. The **Bridgestone Winter Driving School** (✉ 1850 Ski Time Square Dr. ☎ 970/879–6104 or 800/949–7543) has half-day and full-day winter driving courses, as well as special, women-only programs.

RAFTING **High Adventures** (✉ 729 Lincoln St. ☎ 970/879–8747) runs rafting excursions to the Yampa, Elk, and Eagle rivers. Half-day to two-week trips are available for all levels.

SNOWMOBILING Explore the forests and meadows of the Medicine Bow/Routt National Forest with **Steamboat Powder Cats** (☎ 970/879–5188). **Steamboat Snowmobile Tours** (☎ 970/879–6500) has guided tours. A shuttle serves most hotels.

Where to Stay & Eat

★ $$$–$$$$ ✕ **L'Apogée.** Steamboat's most intimate restaurant, L'Apogée charms you with rose-color walls, flickering candlelight, and hanging plants. The classic French cuisine, with subtle Asian influences, is well crafted. Especially fine are the half roast duckling glazed with orange-blossom honey, the Alaskan King–crab cakes, and pan-seared foie gras topped with warm chèvre. Still, the menu takes a back seat to the admirable wine list. Oenophile alert: owner Jamie Jenny is a collector whose magnificent wine cellar—cited by *Wine Spectator* as one of America's best—contains more than 10,000 bottles. ✉ *911 Lincoln Ave.* ☎ *970/ 879–1919* ▤ *AE, DC, MC, V.*

$$–$$$$ ✕ **Antares.** The owners of this hot spot cut their culinary teeth at some of Steamboat's finest restaurants, including Harwig's and L'Apogée. With fieldstone walls, pressed-tin ceilings, and beautiful stained-glass windows, the splendid Victorian building attracts all the attention at first. Then Paul LeBrun's exciting, eclectic dishes arrive. You might feast on elk medallions with a Bing cherry–merlot sauce, or Maine lobster over chili pepper linguine. Doug's encyclopedic knowledge of wines is reflected in the comprehensive, fairly priced list. ✉ *57½ 8th St.* ☎ *970/879–9939* ✍ *Reservations essential* ▤ *AE, MC, V* ⊘ *No lunch.*

$$–$$$ ✕ **Harwig's Grill.** In a historic building that once housed Harwig's Saddlery and Western Wear, this popular eatery is run by the same team as neighboring L'Apogée. The bar serves 40 wines by the glass, including many lesser-known labels. If you don't see one you like, you can order something from L'Apogée's cellar. The menu reflects owner Jamie Jenny's love of travel, so you'll find confidently prepared specialties from around the world. There's everything from home-cured salmon pastrami to raclette, jambalaya to dim sum. The desserts are predictably sinful. ✉ *911 Lincoln Ave.* ☎ *970/879–1980* ▤ *AE, MC, V* ⊘ *No lunch.*

$$–$$$ ✕ **Riggio's.** In a dramatic industrial space, this Italian eatery evokes the old country with tapestries, murals, and landscape photos. The menu includes tasty pizzas (with toppings such as goat cheese and clams) and pasta dishes (*sciocca,* with rock shrimp, eggplant, tomatoes, and basil, is superb). Standards such as manicotti, chicken cacciatore, and saltimbocca are also well prepared. Try the house salad with Gorgonzola vinaigrette. ✉ *1106 Lincoln Ave.* ☎ *970/879–9010* ▤ *AE, D, DC, MC, V* ⊘ *No lunch.*

$–$$$ ✕ **La Montaña.** This Tex-Mex establishment is among Steamboat's most popular restaurants, and with good reason. The kitchen incorporates indigenous specialties into the traditional menu. Among the standouts are sunflower-seed-crusted tuna with a margarita beurre blanc, enchiladas layered with Monterey Jack and goat cheese and roasted peppers, and elk loin crusted with pecan nuts and bourbon cream sauce. ✉ *Après Ski Way and Village Dr.* ☎ *970/879–5800* ▤ *AE, D, MC, V* ⊘ *No lunch.*

$$ ✕ **Yama-Chans.** Many believe that you can't get good sushi in Colorado, but Yama-Chans proves them wrong. Somehow, the yellowfin tuna tastes fresher in the crisp mountain air at this simple, superlative Japanese restaurant. The rest of the menu is equally well presented and prepared. ✉ *Old Town Sq., 635 Lincoln Ave.* ☎ *970/879–8862* ▤ *AE, MC, V* ⊘ *Closed Mon. year-round; closed Sun. mid-Nov.–mid-Apr. No lunch weekends.*

★ **$$$$** ⊞ **Home Ranch.** You won't be roughing it at this all-inclusive retreat, a Relais & Chateaux property nestled among towering stands of aspen north of Steamboat near Clark. With a magnificent fieldstone fireplace surrounded by plush leather armchairs and sofa, the main room couldn't be cozier. The dining room, where Clyde Nelson turns out gourmet Southwestern fare, has soaring ceilings and wonderful views. Accommodations are in the main lodge or in individual cabins with terraces and private hot tubs. The decor leans toward Native American rugs and prints, lace curtains, terra-cotta tile or hardwood floors, and stenciled walls. A seven-night minimum stay is required. ⊠ *54880 County Rd. 129, Clark 80428* ☎ *970/879–1780* ⊕ *www.homeranch.com* ➷ *6 rooms, 8 cabins* ⚭ *Dining room, pool, hot tub, fishing, horseback riding, cross-country skiing, ski shop, lounge* ⊟ *AE, D, MC, V* ☉ *Closed late Mar.–early June and early Oct.–late Dec.* ¶◎¶ *FAP.*

$$$$ ⊞ **Vista Verde Guest Ranch.** Set on a working ranch, the luxurious Vista Verde provides city slickers with an authentic Western ambience. Lodge rooms are huge and beautifully appointed, with lace curtains, Western art, and lodgepole furniture. Cabins are more rustic, with pine paneling and old-fashioned wood-burning stoves, plus refrigerators, coffeemakers, and porches. Three-, five- and seven-night packages are available. ⊠ *3100 County Rd. 64, 80477* ☎ *970/879–3858 or 800/526–7433* ⊟ *970/879–1413* ⊕ *www.vistaverde.com* ➷ *3 rooms, 9 cabins* ⚭ *Dining room, gym, 10 hot tubs, sauna, fishing, horseback riding, cross-country skiing* ⊟ *No credit cards* ☉ *Closed mid-Mar.–May and Oct.–Nov.* ¶◎¶ *FAP.*

$$–$$$$ ⊞ **Sheraton Steamboat Resort & Conference Center.** This bustling high-rise is Steamboat's only true ski-in/ski-out property. The amenities are classic resort-town, with a ski shop, golf course, and four rooftop hot tubs with sweeping views of the surrounding ski slopes. The large rooms in the main building are standard issue, with muted color schemes and comforts like refrigerators. ⊠ *2200 Village End Ct., 80477* ☎ *970/879–2220 or 800/848–8877* ⊟ *970/879–7686* ⊕ *www.steamboat-sheraton.com* ➷ *317 rooms* ⚭ *2 restaurants, in-room safes, refrigerators, cable TV, 18-hole golf course, pool, 4 hot tubs, sauna, steam room, ski shop, bar, meeting room* ⊟ *AE, D, DC, MC, V.*

$$–$$$ ⊞ **Best Western Ptarmigan Inn.** Situated on the slopes, this laid-back lodging couldn't have a more convenient location. The steeply sloped roof and wood railings add a touch of Western charm. The modest rooms, decorated in pleasing pastels, have balconies with views of the surrounding mountains. ⊠ *2304 Après Ski Way, Box 773240, 80477* ☎ *970/879–1730 or 800/538–7519* ⊟ *970/879–6044* ⊕ *www.bestwestern.com* ➷ *77 rooms* ⚭ *Restaurant, in-room data ports, refrigerators, cable TV, in-room VCRs, pool, hot tub, sauna, ski shop, bar* ⊟ *AE, D, DC, MC, V.*

$$ ⊞ **Rabbit Ears Motel.** The playful, pink-neon bunny sign outside this motel has been a local landmark since 1952, making it an unofficial gateway to Steamboat Springs. The location is ideal if you're visiting the springs (across the street); the ski area (the bus stops outside); and the downtown shops, bars, and restaurants. All the rooms are clean and attractive, and most have balconies with views of the Yampa River. Continental breakfast is included in the rate. ⊠ *201 Lincoln Ave., 80477* ☎ *970/879–1150 or 800/828–7702* ⊟ *970/870–0483* ⊕ *www.rabbitearsmotel.com* ➷ *66 rooms* ⊟ *AE, D, DC, MC, V* ¶◎¶ *CP.*

$$ ⊞ **Steamboat B&B.** This custard-and-blue Victorian, originally a church, was converted by owner Gordon Hattersley into the area's nicest B&B. He cleverly retained the arched doorways and stained-glass windows. The cozy, comfy rooms have floral wallpaper, lace curtains, potted geraniums, polished hardwood floors, and lovely period antiques. A full breakfast is included. ⊠ *442 Pine St., 80477* ☎ *970/879–5724* 🖶 *970/870–8787* ⤴ *7 rooms* ⛴ *Dining room, hot tub* ▤ *AE, D, MC, V* �𝍖 *BP.*

CONDOMINIUMS **Torian Plum**, one of the properties managed by **Resort Quest Steamboat** (⊠ 1855 Ski Time Sq., 80487 ☎ 970/879–8811 or 800/228–2458 🖶 970/879–8485), has elegant one- to three-bedroom units in a ski-in/ski-out location. Hot tubs are available. **Mountain Resorts** (⊠ 2145 Resort Dr., Suite 100, 80487 ☎ 800/525–2622 🖶 970/879–3228 ⊕ www.mtn-resorts.com) manages condominiums at more than 15 locations. **Steamboat Resorts** (🖃 Box 2995, 80477 ☎ 800/525–5502 🖶 970/879–8060 ⊕ www.steamboatresorts.com) rents plenty of properties near the slopes.

Nightlife

Mahogany Ridge Brewery & Grill (⊠ 5th St. and Lincoln Ave. ☎ 970/879–2233) serves superior pub grub and pours an assortment of homemade ales, lagers, porters, and stouts. The **Old Town Pub** (⊠ 600 Lincoln Ave. ☎ 970/879–2101) has juicy burgers and music from some great bands. On the mountain, **The Tugboat** (⊠ Ski Time Sq. ☎ 970/879–7070) is the place for loud rock-and-roll. You can also challenge locals to a game of pool.

Shopping

At the base of the ski area are three expansive shopping centers—Ski Time Square, Torian Plum Plaza, and Gondola Square. Downtown Steamboat's **Old Town Square** (⊠ 7th St. and Lincoln Ave.) is a collection of upscale boutiques and retailers. There are also plenty of places to get a good cup of coffee.

BOOKS **Off the Beaten Path** (⊠ 56 7th St. ☎ 970/879–6830) is a throwback to the Beat Generation, with poetry readings, lectures, and concerts. It has an excellent selection of New Age works, in addition to the usual bestsellers and travel guides.

BOUTIQUES In Torian Plum Plaza, **The Silver Lining** (⊠ 2748 Ski Time Square Dr. ☎ 970/879–7474) displays art, crafts, and clothing from around the world, including Balinese cradle watchers, carved wooden figures believed to keep evil spirits away from sleeping children. You can make your own earrings at the bead counter.

GALLERIES **White Hart Gallery** (⊠ 843 Lincoln Ave. ☎ 970/879–1015) is a magnificent clutter of Western-theme paintings and objets d'art.

Native American images adorn the walls of the **Wild Horse Gallery** (⊠ 2200 Village End Ct. ☎ 970/879–7660). This shop inside the Sheraton Steamboat is the place to buy artwork, jewelry and blown glass.

SPORTING GOODS You can rent or buy the latest ski equipment at **Christy Sports** (⊠ 1724A Mt. Werner Circle ☎ 970/879–9001). **Straightline Sports** (⊠ 744 Lincoln Ave. ☎ 970/879–7568) is a good bet for downhill necessities. **Ski Haus** (⊠ 1457 Pine Grove Rd. ☎ 970/879–0385) can outfit you for the slopes.

WESTERN PARAPHERNALIA Owned by the same family for four generations, **F. M. Light and Sons** (⊠ 830 Lincoln Ave. ☎ 970/879–1822) caters to the Marlboro man in us all. If you're lucky you'll find a bargain—how about cowboy hats for $4.98? **Into the West** (⊠ 807 Lincoln Ave. ☎ 970/879–8377) is owned by Jace Romick, a former member of the U.S. ski team and a veteran of the rodeo circuit. He crafts splendid, beautifully textured lodgepole furniture. There are also antiques (even ornate potbellied stoves), cowhide mirrors, and handicrafts such as Native American–drum tables and fanciful candleholders fashioned from branding irons. **Two Rivers Gallery**

(✉ 56 9th St. ☎ 970/879–0044) sells such cowboy collectibles as antler chandeliers and cow-skull lamps, as well as vintage photographs, prints, sculpture, and paintings.

en route   Head west on I–70 to reach 15-mi-long **Glenwood Canyon.** Nature began the work as the Colorado River carved deep granite, limestone, and quartzite gullies—buff-tint walls brilliantly streaked with lavender, rose, and ivory. This process took a half billion years. Then man stepped in, seeking a more direct route west. In 1992 the work on I–70 through the canyon was completed, at a cost of almost $500 million. Much of the expense was attributable to the effort to preserve the natural landscape as much as possible. When contractors blasted cliff faces, for example, they stained the exposed rock to simulate nature's weathering. Biking trails were also created, providing easy access to the hauntingly beautiful **Hanging Lake Recreation Area.** Here Dead Horse Creek sprays ethereal flumes from curling limestone tendrils into a startlingly turquoise pool, as jet-black swifts dart to and fro. It's perhaps the most transcendent of several idyllic spots in the canyon reachable on bike or foot. The intrepid can scale the delicate limestone cliffs, pocked with caverns and embroidered with pastel-hue gardens.

ROARING FORK VALLEY

Roaring Fork Valley stretches nearly 50 mi, from Glenwood Springs to Aspen, with tiny towns and backcountry hamlets dotting the highway between. The valley's original inhabitants, the Ute people, were supplanted in the mid-1800s by gold prospectors and silver miners, who came to reap the region's bounty. But with the demonetization of silver in 1893 came the quiet years, as the population dwindled and ranching became a way of life. Nearly half a century later, the tides would turn again as downhill skiing gave new life to Aspen, and thus its downstream neighbors. Today, the Roaring Fork Valley weaves together its past and present through a unique blend of small-town charm and world-class amenities, all surrounded by the majestic beauty of central Colorado's 2-million-acre White River National Forest.

Glenwood Springs

🕧 *110 mi from Steamboat Springs via U.S. 131 south and I–70 west; 160 mi from Denver via I–70 west.*

Interstate 70 snakes through Glenwood Canyon on its way to a famed spa that forms the western apex of a triangle with Vail and Aspen. Once upon a time, Glenwood Springs was every bit as tony as those chic resorts are today, attracting a faithful legion of the pampered and privileged who came to enjoy the waters of the world's largest natural hot springs, said to cure everything from acne to rheumatism.

Today the entrance to town is marred by the proliferation of strip malls, chain motels, and fast-food outlets. Remnants of her glory days can still be seen in the grand old **Hotel Colorado** (✉ 526 Pine St.), regally commanding the vaporous pools from a patrician distance. Modeled after the Villa de Medici in Italy, the property opened its doors in 1893. Teddy Roosevelt even made it his unofficial "Little White House" in 1905.

Hot Springs Pool, formerly called Yampah Hot Springs, was discovered by the Utes (Yampah is Ute for "big medicine"). Even before the heyday of the hotel, Western notables from Annie Oakley to Doc Holliday

in Aspen, serves up dishes so authentic that you'll swear you're in the high Himalayas. Try fish *kawab* (marinated overnight and then baked in a tandoor) with a side of garlicky *naan* (spongy flat bread) if you're skeptical. ⊠ *6824 Hwy. 82* ☎ *970/945–8803* ▭ *AE, MC, V* ☉ *No lunch Sun.*

¢ ✕ **Daily Bread.** For years, locals have been packing this little café, where you can get some of the best food at the best prices in town. Hearty breakfasts such as the veggie skillet, breakfast burrito, and cinnamon-roll french toast are favorites, and lunch features creative sandwiches, soups, and burgers. Many items are low-fat or vegetarian. The bakery also sells its baked goods to go. ⊠ *729 Grand Ave.* ☎ *970/945–6253* ▭ *D, MC, V* ☉ *No dinner. Closed Sun.*

$$ ▣ **Hotel Colorado.** When you catch sight of the graceful sandstone colonnades and Italianate campaniles of this exquisite building, you won't be surprised it is listed in the National Register of Historic Places. The impression of luxury continues in the imposing yet gracious marble lobby and public rooms. The sunny, individually decorated rooms and suites—most with high ceilings, fireplaces, gorgeous period wainscoting, deluxe marble bathrooms, and balconies affording superlative vistas—are designed to match. Everyone, whether notable or notorious, from Teddy Roosevelt to Al Capone, stayed here in its halcyon days. The on-site bike shop and white-water-rafting outfitter can get you geared up for adventures outside the hotel. ⊠ *526 Pine St., 81601* ☎ *970/945–6511 or 800/544–3998* ♨ *970/945–7030* ⊕ *www.hotelcolorado.com* ➴ *129 rooms, 32 suites* ♨ *Restaurant, café, gym, hair salon, meeting room* ▭ *AE, D, DC, MC, V.*

$–$$ ▣ **Hot Springs Lodge.** This lodge is perfectly located, just steps from the Hot Springs Pool (which is also used to heat the property). The attractive rooms, decorated in jade, teal, buff, and rose, stress a Southwestern motif. Deluxe rooms offer a small refrigerator and tiny balcony, in addition to standard conveniences such as cable TV. Breakfast is included. ⊠ *415 E. 6th St., 81601* ☎ *970/945–6571 or 800/537–7946* ♨ *970/947–2950* ⊕ *www.hotspringspool.com* ➴ *107 rooms* ♨ *Snack bar, some refrigerators, cable TV, pool, hot tub, bar, business services, meeting rooms* ▭ *AE, D, DC, MC, V* ⑩ *CP.*

$–$$ ▣ **Hotel Denver.** Although this hotel was built in 1806, its most striking features are the numerous art-deco touches throughout. Most rooms open onto a view of the nearby springs or a three-story New Orleans–style atrium bedecked with colorful canopies. The accommodations are a bit dated, but comfortable, and so quiet it's hard to believe you're only footsteps from the train station. Glenwood's only microbrewery—the Glenwood Canyon Brewing Company—is the hotel restaurant. ⊠ *402 7th St., 81601* ☎ *970/945–6565 or 800/826–8820* ♨ *970/945–2204* ⊕ *www.thehoteldenver.com* ➴ *78 rooms* ♨ *Restaurant, gym, hair salon, bar, meeting room* ▭ *AE, D, DC, MC, V.*

$ ▣ **Sunlight Mountain Inn.** This charming traditional ski lodge is a few hundred feet from the Sunlight Mountain Resort lifts. It brims with a country ambience, from the delightful lounge (with a carved fireplace and wrought-iron chandeliers) and Western-flair restaurant to the cozily rustic rooms, all with pine-board walls and rough-hewn armoires. The restaurant, open in winter only, specializes in apple dishes, made from local fruit in season; the bar is a perfect place to end your day. This is a true get-away-from-it-all place, so there are no TVs to distract you. A full breakfast is included. ⊠ *10252 County Rd. 117, 81601* ☎ *970/945–5225 or 800/733–4757* ♨ *970/947–1900* ⊕ *www.sunlightinn. com* ➴ *20 rooms* ♨ *Restaurant, hot tub, bar; no room TVs* ▭ *AE, D, MC, V* ⑩ *BP.*

en route | At Carbondale, Highway 82 splits and continues southeast, skirting the Roaring Fork River on its way to Aspen and Snowmass Village. Highway 133 veers south on its way to Redstone.

Redstone

16 *29 mi from Glenwood Springs via Hwy. 82 east and Hwy. 133 south.*

Redstone is a charming artists' colony whose streets are lined with pretty galleries and boutiques, and whose boundaries are ringed by the impressive sandstone cliffs from which the town draws its name. Summer sees streams of visitors strolling the main drag, Redstone Boulevard; in winter, horse-drawn carriages carry people along the snow-covered road.

Redstone's history dates to the late 19th century, when J. C. Osgood, director of the Colorado Fuel and Iron Company, built Cleveholm Manor, now known as **Redstone Castle** (⌧ 58 Redstone Blvd. ☎ 970/963–2526). Here he entertained other titans of his day, such as John D. Rockefeller, J. P. Morgan, and Teddy Roosevelt. Among the home's embellishments are gold-leaf ceilings, maroon velvet walls, silk brocade upholstery, marble and mahogany fireplaces, Persian rugs, and Tiffany chandeliers. Although the Castle has been closed as a public lodge for several years, Redstone Historical Society is overseeing operations so that you can still catch a glimpse of the baronial splendor during sporadic tours.

A few miles up Highway 133 is **Marble,** a sleepy town that's undergoing a small renaissance as seekers of rural solitude are making it their summer residence and winter retreat. Incorporated in 1899 to serve workers of the Colorado Yule Marble Quarry, the tiny hamlet includes many historic sites, including the old quarry (marble from this spot graces the Lincoln Memorial and Tomb of the Unknowns in Washington, D.C.), a one-room schoolhouse that houses the Marble Historical Society Museum, and the quaint Marble Community Church. Marble is also the gateway to one of Colorado's most photographed places: the **Crystal Mill.** Set on a craggy cliff overlooking the river, the 1917 mill harkens back to the area's mining past; it is also the perfect place to enjoy a picnic lunch in the solitude of the Colorado Rockies. A four-wheel-drive vehicle is needed to get you here in good weather (your feet will have to do on rainy days when the road isn't passable).

Sports & the Outdoors

GOLF **River Valley Ranch** (⌧ 303 River Valley Ranch Dr., Carbondale ☎ 970/963–3625) is a solid course designed by Jay Moorish that sits on the banks of the Crystal River. There is lots of water, a constant breeze, and superb—if not distracting—views of Mt. Sopris.

HORSEBACK RIDING **Chair Mountain Stables** (⌧ 0178 County Rd. 3, Marble ☎ 970/963–1232) offers daily one-hour rides, as well as dinner tours, all-day adventures, and overnight stays in the surrounding backcountry.

NORDIC SKIING **Ute Meadows Nordic Center** (⌧ 2880 County Rd. 3 ☎ 970/963–5513, 970/948–1895 for snow conditions) is a winter playground with 10 mi of groomed cross-country trails and countless miles of ungroomed skiing and snowshoe trails set in the remote reaches of the Crystal River Valley. A complete rental shop, with services including waxing and tune-ups, is on the premises. Dogs are welcome to accompany skiers and snowshoers (there's a nominal fee).

Where to Stay & Eat

$$–$$$ ✕ **SIX89.** Located in a decidedly unglamorous ranching community just north of Redstone, this funky restaurant is well worth a visit. As chef

Mark Fisher's attempt to provide an "intelligent alternative" to Aspen's posh eateries, the kitchen and wine bar's irreverent menu and whimsical lexicon, coupled with an unusual zinc-topped bar, create a downright delightful dining experience. Follow Fisher's "sharing and grazing" philosophy with dishes like truffled macaroni and cheese or crispy goat cheese gnocchi and you'll get the picture. ⊠ *689 Main St., Carbondale* ☎ *970/963–6890* ⚐ *Reservations essential* ▭ *AE, D, MC, V* ⊘ *No lunch.*

$ ▦ **Redstone Inn.** The inn was originally designed as an elegant lodge for the bachelor employees of the Colorado Fuel and Iron Company. (Owner J. C. Osgood also constructed one of the region's first planned communities, a utopian model in its day.) Eat in the casual poolside Grill or the more formal Redstone Dining Room, where people from miles around come for Sunday brunch. Stay overnight in rooms ranging from the antiques-laden to one-of-a-kind. Many have a veranda with a view. Don't pass up the complimentary wine-and-cheese receptions every afternoon. ⊠ *82 Redstone Blvd., 81623* ☎ *970/963–2526 or 800/748–2524* 🖷 *970/963–2527* ⊕ *www.redstoneinn.com* ⤏ *35 rooms* ♿ *Restaurant, grill, tennis court, pool, hot tub, spa* ▭ *AE, D, MC, V.*

The Arts

The studio gallery and sculpture garden at the **Redstone Arts Center** (⊠ 173 Redstone Blvd. ☎ 970/963–3790) display such art and crafts as sculpture, painting, jewelry, and pottery. Sunday afternoons in summer feature craft workshops of a surprisingly high caliber.

| en route | As you drive down Highway 82 through the bedroom communities of Carbondale and El Jebel on its way to Aspen and Snowmass, a detour through the old railroad town of **Basalt** is well worth the trouble. Basalt, at the confluence of the Fryingpan and Roaring Fork rivers, has the feeling of a ski town without the lift. Walking down its main drag, Midland Avenue, you get a hint of what Aspen must have been like years ago. Browse the town's quaint shops and surprisingly upscale galleries, then dine at one of several new and impressive restaurants. Or, at gateway to Ruedi Reservoir, take to the water for a day of fishing, boating or just relaxing away from the hustle and bustle of the town's noisy neighbors. |

Aspen

⓱ *42 mi from Glenwood Springs via Hwy. 82 east; 200 mi from Denver via I–70 west and Hwy. 82 east; 165 mi from Denver via I–70 west, Hwy. 91 south, and Hwy. 82 west (summer only).*

One of the world's fabled resorts, Aspen practically defines glitz, glamour, and glorious skiing. To the uninitiated, Aspen and Vail are synonymous. To residents, a rivalry exists, with locals of each claiming to have the state's most epic skiing, finest restaurants, and hottest nightlife. The most obvious distinction is the look: Vail is a faux-Bavarian development, whereas Aspen is an overgrown mining town. Vail is full of politicians: it's where Gerald Ford, Dan Quayle, and John Sununu fled to escape the cares of state, whereas Aspen is popular with singers and movie stars. Don Johnson and Melanie Griffith married (and divorced) here, and Barbra Streisand took a stand against state legislation that discriminated against gay people.

Between the galleries, museums, music festivals, and other glittering social events, there's so much going on in Aspen that even in winter many people come simply to "do the scene"—many never make it to the slopes. High-end boutiques have been known to serve free Campari-and-sodas après-ski, a practice so brazenly elitist that there's a certain charm to it. At the same time, Aspen is a place where people live fairly average lives, sending their children to school and working at jobs that may or may not have to do with skiing. It is, arguably, America's original ski-bum destination, a fact that continues to give the town's character an underlying layer of humor and texture. You can come to Aspen and have a reasonably straightforward, enjoyable ski vacation, because once you've stripped away the veneer, Aspen is simply a great place to ski.

Aspen has always been a magnet for cultural and countercultural types. Bad-boy gonzo journalist Hunter S. Thompson is one of the more visible citizens of the nearby community of Woody Creek. One of Aspen's most amusing figures is Jon Barnes, who tools around in his "Ultimate Taxi" (it's plastered with 3-D glasses, crystal disco balls, and neon necklaces and is redolent of dry ice and incense). You'll find everyone from socialites with *Vogue* exteriors and vague interiors to long-haired musicians in combat boots and fatigues. Ultimately, it doesn't matter what you wear here, as long as you wear it with conviction.

Originally called Ute City (after its displaced former residents), Aspen was founded in the late 1870s during a silver rush. The most prominent early citizen was Jerome Wheeler, who opened two of Aspen's enduring landmarks, the Hotel Jerome and the Wheeler Opera House. The silver market crashed in 1893, and Aspen's population dwindled from 15,000 to 250 by the end of the Depression. In the late 1930s, the region struck gold when Swiss mountaineer and ski consultant Andre Roche determined that Aspen Mountain would make a prime ski area. By 1941 it had already landed the U.S. Nationals, but Aspen was really put on the world map by Walter Paepcke, who developed the town as a cultural mecca. In 1949 he helped found the Aspen Institute for Humanistic Studies, and subsequently organized an international celebration to mark Johann Wolfgang von Goethe's 200th birthday. This event paved the way for such renowned annual festivities as the Aspen Music Festival and the International Design Conference.

Downtown Aspen is easily explored on foot. It's best to wander without a planned itinerary. You can spend an afternoon admiring the sleek window displays and graceful Victorian mansions, many of which now house fine boutiques and restaurants.

In summer, grab a bench near the town's focal point, the **Aspen Fountain** (✉ Mill St. and Hyman Ave.). Jets of water shoot up at random, soaking anyone who happens to be in the way. It's a great spot for people-watching during the day and listening to musicians in the evenings.

Many of Aspen's beautiful buildings were constructed in the 1880s, when the surrounding mines were overflowing with silver. Jerome Wheeler, one of the town's most prominent citizens, constructed the 1889 **Hotel Jerome** (✉ 330 E. Main St. ☎ 970/920–1000). Peek into the ornate lobby to get a sense of turn-of-the-20th-century living. Built in the same year, the elegant **Wheeler Opera House** (✉ 320 E. Hyman Ave. ☎ 970/920–5770) still serves as a concert venue.

You can get a taste of Victorian high life at the Queen Anne–style **Wheeler-Stallard House Museum**, which displays memorabilia collected by the Aspen Historical Society. While you're there, ask about the organization's newest endeavor, the Holden/Marolt Ranching and Mining Museum, a hands-on exploration of Aspen's past, housed in an old barn on the western edge of town. ✉ *620 W. Bleeker St.* ☎ *970/*

COLORADO'S FRAGILE WILDERNESS

MORE THAN 1,500 PEAKS PIERCE THE COLORADO SKYLINE, creating one of the most extensive and pristine alpine landscapes in the United States. It is a treeless landscape that has changed little in thousands of years; summer storms bury prehistoric glaciers, colorful wildflowers push up through snowy meadows, and ice-covered mountains fill 100-mi views.

But time is catching up with this ice-age wilderness. The very characteristics that once preserved the panoramic heights from human impact—rugged peaks, polar weather, barren vistas—are the same ones that today threaten it. Growing environmental pressures from recreational use, industrial pollution, and changing land-use patterns are taking a toll on this surprisingly fragile ecosystem.

Colorado's burgeoning population is increasing at an annual rate of 3 percent, a rate not seen since since the gold rush days of 1859. Many who move to the Mile High State enjoy an outdoor lifestyle that includes hiking. A popular pastime for many has been tackling the "Fourteeners," the state's 54 peaks that top 14,000-feet. As more and more hikers trample up these mountains, they gouge new trails, compact thin soil, and crush root systems. This damage can take a surprisingly long time to heal. Trails across the tundra near Rocky Mountain National Park that were carved out by Ute and Arapaho scouts hundreds of years ago are still visible today.

Less subtle than erosion, and equally devastating, is the harm caused by industrial pollution. Western Slope power plants in Craig and Hayden burn low-sulfur coal. Scientists believe the resulting sulfur and nitrogen emissions may be creating acid snow in the alpine watersheds, the same watersheds that pour forth several of the great American rivers, including the Colorado, Rio Grande and Arkansas.

Ironically, one of the greatest threats to the alpine tundra comes from attempts at preserving native wildlife. With wolves and grizzlies extinct in Colorado and hunting banned in Rocky Mountain National Park, the elk population has exploded from a handful of over-hunted animals to more than 2,500. Their sharp hooves trample summer pastures above the timberline and destroy many of the arctic willow stands that provide food and shelter for other wildlife, including the white-tailed ptarmigan.

Despite tales told to the tourists who admire its raw beauty in record numbers, Colorado's alpine wilderness is not the land that time forgot. In an amazing wilderness that has been around for more than 100 centuries, the clock is still ticking.

—by Jad Davenport

925–3721 ⊕ www.aspenhistory.org ✉ $6 ☉ Tues. and Thurs.–Sat. 1–5, Wed. 1–8.

Works by top regional and national artists are exhibited at the **Aspen Art Museum.** The complimentary wine-and-cheese reception held every Thursday at 5 is the best time to visit. ✉ 590 N. Mill St. ☎ 970/925–8050 ⊕ www.aspenartmuseum.org ✉ $5, free on Fri. ☉ Tues., Wed., Fri., and Sat. 10–6, Thurs. 10–7, Sun. noon–6.

With a trail that winds through gravestones dating to the 1800s, **Ute Cemetery** (✉ next to Ute Park off Ute Ave.) is a reminder that Aspen's roots go back deep into the nation's history.

Downhill Skiing & Snowboarding

Aspen is really four ski areas rolled into one resort. Aspen Highlands, Aspen (or Ajax) Mountain, Buttermilk, and Snowmass can all be skied with the same ticket. Aspen, Aspen Highlands, and Buttermilk are clustered close to downtown Aspen, whereas Snowmass is down the valley near Snowmass Village. A free shuttle system connects the four.

FodorśChoice ★

Aspen Highlands is essentially one long ridge with trails dropping off either side. Over the past few years the antiquated lift system has been replaced by three high-speed quads, and a massive base-area village has risen, turning the "maverick" ski hill into a destination in and of itself. Aspen Highlands has thrilling descents at Steeplechase, Olympic Bowl, and now, Highland Bowl, a hike-in experience unlike any in Colorado. The steep and often bumpy cluster of trails around Steeplechase and Highland Bowl makes this mountain one of the best places to be on a good powder day. Aspen Highlands has a wide-open bowl called Thunder that's popular with intermediate skiers, as well as plenty of lower-mountain blue runs. Besides the comparatively short lift lines and some heart-pounding runs, a highlight of Aspen Highlands is your first trip to the summit. The view, which includes the Maroon Bells and Pyramid Peak, is the most dramatic in the area and one of the best in the country. ⊠ *Maroon Creek Rd.* ☎ *970/925–1220 or 800/525–6200* ⊕ *www.aspensnowmass.com* ☉ *Early Dec.–early Apr., daily 9–4.*

Aspen Mountain is a dream destination for any mogul skier. Nearby Bell Mountain provides some of the best bump skiing anywhere, followed by Walsh's, Hyrup's, and Kristi's. Those wanting long cruisers head to the ridges or valleys: Ruthie's Run, Buckhorn, and International are the classics. Newcomers should note that there are no novice-level runs here. This is a resort where 65% of the trails are rated advanced or expert. A black diamond trail here might rank as a double diamond elsewhere. The narrow ski area is laid out on a series of steep, unforgiving ridges with little room for error. Most skiers spend much of the morning on intermediate trails off the upper-mountain quad. Then they head for lunch on the deck of Bonnie's, the mid-mountain restaurant that on sunny days is one of the great people-watching scenes in the skiing world. After a big storm, there's snow cat skiing on the back side of the mountain. The biggest drawback to skiing at Aspen Mountain is that too many trails funnel into Spar Gulch, making the end-of-day rush to the bottom chaotic and often dangerous—a situation that has become increasingly tense because snowboarders are now part of the mix. ⊠ *Durant St.* ☎ *970/925–1220 or 800/525–6200* ⊕ *www.aspensnowmass.com* ☉ *Late Nov.–mid-Apr., daily 9–4.*

Buttermilk—a place where it is virtually impossible to get into trouble—is terrific for novices, intermediates, and, thanks to its halfpipe and 2-mi long Crazy T'rain Park, snowboarders. It's a low-key, lighthearted sort of place, and an antidote to the kind of hotdogging you might encounter at Aspen Mountain. Among the featured attractions is a hangout for children named Ft. Frog. The Tiehack section to the east, with sweeping views of Maroon Creek Valley, has several advanced runs (though nothing truly expert). It also has superb powder, and the deep snow sticks around longer because so few serious skiers realize what they're missing. If you're looking for an escape from the hustle and bustle of Aspen, spend a day at Buttermilk. ⊠ *West Buttermilk Rd.* ☎ *970/925–1220 or 800/525–6200* ⊕ *www.aspensnowmass.com* ☉ *Late Nov.–early Apr., daily 9–4.*

FACILITIES

Aspen Highlands: 3,635-foot vertical drop; 790 skiable acres; 131 trails; 18% beginner, 30% intermediate, 16% advanced, 36% expert; 3 high-speed quad chairs, 1 triple chair.

Aspen Mountain: 3,267-foot vertical drop; 673 skiable acres; 76 trails; 48% intermediate, 26% advanced, 20% expert; one 6-passenger gondola, 1 high-speed quad chair, 2 quad chairs, 1 high-speed double chair, 3 double chairs.

Buttermilk: 2,030-foot vertical drop; 429 skiable acres; 41 trails; 35% beginner, 39% intermediate, 26% advanced; 1 high-speed quad chair, 5 double chairs, 1 surface lift.

LESSONS & PROGRAMS **Aspen Skiing Company** (☎ 970/925–1220 or 800/525–6200) gives lessons at all four mountains. Half-day group lessons start at $64, and a private half-day lesson will cost you $329. A noteworthy deal is the three-day guaranteed learn-to-ski or learn-to-snowboard package at Buttermilk, which include lessons and lift tickets for $308. The company also runs snow cat trips on Aspen Mountain.

Aspen Mountain Powder Tours (☎ 970/925–1220) provides access to 1,500 acres on the back side of Aspen Mountain via snowcats. Most of the terrain is negotiable by confident intermediates, with about 10,000 vertical feet constituting a typical day's skiing. Reservations are required at least a day in advance, but you should book as early as possible. Trips cost $275.

LIFT TICKETS Lift tickets are $72, but almost nobody pays full price thanks to multi-day savings, early- and late-season specials, and other discounts.

RENTALS Numerous ski shops in Aspen rent equipment. Rental packages (skis, boots, and poles) start at around $18 per day and rise to $40 or more for the latest and greatest equipment. Snowboard packages (boots and boards) run about $25. Bargain shopping at stores around town may turn up better deals. **Aspen Sports** (✉ 408 E. Cooper Ave. ☎ 970/925–6331) has plenty of gear to choose from. **Durrance Sports** (✉ 4102 Trailhead Lodge ☎ 970/429–0101), in Aspen Highlands Village, has equipment from many companies. **Pomeroy Sports** (✉ 614 E. Durrant Ave. ☎ 970/925–7875), at the base of Aspen Mountain gondola, has good deals on equipment.

Nordic Skiing

BACKCOUNTRY SKIING The **Alfred A. Braun Hut System** is one of Aspen's major backcountry networks. The trailhead leads from the Ashcroft Ski Touring Center into the Maroon Bells–Snowmass Wilderness. Take the usual precautions, because the trails cover terrain prone to avalanche. Huts sleep 7 to 14 people. They're open in winter only, and reservations can be made beginning May 1. ✍ *Box 7937, 81612* ☎ *970/925–5775* 🖅 *$25 per night.*

The **10th Mountain Hut & Trail System,** named in honor of the U.S. Army's 10th Mountain Division, includes 10 huts along the trail connecting Aspen and Vail. The main trail follows a generally avalanche-safe route in altitudes from 8,000 feet to 12,000 feet. This translates to a fair amount of skiing along tree-lined trails and a good bit of high-alpine ups and downs. You must be in good shape, and some backcountry skiing experience is extremely helpful. Accommodations along the trail vary, but this system does include the Ritz-Carltons of backcountry huts, supplied with mattresses and pillows, pre-cut logs for wood-burning stoves, and utensils for cooking. Huts sleeps from 6 to 16 people (more if you're willing to cuddle). Reservations are accepted beginning in March; weekends in peak ski season fill up quickly. ✉ *1280 Ute Ave., 81611* ☎ *970/ 925–5775* 🖅 *$26 per night.*

If you're either unfamiliar with the hut system or inexperienced in backcountry travel, you should hire a guide. One reliable company is **Aspen Alpine Guides** (✍ Box 659, 81612 ☎ 970/925–6618 or 800/643–8621 ⊕ www.aspennordic.com). In Aspen, the best place for backcountry-gear rentals (including ski equipment, climbing skins, packs, sleeping bags, and mountaineering paraphernalia) is the **Ute Mountaineer** (✉ 308 S. Mill St. ☎ 970/925–2849).

TRACK SKIING There is something to be said for maintaining a wealthy tax base. Subsidized by local taxes, the **Aspen/Snowmass Nordic Council** (✉ Box 10815, 81612 ☎ 970/544–9246) charges no fee for the 48 mi of maintained trails in the Roaring Fork Valley, making it the largest free groomed Nordic-trail system in North America. For a longer ski try the Owl Creek Trail, connecting the Aspen Cross-Country Center trails with the Snowmass Club–trail system. More than 10 mi long, the trail leads through some lovely scenery.

Lessons and rentals are available at the **Aspen Cross-Country Center** (✉ 39551 Hwy. 82 ☎ 970/544–9246). Diagonal, skating, racing, and light-touring setups are available.

About 12 mi from Aspen, the **Ashcroft Ski Touring Center** (✉ 11399 Castle Creek Rd. ☎ 970/925–1971) is sequestered in a high alpine basin up Castle Creek, which runs between Aspen Mountain and Aspen Highlands. The 25 mi of groomed trails are surrounded by the high peaks of the Maroon Bells–Snowmass Wilderness, and crisscross the ghost town of Ashcroft. This is one of the most dramatic cross-country sites in the High Rockies.

Other Sports & the Outdoors

Aspen Center for Environmental Studies (✉ 100 Puppy Smith St. ☎ 970/925–5756) is a research center and wildlife sanctuary where children and adults alike can take refuge. The facility sponsors snowshoe walks with naturalist guides in winter, and wildlife workshops that teach everything from how to create a small wildlife sanctuary in your own backyard to what animals you might find on local trails. In summer there are bird-watching hikes and "special little naturalist" programs for four- to seven-year-olds, which include nature walks and arts and crafts.

Aspen is equally popular in summer and winter; in warm weather there's plenty of hiking and biking opportunities throughout the **White River National Forest.** A favorite jaunt through the forest is to the majestic Maroon Bells, twin peaks more than 14,000 feet high. The colorful peaks, thanks to mineral streaking, is so vivid you'd swear they were blanketed with primrose and Indian paintbrush. It's one of the most photographed spots in the state. Cars are allowed only part-way, but the Roaring Fork Transit Agency provides shuttle buses that leave regularly in summer months from the Rubey Park Transportation Center in downtown Aspen. A convenient pass, available for $18.50, includes one trip to the Maroon Bells and one ride up Aspen Mountain's Silver Queen Gondola, where concerts, nature walks, and other activities await you.

BICYCLING **Aspen Sports** (✉ 408 E. Cooper Ave. ☎ 970/925–6331) has the area's widest selection of rental bikes, including tandems and all types of carriers for kids. **Blazing Pedals** (✉ Mill St. and Hyman Ave. ☎ 970/923–4544 or 800/282–7238) leads downhill bicycle tours through Aspen and the surrounding valleys. **The Hub of Aspen** (✉ 315 E. Hyman Ave. ☎ 970/925–7970) gives mountain-biking lessons through the Aspen Cycling School.

FISHING **Aspen Trout Guides** (✉ 516 E. Durant Ave. ☎ 970/925–7266) runs fly-fishing tours of local waterways. The company is located inside the Stefan Kaelin Pro Shop. **Taylor Creek Fly Shop** (✉ 408 E. Cooper Ave. ☎ 970/920–1128) has the town's best selection of flies and other supplies.

FITNESS The **Aspen Athletic Club** (✉ 720 E. Hyman Ave. ☎ 970/925–2531) is a fully equipped gym with a steam room and sauna. There's also a tanning salon and massage therapy. The upscale **Aspen Club & Spa** (✉ 1450 Crystal Lake Rd. ☎ 970/925–8900) has plenty of weight-training and cardiovascular equipment, as well as indoor courts for squash, basketball, and other sports. It's also home to Carmichael Training Systems bicycle performance and testing center and John Clendenin's "Ski Doctor" indoor ski simulator. When you're finished getting all sweaty, relax in the luxurious full-service spa.

GOLF **The Aspen Golf Course** (✉ 39551 Hwy. 82 ☎ 970/925–2145) is a fine 18-hole municipal facility, with a driving range, a pro shop, and an outstanding restaurant.

HORSEBACK RIDING For day or overnight horseback tours into the spectacular Maroon Bells–Snowmass Wilderness, try **T Lazy Seven Ranch** (✉ 3129 Maroon Creek Rd. ☎ 970/925–4614). In winter there's snowmobiling.

ICE SKATING The **Aspen Recreation Center** (✉ Castle Creek Rd. ☎ 970/544–4100) is home to an indoor ice rink big enough for National Hockey League games. There's also an Olympic-size swimming pool. If you prefer outdoor skating, try the **Silver Circle** (✉ 433 E. Durant Ave. ☎ 970/925–6360).

PARAGLIDING To see the resort from a different point of view, contact **Aspen Paragliding** (✉ 406 S. Spring St. ☎ 970/925–7635). The company sends you soaring through the skies above Aspen—in winter or summer—on a tandem paraglider with a professional pilot.

RAFTING For the truly adventurous, **Ajax Whitewater** (✉ 31300 Hwy. 82 ☎ 970/948–3797 🌐 www.ajaxwhitewater.com) rents inflatable kayaks perfect for running the rapids. The company also offers lessons. **Blazing Paddles** (✉ Mill St. and Hyman Ave. ☎ 970/923–4544 or 800/282–7238) runs trips to rivers and streams in and around Aspen. **Colorado Riff Raft** (✉ 555 E. Durant Ave. ☎ 970/925–5405 or 800/759–3939) runs mild to wild excursions on the Shoshone, Upper Roaring Fork, and lower Colorado rivers.

Where to Stay & Eat

$$$$ ✕ **Century Room.** Everything about the Hotel Jerome is exquisite, and dinner at the Century Room is no exception. With its high, vaulted ceilings, massive stone-and-marble fireplace, and comfortable wingback chairs, it is at once impressive and intimate. Chef Todd Slossberg's signature dishes, such as lobster-and-crab cakes, complement more traditional fare, such as Colorado rack of lamb. ✉ *330 E. Main St.* ☎ *970/ 920–1000* ⚖ *Reservations essential* ▭ *AE, DC, MC, V* ⊗ *No lunch.*

$$$$ ✕ **Matsuhisa.** Renowned in Los Angeles, New York, London, and Tokyo, Nobu Matsuhisa brings his nouveau-Japanese cuisine to Aspen. Although you shouldn't expect to see Nobu in the kitchen, his recipes and techniques are unmistakable. His jalapeño yellowtail is scrumptious, his anticucho beef is delicious, his new-style sashimi marvelous, and his prices astronomical. Check out Matsuhisa Lounge upstairs for cocktails and a limited sushi menu. ✉ *303 E. Main St.* ☎ *970/544–6628* ⚖ *Reservations essential* ▭ *AE, MC, V* ⊗ *No lunch.*

★ $$$$ ✕ **Pine Creek Cookhouse.** Strap on cross-country skis or board a horse-drawn sleigh (or hike during the summer) to get to this homey log cabin. The emphasis is on game specialties, including quail, elk, and wild boar. Lunch offerings include hot smoked-salmon salad, spinach crepes, and Hungarian goulash. In winter or summer, shoot for a seat on the deck for breathtaking views of the Elk Mountains. ✉ *11399 Castle Creek* ☎ *970/925–1044* 🌐 *www.pinecreekcookhouse.com* ⚖ *Reservations essential* ▭ *AE, MC, V.*

$$$$ ✕ **Piñons.** The Southwestern ranch-style dining room has leather-wrapped railings, a teal green ceiling, and upholstered walls. The contemporary

American menu scores high on creativity: For an appetizer, try the lobster strudel, a mainstay of chef Rob Mobillian. For your entrée, try the foie-gras topped beef fillet. The service and wine list are impeccable. ⊠ *105 S. Mill St.* ☎ *970/920–2021* ⚑ *Reservations essential* ☰ *AE, MC, V* ⊘ *No lunch.*

★ $$$$ ✕ **Syzygy.** Personable owner Walt Harris succeeds at providing a harmony of expressive cuisine (the name refers to the alignment of heavenly bodies) thanks to a sterling, unusually helpful waitstaff and the assured, sublimely seasoned creations of chef Morton Oswald. The food is crisply flavored and sensuously textured, floating from French to Asian to Southwestern influences without skipping a beat. Standouts include the Szechuan tempura lobster with grilled pineapple and Asian-vegetable salad, and main courses such as elk tenderloin with sun-dried fig chutney and chile aioli. The patient and knowledgeable will find a few good buys on the extensive wine list; enjoy a glass while listening to Aspen's best live jazz. ⊠ *520 E. Hyman Ave.* ☎ *970/925–3700* ⚑ *Reservations essential* ☰ *AE, D, DC, MC, V* ⊘ *No lunch.*

$$$–$$$$ ✕ **Kenichi.** This Asian restaurant gets the nod for its delectable bamboo salmon and Oriental roast duck served Peking style. Blackened sea bass is popular, as is everything from the sushi bar. With a crowd? Book one of the private tatami rooms. ⊠ *533 E. Hopkins Ave.* ☎ *970/920–2212* ☰ *AE, D, DC, MC, V* ⊘ *No lunch.*

$$–$$$$ ✕ **Ajax Tavern.** The brains behind Mustards Grill and Tra Vigne, two of Napa Valley's finest eateries, have created this bright, pleasant restaurant, with mahogany paneling, diamond-pattern floors, leather banquettes, open kitchen, and an eager, unpretentious waitstaff. Try the grilled lamb chops with seasonal vegetables. The wine list, showcasing Napa's best, is almost matched by the fine selection of microbrews. Enjoy outstanding lunch offerings on the spacious, sunny patio, which abuts Aspen Mountain. ⊠ *685 E. Durant Ave.* ☎ *970/920–9333* ⊕ *www.ajaxtavern.com* ⚑ *Reservations essential* ☰ *AE, D, DC, MC, V.*

$$–$$$$ ✕ **Cache Cache.** The sunny flavors of Provence explode on the palate, thanks to chef Christopher Lanter's savvy use of garlic, tomato, eggplant, fennel, and rosemary. The osso buco in marsala sauce is sublime; salads and rotisserie items are sensational; desserts are worth leaving room for. The bar menu offers a budget-conscious way to sample this outstanding cuisine. ⊠ *205 S. Mill St.* ☎ *970/925–3835 or 888/511–3835* ⊕ *www.cachecache.com* ☰ *AE, DC, MC, V* ⊘ *No lunch.*

$$–$$$$ ✕ **L'Hostaria.** This subterranean hotspot is sophisticated yet rustic, with an open-beam farmhouse ceiling, sleek blond-wood chairs, contemporary art, and a floor-to-ceiling glass wine cooler in the center of the room. The menu relies on simple, subtle flavors in specialties such as goat-cheese flan on mixed greens, gnocchi with duck ragout, risotto with veal sauce, and a delectable veal Milanese. For a change of pace, check out the carpaccio bar, which features wonderful cured meats and fish. ⊠ *620 E. Hyman Ave.* ☎ *970/925–9022* ☰ *AE, MC, V.*

★ $$$ ✕ **Toppers.** Cheerful Greg Topper, previously the esteemed chef of the Ajax Tavern, has opened a fuss-free café and take-out shop with first-rate American food. He serves fresh salads, soups, and fancy pizzas (think truffle oil), and the best sandwiches in town. Locals love the $9.95–$10.95 Aspen Bowls: you mix and match main items, such as fennel-spiced pork stew and red snapper and rock shrimp vegetable curry, with various sides. If you come for dinner, get the succulent, slow-braised short ribs. Also popular are venison chili, rotisserie chicken, trout puttanesca, and Colorado lamb. ⊠ *300 Puppy Smith St.* ☎ *970/920–0069* ☰ *MC, V.*

$$–$$$ ✕ **Poppies Bistro Cafe.** Ask 20 Aspenites where to find the most romantic meal in Aspen, and 19 of them will tell you to go to Poppies (the other one probably works at the competition). Its out-of-the-way loca-

tion, on the tranquil, westernmost edge of town, makes it feel like a secret retreat, and the intimate atmosphere, loaded with Victorian charm, just begs you to play Casanova. The cuisine ranges from classic bistro entrées such as steak au poivre in a cognac cream sauce to house specialties like spicy Anaheim peppers stuffed with lobster and goat cheese. It's cozy in winter, but even better in summer after an afternoon concert at the nearby music tent. ⊠ *834 W. Hallam St.* ☎ *970/925–2333* ⊟ *AE, MC, V* ☺ *No lunch.*

$–$$$ ⨯ **Little Annie's Eating House.** Everything at this charmer is ultra simple, from the wood paneling and red-and-white checked tablecloths to the fresh fish, barbecued ribs and chicken, and Colorado lamb. Annie's is a big favorite with locals, who like the relaxed atmosphere, dependable food, and reasonable prices, not to mention the Bundt cake and "shot and a beer" special. ⊠ *517 E. Hyman Ave.* ☎ *970/925–1098* ⊟ *AE, DC, MC, V.*

$–$$$ ⨯ **Main Street Bakery & Café.** Perfectly brewed coffee and hot breakfast buns and pastries are served at this café, along with a full breakfast menu that includes homemade granola. On sunny days, head out back to the deck for the mountain views. This is also a good spot for lunch and dinner (it's a quiet respite during the heart of the season). Try the Yankee pot roast, chicken potpie, and homemade soups. ⊠ *201 E. Main St.* ☎ *970/925–6446* ⊟ *AE, MC, V* ☺ *No dinner Apr.–June and Sept.–Nov.*

★ $$ ⨯ **Farfalla.** This sleek, L.A.-style northern Italian eatery is well lit and adorned with fine art. Specialties include homemade tortellini with asparagus and goat cheese in walnut sauce, an outstanding veal chop, wood-fired pizzas, and one of the town's best selections of grappa. ⊠ *415 E. Main St.* ☎ *970/925–8222* ⊟ *AE, DC, MC, V.*

¢–$$ ⨯ **Boogie's Diner.** This cheerful spot filled with diner memorabilia and an outrageous waitstaff resounds with rock-and-roll faves from the 1950s and '60s. The menu has true diner range—from vegetarian specialties to grilled cheese and half-pound burgers (including turkey). Other items are excellent soups, a monster chef salad, meat loaf and mashed potatoes, and a hot turkey sandwich. There's even a potato bar with one-pound taters and many toppings. Save room for a gigantic milk shake, malted, or float. ⊠ *534 E. Cooper Ave.* ☎ *970/925–6610* ⊟ *AE, MC, V.*

¢–$$ ⨯ **Hickory House Ribs.** Tie on your bib and dig in. No one will mind if your hands and face are covered in the secret sauce that tops the slow-cooked meats and chicken. These hickory-smoked baby-back ribs have won more than 40 national competitions. The rustic Hickory House is also home to Aspen's only Southern-style breakfast, grits and all. And for a hangover, nothing beats a good helping of ribs and eggs. ⊠ *730 W. Main St.* ☎ *970/925–2313* ⊟ *D, MC, V.*

$ ⨯ **La Cocina.** For good inexpensive eats, follow the locals. They'll lead you to this small Mexican restaurant (although no one can explain the garlic bread that comes with every dish). You'll order by the number and receive some combination of beans, rice, chicken, tortilla, and chile verde. Almost every night the house is packed full. If the wait is too long, you'll likely cop a complimentary bean dip or margarita for your trouble. ⊠ *308 E. Hopkins Ave.* ☎ *970/925–9714* ⌲ *Reservations not accepted* ⊟ *MC, V* ☺ *No lunch.*

¢ ⨯ **Charcuterie Cheese Market.** This take-out shop has dozens of hot and cold sandwich options, and a wide selection of fine cheeses. Feel free to mix and match ingredients and breads. The store also carries crackers, cookies, jams, and other food items to arm you for your picnic. It's near the base of Aspen Mountain, just east of the gondola. Hours are limited in the off-season. ⊠ *665 E. Cooper Ave.* ☎ *970/925–8010* ⊟ *AE, MC, V* ☺ *No dinner.*

$$$$ ⊞ **Hotel Aspen.** Just a few minutes from the mall and the mountain, this hotel on the town's main drag is a good find. The modern exterior is opened up with huge windows that take full advantage of the view; the lobby reveals a Southwestern influence. Rooms are comfortable, if not luxurious, with plenty of down pillows and comforters. Most have balconies or terraces, and a few have hot tubs. A Continental breakfast is included in the room rate, as is après-ski wine and cheese. ⊠ *110 W. Main St., 81611* ☎ *970/925–3441 or 800/527–7369* 🖷 *970/920–1379* ⊕ *www.hotelaspen.com* ⤺ *37 rooms, 8 suites* ⚷ *Refrigerators, microwaves, in-room VCRs, pool, 2 outdoor hot tubs, airport shuttle* ▤ *AE, D, DC, MC, V* ⎪⎤⎪ *CP.*

★ **$$$$** ⊞ **Hotel Jerome.** One of the state's truly grand hotels since it opened in 1889, Hotel Jerome is a treasure trove of Victoriana. The sumptuous public rooms have five kinds of wallpaper, antler sconces, and more than $60,000 worth of rose damask curtains, as well as crystal chandeliers, intricate woodwork, and gold-laced floor tiling. Guest rooms are generously sized, with high ceilings, sprawling beds, and huge bathtubs. The restaurants are held in high regard, and the J-Bar is legendary. Ask about "ski free" packages. ⊠ *330 E. Main St., 81611* ☎ *970/920–1000 or 800/331–7213* 🖷 *970/925–2784* ⊕ *www.hoteljerome.com* ⤺ *76 rooms, 16 suites* ⚷ *2 restaurants, room service, in-room data ports, in-room VCRs, minibars, cable TV, pool, gym, 2 outdoor hot tubs, 2 bars, business services, convention center, meeting room, airport shuttle* ▤ *AE, DC, MC, V.*

$$$$ ⊞ **Hotel Lenado.** The focal point of this dramatic inn is a very modern, 28-foot-tall stone-and-concrete fireplace. The smallish but quaint rooms contain either intricate carved applewood or ironwood beds (*lenado* is Spanish for wood, and much of it appears throughout the hotel). You'll also find antique armoires and wood-burning stoves, in addition to modern amenities such as cable TV. Rates include a full breakfast, served in the urbane bar area, which is also a great place to enjoy an evening aperitif. ⊠ *200 S. Aspen St., 81611* ☎ *970/925–6246 or 800/321–3457* 🖷 *970/925–3840* ⊕ *www.hotellenado.com* ⤺ *19 rooms* ⚷ *Hot tub, cable TV, lobby lounge, meeting rooms* ▤ *AE, DC, MC, V* ⎪⎤⎪ *BP.*

★ **$$$$** ⊞ **Little Nell.** The Nell is the only true ski-in/ski-out property in Aspen. Belgian wool carpets and overstuffed couches distinguish the lobby. The luxurious rooms have fireplaces, beds piled with down comforters, and large marble baths. Equally superior is the staff, which anticipates your needs. The unpretentious Montagna restaurant is worth a splurge; even your dog can enjoy a gourmet meal. The bar hosts one of town's most fashionable après-ski scenes. ⊠ *675 E. Durant Ave., Aspen 81611* ☎ *970/920–4600 or 888/843–6355* 🖷 *970/920–4670* ⊕ *www. thelittlenell.com* ⤺ *77 rooms, 15 suites* ⚷ *2 restaurants, room service, in-room safes, minibars, in-room VCRs, pool, health club, outdoor hot tub, bar, concierge, meeting rooms, airport shuttle, pets allowed* ▤ *AE, D, DC, MC, V.*

★ **$$$$** ⊞ **St. Regis Aspen.** This hotel is a memorable one, even by Aspen's exacting standards. The august reception area is comfortably furnished with overstuffed chairs with soft suede pillows, leather-topped tables, and rawhide lamp shades. The rooms follow suit with dark-wood furniture, muted colors, and such signature touches as bowls of fresh fruit. Luxurious baths are stocked with Bijan toiletries. The house restaurant is Olives, owned by celebrity chef Todd English; Whiskey Rocks, a cousin to L.A.'s Sky Bar, is the chic place to imbibe. ⊠ *315 E. Dean St., 81611* ☎ *970/920–3300 or 888/454–9005* 🖷 *970/925–8998* ⊕ *www. stregisaspen.com* ⤺ *224 rooms, 33 suites* ⚷ *Restaurant, room service, in-room safes, minibars, in-room VCRs, pool, health club, hair salon, outdoor hot tub, sauna, steam room, ski shop, bar, lobby lounge, meet-*

ing room, airport shuttle, business services, meeting room ☰ AE, D, DC, MC, V.

$$$$ 🏨 **Sky Hotel.** Aspen's hippest new hotel, the Sky has a sleek style and slopeside locale that make it ideal for those in search of something a bit different. The lobby, with its black walls and oversized white leather chairs—think *Alice in Wonderland*—leads to the ultra-cool and ultra-crowded 39 Degrees bar and the daily "altitude adjustment" happy hour with complimentary wine. Rooms, though small, are unforgettable because of their yellow walls, white headboards, and black accents. Signature touches like Frette linens, Aveda bath products, and your own bottle of oxygen make the Sky stand out from the rest. ⊠ *709 E. Durant Ave., 81611* ☎ *970/925–6778 or 800/474–1970* 🖷 *970/920–1379* ⊕ *www.theskyhotel.com* ↪ *90 rooms* ᕕ *Restaurant, room service, minibar, in-room VCRs, pool, health club, outdoor hot tub, ski shop, bar, concierge, meeting rooms, airport shuttle, business services, pets allowed* ☰ *AE, D, DC, MC, V.*

$$$–$$$$ 🏨 **Boomerang Lodge.** This comfortable inn has a wide range of accommodations, from somewhat drab rooms to smartly appointed apartments. The nicest lodgings are the deluxe units, decorated with a Southwestern flair, each with a fireplace, a wet bar, and a balcony with views of the surrounding mountains. The lobby fireplace becomes a social scene during afternoon tea. A Continental breakfast is included in the rate. ⊠ *500 W. Hopkins Ave., 81611* ☎ *970/925–3416 or 800/992–8852* 🖷 *970/925–3314* ⊕ *www.boomeranglodge.com* ↪ *32 rooms, 2 apartments* ᕕ *Refrigerators, pool, outdoor hot tub, sauna* ☰ *AE, D, DC, MC, V* ⦿ *CP.*

$$$–$$$$ 🏨 **Limelite Lodge.** It began as a nightclub, but this little lodge's party days are in the past. Today it's a good choice for skiers because of its prime location, just two blocks from the mall and three blocks from Lift 1A on Aspen Mountain. The somewhat dated rooms are furnished with pretty brass or cherrywood beds. All rooms are accessible from the outside, which makes the lodge convenient for families. Nine apartments with full kitchens and two log cabins are also available. ⊠ *228 E. Cooper St., 81611* ☎ *970/925–3025 or 800/433–0832* 🖷 *970/925–5120* ⊕ *www.limelitelodge.com* ↪ *63 rooms, 9 apartments* ᕕ *Refrigerators, 2 pools, 2 outdoor hot tubs, sauna, ski storage, pets allowed* ☰ *AE, D, DC, MC, V* ⦿ *CP.*

$$$ 🏨 **Snowflake Inn.** This motel has a great location in the heart of Aspen, but its rooms, with rough-wood paneling and dated furniture, are in need of a face-lift. The reasonable prices make it a good choice for a family on a budget; many of the rooms are quite large. The rustic lobby with its stone fireplace and wood beams is a convivial gathering place for the complimentary Continental breakfast and afternoon tea. ⊠ *221 E. Hyman Ave., 81611* ☎ *970/925–3221 or 800/247–2069* 🖷 *970/925–8740* ⊕ *www.snowflakeinn.com* ↪ *14 rooms, 24 suites* ᕕ *Kitchenettes, pool, outdoor hot tub, sauna, airport shuttle* ☰ *AE, D, DC, MC, V* ⦿ *CP.*

$$–$$$ 🏨 **Gems of Aspen.** Not one lodge, but a collection of a dozen family-owned inns, this is the place to turn for an affordable vacation. All accommodations are within walking distance of downtown and most include breakfast. Amenities vary, but what these properties lack in luxuries they make up twofold in charm, personality, and personal attention. ⊠ *Box 408, 81612* ☎ *970/925–9000 or 800/290–1325* ⊕ *www.gemsofaspen.com.*

CONDOMINIUMS **Aspen Alps** (⊠ 777 Ute Ave., 81611 ☎ 970/925–7820 or 800/228–7820 🖷 970/920–2528) has nicely appointed condos at the base of Aspen Mountain. **The Gant** (⊠ 610 W. End St., 81611 ☎ 970/925–5000 or 800/

345–1471 ☎ 970/925–6891 ⊕ www.www.gantaspen.com) has impressive accommodations with an excellent pool and meeting space. **Coates, Reid & Waldron** (✉ 720 E. Hyman Ave., 81611 ☎ 970/925–1400 or 800/222–7736 ☎ 970/920–3765) rents everything from studios to large homes. **Frias Properties** (✉ 730 E. Durant Ave., 81611 ☎ 970/920–2010 or 800/633–0336 ☎ 970/920–2020 ⊕ www.friaspropeties.com) has lavish homes in the mountains.

Nightlife & the Arts

THE ARTS   The **Aspen Music Festival and School** (☎ 970/925–3254), focusing on chamber music to jazz, runs from late June to mid-August. **Jazz Aspen Snowmass** (☎ 970/920–4996) has festivals in June and September, and also sponsors free Thursday-night concerts in summer. **Wheeler Opera House** (✉ 320 E. Hyman Ave. ☎ 970/925–5770) presents big-name classical, jazz, pop, and opera performers, especially in summer.

The **Aspen Writers' Foundation** (☎ 970/925–3122) has everything from a weekly writers' group (visitors welcome) to a summer literary festival.

BARS & LOUNGES   East Hyman Avenue is the best place for bar-hopping—a cluster of four nightspots share the same address. **Aspen Billiards** (✉ 315 E. Hyman Ave. ☎ 970/920–6707) is the town's most upscale pool hall. Challenge the locals to a game of eight ball. The smoky **Cigar Bar** (✉ 315 E. Hyman Ave. ☎ 970/920–4244) is a dimly-lit joint straight from Humphry Bogart movies. Overstuffed chairs and sofas and velvet curtains set the mood. Whiskey—and lots of it—is the claim to fame of **Eric's Bar** (✉ 315 E. Hyman Ave. ☎ 970/920–6707), a hip little watering hole, attracts a rowdy crowd. There's a varied lineup of imported beers on tap. **Su Casa** (✉ 315 E. Hyman Ave. ☎ 970/920–1488) is the place to get your fill of margaritas or sangria.

Inside Hotel Jerome, the **J-Bar** (✉ 330 E. Main St. ☎ 970/920–1000) is a fun, lively spot. You can't say you've seen Aspen until you've set foot in this place. The other watering hole inside Hotel Jerome, the mellow **Library Bar** (✉ 330 E. Main St. ☎ 970/920–1000), is the perfect capper to a long day on the slopes or night on the town. If you want to see the stars (and we're not talking about astronomy), head to **Whiskey Rocks** (✉ 315 Dean St. ☎ 970/920–3300). Lots of A-listers hang out in this bar at the St. Regis Aspen.

By its own admission, the **Woody Creek Tavern** (✉ 0002 Woody Creek Plaza, Woody Creek ☎ 970/923–4585) has "no redeeming features." This may be true, except that it's a great place to socialize. A grungy atmosphere, assorted bar games, and notable visitors such as Don Johnson and Hunter S. Thompson attract the crowds. Join the masses by riding your bike here in summer via the Rio Grande Trail.

CABARET   The **Crystal Palace** (✉ 300 E. Hyman Ave. ☎ 970/925–1455) is an Aspen fixture, offering two seatings nightly with fine food and fiercely funny, up-to-the-minute satire.

MUSIC & DANCE   Jazz is all that's needed to draw crowds to the cozy but crowded bar at CLUBS   **Little Nell** (✉ 675 E. Durant Ave. ☎ 970/920–4600). For late-night jazz of truly astounding quality, head to **Syzygy** (✉ 520 E. Hyman Ave. ☎ 970/925–3700).

Acoustic music by local and visiting musicians enlivens the **Main Street Bakery** (✉ 201 E. Main St. ☎ 970/925–6466). The place has an evening "listening room" that's ideal. Once a country and western saloon and now a full-on disco, **Shooters** (✉ Galena and Hopkins Sts. ☎ 970/925–4567) is the only place in town to shake it up on the dance floor.

Shopping

Downtown Aspen is an eye-popping display of conspicuous consumption. For an eclectic mix of glitz and glamour, T-shirts and trinkets, stroll past the shops lining Cooper Street. For chic boutiques, check out the **Brand Building** (⊠ Hopkins Ave. between Mill and Galena Sts.). This edifice is home to Gucci, Louis Vuitton, and Christian Dior, as well as local lions like Cashmere Aspen. For something silly for the folks back home, your best bet is the **Hyman Avenue Mall** (⊠ Hyman Ave. between Mill and Galena Sts.).

ANTIQUES **Fetzer Antiques** (⊠ 113 Aspen Airport Business Center ☎ 970/925–
DEALERS 5447) carries the community's finest antiques. The shop specializes in 18th- and 19th-century English and European items. **Little Bear Antiques & Uniques** (⊠ 415 Spring St. ☎ 970/925–3750) is jam-packed with European and American antique furniture and accessories.

ART GALLERIES **Baldwin Gallery** (⊠ 209 S. Galena St. ☎ 970/920–9797) is the place to see and be seen at receptions for nationally known artists. **David Floria Gallery** (⊠ 312 S. Mill St. ☎ 970/544–5705) exhibits the hottest new artists. **Galerie Maximillian** (⊠ 602 E. Cooper Ave. ☎ 970/925–6100) is the place to find high-quality paintings and sculpture.

Joel Soroka Gallery (⊠ 400 E. Hyman Ave. ☎ 970/920–3152) specializes in rare photos. **Magidson Fine Art** (⊠ 525 E. Cooper Ave. ☎ 970/920–1001) is known for its well-rounded collection of contemporary art. For offbeat exhibits, including works by such notables as Hunter S. Thompson and Andy Warhol, drive to the **Woody Creek Store** (⊠ 0006 Woody Creek Plaza, Woody Creek ☎ 970/922–0990).

BOUTIQUES In downtown Aspen, **Boogie's** (⊠ 534 E. Cooper Ave. ☎ 970/925–6111) sells everything from jeans to jewelry. **Chepita's** (⊠ 525 E. Cooper Ave. ☎ 970/925–2871) calls itself a "toy store for adults," which means it sells kinetic clothing and designer watches and jewelry. **Funky Mountain Threads** (⊠ 520 E. Durant Ave. ☎ 970/925–4665) offers just that: colorful clothes, festive hats, extravagant beadwork, and imaginative jewelry. **Scandinavian Designs** (⊠ 607 E. Cooper Ave. ☎ 970/925–7299) features some of Aspen's finest hand-knit sweaters, as well as everything Scandinavian, from Swedish clogs to Norwegian trolls.

CRAFTS **Aspen Potters** (⊠ 231 E. Main St. ☎ 970/925–8726) sells the latest designs from local artisans. To create your own art, visit the **Kolor Wheel** (⊠ 720 E. Durant Ave. ☎ 970/544–6191), a paint-it-yourself pottery studio.

Heather Gallery (⊠ 555 E. Durant Ave. ☎ 970/925–6170) features an enchanting mix of merchandise, including Janna Ungone's hand-painted lamp shades and animal clocks made by a local. You can even commission a portait of Fido or Fifi.

SPORTING GOODS **Aspen Sports** (⊠ 408 E. Cooper Ave. ☎ 970/925–6331) is the biggest sporting goods store in town. It stocks a full line of apparel and equipment for all sports. **Ute Mountaineer** (⊠ 308 S. Mill St. ☎ 970/925–2849) has Aspen's best selection of mountaineering clothes and equipment. The experienced staff makes sure you get what you need.

Snowmass

⑱ *42 mi from Glenwood Springs via Hwy. 82 east; 200 mi from Denver via I–70 west and Hwy. 82 east; 165 mi from Denver via I–70 west, Hwy. 91 south, and Hwy. 82 west (summer only).*

Heading east along Highway 82 toward Aspen you'll spot the turnoffs (Brush Creek and Owl Creek roads) to the Snowmass Ski Area, one of four ski mountains owned by the Aspen Skiing Company. The town at the mountain's base, Snowmass Village, has a handful of chic boutiques and eateries, but it's more down-to-earth and much slower-paced than Aspen.

Snowmass was built in 1967 as Aspen's answer to Vail—a ski-specific resort—and although it has never quite matched the panache or popularity of Vail, it has gained a certain stature with age. But the town struggles with finding its identity, a difficult proposition since it often calls itself Snowmass Village at Aspen. And the town's latest battle—what to do with its outdated base area—is another problem.

Still, an effort has been made to breathe a little life into Snowmass Village, and the effect has been noticeable. Better restaurants and a livelier après-ski scene give people something to do after the lifts close. In general, Snowmass is the preferred alternative for families with young children, leaving the town of Aspen to a more up-at-the-crack-of-noon kind of crowd. The selling points of Snowmass as an alternative to Aspen are lots of ski-in/ski-out lodging, a slower pace, and one of the best intermediate ski hills in the country.

Downhill Skiing & Snowboarding

Snowmass is the biggest of the four ski areas in the Aspen area. Aspen Highlands, Aspen Mountain, Buttermilk, and Snowmass can all be skied with the same ticket. A free shuttle system connects all four.

Snowmass is a sprawling ski area. There are six distinct sectors: Elk Camp, High Alpine/Alpine Springs, Big Burn, Sam's Knob, Two Creeks, and Campground. Except for the last two, all these sectors funnel into the pedestrian mall at the base. Snowmass is probably best known for the Big Burn, itself a great sprawl of wide-open, intermediate skiing. Experts head to such areas as Hanging Valley and the Cirque for the best turns.

At Snowmass, 55% of the 3,010 skiable acres are designated for intermediate-level skiers. The route variations down Big Burn are essentially inexhaustible, and there are many other places on the mountain for intermediates to find entertainment. The novice and lower-intermediate terrain on the lower part of the mountain makes Snowmass a terrific place for younger children.

But don't overlook the fact that Snowmass is four times the size of Aspen Mountain, and has triple the black- and double-black-diamond terrain of its famed sister, including several fearsomely precipitous gullies at Hanging Valley. Although only 38% of the terrain is rated advanced or expert, this huge mountain has enough difficult runs to satisfy all but the most demanding skiers.

Snowboarders take note: this mountain has one of the most comprehensive snowboarding programs in the country. A special terrain map points out the numerous snowboard-friendly trails and terrain parks while steering riders away from flat spots. You'll want to visit Trenchtown in the Coney Glade area, which has two lift-accessed pipes, video evaluation, piped-in music, and a yurt hangout complete with couches and snacks. ⊠ *Via Brush Creek Rd. or Owl Creek Rd.* ☎ *970/925–1220 or 800/525–6200* ⊕ *www.aspensnowmass.com* ☉ *Late-Nov.–mid-Apr., daily 9–4.*

FACILITIES   4,406-foot vertical drop; 3,010 skiable acres; 7% beginner, 55% intermediate, 18% advanced, 20% expert; 20 lifts, 7 high-speed quad chairs, 6 double chairs, 2 triple chairs, and 6 surface lifts.

LESSONS & PROGRAMS   **Aspen Skiing Company** (⊠ Snowmass Village Mall ☎ 970/925–1220 or 800/525–6200) gives lessons at Snowmass and Aspen's other mountains.

LIFT TICKETS Lift tickets are $72, but almost nobody pays full price thanks to multi-day savings, early- and late-season specials, and prepurchase discounts.

RENTALS Snowmass has numerous ski shops offering rental packages (skis, boots, and poles). **Aspen Sports** (✉ 70 Snowmass Village Mall ☎ 970/923–6111) is one of the best-known outfitters in Snowmass. **Incline Sports** (✉ Snowmass Village Mall ☎ 970/923–4726) is conveniently located just steps from the shuttle bus stop.

Nordic Skiing

TRACK SKIING **Aspen/Snowmass Nordic Council** (✉ Box 10815, Aspen 81612 ☎ 970/544–9246) has 48 mi of maintained trails in the Roaring Fork Valley. Probably the most varied, in terms of scenery and terrain, is the 18-mi Snowmass Club–trail network. For a longer ski, try the Owl Creek Trail, connecting the Snowmass Club–trail system and the Aspen Cross-Country Center trails. More than 10 mi long, the trail provides both a good workout and a heavy dosage of woodsy beauty, with many ups and downs across meadows and aspen-gladed hillsides. Best of all, you can take the bus back to Snowmass Village when you're finished.

Nordic-skiing equipment is available at the **Snowmass Cross-Country Center** (✉ 239 Snowmass Village Circle ☎ 970/923–3148).

Other Sports & the Outdoors

BALLOONING **Snowmass Mountain Outfitters** (☎ 970/923–8647) offers sunrise flights over the Roaring Fork Valley that end with a champagne toast. **Unicorn Balloon Company** (☎ 970/925–5752) flies you over the slopes of Aspen, and gives you a personal flight video as a keepsake.

BICYCLING **Aspen Sports** (✉ 70 Snowmass Village Mall ☎ 970/923–6111) has the widest selection of rental bikes in town, plus carriers for the kids. **Aspen Skiing Company** (✉ Snowmass Village Mall ☎ 970/925–1220) can give you a map of area trails, including the terrain park accessed by the Burlingame Lift. The company can also sell you a lift ticket so you won't have to ride uphill.

DOGSLEDDING With about 200 dogs ready to go, **Krabloonik** (✉ 4250 Divide Rd., Snowmass Village ☎ 970/923–3953), can always put together a half-day ride. These trips, beginning at 8:30 AM and 12:30 PM, include lunch or dinner at the Krabloonik restaurant, one of the best in the area. In summer, meet the dogs during daily kennel tours.

FISHING **Snowmass Mountain Outfitters** (✉ Snowmass Village Mall ☎ 970/923–8647) leads trips on the Colorado, Roaring Fork, and Fryingpan rivers. The company can also rent you all the gear you need to strike out on your own.

GOLF **Snowmass Club Golf Course** (✉ 239 Snowmass Village Circle ☎ 970/923–3148) is an 18-hole, 6,900-yard championship course designed by golf legends Arnold Palmer and Ed Seay. There's also a driving range, pro shop, and snack bar on the premises. Didn't bring your clubs? You can rent some here.

Where to Stay & Eat

★ $$$$ ✕ **Krabloonik.** Owner Dan MacEachen has a penchant for dogsled racing, and Krabloonik (Eskimo for "big eyebrows," and the name of his first lead dog) helps subsidize his expensive hobby. This rustic yet elegant cabin is on the slopes, which means you'll be treated to wonderful views on your way there. Although you can drive to the restaurant, the best—and most memorable—way to arrive is by dogsled. You'll dine sumptuously on some of the best game in Colorado—caribou and wild boar, for starters. Wash it all down with a selection from Snowmass's most extensive wine list. ⊠ *4250 Divide Rd., Snowmass Village* ☎ *970/ 923–3953* ⌕ *Reservations essential* ⊟ *AE, MC, V.*

★ **$$–$$$$** ✕ **Butch's Lobster Bar.** Once a lobsterman off Cape Cod, Butch Darden knows his lobster, and serves it up countless ways. The menu also includes plenty of other seafood favorites, including crab legs, shrimp, and steamers. There's also the obligatory steak, and chicken dishes. Although the atmosphere isn't fancy and the service isn't doting, this is the best place in town to get your seafood fix. ⊠ *Parking Lot 13, Snowmass Village* ☎ *970/923–4004* ⌕ *Reservations essential* ⊟ *AE, MC, V* ☾ *No lunch.*

$$–$$$$ ✕ **Il Poggio.** In the cutthroat competition between resort-town restaurants, this unassuming Italian place is smart enough to let the big boys duke it out. It wins in the end, as it's possibly the best casual restaurant in the village. The classic Italian food is well received by the après-ski crowd. Try one of the hearth-baked pizzas, a hearty pasta dish, or any beef or chicken entrée. ⊠ *73 Elbert La., Snowmass Village* ☎ *970/923– 4292* ⊟ *AE, DC, MC, V* ☾ *No lunch.*

$–$$ ✕ **The Stewpot.** There's a lot more than stew on the menu here, but stick to the namesake dish. A hearty bowl of beef or chicken stew served with homemade bread is hard to beat. This is an ideal spot for lunch after a long morning on the slopes. Daily soup specials—tomato cheddar is a winner, as is chicken vegetable barley—and a selection of sandwiches are also on the menu. The two-story restaurant has windows overlooking the mall and walls hung with photographs by local artists. ⊠ *62 Snowmass Village Mall, Snowmass Village* ☎ *970/923–2263* ⊟ *MC, V.*

★ **$$$$** ▦ **Stonebridge Inn.** Slightly removed from the hustle and bustle of the Village Mall, the Stonebridge Inn's boxy exterior does little to reveal its true character. It's one of the nicest lodging options in Snowmass. The lobby and bar are streamlined and elegant; the window-ringed restaurant offers regional cuisine in the dining room and on the terrace in summer. Rooms, all with two queen beds, aren't fancy, but are comfortably appointed. A Continental breakfast is included in the rate. The Stonebridge also rents out the adjacent two- and four-bedroom Tamarack Townhouses. Ask about "stay and ski' packages. ⊠ *300 Carriage Way, Snowmass Village 81615* ☎ *970/923–2420 or 800/922–7242* 🖷 *970/ 923–5889* ⊕ *www.stonebridgeinn.com* ⇜ *90 rooms, 5 suites, 28 condos* ⌕ *Restaurant, minibars, pool, gym, 2 outdoor hot tubs, sauna, bar, meeting rooms, airport shuttle* ⊟ *AE, D, DC, MC, V.*

$$$–$$$$ ▦ **Silvertree Hotel.** This ski-in, ski-out property, under the same management as the Wildwood Lodge next door, is built into Snowmass Mountain. It's a sprawling complex—virtually everything you need is under one roof. After a morning on the slopes, warm up in one of the hot tubs or the steam room. Rooms and suites feature subdued but attractive decor, with all the expected amenities. Condos are also available, with full use of facilities. ⊠ *100 Elbert La., Snowmass Village 81615* ☎ *970/923– 3520 or 800/525–9402* 🖷 *970/923–5192* ⊕ *www.silvertreehotel.com* ⇜ *262 rooms, 15 suites, 200 condos* ⌕ *2 restaurants, in-room safes, minibars, in-room VCRs, 2 pools, health club, 2 outdoor hot tubs, spa, steam room, sauna, ski shop, bar, lobby lounge, meeting room, airport shuttle* ⊟ *AE, D, DC, MC, V.*

★ **$–$$$** ▦ **Snowmass Inn.** This family-owned lodge is one of the original properties at Snowmass; it commands a prime location in the middle of the Snowmass Village Mall. It's also a short stroll from the slopes. Rooms are spacious and comfortable, although some are showing signs of wear. Still, this is the perfect place for those on a budget or those looking to be in the middle of the action. ⊠ *67 Daily La., Snowmass Village 81615* ☎ *970/923–4204 or 800/635–3758* 🖷 *970/923–2819* ⊕ *www.*

snowmassinn.com ✒ *39 rooms* ⚙ *Refrigerators, pool, outdoor hot tub, airport shuttle* ▤ *AE, D, DC, MC, V* ⦿ *CP.*

CONDOMINIUMS **Snowmass Lodging Company** (⌂ 425 Wood Rd., Snowmass Village 81615 ☎ 970/923–3232 or 800/365–0410 🖷 970/923–5740) rents a wide variety of condominiums. **Village Property Management** (⌂ 100 Elbert La., Snowmass Village 81615 ☎ 970/923–4350 or 800/525–9402 🖷 970/923–5192) has everything from studio apartments to fully stocked homes. **Stay Aspen Snowmass** (☎ 888/290–1325 ⊕ www. stayaspensnowmass.com) is the central lodging service for the area.

Nightlife

BARS & LOUNGES **The Cirque Café** (✉ 105 Snowmass Village Mall ☎ 970/923–8686) has the most happening après-ski scene, with live music most evenings. The sun-soaked deck is a popular place in summer. For a mellow experience, try the **Conservatory** (✉ 100 Elbert La. ☎ 970/923–3520). It has a dark, moody atmosphere and occasional live music. **Zane's Tavern** (✉ 10 Snowmass Village Sq. ☎ 970/923–3515) is your classic mountain-town bar, with loud music, pool tables, and beer by the pitcher.

CABARET The **Tower** (✉ 45 Snowmass Village Mall ☎ 970/923–4650) hosts hokey but hilarious magic and juggling acts.

Shopping

ART GALLERIES **Anderson Ranch Arts Center** (✉ 5263 Owl Creek Rd. ☎ 970/923–3181) exhibits the work of resident artists. It also hosts lectures, workshops, and other special events.

SPORTING GOODS **Aspen Sports** (✉ 70 Snowmass Village Mall ☎ 970/923–6111) is the biggest store around, with a full line of apparel and equipment for all sports.

I–70 & THE HIGH ROCKIES A TO Z

To research prices, get advice from other travelers, and book travel arrangements, visit www.fodors.com.

AIR TRAVEL

CARRIERS Aspen Airport is served daily by United Express, America West Express/ Mesa, and Northwest Express/Mesaba, and has nonstop United service to Los Angeles in ski season. American, Continental, Northwest, TWA, and United Express fly nonstop from various gateways during ski season to Steamboat Springs' Yampa Valley Airport. The Vail Valley is served by Eagle County Airport, 35 mi west of Vail. During ski season, American, Continental, Delta, United, and Northwest have nonstop flights from several gateways. United is the only airline that flies year-round.
🗐 **Airlines & Contacts America West Express** ☎ 800/235-9292 ⊕ www.americawest. com. **Northwest Express** ☎ 800/225-2525 ⊕ www.nwa.com. **United** ☎ 800/241-6522 ⊕ www.united.com.

AIRPORTS

There's no mistaking the Denver International Airport (DIA), with its tented white canopy and spacious terminals. This is the gateway to the High Rockies. Fast, efficient, clean, and full of great shops, the airport is located just east of Denver, about a 20-minute taxi ride from the city center and an hour's drive from the Continental Divide. From here you can hop commuter flights to all of the ski resorts on the west side of the Continental Divide. Pitkin County Airport is 3 mi from Aspen, and Yampa Valley Airport is 22 mi from Steamboat Springs. Eagle County Airport is 35 mi west of Vail.

Most of the I–70 corridor is served via Denver and its airports. This used to be the surer choice because flying into the smaller airports in winter was always iffy, but with jets making nonstop flights to many of those smaller airports, the decision of which airport to use depends more on where you're coming from and which flights are convenient.
📍 **Pitkin County Airport** ☎ 970/920-5385 ⊕ www.aspenairport.com. **Denver International Airport** ☎ 800/247-2336 ⊕ www.flydenver.com. **Eagle County Airport** ☎ 970/524-9490 ⊕ www.eagle-county.com/airport. **Yampa Valley Airport** ☎ 970/276-3669.

TRANSFERS

To and from Aspen and Snowmass Village, your best bet is Roaring Fork Transit Agency, which provides bus service from Pitkin County Airport to the Rubey Park bus station. Colorado Mountain Express connects Aspen with Denver, Grand Junction, and the Eagle County airport. High Mountain Taxi will also provide charter service outside the Roaring Fork Valley.

To and from Summit County (Breckenridge, Copper Mountain, Dillon, Frisco, Keystone), use Resort Express or Colorado Mountain Express, which have regular service to and from Denver airports. Rainbow Taxi provides local service in Summit County.

To and from Steamboat Springs, take Alpine Taxi or Steamboat Taxi. Both have special rates to Vail, Boulder, and Denver.

To and from Vail and Beaver Creek, try Colorado Mountain Express or Vail Valley Taxi. Home James Transportation and Greyhound travel between Winter Park and Denver.
📍 Shuttle Information **Alpine Taxi** ☎ 970/879-2800. **Colorado Mountain Express** ☎ 970/949-4227 or 800/525-6353. **Greyhound Lines** ☎ 800/231-2222. **High Mountain Taxi** ☎ 970/925-8294 or 800/528-8294. **Home James Transportation** ☎ 970/726-5060 or 800/451-4844. **Resort Express** ☎ 970/468-7600 or 800/334-7433. **Rainbow Taxi** ☎ 970/453-8294. **Roaring Fork Transit Agency** ☎ 970/925-8484. **Steamboat Taxi** ☎ 970/879-3335. **Vail Valley Taxi** ☎ 970/476-8294 or 800/882-8872.

BICYCLING

Biking in the High Rockies requires more planning than a similar excursion at sea level. The weather in the mountains changes without warning in summer, so bring along adequate clothing for rain and even snow. Bring lots of water and stuff a few extra energy bars in your pack. And don't forget sunscreen—at these altitudes, you need it even on cloudy days. Always carry a map if you're hiking in the high-country forests or riding on mountain trails, even if you are planning a short journey. Signage is better in some places than others, making it easy to ride down the wrong path.

If you're mountain-biking during hunting season—roughly mid-September to October—wear bright colors and stay on well-traveled trails in open areas. When exploring, keep far away from the many open mine shafts that dot the mountains. These remnants of the region's mining heritage may be unstable, and the shafts may drop hundreds of feet. The long-abandoned mining structures are also dangerous.

When choosing a route, touch base with someone at one of the local bike shops. They can tell you if the route is appropriate for someone of your physical condition and ability. Many paths are rated—easy, more difficult, or difficult.

BUS & SHUTTLE TRAVEL

Greyhound Lines has regular service from Denver to several towns along I–70. The company also runs intercity bus service. All the resorts run free or inexpensive shuttles between the ski villages and the slopes, and between ski areas in Summit County.

🚍 Aspen/Snowmass Information **Roaring Fork Transit Agency** ☎ 970/925-8484.

🚍 Steamboat Springs Information **Steamboat Springs Transit** ☎ 970/879-5585.

🚍 Summit County Information **Breckenridge Free Shuttle** ☎ 970/547-3140. **KAB Express** ☎ 970/468-4200. **Keystone Resort Shuttle Service** ☎ 970/468-2316. **Summit Stage** ☎ 970/668-0999.

🚍 Vail/Beaver Creek Information **Avon Beaver Creek Transit** ☎ 970/748-4120. **Beaver Creek Dial-A-Ride** ☎ 970/949-1938. **Resort Express** ☎ 970/468-7600. **Town of Vail** ☎ 970/479-2100.

🚍 Winter Park Information **Winter Park Lift** ☎ 970/726-4163.

CAR RENTAL

The most convenient place for visitors to rent a car is at the DIA. Alamo, Avis, Budget, Hertz, and National have offices in the smaller regional airports as well.

🚗 **Alamo** ☎ 800/462-5266 ⊕ www.alamo.com. **Avis** ☎ 800/230-4898 ⊕ www.avis.com. **Budget** ☎ 800/527-0700 ⊕ www.budget.com. **Hertz** ☎ 800/654-3131 ⊕ www.hertz.com. **National** ☎ 800/227-7368 ⊕ www.nationalcar.com.

CAR TRAVEL

The hardest part about driving in the High Rockies is keeping your eyes on the road. A glacier-carved canyon off to your left, a soaring mountain ridge to your right, and there, standing on the shoulder, a bull elk. Some of the most scenic routes aren't necessarily the most direct. The Eisenhower Tunnel sweeps thousands of cars daily beneath the mantle of the Continental Divide, whereas only several hundred drivers choose the slower, but spectacular, Loveland Pass. Some of the most beautiful byways, like the Mt. Evans Scenic and Historic Drive, are one-way roads.

Although it is often severely overcrowded, I–70 is still the quickest and most direct route from Denver to the High Rockies. It slices through the state, separating it into northern and southern halves. Idaho Springs, Summit County, Vail Valley, and Glenwood Springs are all along I–70. Winter Park is north of I–70, on U.S. 40, which has several hairpin turns. Berthoud Pass, a particularly lovely stretch of U.S. 40, can be treacherous when a winter storm blows in. Leadville and Ski Cooper are south of I–70 along U.S. 24 and Route 91.

Generally speaking, driving to Aspen from Denver during winter is more trouble than it's worth, unless you are on an extended vacation and plan to stop along the way. With Independence Pass closed in winter, the drive west on I–70 and east on Route 82 takes more than three hours at best, depending on road and weather conditions. On the other hand, the drive from the west is relatively easy, with no high-mountain passes to negotiate. Take the Route 82 exit off I–70 at Glenwood Springs.

Steamboat Springs is about a three-hour drive from Denver via I–70 west and U.S. 40 north. The route traverses some high-mountain passes, so it's a good idea to check road conditions before you travel.

Gasoline is readily available along I–70 and its arteries, but when venturing into more remote areas like Mount Evans and Guanella Pass be sure you have enough fuel to get there and back. Blinding snowstorms can appear out of nowhere on the high passes at any time of the year. Chains aren't normally required for passenger vehicles on highways, but it's a good idea to carry them in bad weather. A shovel isn't a bad idea, either. Keep your eyes peeled for wildlife, especially along the stretch of

I–70 from Idaho Springs to the Eisenhower Tunnel. Bighorn sheep and deer frequently graze along the north side of the highway.

🚔 **Colorado State Patrol** ☎ 303/239–4500 ⊕ www.csp.state.co.us.

🚔 **Colorado Road Condition Hotline** ☎ 303/639–1111 near Denver, 303/639–1234 statewide.

EMERGENCIES

🚔 **Ambulance or Police Emergencies** ☎ 911.

🚔 **24-Hour Medical Care Aspen/Snowmass: Aspen Valley Hospital** ⊠ 0401 Castle Creek Rd. ☎ 970/925–1120. **Glenwood Springs: Valley View Hospital** ⊠ 1906 Blake St. ☎ 970/945–6535. **Steamboat Springs: Routt Memorial Hospital** ⊠ 1024 Central Dr., Steamboat Springs ☎ 970/879–1322. **Summit County: Summit Medical Center** ⊠ Rte. 9 and School Rd., Frisco ☎ 970/668–3300. **Vail Valley: Beaver Creek Village Medical Center** ⊠ 1280 Village Rd., Beaver Creek ☎ 970/949–0800. **Vail Valley Medical Center** ⊠ 181 W. Meadow Dr., Vail ☎ 970/476–2452. **Winter Park: Seven Mile Medical Center** ⊠ Base of Winter Park ski area, Winter Park ☎ 970/726–8066.

LODGING

Despite the abundant amount of federal and state land that checkerboards the High Rockies, finding an established campsite is surprisingly difficult along the I–70 corridor. From Memorial Day to Labor Day campsites fill up quickly, especially on weekends and holidays. To improve your chances, call to reserve a campsite or arrive early in the day. Established car-camping sites generally have rest rooms, water pumps, trash cans, and fire pits. Open fires are only allowed when the danger of wildfires is low. Wilderness devotees who don't relish the idea of a neighborhood of tents can escape into the vast backcountry. The Indian Peaks Wilderness Area—a string of 13,000-foot-high peaks that brace the Continental Divide north of I–70—offers limitless opportunities. As long as you are 200 feet away from a water source, you can pitch your tent anywhere.

🚔 **Colorado Campground and Lodge Owners Association** ☎ 970/247–5406 ⊕ www.campcolorado.com.

TOURS

In Aspen, a romantic way to orient yourself to the backcountry is by taking the T Lazy Seven Ranch private sleigh ride. Aspen Carriage Co. has stagecoach tours around downtown and the historic West End. From the beginning of summer through mid-October, narrated bus tours from Aspen to the Maroon Bells are available.

The Summit Historical Society leads lively 1½-hour tours of downtown Breckenridge, Colorado's largest National Historic District, Monday to Saturday at 10 AM. Steamboat's Sweet Pea Tours visits nearby hot springs. Vail's Nova Guides runs Jeep and all-terrain-vehicle tours, as well as rafting, fishing, snowmobiling, and hiking expeditions.

Mad Adventures has Continental Divide van tours from Winter Park. If rafting is your choice, Mad Adventures can help you shoot the rapids of the North Platte, Colorado, and Arkansas rivers. Timberline Tours runs rafting trips and Jeep tours throughout the region.

🚔 **Tour Operators Aspen Carriage Co.** ⊠ Aspen ☎ 970/925–3394. **Mad Adventures** ⊠ Winter Park ☎ 970/726–5290 or 800/451–4844. **Maroon Bells Bus Tour** ⊠ Aspen ☎ 970/925–8484. **Nova Guides** ⊠ Vail ☎ 970/949–4232. **Summit Historical Society** ☎ 970/453–9022. **Sweet Pea Tours** ⊠ Steamboat Springs ☎ 970/879–5820. **T Lazy Seven Ranch** ⊠ Aspen ☎ 970/925–4614. **Timberline Tours** ⊠ Vail ☎ 970/476–1414.

TRAIN TRAVEL

Amtrak has service from Denver's Union Station to the Winter Park Ski Area station in nearby Fraser (where shuttles to the area are available). Glenwood Springs is on the *California Zephyr* route.

The nonstop Ski Train leaves Denver's Union Station every Saturday and Sunday morning, chugging through 29 tunnels before depositing passengers only 50 yards from Winter Park's lifts.

🚆 Train Information **Amtrak** ☎ 800/872-7245 ⊕ www.amtrak.com.

VISITOR INFORMATION

If you're ready to take to the slopes, the first thing you will need to know is whether there is plenty of snow. Each resort has its own hot line with the latest on weather conditions.

🚆 Snow reports **Aspen** ☎ 800/525-6200. **Breckenridge** ☎ 800/789-7669. **Copper Mountain** ☎ 970/968-2100. **Keystone** ☎ 970/468-2316. **Steamboat Springs** ☎ 970/879-7300. **Vail** ☎ 970/476-4888. **Winter Park** ☎ 970/726-7669.

🚆 **Aspen Chamber Resort Association** ✉ 425 Rio Grande Pl., 81611 ☎ 970/925-1940 or 800/262-7736 ⊕ aspenchamber.org. **Breckenridge Resort Chamber** ✉ 309 N. Main St., 80424 ☎ 970/453-6018 ⊕ gobreck.com. **Copper Mountain Resort** ✒ Box 3001, 80443 ☎ 970/968-2882 or 800/458-8386 ⊕ www.coppercolorado.com. **Glenwood Springs Chamber Resort Association** ✉ 806 Cooper Ave., 81601 ☎ 970/945-6589 or 800/221-0098 ⊕ glenwoodchamber.com. **Keystone Resort** ✒ Box 38, Keystone 80435 ☎ 970/468-2316 ⊕ keystoneresort.com. **Leadville Chamber of Commerce** ✉ 809 Harrison St., 80461 ☎ 719/486-3900 ⊕ leadvilleusa.com. **Steamboat Ski & Resort Corporation** ✉ 2305 Mt. Werner Circle, Steamboat Springs 80487 ☎ 970/879-6111 ⊕ steamboat.com. **Steamboat Springs Chamber Resort Association** ✉ 1255 S. Lincoln Ave., 80477 ☎ 970/879-0880 or 800/922-2722 ⊕ steamboatchamber.com. **Summit County Chamber of Commerce** ✒ Main St., Frisco 80443 ☎ 970/668-5000 or 800/530-3099 ⊕ www.summitchamber.org. **Vail Resorts, Inc.** ✒ Box 7, Vail 81658 ☎ 970/476-5601 ⊕ vail.com. **Vail Valley Tourism and Convention Bureau** ✉ 100 E. Meadow Dr., Vail 81658 ☎ 970/476-1000 or 800/824-5737 ⊕ www.visitvailvalley.com. **Winter Park Resort** ✒ Box 36, Winter Park 80482 ☎ 970/726-5514 ⊕ www.winterparkresort.com. **Winter Park/Fraser Valley Chamber of Commerce** ✒ Box 3236, Winter Park 80482 ☎ 970/726-4118 or 800/903-7275 ⊕ www.winterpark-info.com.

SOUTHWEST COLORADO

FODOR'S CHOICE

Black Canyon of the Gunnison National Park, *Montrose*
Durango & Silverton Narrow Gauge Railroad, *Durango*
Mesa Verde National Park
Red Mountain Pass, *Ouray*
Strater Hotel, *Durango*
The Town of Telluride
Yankee Boy Basin, *Ouray*

HIGHLY RECOMMENDED

SIGHTS Anasazi Heritage Center, *Dolores*
Underground Mining Museum, *Creede*

OUTDOORS Rafting on the Gunnison River, *Montrose*
Mountain Biking in Crested Butte
Silverton Mountain Ski Area, *Silverton*
Wolf Creek Ski Area, *Pagosa Springs*

Many other great hotels and restaurants enliven this area. For other favorites, look for the black stars as you read this chapter.

Revised &
Updated by
Claire Walter

THE RUDDY OR RED-HUED ROCKS found in much of the state, particularly in the Southwest, give Colorado its name. The region's terrain varies widely—from yawning black canyons and desolate monochrome moonscapes to pastel deserts and mesas, glistening sapphire lakes, and wide expanses of those stunning red rocks. It's so rugged in the southwest that a four-wheel-drive vehicle or hiker's sturdiness is necessary to explore much of the wild and beautiful backcountry.

The region's history and people are as colorful as the landscape. Southwestern Colorado, as well as the "Four Corners" neighbors of northwestern New Mexico, northeastern Arizona, and southeastern Utah, was home to the Ancestral Puebloan peoples formerly known as Anasazi, meaning "ancient ones." They constructed impressive cliff dwellings in what are now Mesa Verde National Park, Ute Mountain Tribal Park, and other nearby sites. This wild and wooly region, dotted with rowdy mining camps and boomtowns, also witnessed the antics of such notorious outlaws as Butch Cassidy, who embarked on his storied career by robbing the Telluride Bank in 1889, and Robert "Bobby" Clark, who hid out in Creede from the James Gang after he shot Jesse in the back. Even today, the more ornery, independent locals, disgusted with the political system, periodically talk of seceding from the union. They can be as rough as the country they inhabit.

Southwest Colorado offers such diversity that, depending on where you go, you can have radically different vacations. You can spiral from the towering peaks of the San Juan range to the plunging Black Canyon of the Gunnison, taking in alpine scenery along the way, as well as the eerie remains of old mining camps, before winding through striking desert landscapes, the superlative Ancestral Puebloan ruins, and the Old West railroad town of Durango. If you're not here to ski or golf in the world-class resorts of Crested Butte, Purgatory, or Telluride, there is still much to experience in this part of the state.

Exploring Southwest Colorado

Southwest Colorado is the land beyond the interstates. It is a landscape of towering mountains, arid mesa-and-canyon country, and roiling rivers. Old mining roads, legacies of the late 19th and early 20th centuries when gold and silver mining was ascendant, lead through drop-dead gorgeous mountain valleys to the rugged high country. However, much of this part of the state is designated as wilderness area—including the nearly 1-million-acre Weminuche Wilderness, the state's largest protected area—which means that no roads may be built and no wheeled or motorized vehicles are permitted. This is a region where some state highways are unpaved, a federal highway known as U.S. 550 corkscrews over a high mountain pass known for heavy snows and a lack of guardrails, and snowmobiles regularly replace other motor vehicles as winter transportation. High-clearance, four-wheel-drive vehicles in summer and snowmobiles in winter are required for backcountry exploration, but regular passenger cars can travel most roads.

About the Restaurants

With dining options ranging from creative contemporary cuisine in the posh ski resorts of Telluride (and to a lesser extent in Crested Butte and Durango) to no-frills American fare in down-home ranching communities, no visitor has any excuse to visit a chain restaurant here. The leading chefs are tapping into the region's local bounty, so you'll find innovative recipes for ranch-raised game, lamb, and trout. Seasonal produce is always highlighted on the best menus.

About the Hotels

No matter what you're looking for in vacation lodging—luxurious slope-side condominium, landmark inn in a historic town, riverside cabin, quaint bed-and-breakfast inn, budget motel, or chockful-of-RVs campground—southwest Colorado has it in abundance. In ski resorts, especially, the rates vary from season to season. Some properties close in the fall once the aspens have shed their golden leaves, open in winter when the lifts begin running, close in the spring after the snow melts, and open again in mid-June.

WHAT IT COSTS				
$$$$	**$$$**	**$$**	**$**	**¢**
RESTAURANTS over $25	$19–$25	$13–$18	$8–$12	under $8
HOTELS over $200	$151–$200	$111–$150	$70–$110	under $70

Restaurant prices are for a main course at dinner, excluding sales tax of 6.75%–8%. Hotel prices are for two people in a standard double room in high season, excluding service charges and 5.4%–9.8% tax.

Timing

Southwest Colorado, like the rest of the state, is intensely seasonal. Snow begins falling in the high country in late September or early October, and by Halloween seasonal closures turn most unpaved roads into routes for snowmobiles. The San Juan Mountains are the snowiest region of the Colorado Rockies, with average annual snowfalls approaching 400 inches in some spots. Skiers and snowboarders treasure this abundance of white gold. Winter lingers well into the season that is called spring on the calendar. In fact, the greatest snowfalls generally occur in March and April. Skiing winds down in early to mid-April, and ski towns virtually shut down until the summer sun draws hikers and bikers. Gunnison and Durango, being college towns, keep rolling throughout the year.

At about the same time skiers are packing up their poles, the snow in the higher elevations begins to melt. Cresting streams offer thrilling, if chilling, white-water rafting and kayaking. Snowplows begin busting through the drifts on unpaved roads, restoring them to motor vehicle use. Hiking trails become accessible, and wildflowers begin their short, intense season of show. Summer is glorious in the mountains, with brilliant sunshine in cobalt blue skies. Late summer brings brief and often intense showers on many an August afternoon, sometimes accompanied by dramatic thunder and lightning. Summer tourism winds down after Labor Day and shuts down completely after the last leaf has drifted to the ground in October and the cycle begins again. In the harsh dry climate of the mesa-and-canyon country around the Four Corners, summers are brutally hot, winters can be windy and cold, and spring and fall are the best times to visit.

GUNNISON RIVER BASIN

Crested Butte

❶ *90 mi from Glenwood Springs via Rtes. 82 east, 133 south, and Rte. 135 (over Kebler Pass, summer only); 110 mi from Aspen via Rte. 82 west, Rte. 133 south, and Rte. 135 (summer only); 190 mi from Glenwood Springs, south via Rte. 82 east, 133 south, Rte. 92 south, U.S. 50 east, and Rte. 135 north; 210 mi from Aspen via Rte. 82 west, south on Rte. 133, Rte. 92 south, U.S. 50 east, and Rte. 135 north.*

4

Numbers in the text correspond to numbers in the margin and on Southwest Colorado map.

If you have 3 days

From 🚩 **Ridgway** ④, drive south for 10 mi to visit **Ouray** ⑥, a Victorian-era gem along the stupendously beautiful San Juan Skyway. Retrace your route, then head to **Telluride** ⑤ for lunch and a gondola ride up the mountain. Continue over Lizard Head Pass, stopping at the Anasazi Heritage Center in **Dolores** ⑬ before spending the night in 🚩 **Cortez** ⑫ or Mancos. Start early the next morning so you can explore **Mesa Verde National Park** ⑪ before the peak heat of the day. Drive east to 🚩 **Durango** ⑩, a good place to spend the night. The next morning, board the Durango & Silverton Narrow Gauge Railroad, one of the state's must-see attractions. Spend a few hours in **Silverton** ⑧, and return for dinner at one of Durango's world-class restaurants.

If you have 5 days

Begin your trip in **Gunnison** ②, passing Blue Mesa Reservoir on your way to the Black Canyon of the Gunnison National Park. Spend the night in 🚩 **Montrose** ③ or 🚩 **Ridgway** ④ before hooking into the three-day itinerary above. After your return to Durango, drive east via **Pagosa Springs** ⑭ and over Wolf Creek Pass. Depending on where you wish to finish your journey, continue north through **Creede** ⑮ and **Lake City** ⑦ to return to Blue Mesa Reservoir, or continue east to **Del Norte** ⑯ or **Alamosa** ⑰ and into the broad San Luis Valley and **Great Sand Dunes National Monument & Preserve** ⑱ before ending your journey.

If you have 7 days

Start your itinerary in 🚩 **Crested Butte** ①, spending a day hiking amid the wildflowers, fishing in the crystal-clear streams, or just exploring this quaint mountain town. Spend a night there or in nearby 🚩 **Gunnison** ②, and then follow the suggested five-day itinerary above, leaving enough time to visit Yankee Boy Basin, soak in the hot springs of either 🚩 **Ouray** ⑥ or 🚩 **Ridgway** ④, and overnight in either of those towns before driving to **Telluride** ⑤.

Crested Butte is just over the mountain from Aspen, but a short drive in summer turns into a four-hour trek by car in winter, when Kebler Pass (on Route 135) is closed and it is necessary to drive a circuitous route. Both Aspen and Crested Butte are surrounded by designated wilderness areas, which means that few roads pass through this region.

The ski resort, at the base of the lifts a couple of miles uphill from the old town, is properly called Mt. Crested Butte. When people talk about Crested Butte, they might be referring to the old town, the ski resort, or both. You'll have to figure it out from the context. Like Aspen, the town of Crested Butte was once a quaint mining village. The Victorian gingerbread-trim houses remain—albeit painted in whimsical shades of hot pink, magenta, and chartreuse. Unlike Aspen, however, Crested Butte never became chic. A controversial ad campaign for the ski area touted it as "Aspen like it used to be, and Vail like it never was."

Locals are proud and independent, and share a puckish sense of humor seen most clearly when they streak down the mountain nude on the last day of ski season. The authorities periodically try to squelch such merriment, but nobody really pays attention. Like so many other Colorado ski resorts where posh real estate developments have gobbled up ranches and other open areas, Crested Butte has become an escape for the wealthy, losing some of its reputation as a holdout of renegades. The fact remains that no matter what your budget or lifestyle, you'll find Crested Butte is just about the friendliest ski town around.

Crested Butte has always been cutting edge when it comes to embracing new ways to take advantage of the powdery snow. It was an early hotbed of telemark skiing, a graceful, free-heel way of cruising downhill, and was popular with snowboarders back when few people had heard of the sport. But it is as an extreme-skiing mecca that Crested Butte earned its reputation with some of the best skiers in the land. Although many resorts are limiting their "out-of-bounds" terrain owing to increasing insurance costs and lawsuits, Crested Butte has steadily increased its extreme skiing terrain to 550 ungroomed acres. The Extreme Limits and The North Face should only be attempted by advanced or expert skiers, but there are plenty of cruise-worthy trails for skiers of all levels.

Crested Butte is just as popular in the summer. Blanketed with columbine and Indian paintbrush, the landscape is mesmerizing. It has grown into one of the country's major mountain biking centers. Once the snow melts, mountain bikers challenge the hundreds of miles of trails surrounding the town. If you're lucky, you'll visit during one of the annual celebrations, like the popular Wild Mushroom Festival that pops up in August.

There is reliable shuttle-bus service between the town and the resort, which are about 3 mi apart. However, because most lodging is at the resort and the better restaurants and shops (and general atmosphere) are in town, you can expect to make many round-trip journeys. Although a car is unnecessary and even unnerving for those not comfortable with driving on snow and ice, having one makes the going much easier. The town more or less shuts down between mid-April and Memorial Day, and again between October and the start of ski season in mid-December. Businesses may stay shuttered for a month or more.

The **Mountain Bike Hall of Fame & Museum,** housed in a landmark general store on the main drag, has amassed hundreds of items of mountain-bike memorabilia. It's open during the summer, Tuesday to Sunday from noon to 8. Admission is $3. ✉ *331 Elk Ave.* ☎ *970/369–6817* ⊕ *www.mtnbikehalloffame.com.*

Downhill Skiing & Snowboarding

Crested Butte skiing has a split personality, which is plain to see when you check out the skiers who come here year after year. Its more sedate side is the traditional trail network, characterized by long lower-intermediate and intermediate runs. This is the sort of skiing that attracts casual skiers and snowboarders who take to the snow once or twice a winter. There's a wonderful expanse of easy terrain from the Keystone lift—not just a trail network but rolling, tree-dotted meadows with plenty of opportunities to poke around off the beaten track. Families flock to Crested Butte for the excellent slopeside child-care and children's ski school facilities, as well the the resort's laid-back and friendly ambience.

The wilder side of Crested Butte's personality is the Extreme Limits, several hundred acres of steep bowls, gnarly chutes, and tight tree skiing. It's no surprise that Crested Butte has hosted the U.S. Extreme Freeskiing Championship and the U.S. Extreme Borderfest, both nationally televised events full of thrills and spills. That's not to say you have to be a hot shot to enjoy Crested Butte's often steep and challenging terrain. You do, however, need to be able to handle snow that hasn't been groomed.

4

The Anasazi Trail

Steep yourself in the mysterious and compelling legacy of the Anasazi, the popular name given to the Ancestral Puebloan people of the Four Corners area. Orient yourself at the Anasazi Heritage Center in Dolores, which includes some nearby ruins. Then craft an itinerary that includes Mesa Verde National Park and its phenomenal sites and the Canyons of the Ancients National Monument & Preserve. Be sure to visit Hovenweep National Monument and Lowry Pueblo while you are there. Also on the must-see list is Crow Canyon Archeological Center and Chimney Rock Archeological Area.

Four-Wheel-Drive Tours

Southwest Colorado boasts Colorado's greatest concentration of old mining roads, which is good news for four-wheel-drive fans. Whether you commandeer your own 4x4, rent one from the dozens of dealers around the region, or take a trip with a tour company, you will experience an unsurpassed combination of thrilling drives, gorgeous scenery, and history when you travel the state's rugged backcountry roads. Among the highlights are the stretch of the Alpine Loop between Ouray and Lake City, Imogene Pass between Ouray and Telluride, Animas Forks north of Silverton, and Tomboy Road near Telluride. A high-clearance vehicle is almost a necessity if you want to visit Yankee Boy Basin near Ouray or drive over Ophir Pass between Telluride and Silverton. In winter, put away the car keys. Snowmobiles take over some of these routes.

The best skiing on the main trail network is on the front side of the mountain. The Silver Queen high-speed quad shoots you up 2,000 vertical feet in one quick ride. From there, you have a choice of lifts and runs, roughly segmented by degree of challenge, with the steep twisters off to the right, the easier cruisers concentrated on the left, and the gnarly steeps above. The Teocalli lift brings you directly to Crested Butte's half-pipe, and the best intermediate terrain.

The Extreme Limits is backcountry-style skiing and riding that is not for the faint of heart. If you're lucky enough to have good snow, skiing in this steep and rocky region will be the thrilling highlight of your visit. Strong, confident skiers and riders ready to tackle this terrain should sign up for a group tour. ⊠ *17 Emmons Loop, Mt. Crested Butte 81225* ☎ *970/349–2222* 🖷 *970/349–2270* ⊕ *www.skicb.com* ☻ *Open mid-Nov. or mid-Dec.–mid-Apr., daily 9–4.*

FACILITIES   2,775-foot vertical drop; 1,058 skiable acres; 15% beginner, 44% intermediate, 10% advanced, 31% expert; 3 high-speed quad chairs, 3 triple chairs, 3 double chairs, 3 surface lifts, and 2 "moving carpets" (beginners' lifts).

LESSONS & PROGRAMS   The Beginner's Shortcut is a three-hour lesson and lift ticket that costs $80; the 5½-hour lesson and lift ticket costs $95, and practically guarantees you'll be skiing green runs by the end of the day. For kids from 3 through 16, all-day lessons are $92 and half-day lessons are $83. For more information, contact the **Crested Butte Ski & Snowboard School** (⊠ Gothic Bldg. ☎ 970/349–2252 or 800/444–9236 ⊕ www.skicb.com). One program of note is Kim Reichhelm's **Women's Ski Adventures** (⊠ 2335 Honolulu Ave., Montrose 91020 ☎ 888/444–8151 ⊕ www.skiwithkim.

com). Reichhelm, a former member of the U.S. Olympic Ski Team and a one-time extreme-skiing champion, leads four-day workshops aimed at "breakthrough" experiences for women of all skill levels.

LIFT TICKETS The walk-up rates for lift tickets range from $63 for one day to $378 for a week; prices are less early and late in the season. Children under four ski free, and those ages 5 through 16 "pay their age." This means that a 7-year-old pays $7 a day and a 14-year-old skis or rides for just $14, considerably less than the adult ticket rate imposed on youngsters at many other resorts.

RENTALS Full-rental packages (including skis, boots, and poles), as well as touring and telemark equipment, are available through **Crested Butte Ski & Snowboard Rental** (⊠ 17 Emmons Loop Rd. ☎ 970/349–2241). Rates start at $14 per day. Substantial discounts are available for multiday rentals.

Nordic Skiing

BACKCOUNTRY SKIING Crested Butte abounds with backcountry possibilities. Skiing or snowshoeing on the old mining roads that radiate from town are a few of the most popular pastimes. Washington Gulch, Slate River Gulch, and Gothic Road are among the most accessible routes. Dogs are permitted, and you'll have to contend with snowmobiles on some trails. Hardy locals hike up the slopes for above-tree-line telemarking, but this requires strong legs, strong lungs, and real avalanche awareness. You'll need the right equipment, including a functioning beacon and a shovel. Make sure you ski with a group—this is territory where going it alone is asking for trouble. Keep in mind that this is the high country (the town itself is around 9,000 feet, and things go up from there). Weather conditions can change with little or no warning.

To play it safe, confine your backcountry experiences to the lift-served terrain or arrange a guided tour with the **Crested Butte Nordic Center** (✉ 602 2nd St. ☎ 970/349–1707 ⊕ www.cbnordic.org). The center has details about the annual Alley Loop Marathon, held in early February. During this cross-country race through the town's snow-covered streets and alleys, spectators line the route as participants race past homes and restaurants, cross pedestrian bridges, and cruise down the scenic trails along the edge of town. The **Alpineer** (✉ 419 6th St. ☎ 970/349–5210) rents top-notch backcountry equipment and provides information on routes and snow conditions.

TRACK SKIING Three loops of classic cross-country tracks and skate–skiing lanes totaling approximately 31 mi are maintained by the **Crested Butte Nordic Center** (✉ 602 2nd St. ☎ 970/349–1707 ⊕ www.cbnordic.org). The largest of the three, Red Lady Loop, covers mostly flat and moderately rolling terrain across meadows and through aspen groves near the valley floor. The views of some of the distant peaks are stunning. The Bench trail network includes a steep loop through the trees of Gibson Ridge— close to town but seemingly far away in the woods. A groomed trail measuring 2½ mi links Crested Butte and Mt. Crested Butte. Town Ranch Loop on the valley floor is flat, friendly, and free—and there's no problem if you want to bring your dog. The center allows snowshoers, but not on all tracks.

SNOWSHOEING A great way to experience the side of Crested Butte that fast-moving skiers and snowboarders speed past is via a guided snowshoe tour. Tours depart daily at 9:45 AM and 1:15 PM from **Crested Butte Ski & Snowboard Rental** (✉ 602 2nd St. ☎ 970/349–2241 or 888/280–5728). Groups ride up the Keystone lift and make an easy loop with spectacular views of the Elk Mountain Range. On moonlight tours, groups ascend in a heated snow cat to the Twister Warming House for hot cocoa and cold ice cream before trudging back down to the base.

Other Sports & the Outdoors

Alpine Outside (✉ 315 6th St. ☎ 970/349–5011 or 888/761–3474) can arrange myriad outdoor activities, including scenic river floats, white-water rafting, fly fishing, kayak lessons, horseback riding, and pack trips. The company offers four-wheel-drive tours in summer and snowmobile rides, sleigh rides, ice fishing, and balloon rides in the winter.

Three Rivers Resort & Outfitting (✉ 130 Country Rd. 742, Almont ☎ 970/641–1303 or 888/761–3474 ⊕ www.3riversresort.com) offers guided fly-fishing excursions, kayaking lessons, and white-water-rafting trips.

FISHING At Almont, south of Crested Butte, the East and Taylor rivers join to form the Gunnison River, making this tiny angler-oriented hamlet one of Colorado's top fly-fishing centers. Local fishing outfitters rent equipment, teach fly fishing, and lead guided wading or float trips both to public and private waters.

Almont Anglers (✉ 10209 Hwy. 135, Almont ☎ 970/641–7404 ⊕ www.almontanglers.com) offers guided wading and float-fishing trips on the East, Taylor, and Gunnison rivers.

Dragonfly Anglers (✉ 307 Elk Ave. ☎ 970/349–1228 or 800/491–3079 ⊕ www.dragonflyanglers.com) is Crested Butte's oldest year-round guide service and fly fishing outfitter.

At Three Rivers Resort & Outfitting, **Willowfly Anglers** (✉ 130 County Rd. 742, Almont ☎ 970/641–1303 or 888/761–3474 ⊕ www.3riversresort.com) provides the gear for anglers of all skill levels.

GOLF **The Club at Crested Butte** (✉ 385 Country Club Dr. ☎ 970/349–6127) is known for its ravishing 18-hole course designed by golf legend Robert Trent Jones Jr. The course belongs to the country club, but it is open to the public.

HIKING Near three designated wilderness areas (Maroon Bells–Snowmass to the north, Raggeds to the west, and Collegiate Peaks to the east), as well as other areas with equally stunning scenery, Crested Butte offers an extensive system of trails. In wilderness areas, you'll find splendid trails far off the beaten path. Outside of these protected areas, you may have to share routes with mountain bikers and even four-wheel-drive vehicles. One of the easiest trails is a 2-mi round-trip from the Gothic Campground north of Crested Butte to **Judd Falls**. Another easy trail is a 5-mi round-trip from the Lost Lake Slough Campground, off the Kebler Pass Road about 19 mi from town, to **Beckwith Pass**. For an even easier route, hop onto the Silver Queen chairlift and explore the hiking trails on **Mt. Crested Butte**.

The surrounding mountains are carpeted with such abundant growth that Crested Butte has been nicknamed "The Wildflower Capital of Colorado." For one glorious week in mid-July, the town celebrates this beautiful bounty with the **Crested Butte Wildflower Festival** (☎ 970/349–2571). There are guided wildflower walks, wildflower identification workshops, wildflower cooking classes, and wildflower art exhibits.

HORSEBACK One of the best ways to see Crested Butte is from atop a horse. **Fantasy**
RIDING **Ranch** (✉ Gothic Rd. ☎ 970/349–5425) rents horses for tours of the surrounding mountains.

HOT-AIR The conditions must be just right, but on a clear, windless morning, this
BALLOONING wide-open basin, surrounded by mountain ranges, must surely be one of the country's best places to be aloft in a balloon. For information on these flights of fancy, contact **Big Horn Balloon Company** (☎ 970/240–4530 ⊕ www.balloon-adventures.com). Trips are $170 for adults and $110 for children, and group discounts are available.

ICE SKATING If you're eager to practice a figure eight, the **Crested Butte Nordic Center** (✉ 602 2nd St. ☎ 970/349–1707 ⊕ www.cbnordic.org.) operates the adjacent skating rink. The lodge rents skates for $8 for adults, $6 for children.

MOUNTAIN Crested Butte is probably the mountain-biking center of Colorado. This
BIKING is a place where there are more bikes than cars, and probably more bikes
★ than residents. Many people own two mountain bikes: a town bike for hacking around and a performance bike for *serious* hacking around. Mountain-bike chroniclers say that **Pearl Pass** is the route that got the mountain-biking craze started in the mid-1970s. After a group of Aspen motorcylists rode the rough old road over Pearl Pass to Crested Butte, that town's mountain bikers decided to retaliate and ride to Aspen. They hopped on board their clunky two-wheelers—a far cry from the sophisticated machinery of today—and with that, a sport was born. The 40-mi trip over Pearl Pass can be done in a day, but you must be in excellent condition and acclimatized to the elevation to have a chance of finishing. Altitude is your main foe; the pass crests at 12,700 feet. The trip is daunting and not to be undertaken lightly. One option for your return journey to Crested Butte is a scenic two-day ride along the road—better than retracing your route over the pass. Otherwise you'll need to make arrangements to travel by car or even by plane.

Stocking all the gear you'll need, the **Alpineer** (✉ 419 6th St. ☎ 970/349–5210 ⊕ www.alpineer.com) is a good place to rent mountain bikes.

Guided tours of nearby trails are available through **Crested Butte Mountain Guides** (✉ Box 1061 ☎ 970/349–5430 ⊕ www.crestedbutteguides. com).

Each summer, mountain biking enthusiasts roll in for the **Fat Tire Bike Week** (✍ Crested Butte Chamber of Commerce, Box 1288, 81224 ☎ 800/545–4505 or 970/349–6438 ⊕ www.cbchamber.com), the country's longest-running mountain-bike festival. The event is a solid week of racing, touring, silly competitions, and mountain-biker bonding.

TENNIS   Golfers find that their balls fly farther because of the lofty elevation and thin air, and so do tennis players. The **Crested Butte Town Courts** (✉ 6th St. and Elk Ave. ☎ 970/349–5338) are free.

WATER SPORTS   The rivers around Crested Butte are at their best from May through September. **Three Rivers Resort & Outfitting** (✉ 130 Country Rd. 742, Almont ☎ 970/641–1303 or 888/761–3474 ⊕ www.3riversresort.com) takes you on rafting trips and gives kayaking lessons on the Gunnison River.

Where to Stay & Eat

★ $$$–$$$$ ✗ **Soupçon.** Soupçon ("soup's on," get it?) occupies two intimate rooms in a delightful log cabin—and a cozier place doesn't exist in this town. Chef Scott Greene serves American dishes with a strong French accent. His menu, which changes nightly, includes innovative takes on classic bistro fare. Roast duckling topped with an impeccable hoisin glaze, succulent grilled elk tenderloin, tandoori-style rack of lamb, and the fresh fish dishes are sublime. Desserts really shine; order the homemade ice cream or crème brûlée. ✉ 2nd St. behind Kochevar's ☎ 970/349–5448 ⚲ Reservations essential ▭ AE, MC, V ☉ No lunch. Closed early Oct.–early Dec. and Apr.–early June.

$$–$$$$ ✗ **Timberline.** This elegant dining room serves a more than respectable fettuccine Alfredo and a tasty sesame ahi tuna. Don't pass up the salmon with chanterelle-mushroom sauce or the veal chop accompanied by risotto with local wild mushrooms. Smoked trout with local tomatoes is a signature dish. The handsome bar is a great place to discuss your triumphs on the slopes. ✉ 21 Elk Ave. ☎ 970/349–9831 ⚲ Reservations essential ▭ AE, MC, V ☉ No lunch Sat. Closed Sun. Closed Labor Day–mid-Dec. and Apr.–June.

★ $$–$$$ ✗ **Slogar.** Set in a lovingly renovated Victorian tavern awash in handmade lace and stained glass, this restaurant is just plain cozy. Slogar's turns out some of the plumpest, juiciest fried chicken west of the Mississippi. The fixings are sensational: flaky biscuits fresh from the oven, creamy mashed potatoes swimming in hearty chicken gravy, and unique sweet-and-sour coleslaw from a Pennsylvania Dutch recipe that dates back nearly two centuries. Served family-style, you get all that and more, including ice cream, for just $13.45 (if you'd prefer a steak, it's $22.95). For down-home cooking and a friendly atmosphere, Slogar's is hard to beat. ✉ 2nd and Whiterock Sts. ☎ 970/349–5765 ▭ MC, V ☉ No lunch. Closed late Sept.–mid-Dec. and mid-Apr.–mid-June.

$$–$$$ ✗ **Swiss Chalet.** If you're in search of an authentic alpine experience, this place is perfect, right down to the Bierstube (pub) where you can order a Paulaner on tap. The kalbsgeschnetzeltes (minced veal loin sautéed with mushrooms and shallots in white-wine cream sauce), raclette, and fondue are luscious, as are such hard-to-find specialties as Bündnerfleisch (savory air-dried beef). ✉ 621 Gothic Rd., Mt. Crested Butte ☎ 970/ 349–5917 ▭ AE, MC, V ☉ No lunch. Closed Apr. 15–June 15 and Sept. 15–mid-Nov. or mid-Dec.

★ $–$$$ ✗ **Powerhouse.** Housed in Crested Butte's original electricity-generating plant, the Powerhouse is popular because of its "haute Mexican" cuisine. In addition to such classics as grilled steaks, chicken, and pork tenderloin, the restaurant scores with seafood specials inspired by dishes from the Yucatán and the Caribbean. A knockout list of more than 100 tequilas means there's an enormous variety of margaritas. ✉ *130 Elk Ave.* ☎ *970/349–5494* ✍ *Reservations not accepted* 💳 *AE, D, DC, MC, V* ⏲ *No lunch.*

$–$$ ✕ **Donita's Cantina.** This down-home Mexican restaurant is hard to miss; it's in a building painted shocking pink. The food isn't nearly as showy—it's simply good, solid standards such as fajitas and enchiladas served with tangy salsa. Between the bargain prices and the killer margaritas the crowds here are always jovial. ✉ *330 Elk Ave.* ☎ *970/349–6674* ✍ *Reservations not accepted* 💳 *AE, D, MC, V* ⏲ *No lunch.*

$$$$ **Club Med Crested Butte.** This sprawling complex is nestled at the base of Crested Butte's ski lifts, a hard-to-beat location. The only Club Med in North America, it has all-inclusive rates that include lodging, three meals a day, lift tickets, ski instruction, entertainment, and such on-site amenities as an exercise room, indoor pool, hot tub, and sauna. Because it's a "family club," there's a children's program to give parents time to themselves. ✉ *Mt. Crested Butte 81224* ☎ *970/349–8700 or 800/258–2633* 🌐 *www.clubmed.com* ♨ *Dining room, indoor pool, hot tub, sauna, gym, ski shop, bar, lounge.*

$$$–$$$$ **Crested Butte Club.** This quaint, stylish inn is a Victorian dream: each sumptuous, individually furnished room contains a gas fireplace, brass or mahogany bed, and cherry-wood antiques or good-quality reproductions. All have spacious modern baths with such little extras as footed copper and brass tubs. The downstairs bar is similarly delightful, but best of all is the full-service health club. The complimentary Continental breakfast always includes a few extras. ✉ *512 2nd St., 81224* ☎ *970/349–6655 or 800/815–2582* 📠 *970/349–7580* 🌐 *www.crestedbutteclub.com* ⇨ *8 rooms* ♨ *Indoor pool, health club, bar* 💳 *D, MC, V* 🍽 *CP.*

$$–$$$ **Nordic Inn.** This slope-side inn with alpine-style trim is one of the last old-style ski lodges in a sea of cookie-cutter condominiums. Spacious but simply decorated rooms, a cozy lobby perfect for lounging, and an inviting breakfast room are reminders of the way mountain vacations used to be. An outdoor hot tub on a modest deck is about all there is in the way of amenities. ✉ *14 Treasury Rd., Mt. Crested Butte 81224* ☎ *800/542–7669* 🌐 *www.nordicinncb.com* ♨ *Breakfast room, in-room data ports, some kitchenettes, hot tub* 💳 *AE, MC, V* 🍽 *CP.*

$–$$$ **Sheraton Crested Butte Resort.** This ski-in/ski-out property, only 200 yards from the lift, offers all the amenities and facilities of Crested Butte's other luxury hotels. The difference is down-to-earth prices. A warm, stone-log lobby welcomes you when you check in. Huge rooms are decorated in muted earth and pastel tones with copper accents. ✉ *6 Emmons Loop, Mt. Crested Butte 81225* ☎ *970/349–7561 or 800/544–8448* 📠 *970/349–2270* 🌐 *www.skicb.com* ⇨ *248 rooms, 106 suites* ♨ *Restaurant, in-room data ports, indoor-outdoor pool, gym, outdoor hot tub, bar, recreation room, laundry service, meeting room* 💳 *AE, D, DC, MC, V* ⏲ *Closed mid-Apr.–mid-June and mid-Aug.–mid-Dec.*

$ **Cristiana Guesthouse.** This alpine-style ski lodge with a sun deck and a huge stone fireplace in the beamed lobby provides a cozy, unpretentious haven for those who love mountain sports. Wood-paneled rooms are decorated in soothing neutrals with traditional country pine furnishings. The lodge is within walking distance of the historic downtown, and is close to hiking and Nordic-ski trails. ✉ *621 Maroon Ave., 81224* ☎ *970/349–5326 or 800/824–7899* 📠 *970/349–1962* 🌐 *www.cristianaguesthouse.com* ⇨ *21 rooms* ♨ *In-room data ports, hot tub,* *sauna* ▤ *AE, D, MC, V* ⊘ *Closed early Nov. and mid-Apr.–mid-May* ⦿ *CP.*

$ ▣ **Pioneer Guest Cabins.** Surrounded by the Gunnison National Forest, this dream getaway is about 10 mi from town. Rustic log cabins from the 1930s have been appointed with everything from down comforters to antique furnishings. You can hear the stream that runs through the property coming from every cabin. Each cabin has its own personality and comes with a fully equipped kitchen, as well as a fireplace or wood-burning stove. East River, 2 mi away, is a world-class fishing stream. A resident guide conducts mountain bike tours in summer and snow-shoeing and Nordic-ski tours in winter. ⊠ *Cement Creek Rd., 81224* ☎ *970/349–5517* ⊕ *www.thepioneer.net* ⇄ *8 cabins* ⚬ *Kitchenettes, hiking, cross-country skiing, snowshoeing, ski shop* ▤ *MC, V.*

CONDOMINIUMS **Crested Butte Vacations** (⬚ Box 5700, Mt. Crested Butte 81225 ☎ 800/544–8448 ☎ 970/349–2270) can make arrangements for all condominiums on the mountain.

Nightlife & the Arts

THE ARTS The **Crested Butte Center for the Arts** (⊠ 606 6th St. ☎ 970/349–7487 ⊕ www.visitcrestedbutte.com/cftarts) is a 215-seat theater that hosts local and touring concerts, theater, dance, movies and more. Upstairs, the Piper Gallery is a multimedia art space where local artists display their work.

NIGHTLIFE **Kochevar's** (⊠ 127 Elk Ave. ☎ 970/349–6745), a hand-hewn 1896 log cabin, is a classic saloon. Locals stop by to play pool. The popular **Wooden Nickel** (⊠ 222 Elk Ave. ☎ 970/349–6350) is packed for happy hour each day from 4 to 6.

Shopping

Cookworks (⊠ 321 Elk Ave. ☎ 970/349–7398 or 800/765–9511 ⊕ www.cookworks.com) is a delightful cookware and tableware shop housed in a quaint Victorian home. **Creekside Pottery** (⊠ 126 Elk Ave. ☎ 970/349–6459) showcases local artist Mary Jursinovic's imaginative pottery and lamps.

en route Scenic Route 135 runs northwest from Crested Butte over Kebler Pass to Paonia, and south to Gunnison through the banks of cottonwoods that line the Gunnison River. The Crested Butte–Paonia section of the road is unpaved and closed to motor vehicles in winter; the Crested Butte–Gunnison section is a paved road open year-round.

Gunnison

❷ *28 mi from Crested Butte via Rte. 135 south.*

At the confluence of the Gunnison River and Tomichi Creek, Gunnison is a traditional ranching community that has been adopted by nature lovers because of the excellent fishing and hunting nearby. In fact, long before these types arrived, the Utes used the area as summer hunting grounds. Gunnison provides economical lodging and easy access to Crested Butte and Blue Mesa Reservoir. Gunnison's other claim to fame is that it has recorded some of the coldest temperatures ever reported in the continental United States.

Western State College announces its presence with a 320-by-420-foot white-washed rock that's shaped like a W on Tenderfoot Mountain, just to the north of the campus.

Those interested in the region's history can stop by the **Pioneer Museum.** The complex includes several buildings dating from the late 19th century. ⊠ *U.S. 50 and S. Adams St.* ☎ *970/641–4530* ⊡ *$3* ⊙ *Memorial Day–Labor Day, Mon.–Sat. 9–5, Sun. noon–5.*

The **Gunnison County Chamber of Commerce** (⊠500 E. Tomichi Ave. ☎970/641–1501 ⊕ www.gunnisonchamber.com) prints a visitors' guide to Gunnison County and provides information about the entire county.

Nine miles west of Gunnison is the **Curecanti National Recreation Area,** set amid a striking eroded volcanic landscape and stretching for more than 60 mi. Dams built along the Gunnison River during the 1960s created three reservoirs, including **Blue Mesa Reservoir,** the state's largest body of water. Here you can fish, swim, or even windsurf. The reservoirs provide a wealth of recreational opportunities, including fine camping and hiking. Rangers lead education programs, including twice-daily boat tours of the Upper Black Canyon of the Gunnison River. At the western entrance to the Curecanti National Recreation Area, the **Cimarron Visitor Center** (⊠U.S. Hwy. 50 ☎970/249–4074 ⊙ June–Sept., daily 8–4:30) displays vintage locomotives, a reconstructed stockyard, and an 1882 trestle that's listed on the National Register of Historic Places. ⊠ *102 Elk Creek* ☎ *970/641–2337* ⊕ *www.nps.gov/cure.*

Sports & the Outdoors

GOLF Water hazards make for challenging play on 17 of the 18 holes at **Dos Rios Golf Club** (⊠ 501 Camino del Rio, 2 mi west of Gunnison ☎ 970/641–1482).

HORSEBACK **Lazy F Bar Outfitters** (⊠2991 County Rd. 738 ☎970/641–0193 ⊕ www.
RIDING lazybarfranch.com) rents horses for rides in the high country from June to early September and sleigh rides in the valleys from December to early April.

WATER SPORTS At 26 mi long, Blue Mesa Reservoir ranks as Colorado's largest body of water. Created in the mid-1960s when the state dammed the Gunnison River in three places, the lake is some 7,500 feet above sea level. It has become a mecca for water-sports enthusiasts, including boaters, kayakers, waterskiers, windsurfers, anglers, and occasionally even scuba divers. (Jet Skis and other personal watercraft are prohibited on the reservoir.) In addition to the Cimarron Visitor Center at Curecanti National Recreation Area, there are smaller seasonal ranger stations at Lake Fork, Cimarron, and East Portal.

Elk Creek Marina (⊠east side of the lake ☎ 970/641–0707 or 970/641–5387 ⊕ www.whresorts.com), about 15 mi from Gunnison, rents pontoon boats, rowboats, and aluminum fishing boats from May 1st to October 1st. The marina also runs guided fishing trips to Blue Mesa, Morrow Point, and Crystal reservoirs.

If you have your own boat, you can use the ramps at Ponderosa (northern end at Soap Creek Arm), Stevens Creek (eastern end of the north shore), and Lola (eastern end on the south shore). A two-day boat permit is $4, and a two-week permit is $10.

Where to Stay & Eat

$$ ✕ **Garlic Mike's.** For upscale Italian, give this cheerful spot a try. Don't miss the homemade ravioli, pizza, and eggplant Parmesan. The marinated sirloin steak carbonara wins hands-down as the house favorite. The menu is a welcome change of pace from those at the burger and fast-food joints that abound in the area. ⊠ *2674 Hwy. 135* ☎ *970/641–2493* ▭ *AE, D, MC, V* ⊙ *No lunch.*

$–$$ ▣ **Mary Lawrence Inn.** This restored Victorian is an unexpected delight. Large rooms are furnished with tasteful antiques and thoughtful touches such as lace curtains, stenciled walls, handmade quilts, and bowls of pot-pourri. A complimentary breakfast is offered each morning, along with a smile and advice for the day's adventures from helpful innkeeper Janette McKinny. ⊠ *601 N. Taylor St., 81230* ☎ *970/641-3343 or 888/ 331-6863* 🖷 *970/641-6719* ⊕ *www.commerceteam.com/mary.html* ↪ *7 rooms* ⚬ *Breakfast room, hot tub* ▤ *AE, D, DC, MC, V* ⏅ *BP.*

Shopping

Save time to browse the 2,000 square feet of seasonal decorations, linens, floral arrangements, pottery, handmade lace, and candles at **Let's Go Country** (⊠ 234 N. Main St. ☎ 970/641-1638). **The Corner Cupboard** (⊠ 101 N. Main St. ☎ 970/641-0313) has a nifty selection of specialty food items, kitchen aids, and gift items. On the northwest corner of the intersection of U.S. 50 and Highway 135, it occupies the most promi-nent location in town.

Montrose

❸ *65 mi west of Gunnison via U.S. 50.*

The self-described "Home of the Black Canyon" sits amid glorious sur-roundings, but it's an otherwise nondescript town with little more than a collection of truck stops, trailer parks, strip malls, and big-box stores frequented by area residents. Montrose also has a small airport that is a good gateway for skiers heading to Telluride, whose airport is often closed due to weather. Montrose is perfectly placed for exploring the Black Canyon of the Gunnison and Curecanti National Recreation Area to the east; the San Juan Mountains to the south; the world's largest flattop mountain, Grand Mesa, to the north; and the fertile Uncompahgre Plateau to the west.

If you're interested in the lives of the region's original residents, stop by the excellent **Ute Indian Museum**, 3 mi south of town on U.S. 550. The museum contains several dioramas and the most comprehensive collection of Ute materials and artifacts in Colorado. ⊠ *17253 Chipeta Rd.* ☎ *970/249-3098* 🎫 *$3* ⏱ *Mon.–Sat. 9–4:30, Sun. 11–4:30.*

FodorsChoice ★

The Gunnison River slices through one of the state's most awe-inspir-ing attractions, the **Black Canyon of the Gunnison National Park.** This 2,000-foot-deep gash in the earth's crust is 1,000 feet wide at its rim and only 40 feet wide at the bottom. The canyon's name comes from the fact that so little sunlight penetrates its depths, and the eternal shadows permit scant plant growth on its steep walls. This spectacular sight was elevated from national monument to national park status in 2000. To reach the south rim of this forbidding chasm, take U.S. 50 east from Montrose (or west from Gunnison) and head north on Route 347. Most visitors drive along the 7-mi paved road on the southern rim and stare down into the canyon from the 10 scenic overlooks. One mile from the park entrance is a fine visitor center with exhibits on the region's geology, history, and flora and fauna. The south rim road is not plowed past the visitor center but is used by cross-country skiers and snowshoers. ⊠ *Hwy. 347* ☎ *970/641-2337* ⊕ *www.nps.gov/blca* 🎫 *$7 per vehi-cle* ⏱ *Park daily 8–5; visitor center June–Sept., daily 8–6, Oct.–May, daily 8:30–4.*

Sports & the Outdoors

BOATING The **Lake Fork Marina** (⊠ west side of the lake ☎ 970/641-0707 or 970/ 641-5387 ⊕ www.whresorts.com) rents all types of boats. If you have your own boat, there is a ramp at the marina. A two-day boat permit is $4, whereas a two-week permit is $10.

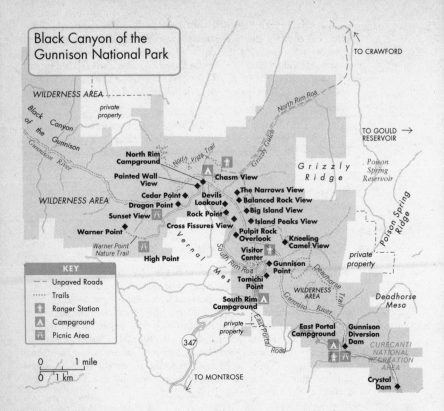

Black Canyon of the
Gunnison National Park

TO CRAWFORD

WILDERNESS AREA

private property

Black Canyon of the Gunnison River

WILDERNESS AREA

TO GOULD RESERVOIR →

Poison Spring Reservoir

Grizzly Ridge

North Rim Road

Grizzly Gulch

North Vista Trail

North Rim Campground

Painted Wall View

Chasm View

Cedar Point
Dragon Point
Sunset View

Devils Lookout
Rock Point
Cross Fissures View

The Narrows View
Balanced Rock View
Big Island View
Island Peaks View

Pulpit Rock Overlook

Kneeling Camel View

Warner Point

Warner Point Nature Trail

High Point

Visitor Center

Gunnison Point

Tomichi Point

South Rim Road

Vernal Mesa

Poison Spring Ridge

private property

Deadhorse Trail

Deadhorse Mesa

WILDERNESS AREA

Gunnison River

South Rim Campground

private property

347

East Portal Road

East Portal Campground

Gunnison Diversion Dam

CURECANTI NATIONAL RECREATION AREA

TO MONTROSE →

Crystal Dam

KEY
- - Unpaved Roads
..... Trails
Ranger Station
Campground
Picnic Area

0   1 mile
0   1 km

CANOEING & KAYAKING

★

The spectacular 12-mi stretch of the Gunnison River that passes through the Black Canyon is so narrow in some sections that the rim seems to be closing up above your head. In fact, the Black Canyon earned its name because in many places very little sunlight reaches the bottom. The Gunnison River is one of the premier kayak challenges in North America, with plenty of Class IV and Class V rapids. Early visitors to the canyon declared this section unnavigable, and for all practical purposes, they were right. No commercial trips run through this section. Once you are downstream from the rapids, the canyon opens up into what is called the Gunnison Gorge. The rapids ease considerably, and the trip becomes more of a quiet float on Class I to Class III water. The Gunnison Gorge National Conservation Area is under the jurisdiction of the **Bureau of Land Management** (⊠ 2465 S. Townsend St., Montrose 81401 ☎ 970/240–5300 ⊕ www.blm.gov/ggnca).

Gunnison River Expeditions (⌂ 317 E. Main St., Box 315, Montrose 81402 ☎ 970/249–4441 ⊕ www.gunnisonriverexpeditions.com) specializes in white-water-rafting trips. The company also offers float trips on the river's quieter sections.

FISHING

Only 168 mi of Colorado's nearly 9,000 mi of streams and rivers have been designated as "gold medal" waters by the Colorado Wildlife Commission. The second-longest stretch is the 126 mi beginning with the upper section of the Black Canyon of the Gunnison. Kokanee salmon and rainbow, brown, and lake trout are plentiful in the area. Many local companies, including **Gunnison River Expeditions** (⌂ 317 E. Main St., Box 315, Montrose 81402 ☎ 970/249–4441 ⊕ www.gunnisonriverexpeditions. com), offer guided fishing expeditions.

BLACK CANYON WILDLIFE

SPRING AND EARLY SUMMER are the best times for birdwatching: you may spot peregrine falcons nesting in May and June, especially in the vicinity of Painted Wall, or other birds of prey such as red-tailed hawks, Cooper's hawks, and golden eagles circling overhead at any time of year. In summer, turkey vultures join the flying corps, and in winter, bald eagles. Also keep an eye out for blue grouse, which frequent the trails and roadsides.

Mule deer, elk (most commonly seen in winter), and bobcat (occasionally glimpsed in fall, winter, and spring) also call the park home. In spring and fall, you may see a porcupine among pinyon trees on the rims. Listen for the distinctive, high-pitched chirp of the yellow-bellied marmot, which hangs out on sunny, rocky outcrops near South Rim visitor center, Oak Flat Trail, and Chasm View lookout. From the campgrounds at night, you're likely to hear the spine-tingling yips of coyotes, as they gather on the rim. Mountain lions also live in the park (though they're rarely seen), as do black bears, which are sometimes spotted in dry years, when they have to forage more widely for food.

To learn the rules and regulations regarding a fishing license, contact the **Colorado Division of Wildlife** (✉ 2300 S. Townsend Ave., Montrose 81401 ☎ 970/249–3431).

HIKING For information on backcountry hiking in the Uncompaghre Plateau and other nearby wilderness areas, contact the district office of the **Grand Mesa, Uncompahre, and Gunnison National Forests** (✉ 2250 U.S. 50, Delta 81416 ☎ 970/641–6660 ⊕ www.fs.fed.us/r2/gmug).

Where to Stay & Eat

$ ✗ **Sally's Café.** Friendly waitresses serve huge portions of gravy-laden food at Sally's Café. The menu has it all, from patty melts, chicken-fried steak, and grilled peanut butter and jelly sandwiches to Duncan Hines cakes and big cups of piping hot coffee (no espresso here). The down-home decor reflects Sally's quirky sense of humor, so it's no surprise to see a reindeer made out of an old clock hanging on the wall during the Christmas season. And those decorative dishes are from Sally's own collection ("I like my dishes," she says with typical understatement). ✉ 715 S. Townsend Ave. ☎ 970/249–6096 ⊟ No credit cards ☉ Closed Wed. and Thurs.

¢–$ ✗ **Fiesta Guadalajara.** Hefty portions of authentic Mexican fare like quesadillas, tostadas, and enchiladas are the draw at this local favorite. Take our advice and opt for the shrimp fajitas. The festive atmosphere will make you think you've been transported south of the border. ✉ 147 S. Main St. ☎ 970/249–2460 ⊟ AE, MC, V.

$$ ▥ **Best Western Red Arrow Motor Inn.** This low-key establishment is one of the nicest lodgings in the area, mainly because of the large, prettily appointed rooms filled with handsome mahogany furnishings. The full baths include soothing whirlpool tubs. ✉ 1702 E. Main St., 81401 ☎ 970/

249–9641 or 800/468–9323 ⊜ 970/249–8380 ⊕ *www.bestwestern. com* ↩ *60 rooms* ♨ *Gym, hot tub, laundry service, meeting room* ⊟ *AE, D, DC, MC, V.*

¢ ⊡ **Colorado Inn.** This friendly place offers pleasant, good-size rooms with such amenities as a pool and a hot tub. What sets the Colorado Inn apart from its competitors is that is has considerably lower rates. Another draw is the free Continental breakfast. ⊠ *1417 E. Main St., 81401* ☎ *970/ 249–4507* ↩ *71 rooms* ♨ *Restaurant, pool, hot tub, sauna, bar, laundry facilities* ⊟ *AE, D, DC, MC, V* ⍟ *CP.*

The Arts

The **Montrose Pavilion** (⊠ 1800 Pavilion Dr., Montrose ☎ 970/249–7015) is a 602-seat auditorium where well-known musicians, comedians, dance companies, and regional orchestras often perform.

Shopping

Got a sweet tooth? The **Russell Stover Factory Outlet** (⊠ 2200 Stover ☎ 970/249–5372 ☉ Daily 9–6) sells fresh chocolates made in the factory across the street. The store is easy to find—it's south of downtown off U.S. 550.

SAN JUAN MOUNTAINS

Ridgway

❹ *26 mi south of Montrose via U.S. 550.*

The 19th-century railroad town of Ridgway has been the setting for some classic Westerns, including *True Grit* and *How the West Was Won.* Though you'd never know it from the rustic town center, the area is also home to many swank ranches, including one belonging to fashion designer Ralph Lauren.

The **Ridgway Railroad Museum** (⊠ Box 588, Ridgway 81432 ⊕ www. ridgwayrailroadmuseum.org ☒ Free) celebrates the town's importance during the heyday of the railroad. The first exhibits were rolling stock, including a wooden boxcar built for the filming of *Butch Cassidy and the Sundance Kid.*

Sports & the Outdoors

GOLF **Fairway Pines Golf Club** (⊠ 117 Ponderosa Dr., Ridgway ☎ 800/443–7760 or 970/626–5584) is an 18-hole golf course and driving range open from April to October. Greens fees are $54 to $64, depending on the season. Cart rental is $15.

WATER SPORTS At the **Ridgway State Park & Recreation Area** (⊠ 2855 U.S. 550, Ridgway 81423 ☎ 970/626–5822 ⊕ www.parks.state.co.us), 12 mi north of Ridgway, the reservoir is stocked with plenty of rainbow trout, as well as the larger and tougher German brown. Anglers also pull up kokanee, yellow perch, and the occasional large-mouth bass. The park also has hiking trails and areas reserved for camping.

Ridgway Marina (⊠ U.S. 550 ☎ 970/626–5094 or 970/626–5538 ⊕ www.ridgwaymarina.com) rents fishing boats, pontoon boats, kayaks, and small sailboats.

Where to Stay & Eat

$–$$ ✕ **True Grit.** Scenes from *True Grit* were filmed here, and the local hangout is a shrine to the film and its star, John Wayne. This neighborhood pub serves standard fare—burgers, nachos, and delicious chicken fried steak. ⊠ *123 N. Lena Ave.* ☎ *970/626–5739* ⊟ *D, MC, V.*

ADVENTURES IN SAVINGS

The canyons of the Colorado National
Monument are spectacular all year round.
Drive through stunning scenery or explore miles
of hiking trails at your leisure. For value-priced
accomodations and special package rates,
go to www.visitgrandjunction.com

GRAND JUNCTION
Colorado's Wine Country

800.962.2547
www.visitgrandjunction.com

Find America *with a Compass*

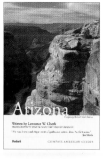

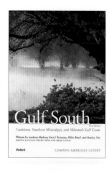

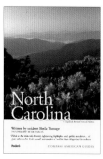

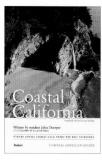

Written by local authors and illustrated throughout
with spectacular color images, Compass American
Guides reveal the character and culture of more than
40 of America's most fascinating destinations. Perfect
for residents who want to explore their own backyards
and for visitors who want an insider's perspective
on the history, heritage, and all there is to see and do.

Fodor's COMPASS AMERICAN GUIDES

At bookstores everywhere.

★ **$$** ⬚ **Chipeta Sun Lodge & Spa.** Owners Jack and Patsy Young recently purchased the most acclaimed lodging in Ridgway. The dramatic Southwestern-style adobe's rooms have rough-hewn log beds, hand-painted Mexican tiles, and stunning views from the decks. The inn is a stone's throw from the year-round outdoor activities in this stretch of the San Juan Mountains. When you're finished hiking or biking, return to the spa for a little pampering. The hearty complimentary breakfast is served in a sunny solarium. ⊠ *304 S. Lena St., 81432* ☎ *970/626–3737 or 800/633–5868* 🖷 *970/626–3715* ⊕ *www.chipeta.com* 🛏 *23 rooms* ⚲ *Hot tubs, spa* ▭ *MC, V* ⧂ *BP.*

Shopping

Unicas Southwest (⊠ 109 N. Lena St. ☎ 970/626–5723 ⊕ www.uincas. com) sells colorful clothing, folk art, and handicrafts from around the world, with an emphasis on the Southwest.

en route U.S. 550 and Route 62 fan out from Ridgway to form one of the country's most stupendously scenic drives, the **San Juan Skyway.** The roadway weaves through a series of "fourteeners" (a Rockies term for peaks reaching more than 14,000 feet) and picturesque mining towns. U.S. 550 continues south to historic Ouray and over Red Mountain Pass to Silverton and Durango. Take Route 62 west and Route 145 south to see the extraordinary cliff dwellings of Mesa Verde National Park. U.S. 160 completes the San Juan Skyway circuit to Durango. In late September and early October this route offers some of the most spectacular aspen viewing in the state.

Telluride

❺ *45 mi from Ridgway via Rte. 62 west and Rte. 145 east.*

Fodor'sChoice
★

Tucked like a jewel in a tiny valley caught between azure sky and gunmetal mountains is Telluride, once so inaccessible that it was a favorite hideout for desperadoes such as Butch Cassidy, who robbed his first bank here in 1889. The savage but beautiful terrain now attracts mountain people of a different sort—alpinists, snowboarders, freestylers, mountain bikers, and freewheeling four-wheelers—who attack any incline, up or down, and do so with abandon.

The town's independent spirit is shaped not only by its mining legacy, but by the social ferment of the 1960s and early '70s. Before the ski area opened in 1971, Telluride had been as remote as it was back in Cassidy's day. It was even briefly included on the "Ghost Town Club of Colorado" itinerary, but that was before countercultural types moved in, seeking to lose themselves in the wilderness. By 1974 the town's orientation had changed so radically that the entire council was composed of hippies. An enduring Telluride tradition called the Freebox (Pine St. and Colorado Ave.), where residents can sort through and take whatever used clothing and appliances they need, remains as a memento of those times. (One memorable day, just after a fur shop had the temerity to open in town, surprised residents found a wide selection of minks, sables, and chinchillas at the Box. After the mysterious break-in, the furriers got the point and moved on.)

Despite such efforts at keeping visible signs of wealth away, more and more locals are finding they can no longer afford to live here. And thanks to the construction of the Telluride Regional Airport in the mid-1980s, it has drawn more and more people. Today Telluride is an upscale alternative to Vail and Aspen, and celebrities who need only be identified by their first names (Arnold and Oprah, for example) have been spotted here.

Telluride is chic, which thrills some and dismays others. Many townies deplore the over-the-top Telluride Mountain Village development in the heart of the ski area, and some bitterly resent the construction of the glamorous Wyndham Peaks Resort. The ambivalence felt about the influx of wealth and new buildings brings into question whether development is inevitable, whether the pristine can be preserved in this fast-paced world. For better or worse, Telluride is gorgeous. The San Juans loom over town either menacingly or protectively, depending on the lighting.

Although the resort and the town are distinct areas, you can travel between them via a 2½-mi, over-the-mountain gondola, one of the most beautiful commutes in Colorado. The gondola makes a car unnecessary for local transportation; both the village and the town are pedestrian-friendly. This innovative form of public transportation operates summer and winter from early morning until late at night, and unless you have skis or a snowboard, the ride is free.

Telluride magazine prints an excellent historic walking tour in its "Visitors' Guide" section. The town offers one pastel Victorian residence or frontier trading post after another. It's hard to believe that the lovingly restored shops and restaurants once housed gaming parlors and saloons known for the quality of their "waitressing." That party-hearty spirit lives on, evidenced by numerous annual summer celebrations. Highly regarded wine and wild-mushroom festivals alternate with musical performances celebrating everything from bluegrass to jazz to chamber music. And the Telluride Film Festival is one of the world's leading showcases for the latest releases. Displaying a keen sense of humor, the town even promotes a No Festival Weekend, when nothing whatsoever is on the calendar.

Telluride has two off-seasons, when most restaurants and many lodgings are closed. Nearly everyone flees town after the ski area shuts down in mid-April, to return in early or mid-June. (But with the growing renown of Mountainfilm, a Memorial Day celebration of mountain sports and mountain culture, more and more places are opening then.) The town closes up from late September or early October until ski season gets going in late November to early December.

The 1887 brick **San Miguel County Courthouse** (⊠ 301 Colorado Ave.) was the county's first courthouse, and it still operates as one today. William Jennings Bryan spoke at the **New Sheridan Hotel & Opera House** (⊠ 231 W. Colorado Ave. ☎ 970/728–4351) during his 1896 presidential campaign. The opera house, added in 1914 and completely redone in 1996, is now home to the thriving Sheridan Arts Foundation.

In the old Miner's Hospital, **Telluride Historical Museum** (⊠ 201 W. Gregory Ave. ☎ 970/728–3344 ⊕ wwww.telluridemuseum.com) was constructed in 1888 and carefully restored in 2000. Exhibits on the town's past, including work in the nearby mines and techniques practiced by doctors who once practiced here, are on display. It's open Tuesday to Saturday noon to 5. Admission is $5.

Downhill Skiing & Snowboarding

Telluride is really two ski areas in one. For many years, Telluride had a reputation as being an experts-only ski area. Indeed, the north-facing trails are impressively steep and long, and by spring the moguls are massive. The terrain accessed by Chairlift Nine, including the famed Spiral Staircase and The Plunge, is for experts only (although one side of The Plunge is groomed so advanced skiers can have their turn).

But then there is the other side—literally—of the ski area, the gently sloping valley called Goronno Basin, with long runs excellent for intermediates and beginners. On the ridge that wraps around the ski area's core is the aptly named See Forever, a long cruiser that starts at 12,255 feet. and seems to go on and on. Below that are numerous intermediate runs and a phenomenal terrain park called Sprite Air Garden, designed for snowboarders. Near Goronno Basin is another section that includes super-steep, double-diamond tree runs on one side and glorious cruisers on the other.

Slide through a Western-style gate and you come to Prospect Bowl, a 733-acre expansion that includes three chairlifts and a network of runs subtly cut around islands of trees. One cluster of intermediate runs is served by a swift high-speed quad. The terrain runs the gamut from almost flat beginner terrain to double-diamond fall-away chutes, cliff bands, and open glades. ⊠ *565 Mountain Village Blvd., 81435* ☎ *970/ 728–6900 or 866/287–5016* ⊕ *www.tellurideskiresort.com* ☉ *Late Nov.–early Apr., daily 4 AM–4 PM.*

FACILITIES 3,535-foot vertical drop; 1,700 skiable acres; 24% beginner, 38% intermediate, 38% advanced/expert; 2 gondolas, 7 high-speed quad chairs, 2 triple chairs, 2 double chairs, 2 surface lifts, 1 moving carpet. **Snow report:** (☎ 970/728–7425).

LESSONS & The **Telluride Ski & Snowboard School** (⊠ 565 Mountain Village Blvd.
PROGRAMS ☎ 800/801–4832) offers half-day group clinics beginning at $45. Lessons for first-timers are available for alpine and telemark skiers, as well as snowboarders. A five-hour clinic with rentals and restricted lift tickets costs $99.

Beginner lessons are available for alpine and telemark skiers, as well as snowboarders. A five-hour clinic with rentals and restricted beginner lift tickets costs $95. Children's programs for ages 3 to12 are $95 a day for lifts, lessons, and lunch. Telluride was a pioneer in creating Women's Week programs, five days of skills-building classes with female instructors. Sessions are scheduled for January, February, and March.

LIFT TICKETS The walk-up rate is $69. On multiday, advance-purchase tickets the daily rate can drop as low as $59.

RENTALS Equipment rentals are available at **Paragon Ski and Sport** (⊠ 236 S. Oak St. ☎ 970/728–4525 ⊕ www.paragon telluride.com). Beginner packages (skis, boots, and poles) are $19 a day, and top-of-the-line packages are $39 a day. Paragon also rents telemark and cross-country gear, as well as snowshoes and snowblades.

Ski rentals are available from the ubiquitous **Telluride Sports** (⊠ 150 West Colorado Ave. ☎ 800/828–7547 ⊕ www.telluridesports.com). Complete packages (skis, boots, and poles) start at around $25. There are 10 other locations in the area.

Nordic Skiing

BACKCOUNTRY Among the better backcountry skiing routes is the **San Juan Hut System**
SKIING (⊠ 224 E. Colorado Ave., 81435 ☎ 970/626–3033). It leads toward Ridgway along the Sneffels Range. The five huts in the system are about 7 mi apart and are well equipped, with beds, blankets, wood-burning stoves, and cooking stoves. Previous backcountry experience is not essential to ski here, though it is highly recommended. Rental equipment is available, and reservations are recommended at least two weeks in advance. The San Juan Hut System also offers a guide service as an introduction to the backcountry tracks.

TRACK SKIING **Telluride Nordic Center** (✉ Town Park ☎ 970/728–1144) gives you access to 10 mi of cross-country trails. The areas around Molas Divide and Mesa Verde National Park are extremely popular. The center also rents equipment for both adults and children.

The **Topaten Touring Center** (☎ 970/728–7517), near the Chair 10 unload, offers 6¼ mi of trails groomed for cross-country skiing and snowshoeing in a high-mountain setting.

Other Sports & the Outdoors

Telluride Outside (✉ 121 W. Colorado Ave. ☎ 970/728–3895 or 800/831–6230 ⊕ www.tellurideoutside.com) organizes a variety of winter activities in the Telluride area, including hot-air ballooning, sleigh rides, snowmobile tours, mountain-biking trips, and even winter fly-fishing excursions.

FISHING **Telluride Angler** (✉ 121 W. Colorado Ave. ☎ 970/728–0773), Colorado's second largest fishing-guide service, offers guided fly-fishing trips on the beautiful San Miguel and Delores rivers.

FOUR-WHEELING The Tomboy Road, accessed directly from North Fir Street at the edge of town, leads to one of the country's most interesting mining districts. It went down in history in 1901 when the Western Federation of Miners organized a strike at Tomboy Mine. The state militia was eventually called in to put an end to the strike. The ruins of Tomboy Mine, Tomboy Mill, and parts of the town of Tomboy are all that remain of those turbulent times. The road offers fabulous views of Bridal Veil Falls and passes through the Social Tunnel on its way to the high country. After 7½ mi, the road crests over 13,114-foot-high Imogene Pass, the highest pass road in the San Juan Mountains. If you continue down the other side, you will end up near Yankee Boy Basin near Ouray.

Dave's Mountain Tours (✉ Box 2736, 81435 ☎ 970/908–2578 ⊕ www.telluridetours.com) conducts summer jeep tours over Imogene Pass and other historic areas. In winter it offers snowmobile tours.

GLIDER RIDES Offering an unusual look at the San Juans, **Telluride Soaring** (☎ 970/209–3497) operates out of the Telluride Airport. Rates are about $110 per half hour, $160 per hour; rides are offered daily, weather permitting.

GOLF **Telluride Golf Club** (✉ Telluride Mountain Village ☎ 970/728–2606) has breathtaking views of Mt. Wilson and Mt. Sunshine, which dominate this 6,700-yard course. Weather permitting, the course is playable from mid-May to mid-October. Greens fees are $140 to $160, depending on the time of year.

HIKING The peaks of the rugged San Juan Mountains around Telluride require some scrambling, occasionally bordering on real climbing, to get to the top. A local favorite is **Mt. Wilson,** a roughly 4,000-vertical-foot climb for which only the last 400 vertical feet call for a scramble across steep, shale slopes. July and August are the most likely snow-free months on this 8-mi round-trip hike. Sound a bit too grueling? From a trailhead at the foot of Pine Street, an immensely popular 2-mi trail leads to **Bear Creek Falls.** The route is also used by mountain bikers. On the opposite side of the valley, from trailheads leading off Aspen Street and Tomboy Road, the 3-mi **Jud Wiebe Trail** begins as an excellent hike that is often passable from spring until well into the fall. From here you have amazing views of Utah's LaSal Mountains. For more ambitious hikers, the Jud Wiebe Trail links with the 13-mi **Sneffels Highline Trail.** This route leads through wildflower-covered meadows. Another trail leads to 425-foot **Bridal Veil Falls,** the state's highest cascade. It tumbles lavishly from the head of a box canyon. A beautifully restored powerhouse sits beside the falls. For more information, contact **Uncompahgre National Forest** (✉ 2250 U.S. 50, Delta 81416 ☎ 970/874–6600 ⊕ www.fs.fed.us/r2/gmug).

HORSEBACK RIDING
Roudy Roundebush rode through America's living rooms courtesy of a memorable television commercial in which he and his horse, Cindy, trotted right up to the bar at the New Sheridan Hotel. Roudy is now riding Cindy's son, Golly, and you can join them. His slogan has long been "Gentle horses for gentle people, fast horses for fast people, and for people who don't like to ride, horses that don't like to be rode." **Ride with Roudy** (☎ 970/728–9611 ⊕ www.ridewithroudy.com) is in a barn on an old ranch 6 mi from Telluride. Trail rides pass through aspen groves and across open meadows with views of the Wilson Range. Winter rides leave from Roudy's other ranch, in Norwood. Hour-long rides cost about $35.

RAFTING
There are plenty of rapids around Telluride. **Telluride Outside** (✉ 121 W. Colorado Ave. ☎ 970/728–3895 or 800/831–6230 ⊕ www. tellurideoutside.com) explores the Gunnison, Dolores, Colorado, and Animas rivers.

ROCK CLIMBING
Many people would consider being suspended from wall of ice or a sheer cliff to be a bizarre form of torture. For those who think it might be fun, **Fantasy Ridge Mountain Guides** (✉ 28 Village Ct., Box 405, Placerville 81430 ☎ 970/728–3546 ⊕ www.fantasyridge.com) offers introductory ice-climbing and rock-climbing courses. A three-day ice-climbing course costs about $900 (lodging included). Rock-climbing classes range from hourly instruction costing $25 to five-day programs that run about $800. Many use the famous Ophir Wall. Fantasy Ridge also guides fourteener climbs and other expeditions in the San Juan Mountains.

TENNIS
If you want to practice your backhand, **Telluride Town Park** (✉ Eastern end of E. Pacific St. ☎ 970/728–2173) has free public tennis courts. **Wyndham Peaks Resort** (✉ 136 Country Club Dr., 81435 ☎ 970/728–3458) has five tennis courts and two tennis pros. There is a small fee is you are not a resort guest.

Where to Stay & Eat

★ $$$$ ✕ **La Marmotte.** With its rough brick walls, lacy curtains, and baskets overflowing with flowers or strings of garlic bulbs, this romantic bistro would be right at home in Provence. Fish dishes, such as grilled salmon with spinach and olives in a red wine sauce, are particularly splendid. If you like wild game, the loin of venison with braised apple and Jerusalem artichoke is a standout. ✉ *150 W. San Juan Ave.* ☎ *970/728–6232* ⊕ *www.lamarmotte.com* ⌕ *Reservations essential* ⊟ *AE, D, MC, V* ⊘ *No lunch. Closed mid-Apr.–early June, Oct.–late Nov., and Tues. mid-June–Sept.*

★ $$$–$$$$ ✕ **Allred's.** After riding up in the gondola, diners are still astounded by the views from this mountainside eatery. Colorado native chef Bob Scherner, who worked with Charlie Trotter in Chicago, designed a creative menu that should satisfy the most discriminating tastebuds. Try the free-range Canadian veal chop with potato-chanterelle hash, or the seared yellowfin tuna with vegetable risotto, fried oyster mushrooms, and red pepper au jus. The bittersweet chocolate cake and the passion fruit sorbet will send you home smiling. ✉ *Top of San Sophia gondola,* ☎ *970/728–7474* ⊟ *AE, D, MC, V* ⊘ *No lunch. Closed early Apr.–early June and Oct.–late Nov.*

$$$–$$$$ ✕ **Cosmopolitan.** Hotel Columbia, a sleek lodge at the base of the gondola, is home to this elegant eatery. Overseen by chef Chad Scothorn, the kitchen whips up such satisfying dishes as salmon with a spicy dip-

ping sauce and seared tuna with coconut-vanilla rice. An unusual dessert, listed on the menu as "coffee and donuts," is actually scrumptious New Orleans–style beignets with a choice of specialty coffees. For a special evening, book a table for two in the cozy wine cellar. ⊠ *300 W. San Juan Ave.* ☎ *970/728–1292* ⌕ *Reservations essential* ▭ *AE, MC, V* ◷ *No lunch. Closed mid-Apr.–Memorial Day and mid-Oct.–Thanksgiving.*

$$–$$$$ ✕ **221 South Oak Bistro.** In a pretty Victorian cottage, this elegant bistro entices you to linger with its soft peach walls and a blond-wood bar. Soft music wafts through the casually elegant space. Chef-owner Eliza Goodall trained in Paris, New Orleans, and the Napa Valley, and cooks up such dishes as Muscovy duck breast with duck confit, spinach, shiitakes, spinach, and pine nuts; rack of lamb with zucchini and potato-chèvre ravioli; and potato-crusted halibut with asparagus and fennel. Most people come only for the fine food, but some regulars schedule their visits to sample special martinis on Wednesday evenings. ⊠ *221 S. Oak St.* ☎ *970/728–9507* ▭ *AE, MC, V* ◷ *No lunch. Closed Tues., early Apr.–mid-June, and early Oct.–early Dec.*

$$–$$$ ✕ **Roma Bar and Café.** Forget about the walls talking—what you'd really like to tell its tales is the bar, backed by 12-foot-high mirrors, that has dominated this low-key eatery since 1860. It has seen everything, including cowboys riding their mounts right into the restaurant. Flappers even brewed up rotgut whiskey in the cellar during Prohibition. Now, it is a popular spot for families. The pasta specials are a terrific value, as are the pizzas, salads, and slabs of beef. ⊠ *133 E. Colorado Ave.* ☎ *970/ 728–3669* ▭ *AE, MC, V* ◷ *Closed Tues. and Wed. in Nov. No lunch Oct.–May.*

$–$$ ✕ **Fat Alley's BBQ.** Some old skis and other ski paraphernalia are what passes as decor at this popular spot. Messy, mouthwatering ribs and Carolina-style pulled-pork sandwiches are complemented by delectable side dishes such as red beans and rice, baked sweet potatoes, and snap-pea and feta salad. More than a dozen beers, 30 bourbons, and a few wines are available, in addition to homemade iced tea and pink lemonade. A few long tables flanked by benches let you dine family-style. ⊠ *128 S. Oak St.* ☎ *970/728–3985* ⌕ *Reservations not accepted* ▭ *AE, MC, V.*

$–$$ ✕ **Honga's Lotus Petal & Tea Room.** A local favorite, this tearoom serves up Japanese-, Thai-, and Balinese-influenced fare in the vibrant, elegant setting of a restored Victorian. The sushi bar is one of the best in town. Though the place caters mostly to vegetarians, it also puts free-range chicken and organic beef on the menu. Blackened tofu is the signature dish, and the crowds go wild for the crunchy shrimp roll and pineapple-coconut curry. Don't leave town without sampling the addictive potstickers. ⊠ *133 S. Oak St.* ☎ *970/728–5134* ▭ *AE, MC, V* ◷ *Closed early Apr.–early June and mid-Oct.–late Nov.*

$$$$ ▤ **Camel's Garden.** In a curious contradiction, this ultra-modern lodging that is all gleaming glass and sleek surfaces bears the name of one of the town's oldest mines. Fireplaces keep the rooms toasty on winter evenings. There are plenty of nice touches, including stereos and CD players. The Continental breakfast is loaded with fresh-baked pastries from the bakery next door. The hotel is steps away from the Oak Street chairlift. ⊠ *250 W. San Juan Ave., 81435* ☎ *970/728–9300 or 888/772–2635* ⊠ *970/728–0433* ⊕ *www.camelsgarden.com* ⬐ *30 rooms, 7 condos* ⌂ *In-room VCRs, hot tub, steam room, spa* ▭ *AE, D, DC, MC, V* ⧖*CP* ◷ *Closed Oct.–Nov.*

$$$$ ▤ **New Sheridan Hotel.** William Jennings Bryan delivered his rousing "Cross of Gold" speech here in 1896, garnering a presidential nomination in the process. The brick walls are covered with old tintypes, creating just the right mood. Rounding out the decor are antiques such as fringed lamps, marble-top dressing tables, and red velour love seats. The gorgeous Victorian-era bar, a favorite among locals, is the original. A complimentary breakfast and afternoon tea complete the picture of gracious fin-de-siècle living. ⊠ *231 W. Colorado Ave., 81435* ☎ *970/728–4351* 📠 *970/728–5024* ⊕ *www.newsheridan.com* ⇆ *26 rooms, 8 with shared bath; 6 suites* ♿ *Restaurant, in-room data ports, gym, 2 hot tubs, bar, meeting room* ☰ *AE, MC, V* ⦿ *BP* ⊘ *Closed mid-Apr.–mid-May and mid-Oct.–mid-Nov.*

$$$$ 🏨 **Wyndham Peaks Resort & Golden Door Spa.** The somewhat forbidding exterior at this luxury resort no longer seems worth mentioning when you first catch sight of Mt. Wilson, the peak pictured on every can of Coors. Make sure to ask for a room with a balcony. And then there are the invigorating, revitalizing treatments at the five-story Golden Door Spa. More than 55 are offered in the 44 private rooms, from skin-tightening wraps to muscle-taming massages. The rooms are sizable, decorated in Norwegian wood and muted shades of green. The range of activities here is vast, ranging from an indoor pool to tennis courts—there's even an indoor climbing wall. ⊠ *136 Country Club Dr., 81435* ☎ *970/728–6800 or 800/789–2220* 📠 *970/728–6567* ⊕ *www.wyndham.com* ⇆ *174 rooms, 32 suites* ♿ *2 restaurants, in-room data ports, 5 tennis courts, indoor-outdoor pool, gym, hair salon, hot tub, sauna, spa, racquetball, squash, bar, business services, meeting rooms* ☰ *AE, DC, MC, V* ⊘ *Closed early Apr.–mid-May and mid-Oct.–mid-Nov.*

$$$–$$$$ 🏨 **The Ice House.** An appealing blend of Scandinavian and Southwestern decor makes this lodging unique. Native American tapestries and polished wood ceilings are complemented by rich fabrics in shades of beige, green, and maroon. Spacious rooms have balconies that let you enjoy the view, while the baths have oversized tubs. The hotel provides a free Continental breakfast and a place to store your skis. Best of all, the Oak Street lift is a little more than a block away. ⊠ *310 S. Fir St., 81435* ☎ *970/728–6300 or 800/544–3436* 📠 *970/728–6358* ⊕ *www.icehouselodge.com* ⇆ *42 rooms, 16 condos* ♿ *Minibars, cable TV, pool, hot tub, steam room* ☰ *AE, D, DC, MC, V* ⦿ *CP* ⊘ *Closed mid-Apr.–early June.*

★ $$$–$$$$ 🏨 **San Sophia B&B.** Gingerbread trim gives this turreted Victorian-style inn a fanciful feeling. Pristine mountain light streams into the rooms, which are warmly accented with whitewashed-oak woodwork. Rooms have brass beds covered with handmade quilts and tables and chairs crafted by local artisans. The stained-glass windows over the oversize tubs is a nice touch. The inn is known for its fabulous breakfasts and après-ski treats. Owners Alicia Bixby and Keith Hampton are overachievers; they also run a marketing firm in town, sponsor the annual wine festival, and raise two young children, but they still find time to mingle with the guests. ⊠ *330 W. Pacific St., 81435* ☎ *970/728–3001 or 800/537–4781* 📠 *970/728–6226* ⊕ *www.sansophia.com* ⇆ *16 rooms* ♿ *Hot tub* ☰ *AE, MC, V* ⦿ *BP* ⊘ *Closed early Apr.–early May and two weeks in Nov.*

CONDOMINIUMS **Telluride Central Reservations** (☎ 800/525–3455 ⊕ www.visittelluride.com) handles all the properties at Telluride Mountain Village, and several more in town. **Telluride Resort Accommodations** (☎ 800/538–7754) rents several top-notch accommodations.

Nightlife & the Arts

THE ARTS Telluride is home to numerous music festivals during the summer, including monstrous jazz and bluegrass events. The **Telluride Film Festival** (☎ 603/643–1255) in September is considered one of the world's leading showcases for foreign and domestic films.

The **Sheridan Arts Foundation** (✉ 110 N. Oak St. ☎ 970/728–6363) is a mentoring program that brings top actors and singers to town to perform alongside budding young artists in the Sheridan Opera House. The **Telluride Repertory Theatre Company** (☎ 970/728–4539) gives free performances in the town park each summer. The **Lizard Head Theatre Company** (☎ 970/728–3133 ⊕ www.lizardheadtheatre.com) brings big-name actors to perform a summer repertory season at the Sheridan Opera House.

NIGHTLIFE **Allred's** (✉ Top of San Sophia gondola, ☎ 970/728–7474) is a divine après-ski. Take in eye-popping views of the mountains and the lights twinkling in the town below as you enjoy an excellent selection of wines by the glass. Appetizers can make for an early dinner.

Excelsior Café (✉ 200 W. Colorado Ave. ☎ 970/728–4250) is the spot to hear the best folk-rock. The **Fly Me to the Moon Saloon** (✉ 132 E. Colorado Ave. ☎ 970/728–1942) has live music—jazz, blues, funk, ska, rock, you name it—most nights. The action gets wild on the spring-loaded dance floor.

The **Last Dollar Saloon** (✉ 100 E. Colorado Ave. ☎ 970/728–4800) has a jukebox filled with old favorites. The century-old bar at the **New Sheridan Hotel** (✉ 231 W. Colorado Ave. ☎ 970/728–4351) is a favorite hangout for skiers returning from the slopes. Prime time is between 4 PM and 8 PM. In summer, folks gather to socialize and watch the world go by. On July 4th, a cowboy named Rowdy is known to ride into the bar and enjoy his drink while astride his horse.

Shopping

BOOKS **Between the Covers Bookstore & Coffee House** (✉ 224 W. Colorado Ave. ☎ 970/728–4504) has the perfect ambience for browsing through the latest releases while sipping a foam-capped cappuccino.

BOUTIQUES The **Bounty Hunter** (✉ 226 W. Colorado Ave. ☎ 970/728–0256 ⊕ www.bountyhuntertelluride.com) is the spot for leather items, especially boots, hats, and vests. It also has an astonishing selection of hats, among them Panama straw, beaver felt, Australian Outback, and just plain outrageous.

CRAFT & ART **Hell Bent Leather & Silver** (✉ 209 E. Colorado Ave. ☎ 970/728–6246
GALLERIES ⊕ www.hellbentleather.com) is a fine source for Native American arts and crafts. **The Potter's Wheel** (✉ 221 E. Colorado Ave. ☎ 970/728–4912) has decorative and functional pottery crafted by local artisans.

SPORTING GOODS **Telluride Sports** (✉ 150 W. Colorado Ave. ☎ 970/728–4477) has equipment and clothing for all seasons.

Ouray

⑥ *10 mi from Ridgway on U.S. 50 south; 23 mi from Silverton via U.S. 550 north.*

The town of Ouray is trapped in a narrow, steep-wall valley in the bullying shadow cast by rugged peaks of the San Juan Mountains. It was named for the great Southern Ute chief Ouray, labeled a visionary by the U.S. Army and branded a traitor by his people because he attempted to assimilate the Utes into white society. The former mining town is the proud owner of a National Historic District, with lavish old hotels, commercial buildings, and residences. The town's ultimate glory lies in its surroundings, and it has become an increasingly popular destination for climbers (both the mountain and ice varieties), mountain-bike fanatics, and hikers.

More than 25 classic edifices are included in the walking-tour brochure issued by the Ouray County Historical Society. Among the points of

CHIEF OURAY

CRAWLING WITH PROSPECTORS AND SETTLERS in search of their fortunes, Colorado was undergoing great social and political change in the mid-1800s. The Ute Indians, who until then occupied all of Colorado except for the eastern slope, wanted nothing to do with the newcomers.

Chief Ouray (whose Ute name means arrow) found himself caught in the middle. On the one hand, if he didn't learn the white man's politics, what chance did he stand of striking a deal with the United States government to save the best part of his people's land? On the other hand, would his people think he was a traitor if he negotiated with the white man and adopted his ways?

One of Ouray's major accomplishments was the negotiation of the Great Ute Treaty of 1868, which granted some 6 million acres of land to the Ute. The treaty was considered to be the most favorable ever negotiated with the U.S. government by an Indian tribe. But it wouldn't last. By 1874, discontent among the Ute was rising after the discovery of gold in the San Juan Mountains attracted fortune seekers by the dozens to Ute land. While most of the Ute favored violent retaliation, Ouray insisted on peaceful negotiation. The United States drew up another treaty, proposing that the Ute give up almost 4 million acres of their land in return for some $60,000 in annuities and allotments. Ouray, who was still convinced that cooperation with the U.S. government was best for his people, reluctantly signed the agreement, known as the Brunot Treaty. The tribe never received any money from the United States.

The Brunot Treaty recognized Ouray as head chief of the entire Ute nation and granted him an annual salary of $1,000. Even though he preferred the traditional ways, Ouray knew his people could not stop the march of history, something he believed his fellow Ute would never understand. He took up residence with his wife, Chipeta, on a small government-owned farm south of Montrose to show his people that it was possible for them to adjust to white ways. The couple adopted Euro-American customs, furnishing their home with curtains, china, and teapots. Ouray even wore the white man's broadcloth and boots for a time, but he refused to cut his long hair, which he wore in braids that hung down on his chest in typical Ute fashion. Most Ute felt Ouray had sold out to the whites. He was even accused of treason and several attempts were made on his life.

Ouray, who was instrumental in negotiating the release of white hostages kidnapped during the Meeker Massacre in 1879, continued to act as a negotiator between his people and the government until his death in 1880. A great negotiator, Ouray is remembered as a man who believed in peace more than war.

---

interest are the grandiose Wright's Opera House, the Western Hotel, and the St. Elmo Hotel. One of the loveliest buildings in town is the **Beaumont Hotel** (✉ 505 Main St. ☎ 970/325–7000). This 1887 landmark, a confection of French, Italian, and Romanesque Revival design, stood vacant for years before Dan and Mary King set about restoring it. The project cost millions of dollars—the owners strove for perfection at every step. The building was added to the National Register of Historic Places in 1973.

The **Ouray County Museum** preserves the history of the San Juan Mountains and of Ouray. Mining equipment, railroad paraphernalia, and commercial artifacts are carefully arranged in the former St. Joseph's Hospital, built in 1887. ✉ 420 Sixth Ave. ☎ 970/325–4576 ⊙ Call for hrs 🖾 $5.

Ouray is also the northern end of the Million Dollar Highway, the awe-

Fodor's Choice ★ some stretch of U.S. 550 that climbs over **Red Mountain Pass.** As it ascends steeply from Ouray, the road clings to the cliffs hanging over the
Uncompaghre River far below. This two-laner bears little resemblance
to the image one usually has of U.S. highways. Guardrails are few, hairpin turns are many, and behemoth RVs often seem to take more than
their share of road. It earned its nickname either because the crushed
ore used for the roadbed was rumored to contain gold and silver, or because of the fortune that 19th-century roadbuilder Otto Mears spent to
create it. This priceless road is kept open all winter by heroic plow crews.
The Ouray side, on the whole, is steeper and narrower than the Silverton side. It is the most spectacular part of the 236-mi **San Juan Skyway,**
designated as an All-American Road for its scenic splendor and historic
significance.

One particularly gorgeous jaunt is to **Box Canyon Falls.** The turbulent
waters of Clear Creek thunder 285 feet down a narrow gorge. A steel
suspension bridge and well-marked trails afford breathtaking vistas. Birders flock to the park, and a visitor center has interpretive displays.
✛ *West end of Third Ave., off U.S. 550* ☎ *970/325–4464* ☉ *mid-
Oct.–mid-May, daily 10–10; mid-May–mid-Oct., daily 8 AM–dusk* ☜ *$3.*

Another option is to immerse yourself in nature at the area's various hot
springs. At **Ouray Hot Springs Pool** it's hard to tell which is more refreshing;
the pools brimming over with 96- to 106-degree water or the views of
surrounding peaks. There is a fitness center in the bathhouse. ⊠ *U.S. 550
at the north end of town* ☎ *970/325–4638* ☜ *$9* ☉ *Daily 10–10.*

The Historic Wiesbaden Hot Springs Spa & Lodge is at the source of the
springs. In an underground chamber, you can soak in the steamy pools
and inhale the pungent vapors. There is also an outdoor pool with
views of the trees. Massage and mud wraps are offered at the spa.
⊠ *625 5th St.* ☎ *970/325–7037* ⊕ *www.wiesbadenhotsprings.com*
☜ *$9* ☉ *Daily 8 AM–9:45 PM.*

On the **Bachelor-Syracuse Mine Tour,** a mine train hauls visitors down 3,500
feet into one of the region's great mines. Explanations of mining techniques, a visit to a blacksmith shop, and panning for gold are part of
the experience. Tours depart every half hour. ⊠ *1222 County Rd. 14*
☎ *970/325–0220 or 888/227–4584.*

Sports & the Outdoors

FOUR-WHEELING Off-roaders delight in the more than 500 mi of four-wheel-drive roads
around Ouray. Popular routes include the Alpine Loop Scenic Byway
to the Silverton and Lake City areas, and Imogene Pass or Black Bear
Pass to Telluride. Figure on the four-wheeling season running from May
to September, but you'll have to keep an eye on the weather.

Fodor's Choice ★ About the first 7 mi of the road to **Yankee Boy Basin** are accessible by
regular cars, but it takes a 4x4 to reach the heart of this awesome alpine
landscape. The route, designated County Road 361, veers off U.S. 550
just south of Ouray and climbs west into a vast basin ringed with soaring summits and carpeted with one of Colorado's most lavish displays
of wildflowers. This is one of the region's premier day-trip destinations.
Contact the **Ouray Ranger District** (⊠ County Rd. 361 ☎ 970/240–5300
⊕ www.fs.fed.us/r2/gmug).

If you have the skill and confidence but not the right vehicle, you can rent
one from **Switzerland of America Tours** (⊠ 226 7th Ave. ☎ 970/325–4484
or 800/432–5337 ⊕ www.soajeep.com). The company also offers guided
tours in open-air six-passenger jeeps. Full-day tours cost $90 to $95.

ICE CLIMBING Ouray is known in ice-climbing circles for its abundance of frozen waterfalls. The Ouray Ice Festival, held each January, helped to cement its reputation. The **Ouray Ice Park** (⌂ Box 1058 ☎ 970/325–4288 ⊕ www. ourayicepark.com) is the world's first facility dedicated to ice climbing. Located in the Uncompahgre Gorge south of town, the Ice Park has three main climbing areas with more than 40 routes. **Ouray Mountain Sports** (✉ 722 Main St. ☎ 970/325–4284 ⊕ www.ouraysports.com) arranges lessons and guided climbs.

NORDIC SKIING About 9 mi south of Ouray, Ironton Park is a marked trail system for Nordic skiers and snowshoers. Several interconnecting loops let you spend a day on the trails. Local merchants stock trail maps. For information, contact **Ouray County Nordic Council** (⌂ Box 469, Ouray 81427 ☎ 970/ 325–4932).

TENNIS Free public tennis courts are located at **Ouray Hot Springs Pool** (✉ 1220 Main St. ☎ 970/325–4638).

Where to Stay & Eat

$$$-$$$$ ✕**Tundra Restaurant at the Beaumont.** Well before the hotel itself was ready for guests, this second-floor restaurant was serving upscale "high-altitude" cuisine in an elegant, high-ceilinged setting. Look for regional specialties served with a little added flair. The restaurant has won awards for its stellar wine cellar, and proves it with a Thursday evening tasting. ✉ *505 Main St.,* ☎ *970/325–7040* ⚐ *Reservations essential* ☰ *MC, V* ☉ *Closed Mon. and Tues.*

$$-$$$ ▦ **Box Canyon Lodge & Hot Springs.** The private mineral spring here was used first by the Utes and later by the Cogar Sanitarium. Soak away your cares in four redwood tubs full of steaming 103° to 107° water, with mountain views around you. The rooms are nondescript, but modern and comfortable. Two-room suites are also available. ✉ *45 3rd Ave., 81427* ☎ *970/325–4981 or 800/327–5080* ☐ *970/325–0223* ⊕ *www.boxcanyonouray.com* ⇆ *38 rooms* ⚐ *Kitchens, cable TV* ☰ *AE, D, DC, MC, V.*

★ $-$$$ ▦ **China Clipper Inn.** A welcome departure from the typical Western- and Victorian-style inns in this area, the China Clipper is tastefully decorated with Asian antiques. Most rooms open onto a charming flower-filled patio and hot tub. The inn was built almost entirely—with great attention to detail—by a retired Navy commander from Louisville, Kentucky. Full breakfast and afternoon tea are included in the rate. ✉ *525 2nd St., 81427* ☎ *970/325–0565 or 800/315–0565* ☐ *970/325–4190* ⊕ *www. chinaclipperinn.com* ⇆ *12 rooms* ⚐ *Hot tub* ☰ *AE, D, MC, V* ❏ *BP.*

★ $-$$ ▦ **St. Elmo Hotel.** This tiny 1898 hostelry was originally a haven for "miners down on their luck," or so the story goes. Its original owner was Kitty Heit, who couldn't resist a sob story. Family ghosts reputedly hover about protectively. The rooms are graced with stained-glass windows, marble-top armoires, brass or mahogany beds, and other antiques. A complimentary breakfast buffet is served in a sunny parlor. The Bon Ton restaurant serves fine Continental cuisine with an Italian flair. The staff will recommend something from the sophisticated wine list. ✉ *426 Main St., 81427* ☎ *866/243–1502 or 970/325–4951* ☐ *970/325–0348* ⊕ *www.stelmohotel.com* ⇆ *7 rooms, 2 suites* ⚐ *Restaurant, hot tub, sauna* ☰ *AE, D, DC, MC, V* ❏ *BP.*

$-$$ ▦ **Riverside Inn.** A comfortable stop beside the Uncompahgre River, this welcoming motel has been completely redecorated and features handmade log furniture. The cabins are popular with ice-climbers and other sports hounds. ✉ *1805 N. Main St., 81427* ☎ *970/325–4061 or 800/432–4170* ☐ *970/325–7302* ⊕ *www.ourayriversideinn.com* ⇆ *18 rooms, 4 suites, 10 cabins* ⚐ *Kitchenettes* ☰ *AE, D, MC, V.*

In the restored Beaumont Hotel, **Buckskin Booksellers** (⊠ 505 Main Ave. ☎ 970/325–4044) has books about such topics as mining, railroading, and ranching, as well as collectibles and Native American items. **North Moon** (⊠ 801 Main St. ☎ 970/325–4885) carries irresistible pieces of jewelry. **Ouray Glassworks** (⊠ 619 Main St. ☎ 800/748–9421) sells exquisite handblown glass created by Sam Rushing and leatherwork crafted by Robert Holmes.

Lake City

❼ *45 mi from Ouray via the Alpine Loop Scenic Byway (summer only); 55 mi from Gunnison via U.S. 50 west and Rte. 149 south; 49 mi from Creede via Rte. 149 north.*

Lake City—with its collection of lacy gingerbread-trim houses and false-front Victorians—claims to have the largest National Historic District in Colorado. But the history the town is perhaps best-known for is the lurid story of a notorious rogue named Alfred Packer. Packer led a party of six prospectors who camped near Lake San Cristobal during the winter of 1874. That spring, only Packer emerged from the mountains, claiming that after he had been deserted by the rest he subsisted on roots and rabbits. Soon after, a Ute traveling near Lake San Cristobal came across a grisly pile of human flesh and crushed skulls. Packer protested his innocence and fled, but a manhunt ensued. He was caught nine years later and sentenced to life in prison.

Lake City is the point of departure for superb hiking and fishing in the Gunnison National Forest. A geological phenomenon known as the Slumgullion Earthflow occurred some 800 years ago, when a mountainside sloughed off into the valley, blocking the Lake Fork of the Gunnison River and creating Lake San Cristobal, the state's second-largest natural lake. There is a scenic overlook along Highway 149, just south of town, with a sign explaining how this happened.

Lake City is the northern tip of the **Silver Thread Scenic Byway,** whose tail is 75 mi south in Southfork. The route, also called Highway 149, climbs over Slumgullion Pass from Lake City, overlooks the headwaters of the Rio Grande, and then drops down into the lush Rio Grande Valley. It is paved, so passenger cars have no problem getting through.

The inspiring **Alpine Loop Scenic Byway** joins Lake City with Ouray and Silverton. This part of the route is only open in summer and is not paved over Cinnamon Pass and Engineer Pass. However, this is heaven for four-wheelers, dizzily spiraling from 12,800-foot-high passes to gaping valleys.

Sports & the Outdoors

FISHING Numerous high alpine lakes and mountain streams make Lake City a fisherman's heaven. Lake San Cristobal is known around the region for its rainbow and brown trout. The Lake Fork of the Gunnison offers anglers rainbow and brook trout. For information about guided trips, fishing licenses, or renting gear, check with **Dan's Fly Shop** (⊠ 723 Gunnison Ave. ☎ 970/944–2281 ⊕ www.dansflyshop.com).

HIKING Hikers often overnight in Lake City to depart for three of Colorado's easier fourteeners—meaning peaks higher than 14,000 feet. Sunshine and Redcloud are generally climbed together, and Handies is across the valley. This means it is fairly easy for fit hikers to bag three fourteeners in just two days.

Where to Stay & Eat

$ ⊡ **Old Carson Inn.** This peaceful A-frame log cabin is nestled among stands of towering aspen and spruce. The seven rooms are brimming with rustic charm and are nicely appointed with down comforters. The complimentary country breakfast, served family style, should get you off to a good start. ⌖ *Box 144, County Rd. 30, 81235* ☏ *970/944–2511* 🖷 *970/944–0149* ⊕ *www.oldcarsoninn.com* ⊸ *7 rooms* ⌂ *Hot tub* ⊟ *AE, D, MC, V* ⏸ *BP.*

Silverton

❽ *23 mi from Ouray via U.S. 550 north, 20 mi from Purgatory via U.S. 550 north.*

Glorious peaks surround Silverton, an isolated, unspoiled old mining community. It reputedly got its name when a miner exclaimed, "We ain't got much gold but we got a ton of silver!" Silverton is the county seat, as well as the only remaining town, in San Juan County. The last mine went bust in 1991 (which is recent as such things go), leaving Silverton to boom only during the summer when the Durango & Silverton Narrow Gauge Railroad deposits four trainloads of tourists a day. With the recent opening of the Silverton Mountain ski area, Silverton is beginning to shake off its long slumber, and more businesses are finding it worthwhile to stay open year-round.

Silverton's hardy and spirited populace still commemorates its rowdy past. At 5:30 PM on Thursday through Sunday evenings, a gunfight erupts at the corner of Blair and 12th streets. Of course the good guys always win. At 6 PM the town's much-ballyhooed brass band plays old favorites.

The downtown area has been designated a National Historic Landmark District. Be sure to pick up the walking-tour brochure that describes— among other things—the most impressive buildings lining Greene Street: **Miners' Union Hall, Teller House,** the **Town Hall,** the **San Juan County Courthouse** (home of the county historical museum), and the **Grand Imperial Hotel.** These structures have historical significance, but more history was probably made in the raucous red-light district along Blair Street.

The **San Juan County Historical Museum** is in the old San Juan County Jail. It was erected in 1902 from prefabricated parts that were shipped by train from St. Louis. The museum houses a mineral collection, mining memorabilia, and local artifacts. ⊠ *1559 Greene St.* ☏ *970/387– 5838 or 970/387–5609* ⊕ *www.silvertonhistoricalsociety.org* ⊗ *Daily 9–5* ▣ *$4.*

Ask at the **Chamber of Commerce** about a Heritage Pass, good for savings on admission to the Silverton Jail and Museum, Old Hundred Gold Mine, and Mayflower Mill. ⊠ *414 Greene St.* ☏ *970/387–5654 or 800/752–4494* ⊕ *www.silvertoncolorado.org* ⊗ *May, June, Oct. daily 9–5; July–Sept. daily 9–6; Nov.–Apr. daily 10–4.*

A tram takes visitors 1,500 feet into the **Old Hundred Gold Mine** for a tour of one of the town's oldest mining facilities. Old Hundred operated for about a century, from the first strike in 1872 until the last haul in the early 1970s. ⊠ *5 mi north of Silverton on Hwy. 110, then County Rd. 4* ☏ *970/387–5444 or 800/872–3009* ⊕ *www.minetour.com* ▣ *$15* ⊗ *May–mid-Oct., daily 10–4.*

The nearby **Mayflower Mill** has been designated a National Historic Landmark. Tours explain how precious metals are extracted from the earth. ⊠ *5 mi north of Silverton on Hwy. 110* ☏ *970/387–0294* ⊕ *www. silvertonhistoricalsociety.org* ▣ *$7* ⊗ *Memorial Day–mid-Oct.*

If you look north toward Anvil Mountain, you'll see the community's touching tribute to miners, the **Christ of the Mines Shrine.** It was built in the 1950s out of Carrara marble. A moderately strenuous 1-mi hike leads to the shrine, which has memorable views of the surrounding San Juan Mountains.

Sports & the Outdoors

DOWNHILL SKIING & SNOWBOARDING

Run by the town, **Kendall Mountain** (☎ 970/387–5522 ✉ $6) is a single-tow ski center open weekends during ski season, weather permitting. It's not a challenging slope, so its perfect for beginners. Sledding and tubing are also permitted.

★ About 6 mi north of town, **Silverton Mountain** is one of the country's simplest yet most innovative ski areas. With a single lift accessing the never-groomed backcountry steeps and a maximum of 40 people per day allowed on the vast and challenging terrain, Silverton Mountain gained instant cult status with some of the country's best skiers. Fans say the experience is like heli-skiing without a chopper. From the 10,400-foot base, the lift ascends to 12,300 feet, and you can hike up to 13,300 feet if you want an extra-long run. ✉ *Route110A* ☎ *970/387–5706* ⊕ *www. silvertonmountain.com* ✉ *$99.*

ICE SKATING

At the Kendall Mountain Recreation Area, the **Silverton Town Rink** (✉ 14th St. ☎ no phone) lets you skate for free, weather permitting. You can rent skates at the visitor center.

FOUR-WHEEL DRIVING

Silverton provides easy access to such popular four-wheel-drive routes as Ophir Pass to the Telluride side of the San Juans, Stony Pass to the Rio Grande Valley, and Engineer and Cinnamon Passes, components of the Alpine Loop. With an all-terrain vehicle you can see some of Colorado's most famous ghost towns, remnants of mining communities, and jaw-dropping scenery. The four-wheeling season is May to mid-October, weather-permitting. In winter, these unplowed trails are transformed into fabulous snowmobile routes.

Silver Summit RV Park (✉ 640 Mineral St. ☎ 800/352–1637 or 970/387–0240 ⊕ www.silversummitrvpark.com) rents four-wheelers for about $150. Full-day tours with a guide cost about $100 per person. **Triangle Jeep Rental** (✉ 864 Greene St. ☎ 970/387–9990 or 877/522–2354 ⊕ www.trianglejeeprental.com) rents four-wheel-drive vehicles for about $125 a day.

NORDIC SKIING

The local snowmobile club grooms a cross-country skiing and snowshoeing loop completely around Silverton, so the route is flat, easy, and safe. Molas Pass, 6 mi south of Silverton on U.S. 550, offers a variety of Nordic routes, from easy half-milers in broad valleys to longer, more demanding ascents.

St. Paul Lodge (✉ Box 463, Silverton 81433 ☎ 970/387–5494) is an incredible find for anyone enchanted by remote high country. Above 11,000 feet and about a half-hour ski-in from the summit of Red Mountain Pass between Ouray and Silverton, the lodge (a converted mining camp) provides access to a series of above-treeline bowls and basins. Included in the lodge rates are guide service (essential in this area), ski equipment, and telemark lessons, along with meals and lodging. Be prepared for rather primitive facilities.

Where to Stay & Eat

$–$$ ✗ **Handlebars.** As much a museum as an eatery, the restaurant is crammed with mining artifacts, odd antiques, and mounted animals—including a full-grown elk. One specialty you shouldn't pass up is the huge platter of baby-back ribs basted with the restaurant's barbecue sauce. (If you like the sauce as much as the locals do, buy a bottle). The hearty menu also includes steaks, hamburgers, chicken, pasta, mashed potatoes, and more. On weekends, the action heats up on the dance floor with rock and country bands. ✉ *117 13th St.* ☎ *970/387–5395* ▭ *D, MC, V* ☺ *Closed Nov.–Apr.*

$ ✕ **Avalanche Coffee House.** This warm and cozy hangout is the place for delicious coffees, freshly made baked goods, and a chance to mingle with the locals. House-made deli sandwiches, soups, and quiches make for filling lunches. More substantial fare is served Friday and Saturday evening. Happy hour starts at 5:30, so be sure to grab your seat at the bar. ✉ *1067 Blair St.* ☎ *970/387–5282* ▭ *No credit cards* ☺ *Closed Mon. No dinner Sun.–Thurs.*

$$–$$$ 🏨 **Wyman Hotel & Inn.** Listed on the National Register of Historic Places, this wonderful red-sandstone building dates from 1902. It has 24-inch-thick walls, so the builders obviously expected it to last a while. The attractive rooms, many with beautiful arched windows, are filled with period antiques. Five have whirlpool tubs, where you can soak after a morning on the slopes. In summer, you can opt to stay in a romantically refurbished caboose with private hot tub. Full breakfast and afternoon tea are included. The dining room serves some of Silverton's best and most interesting cuisine. ✉ *1371 Greene St., 81433* ☎ *970/387–5372 or 800/609–7845* 🖷 *970/387–5745* ⊕ *www.thewyman.com* ⬗ *13 rooms, 4 suites* ⬙ *In-room VCRs* ▭ *AE, D, MC, V* ⊦⊙⊣ *BP.*

$–$$ 🏨 **Wingate House Bed & Breakfast.** Owner Judy Graham, a prominent landscape artist, adorns the walls of this beautifully restored inn with her own work and family photos dating from the Civil War. The effect is both sophisticated and homey. The breezy front porch overlooks Kendall Mountain, a majestic "thirteener" (a mountain higher than 13,000 feet). Large, sunny rooms are filled with antiques and beds piled with down pillows and comforters. An eclectic library stocks books culled from Judy's journeys. A well-set dining room table is the scene of breakfast, with freshly ground coffee and home-baked treats. ✉ *1045 Snowden St., 81433* ☎ *970/387–5520* 🖷 *970/387–5520* ⊕ *www. wingatehouse.com* ⬗ *5 rooms, 3 with bath* ⬙ *Dining room, hot tub* ▭ *MC, V* ⊦⊙⊣ *CP.*

The Arts

In the Miners Union Theatre, **A Theatre Group** (✉ 1069 Greene St. ☎ 970/387–5337 or 800/752–4494) stages a summer repertory season running from May to October and a winter season lasting from December to April.

Shopping

Remember that the majority of Silverton's retail establishments only operate in the months when the Durango & Silverton Narrow Gauge Railroad is operating. **Blair Street Emporium** (✉ 1147 Blair St. ☎ 970/ 387–5323) specializes in all manner of Christmas ornaments, lights, and decorations. The gift shop **My Favorite Things** (✉ 1145 Greene St. ☎ 970/ 387–5643) stocks porcelain dolls, antique jewelry, and romantic, lacy wearables.

en route   The tortuous route between SIlverton and Purgatory includes a dizzying series of switchbacks as it climbs over Coal Bank Pass and Molas Pass and past splendid views of the Grand Turks, the Needles Range, and Crater Lake. This is prime mountain-biking and four-wheeling territory.

Purgatory

❾ *20 mi from Silverton via U.S. 550 north; 25 mi from Durango via U.S. 550 north.*

North of the U.S. 160 and U.S. 550 junction are two well-known recreational playgrounds: the ravishing golf course and development at the Lodge at Tamarron, and Purgatory at Durango Mountain Resort. Purgatory, as everyone still calls this ski area despite its recent name change, is about as down-home as a ski resort can get. The clientele includes cowboys, families, and college students on break.

Downhill Skiing & Snowboarding

Purgatory at Durango Mountain Resort (formerly known simply as Purgatory) has plenty of intermediate runs and glade and tree skiing. What's unique about Purgatory is its stepped terrain: lots of humps and dips and steep pitches followed by virtual flats. This trail profile makes it easier for skiers and snowboarders to stay in control (or simply get their legs back under them after they've conquered a section a little steeper than they might be accustomed to). A great powder day on the mountain's backside will convince anyone that Purgatory isn't just "Pleasant Ridge," as it's somewhat condescendingly known in Crested Butte and Telluride.

The truth is that Purgatory is just plain fun, and return visitors like it that way. The ski area is perfect for families and those who enjoy skiing or snowboarding but are open to other diversions. Purgatory's innovative Total Adventure Ticket lets you trade a portion of the multiday lift ticket for a guided snowshoe tour, a ride on the Durango & Silverton Narrow Gauge Railroad, an afternoon of cross-country skiing, an excursion to the Sky Ute Casino, a soak and massage at Trimble Hot Springs, or a horse-drawn dinner sleigh ride.

For a bit more money, skiers and snowboarders can explore 35,000 acres of untamed wilderness with the San Juan Ski Company's snow cat operation. For a gentler diversion, there's cross-country skiing on 26 mi of machine-groomed trails just outside the main ski area. ⊠ *U.S. 550* ☎ *970/247–9000 or 800/568–3275* ⊕ *www.durangomountainresort. com* ☉ *Late Nov.–early Apr., daily 9–4.*

FACILITIES 2,029-foot vertical drop; 1,200 skiable acres; 23% beginner, 51% intermediate, 26% advanced; 1 high-speed 6-passenger chair; 1 high-speed quad chair, 4 triple chairs, 3 double chairs, 1 surface lift, and 1 moving carpet (beginners' lift).

LESSONS & Purgatory's **Adult Adventure School** (☎ 970/385–2149) offers 2½-hr
PROGRAMS group lessons for everyone from newcomers to experts at 9:45 and 1:15 each day during the season. The cost is $35. There are also daily lessons in snowbiking and twice-monthly lessons in telemark skiing.

Teaching children to ski or snowboard is a cinch at **Kids Mountain Adventure** (☎ 970/385–2149). There are three age-appropriate classes for kids 3 to 12 years old. There's also child care for those between 2 months and 3 years. A full day costs $75.

LIFT TICKETS The at-the-window rates are $52 to $55 for a one-day lift ticket. An All-Mountain Ski Package is a good deal for experienced skiers, as it combines a half-day morning or afternoon ski lesson, rental of skis, and an all-day lift ticket. The cost is $99.

RENTALS **Bubba's Boards** (⊠ Village Plaza ☎ 970/259–7377) is Durango Mountain Resort's full-service snowboard shop. Rentals begin at $32 per day.

Performance Peak (☎ 970/247–9000) rents top-of-the-line demo and retail skis and boots from K2, Salomon, Dynastar, Volkl, Nordica, Dolomite, and Rossignol; full packages (skis, boots, and poles) begin at $39. Snowshoe rentals are $12. The shop also offers custom boot fitting, ski tuning, and equipment repair.

Purgatory Rentals (✉ Village Center ☎ 970/385–2182) offers skis, boots, and poles, as well as other equipment. Rates begin at $21 per day for the basic package, rising to $29 for the high-performance package.

Other Sports & the Outdoors

GOLF The splendid **Glacier Club at Tamarron** (✉ 40290 U.S. 550 N ☎ 970/382–6700 or 866/375–8300) has 27 holes of scenic masters-level golf near the spectacular Hermosa Cliffs. This club, part of the Lodge at Tamarron, is considered one of the country's top resort courses. Public greens fees are $60 to $109, including cart rental.

SNOWMOBILING **Snowmobile Adventures** (✉ Village Center ☎ 970/247–9000 or 970/385–2110) offers guided snowmobile tours on more than 60 mi of nearby trails.

Where to Stay & Eat

$$$$ ✕ **Café Cascade.** Many locals say this is the best restaurant on the mountain, if not in the entire region. The intimate, split-level eatery features the Southwestern stylings of chef Roy Griffiths. The menu has become more affordable in recent years. Try the roast Colorado lamb accompanied by grilled Anasazi beans, or grilled elk tenderloin served over wild mushrooms in a lingonberry-merlot sauce. Served with peanut sauce, the rabbit *satay* (Thai-style barbecue) is a sterling starter. ✉ *50827 U.S. 550 N, 1 mi north of Purgatory, Cascade Village* ☎ *970/259–3500* 🚫 *AE, D, DC, MC, V* ⊘ *No lunch.*

★ $$$$ ✕ **Sow's Ear.** It's a toss-up between the Ore House in downtown Durango and this watering hole in the Silverpick Lodge for the area's "best steak house" award. The Sow's Ear has the edge, though, for its great views of the mountain. If you prefer more action, there's also an open kitchen in the dining area where you can view your meal being prepared. The mouthwatering, fresh-baked jalapeño-cheese rolls and honey-wheat rolls, and creative entrées such as blackened filet mignon are a few more reasons Sow's Ear leads the pack. Complement your meal with a selection from their extensive domestic wine list. ✉ *48475 U.S. 550 N.* ☎ *970/247–3527* ⚭ *Reservations essential* 🚫 *AE, D, MC, V* ⊘ *Closed mid-Mar.–Memorial Day and Labor Day–mid-Dec.*

$$$$ ▦ **The Lodge at Tamarron.** This handsome lodge, on 750 acres surrounded by the San Juan National Forest, fits in beautifully with the natural environment. The sprawling main lodge seems to be an extension of the nearby Hermosa Cliffs. The well-appointed rooms are a blend of frontier architecture and Southwestern decor, and nearly all feature a fireplace, a full kitchen, and a private terrace. The lodge is famed for having one of the country's most beautiful championship golf courses, and tennis and horseback riding are also popular pastimes. ✉ *18 mi north of Durango on U.S. 550* 🗄 *Drawer 3131, 81302* ☎ *970/259–2000 or 800/678–1000* 🖷 *970/382–7899* 🌐 *www.tamarron.com* 🛏 *412 rooms* ♿ *2 restaurants, 27-hole golf course, 3 tennis courts, indoor-outdoor pool, hot tub, spa, horseback riding, bar* 🚫 *AE, D, DC, MC, V.*

$–$$$ ▦ **Durango Mountain Resort.** This comfortable slopeside lodging has generously proportioned rooms decorated with Native American rugs and prints. If you want a bit of pampering, the one- and two-bedroom condos have wood-burning fireplaces and whirlpool baths. ✉ *5 Skier Pl., 81302* ☎ *970/385–2100 or 800/693–0175* 🖷 *970/382–2248*

⊕ www.durangomountainresort.com ⤏ 133 rooms ⌂ 2 restaurants, some kitchens, pool, 2 hot tubs, bar ⊟ AE, D, MC, V.

CONDOMINIUMS There are 110 beautiful apartments at **Cascade Village** (⊠ 50827 U.S. 550 N, 81301 ☎ 970/259–3500 or 800/525–0896), about 1½ mi north of the ski area.

Nightlife

Check out **Purgy's** (⊠ Village Center ☎ 970/247–9000), which attracts a lively, youthful crowd and hosts bands on weekends.

Shopping

Honeyville (⊠ 33633 U.S. 550 N, Hermosa ☎ 800/676–7690) south of Durango Mountain Resort, sells jams, jellies (try the chokecherry), condiments, and, of course, honey. You can watch how the bees go about their work in glass hives and listen to a lecture by a fully garbed beekeeper.

en route · U.S. 550 toward Durango parallels the Animas River and the tracks of Durango & Silverton Narrow Gauge Railroad. The famous *Butch Cassidy and the Sundance Kid* scene in which the outlaws, with pursuers hot on their trail, leap from a high cliff into the river far below was filmed in this canyon.

FOUR CORNERS

Durango

🔟 *25 mi from Purgatory via U.S. 550 north; 45 mi from Cortez via U.S. 160 east; 62 mi from Pagosa Springs via U.S. 160 west.*

Wisecracking Will Rogers had this to say about Durango: "It's out of the way and glad of it." His statement is a bit unfair, considering that as a railroad town Durango has always been a cultural crossroads and melting pot (as well as a place to raise hell). It was founded in 1879 by General William Palmer, president of the all-powerful Denver & Rio Grande Railroad, when nearby Animas City haughtily refused to donate land for a depot. Within a decade Durango had completely absorbed its rival. The booming town quickly became the region's main metropolis and a gateway to the Southwest. A walking tour of the historic downtown bears eloquent witness to Durango's prosperity during the late 19th century. The northern end of Main Avenue offers the usual assortment of cheap motels and fast-food outlets, all evidence of Durango's present status as the major hub for tourism in the area.

The intersection of 13th Avenue and Main Avenue (locals also refer to it is Main Street) marks the northern edge of Durango's **National Historic District**. Old-fashioned streetlights line the streets, casting a warm glow on the elegant Victorians now filled with upscale galleries, restaurants, and the occasional factory outlet store. The three-story sandstone **Newman Building** (⊠ 8th St. and Main Ave.) is one of the elegant edifices restored to their original grandeur. Dating from 1887, the **Strater Hotel** (⊠ 7th St. and Main Ave.) is a reminder of when this town was a stop for many people headed west. Awash in flocked wallpaper and lace, the hotel's Diamond Belle Saloon is dominated by a gilt-and-mahogany bar. A player piano and scantily clad waitresses call to mind an old-time honky-tonk. The **Durango Depot** (⊠ 4th St. and Main Ave.), dating from 1882, is a must for those who dream of riding the rails.

The **Third Avenue National Historic District** (known simply as "The Boulevard"), two blocks east of Main Avenue, contains several Victorian residences, ranging from the imposing mansions built by railroad barons to more modest variations erected by well-to-do merchants. The hodge-podge of styles veers from Greek revival to Gothic revival to Queen Anne to Spanish Colonial and Mission designs.

The most entertaining way to relive the halcyon days of the Old West is to take a ride on the **Durango & Silverton Narrow Gauge Railroad,** a 9-hour, round-trip journey along the 45-mi railway to Silverton. You'll travel in comfort in lovingly restored coaches or in the open-air cars called gondolas as you listen to the train's shrill whistle as it chugs along. You get a good look at the Animas Valley, which in some parts is broad and green and in others is narrow and rimmed with rock. The train runs from mid-May to late October, with four departures daily between June and August and one daily at other times. A shorter excursion—to Cascade Canyon—is available in winter. ⊠ *479 Main Ave.* ☎ *970/247–2733 or 888/872–4607* ⊕ *www.durangotrain.com* ✉ *$60.*

About 7 mi north of Durango, **Trimble Hot Springs** is a great place to soak your aching bones, especially if you've been doing some hiking. The complex includes an Olympic-size swimming pool and three natural mineral pools ranging from 83° to 107°. Massage and spa treatments are also available. ⊠ *County Rd. 203, off U.S. 550* ☎ *970/247–0111* ⊕ *www.trimblehotsprings.com* ☉ *Daily 8–11* ✉ *$9.*

High on a mesa southeast of Durango, **Fort Lewis College,** brings a bit of culture to the Four Corners area. The Center for Southwest Studies gallery has rotating exhibitions of contemporary artists, Native American treasures, and Western-cultural collections. **The Art Gallery** (☎ 970/247–7167 ☉ Weekdays 10–4) is a beautifully lighted contemporary space showcasing the creations of a creative and diverse student body. ⊠ *1000 Rim Dr.* ☎ *970/247–7456* ⊕ *www.fortlewiscollege.edu.*

Sports & the Outdoors

The **San Juan Public Lands Center** (⊠ 15 Burnett Ct., 80301 ☎ 970/247–4874 ☉ Weekdays 8–5) gives out information on hiking, fishing, and camping, as well as cross-country skiing, snowshoeing, and snowmobile routes. This office also stocks maps and guidebooks. Contact the rangers of the **San Juan National Forest** (⊠ 15 Burnett Ct., Durango 80301 ☎ 970/247–4874 ⊕ www.fs.fed.us/r2/sanjuan) for information about rock-climbing and other outdoor activities in the San Juan Mountains.

BICYCLING Being a college town, Durango is extremely bike-friendly. Many locals consider bikes to be their main form of transportation, and mountain biking is a particularly popular recreational activity. **Mountain Bike Specialists** (⊠ 949 Main Ave. ☎ 970/247–4066 ⊕ www.mountainbikespecialists.com) rents bikes and arranges tours of the area.

CLIMBING **Southwest Adventures** (⊠ 1205 Camino del Rio ☎ 970/259–0370 ⊕ www.mtnguide.net) is a climbing school that takes you to some of the area's most beautiful peaks. Other programs include rock climbing, ice climbing, Nordic skiing, snowshoeing, and mountaineering.

FISHING In business since 1983, **Duranglers** (⊠ 923 Main Ave. ☎ 970/385–4081 ⊕ www.duranglers.com) sells rods and reels, gives fly-fishing lessons, and runs custom trips to top fishing spots in the area, including the San Juan River in nearby northern New Mexico.

GOLF About 6 mi north of Durango, the **Dalton Ranch Golf Club** (⊠ 589 County Rd. 252, off U.S. 550 ☎ 970/247–7921 ⊕ www.daltonranch.com) is a Ken Dye–designed 18-hole championship course with inspiring panoramas of red-rock cliffs. Dalton's Grill has become a popular hangout for locals who like watching the resident elk herd take its afternoon stroll, especially in late fall and winter. The golf season here is mid-March to late October, weather permitting. Greens fees are $79.

The **Hillcrest Golf Course** (⊠ 2300 Rim Dr. ☎ 970/247–1499) is an 18-hole public course perched on a mesa near the campus of Fort Lewis College. The course is open from March to December, weather permitting. Greens fees are $25.

HORSEBACK RIDING **Southfork Stables & Outfitters** (⊠ 28481 U.S. 160 ☎ 970/259–4871 ⊕ www.durangohorses.com) offers guided trail rides in summer and one-hour trips to view an elk herd in winter. You can also take part in cattle drives.

RAFTING **Durango Rivertrippers** (⊠ 720 Main Ave. ☎ 970/259–0289 ⊕ www.durangorivertrippers.com) runs two- and four-hour trips down the Animas River, as well as 2- to 10-day wilderness expeditions on the Dolores River.

TENNIS There are 10 free public tennis courts in Durango: six at Durango High School (2390 N. Main Ave.) and two at Needham Elementary School (2425 W. Third St.) and at the Mason Center (301 E. 12th St.). Information is available from **Durango Parks and Recreation Department** (☎ 970/385–2950 ⊕ www.durango.gov.org).

Where to Stay & Eat

$$–$$$$ ✕ **Ore House.** Durango is a meat-and-potatoes kind of town, and this is Durango's idea of a steak house. The aroma of beef smacks you in the face as you walk past. This local favorite serves enormous slabs of aged Angus that are hand-cut daily. If you are watching your cholesterol, better steer clear. ⊠ *147 E. College Dr.* ☎ *970/247–5707* ▭ *D, MC, V.*

$$–$$$$ ✕ **The Red Snapper.** If you're in the mood for fresh fish, head to this congenial place, which is full of saltwater aquariums. Try the oysters Durango, with jack cheese and salsa; salmon Wellington; or snapper Monterey, with jack cheese and tarragon. Delicious steaks and prime rib are also available. The salad bar is enormous. ⊠ *144 E. 9th St.* ☎ *970/259–3417* ▭ *AE, MC, V* ☉ *No lunch.*

$–$$$ ✕ **Ariano's.** This popular northern Italian restaurant occupies a dimly lit room plastered with local art. It offers a selection of pastas that are made fresh daily. Try the veal scallopini with fresh sage and garlic or the fettuccine Alfredo. ⊠ *150 E. College Dr.* ☎ *970/247–8146* ▭ *AE, D, DC, MC, V* ☉ *No lunch.*

★ $–$$ ✕ **Ken & Sue's Place.** This might well be Durango's favorite restaurant. Locals are wild for the artfully prepared contemporary cuisine enlivened with a light touch of Asian and Southwestern accents. Try the pistachio nut–crusted grouper with vanilla-rum butter, or lemon-pepper linguine. ⊠ *937 Main Ave.* ☎ *970/259–2616* ☉ *No lunch weekends* ▭ *AE, D, DC MC, V.*

$ ✕ **Carver's Bakery & Brew Pub.** This microbrewery run by the "Brews Brothers," Bill and Jim Carver, has about eight beers on tap at any given time, including such flavors as Raspberry Wheat Ale, Jackrabbit Pale Ale, and Colorado Trail Nut Brown Ale. If you're feeling peckish, try one of the bread bowls filled with soup or salad. There's a patio out back where you can soak up the sun. From breakfast to the wee hours, the place is always hopping. ⊠ *1022 Main Ave.* ☎ *970/259–2545* ⌂ *Reservations not accepted* ▭ *AE, D, MC, V.*

$–$$$$ ▤ **Strater Hotel.** This grand dame opened for business in 1887, and a
Fodor'sChoice loving restoration has restored her luster. Inside, the Diamond Belle
★ Saloon glitters with crystal chandeliers, beveled-glass windows, rustic oak beams, flocked wallpaper, and plush velvety curtains. The individually decorated rooms are swooningly exquisite: after all, the hotel

owns the country's largest collection of Victorian walnut antiques and has its own wood-carving shop to create exact period reproductions. Your room might have entertained Butch Cassidy, Louis L'Amour (he wrote *The Sacketts* here), Francis Ford Coppola, John Kennedy, or Marilyn Monroe (the latter two stayed here at separate times). ✉ *699 Main Ave., 81301* ☎ *970/247–4431 or 800/247–4431* 🖷 *970/259–2208* ⊕ *www.strater.com* ⇥ *93 rooms* ⚴ *Restaurant, hot tub, bar* ⊟ *AE, D, DC, MC, V.*

$$–$$$ 🏨 **New Rochester Hotel.** This one-time flophouse is funky yet chic, thanks to the mother-and-son team of Diane and Kirk Komick, who rescued some of the original furnishings. Steamer trunks, hand-painted settees, wagon-wheel chandeliers, and fluffy quilts contribute to the authentic feel. Windows from Denver & Rio Grande Railroad carriages convert the back porch into a parlor car, and gas lamps beneath the towering maple trees add a warm glow to the courtyard. If there's no room here, the owners also run the nearby Leland House B & B. A full gourmet breakfast is served to guests of both establishments. ✉ *726 E. 2nd Ave., 81301* ☎ *970/385–1920 or 800/664–1920* 🖷 *970/385–1967* ⊕ *www.rochesterhotel.com* ⇥ *17 rooms, 8 suites* ⚴ *Restaurant, kitchenettes, massage* ⊟ *MC, V* ❄ *BP.*

★ $$ 🏨 **Apple Orchard Inn.** About 8 mi from downtown Durango, this little gem sits on five acres in the lush Animas Valley. The main house and six cottages surround a flower-bedecked pond, complete with friendly geese. Cherry-wood antiques, fluffy feather beds, and handcrafted armoires add a graceful touch to the handsome rooms. In the evening, relax on your cottage swing, enjoying views of the surrounding cliffs. The owners' experience at European cooking schools is evident in the breakfasts—and in the "train cookies" sometimes sent along with guests who make the journey to Silverton. ✉ *7758 County Rd. 203, 81301* ☎ *970/247–0751 or 800/426–0751* 🖷 *970/385–6976* ⊕ *www.appleorchardinn. com* ⇥ *10 rooms* ⚴ *Hot tub* ⊟ *D, MC, V* ❄ *BP.*

$–$$ 🏨 **Comfort Inn.** This is one of the nicer properties along Durango's strip, because it's clean, comfortable, and has sizable rooms. The hot tubs are nice after a day on the slopes. ✉ *2930 N. Main St., 81301* ☎ *970/259–5373* 🖷 *970/259–1546* ⊕ *www.choicehotel.com/durangohotel.com* ⇥ *48 rooms* ⚴ *Pool, 2 hot tubs* ⊟ *AE, D, DC, MC, V.*

Nightlife & the Arts

THE ARTS   The **Diamond Circle Theater** (✉ 699 Main Ave. ☎ 970/247–4431) stages rip-roaring melodramas all summer long. The **Durango Lively Arts Co.** (✉ 802 2nd Ave. ☎ 970/259–2606) presents fine community theater productions.

The **Fort Lewis College Community Concert Hall** (☎ 970/247–7162) is a modern 600-seat auditorium that hosts local, regional, and touring performers. The college's outdoor amphitheater is the setting for the **Durango Shakespeare Festival** (☎ 970/247–7410).

BARS & CLUBS   Even though it opened more than a century ago, the hottest spot in town is still the **Diamond Belle Saloon** (✉ 699 Main Ave. ☎ 970/247–4431). The honky-tonk player piano and waitresses dressed as 1880s saloon girls pack them in to this spot in the Strater Hotel. **Lady Falconburgh's Barley Exchange** (✉ 640 Main Ave. ☎ 970/382–9664) is a favorite with locals. The pub serves more than 140 types of beer.

CASINOS   About 25 mi southeast of Durango, the **Sky Ute Casino & Lodge** (✉ 14826 Hwy. 172 N, Ignacio ☎ 970/563–3000 or 800/876–7017 ⊕ www. skyutecasino.com), offers limited-stakes gambling. There are 400 slot machines and tables for blackjack, poker, and bingo. Call for free shuttle service from Durango.

DINNER SHOWS   The **Bar D Chuckwagon** (✉ 8080 County Rd. 250, East Animas Valley
☎ 970/247–5753) serves up mouthwatering barbecued beef, beans,
and biscuits. Many people head to this spot 9 mi from Durango to hear
the Bar D Wranglers sing.

Shopping

BOOKS   **Maria's Bookshop** (✉ 960 Main Ave. ☎ 970/247–1438 ⊕ www.
mariasbookshop.com) specializes in regional literature and nonfiction.

BOUTIQUES   **Appaloosa Trading Co.** (✉ 501 Main Ave. ☎ 970/259–1994 ⊕ www.
appaloosadurango.com) is one of the best venues for all things leather,
from purses to saddles, hats to boots. The exotic belts are especially nice
when paired with sterling silver buckles. The shop also sells locally produced weavings and other handicrafts. **O'Farrell Hatmakers of Durango**
(✉ 399 Camino Iglesia ☎ 970/259–5900 ⊕ www.offarrellhats.com)
makes fine custom hats made of everything from straw to palm leafs to
beaver pelts. Your best bet is probably an old-fashioned cowboy hat or
fedora. **Shirt Off My Back** (✉ 680 Main Ave. ☎ 970/247–9644) sells T-
shirts silk-screened while you wait. You have your choice of some 60
images of elk, horses, bears, mountains, and wildflowers.

GALLERIES   The selection of arts and crafts from Mexico and elsewhere is remarkable at **Artesanos** (✉ 700 E. 2nd Ave. ☎ 970/259–5755 ⊕ www.
artesanosdesign.com). **Dietz Market** (✉ 26345 U.S. 160 ☎ 970/259–
5811 or 800/321–6069) carries pottery, metalwork, candles, weavings,
and foodstuffs, all celebrating the region. **Hellbent Leather & Silver** (✉ 741
Main Ave. ☎ 970/247–9088 ⊕ www.hellbentleather.com) makes its
own leather handbags and also sells imported pottery and tiles and other
handicrafts.

Toh-Atin Gallery (✉ 145 W. 9th St. ☎ 970/247–8277 ⊕ www.toh-atin.
com) is one of the best Native American galleries in Colorado, specializing in Navajo rugs and weavings. There is also a wide range of paintings, pottery, and prints.

en route   At the junction of U.S. 550 and U.S. 160 you have three options:
pick up U.S. 550 north toward Purgatory, head U.S. 160 west
toward Cortez, or follow U.S. 160 east toward Pagosa Springs.
About 35 mi east of Durango is the Highway 151 turnoff south to
Chimney Rock Archeological Area (☎ 970/264–2268 ⊕ www.
chimneyrockco.org). Twin spires of rock loom over pueblo ruins
that architecturally are more closely related to the sites around
Chaco Canyon in New Mexico than to those in Mesa Verde
National Park. Anthropologists debate whether the structures served
as a trading post or an astronomical observatory, but archeologists
have determined that this high mesa was also an active agricultural
area. Whatever their heritage, many believe that the ruins retain
their power and resonance. Between May 1 and September 15,
access to the site is possible only with a U.S. Forest Service guide.
Reservations are necessary for the free tour. Monthly programs
include four to six hour interpretive hikes to unexcavated sites and
full-moon tours of the ruins. Sunrise programs at summer solstice
and autumn equinox are special times to visit. In the off-season, you
can walk, ski, or snowshoe up the 3-mi unplowed road to the ruins.

Mesa Verde National Park

⓫ *10 mi from Cortez via U.S. 160 east.*

FodorsChoice
★   Cortez is the western gateway to Mesa Verde National Park, an 80-square-
mi nature preserve that is one of the nation's most riveting attractions.

In 1888, two ranchers—Richard Wetherill and Charlie Mason—set off in search of stray cattle and stumbled upon the remarkable and perfectly preserved Cliff Palace, apartment-style cliff dwellings built into the canyon walls. By the end of the next day they had discovered two more major sites: Spruce Tree House and Square Tower House. Excitement over their find culminated in the 1906 creation of the national park, making it the nation's first park established to preserve the works of humans.

Mesa Verde is one of the state's highlights, so it's not surprising that it is often packed. Consider visiting in the spring or fall (although some of the ruins are closed then) or overnighting in the park so that you can avoid the crowds. If you must visit in mid-summer, arrive early in the day to avoid the mid-day heat. You can pick up information on the park and accommodations at the entrance on U.S. 160. From here a 15-mi drive corkscrews up the mesa, skirting canyons and plateaus, to the Far View Visitor Center. Here you can head in one of two directions. The scenic route to **Wetherill Mesa,** open Memorial Day to Labor Day, has great views of the Shiprock Formation in New Mexico and Monument Valley in Arizona and Utah. A tram that takes you to the ruins departs every half hour between 8:55 AM and 4:55 PM from the Wetherill Mesa parking lot. Self-guided and ranger-led tours of Long House, the second-largest dwelling in the park, are also options. The other route from the Far View Visitor Center, **Ruins Road,** accesses the major sites on Chapin Mesa. If you don't want to hike down into the canyons to view the ruins up close (which requires a free ticket available at the visitor center), this drive still offers several strategically placed scenic overlooks.

The first stop on the Ruins Road is the park's informative archaeological museum, which traces the development of an Ancestral Puebloan culture. It's a short walk from the museum to one of the most extraordinary sites, **Spruce Tree House,** the only ruin that is open year-round. Climb down into an excavated kiva, symbolic of the womb of Mother Earth, for a better sense of how the Ancestral Puebloans worshipped.

From the museum trailhead, one loop leads to the most famous ruin, the **Cliff Palace,** the largest dwelling of its kind in the world. It's accessible by a moderately strenuous 15-minute hike. It also leads to the more remote Balcony House, reached by an arduous trek into the canyon below. Ranger-led tours are available. The other loop brings you to two major ruins, **Sun Temple** and **Square Tower House,** both involving a significant amount of walking and climbing. ⊠ *U.S. 160* ☎ *970/529–4465* ⊕ *www.nps.gov/meve* ⊠ *$10 per vehicle* ⊙ *Park late May–early Sept., daily 8–6:30; early Sept.–mid-Oct., daily 9–6:30; mid-Oct.–early Apr., daily 9–5; early Apr.–early May, daily 9–6:30. Visitor Center May–Sept., daily 8–5.*

off the beaten path

MUD CREEK HOGAN – Driving east on U.S. 160 from Mesa Verde National Park will take you past this endearing bit of classic American kitsch. More than a dozen enormous arrows stuck in the ground mark the spot of this hokey trading post and museum, where you get the feeling that everything is for sale. The grounds are adorned with tepees and a giant plastic horse. Beside the shop is a recreation of a frontier town, complete with saloon, hotel, bank, jail, and livery station. Don't breathe too hard or you'll blow the town over: the paper-thin buildings don't exist past the facades. ⊠ *U.S. 160* ☎ *970/533–7117.*

Sports & the Outdoors

CAMPING Plenty of campsites are available in Mesa Verde. Contact the **National Park Service** (⌂ Box 8, Mesa Verde 81330 ☎ 970/529–4461 ⊕ www. nps.gov/meve). About 4 mi from the park's entrance, **Morefield Campground** (⌂ Box 277, Moncos 81328 ☎ 970/533–1944 or 800/449–2288 ⊕ www.visitmesaverde.com) has campsites on a first-come, first-served basis. Amenities include a general store, gas station, coin laundry, gift shop, and snack bar.

HORSEBACK **Rimrock Outfitters** (✉ 1275 County Rd. 44, Mancos 81328 ☎ 970/533–
RIDING 7588 ⊕ www.rimrockoutfitters.com) provides horses for tours ranging from gentle one-hour rides to more strenuous overnight excursions. Evening rides including steak dinners served on the open range. Rates begin at $20.

Where to Stay & Eat

$–$$ ✕ **Millwood Junction.** Folks come from four states (no fooling) for the phenomenal Friday-night seafood buffet at Millwood Junction. If that wasn't enough, there's also a 25-item salad bar. Steaks are grilled to perfection in this upscale eatery. ✉ *U.S. 160 and Main St., Mancos* ☎ *970/ 533–7338* ▭ *MC, V.*

★ $$ ⊡ **Far View Lodge.** Talk about a view—this lodge has balconies where you can admire the neighboring states of Arizona, Utah, and New Mexico. Soothing desert pastels predominate in the nicely decorated rooms. Another draw here is the hotel's enthusiastic guided tours of Mesa Verde National Park. There are also nightly talks by experts on Native American culture and a multimedia show on the Ancestral Puebloan people. The Metate Room, the lodge's main dining room, is acclaimed for its fine steaks and excellent Southwestern fare. ⌂ *Box 277, Mancos 81328* ☎ *970/529–4421 or 800/449–2288* ⊟ *970/529–4411* ⊕ *www. visitmesaverde.com* ⊷ *150 rooms* ⚮ *Restaurant, travel services* ▭ *AE, D, DC, MC, V* ☉ *Closed mid-Oct.–mid-Apr.*

Cortez

⑫ *45 mi from Durango via U.S. 160 west; 10 mi from Dolores via Rte. 145 south and U.S. 160 west.*

The northern escarpment of Mesa Verde and the volcanic blisters of the La Plata Mountains to the west dominate sprawling Cortez. A series of Days Inns, Dairy Queens, and Best Westerns, the town has a layout that seems to have been determined by neon-sign and aluminum-siding salesmen of the 1950s. Hidden among these eyesores, however, are fine galleries and a host of second-hand shops that can yield surprising finds.

The exterior of the excellent **Cortez Cultural Center** has been painted to resemble the cliff dwellings of Mesa Verde. Exhibits focus on regional artists and artisans, the Ute Mountain branch of the Ute tribe, and various periods of Ancestral Puebloan culture. The Cultural Park at the Cortez Cultural Center contains an authentic Navajo hogan and a Ute tepee. The park itself is open 9 to 5; admission is free. Summer evenings there are Native American dances; sandpainting, rug weaving, and pottery-making demonstrations; theatrical events; and storytelling. ✉ *25 N. Market St.* ☎ *970/565–1151* ⊕ *www.cortezculturalcenter.org* ▨ *Free* ☉ *June–Aug., Mon.–Sat. 10–10; Sept.–May, Mon.–Sat. 10–5.*

Visitor information is available at the **Colorado Welcome Center** (✉ Cortez City Park, 928 E. Main St. ☎ 970/565–3414 or 800/253–1616 ⊕ www. mesaverdecountry.com).

off the
beaten
path

FOUR CORNERS MONUMENT – A brass plaque set on a granite platform surrounded by four state flags marks the only spot where four states—Colorado, Arizona, Utah, and New Mexico—meet at a single point. This is photo-op country. Snacks and souvenirs are sold by Native Americans from rickety wood booths. To get here, travel south from Cortez on U.S. 160 for about 40 mi. You can't miss the signs. ✛ *U.S. 160* ☎ *no phone* ⊕ *www.navajonationparks.org* ☒ *$2 per vehicle* ☉ *Daily 8–6.*

Sports & the Outdoors

GOLF The **Conquistador Golf Course** (☒ 2018 N. Dolores Rd., Cortez ☎ 970/565–9208 ⊕ www.buydurango.com/conquistador.htm) is an 18-hole public course with sweeping views of Mesa Verde and Sleeping Ute Mountain. Greens fees are a modest $15, and an additional $19 gets you a golf cart.

Where to Stay & Eat

¢ ✕ **M&M Family Restaurant & Truck Stop.** Semis and RVs jammed into the parking lot attest that M&M is the real McCoy. If crispy chicken-fried steak and overstuffed enchiladas are your fancy, you'll be thrilled to eat here. Many people return again and again for the huge breakfasts, served 24 hours a day. There are posher restaurants in town, but none better—certainly not at these prices. ☒ *7006 U.S. 160, Cortez* ☎ *970/565–6511* ⌖ *Reservations not accepted* ▭ *AE, D, DC, MC, V.*

$ ▨ **Anasazi Motor Inn.** This is definitely the nicest motel on the strip, mostly because its air-conditioned rooms are spacious and pleasantly decorated in desert colors. The pool is a godsend after a long drive. ☒ *640 S. Broadway, 81312* ☎ *970/565–3773 or 800/972–6232* ☐ *970/565–1027* ⇝ *89 rooms* ⌖ *Restaurant, some microwaves, some refrigerators, pool, hot tub, bar, meeting room, airport shuttle* ▭ *AE, D, DC, MC, V.*

Nightlife

At the base of the legendary Sleeping Ute Mountain, the state's largest casino rings with the sound of more than 500 slot machines. **Ute Mountain Casino** (☒ 3 Weeminuche Dr., Towaoc ☎ 970/565–8800 ⊕ www.utemountainute.com) also draws the crowds bingo, blackjack, and poker (both the live and the video versions). Near Four Corners, the casino is 11 mi south of Cortez on U.S. 160. If you're planning on staying a while, Kuchu's Restaurant and a full-service RV park are next door.

Shopping

Mesa Indian Trading Company (☒ 27601 U.S. Hwy. 160 E ☎ 970/565–4492) sells ceramics from most Southwestern tribes. **Clay Mesa Art Gallery and Studio** (☒ 29 E. Main St. ☎ 970/565–1902) showcases original works by local artists Richard St. John and Lesli Diane. **Notah Dineh Trading Company and Museum** (☒ 345 W. Main St. ☎ 800/444–2024 ⊕ www.notahdineh.com) specializes in rugs, hand-carved katsinas, cradleboards, baskets, beadwork, and silver jewelry. Be sure to stop in the free museum to see relics of the Old West, as well as a noteworthy rug in the Two Grey Hills pattern. **Ute Mountain Pottery Plant** (☒ U.S.160 at U.S. 491, Towaoc ☎ 970/565–8548) invites you to watch the painstaking processes of molding, trimming, cleaning, painting, and glazing pottery before adjourning to the showroom so that you can buy pieces straight from the source.

Dolores

⑬ *75 mi from Telluride via Rte. 145 south; 10 mi from Cortez via U.S. 160 east and Rte. 145 north.*

In 1968, state officials approved the construction of an irrigation dam across the Dolores River, forming the **McPhee Reservoir.** An environmental-impact study concluded that hundreds of potentially valuable archaeo-logical sites would be flooded. This led to federally funded excavations that uncovered the cliff dwellings of Ancestral Puebloan peoples. No one knows for sure why these people abandoned their homes, but most an-thropologists surmise that a combination of drought and overfarming sent them off in search of greener pastures. One current school of thought is that they never disappeared; rather, they live on in the mod-ern Pueblo Indians. Striking similarities between the artwork and cus-toms of the two cultures seem to support this line of thought.

★ ☾ The **Anasazi Heritage Center** houses the finest artifacts culled from more than 1,500 excavations in the region. A full-scale replica of an Ances-tral Puebloan pit-house dwelling that illustrates how the people lived around AD 850. The first explorers to stumble upon Ancestral Puebloan ruins were the Spanish friars Dominguez and Escalante, who set out in 1776 from Santa Fe to find a safe route west to Monterey. The two major ruins at the Anasazi Heritage Center are named for the pair. The Dominguez site is the less impressive of the two, although it is of great archaeological interest because here scientists uncovered extremely rare evidence of a "high-status burial." The Escalante site is a 20-room ma-sonry pueblo standing guard over the McPhee Reservoir. ✉ *27501 Rte. 184, 3 mi west of Dolores* ☎ *970/882–4811* ⊕ *www.co.blm.gov/ahc* 🖃 *$3* ☾ *Mar.–Oct. 9–5, Nov.–Feb. 9–4.*

The gentle rising hump to the southwest of town is **Sleeping Ute Moun-tain,** which resembles the reclining silhouette of a Native American re-plete with headdress. The site is revered by the Ute Mountain tribe as a great warrior god who, mortally wounded in a titanic battle with the evil ones, lapsed into eternal sleep, his flowing blood turning into the life-giving Dolores and Animas rivers.

In town, the enchanting **Galloping Goose Museum** (✉ 5th St. at Rte. 145 ☎ 970/882–7082 ⊕ www.doloresgallopinggoose5.org) is a replica of an 1881 train station that contains an original narrow-gauge railcar. This distinctive vehicle connected Telluride with the rest of the world in the declining years of rail travel.

off the beaten path

CANYONS OF THE ANCIENTS NATIONAL MONUMENT – Spread across 164,000 acres of arid mesa-and-canyon country, Canyons of the Ancients holds more than 20,000 known archaeological sites, the greatest concentration anywhere in the United States. There are 40, 60, or sometimes even 100 sites per square mi. Some, like apartment-style cliff dwellings and hewn-rock towers, are impossible to miss. Others are as subtle as evidence of agricultural fields, springs, and water systems. They are powerful evidence of the complex and mystical civilization of the Anasazi, "the ancient ones," who inhabited the area between AD 450 and 1300 and are believed to have been the ancestors of today's Pueblo peoples.

The national monument includes several sites previously under federal protection: **Hovenweep National Monument,** straddling the Colorado-Utah border, is known for distinctive square, oval, round, and D-shaped towers that were engineering marvels when they were built around AD 1200. **Lowry Pueblo,** in the northern part of the monument, is a 40-room pueblo. It features eight kivas (round chambers thought to have been used for sacred rituals). Its Great Kiva is one of the largest yet discovered in the Southwest. Also look for the Painted Kiva, which provides insight into Ancestral Puebloan decorative techniques.

Located in the vast and rugged backcountry area west of Mesa Verde National Park, the monument is a must if you're fascinated by the culture of the Ancestral Puebloans. The going may be rough, however. Roads are few, hiking trails are sparse, and visitor services are all but non-existent. The Anasazi Heritage Center at Lowry Pueblo serves as the visitor center for the Canyon of the Ancients National Monument. A brochure, which details the self-guided tour, is available at the entrance to the site. ⊠ *From Dolores, take Hwy. 184 west to U.S. 491, then head west onto County Rd. CC for 9 mi* ☎ *970/562–4282* ⊕ *www.co.blm.gov/canm* ⊠ *$6 per vehicle* ⊙ *Daily 8–4.*

Sports & the Outdoors

FISHING & BOATING   McPhee Reservoir, filled in 1987, is popular with boaters and anglers. The Colorado Division of Wildlife stocks this large artificial lake with plenty of trout. Other species found here include bass, bluegills, crappies, and kokanee salmon. The most easily reached fishing access spot is at the end of Hwy. 145, west of downtown Dolores. **McPhee Marina** (⊠ 25021 Hwy. 184, Dolores ☎ 970/882–2257) has boat ramps, boat slips, and other amenities. You can also sign up for fishing licenses here.

RAFTING   Beginning in the San Juan Mountains of southwestern Colorado, the Dolores River runs north for more than 150 mi before joining the Colorado River near Moab, Utah. This is one of those rivers that tend to flow madly in spring and diminish considerably by midsummer, and for that reason rafting trips are usually run between April and June. Sandstone canyons, Ancestral Puebloan ruins, and the spring bloom of wildflowers and cacti are trip highlights. The current's strength depends mostly on how much water is released from McPhee Reservoir, but for the most part this trip is a float interrupted by rapids that—depending on the flow level—can rate a Class IV.

Pagosa Springs

⑭ *62 mi from Durango via U.S. 160 east.*

Although not a large town, Pagosa Springs has become a major center for outdoor sports. Hiking, biking, and cross-country-skiing opportunities abound not far from the excellent ski area of Wolf Creek. It has no lodging facilities, so Pagosa Springs is a logical place to stay. A bonus is the hot mineral baths found in the middle of town. **The Springs,** consisting of 13 outdoor tubs with temperatures ranging from 90°F to 110°F. Locals swear the waters have healing properties. ⊠ *165 Hot Springs Blvd.* ☎ *970/264–2284* ⊠ *$12* ⊙ *5 AM–1 PM* ▣ *AE, D, DC, MC, V.*

With water ranging in temperature from 84°F to 114°F, the **Springs Resort** is a great place to relax. There are 17 outdoor tubs, a Mediterranean-style bathhouse, private rooms for massage therapy and spa treatments, a mountain sports shop, and an organic café. ⊠ *165 Hot Springs Blvd.* ☎ *800/225–0934* ⊕ *pagosahotsprings.com* ⊙ *Daily 7–11* ⊠ *Sun.–Thurs. $13; Fri. and Sat. $15* ▣ *AE, D, DC, MC, V.*

Sports & the Outdoors

DOWNHILL
SKIING
★
With five lifts, 800 acres, and a 1,425-foot vertical drop, **Wolf Creek** is one of Colorado's best-kept secrets and a powder hound's dream: it's not crowded, has no lift lines, and it gets phenomenal snow (averaging more than 450 inches a year). The 50 trails run the gamut from wide-open bowls to steep glades. ⊠ *U.S. 160, at the top of Wolf Creek Pass* ☎ *970/264–5629* ⊘ *Early Nov.–mid-Apr., daily 9–4.*

GOLF
About 3 mi west of town, **Pagosa Springs Golf Club** (⊠ 1 Pine Club Pl. ☎ 970/731–4755 ⊕ www.golfpagosa.com) has 27 championship holes that can be played in three combinations, essentially creating three 18-hole courses. A bonus is the gorgeous mountain scenery. The regular season runs from May 15th to October 1st. The greens fees are $44 for 18 holes, dropping to $24 in the off-season. Cart rental is $13 for 18 holes.

Where to Stay & Eat

¢ ✕ **Elkhorn Café.** Filling and fiery Mexican fare (try the stuffed sopaipillas), as well as the usual burgers and chile fries, makes this a popular drop-in spot for locals. Fill up on a breakfast burrito before attacking the Wolf Creek bowls. ⊠ *438 Main St.* ☎ *970/264–2146* ⊟ *AE, D, MC, V.*

$ ▥ **Davidson's Country Inn B&B.** This three-story log cabin is on a 32-acre working ranch in the middle of Colorado's San Juan Mountains. It's just north of Pagosa Springs, meaning you can stay here and still enjoy the slopes at the Wolf Creek Ski Area. Rooms are comfortable and crammed with family heirlooms and antiques. A full breakfast is included. ⊠ *2763 U.S. 160 E, 81147* ☎ *970/264–5863* ☒ *970/264–5492* ⊠ *9 rooms, 4 with shared bath* ⊘ *Recreation room* ⊟ *AE, D, MC, V* ⊺⊝*BP.*

THE SAN LUIS VALLEY

The San Luis Valley is technically not in Southwest Colorado at all. In fact, it is in the middle of the south-central part of the state. But in many ways, it *feels* like the Southwest. At 8,000 square mi, the San Luis Valley is the world's largest alpine valley, sprawling on a broad, flat, dry plain between the San Juan and La Garita mountains to the west and the Sangre de Cristo range to the east. But equally important is that the valley, like the Southwest, remains culturally rooted in the early Hispanic tradition rather than the Northern European one that early prospectors and settlers brought to central and northern Colorado.

Despite its average elevation of 7,500 feet, the San Luis Valley's sheltering peaks help to create a relatively mild climate. The area is one of the state's major agricultural producers, with huge annual crops of potatoes, carrots, canola, barley, and lettuce. In many ways, it is self-sufficient to the point that local business owners threatened to secede in the 1950s to prove that the state couldn't get along without the valley and its valuable products. Half a century later, however, the reality is that the valley is economically disadvantaged and contains two of the state's poorer counties. The large and sparsely populated valley contains some real oddities, including an alligator farm, a UFO-viewing tower, and the achingly New Age town of Crestone.

Watered by the Rio Grande and its tributaries, the San Luis Valley also supports a magnificent array of wildlife, including flocks of birds, such as migrating sandhill cranes. The range of terrain is equally impressive, from soaring fourteeners, to the stark moonscape of the Wheeler Geologic Area, to the undulating landscape of the Great Sand Dunes National Monument and Preserve. The valley's natural beauty is simply awe-inspiring.

This area was settled first by the Ute, then by the Spanish, who left their indelible imprint in the town names and architecture. The oldest town (San Luis), the oldest military post (Ft. Garland), and the oldest church (Our Lady of Guadalupe in Conejos) in the state are in this valley.

World-class climbing can be found outside Del Norte in the Penitente Canyon and in the Wheeler Geologic Area outside Creede. Great Sand Dunes National Monument and Preserve, poised to be elevated to national park status, is a draw for hikers. The Rio Grande National Forest west of the valley and the San Isabel National Forest to the east offer millions of acres of backcountry pleasures.

Creede

⓯ *105 mi from Gunnison via U.S. 50 west and Rte. 149 south; 49 mi from Lake City via Rte. 149 south.*

Creede once earned a reputation as Colorado's rowdiest mining camp and was immortalized in an evocative poem by the local newspaper editor, Cy Warman. "It's day all day in daytime," he wrote, "and there is no night in Creede." Every other building back then seems to have been a saloon or bordello. Bob Ford, who killed Jesse James, was himself gunned down here; other notorious residents included Calamity Jane and Bat Masterson. As delightful as the town is today, its location is even more glorious. About 96 percent of Mineral County is public land, including the nearby Weminuche Wilderness to the south and west, and the Wheeler Geological Area to the west, where the unusual rock formations resemble playful abstract sculptures or M. C. Escher creations. The Colorado Trail and the Continental Divide Trail, two of the country's most significant long-distance recreational paths, pass through Mineral County.

The **Creede Museum,** occupying the original Denver & Rio Grande Railroad Depot, paints a vivid portrait of those rough-and-tumble days. ⊠ *6th and San Luis Sts.* ☎ *719/658–2374* 🖾 *$1* ⊙ *Memorial Day–Labor Day, Mon.–Sat. 10–5.*

★ The **Underground Mining Museum** is housed in rooms that local miners blasted out of solid rock to commemorate the life of the hard-rock miner. Exhibits tracing the history of mining from 1892 to the 1960s teach you the difference between a *winze* (reinforced shaft leading straight down) and a *windlass* (hand-operated hoist). There are guided tours (at 10 and 2:30 daily), but you can also poke about on your own. After you've toured the mine, ask if you can look into the world's only underground firehouse, directly next door. If a volunteer firefighter is around, he'll gladly show you. Donations are welcome. ⊠ *5034 Service Rd.* ☎ *719/658–0811* ⊙ *Memorial Day–Labor Day, daily 10–4; Labor Day–mid-Oct., Mon.–Sat., 10–3; mid-Oct.–Labor Day, weekdays 10-3* 🖾 *$10 for guided tour; $6 for self-guided tour.*

Where to Stay & Eat

$ 🏨 **Antler's Rio Grande Lodge.** Dating to the late 1800s, this cozy lodge has rooms in the main building as well as rustic cabins at a secluded spot along the river. If you brought your own accommodations, there are also campsites available. The restaurant offers cuisine with a flamboyant flair—European dishes, island fare, and up to five nightly specials. The deck offers fine mountain views. ⊠ *26222 Hwy. 149, 81130* ☎ *719/658–2423* 🖶 *719/658–0804* ⊕ *www.antlerslodge.com* 🛏 *9 rooms, 14 cabins* ⊙ *Closed Sept.–May* ▭ *MC, V.*

$ 🏨 **Creede Hotel.** A relic of silver-mining days, this charming 1890s structure with a street-front balcony has been fully restored. Comfortable rooms offer the usual Victoriana. Excellent lunch and dinner, as well as complimentary breakfast, are served in the gracious dining room. ✉ *120 Main St., 81130* ☎ *719/658–2608* 🖷 *719/658–0725* ⊕ *www.creedehotel. com* 🔌 *4 rooms* ♨ *Restaurant* ➦ *AE, D, DC, MC, V* 🍽 *CP.*

$ 🖼·**Wason Ranch.** Enjoy tranquillity in a spacious riverside cottage or cozy cabin, both with kitchens. The original ranch house, dating from the 1870s, is a local landmark. Set on the Rio Grande, this sprawling spread affords miles of great fly-fishing and spin fishing. ✉ *19082 Hwy. 149, 81130* ☎ *719/658–2413 or 877/927–6626* ⊕ *www.wasonranch.com* 🔌 *9 cottages* ➦ *No credit cards.*

¢–$ 🖼 **Bruces' Snowshoe Lodge and B & B.** On the outskirts of Creede, this century-old lodge has two snug little rooms in the main house. The other rooms are undistinguished. ✉ *202 E. 8th St. on Hwy. 149, 81130* ☎ *719/658–2315 or 866/658–2315* ⊕ *www.creede-co.com/snowshoe* 🔌 *18 rooms* ☉ *Closed Sept.–May* ➦ *AE, D, DC, MC, V.* 🍽 *BP.*

The Arts

Creede Repertory Theatre (🖅 Box 269, 81130 ☎ 866/658–2540 ⊕ www.creederep.com), housed in the beautifully restored 1892 Creede Opera House, has a summer season of up to five shows a week. The fall season is known for productions of works by new playwrights, particularly from the Southwest. The theater adjoins the Creede Hotel on Main Street.

Shopping

San Juan Sports (✉ 102 S. Main St. ☎ 719/658–2359 or 888/658–0851 ⊕ www.sanjuansports.com) specializes in sales and rentals of outdoor gear for hiking, biking, backpacking, camping, and winter backcountry expeditions. There are also good selections of maps, books, and the ubiquitous Colorado T-shirts.

en route Continue along Route 149—the Silver Thread National Scenic Byway—on its impossibly beautiful journey east through South Fork. The road flirts with the Rio Grande and passes near the majestic North Clear Creek Falls. You need a four-wheel-drive vehicle to navigate the 24 mi from Creede to the **Wheeler Geological Area,** distinguished by dramatically eroded pinnacles of volcanic tuff. Once there, exploring is by foot or horseback only.

Del Norte

⑯ *38 mi from Creede via Rte. 149 south and U.S. 160 east.*

In and around Del Norte are several historic sites, one of which is an original 1870s station belonging to the Barlow-Sanderson Stagecoach Line. The **Rio Grande County Museum and Cultural Center** celebrates the region's multicultural heritage with displays of petroglyphs, mining artifacts, early Spanish relics, and rotating shows of contemporary art. ✉ *580 Oak St.* ☎ *719/657–2847* 🎫 *$1* ☉ *June–Sept., Tues.–Sat. 10–5; Oct.–Apr., Tues.–Sat. noon–5.*

Just west of town is the gaping **Penitente Canyon.** Once a retreat and place of worship for a small, fervent sect of the Catholic Church known as Los Hermanos Penitente, it is now a haven for rock climbers. Follow Route 112 about 3 mi from Del Norte, then follow the signs to the canyon.

In the nearby La Garita Wilderness is another marvel—the towering rock formation **La Ventana Natural Arch.**

Sports & the Outdoors

FISHING The Rio Grande River—between Del Norte and South Fork—teems with rainbows and lunker browns. The area is full of "gold medal" waters, designated as great fishing spots by the Colorado Wildlife Commission.

Shopping

Casa de Madera (✉ 680 Grand St. ☎ 719/657–2336) sells designer kitchen items and pretty pieces of pottery. Its sister store, **Casa de Madera Sports** (✉ 660 Grand St. ☎ 719/657–2336), offers camping, climbing, and fishing gear, as well as maps and books about the region. **Cobblestone Corner** (✉ 578 Grand Ave. ☎ 719/657–2322) is the place for antiques, gourmet products, and gift baskets overflowing with goodies. **Haefeli's Honey Farms** (✉ 0041 S. Rd. 1, Monte Vista ☎ 719/852–2301), on the way to Monte Vista, sells delectable mountain-bloom honeys.

Alamosa

🟤 *34 mi from Del Norte via U.S. 160 east.*

The San Luis Valley's major city is best known as a high-altitude training center for long-distance runners. Just outside town is the **Alamosa National Wildlife Refuge.** These natural and man-made wetlands—an anomaly amid the arid surroundings—are an important sanctuary for myriad migrating birds. ✉ *9383 El Rancho La.* ☎ *719/589–4021* 🎫 *Free* ☉ *Daily sunrise–sunset.*

From late February to mid-March, birders flock to nearby Monte Vista to view the migration of the sandhill cranes at the **Monte Vista National Wildlife Refuge.** Nicknamed the Valley of the Cranes, the park is one place where you can see these interesting creatures at close range. Every morning during the Festival of the Cranes, buses shuttle visitors to the refuge from Alamosa. ✉ *6140 Hwy. 15, Monte Vista* 🎫 *Free* ☉ *Daily sunrise–sunset.*

Adams State College contains several superlative examples of 1930s WPA-commissioned murals in its administrative building. The college's **Luther Bean Museum and Art Gallery** displays European porcelain and furniture collections in a handsome, wood-paneled 19th-century drawing room, and changing exhibits of regional arts and crafts. ✉ *Richardson Hall, Richardson and 3rd Sts.* ☎ *719/587–7011* 🎫 *Free* ☉ *Weekdays 1–4:30.*

The **San Luis Valley History Museum** showcases Indian artifacts, photographs, military regalia, and collectibles of early railroading, farming, and ranch life. Exhibits feature the multicultural influence of Hispanic, Japanese-American, Mormon, and Dutch settlers. ✉ *306 Hunt Ave.* ☎ *719/587–0667* 🎫 *Free* ☉ *June–late Sept., daily 10–4.*

> off the
> beaten
> path

MANASSA – Known as the Manassa Mauler, one of the greatest heavyweight boxing champions of all time is honored in his hometown at the **Jack Dempsey Museum** (✉ 401 Main St. ☎ 719/843–5207 ☉ Memorial Day–Sept., Mon.–Sat. 9–5). The town is about 23 mi from Alamosa, south on U.S. 285 and east on Route 142.

Sports & the Outdoors

GOLF The lovely **Cattails Golf Course** (✉ 6615 N. River Rd. ☎ 719/589–9515) is an 18-hole, par-71 course that wraps scenically around the Rio Grande.

Where to Stay & Eat

$–$$ ✕ **True Grits.** At this noisy steak house the cuts of beef are predictably good, but that's not the real draw. As the name implies, the restaurant is really just a shrine to John Wayne. His portraits hang everywhere: the Duke in action; the Duke in repose; the Duke lost in thought. ✉ *Junction U.S. 160 and Rte. 17* ☎ *719/589–9954* ⚑ *Reservations essential* 🖃 *MC, V.*

★ **$$** ▣ **Cottonwood Inn B&B.** This pretty cranberry-and-azure house has been lovingly refurbished. Public rooms are decorated in Arts and Crafts style and feature original and reproduction woodwork and furnishings. Pretty watercolors (most of them for sale) grace the walls. In the quintet of sunny rooms you'll find country-French washed walls, hand-painted florets, lacey curtains, and airy wicker furnishings. There are also four suites, all with old-fashioned claw-foot tubs. A complimentary breakfast is provided. Cooking workshops are offered monthly. ✉ *123 San Juan Ave., 81101* ☎ *719/589–3882 or 800/955–2623* 🖷 *719/589–6437* ⊕ *cottonwoodinn.com* ⇆ *5 rooms, 4 suites* 🖃 *AE, DC, MC, V* ⍟*BP.*

$ ▣ **Best Western Alamosa Inn.** This sprawling, well-maintained complex is your best bet for budget lodgings. Rooms are spacious and offer the standard amenities. The Grizzly Inn Restaurant and Pub next door is a great place for dinner. ✉ *1919 Main St., 81101* ☎ *719/589–3567* 🖷 *719/589–0767* ⊕ *www.bestwestern.com/alamosainn* ⇆ *53 rooms* ⚑ *Restaurant, bar, indoor pool, hot tub* 🖃 *AE, D, DC, MC, V.*

$ ▣ **Conejos River Guest Ranch.** On the Conejos River, this peaceful, family-friendly retreat is about 32 mi south of Alamosa. One of the draws is the great fishing in the area. The cabins and eight guest rooms are pleasantly outfitted with ranch-style decor, including lodgepole pine furnishings. Breakfast is complimentary. ✉ *25390 Hwy. 17, Antonito 81120* ☎ *719/ 376–2464* ⊕ *www.conejosranch.com* ⇆ *8 rooms, 7 cabins* ⚑ *Restaurant, fishing, horseback riding* 🖃 *D, MC, V* ⊗ *Closed Dec.–Apr.* ⍟ *BP.*

Shopping

Fireworks Gallery (✉ 608 Main St. ☎ 719/589–6064) carries fine art, collectibles, jewelry, weavings, and prints. The San Luis Valley is noted for its produce. Mycophiles should stop by to sample the wide variety at **Rakhra Mushroom Farm** (✉ 10719 Rd. 5 S ☎ 719/589–5882). **The Turquoise Shop** (✉ 423 San Juan Ave. ☎ 719/589–2631) sells sterling-silver and turquoise jewelry and various handicrafts.

In nearby Manassa, **Destiny Pewter** (✉ 419 Main St. ☎ 719/843–0821) fashions seemingly everything—from bolos to belts, charms to figurines—in silky pewter.

Great Sand Dunes National Monument & Preserve

⑱ *35 mi from Alamosa via U.S. 160 east and Rte. 150 north.*

Created by wind swept from the floor of the San Luis Valley, these 750-foot-high sand dunes are an improbable, unforgettable sight. The dunes, as curvaceous as Rubens's nudes, stretch for 55 square mi and are painted with light and shadow that shift through the day. Their very existence seems tenuous, as if they might blow away before your eyes, yet they're solid enough to withstand the stress of hikers and saucer-riding thrill-seekers. The sand is as fine and feathery as you'll find anywhere. In the off-season, this preserve can be a place for contemplation and repose, the silence broken only by passing birds and the faint rush of water from the Medano Creek. In peak season, however, the section of the dunes closest to the parking lots sounds more like a playground than a peaceful place. ✉ *11500 Rte. 150, Mosca* ☎ *719/378–2312* ⊕ *www.nps.gov/ grsa* 🖂 *$3* ⊙ *Visitor center, daily 9–4:30.*

Just outside Great Sand Dunes National Monument is the **Great Sand Dunes Oasis** (✉ 5400 Hwy. 150, Mosca 81146 ☏ 719/378–2222). Here you'll find a restaurant, gift shop, motel, and hook-ups for RVs. This company is also the concessionaire for tours on a rough road toward Mosca Pass that skirts the sand dunes. The two-hour tours are in open-air four-wheel-drive trucks and cost $14.

Sports & the Outdoors

GOLF **Great Sand Dunes Country Club** (✉ 5303 Rte. 150, Mosca ☏ 719/378–2357) is an 18-hole course with the billowing dunes as a backdrop.

San Luis

19 *46 mi from Alamosa via U.S. 160 east and Rte. 159 south; 32 mi from Manassa via Rte. 142 east.*

San Luis, founded in 1851, is the oldest incorporated town in Colorado. Murals depicting famous stories and legends of the area adorn the town's gracious tree-lined streets. A latter-day masterpiece is the Stations of the Cross Shrine, created by renowned local sculptor Huberto Maestas. Perched above town on a mesa called La Mesa de la Piedad y de la Misericordia (Hill of Piety and Mercy), its 15 figures illustrate the last hours of Christ's life. The trail culminates in a tranquil grotto dedicated to the Virgin Mary. San Luis's Hispanic heritage is celebrated in the **San Luis Museum & Cultural Center,** with its extensive collection of *santos* (decorated figures of saints used for household devotions), *retablos* (religious paintings on wood), and *bultos* (carved religious figures). ✉ *401 Church Pl.* ☏ *719/672–3611* ✉ *$2* ☉ *Daily 10–4 in summer, Weekdays 9–4 in winter.*

> off the beaten path

FT. GARLAND – Colorado's first military post, established in 1856 to protect settlers, lies in the shadow of the Sangre de Cristo Mountains. They were named the Blood of Christ Mountains because of their ruddy color, especially at dawn. The legendary Kit Carson commanded the outfit, and the six original adobe structures are still standing. The **Ft. Garland State Museum** features a re-creation of the commandant's quarters, period military displays, and a rotating local folk-art exhibit. The museum is 16 mi north of San Luis via Rte. 159 and 24 mi east of Alamosa via U.S. 160. ✉ *South of intersection of U.S. 160 and Hwy. 159* ☏ *719/379–3512* ✉ *$3* ☉ *Apr.–Oct., daily 9–5; Nov.–Mar., Thurs.–Mon. 8–4.*

SOUTHWEST COLORADO A TO Z

To research prices, get advice from other travelers, and book travel arrangements, visit www.fodors.com.

AIR TRAVEL

CARRIERS The Durango–La Plata Airport is served by American, America West Express, Great Lakes Aviation, and Rio Grande Air. Gunnison County Airport is served by American Airlines, United Express, and Western Express. Montrose Airport is served by American, America West, Continental, and Great Lakes Aviation. Telluride Regional Airport welcomes flights from America West and Great Lakes Aviation.

🛪 Airlines & Contacts **American** ☏ 800/433-7300 ⊕ www.aa.com. **America West** ☏ 800/235-9292 ⊕ www.americawest.com. **Great Lakes Aviation** ☏ 307/432-7000 or 800/554-5111 ⊕ www.greatlakesav.com. **Rio Grande Air** ☏ 877/435-9742 ⊕ www. iflyrga.com. **Skywest/Delta Connection** ☏ 800/453-9417 ⊕ www.skywest.com. **United**

Express ☎ 800/241-6522 ⊕ www.ual.com. **Western Express** ☎ 877/882-2746 ⊕ www. westex.ca.

AIRPORTS

Telluride is notorious for being one of the hardest ski resorts in the country to fly into, mainly because the elevation of Telluride Regional Airport is well above 9,000 feet. A little turbulence, a few clouds, and the next thing you know you're landing at Montrose Airport, 67 mi away, and taking a shuttle to Telluride.

The Gunnison-Crested Butte Regional Airport also serves the nearby resort area. The Durango-La Plata Airport is the gateway to the communities near Four Corners.

🚹 **Durango-La Plata Airport** ☎ 970/247-8143 ⊕ www.durangoairport.com. **Gunnison-Crested Butte Regional Airport** ☎ 970/641-2304. **Montrose Airport** ☎ 970/249-3203 ⊕ www.montrose-colo.com. **Telluride Regional Airport** ☎ 970/728-5313 ⊕ www.tellurideairport.com.

TRANSFERS Several companies offer transportation between the airports and the resorts. Shuttles average $15–$20 per person. In Crested Butte and Gunniston, try Alpine Express. In Durango, the best service is Durango Transportation. Telluride Express, Skip's Taxi, and Western Express Taxi serve Telluride Regional Airport.

🚹 **Alpine Express** ☎ 970/641-5074 or 800/822-4844. **Durango Transportation** ☎ 970/247-4161 or 800/626-2066. **Skip's Taxi** ☎ 970/728-6667. **Telluride Express** ☎ 970/728-6000 ⊕ www.tellurideexpress.com. **Western Express Taxi** ☎ 970/249-8880.

BUS TRAVEL

If you're traveling between the major towns, Greyhound is your best bet. In Crested Butte, Mountain Express shuttles regularly between the town and the ski area every 15 minutes during ski season. Durango Lift has regular bus service up and down Main Street, as well as to Purgatory during ski season. The Galloping Goose loops around Telluride every 15 minutes in the summer and winter, less often in the off-season.

🚹 **Durango Lift** ☎ 970/259-5438. **Galloping Goose** ☎ 970/728-5700. **Mountain Express** ☎ 970/349-5616.

CAR RENTAL

Avis, Budget, Dollar, Hertz, and National have counters at Durango-La Plata Airport, Gunnison-Crested Butte Regional Airport, and Telluride Regional Airport.

🚹 **Avis** ☎ 800/331-1212 ⊕ www.avis.com. **Budget** ☎ 800/527-0700 ⊕ www.budget.com. **Dollar** ☎ 800/800-4000 ⊕ www.dollar.com. **Enterprise** ☎ 800/325-8007 ⊕ www.enterprise.com. **Hertz** ☎ 800/654-3131 ⊕ www.hertz.com. **National** ☎ 800/227-7368 ⊕ www.nationalcar.com.

CAR TRAVEL

Crested Butte is 230 mi southwest of Denver. Take U.S. 285 south to U.S. 24 south to U.S. 50 west to Gunnison. From Gunnison, take Route 134 north to Crested Butte. Telluride is 330 mi southwest of Denver. There is no such thing as a direct route, but the fastest is probably U.S. 285 south to U.S. 24 south to U.S. 50 west to Montrose. Take U.S. 550 south to Ridgway. From Ridgway, take Route 62 west to Placerville and Route 45 south to Telluride.

Getting to the remote Four Corner region is a bit simpler. If you're entering Colorado from the south, U.S. 550, U.S. 160, and U.S. 491 lead to the Four Corners region. From the east or west, Interstate 70 (U.S. 6) intersects U.S. 50 in Grand Junction; U.S. 50 runs south to the San Juan Mountains and Four Corners. From the Denver area, take Interstate 25 to Interstate 70 west for a long drive to U.S. 50.

The main roads through the region are Route 135 between Crested Butte and Gunnison; U.S. 50 linking Poncha Springs, Gunnison, Montrose, and Delta; Route 149 between Gunnison, Lake City, and Creede; U.S. 550 from Montrose to Ridgway; Route 62 and Route 145 linking Ridgway with Telluride, Dolores, and Cortez; Route 110 running from Ridgway through Ouray and Silverton to Durango; and U.S. 160, the closest thing to a major highway in the area, from Cortez to Durango via the Mesa Verde National Park north entrance.

🚗 **American Automobile Association of Colorado** ☎ 970/245-2236 ⊕ www.aaa.com. **Colorado Road Report** ☎ 877/315-7623 ⊕ www.cotrip.org. **Colorado State Patrol** ☎ 970/249-4392 ⊕ www.csp.state.co.us.

EMERGENCIES

🚑 Ambulance or Police **Emergencies** ☎ 911.

🚑 24-Hour Medical Care **Gunnison Valley Hospital** ⊠ 711 N. Taylor, Gunnison ☎ 970/641-1456 ⊕ www.gunnisonvalleyhospital.org. **Mercy Medical Center** ⊠ 375 E. Park Ave., Durango ☎ 970/247-4311 ⊕ www.mercydurango.org. **Montrose Memorial Hospital** ⊠ 800 S. 3rd St., Montrose ☎ 970/249-2211 ⊕ www.montrosehospital.org. **Southwest Memorial Hospital** ⊠ 1311 N. Mildred St., Cortez ☎ 970/565-6666 ⊕ www.swhealth.org. **Telluride Medical Center** ⊠ 500 W. Pacific Ave., Telluride ☎ 970/728-3848 ⊕ www.telluridemedicalcenter.org.

LODGING

The Colorado Office of Tourism maintains a Web site that includes information about all types of lodging, from quaint B&Bs to massive ski resorts. Representing more than 100 inns, Bed & Breakfast Innkeepers of Colorado maintains rigorous standards. Distinctive Inns of Colorado represents the most luxurious lodgings. The Colorado Hotel & Lodging Association, with more than 500 members, often has deals on its web site.

🏨 **Bed & Breakfast Innkeepers of Colorado** ☎ 877/206-5653 ⊕ www.innsofcolorado.org. **Colorado Hotel & Lodging Association** ☎ 303/297-8335 ⊕ www.coloradolodging.com. **Colorado Office of Tourism** ☎ 800/265-6723 ⊕ www.colorado.com. **Distinctive Inns of Colorado** ☎ 800/866-0621 ⊕ www.bedandbreakfastinns.com.

CAMPING   Camping in the region ranges from rugged back-country camping to developed campsites that generally have electrical hook-ups and visitor center services with flush toilets and showers.

🏕 **Colorado Campground & Lodge Owners Association** ☎ 970/247-5406 ⊕ www.campcolorado.com.

OUTDOORS & SPORTS

FISHING   There is an incredible variety of fishing options in and around the region. Of the 13 rivers designated as "gold medal" waters by the Colorado Wildlife Commission, the Animas, Gunnison, and Rio Grande are all located in Southwest Colorado. For information on fishing licenses, contact the Colorado Division of Wildlife. Additional information can be found at the U.S. Fish and Wildlife Service.

🎣 **Colorado Division of Wildlife** ⊠ 711 Independent, Grand Junction 81505 ☎ 970/255-6100 ⊕ www.wildlife.state.co.us. **U.S. Fish and Wildlife Service** ⊠ 764 Horizon Dr., South Annex A, Grand Junction 81506 ☎ 970/243-2778 ⊕ www.mountain-prairie.fws.gov.

HIKING   Whether you're looking for a short hike or an all-day excursion, you'll find lots of hiking trails throughout the region's national parks and forests. For trail maps, contact the Bureau of Land Management or U.S. Forest Service.

🥾 **Bureau of Land Management** ⊠ 2815 H Rd., Grand Junction 81506 ☎ 970/244-3000 ⊕ www.co.blm.gov/recweb. **Grand Mesa, Uncompahre, and Gunnison National Forests** ⊠ 2250 U.S. 50, Delta 81416 ☎ 970/641-6660 ⊕ www.fs.fed.us/r2/gmug. **Mesa Verde National Park** ✉ Box 8, Mesa Verde Park 81330 ☎ 970/529-4465

⊕www.nps.gov/meve. **San Juan National Forest** ✉15 Burnett Ct., Durango 80301 ☎970/
247-4874 ⊕ www.fs.fed.us/r2/sanjuan.

MOUNTAIN BIKING

Mountain-biking trails are available for people of all abilities throughout the region. For trail maps covering mostly western Colorado and parts of Utah, send $2 to Colorado Plateau Mountain Bike Trail Association. Much useful information is posted online.

🛈 **Colorado Plateau Mountain Bike Trail Association** ✉ Box 4602, Grand Junction 81502 ☎ 970/249-8055 ⊕ www.copmoba.com. **Bureau of Land Management** ✉ 2815 H Rd., Grand Junction 81506 ☎ 970/ 244-3000 ⊕ www.co.blm.gov/recweb.

TAXIS

In most resort towns you'll need to call for a cab. The wait is seldom more than 15 minutes. In Montrose, Western Express Taxi gives you door-to-door service.

🛈 **Local Companies** **Crested Butte Town Taxi** ☎ 970/349-5543. **Durango Transportation** ☎ 970/259-4818. **Telluride Shuttle & Taxi** ☎ 970/728-6667. **Telluride Transit** ☎ 970/728-6000. **Western Express Taxi** ☎ 970/249-8880.

TOURS

Adventures to the Edge creates customized high-country treks, cross-country skiing expeditions, and alpine ascents in the Crested Butte area. ARA Mesa Verde Company runs three- and six-hour tours of Mesa Verde National Park. Mesa Verde Tours arranges tours of the national park and the San Juan Skyway. Operated by local thespian Ashley Boling, Historic Tours of Telluride provides humorous walking tours around the downtown streets, adding anecdotes about infamous figures such as Butch Cassidy and Jack Dempsey.

Crow Canyon Archaeological Center promotes understanding and appreciation of Ancestral Puebloan culture by guiding visitors through excavations and botanical studies in the region. Also included in the weeklong programs are day trips to isolated canyon sites and hands-on lessons in weaving and pottery-making with Native American artisans. Native American guides at Ute Mountain Tribal Park lead grueling hikes into this dazzling repository of Ancestral Puebloan ruins, including the majestic Tree House cliff dwelling and enchanting Eagle's Nest petroglyphs. Tours usually start at the Ute Mountain Pottery Plant, 15 mi south of Cortez, on U.S. 491. Overnight camping can also be arranged.

🛈 **Tour Operators** **Adventures to the Edge** ✉ 308 3rd St., Crested Butte ☎ 970/349-5219 ⊕ www.atedge.com. **ARA Mesa Verde Company** ⊘ Box 277 Mancos ☎ 970/529-4421. **Crow Canyon Archaeological Center** ✉ 23390 County Rd. K, Cortez 81321 ☎ 970/565-8975 or 800/422-8975 ⊕ www.crowcanyon.org. **Mesa Verde Tours** ✉ 547½ E. 2nd St., Durango ☎ 970/259-4818. **Historic Tours of Telluride** ☎ 970/728-6639. **Ute Mountain Tribal Park** ⊘ Box 109 Towaoc 81334 ☎ 970/565-3751 ⊕ www.utemountainute.com.

TRAIN TRAVEL

The Durango & Silverton Narrow Gauge Railroad can take you from Durango to Silverton in lovingly restored coaches. The train runs from mid-May to late-October, with four departures daily from June to August and only one in the other months.

🛈 **Durango & Silverton Narrow Gauge Railroad** ✉ 479 Main Ave. ☎ 970/247-2733 or 888/872-4607 ⊕ www.durangotrain.com ⬚ $60.

VISITOR INFORMATION

🛈 **Crested Butte Information** **Crested Butte-Mt. Crested Butte Chamber of Commerce** ✉ 601 Elk Ave., 81224 ☎ 970/349-6438 or 800/545-4505 ⊕ www.crestedbuttechamber.com. **Crested Butte Mountain Resort** ✉ 500 Gothic Rd., Box A, Mount Crested Butte 81225 ☎ 970/349-2378 or 888/223-3530 ⊕www.crestedbutteresort.

com. **Crested Butte Vacations** ✉ 12 Snowmass Rd., Crested Butte 81224 ☎ 800/544-8448 ⊕ www.visitcrestedbutte.com. **Crested Butte Snow Report** ☎ 888/442-8883.

🛈 Telluride Information **Telluride and Mountain Village Visitor Services** ✉ 630 W. Colorado Ave., Box 653, Telluride 81435 ☎ 800/525-3455 ⊕ www.visittelluride.com. **Telluride Chamber Resort Association** ✉ 666 W. Colorado Ave., 81435 ☎ 970/728-3041 ⊕ www.telluride.com. **Telluride Ski Resort** ✉ 565 Mountain Village Blvd., Telluride 81435 ☎ 970/728-6900 or 866/287-5015 ⊕ www.telski.com. **Telluride Snow Report** ☎ 970/728-7425.

🛈 Tourist Information **Cortez Area Chamber of Commerce** ✉ 928 E. Main St., 81321 ☎ 970/565-3414 ⊕ www.mesaverdecountry.com. **Durango Chamber Resort Association** ✉ 111 S. Camino del Rio, 81302 ☎ 970/247-0312 or 800/525-8855 ⊕ www.durango.org. **Gunnison County Chamber of Commerce** ✉ 500 E. Tomichi Ave., 81230 ☎ 970/641-1501 or 800/274-7580 ⊕ www.gunnisonchamber.com. **Lake City Chamber of Commerce** ✉ 800 N. Gunnison Ave., 81235 ☎ 970/944-2527 ⊕ www.lakecityco.com. **Mesa Verde Country** ⌖ Box HH, Cortez 81321 ☎ 800/253-1616 ⊕ www.mesaverdecountry.com. **Montrose Chamber of Commerce** ✉ 1519 E. Main St., 81401 ☎ 970/249-5000 ✉ 17253 Chipeta Rd., 81401 ☎ 970/249-1726 ⊕ www.montrose.org/chamber2. **Ouray County Chamber** ✉ 1222 Main St., Ouray 81427 ☎ 970/325-4746 or 800/228-1876 ⊕ www.ouraycolorado.com. **Pagosa Springs Chamber of Commerce** ✉ 402 San Juan St., 81147 ☎ 303/264-2360 or 800/252-2204 ⊕ www.pagosa-springs.com. **Silverton Chamber of Commerce** ✉ 414 Greene St., 81433 ☎ 970/387-5654 or 800/752-4494 ⊕ www.silverton.org. **Southwest Colorado Travel Region** ☎ 800/933-4340 ⊕ www.swcolotravel.org.

SOUTH CENTRAL COLORADO

FODOR'S CHOICE

The Broadmoor, *a hotel in Colorado Springs*

The Cliff House, *a hotel in Colorado Springs*

Collegiate Peaks Wilderness Area, *Buena Vista*

North Cheyenne Cañon Park, *Colorado Springs*

Rafting on the Arkansas River, *Buena Vista*

Royal Gorge, *Cañon City*

HIGHLY RECOMMENDED

RESTAURANTS
Briarhurst Manor, *Colorado Springs*

Ianne's Whiskey Ridge, *Pueblo*

Nana and Nano's Pasta House, *Trinidad*

HOTELS
Abriendo Inn, *Pueblo*

Adobe Inn, *Buena Vista*

Briarhurst Manor, *Colorado Springs*

Cañon Inn, *Cañon City*

Liar's Lodge, *Buena Vista*

St. Cloud Hotel, *Cañon City*

Thunder Lodge, *Buena Vista*

Tudor Rose, *Salida*

Victor Hotel, *Victor*

SIGHTS
Bent's Old Fort National Historic Site, *La Junta*

Bishop's Castle, *Pueblo*

Colorado Renaissance Festival

Florissant Fossil Beds National Monument

Corazon de Trinidad, *Trinidad*

Mt. Princeton Hot Springs Resort, *Buena Vista*

Rosemount Victorian Museum, *Pueblo*

San Isabel National Forest

Revised &
Updated by
Eric Peterson &
Robert Ehlert

RUNNING FROM RUGGED HIGH DESERT PLAINS into majestic mountains, south central Colorado was first explored by the United States in 1806, three years after it made the Louisiana Purchase. Zebulon Pike took up the assignment of scout, but he never did climb the peak that is now named for him, nor did he have the scientific background of his contemporaries, the famous explorers Lewis and Clark. Weaving through the southeastern section of the state are the haunting remains of the Santa Fe Trail, which guided pioneers westward beginning in the 1820s. Towns such as Cripple Creek and Trinidad are living history. In fact, residents are so proud of their mining heritage that, despite economic hard times, they've earmarked tax revenues to preserve local landmarks.

At the foot of looming Pikes Peak, Colorado Springs is the region's population center and, bucking the mining-nostalgia trend, a hub of high-tech industry. The city has been a destination for out-of-towners since its founding in 1870, due to the alleged healing power of the local springwater. The gold rush fueled the city's boom through the early 20th century, as the military boom did following World War II. (NORAD— the missile defense complex inside Cheyenne Mountain—and the Air Force Academy are products of the latter.) Now about 400,000 residents strong, the city offers a mix of history and modernity, as well as incredible access to the trails and red-rock scenery of the Rockies.

Surrounding Colorado Springs is a ring of smaller cities and alluring natural attractions. To the southwest, between alpine and desert scenery are the Florissant Fossil Beds and the Royal Gorge, both worth a short visit if not an entire day. Cripple Creek offers low-stakes gambling, Cañon City rafting, and Pueblo a nice dash of public art and history museums. Outdoorsy types love the entire area: camping and hiking are especially superb in the San Isabel and Pike national forests. Climbers head to the Collegiate Peaks around Buena Vista and Salida (west of Colorado Springs) and the Cañon City area for a variety of ascents, from moderate to difficult. A side trip north of Colorado Springs—to Palmer Lake and Larkspur—is another worthwhile excursion, especially for hikers.

Exploring South Central Colorado

South central Colorado is full of surprises, from historic forts, museums, and neighborhoods to pristine natural wonders. It's worth a few days of exploration—embarking on a white-water rafting trip, wandering through the old downtowns, and hiking in the backcountry are all great excursions in these parts. Much of the area has an undiscovered feel, so if it's peace and quiet you're after, staying put in a woodsy cabin here can make for an utterly relaxed week.

The intersection of Interstate 25 and U.S. Highway 24 is vital to the life and commerce of Colorado Springs. The same was true for the Ute Indians who used the same route when they ruled the land for centuries. (That's why the road to the city of Woodland Park is called "Ute Pass.") The crossroads today is vacation junction for travelers headed for high altitude and high adventure, using the Springs as a comfortable base camp. With the Front Range always outlining the West, it's hard to get lost.

About the Restaurants

Many restaurants serve regional trout and game, as well as locally-grown fruits and vegetables. Other than top-notch Mexican eateries, there's not much variety in terms of ethnic foods outside Colorado Springs. Like much of the rest of urban Colorado, Colorado Springs is a champion of chain restaurants, but you will find unique Colorado cuisine that zings taste buds without zapping budgets. Juxtaposed among the Outback

Steakhouse and Black Eyed Pea pit stops are memorable Chinese, Japanese, Thai, Vietnamese, German, Italian, and Mexican restaurants.

About the Hotels

The five-star Broadmoor Hotel in Colorado Springs was built from the booty of the late-19th-century gold-rush days, and predictable boxy-bed motel rooms await travelers at the junction of any major highways. Interspersed are quaint mom-and-pop hotels in tourist districts and small luxury hotels. Pueblo is dominated by chain hotels and motels, but the smaller towns and mountain municipalities offer a blend of roadside motels, Victorian bed-and-breakfasts, and backwoods cabins. You can check into a number of budget accommodations in the region for less than $50 a night, and the priciest hotels run about $150 to $200 a night.

WHAT IT COSTS					
	$$$$	**$$$**	**$$**	**$**	**¢**
RESTAURANTS	over $25	$19–$25	$13–$18	$8–$12	under $8
HOTELS	over $200	$151–$200	$111–$150	$70–$110	under $70

Restaurant prices are for a main course at dinner, excluding sales tax of 6%. Hotel prices are for two people in a standard double room in high season, excluding service charges and 8.1% tax.

Timing

The early summer (when snowmelt-fed rivers are ideal for rafting and angling) and early fall (mild weather and lack of snowpack) are the best times to visit the region. Spring can be muddy or still snowed in, especially in the mountains, whereas summers are hot, and winters unpredictable.

COLORADO SPRINGS & VICINITY

The contented residents of the Colorado Springs area believe they live in an ideal location, and it's hard to argue with them. To the west, the Rockies form a majestic backdrop. To the east, the plains stretch for miles. Taken together, the setting ensures a mild, sunny climate year-round, and makes skiing and golfing on the same day feasible with no more than a two- or three-hour drive. You don't have to choose between adventures here: you can climb the Collegiate Peaks one day, and go white-water rafting on the Arkansas River the next.

The region abounds in natural and man-made wonders, from the eerie sandstone formations of the Garden of the Gods to the space-age architecture of the U.S. Air Force Academy. The most indelible landmark is unquestionably Pikes Peak (14,110 feet), from where Katharine Lee Bates penned "America the Beautiful." The song's lyrics remain an accurate description of south central Colorado's many glories.

Colorado Springs & Manitou Springs Area

68 mi from Denver via I–25.

Pikes Peak, the state's most famous landmark, is a constant reminder that this very contemporary city is still close to nature. Purple in the early morning, snow-packed after winter storms, capped with clouds on windy days, the mountain is a landmark for directions and, when needed, a focus of contemplation. Visitors come as much for the peak and the otherworldly-sounding Cave of the Winds and Garden of the Gods as for the tried-and-true historic neighborhood tours in the city.

Numbers in the text correspond to numbers in the margin and on the South Central Colorado map.

If you have
3 days

Base yourself in ⊞ **Colorado Springs** ❶–⓮. On the first day, take the Pikes Peak Cog Railway to the top of the mountain and explore **Manitou Springs** ⓯–㉑ before and after your trip—it's a great spot for dinner or a night's stay. On day two, check out downtown Colorado Springs and the Cheyenne Mountain area and visit the Broadmoor for a look at its palatial Victorian architecture. On day three, hike the reservoir trails that come out of **Palmer Lake** ㉒. If you prefer something more adventurous, sign up for a full day of white-water rafting out of **Buena Vista** ㉔.

If you have
5 days

Follow the three-day itinerary above, spending the third day in **Palmer Lake** ㉒. Leave Colorado Springs on the fourth day for a white-water rafting trip from ⊞ **Buena Vista** ㉔ or ⊞ **Salida** ㉕. Spend the night in one of those towns, taking your pick of the mom-and-pop motels, campgrounds, and Victorian B&Bs. Exercise your legs the fifth day in the Collegiate Peaks National Wilderness Area or elsewhere in the San Isabel National Forest.

If you have
7 days

Follow the suggested five-day itinerary, and on day six, head to the Royal Gorge and spend the night in ⊞ **Cañon City** ㉖. Visit the Museum of Colorado Prisons or Buckskin Joe Frontier Town and then head south to get an eyeful of Bishop Castle, near Westcliffe. Take Route 96 (Route 78 is partially unpaved) back east to historic ⊞ **Pueblo** ㉗, home to the largest mural in the world, the Pueblo Levee Project.

General William Jackson Palmer, president of the Denver & Rio Grande Railroad, founded Colorado Springs in the 1870s and shaped it as a utopian vision of fine living. Original broad, tree-lined boulevards still grace sections of the city. With the discovery of hot springs in the area, the well-to-do descended on the bustling resort town to take the waters and to enjoy the mild climate and fresh air. It became known as "Saratoga of the West" and "Little London," the latter for the snob appeal of its considerable resident and visiting English population. The discovery of gold at nearby Cripple Creek toward the end of the 19th century signaled another boom for the Springs. In the early part of the 1900s, until the mines petered out just before World War I, the residents' per-capita wealth was the highest in the nation.

After World War II city leaders invited the military to move in, and the Colorado Spring's personality changed drastically. A significant portion of the local economy is dependent on Department of Defense contracts, related to the army's Fort Carson (Colorado's largest military base, just south of downtown Colorado Springs) and the Peterson Air Force Base complex.

If Colorado Springs is anything, it's organized, and it manages all the utilities, one of the hospitals, and the airport (there are advantages and disadvantages to that). The state's second-largest city is known as a politically conservative bastion, and the reputation is somewhat deserved. But consider that the last mayor was a woman and the present one is a

Hispanic man, a former military officer. Tax-raising school bond issues have a hard time at the polls, but this same city voted by a two-to-one margin to fund new open-space initiatives. This is the West, but a West that understands the value of stewardship when it comes to its natural resources.

A Good Tour: Colorado Springs

Begin at the **U.S. Air Force Academy** ❶ ▶. Directly across Interstate 25 from the north gate of the academy is the considerable acreage of the **Western Museum of Mining and Industry** ❷. Continue south along Interstate 25 toward downtown and get off at Exit 147. A bronze rodeo bull lures visitors to the **Pro Rodeo Hall of Fame and Museum of the American Cowboy** ❸. Now take Interstate 25 or Nevada Avenue to the southern end of the city for a glimpse of its posher neighborhoods, where **The Broadmoor Hotel** ❹ stands. From the Broadmoor, make a left onto Mesa Avenue, and then turn right onto Evans. Continue along Evans, and then take the Cheyenne Mountain Zoo Road to begin the ascent of Cheyenne Mountain. Aside from panoramic views of the city and Pikes Peak in the distance, the road leads to the **Cheyenne Mountain Zoo** ❺ and then further spirals to the **Will Rogers Shrine of the Sun** ❻. At the base of the mountain, turn west on Cheyenne Road and follow the signs to **Seven Falls** ❼. Exit Seven Falls on South Cheyenne Cañon Road heading north until it intersects North Cheyenne Cañon Road. There, turn west and enter **North Cheyenne Cañon Park** ❽. Leaving the park, follow North Cheyenne Cañon Road east to a fork with Cheyenne Road. Continue east on Cheyenne Road to Nevada Avenue. Turn north and head back into town.

Colorado Springs's handsome downtown contains many historically significant buildings, including the **Pioneers Museum** ❾. A few blocks north is the **Colorado Springs Fine Arts Center** ❿. Take Nevada Avenue south and Boulder Street east to the **Olympic Training Center** ⓫. Cross under Interstate 25 to Colorado Avenue and take it west, turning left on 21st Street, which you'll follow to **Ghost Town** ⓬ and the **Van Briggle Art Pottery Factory and Showroom** ⓭. Back on Colorado Avenue you'll find yourself in **Old Colorado City** ⓮, once a separate, rowdier town where miners caroused; today it's a National Historic Landmark District whose restored buildings house some of the city's choicest galleries and boutiques.

TIMING These attractions are fairly spread out and it takes at least an hour to tour the Air Force Academy. The Olympic Training Center tours last an hour. Save some time to wander around the Broadmoor, and while you're in the neighborhood, at least drive through Seven Falls. The Fine Arts Center also merits at least 45 minutes.

What to See: Colorado Springs

❹ **The Broadmoor Hotel.** This pink-stucco Italianate complex, built in 1918, remains one of the world's great luxury resorts—a tribute to the foresight of its original owner, the enterprising Spencer Penrose, one of Colorado Springs' wealthiest (and most conspicuously consuming) philanthropists. Having constructed the zoo, the Cheyenne Mountain Highway, and Pikes Peak Cog Railway, Penrose is credited with making the town the tourist mecca it is today. The free **Carriage House Museum** displays Penrose's prodigious carriage collection, from broughams (closed carriages with driver outside) to opera buses. ⊠ *1 Lake Circle* ☎ *719/634–7711 Ext. 5353* ⊠ *Free* ☉ *Museum Mon.–Sat. 10–noon, 1–5; Sun. 1–5.*

❺ **Cheyenne Mountain Zoo.** America's highest zoo, at 6,800 feet, has more than 500 animals amid mossy boulders and ponderosa pines. The

5

Live Like a King of Colorado Springs

The Pioneers Museum and other historical repositories in Colorado Springs give a sense of the life of General William Jackson Palmer, the city founder and an obsessed Europhile. He built the Springs in his image of "Little London" and gave his personal estate, Glen Eyrie, a Scottish name. Though he built his castlelike home for his wife, whom he adoringly called Queen, you could say he was the homemaker in the relationship. Gathering treasures from the four courners of the old country, he was responsible for furnishing and decorating their expansive abode. Despite his preference for all things European, Palmer was as American as any other Andrew Carnegie–era philanthropist. He carefully planned Colorado Springs, donated a fortune in land for parks, and brought cottonwood trees from the Arkansas River Valley to shade the streets. Take a day to trace the good general's steps, spending a night at the castle, just north of the Garden of the Gods. Awaken to the same sight he did: early morning sun lighting the red-rock formations beneath a blue Colorado sky. Then hike a bit on the local trails (you can get permission for this from the present caretakers, the Navigators Christian ministry). Palmer was known to survey the grounds daily, by foot or horseback. Breathe the mountain air and listen to babbling brooks before returning to the landscaped green lawns. When done with your day at Glen Eyrie, drive to the intersection of Platte and Nevada in downtown Colorado Springs, where a statue of the general seems to direct traffic adjacent to Acacia Park, one of many parks that came to be because of his generous land donations. In the cool of the shade, offer the old boy a salute.

Rafting

Held in high regard for its adrenaline-charging rapids that range from Class II to Class V, Colorado's Arkansas River is one of the most commercially rafted rivers in the world. Among the most fabled stretches of the Arkansas are the Narrows, the Numbers, and Browns Canyon, but extreme paddlers tend to jump on trips through the Royal Gorge, which the river has carved out over eons. There are numerous other whitewater opportunities in other areas: Clear and Gore creeks and the Dolores, Gunnison, and Colorado rivers, to name a few.

African Rift Valley opened in May 2003 and features the zoo's signature giraffe herd, said to be one of the most prolific in the world. Other highlights include the primates, wolves, and big cats of Asia. ⊠ *4250 Cheyenne Mt. Zoo Rd.* ☎ *719/633–9925* ✉ *$12* ☉ *May–Sept., daily 9–6; Oct.–Apr., daily 9–5.*

❿ **Colorado Springs Fine Arts Center.** This pueblo-style space includes a performing-arts theater, an art school, and a room devoted to the work and life of famed Western artist Charles Russell. Also at the center are a handsome sculpture garden, a surprisingly fine permanent collection of modern art, and rotating exhibits that highlight the cultural contributions of the area's diverse ethnic groups. ⊠ *30 W. Dale St.* ☎ *719/ 634–5581* ⊕ *www.csfineartscenter.org* ✉ *$5. Sat. free* ☉ *Tues.–Sat. 9–5, Sun. 1–5.*

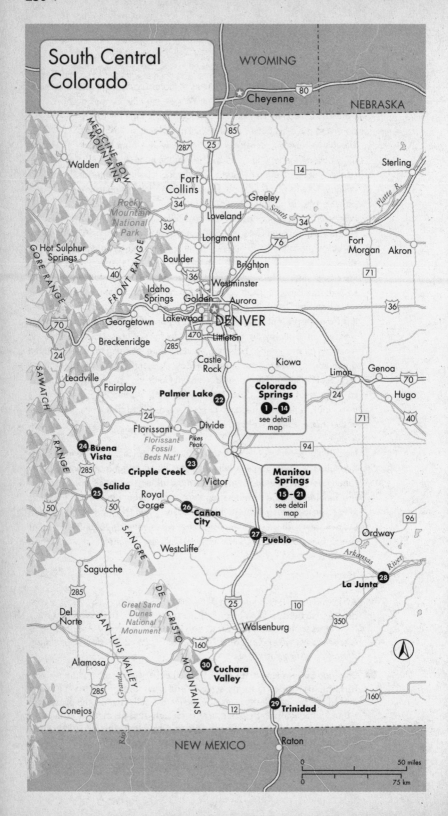

South Central Colorado

WYOMING

★ Cheyenne   80

NEBRASKA

MEDICINE BOW MOUNTAINS

Walden

287   85   25

Sterling

14

Fort Collins

34   Greeley

Loveland

34

Rocky Mountain National Park

36   Longmont

76

Fort Morgan   Akron

Hot Sulphur Springs

GORE RANGE

40   FRONT RANGE

Boulder   36   Brighton

71

Idaho Springs   Westminster

36

70   Georgetown   Golden   Aurora

DENVER

Lakewood   36

Breckenridge   285   470   Littleton

24   SAWATCH   Castle Rock   Kiowa

Leadville   Fairplay   Limon   Genoa   70

Palmer Lake   22   **Colorado Springs**   24   Hugo

40

1 – **14**
see detail map

71

24   Divide

Florissant   Pikes Peak

RANGE   Florissant Fossil Beds Nat'l

94

24 Buena Vista   **23**

285   **Manitou Springs**

Cripple Creek   Victor   **15** – **21**
see detail map

25 Salida   Royal Gorge   **26** Cañon City   96

50   50   Ordway

27   Pueblo

Westcliffe   Arkansas River

SANGRE   Saguache   La Junta   28

285   Great Sand Dunes National Monument   10   350

Del Norte   DE   Walsenburg

CRISTO   160

Alamosa   SAN LUIS VALLEY   MOUNTAINS   **30** Cuchara Valley

285   12   **29** Trinidad   160

Conejos

NEW MEXICO   Raton

0   50 miles
0   75 km

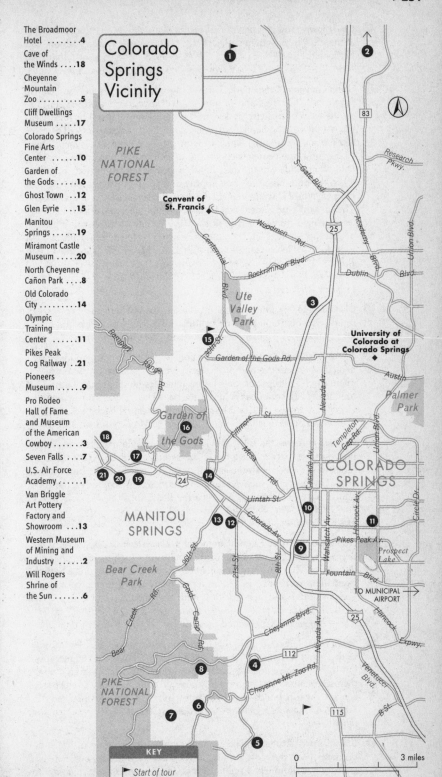

The Broadmoor
Hotel **4**

Cave of
the Winds **18**

Cheyenne
Mountain
Zoo **5**

Cliff Dwellings
Museum **17**

Colorado Springs
Fine Arts
Center **10**

Garden of
the Gods **16**

Ghost Town . .**12**

Glen Eyrie . . .**15**

Manitou
Springs **19**

Miramont Castle
Museum **20**

North Cheyenne
Cañon Park **8**

Old Colorado
City **14**

Olympic
Training
Center **11**

Pikes Peak
Cog Railway . .**21**

Pioneers
Museum **9**

Pro Rodeo
Hall of Fame
and Museum
of the American
Cowboy **3**

Seven Falls **7**

U.S. Air Force
Academy **1**

Van Briggle
Art Pottery
Factory and
Showroom . . .**13**

Western Museum
of Mining and
Industry **2**

Will Rogers
Shrine of
the Sun **6**

**Colorado
Springs
Vicinity**

PIKE
NATIONAL
FOREST

**Convent of
St. Francis**

S. Gate Blvd.

Research Pkwy.

83

Woodmen Rd.

Centennial Blvd.

Rockrimmon Blvd.

Academy Blvd.

Union Blvd.

Dublin Blvd.

25

Ute
Valley
Park

**University of
Colorado at
Colorado Springs**

Garden of the Gods Rd.

Nevada Av.

Austin

Palmer
Park

Bexter

Range Rd.

Garden of
the Gods

Fillmore St.

Mesa Rd.

Cascade Av.

Templeton Gap Rd.

Union Blvd.

COLORADO
SPRINGS

Circle Dr.

24

Uintah St.

Colorado Av.

Wahsatch Av.

Hancock Av.

MANITOU
SPRINGS

21st St.

8th St.

Pikes Peak Av.

Prospect
Lake

Bear Creek
Park

Fountain Blvd.

TO MUNICIPAL
AIRPORT

Bear Creek Rd.

Gold Camp Rd.

Cheyenne Blvd.

Nevada Av.

25

Hancock Expwy.

PIKE
NATIONAL
FOREST

112

Cheyenne Mt. Zoo Rd.

Venetucci Blvd.

B St.

115

KEY

▶ *Start of tour*

0   3 miles
0   2 km

⑫ **Ghost Town.** You can play a real player piano and a nickelodeon at this authentic Western town with a sheriff's office, general store, saloon, and blacksmith. *400 S. 21st St. 719/634–0696 $6 May–Labor Day, Mon.–Sat. 9–6, Sun. 11–5; Labor Day–Apr., Mon.–Sat. 10–6, Sun. noon–5.*

⑧ **North Cheyenne Cañon Park.** This is Colorado Springs at its best. Nearby Seven Falls has the hand of man all over its natural wonders, but the 1,600 acres of this city park manifest nature and natural history without a hint of commercialism—or charge. Start at **Starsmore Discover Center,** at the mouth of the canyon off Cheyenne Boulevard. Open year-round, the center is chock-full of nature exhibits and a climbing wall where kids can try their hands and feet against gravity. In spring when the hummingbirds first appear, and again in August, on National Hummingbird Day, the center educates with fun activities and seminars. The canyon's moderate hikes include Columbine and Cutler trails, each less than a 3-mi round-trip. Both afford a view of the city and a sense of accomplishment. Further into the canyon is Helen Hunt Falls, named for a deceased local naturalist and author. *2110 North Cheyenne Cañon Rd. 719/578–6146 Free Year-round. Discover Center Apr.–Oct., weekdays 9–4:30, Sat. 9–5, Sun. 11–5; Nov.–Mar., Sat. 9–5, Sun. 11–5. Hrs can vary, call ahead.*

Fodor'sChoice ★

⑭ **Old Colorado City.** Once a separate, rowdier town where miners caroused, today it's a National Historic Landmark District whose restored buildings house choice galleries and boutiques. *Colorado Ave.*

⑪ **Olympic Training Center.** America's hopefuls come to train and be tested here, and depending on which teams are in residence at the time, you might catch a glimpse of some future Wheaties-box material. The guided tours every half hour (except during the noon hour) begin with an 8-minute video, and proceed with a 30-minute walk around the facilities. *1750 E. Boulder St. 719/866–4619 Free Mon.–Sat. 9–5, Sun. 10–4.*

⑨ **Pioneers Museum.** Once the Old El Paso County Courthouse, this repository has artifacts relating to the entire Pikes Peak area. It's most notable for the special exhibits it mounts (or receives from institutions such as the Smithsonian), such as a quilt competition commemorating the 100th anniversary of the song "America the Beautiful." *215 S. Tejon St. 719/385–5990 www.cspm.org Free Nov.–Apr., Tues.–Sat. 10–5; May–Oct., Tues.–Sat. 10–5, Sun. 1–5.*

③ **Pro Rodeo Hall of Fame and Museum of the American Cowboy.** Even a tenderfoot would get a kick out of this museum, which includes changing displays of Western art; permanent photo exhibits that capture both the excitement of bronco-bustin' and the lonely life of the cowpoke; gorgeous saddles and belt buckles; and multimedia tributes to rodeo's greatest competitors. *101 Pro Rodeo Dr., Exit 147 off I–25 719/528–4764 www.prorodeo.com $6 Daily 9–5.*

⑦ **Seven Falls.** The road up to this transcendent series of cascades is touted as the "grandest mile of scenery in Colorado." That's an exaggeration, but the red-rock canyon *is* amazing—though no more so than the falls themselves, plummeting into a tiny emerald pool. A set of 224 steep steps leads to the top, but there is an elevator, too. *Cheyenne Blvd. 719/632–0765 $8.25 May–Sept., daily 8:30 AM–10:30 PM; Oct.–Apr., daily 9–4.*

① **U.S. Air Force Academy.** The academy, which set up camp in 1954, has become one of the most popular attractions in Colorado, but increased security has diminished public access. In fact, unless you're on an approved tour such as Gray Line, or a member of your party has a Department of Defense ID, you won't be allowed onto the grounds. Highlights include the futuristic design, 18,000 beautiful acres of land (that have been dedicated as a game preserve), and antique and historic aircraft displays. At the visitor center you'll find photo exhibits, a model of a cadet's room, a gift shop, a snack bar, and a 14-minute film designed to make you want to run out and sign up. Other stops on the tour include a B-52 display, sports facilities, a planetarium, a parade ground (the impressive cadet review takes place daily at noon; other times of day, watch the freshmen square off their corners), and the chapel. The Air Force chapel is easily recognized by its unconventional design, which features 17 spires that resemble sharks' teeth or billowing sails. Catholic, Jewish, and Protestant services can be held simultaneously here. ⊠ *Exit 156B, off I–25 N* ☎ *719/333–7482, Gray Line Tours 719/633–1747* ⊕ *www.asafa.af.mi* ⊠ *Free* ⊙ *Daily 9–5.*

⑬ Van Briggle Art Pottery Factory and Showroom. The Van Briggle factory has been in operation since the turn of the 20th century, and its ceramic work is admired for its graceful lines and pure, vibrant glazes. A free tour of the facility culminates—naturally—in the mind-boggling showroom. ⊠ *600 S. 21st St.* ☎ *719/633–7729* ⊕ *www.vanbriggle.com* ⊠ *Free* ⊙ *Mon.–Sat. 8:30–4.*

❷ Western Museum of Mining and Industry. The rich history of mining is represented through comprehensive exhibits of equipment and techniques and hands-on demonstrations, including gold panning. The 27-acre mountain site has several outdoor exhibits, and is a great spot for a picnic. ⊠ *Exit 156A, off I–25 N* ☎ *719/488–0880* ⊕ *www.wmmi.org* ⊠ *$7* ⊙ *June–Oct., Mon.–Sat. 9–4; Nov.–May, Mon.–Sat. 9–4.*

❻ Will Rogers Shrine of the Sun. This five-story tower was dedicated in 1937 after the tragic plane crash that claimed Rogers's life. Its interior is painted with all manner of Western murals (in which Rogers and Colorado Springs benefactor Spencer Penrose figure prominently) and is plastered with photos and homespun sayings of America's favorite cowboy. In the chapel are 15th- and 16th-century European artworks. ⊠ *Cheyenne Mountain Zoo Rd.* ⊠ *$10 (free with Cheyenne Mountain Zoo ticket)* ⊙ *Memorial Day–Labor Day, daily 9–5:30; Labor Day–Memorial Day, daily 9–4:30.*

A Good Tour: Manitou Springs

The home of Manitou Springs mineral water is set in this quaint National Historic Landmark District, which exudes an informal, if not genteel charm. Antique trolleys ply the streets in summer and the chamber of commerce offers free walking tours of the naturally effervescent springs. Stop by Soda Springs or Twin Springs for an after-dinner spritz (it tastes and acts just like Alka-Seltzer). The strong hardware taste makes for a heavy-metal lemonade. Locals, who swear the spring water is laced with lithium, say that trace element is why they're always so calm, and, ah, smiling. Manitou has a growing artist population; the Manitou Art Project sponsors a year-round public exhibition, and the galleries offer the delightful ArtWalk Thursday evenings in summer.

Take U.S. 24 west from Interstate 25 and 30th Street north to reach the **Glen Eyrie** ⑮ ⌐ estate. Double back on 30th Street to the **Garden of the Gods** ⑯ visitor center. Drive through Garden of the Gods and back onto U.S. 24 west to the **Cliff Dwellings Museum** ⑰ and the **Cave of the Winds** ⑱. On the left of U.S. 24 headed west is **Manitou Springs** ⑲, home of the mineral water. Off Ruxton Avenue, just past downtown, is the **Miramont Castle Museum** ⑳. Continue down Ruxton Avenue to the **Pikes Peak Cog Railway** ㉑.

TIMING You should be able to cover most of the area's attractions on foot in an hour. Exceptions are the Garden of the Gods and the Glen Eyrie estate, which you'll need to drive to. Both are technically in Colorado Springs, but are nearby and handy to include on this tour. The Cave of the Winds tours take 45 minutes; the Glen Eyrie estate tours take about as long. Save some time to hike in the Garden of the Gods and browse in Manitou Springs' downtown.

What to See: Manitou Springs

18 Cave of the Winds. Discovered by two boys in 1880, the cave has been exploited as a tourist sensation ever since. The entrance is through the requisite "trading post," but once inside the cave you'll forget the hype and commercialism. You'll pass through grand chambers with such names as the Crystal Palace, Oriental Garden, the Old Curiosity Shop, the Temple of Silence, and the Valley of Dreams. The cave contains examples of every major sort of limestone formation, from stalactites and stalagmites to delicate cave flowers, rare anthracite crystals, flowstone (rather like candle wax), and cave coral. Enthusiastic guides for the 45-minute tour, most of them members of the Grotto Club (a spelunking group), also run more adventurous cave expeditions with higher degrees of difficulty—and higher prices. Summer evenings, a laser show transforms Williams Canyon, the backdrop for the spectacle. It's an unsurpassed sound-and-light show of massively corny, yet undeniably effective, proportions. ☒ *Cave of the Winds Rd., off Hwy. 24* ☏ *719/685–5444* ☞ *$15* ☉ *Daily 9–9.*

17 Cliff Dwellings Museum. These 40 rooms of prehistoric ruins include ancestral Puebloan cliff dwellings dated to AD 1100. Two rooms of artifacts offer information on the history of the dwellings. Native American dance demonstrations take place several times a day during summer. ☒ *U.S. 24* ☏ *719/685–5242* ⊕ *www.cliffdwellingsmuseum.com* ☞ *$8* ☉ *May–Sept., daily 9–6; Oct.–Apr., daily 9–5.*

16 Garden of the Gods. These magnificent, eroded red-sandstone formations—from gnarled jutting spires to sensuously abstract monoliths—were sculpted more than 300 million years ago. Follow the road as it loops through the Garden of the Gods, past such oddities as the Three Graces, the Siamese Twins, and the Kissing Camels. High Point, near the south entrance, provides camera hounds with the ultimate photo-op: a formation known as Balanced Rock, and jagged formations that frame Pikes Peak. The visitor center has several geologic, historic, and hands-on displays. ☒ *1830 N. 30th St., Colorado Springs* ☏ *719/634–6666* ☞ *Free* ☉ *June–Aug., daily 8–8; Sept.–May, daily 9–5.*

▶ **15 Glen Eyrie.** General William Jackson Palmer, the founder of Colorado Springs, was greatly influenced by European architecture and lifestyle and lived in this evolving mansion-turned-castle from its beginnings in the 1870s until his death in 1909. Original gas lamps and sandstone structures remain. Many of its rocks were hewn with the moss still clinging, to give them an aged look. The period furnishings within the mansion are not original possessions of the general. Try to come here for high tea or at Christmastime, when there's an extravagant drive-through nativity scene. The grandiose estate is maintained by a nondenominational fundamentalist Christian ministry called the Navigators, which publishes religious literary works. ☒ *3820 30th St.* ☏ *719/634–0808* ⊕ *www.gleneyrie.org* ☞ *$5* ☉ *Tours June–Aug., daily at 11 and 1; Sept.–May, daily at 1.*

19 Manitou Springs. The town grew around the springs, so all nine of them are smack in the middle of downtown. Competitions to design the fountains that bring the spring water to the public ensured that each fountain design is unique. It's a bring-your-own cup affair; the water (frequently tested) is potable and free. The Chamber of Commerce publishes a free guide to the springs. ☎ 719/685–5089 ✆ *Free.*

㉒ Miramont Castle Museum. This Byzantine extravaganza was commissioned in 1895 as the private home of French priest Jean-Baptiste Francolon. The museum is a mad medley of exhibits, with 46 rooms offering a wide variety of displays, from original furnishings to antique doll and railroad collections. ✉ *9 Capitol Hill Ave.* ☎ *719/685–1011* ⊕ *www.pikes-peak.com* ✆ *$5* ⊙ *June–Aug., daily 10–5; Sept.–May, daily 11–4.*

㉑ Pikes Peak Cog Railway. The world's highest cog railway departs from Manitou and follows a frolicking stream up a steep canyon, through copses of quaking aspen and towering lodgepole pines, before reaching the timberline and the 14,110-foot summit. ✉ *Ruxton Ave. (depot)* ☎ *719/685–5401* ⊕ *www.cograilway.com* ✆ *$26.50* ⊙ *May–mid-Nov., daily 9–5; call for winter hrs.*

off the beaten path

PIKES PEAK HIGHWAY – You can drive the 19-mi Pikes Peak Highway, which rises nearly 7,000 feet in its precipitous, dizzying climb to the Summit House, a pit-stop café and trading post, in approximately three hours, round-trip. This is the same route that leading race-car drivers follow every July in the famed Pikes Peak Hill Climb, at speeds approaching 100 mi an hour. ✉ *Hwy. 24 west to Cascade (4 mi from Manitou Springs)* ☎ *719/684–9383* ✆ *$10 ($35 maximum fee per carload)* ⊙ *Summit House May–Oct., daily 7–7; Nov.–Apr., daily 9–3.*

Sports & the Outdoors

GOLF **The Broadmoor** (✉ 1 Lake Circle ☎ 719/634–7711) offers 54 splendid holes to guests and members. **Colorado Springs Country Club** (✉ 3333 Templeton Gap Rd. ☎ 719/473–1782) is a fine 18-hole course. The public **Pine Creek Golf Course** (✉ 9850 Divot Terr. ☎ 719/594–9999) has 18 holes.

HIKING Trails in the Pikes Peak area include Barr Trail, which heads up the mountain, and dozens in open spaces and city parks, such as North Cheyenne Cañon Park. Rock climbers test their skills on the stark spires and cliffs of the Garden of the Gods, another city park. Register at the visitor center if you're climbing. The **El Paso County Parks Department** (☎ 719/520–6375) can provide information about facilities in the Colorado Springs/Pikes Peak area. The **Colorado Springs Parks, Recreation and Cultural Services Department** (☎ 719/385–5940) is handy with outdoors information.

HORSEBACK **Academy Riding Stables** (✉ 4 El Paso Blvd., Colorado Springs ☎ 719/
RIDING 633–5667) offers trail rides. **Stables at The Broadmoor** (✉ 1 Lake Circle, Colorado Springs ☎ 719/448–0371) can put you in the saddle for rides in Pike National Forest.

Where to Eat

$$$$ ✕ **Margarita.** Plants, adobe walls, terra cotta tile, and mosaic tables lend an air of refinement to this upscale eatery, whose constantly changing menu is an intriguing hybrid of Mexican and Continental influences. ✉ *7350 Pine Creek Rd.* ☎ *719/598–8667* ▭ *AE, D, DC, MC, V* ⊙ *Closed Mon. No lunch weekends.*

$$–$$$$ ✕ **The Blue Star.** The menu changes in all aspects every Thursday except in the quality, which is fabulous. The kitchen does miraculous things in each meal category, be it meat, seafood, pasta, or the salads and sand-

wiches served in the lively (and less expensive) bar area. Influences can drift from traditional to pan-Asian to Mediterranean and then work their way back around the globe. The line of multigenerational locals—everyone from blue-haired ladies to orange-mohawked punks—forms early on weekends, so it's best to make a reservation. ⊠ *1645 S. Tejon St.* ☎ *719/632–1086* ⊟ *AE, MC, V.*

★ **$$–$$$$** ✕ **Briarhurst Manor.** One of the most exquisitely romantic restaurants in Colorado has several dining rooms, each with its own look and mood. The rich decor includes cherry wood wainscoting, balustrades, and furnishings; Van Briggle wood-and-ceramic fireplaces, tapestries, chinoiserie, and hand-painted glass. Start with the perfectly prepared Chateaubriand or the striped bass. Colorado cuisine—which means a heavy influence on game—is a specialty here, and includes Plains bison. But even non-red-meat eaters make it a point to come here for fish preparations like blackberry salmon. ⊠ *404 Manitou Ave.* ☎ *719/685–1864* ⊟ *AE, MC, V.*

$$–$$$$ ✕ **Craftwood Inn.** This intimate restaurant, more than 50 years old, regularly hosted such luminaries as Cary Grant, Bing Crosby, and Liberace. A delightful Old English feel is achieved through wrought-iron chandeliers, stained-glass partitions, heavy wood beams, and a majestic stone-and-copper fireplace. To start, try the crab and artichoke bisque, pistachio pesto ravioli, or warm spinach salad with wild boar bacon. The mixed game bird and wild grill are particularly memorable entrées, especially when accompanied by a selection from the well-considered and fairly priced wine list. ⊠ *404 El Paso Blvd.* ☎ *719/685–9000* ⊟ *AE, D, DC, MC, V* ☉ *No lunch.*

$$–$$$$ ✕ **La Petite Maison.** This pretty Victorian abode has been divided into several romantic dining rooms. Pale pink walls, floral tracery, Parisian gallery posters, and pots overflowing with flowers create the atmosphere of a French country home. The progressive menu includes a horseradish-crusted Black Angus filet, halibut, roast leg of lamb, and crabcake with crayfish hash. Reservations are recommended. ⊠ *1015 W. Colorado Ave.* ☎ *719/632–4887* ⊟ *AE, D, DC, MC, V* ☉ *Closed Sun. and Mon.*

$$–$$$$ ✕ **Pepper Tree.** From its hilltop position, the Pepper Tree enjoys stellar views of the city that enhance the restaurant's aura of quiet sophistication. It's one of those old-fashioned places were table-side preparations (including the inevitable and delectable pepper steak) are the stock-in-trade, and flambé is considered the height of both elegance and decadence. The chicken marsala and lamb chops are superb and specials might included calamari stuffed with crabmeat and bacon. Reservations are recommended. ⊠ *888 W. Moreno Ave.* ☎ *719/471–4888* ⊟ *AE, DC, MC, V* ☉ *Closed Sun. and Mon. No lunch.*

$–$$ ✕ **Adam's Mountain Café.** With whirring ceiling fans, hanging plants, floral wallpaper, and old-fashioned hardwood tables and chairs, this cozy eatery is reminiscent of someone's great-grandmother's parlor. Come here for smashing breakfasts (fluffy pancakes, muffins, and organic juices); fine pastas (try the baked penne with peperonata and three cheeses); great sandwiches (red-chili-rubbed free-range chicken on grilled polenta with red chili sauce and lime sour cream); and yummy desserts. ⊠ *110 Cañon Ave.* ☎ *719/685–1430* ⊟ *AE, D, MC, V* ☉ *No dinner Sun. and Mon.*

$–$$ ✕ **Saigon Cafe.** Authentic Vietnamese dishes come with that little extra zest, whether from mint, garlic, peppers, or spice. Rice noodle bowls, vegetarian or topped with your choice of meat or seafood, are the most popular orders. The staff is excellent and close tables might make for some elbow-rubbing with your fellow guests. ⊠ *20 E. Colorado Ave.* ☎ *719/633–2888* ⊟ *AE, MC, V* ☉ *Closed Sun.*

¢–$$ ✕**El Tesoro.** At the turn of the 20th century this building served as a brothel, and then for many years it was an artists' atelier. Today, it's a restaurant that doubles as an art gallery. The adobe and exposed brick walls and the tile work are original; rugs, textiles, and the ubiquitous garlands of chili add color. The sterling northern New Mexican food is the real thing—a savvy, savory blend of Native American, Spanish, and Anglo-American influences. The *posole* (hominy with pork and red chili) is magical, the green chili heavenly, and innovative originals such as mango quesadillas (a brilliant pairing of sweet and spicy elements) are simply genius. ✉ *10 N. Sierra Madre St.* ☎ *719/471–0106* ⊟ *AE, D, MC, V* ⊘ *Closed Sun. No dinner Mon. No lunch Sat.*

¢–$ ✕**La Casita Patio Cafe.** Though it's a table-service restaurant serving three meals a day, it feels a bit like a fast-food eatery. Mexican dishes include tacos and fajitas served with beans and rice. The tortillas are homemade and fresh salsa varieties and cilantro top off the fixings bar. The Nevada Avenue location is convenient to the Garden of the Gods. ✉ *3504 N. Academy Blvd.* ☎ *719/574–1499* ⊟ *AE, D, DC, MC, V* ✉ *4295 N. Nevada Ave.* ☎ *719/599–7829* ⊟ *AE, D, DC, MC, V.*

¢ ✕**King's Chef.** With the addition of pink and purple turrets, this original Valentine diner is scarcely recognizable as such. If you finish your order, consisting of a massive mound of home fries or hash browns served alongside an omelet or a red-chili cheeseburger, you'll receive a "clean-plate" award. Come for breakfast all day, humor from behind the counter, and the chance to meet all kinds of locals. ✉ *110 E. Costilla Ave.* ☎ *719/634–9135* ⊟ *No credit cards.*

$ ✕**Old Chicago.** One of many "concept restaurants" popular throughout Colorado, this one has a sports bar in front and a pleasant enclosed atrium and outdoor patio in back. It's a pizza, pasta, and beer (110 varieties) joint, and it scores on all counts. It has several locations in Colorado Springs. ✉ *7115 Commerce Center Dr.* ☎ *719/593–7678* ⊟ *AE, D, MC, V.*

Where to Stay

$$$$ 🛏 **The Broadmoor.** One of America's truly great hotels, the Broadmoor
FodorsChoice celebrates over eight decades of unwaveringly excellent service. Com-
★ pletely self-contained, the hotel has a private lake and its 30 buildings spread majestically across 3,500 acres. The pink-and-ocher main building, crowned by Mediterranean-style towers, has the loveliest rooms, furnished with either period or contemporary furnishings. The resort is renowned for its three world-class championship golf courses and former Davis Cup coach Dennis Ralston's tennis camps. Three of the 10 restaurants (the Tavern, the Penrose Room, and the Charles Court) rank among the state's finest. ✉ *One Lake Circle, Box 1439, 80906* ☎ *719/634–7711 or 800/634–7711* 🖷 *719/577–5700* ⊕ *www.broadmoor.com* ➪ *750 rooms, 110 suites* ⚴ *10 restaurants, 3 18-hole golf courses, 12 tennis courts, 2 pools (1 indoor), hair salon, health club, spa, fishing, horseback riding, 3 bars, cinema, children's programs (ages 4–12), meeting room, car rental* ⊟ *AE, DC, MC, V.*

$$–$$$$ 🛏 **The Cliff House.** This Victorian-era jewel in the emerging class of
FodorsChoice small luxury hotels was built in 1874 as a Manitou Springs stagecoach
★ stop between Colorado Springs and Leadville. Crown princes, U.S. presidents, and famous entertainers have been past guests, and their names live on as monikers for several well-appointed suites: the Theodore Roosevelt, the Buffalo Bill, and the Clark Gable, to name a few. For locals, the Cliff House is a special occasion getaway plump with accoutrements that pamper: two-person spas and steam showers, and even heated toilet seats. The restaurant serves fine Continental cuisine. An attentive wine captain and knowledgeable staff guide you through heavenly selections of drink and menu items such as crab cakes, seafood, steaks, and decadent desserts. ✉ *306 Cañon Ave., 80829* ☎ *719/685–3000 or*

888/212–7000 🖷 719/685–3913 ⊕ *www.thecliffhouse.com* 📎 *38 rooms, 17 suites* ♿ *2 restaurants, room service, in-room data ports, gym, nightclub, meeting rooms* 🖃 *AE, D, MC, V.*

$$–$$$$ 🖾 **Antlers Adams Mark.** With its superb, historic location downtown, two previous incarnations of this hotel competed with the Broadmoor for the business of the rich and famous. William Jackson Palmer built the place to house his antler collection in 1883. The spacious, elegant marble-and-granite lobby strikes an immediate note of class, and the deep-cushioned sofas in the lounge make a comfortable place to read the paper or watch the news. The atrium off the lobby holds a day spa. ⊠ *4 S. Cascade Ave., 80903* ☎ *719/473–5600 or 800/444–2326* 🖷 *719/444–0417* ⊕ *www.adamsmark.com* 📎 *292 rooms, 13 suites* ♿ *2 restaurants, room service, in-room data ports, indoor pool, health club, indoor hot tub, spa, bar, business services, meeting room* 🖃 *AE, D, DC, MC, V.*

$$ 🖾 **Embassy Suites.** This is one of the original properties in this chain, and it's among the best. The airy atrium lobby, crawling with plants, has a stream running through it, stocked with koi. To complete the tropical motif, a waterfall tumbles lavishly into the stream. Suites are comfortable, favoring teal and dusty rose. The pool deck offers a view of Pikes Peak; jazz groups play here every Thursday night in summer. Free breakfast is cooked to order. ⊠ *7290 Commerce Center Dr., 80919* ☎ *719/599–9100 or 800/362–2779* 🖷 *719/599–4644* ⊕ *www. embassysuites.com* 📎 *207 suites* ♿ *Restaurant, indoor pool, gym, hot tub, sauna, bar, meeting room* 🖃 *AE, D, DC, MC, V* ⦿ *BP.*

$$ 🖾 **Holden House.** Innkeepers Sallie and Welling Clark realized their dream when they lovingly restored this 1902 Victorian home and transformed it into a B&B. Two rooms in the main house, two in the adjacent carriage house, and one in the Victorian next door are filled with family heirlooms and antiques. Fireplaces, oversize or claw-foot tubs in the private baths, and down pillows and quilts make guest rooms cozy. A full breakfast is served in the antique-filled dining room. ⊠ *1102 W. Pikes Peak Ave., 80904* ☎ *719/471–3980* 📎 *5 rooms* 🖃 *AE, D, DC, MC, V* ⦿ *BP.*

$$ 🖾 **Red Stone Castle.** This Victorian stone home was built in the 1890s, and a stay here is a fantasy adventure, where you can have a turret of your own. In fact, the entire third floor, called the Inspiration Suite, is your domain. The only other occupants are the owners, the McGrew family, on the second floor. A three-course gourmet breakfast is served in the Victorian-appointed dining room. The private 20-acre estate overlooking Manitou Springs has views of the Garden of the Gods and Colorado Springs. ⊠ *601 S. Side Rd., 80829* ☎ *719/685–5070* ⊕ *www. redstonecastle.cjb.net* 📎 *1 suite* 🖃 *No credit cards* ⦿ *BP.*

$$ 🖾 **Victoria's Keep.** Proud owners Gerry and Donna Anderson preside over this turreted 1891 Queen Anne B&B. The parlor verges on the Dickensian, with its slightly fussy, Victorian clutter. There are carved tile ceilings and intricate tracery. Each Victorian-style room has its own fireplace and some distinguishing feature—a Jacuzzi or stained-glass windows or thrilling views of Miramont Castle. Full breakfasts and afternoon tea and dessert add to the more-than-pleasant guest experience. ⊠ *202 Ruxton Ave., 80829* ☎ *719/685–5354 or 800/905–5337* 🖷 *719/685–5913* ⊕ *www.victoriaskeep.com* 📎 *6 rooms* ♿ *Hot tub, mountain bikes* 🖃 *AE, D, MC, V* ⦿ *BP.*

CAMPING **⚠ Garden of the Gods Campground.** A generally shaded area right in the
¢ city and near natural attractions, this place is loaded with extras—even an indoor whirlpool. ⊠ *3704 West Colorado Ave., just north of U.S. 24* ☎ *800/248–9451 or 719/475–9450* ⊕ *www.coloradocampground. com* ♿ *Flush toilets, full hook-ups, drinking water, laundry facilities, showers, grills, picnic tables, snack bar, electricity, public phones, playground, pool* 📎 *223 full hook-ups, 33 electric and water hook-ups, 57*

tent sites 9 cabins ✉ *Full hook-ups $34, partial hook-ups $32, tents $28, cabins $40* ⌂ *Reservations essential* ▭ *D, MC, V* ☾ *Year-round.*

¢ ⌂ **Pikes Peak RV and Campgrounds.** Set your tent up beneath the shade of large trees along a creek in quaint but busy Manitou Springs. You'll be near natural attractions in the mountains and the quirky tourist strip of the city. ✉ *320 Manitou Ave.* ☎ *719/685–9459* 🖷 *719/685–1871* ⊕*www.rvingusa.com* ⌂ *Flush toilets, full hook-ups, drinking water, showers, general store* ⇩ *60 full hook-ups, 3 partial hook-ups, 6 tent sites* ✉ *Full and partial hook-ups $28, tents $22* ⌂ *Reservations essential* ▭ *MC, V* ☾ *Apr.–Oct.*

Nightlife & the Arts

BARS & LOUNGES   The **Golden Bee** (✉ International Center at the Broadmoor, One Lake Circle ☎ 719/634–7711) is an institution. The gloriously old-fashioned bar, with pressed-tin ceilings and magnificent woodwork, features a piano player leading sing-alongs. Trendy **32 Bleu American Bistro** (✉ 32 S. Tejon, ☎ 719/955–5664) has taken the downtown by storm since its arrival in early 2003. The live music (everything from jazz to rock) and lively spirits are half the reason there's any street traffic in the district on weeknights. Sunday brunch, lunches (think Monte Cristo sandwich) and dinners—contemporary cuisine—strike a note, too. **Judge Baldwin's** (✉ Antlers Adams Mark, 4 S. Cascade Ave. ☎ 719/473–5600) is an excellent brewpub. Some singles head to **Old Chicago** (✉ 118 N. Tejon Ave. ☎ 719/634–8812) for brews. **Phantom Canyon Brewing Co.** (✉ 2 E. Pikes Peak Ave. ☎ 719/635–2800), in a turn-of-the-20th-century warehouse, has rotating art exhibits, billiards, and great pub grub (try the pizzas or the sinful black-and-tan cheesecake brownie).

COMEDY CLUB   **Loonees Comedy Corner** (✉ 1305 N. Academy Blvd. ☎ 719/591–0707) showcases live stand-up comedy Wednesday–Sunday evenings; some of the performers here are nationally known.

DINNER SHOWS   The **Flying W Ranch** (✉ 3330 Chuckwagon Rd. ☎ 719/598–4000), open mid-May–September and weekends during winter, ropes them in for the sensational Western stage show and chuck wagon dinner. The **Iron Springs Chateau** (✉ across from Pikes Peak Cog Railway ☎ 719/685–5104) stages comedy melodramas along with dinner, April–September and between Thanksgiving and New Year's Eve.

MUSIC & DANCE
CLUBS   **Cowboys** (✉ 3910 Palmer Park Blvd. ☎ 719/596–1212) is for hard-core two-steppers. You can dance part of the night away at the Broadmoor's **Stars** (✉ One Lake Circle ☎ 719/634–7711), a sleek, intimate boîte with a striking black granite bar, a black marble floor inlaid with gold stars, and walls covered with photos of celebrities who have stayed at the hotel over the years. There is usually live jazz at the Broadmoor's **Tavern** (✉ One Lake Circle ☎ 719/634–7711) several nights weekly.

The Arts

Colorado Springs' **Pikes Peak Center** (✉ 190 S. Cascade Ave. ☎ 719/520–7469) presents a wide range of musical events as well as touring theater and dance companies.

Shopping

Upscale shopping areas—the kind normally found only in Denver—have moved into Colorado Springs as household incomes have increased. One example is **Shops at Briargate,** which opened in August 2003 across Interstate 25 from the Air Force Academy. Among the tenants are clothiers Ann Taylor, Adrienne Vittadini, Coldwater Creek, and other retailers such as Pottery Barn and Sharper Image.

Charming boutiques and galleries cluster in Old Colorado City and the posh Broadmoor One Lake Avenue Shopping Arcade. The streets of Manitou Springs and Cripple Creek offer one souvenir shop and gallery after another.

The Citadel (✉ N. Academy Blvd. at E. Platte Ave., Colorado Springs), counts JCPenney and Dillard's among its more than 175 stores. **Chapel Hills Mall** (✉ 1710 Briargate Blvd., Colorado Springs), at the north end of town, has a Sears, a Foley's, and a splendid indoor ice arena.

BOUTIQUES **Brok'n Spoke** (✉ 2345 E. Boulder St., Colorado Springs ☎ 719/632–3131) is a bazaar of Western regalia, from square dance outfits to saddles. **The Rhinestone Parrot** (✉ 739 Manitou Ave., Manitou Springs ☎ 719/685–5333) sells brocaded and appliquéd purses, vests, and jackets, and antique costume jewelry. **American Classics Marketplace** (✉ 1815 N. Academy Blvd., Colorado Springs ☎ 719/596–8585) houses dozens of antique and boutique stores and booths in the east-central part of the city and is well worth a visit.

CRAFT & ART **Commonwheel Artists Co-Op** (✉ 102 Cañon Ave., Manitou Springs ☎ 719/
GALLERIES 685–1008) exhibits jewelry and fiber, clay, and glass art. The **Dulcimer Shop** (✉ 740 Manitou Ave., Manitou Springs ☎ 719/685–9655) sells these stringed instruments. **The Flute Player Gallery** (✉ 2511 W. Colorado Ave., Colorado Springs ☎ 719/632–7702) carries southwest Native American art. **Helstrom Studios** (✉ 712 W. Colorado Ave., Colorado Springs ☎ 719/473–3620) showcases pottery and ethnic treasures. **Michael Garman Gallery** (✉ 2418 W. Colorado Ave., Colorado Springs ☎ 719/471–1600) offers Western-style paintings and contemporary sculpture.

Simpich Character Dolls (✉ 2413 W. Colorado Ave., Colorado Springs ☎ 719/636–3272) fashions detailed ceramic figurines and fabric dolls and displays extraordinary marionettes. After a free tour of the **Van Briggle Art Pottery Factory and Showroom** (✉ 600 S. 21st St., Colorado Springs ☎ 719/633–7729) you can better appreciate the pieces for sale. Wood-carver Sophie Cowman's evocative creations—from spoons to sculpture, made out of scrub oak, fragrant cedar, and cottonwood—are for sale at the **Wood Studio** (✉ 725 Manitou Ave., Manitou Springs ☎ No phone).

FOOD **Patsy's Candies** (✉ 1540 S. 21st St., Colorado Springs ☎ 719/633–7215) is renowned for its saltwater taffy and chocolate. In 2003 it celebrated its 100th anniversary. **Pikes Peak Vineyards** (✉ 3901 Janitell Rd., Colorado Springs ☎ 719/576–0075) offers tastings of its surprisingly fine wines, including merlots and chardonnays. **Rocky Mountain Chocolates** (✉ 2431 W. Colorado Ave., Colorado Springs ☎ 719/635–4131) tempts with chocolates of every variety, in delightful seasonal and holiday arrangements.

Palmer Lake

㉒ *25 mi north of Colorado Springs via I–25 and Hwy. 105.*

The idyllic town of Palmer Lake developed around the railroad tracks that were laid here in 1871—its lake was used as a refueling point for steam engines. Photogenic, artsy, and a bit sleepy, Palmer Lake is a magnet for hikers who set out for the evergreen-clad peaks at several in-town trailheads. The town is also home to more good restaurants and working artists than one would expect from a population of 1,500.

Every year since 1934, the 500-foot-tall, 91-bulb Palmer Lake Star lights up the face of Sundance Mountain above Palmer Lake. The town lights it the day after Thanksgiving and keeps it up through New Year's, attracting numerous sightseers.

In a landmark Kaiser-Frazer building on the north fringe of town, the **Tri-Lakes Center for the Arts** hangs rotating exhibits in its auditorium-gallery that also serves as a venue for music and theater. Classes and workshops are offered and several resident artists work from studios on-site. ⊠ *304 Hwy. 105* ☎*719/481–0475* ⊕*www.trilakesarts.com.* ⊠*Free* ⊙*Hrs vary.*

Sports & the Outdoors

FISHING Every June, the trout-stocked waters of **Palmer Lake** (☎ 719/481–2953) attract a horde of youngsters to an annual kids' fishing derby. A more secluded angling spot, the **Upper Palmer Lake Reservoir** (☎ 719/481–2953) offers a mix of trout and bottom-feeders in a peaceful mountain setting.

HIKING One of the most popular hiking trails between Denver and Colorado Springs, the **Palmer Lake Reservoirs Trail** (☎ 719/481–2953) begins near Glen Park. After a fairly steep incline, the 3-mi trail levels out and follows the shorelines of two reservoirs tucked between forested mountains. Bikes and leashed dogs are permitted. The **Santa Fe Regional Trail** (☎ 719/520–6375) begins on the shores of Palmer Lake and continues south for 14 mi, following an abandoned railroad right-of-way. The trail is also popular with equestrians and bikers, as well as cross-country skiers and snowshoers. To the west, the million-acre **Pike National Forest** (☎ 719/545–8737) is a camping and hiking destination. ·

Where to Stay & Eat

$$ ✕ **B & E Filling Station.** Casually elegant dining is the name of the game at the B & E Filling Station. With stained glass windows, mountain views, and local art on the walls, the place is easy on the eyes, and the food is easy on the palate. The best dishes are the crab cakes, bacon-wrapped beef tenderloin, and the daily fresh fish special. Reservations are recommended. ⊠*25 Hwy. 105* ☎*719/481–4780* ▭*D, MC, V* ⊙*No lunch. Closed Sun and Mon.*

¢ 🏨 **Falcon Inn Resort.** Just east of Interstate 25 (Exit 161), this reasonably well-maintained independent motel is the nearest lodging to Palmer Lake. The establishment is mainly of interest to those who realize halfway that they cannot drive the 50 mi between Denver and Colorado Springs, due to fatigue or, more commonly, snow. ⊠ *1865 Woodmoor Dr., Monument 80132* ☎ *719/481–3000* 🖶 *719/488–6645* ⟿ *120 rooms* ⚐ *Restaurant, pool* ▭ *AE, D, DC, V, MC.*

Nightlife & the Arts

NIGHTLIFE A roadhouse eatery where you get to play chef (patrons can cook steaks to their liking on a communal grill), **O'Malley's Steak Pub** (⊠ 104 Hwy. 105 ☎ 719/488–0321) is the most reliable nightlife in the area, with an upstairs poolroom, occasional bands, and plenty of local color.

THE ARTS This is a town that takes Christmas seriously. Like the Palmer Lake Star, the **Palmer Lake Yule Log Hunt** (☎ 719/481–2953) has been a town tradition since the 1930s, drawing hundreds of participants the third Sunday of every December. Whoever finds the large ribboned log hidden in the forested Glen area straddles it for a ride back into town (other participants get to pull). Once in town, the log serves as fuel for a ceremonial fire.

The **Tri-Lakes Center for the Arts** (⊠ 304 Hwy. 105 ☎ 719/481–0475) is the premier arts facility in the Palmer Lake area.

Larkspur (7 mi north of Palmer Lake, accessible via Interstate 25, Exit 173) is home to just 250 residents, but it knows how to throw a heck of a party—and a medieval one at that. For more than 20 summers, the **Colorado Renaissance Festival** has thrown open its gates to throngs of families, chain-mail-clad fantasy enthusiasts, tattooed bikers, and fun lovers of every other kind. Within the wooded, 350-acre "kingdom," there are performers who deliver everything from juggling stunts and fire-eating to hypnotism and comedy (don't miss the antics of Puke and Snot, the long-time stars of the festival). The big event happens three times a day, when knights square off in the arena for a theatrical joust. There are also over 200 artisans selling their wares (from hammocks to stained glass "Sunsifters"), games, rides, and a myriad of food and drink booths. It's a great way to while away a summer day, but it can be a bit much to handle on the hottest days. Admission is $8 for kids 5 to 12. Those under 5 may enter the realm for free. ☎ *303/688–6010* ⊕ *www.coloradorenaissance. com* ✉ *$15.95* ☉ *Mid–June–early Aug., weekends 10–6:30.*

Shopping

The fun and eclectic **Finders Keepers** (✉ 91 Hwy. 105, ☎ 719/487–8020) sells a variety of gifts, antiques, jewelry, and local arts and crafts.

COLORADO SPRINGS & VICINITY A TO Z

To research prices, get advice from other travelers, and book travel arrangements, visit www.fodors.com.

AIR TRAVEL

CARRIERS There are two ways to get to the Pikes Peak Region by air. If you've flown to Colorado Springs Airport (COS), chances are good you'll have made at least one connecting flight. (There are more than a dozen non-stop destinations, including Atlanta, Chicago, Dallas, Los Angeles, and Minneapolis.) Or, you can choose to fly to Denver International Airport (DIA). It's an 80-mi drive from DIA to the Springs, but it'll take you a solid two hours on the road, whether with your own car or one of the Denver–Colorado Springs shuttles.

🛪 Airlines & Contacts **Allegiant Air** ☎ 888/594-6937 ⊕ www.allegiant-air.com. **America West** ☎ 800/235-9292 ⊕ www.americawest.com. **American Airlines** ☎ 800/433-7300 ⊕ www.aa.com. **Continental Airlines** ☎ 800/525-0280 ⊕ www.continental. com. **Delta Airlines** ☎ 800/221-1212 ⊕ www.delta.com. **Mesa Airlines** ☎ 800/637-2247 ⊕ www.mesa-air.com. **Northwest Airlines** ☎ 800/225-2525 ⊕ www.nwa.com. **Skywest Delta Connection** ☎ 800/453-9417 ⊕ www.skywest.com. **United Airlines** ☎ 800/241-6522 ⊕ www.ual.com.

AIRPORTS & TRANSFERS

The company Ground Transportation offers service from the Colorado Springs Airport (COS) and downtown. For taxi service, try Yellow Cab.

🛪 Airport Information **Colorado Springs Airport** ☎ 719/550-1900 ⊕ www.flycos.com. **Denver International Airport** ☎ 303/342-2000 ⊕ www.flydenver.com.

🛪 Taxis & Shuttles **Ground Transportation** ☎ 719/597-4682. **Yellow Cab** ☎ 719/634-5000. **Denver Mountain Express** ☎ 877/933-4362.

BUS TRAVEL

Greyhound Lines and TNM & O Coaches both serve Colorado Springs.

🛪 **Greyhound Lines** ☎ 800/231-2222. **TNM & O Coaches** ☎ 719/635-1608.

CAR RENTAL

Colorado Springs has the typical line-up of car rental agencies. If you're considering flying to Denver and renting a car there, do some cost-comparison shopping. All of the car rental companies listed below, except Advantage, Enterprise, and Thrifty, have locations at the Colorado Springs Airport.

🛪 **Advantage** ☎ 719/574-1144 or 800/777-5500 ⊕ www.arac.com. **Alamo** ☎ 719/574-8579 ⊕ www.alamo.com. **Avis** ☎ 719/596-2571 ⊕ www.avis.com. **Budget** ☎ 719/

597-1271 ⊕ www.budget.com. **Dollar** ☎ 719/573-9990 ⊕ www.dollar.com. **Enterprise** ☎ 719/591-6644 or 800/736-8222 ⊕ www.enterprise.com. **Hertz** ☎ 719/596-1863 ⊕ www.hertz.com. **National** ☎ 719/596-1519 ⊕ www.nationalcar.com. **Thrifty** ☎ 719/390-9800 ⊕ www.thrifty.com.

CAR TRAVEL

Running north–south from Wyoming to New Mexico, Interstate 25 bisects Colorado and is the major artery into the area. In Colorado Springs, the main north–south roads are Interstate 25, Academy Boulevard, Nevada Avenue, and Powers Boulevard, and each will get you where you want to go in good time; east–west routes along Woodmen Road (far north), Austin Bluffs Parkway (north-central), and Platte Boulevard (south-central) can get backed up.

🔲 **AAA Colorado** ☎ 719/591-2222, or 719/632-8800 for emergency road service. **Colorado State Patrol** ☎ 719/635-0385, or 303/693-1111 for weather conditions in the state.

EMERGENCIES

🔲 Ambulance or Police **Emergencies** ☎ 911.
🔲 24-Hour Medical Care **Colorado Springs Memorial Hospital** ✉ 1400 E. Boulder St., Colorado Springs ☎ 719/365-5000. **Memorial Hospital Briargate Medical Campus** ✉ 8890 N. Union Blvd., Colorado Springs ☎ 719/365-2888. **Penrose Hospital** ✉ 2215 Cascade Ave., Colorado Springs ☎ 719/776-5000. **Penrose Community Hospital** ✉ 3205 N. Academy Blvd., Colorado Springs ☎ 719/776-3000.

WHERE TO STAY

🔲 **Colorado Springs Convention and Visitors Bureau** ☎ 800/368-4748 or 877/745-3773 ⊕ www.coloradosprings-travel.com. **Colorado Tourism Office** ☎ 800/265-6723 ⊕ www.colorado.com.

CAMPING The majority of tent wilderness camping opportunities are in outlying areas. RV parks are more common in the city.

🔲 **Coachlight Motel and RV Park** ☎ 719/687-8732 ⊕ www.coachlight.net. **Colorado State Parks** ☎ 800/678-2267 ⊕ www.parks.state.co.us. **Garden of the Gods Campground** ☎ 719/475-9450 ⊕ www.coloradocampground.com. **Pikes Peak RV and Campgrounds** ☎ 719/685-9459 ⊕ www.rvingusa.com. **KOA Kampground of Colorado Springs-South** ☎ 719/382-7575 ⊕ www.koa.com/where/CO/06253.htm. **U.S Forest Service** ☎ 719/636-1602 ⊕ www.fs.fed.us/r2/psicc/pp.

MEDIA

NEWSPAPERS & MAGAZINES The authoritative print source for news and information is the *Colorado Springs Gazette*.

TELEVISION & RADIO Colorado Springs's broadcast offerings, combined with those available from Denver, make for plenty of news and entertainment on the dials. The major TV networks are KOAA (NBC), channels 5 and 30; KTSC (PBS), channel 8; KKTV (CBS), channel 11; KRDO (ABC), channel 13; and KXRM (FOX), channel 21.

On AM radio, tune to KVOR 740 for news and KRDO 1240 for sports. On the FM dial, National Public Radio is broadcast on KRCC 91.5; KRDO 95.1 plays adult contemporary; KKCS 101.9 is home to modern country; and KSAX 105.5 plays smooth jazz.

SPORTS & THE OUTDOORS

ADVENTURE TOURS A number of activities are within an hour or two of Colorado Springs, including hot-air ballooning, white-water rafting, and access jeep tours. Jeep trips can include some time to stretch your legs—over a horse for some more backcountry exploring.

🔲 **Echo Canyon River Expeditions** ✉ 45000 U.S. Highway 50 West, Cañon City ☎ 800/590-3246 ⊕ www.raftecho.com. **Adventures Out West/Colorado Springs** ✉ 3120 Bonnevisa Dr., Colorado Springs ☎ 719/578-0935.

HIKING &
MOUNTAIN
BIKING
The mountains are waiting for you: it's just a matter of how you'll access them. Each August during the Pikes Peak Ascent and Marathon, hundreds run up Pikes Peak. If you want to hike it you have to train and prepare, and thousands do it every year—many of them flatlanders. Halfway up the Barr Trail to Pikes Peak is Barr Camp, where many hikers spend the night. The 12.6-mi hike gains 7,510 feet in elevation before you reach the summit. Outfitters drive bikers up to the peak too. **Barr Camp Caretakers** ⊠ 245 Raven Hills Rd. ☎ 719/264-1489 ⊕ www.barrcamp. com. **Pikes Peak Mountain Bike Tours** ☎ 888/593-3062 ⊕ www.biketours.com.

PUBLIC TRANSIT

Colorado Springs Transit serves most of the metropolitan area, including Manitou Springs.
Colorado Springs Transit ☎ 719/385-7433.

TOURS

Gray Line offers tours of the Colorado Springs area, including Pikes Peak and Manitou Springs, as well as jaunts to Cripple Creek. If you don't have a Department of Defense ID, a Gray Line tour is probably your sole means of visiting the Air Force Academy.
Tour Operators Gray Line ☎ 719/633-1181.

TRAIN TRAVEL

Amtrak ☎ 800/872-7245 ⊕ www.amtrak.com.

VISITOR INFORMATION

Colorado Springs Convention and Visitors Bureau ⊠ 104 S. Cascade Ave., Suite 104, 80903 ☎ 719/635-7506 or 800/368-4748 ⊕ www.coloradosprings-travel.com. **Manitou Springs Chamber of Commerce** ⊠ 354 Manitou Ave., 80829 ☎ 719/685-5089 or 800/642-2567. **Tri-Lakes Chamber of Commerce (Palmer Lake)** ⊠ 300 Hwy. 105, Monument 80132 ☎ 719/481-3282 ⊕ www.trilakes.net.

SOUTH CENTRAL COLORADO

The most direct route from Colorado Springs to the state's southern border is Interstate 25, but it's certainly not the most interesting. Instead, make a loop to the west, starting in Cripple Creek and taking in Florissant Fossil Beds, Buena Vista, Salida, and Cañon City and ending up in Pueblo, to hook up with Interstate 25 again. From here, you can detour to the east to La Junta, and then rejoin Interstate 25 in Trinidad. Finally, travel west to the lovely Cuchara Valley, and you will have experienced most of south central Colorado's charms.

Pike, bass, and trout are plentiful in this region: popular fishing spots include Trinidad Lake, Spinney Mountain Reservoir (between Florissant and Buena Vista), and the Arkansas and South Platte rivers.

Cripple Creek

②③ *46 mi from Colorado Springs via U.S. 24 west and Rte. 67 south.*

Colorado's third legalized gambling town, Cripple Creek once had the most lucrative mines in the state—and 10,000 boozing, brawling, bawdy citizens. Today, its old mining structures and the stupendous curtain of the Collegiate Peaks are marred by slag heaps and parking lots. Although the town isn't as picturesque as Central City or Black Hawk, the other gambling hot spots, Cripple Creek—a little rougher and dustier—feels more authentic.

The **Cripple Creek District Museum** provides a glimpse into mining life at the turn of the 20th century. ⊠ *East end of Bennett Ave.* ☎ *719/689-*

2634 ⊟ *$2.50* ⊙ *Late-May–mid-Oct., daily 10–5; mid-Oct.–late May, weekends noon–4.*

The **Mollie Kathleen Gold Mine Tour** descends 1,000 feet into the bowels of the earth in a mine that operated continuously from 1892 to 1961. ⊠ *Rte. 67, north of town* ☎ *719/689–2466* ⊟ *$15* ⊙ *Apr.–Oct., daily 9–4; tours every 20 min.*

Peek into the mining era's high life at the **Imperial Hotel and Casino** and spin the wheel of fortune. ⊠ *123 N. 3rd St.* ☎ *719/689–7777.*

The **Cripple Creek and Victor Narrow Gauge Railroad** weaves past abandoned mines to Cripple Creek's former rival, Victor, 6 mi to the south. In the boom days of the 1870s through the silver crash of 1893, more than 50 ore-laden trains made this run daily. Today, Victor is a sad town, virtually a ghost of its former self; walking the streets—past several abandoned or partially restored buildings—is an eerie experience that does far more to evoke the mining (and post-mining) days than tarted-up Cripple Creek. ⊠ *520 E. Carr St., at Bennett Ave.* ☎ *719/689–2640* ⊟ *$8.75* ⊙ *Memorial Day–Oct., daily 10–5; departs every 45 min.*

Where to Stay & Eat

Most of the casinos on East Bennett Avenue house predictable (albeit inexpensive) restaurants. Beef is the common denominator across all of the menus. Otherwise, there isn't much of a culinary scene in Cripple Creek proper.

★ $ ✕▥ **Victor Hotel.** Listed on the National Register of Historic Places, the Victor Hotel isn't in Cripple Creek, but it is the nicest place to stay in the area. Public spaces evoke Victorian splendor, and guest rooms have mountain views. Unfortunately, aside from the original open brickwork and a few old-fashioned tubs and radiators, decor and furnishings in rooms are prosaically modern, and bathrooms are tiny. The Bird Cage Café ($; open June–September) serves steak and seafood. ⊠ *4th and Victor Sts., Victor 80860, 6 mi southeast of Cripple Creek* ☎ *719/689–3553 or 800/713–4595* 🖷 *719/689–4197* ⊕ *www.victorhotel.com* ✍ *20 rooms* ⌂ *Restaurant* ⊟ *AE, D, MC, V.*

Nightlife & the Arts

NIGHTLIFE   The bar scene in Cripple Creek is dominated by casinos, where limited-stakes gambling is allowed (up to $5 per bet). The Rocky Mountain Victorian look of **The Gold Rush Hotel & Casino** (⊠ 209 E. Bennett Ave. ☎ 719/689–2646 or 800/235–8239) is fairly typical of the establishments that line historic East Bennett Avenue.

THE ARTS   Musical melodrama is the domain of **The Cripple Creek Players** (⊠ Butte Opera House, E. Bennett Ave. ☎ 719/689–2513 or 800/500–2513 ⊕ www.cripplecreekplayers.com), who perform eight shows weekly during summer.

Shopping

Victor Trading Co. & Manufacturing Works (⊠ 114 S. 3rd St., Victor ☎ 719/689–2346) has everything from beeswax candles to 43 styles of handmade brooms.

off the beaten path

FLORISSANT FOSSIL BEDS NATIONAL MONUMENT – A primeval rain forest was perfectly preserved by volcanic ash 35–40 million years ago, making this little-known site a treasure trove for paleontologists. The visitor center offers guided walks into the monument, or you can follow the well-marked hiking trails and lose yourself in the Oligocene epoch, among 300-foot petrified redwoods. ⊠ *26 mi north of Cripple Creek via Rte. 67 and U.S. 24 (east); 3 mi*

*south of Florissant, off U.S. 24, follow signs ☎ 719/748–3253
⊕ www.nps.gov/flfo ⊠ $3 ⊙ May–Sept., daily 8–7; Oct.–Apr.,
daily 8–4:30.*

Buena Vista

㉔ *112 mi from Cripple Creek via Rte. 67 north and U.S. 24 west.*

Sky-scraping mountains, the most impressive being the Collegiate Peaks,
ring Buena Vista (pronounced *byoo*-na *vis*-ta by locals). The 14,000-
foot whitecaps were first summited by alumni from Yale, Princeton, Harvard, and Columbia, who named them for their respective alma maters.
A small mining town–turned–resort–community, Buena Vista offers the
usual historic buildings alternating with inexpensive roadside motels.
The town is also a hub for the white-water rafting industry that plies
its trade on the popular Arkansas River.

Fodor'sChoice
★

Taking its own name from the many peaks named after famous uni-
versities, the 167,714-acre **Collegiate Peaks Wilderness Area** includes
more 14,000-foot-high mountains (eight) than any other wilderness
area in the lower 48 states, and six more peaks with summits above 13,800
feet. Forty miles of the Continental Divide snake through the area as
well. The most compelling reason to visit Buena Vista is for the almost
unequaled variety of hikes, climbs, and biking trails here. The office han-
dling inquiries about the park is in Leadville. ⊠ *Leadville Ranger District, 2015 N. Poplar St., Leadville* ☎ *719/486–0749.*

★

After a full day of activities, check out the **Mt. Princeton Hot Springs Resort** for a restorative soak. The springs have three swimming pools and
several "hot spots in the creek"—the water temperature ranges between 85°F and 105°F. The resort here also has 40 rooms ($) and a restau-
rant. ⊠ *5 mi west of Nathrop, County Rd. 162* ☎ *719/395–2447*
⊠ *$6* ⊙ *Mon.–Thurs. 9–9; Fri.–Sat. 9–11.*

Before leaving downtown, meander through the four rooms of the
Buena Vista Heritage Museum. Each room is devoted to an aspect of regional history: one to mining equipment and minerals, another to fashions and household utensils, a third to working models of the three
railroads that serviced the area in its heyday, and the last to historical
photos. ⊠ *512 E. Main St.* ☎ *719/395–8458* ⊠ *$3* ⊙ *Memorial
Day–Labor Day, daily 10–5.*

Sports & the Outdoors

BICYCLING
Cycling is popular in the **Collegiate Peaks Wilderness Area,** around Buena
Vista and Salida. **Absolute Bikes** (⊠ 330 W. Sackett St., Salida ☎ 719/
539–9295) provides mountain-bike rentals. **Rocky Mountain Outdoor
Center** (⊠ 228 N. F St., Salida ☎ 800/255–5784) organizes tours.

RAFTING
Fodor'sChoice
★
The rafting and kayaking on the **Arkansas River** can be the most chal-
lenging in the state, ranging from Class II to Class V, depending on the
season. Contact **Wilderness Aware** (☎ 719/395–2112 or 800/462–7238),
Rocky Mountain Outdoor Center (☎ 800/255–5784) or **Dvorak Kayak &
Rafting Expeditions** (☎ 800/824–3795).

Where to Stay & Eat

¢–$ ╳ **Casa del Sol.** Inhabiting an old blacksmith's shop (1890), this stucco-
clad restaurant has a quasi–tiki-hut feel inside and a gorgeous outdoor
seating area. The smothered burritos are tasty and hearty, the salsa is
hot and homemade, and the service is quick and friendly. The full-service bar here specializes in tart but potent margaritas. ⊠ *333 U.S. 24
N* ☎ *719/395–8810* ⊟ *MC, V.*

★ ¢–$ 🏨 **Adobe Inn.** The sister property of the restaurant Casa del Sol, this adobe hacienda has five charming rooms, each named for its predominant decorative motif: antique, Mexican, Native American, Mediterranean, and wicker. Some rooms have a fireplace. The airy solarium is dominated by a magnificent kiva. Breakfast is included in the room rate. ⊠ *303 U.S. 24 N, 81211* ☎ *719/395–6340 or 888/343–6340* ⊕ *www.bbonline. com/colorado/adobe* ↪ *4 rooms* ♨ *Hot tub* ▤ *MC, V* ⊠ *BP.*

★ $$ 🏨 **Liar's Lodge.** Right on the banks of the Arkansas River, the Liar's Lodge is a rugged, rustic B&B surrounded by 23 acres of woodland. The Great Room, under 25-foot-high ceilings, is centered around a huge river-rock fireplace, and the rooms are uniquely decorated (and named): the Pinball Room has a queen bed, a sleeping loft, and a two-person hot tub (but alas, no pinball machine); the Frog Rock Room has a queen and a twin and opens onto a river deck. Larger groups might opt for the 1,200-square-foot house that overlooks the river ($175 a night or $975 a week). ⊠ *30000 CR 371, 81211* ☎ *719/395–3444 or 888/542–7756* ⊕ *www.liarslodge.com* ↪ *5 rooms* ♨ *In-room hot tubs; no room phones* ▤ *MC, V* ⊠ *BP.*

★ ¢–$ 🏨 **Thunder Lodge.** On Cottonwood Creek, this collection of Western-decorated cabins is a great spot for families and is among the nicest cabin resorts in the area. All units have kitchenettes and private baths. The newest cabin, Mountain View, is a stunner, nestled off the property in a pine and aspen forest and featuring a grand fireplace and picture windows (there's a four-night minimum stay). ⊠ *207 Brookdale Ave., 81211* ☎ *719/395–2245 or 800/330–9194* ⊕ *www.thunderlodge.com* ↪ *8 cabins* ♨ *Kitchenettes, cable TV, fishing, hiking, some pets allowed; no a/c, no room phones* ▤ *D, MC, V.*

Nightlife & the Arts

NIGHTLIFE Head to the **Green Parrot** (⊠ 304 Main St. ☎ 719/395–9046), a long-standing Buena Vista watering hole with live music, DJs, and karaoke on weekends.

THE ARTS In a former judicial building, the **Old Courthouse Gallery** houses rotating art exhibits. (⊠ 511 E. Main St. ☎ 719/395–8372 ⊡ Free)

Shopping

The **Trembling Aspen Gallery** (⊠ 321 W. Main St. ☎ 719/395–4800) sells handmade aspen gifts, art, and jewelry.

Salida

㉕ *25 mi from Buena Vista via U.S. 24 and 285 and Rte. 291 south.*

Imposing peaks, including 14,000-plus-foot **Mt. Shavano,** dominate the town of Salida, which is on the Arkansas River. Salida draws some of the musicians who appear at the Aspen Music Festival—classical pianists, brass ensembles, and the like—for its Salida–Aspen Series Concerts in July and August. The town's other big event is the annual kayak and rafting white-water rodeo in June, on a section of river that cuts right through downtown. It's been taking place for over 40 years.

Sports & the Outdoors

FISHING The Arkansas River, as it spills out of the central Colorado Rockies on its course through the south-central part of the state, reputedly supports a brown-trout population exceeding 3,000 fish per mi. Some of the river's canyons are deep and some of the best fishing locations difficult to access, making a guide or outfitter a near necessity. **Browner's Fly Shop and Guide Service** (⊠ 3745 Hwy. 50, Salida ☎ 719/539–9350) is more than just a local fly shop with good advice. Guided trips on the Arkansas, as well as trips into the backcountry of the Sangre de Cristo Mountains, some of Colorado's most ruggedly beautiful, are among services rendered. **ArkAnglers** (⊠ 7500 W. Hwy. 50, Salida ☎ 719/539–4223) is a good fly shop with an experienced staff of guides, offering guided float and wade trips, fly fishing lessons, and equipment rentals.

BICYCLING **Absolute Bikes** (⊠ 330 W. Sackett Ave. ☎ 719/539–9295) rents cruisers and mountain bikes for $10 to $50 a day, and provides repair service, maps, advice, and equipment for sale. The **Banana Belt Bicycle Weekend** (☎ 719/539–2068 or 877/772–5432) is a two-day mountain-bike race held every September at Riverside Park in downtown Salida.

HORSEBACK **High Country Trail Rides** offers scenic guided trail rides near Monarch ski
RIDING area. ⊠22763 W. U.S. 50 (18 mi west of Salida) ☎719/539–9819 ☜$25 for 1 hr to $115 per day.

RAFTING The Salida area is a magnet for rafting aficionados, and there are dozens of outfitters. Salida is constantly jockeying with Buena Vista for the title of "Colorado's Whitewater Capital." The largest company in the state specializing in white-water rafting on the Arkansas is **Black Diamond River Runners** (☎ 800/525–2081). **Canyon Marine Expeditions** (☎ 719/539–7476) takes families on exciting river expeditions. **Independent Whitewater** (☎ 719/539–7737 or 800/428–1479) focuses on intermediate and advanced outings.

SKIING **Monarch** has 5 chairlifts, 54 trails, 670 acres, and a 1,170-foot vertical drop. The service is exceptional. Lift lines and lift ticket prices are nominal compared to other ski areas in the state. ⊠ U.S. 50, 18 mi west of Salida ☎ 719/539–3573 ☜ $36 ⊙ Mid-Nov.–mid-Apr., daily 9–4.

SNOWMOBILING **Monarch Tours** takes customers on winter excursions around Monarch Park. ⊠ Garfield, 18 mi west of Salida ☎ 719/539–2572 or 800/539–2573 ☜ $25 for a 1-hr single ride to $60 for a 2½-hr double ride.

Where to Stay & Eat

$–$$$ ✕ **Dakota's Bistro.** In the oldest building in Chaffee County (1880), this sleek downtown eatery offers some imaginative spins on regional fare, as well as a few healthful entrées. Start with snow crab quesadilla or Caesar salad, move on to a T-bone or a rosemary- and garlic-crusted roast lamb, or red-chili–glazed rainbow trout over wild rice. ⊠ 122 N. F St. ☎ 719/530–9909 ☰ AE, D, MC, V ⊙ Closed Sun. and Mon. Oct.–Apr.

¢–$$ ✕ **First Street Café.** This café in the historic district serves creative heart-healthy and vegetarian specials, in addition to robust Mexican-American fare. It's open for breakfast, lunch, and dinner. ⊠137 E. 1st St. ☎719/539–4759 ☰ AE, D, MC, V.

★ $–$$$ ▦ **Tudor Rose.** Built as a private residence in 1979, this isolated, idyllic B&B sits on a 37-acre spread of pine forest and mountain ridges. The proprietors, John and Terré Terrell, redid the place as a luxury mountain inn in 1995. An oak staircase with a two-story waterfall cascading down the adjacent wall to the foyer is the centerpiece, but the deck overlooking the nearby Mosquito Range is a close second. The rooms have a Victorian feel, but without an overload of frill and lace, and many modern details. All have phones; most have TVs and VCRs, CD players, and minifridges. ⊠ 6720 County Rd. 104, 81201 ☎ 719/539–2002 or 800/379–0889 ⊕ www.thetudorrose.com ➶ 6 rooms ♨ Some in-room VCRs, hot tub; no TVs in some rooms ☰ D, MC, V ꙳ BP.

$ ▦ **River Run Inn.** On the Arkansas River, this gracious Victorian home has breathtaking mountain prospects. Rooms are filled with antiques and family memorabilia, and a complimentary breakfast is provided. ⊠8495 County Rd. 160, 81201 ☎ 719/539–3818 or 800/385–6925 ⊕ www.riverruninn.com ➶ 7 rooms, 6 with bath ☰ AE, D, MC, V ꙳ BP.

¢–$ ▣ **Woodland Motel.** Since 1975, Steve and Viva Borbas have run this impeccable mom-and-pop motel on the outskirts of downtown Salida. Standard rooms are smallish but very clean and have nice furnishings and amenities for the price. The more expensive rooms—condominium units and efficiency studios—are larger and have kitchenettes. Dogs are treated like kings here: treats and freshly laundered doggie beds are included in the rate. ✉ *903 W. 1st St., 81201* ✆ *719/539–4980 or 800/488–0456* ⓕ *www.woodlandmotel.com* ↳ *18 rooms* ♧ *In-room data ports, some kitchenettes, cable TV, hot tub, some pets allowed* =*AE, D, MC, V* Ⓟ*BP.*

Nightlife & the Arts

NIGHTLIFE A watering hole with character, **The Lariat Bar** (✉ 206 E. Main St. ✆ 719/395–9494) is housed in Salida's historic former post office and has a wide selection of microbrews. Pool, video games, and darts are the primary diversions. **Salida Steam Plant Theater** (✉ Sackett and G Sts. ✆ 719/530–0933) puts on several productions each summer, ranging from drama to comedy to music to cabaret, on a stage in Salida's former steam plant.

THE ARTS First Street is home to about 10 galleries, including specialists in contemporary art, photography, and jewelry. The annual Salida ArtWalk takes place in late June. Ask the chamber of commerce for an *Art in Salida* brochure.

Soho (✉ 112 E. 1st St. ✆ 719/530–0130) features bright and colorful paintings, jewelry, and custom furnishings. **On Fire Glassworks** (✉ 246½ 1st St. ✆ 719/221–3355) specializes in fine lamp-worked glass art.

Shopping

Fabulous Finds Emporium (✉ 243 F St. ✆ 719/530–0544) is a multidealer antique mall with over 7,500 square feet of floor space. **Prospector Village** (✉ 17897 U.S. 285 ✆ 719/539–2019), midway between Salida and Buena Vista, is an enormous rock shop with gold-panning equipment, metal detectors, and rock art. The shop also gives gold-panning lessons.

Cañon City

Ⓜ *50 mi east of Salida via U.S. 50.*

Cañon City is an undeniably quirky town—and proud of it. Where else would you find a shop entitled "Fluff 'em, Buff 'em, Stuff 'em"? Would you have guessed the services it provides: hairstyling, car waxing, and taxidermy? From its aggressive, even tacky, strip-mall veneer (softened, fortunately, by some handsome old buildings) you'd think Cañon City existed solely for tourism. Nothing could be further from the truth. Cañon City's livelihood stems from its lordly position as "Colorado's Prison Capital." There are 10 prisons in the vicinity, all of which the citizens lobbied to get. It might seem a perverse source of income to court, but consider that the prisons have pumped nearly $200 million into the local economy, and, as an affable former mayor states, "You got these people walking around Denver and the Springs; here at least they're locked up." Temperate year-round weather draws droves of retirees.

Morbid curiosity seekers and sensationalists will revel in the **Museum of Colorado Prisons,** which formerly housed the Women's State Correctional Facility. Now it exhaustively documents prison life in Colorado, through old photos and newspaper accounts, as well as with inmates' confiscated weapons, contraband, and one warden's china set. The cell exhibits were funded by local businesses and civic organizations. There's also a video room where you can view titles such as *Prisons Ain't What They Used*

SPENDING TIME IN FLORENCE

EAST OF CAÑON CITY down Highway 115 and U.S. 50, the tiny, main-street town of Florence chalks up just about one of everything: one coffeeshop, one diner, one bookstore. But when it comes to prisons, it's got a bounty. Edge up to the city's eastern perimeter and you'll find the town is well equipped with a sprawling complex of four correctional facilities, including the ADX Supermax, the toughest joint in the nation, where an unruly population passes time in 23-hour lockdown. The facility has drawn its share of criticism from prisoners' rights advocates, but within the town itself, it's viewed as an economic godsend. It employs approximately one-third of Florence's 3,000 citizens, most of whom are quite comfortable living in the proximity of hardened criminals. History has perhaps conditioned residents to be so hard to ruffle—the site of the first state prison, Florence has been a "corrections community" since 1894.

Although high-profile celebrities have become full- or part-time residents of Colorado—including Melanie Griffith and Antonio Banderas, Tom Cruise, and Oprah Winfrey, who maintain homes in tony ski towns like Telluride and Aspen—the ADX is home to plenty of men with their own claims to fame, however sinister. John Gotti, Ted Kazinski, and Timothy McVeigh are former residents, and Ramsey Yusef, the alleged architect of the 1993 bombing of the World Trade Center, and Richard Reid, aka "The Shoebomber," are current guests. The Supermax clan may be the only group of visitors that'd prefer to cut their time in beatific Fremont County as short as possible.

---

to Be and *Drug Avengers.* The gas chamber sits in the courtyard. This museum is grim, grisly, gruesome, and fascinating. ⊠ *201 N. 1st St.* ☎ *719/269–3015* ⊕ *www.prisonmuseum.org* ⊠ *$6* ⊗ *May–Oct., daily 8:30–6; Nov.–Apr., Fri.–Sun. 10–5.*

Ⓒ Not only is **Buckskin Joe Frontier Town** the largest Western-style theme park in the region, but it's also an authentic ghost town that was moved here from 100 mi away. Such famous films as *True Grit* and *Cat Ballou* were shot in this place, which vividly evokes the Old West, especially during the re-created gunfights and hangings that occur daily. Children love the horse-drawn trolley rides, horseback rides, and gold panning, while adults appreciate live entertainment in the Crystal Palace and Saloon. The complex includes a scenic railway that travels to the rim of Royal Gorge. ⊠ *Cañon City, off U.S. 50* ☎ *719/275–5149* ⊕ *www.buckskinjoe.com* ⊠ *Combination ticket for all attractions $16* ⊗ *May–Sept., daily 9–6:30.*

Ⓒ Cañon City is also the gateway to the 1,053-foot-deep **Royal Gorge,** which
Fodor'sChoice was carved by the Arkansas River more than 3 million years ago. The
★ gorge is a commercially-run site and is spanned by the world's highest **suspension bridge.** Near the bridge, hubristic signs trumpet, "Who says you can't improve on Nature?" Never intended for traffic, it was constructed in 1929 as a tourist attraction. More than half a million visitors come annually, causing a fair amount of wear and tear the area. Families love crossing the bridge, particularly on gusty afternoons when it sways, adding to the thrill.

You can also ride the astonishing aerial tram (2,200 feet long and 1,178 feet above the canyon floor, across from the bridge) or descend the **Royal Gorge Bridge and Park** (the world's steepest-incline rail line) to stare at the bridge from 1,000 feet below. Also on hand are a theater that presents a 25-minute multimedia show, outdoor musical entertainment in summer, and the usual assortment of food concessions and gift shops.

The famed Royal Gorge War between the Denver & Rio Grande and Santa Fe railroads occurred here in 1877. The battle was over the right-of-way through the canyon, which could only accommodate one rail line. Rival crews would lay tracks during the day and dynamite each other's work at night. The dispute was finally settled in court—the Denver & Rio Grande won. ⊠ *Royal Gorge Bridge, 12 mi west of Cañon City* ☎ *719/275–7507* ⊕ *www.royalgorgebridge.com* 🖃 *$19* ⊙ *Daily 9–7.*

off the
beaten
path

THE WINERY AT HOLY CROSS ABBEY – The seven Benedictine monks cloistered in the Holy Cross Abbey come to Cañon City for spiritual repose. But for the faithful who frequent the winery on the eastern edge of the monastery's property, redemption is more easily found in a nice bottle of chardonnay, or merlot, or a two-year-old riesling. Members of the abbey have been bottling wine here for more than 75 years, but it wasn't until the arrival of Napa Valley wine makers Matt and Sally Cookson that the sacred space got serious about making and marketing its own vino. In 2001, the Cooksons planted a few acres of grapes and soon began harvesting a regional crop of inexpensive, and sublime, wines—all of which can be sampled during self-guided tours of the Abbey's lower levels and its Indian lore museum. During summer, sampling moves to a courtyard garden where vineyards climb heavenward and statues of Mary and the saints face the peaks in the Sangre de Cristo mountain range. It's divine. ⊠ *3011 E. Hwy. 50, Cañon City* ☎ *719/276–5191 or 877/422–9463* ⊕ *www.abbeywinery.com* 🖃 *Free* ⊙ *Mon.–Sat. 10–6, Sun. noon–5.*

Sports & the Outdoors

HIKING Cañon City–owned **Redrocks Park,** 12 mi north of town, offers splendid hiking among the sandstone spires.

RAFTING Rafting through the Royal Gorge is not an experience for the faint of heart, as you pass between narrow canyon walls through rolling Class IV and V waves, with hordes of tourists watching from the suspension bridge above. Several outfitters line U.S. 50. **Raft Masters** (⊠ 2315 E. Main St. ☎ 800/568–7238 ⊕ www.adventuresports.com) offers full- and half-day trips into Royal Gorge and Bighorn Sheep Canyon.

Where to Stay & Eat

$–$$$ ✕ **Merlino's Belvedere.** This Italian standby has ritzy coffee-shop decor, with floral banquettes, centerpieces, and a rock grotto. Locals swear by the top-notch steaks, seafood, and pasta. It's the usual choice in town for a big evening out. ⊠ *1330 Elm Ave.* ☎ *719/275–5558* ▤ *AE, D, DC, MC, V.*

¢–$ ✕ **El Caporal.** With Santa Fe style and a comfortable outdoor patio, this is a fun and casual spot for an inexpensive lunch or dinner. Mexican combination plates dominate the menu, and there is a standout dessert selection, including flan and fried ice cream. The bar makes more than 10 flavors of succulent margaritas and the proprietor, Miguel Lopez, is constantly coming up with new tequila-based concoctions. ⊠ *1028 Main St.* ☎ *719/276–2001* ▤ *AE, D, MC, V.*

¢ ✕ **Downtown Café.** A nostalgic greasy spoon on historic Main Street, the café specializes in big, fluffy omelettes and Southern specials like biscuits and gravy. It's open until noon, and the attached bar—Manhattan's—starts serving its bar menu at 4 PM. ⊠ *331 Main St.* ☎ *719/276–7299* ⊙ *No lunch or dinner* ▤ *MC, V.*

THE WELCOME WAGON FROM NEW YORK

A FORMER NEW YORKER WHO FLED the big city in the 1970s, Janey Workman was the visionary owner and namesake behind Janey's Chile Wagon, a quintessential greasy spoon that's been a 25-year staple among Cañon City locals and tourists. After working for decades as a bartender and waitress, Workman opened the Wagon in 1979 at the age of 53, eventually turning an $800 investment into a wildly successful café that caught the attention of the National Enquirer. The article's headline put it simply: "Waitress Builds Diner into $350,000 Restaurant!" Janey's is famous for its huge portions, delicious burritos smothered in "green chile that won't stay with you all night, hon," and an unabashedly kitschy interior. Velvet paintings and thrift-store tchotchkes, most gifts from friends and customers, line the walls, nooks, and crannies.

But nothing was as colorful as Janey, who cooked, tended bar, and greeted patrons, most of whom she knew by name. When she died in May 2003, many regulars assumed the Wagon would close for good. But Workman's daughter, Diane, has kept things rolling. Having spent 24 years cooking in the back, Diane now owns the business and emulates Janey's hands-on approach. The paintings will stay on the walls, and the red and green chili will remain the menu's main attraction, but Diane has added a little bit of her own flavor. "It was her place, her life, and she built it in a way that it now runs pretty well," the younger Workman says. "But there are some little things I've updated. Customers have told me, 'It tastes even better now! But I hope your mom can't hear me say that!'"

Janey's Chile Wagon ⊠ 807 Cyanide Ave. ☎ 719/275–4885 ⊟ No credit cards ⊗ Closed Sun. and Mon. Main courses at dinner, $3 to $8.

★ ¢-$ 🏨 **Cañon Inn.** Some of the famous people who have stayed here—John Belushi, Tom Selleck, Jane Fonda, John Wayne, Glenn Ford, and Goldie Hawn among them—now have their names emblazoned on the door of a hotel room. Spacious and ultra-comfortable, basic accommodations are offered in the two wings. ⊠ U.S. 50 and Dozier St., 81212 ☎ 719/275–8676 or 800/525–7727 🖨 719/275–8675 ⊕ www.canoninn.com ⊐ 152 rooms ⚭ Restaurant, pool, 6 hot tubs, bar ⊟ AE, D, DC, MC, V.

¢-$ 🏨 **Colorado Inn.** A clean, friendly, and affordable independent motel, the Colorado Inn was renovated in the late 1990s and has been well cared for since. Rooms are large and decorated with modern furnishings. ⊠ 1031 Royal Gorge Blvd., 81212 ☎ 719/275–9601 ⊐ 12 rooms ⚭ Microwaves, refrigerators, cable TV; no smoking ⊟ AE, D, MC, V ⵗ CP.

★ ¢-$ 🏨 **St. Cloud Hotel.** Established during the silver boom in 1883, the St. Cloud still has a functioning Otis elevator guests take to their rooms.

The rooms retain a historic ambiance, with clawfoot tubs. During the heyday of the Hollywood Western, John Wayne, Tom Mix, and Charles Bronson stayed here. ✉ *631 Main St., 81212* ☎ *719/276–2000 or 800/405–9666* ⊕ *www.stcloudhotel.com* ⟿ *33 rooms, 2 suites* ♨ *Restaurant, cable TV, bar; no smoking* ☰ *AE, D, MC, V.*

CAMPING ♨ ¢ △ **Yogi Bear's Jellystone Park Camp Resort.** A great spot for families, this kitschy campground and cabin resort is just 5 mi northwest of the Royal Gorge. There are some shady campsites, and the grounds are well-kept. The facilities include pedal-cart rentals, a hot tub, and volleyball and horseshoe courts. ✉ *43595 U.S. 50* ☎ *800/341–4471, reservation code 188* ⊕ *www.royalgorgejellystone.com* ♨ *Flush toilets, full hook-ups, dump station, drinking water, grills, picnic tables, public telephone, general store, playground, pool* ⟿ *74 sites with full hook-ups, 28 cabin tents, 11 cabins* ▨ *Full hook-ups $30, cabins $43–$110* ☰ *AE, D, MC, V.*

Nightlife & the Arts

NIGHTLIFE With DJs spinning dance records and bands playing country and classic rock, **Manhattan's** (✉ 331 Main St. ☎ 719/276–7299) is a popular downtown bar and grill.

THE ARTS A decidedly different pottery studio, **Picasso's Plate** (✉ 610 Main St. ☎ 719/276–1188) invites customers to paint their own pottery and bring in their own food and drink.

Shopping

Nearby Florence is home to several notable antique dealers. With 2,800 square feet of floor space, **Trails End Antiques** (✉ 202 S. 10th St. ☎ 719/269–1351) is Cañon City's largest antique store.

Pueblo

❷⓻ *40 mi east of Cañon City via U.S. 50; 42 mi south of Colorado Springs via I–25.*

Pueblo is a city divided: it can't make up its mind whether to promote its historic origins or the active lifestyle it offers, with biking in the mountains and golfing in the desert. A working-class, multiethnic steel town, Pueblo lacks the glamour of such towns as Aspen, whose wealth came from gold and silver. Though sizable, it remains in the shadow of Colorado Springs.

The **Union Avenue Historic District** is a repository of century-old stores and warehouses that make for a fashionable commercial district. Among the landmarks are the glorious 1889 sandstone-and-brick Union Avenue Depot; and Mesa Junction, at the point where two trolleys met, which celebrates Pueblo as a crossroads. Pitkin Avenue, lined with fabulous gabled and turreted mansions, attests to the town's more prosperous times. Walking-tour brochures of various districts are available at the **Chamber of Commerce** (✉ 210 N. Santa Fe Ave. ☎ 719/542–1704).

The **El Pueblo Museum** is ostensibly a holding place for the city's history, but it extends its scope to chronicle life on the plains since the prehistoric era, as well as Pueblo's role as a cultural and geographic crossroads, beginning when it was a trading post in the 1840s. The collection is in temporary quarters while a new museum is under construction. ✉ *119 Central Plaza* ☎ *719/583–0453* ▨ *$2.50* ☉ *Mon.–Sat. 10–3, Sun. noon–3.*

★ Unquestionably, the glory of Pueblo is the **Rosemount Victorian Museum,** one of Colorado's finest historical institutions. This splendid 24,000-square-foot, 37-room mansion, showplace of the wealthy Thatcher family, gleams with exquisite maple, oak, and mahogany woodwork throughout, with ivory glaze and gold-leaf trim. Italian marble fireplaces, Tiffany-glass fixtures, and frescoed ceilings complete the opulent look, and rooms seem virtually unchanged. The top floor—originally servants' quarters—features the odd Andrew McClelland Collection: objects of curiosity this eccentric philanthropist garnered on his worldwide travels, including an Egyptian mummy. ⊠ *419 W. 14th St.* ☎ *719/545–5290* ⊕ *www.rosemount.org* ✉ *$6* ⊙ *Tues.–Sat. 10–4; tours every half hour.*

Pueblo's equally vital concern with the present is documented in the gleaming **Sangre de Cristo Arts Center,** where several rotating exhibits in a well-thought-out space celebrate regional arts and crafts. The center also houses the superb Western art collection donated by Francis King; a performing arts theater; and the **Buell Children's Museum,** which provides fun, interactive audiovisual experiences. ⊠ *210 N. Santa Fe Ave.* ☎ *719/295–7200 or 719/543–0130* ✉ *$4* ⊙ *Tues.–Sat. 11–4.*

The uncommonly fine **City Park** (⊠ Pueblo Blvd. and Goodnight Ave.) has fishing lakes, playgrounds, kiddie rides, tennis courts, a swimming pool, and the excellent **Pueblo Zoo** (☎719/561–9664 ⊕www.pueblozoo. org ✉ *$6* ⊙ Daily 10–5)—a biopark that includes an ecocenter with a tropical rain forest, black-footed penguins, ring-tail lemurs, and green-tree pythons.

At the airport, the **Pueblo-Weisbrod Aircraft Museum** traces the development of American military aviation with more than two dozen aircraft in mint condition, ranging from a Lockheed F-80 fighter plane to a Boeing B-29 Super Fortress of atomic-bomb fame. ⊠ *31001 Magnuson, Pueblo Memorial Airport* ☎ *719/948–9219* ⊕ *www.co.pueblo.co.us/ pwam* ✉ *$4* ⊙ *Weekdays 10–4, Sat. 10–2, Sun. 1–4.*

off the
beaten
path

★

BISHOP CASTLE – An elaborate re-creation of a medieval castle replete with turrets, buttresses, and ornamental iron is the prodigious (some might say monomaniacal) one-man undertaking of Jim Bishop, who began work in 1969 and has hauled nearly 50,000 tons of rock used for the construction. A self-taught architect, Bishop has cobbled a structure that suggests a kitchen-sink combination of Antonio Gaudi's Casa Batllo building in Barcelona and the outsider environments of other visionary artists, like the Reverend Howard Finster's Paradise Garden in Georgia.

Not yet complete, Bishop Castle soars three stories and nearly 75 feet, and Bishop has plans to build a drawbridge and moat. The objective is not to keep invaders out, but to draw carloads of the curious in: once considered a blight on pastoral Route 75, which winds through the San Isabel Forest, the structure is now one of southern Colorado's most oft-visited attractions. It isn't, however, for the meek. The brave souls who endeavor to climb into the structure, which slopes precariously in spots and has uneven floors and ceilings throughout, are required to sign a waiver, thereby relieving Bishop of any liability.

Bishop finances this enormous endeavor through donations and a gift shop—which carries everything from Castle-boosting bumper stickers to a solo CD Bishop released last fall. Anyone can stop by at any time; if you're lucky he'll be there, railing against the Establishment (numerous posted signs graphically express his sentiments). ⊠ *Rte. 75* ☎ *719/485–3050* ⊕ *www.bishopcastle.org* ✉ *Free* ⊙ *Daily, hrs vary.*

PUEBLO LEVEE PROJECT: IT ALL BEGAN WITH A FISH IN THE NIGHT

N 1978, A GROUP OF *University of Southern Colorado art students headed out in the cover of night, set up lookouts, and lowered themselves over the wall of the Pueblo Levee. Fashioned with makeshift rope-suspension devices and armed with buckets of paint, the students spent the wee hours crafting a large blue cod on the levee's concrete wall, watching for police as they mixed up their acrylics. Overnight, the waterway— which directs the Arkansas River through the center of town—became home to a public art project that would eventually capture the imagination of the Pueblo community, as well as the attention of the art world and the Guinness Book of World Records. Pueblo Levee is a fantastic, colorful vision field that sprawls over 175,000 square feet, stretches for a mile, and is recognized as the largest mural in the world.*

Organizers estimate that more than 1,000 painters have contributed to the mural— everyone from self-taught father-and-son teams who come to paint on weekends, to the entire members of fire precincts, to classically trained muralists and art students from New York and Chicago. Witty graffitti, comic illustrations, narrative scenes, and cartoons line the levee, which is visible to passengers zooming along Interstate 25. Cynthia Ramu, an elementary-school art teacher, oversees maintenance of the mural and coordinates efforts to restore portions that have faded. Everyone is welcome to join in, though aspiring participants are supposed to check with Ramu before they pick up their brushes. She concedes that she is occasionally met with surprise artistic "statements." Usually, she lets them stay.

"We want it to be an open forum for expression, for people in the community to share something," she says. "But we have had some instances where people have pushed it. One guy used a bunch of white paint to paint the Ku Klux Klan! But most people are respectful, and they come up with great stuff. We've had everything from family portraits to historical murals and photographic transfers."

A few years ago, the City of Pueblo embarked on an extensive beautification plan and asked citizens and leaders to give of their time and talents—building on a model loosely forged by the grassroots Levee Project, which has never received any funding and relies on volunteers and donations. A splendid riverwalk, completed in 2000, has been added to the stretch of the Arkansas River perpendicular to the Historic Union Avenue District. That district holds street fairs and classic car shows on summer weekends that draw what seems like the entire town. Still, the Levee Project remains the area's most beautifully realized attraction—not to mention the working-class city's only true claim to international fame.

Sports & the Outdoors

More than 110 parks, in addition to hiking and biking trails, help to define Pueblo as a sports and recreation center. You can cycle, hike, and canoe in the **Greenway and Nature Center** (⊠ off 11th St. ☎ 719/549–2414) that runs along the Arkansas River. A small interpretive center describes the flora and fauna unique to the area, and a **Raptor Rehabilitation Center,** part of the nature center, cares for injured birds of prey.

There is excellent camping and fishing at **Lake Pueblo State Park** (⊠ off U.S. 50 W ☎ 719/561–9320), as well as many other outdoor activities. The **south shore marina** (☎ 719/564–1043) rents pontoon boats. You can hike in relative solitude in **San Isabel National Forest** (☎ 719/545–8737), 20 mi southwest of Pueblo.

BICYCLING Pueblo has an extensive **Bike Trail System,** which loops the city, following the Arkansas River part way, and then goes out to the reservoir. There are popular in-line skating routes along these trails, too. The **Pueblo Parks and Recreation Department** (☎ 719/566–1745) can provide information.

GOLF **Desert Hawk Golf Course** (⊠ Pueblo West Development, 8 mi west of town on U.S. 50 ☎ 719/547–2280) is an 18-hole championship course. **Pueblo City Golf Course** (⊠ City Park ☎ 719/561–4946) is a handsome, highly rated 18-hole course. **Walking Stick Golf Course** (⊠ 4301 Walking Stick Blvd. ☎ 719/584–3400), an 18-hole course, is perennially ranked in the top 50 American courses by *Golf Digest.*

Where to Stay & Eat

$–$$$$ ✕ **La Renaissance.** This converted church and parsonage is the most imposing and elegant space in town, and the impeccably attired, unfailingly courteous waitstaff completes the picture. Standbys are filet mignon in mushroom sauce, superb baby-back ribs, and New Zealand deep sea bass fillet. The dinner price includes appetizer, soup, salad, and a sinful dessert. ⊠ 217 E. Routt Ave. ☎ 719/543–6367 ▭ AE, D, DC, MC, V ⊘ Closed Sun. and Mon. No lunch Sat.

★ $–$$$ ✕ **Ianne's Whiskey Ridge.** In a beautiful Southwest-deco structure on the way to Pueblo Reservoir, this family-owned and -operated Italian eatery is one of Pueblo's longest-standing dining establishments, serving grateful patrons pasta and seafood for over 50 years. Ravenous couples can order the monstrous steak and lobster plate, priced reasonably at $42. Everything that comes out of the kitchen is prepared from scratch. A brunch is served on Sunday. ⊠ 4333 Thatcher Ave. ☎ 719/564–8551 ▭ AE, D, MC, V ⊘ No lunch. Closed Mon. No dinner Sun.

$–$$$ ✕ **La Tronica's.** Although it's dressed like a saloon, with mirror beer signs and Christmas lights draping the bar, this sectarian restaurant is real "Mamma Mia" Italian. The waitresses, who invariably call you "sweetheart," have been here for as long as anyone can remember. Steak, seafood, scrumptious fried chicken, and homemade pastas are the lure. ⊠ 1143 E. Abriendo Ave. ☎ 719/542–1113 ▭ AE, D, MC, V ⊘ Closed Sun. and Mon. No lunch.

$–$$ ✕ **Irish Brew Pub & Grill.** This consistently jam-packed hot spot is a bar and grill with a difference: it has a good kitchen. The owner *loves* food, and he has elevated pub grub to an art form. Even the house salad—field greens studded with pine nuts and blue cheese—is imaginative. Sandwiches are equally creative; try the buffalo burger or beaver (yes, beaver) sandwich. Dinner entrées include a dazzling prime rib and a "border grill" turkey breast lightly dusted in flour, grilled, and then poached in chicken broth and raspberry vinaigrette. And of course, they brew their own beer—nine varieties. ⊠ 108 W. 3rd St. ☎ 719/542–9974 ▭ AE, D, DC, MC, V ⊘ Closed Sun.

¢–$ ✕ **Grand Prix Restaurant & Lounge.** A neon sign announces the location of this authentic Mexican restaurant run by the Montoya family. Red neon lights and a painted false ceiling relieve the otherwise spartan decor. The food is classic: pork, chorizo, burritos, and Mexican steak, served with the flavorful local Pueblo chili and heaps of rice and beans. ⊠ 615 E. Mesa St. ☎ 719/542–9825 ▭ MC, V ⊘ Closed Mon. No lunch Sat.

★ $–$$ 🏠 **Abriendo Inn.** This exquisite 1906 home, listed on the National Register of Historic Places, overflows with character. Gracious owner Kerrelyn Trent did most of the painting, papering, and refurbishing. The house now gleams with its original, lovingly restored parquet floors, stained glass, and Minnequa oak wainscoting. The 10 no-smoking rooms are richly appointed with antiques, oak armoires, quilts, crocheted bedspreads, and either brass or four-poster beds. Fresh fruit and cookies are left out for nibbling, and gourmet breakfasts are included in the rate. ⊠ *300 W. Abriendo Ave., 81004* ☎ *719/544–2703* 🖷 *719/542–6544* ⊕ *www.abriendoinn.com* 🖵 *10 rooms* ⚬ *In-room data ports, cable TV; no smoking* ⊟ *AE, DC, MC, V* †⊖| *BP.*

¢ 🖥 **Inn at Pueblo West Best Western.** This handsome, sprawling resort is a notch above most Best Westerns. It's about 15 minutes by car to town, but the golf course and activities on nearby Lake Pueblo keep guests busy. Rooms are large, have terraces, and are done in Southwestern earth tones. ⊠ *201 S. McCulloch Blvd., 81007* ☎ *719/547–2111 or 800/448–1972* 🖷 *719/547–0385* 🖵 *80 rooms* ⚬ *Restaurant, 4 tennis courts, pool* ⊟ *AE, D, DC, MC, V.*

Nightlife & the Arts

NIGHTLIFE **Gus' Place** (⊠ 1201 Elm St. ☎ 719/542–0756) is a local hangout that
★ once held a record for the most kegs emptied in an evening. The **Irish Brew Pub & Grill** (⊠ 108 W. 3rd St. ☎ 719/542–9974) is always hopping after work hours. **Peppers Niteclub** (⊠ 4109 Club Manor Dr. ☎ 719/542–8629) has something going on every evening, from oldies nights to stand-up comedy.

THE ARTS **Broadway Theatre League** (⊠ 210 N. Santa Fe Ave. ☎ 719/545–4721) presents touring shows and specialty acts. The **Pueblo Symphony** (⊠ 2200 Bonfort Blvd. ☎ 719/549–2385) performs music, from cowboy to classical, throughout the year. **Sangre de Cristo Arts and Conference Center** (⊠ 210 N. Santa Fe Ave. ☎ 719/295–7200) presents local and touring acts.

Shopping

Pueblo's beautifully restored and renovated **Union Avenue Historic District** and **Mesa Junction** contain several fine antiques shops and boutiques. The **Midtown Center** (⊠ 1000 W. 6th St.) mall includes chains such as Sears. There is a flea market every weekend at the **Pueblo Fairgrounds** (⊠ 1001 Beulah Ave.)

ANTIQUES **Tivoli's Antique Gallery** (⊠ 325 S. Union Ave. ☎ 719/201–2089) sells antique furniture.

BOUTIQUES **Gotcha Covered** (⊠ 111 W. B St. ☎ 719/544–6833) stocks unique clothing from around the world. **Razmataz** (⊠ 335 S. Union Ave. ☎ 719/544–3721) carries creative clothing by local artists.

CRAFT & ART **John Deaux Art Gallery** (⊠ 221 S. Union Ave. ☎ 719/545–8407 or 877/
GALLERIES 888–8580) specializes in contemporary art by southern Colorado artists. **Latka Pottery** (⊠ 229 Midway St. ☎ 719/543–0720) features the designs of Tom and Jean Latka.

FOOD See what's possible to cook up with kitchenware and delicacies from **Seabel's Baskets and Gifts** (⊠ 105 W. C St. ☎ 719/543–2400).

---

en route | If you head east on U.S. 50, leaving the Rockies far behind, you'll be traveling toward the eastern plains, where rolling prairies of the northeast give way to hardier desert blooms and the land is stubbled with sage and stunted piñons. One fertile spot—50 mi along the highway—is the town of **Rocky Ford**, dubbed the "Melon Capital of the World" for the famously succulent cantaloupes grown there.

La Junta

🕮 *65 mi east of Pueblo via U.S. 50.*

Wholesome La Junta was founded as a trading post in the mid-19th century. The town is notable for its **Koshare Indian Museum**, which contains extensive holdings of Native American artifacts and crafts (Navajo silver, Zuni pottery, Shoshone buckskin clothing), as well as pieces from Anglo artists, such as Remington, known for their depictions of Native Americans. The Koshare Indian Dancers (actually a local Boy Scout troop) perform regularly. ✉ *115 W. 18th St.* ☎ *719/384–4411 or 800/693–5482* ⊕ *www.koshare.org* ✉ *$4* ⊙ *Mon. and Wed. 10–9; Tues. and Thurs.–Sun. 10–5.*

★ The splendid **Bent's Old Fort National Historic Site** is a perfect example of a living museum, with its painstaking re-creation of the original adobe fort. Founded in 1833 by savvy trader William Bent, one of the region's historical giants, the fort anchored the commercially vital Santa Fe Trail, providing both protection and a meeting place for the soldiers, trappers, and traders of the era. The museum's interior includes a smithy and soldiers' and trappers' barracks. The guided tour is most informative. ✉ *35110 Hwy. 194 E* ☎ *719/383–5010* ✉ *$3* ⊙ *June–Labor Day, daily 8–5:30.*

off the beaten path

SANTA FE TRAIL'S MOUNTAIN BRANCH – This area of Colorado played a major role in opening up the West, through the Mountain Branch of the Santa Fe Trail. Bent's Fort was the most important stop between the route's origin in Independence, Missouri, and its terminus in Santa Fe, New Mexico. U.S. 50 roughly follows its faded tracks from the Kansas border through the pioneer towns of Lamar and Las Animas to La Junta, where U.S. 350 picks up the trail, traveling southwest to Trinidad. If you detour onto the quiet county roads, you can still discern its faint outline over the dip of arroyos. Here, amid the magpies and prairie dogs, it takes little imagination to conjure visions of the pioneers, struggling to travel just 10 mi a day by oxcart over vast stretches of territory.

Sports & the Outdoors

HIKING There are a few trails through the **Comanche National Grassland** (✉ 1420 E. 3rd St. ☎ 719/384–2181), including a pair of canyon loops where there is a fair amount of rock art. There are picnic tables but camping is prohibited. **Picketwire Canyonlands** is where the largest documented set of fossilized dinosaur tracks in the United States are set in stone. There are also works of rock art and other cultural artifacts. In addition to touring here by car, hiking, mountain biking, and horseback riding are also popular. Contact the **Comanche National Grassland** (✉ 1420 E. 3rd St. ☎719/539–5106) office in La Junta for information on the canyonlands. **Purgatoire Adventures** (✉ 38700 Country Rd. 1654 ☎ 719/384–5813) takes customers on guided one- to four-day horseback trips in the area.

Nightlife & the Arts

A watering hole with a quirky personality, the **Hog's Breath Saloon** (✉ 808 E. 3rd St. ☎ 719/364–7879) is a local institution and a good dinner spot.

The hub for La Junta's arts scene is the **Picketwire Center for Performing and Visual Arts** (✉ 802 San Juan Ave. ☎719/384–8320), which has staged nearly 100 productions since its inception in 1968.

Trinidad

❷❾ *80 mi southwest of La Junta via U.S. 350.*

Founded as a rest-and-repair station along the Santa Fe Trail, Trinidad boomed with the discovery of coal in the area in 1861, followed inevitably by the construction of the railroad. The period from 1880 to 1910 saw major building and expansion. The advent of natural gas, coupled with the Depression, ushered in a gradual decline in population, but did not begin a freefall to stagnation and resignation. Trinidad's citizens contribute 1% of a 4% sales tax to the upkeep of the city's rich architectural heritage. That civic pride is clearly demonstrated in the town's four superb museums, a remarkably large number for a small town. Newcomers are moving in, and Trinidad's downtown is coming to life again, with restaurants, cafés, and galleries.

★ Downtown, called the **Corazon de Trinidad** (Heart of Trinidad), is a National Historic Landmark District with original brick-paved streets, splendid Victorian mansions, churches, and the glorious, bright red domes and turrets of Temple Aaron, Colorado's oldest continuously used synagogue. The **Chamber of Commerce** (✉ 309 Nevada St. ☎ 719/846–9285) publishes an excellent walking tour for Corazon de Trinidad.

The **Baca House/Bloom House/Pioneer Museum Complex** represents the most significant aspects of Trinidad's history. Felipe Baca was a prominent Hispanic trader whose 1870 residence, **Baca House,** is replete with original furnishings in the parlor, sitting room, kitchen, dining room, and bedrooms. Displays convey a mix of Anglo (clothes, furniture) and local Hispanic (santos, rosaries, textiles) influences. Next door, **Bloom House** provides an effective contrast to the Baca House. Frank Bloom made his money through ranching, banking, and the railroad, and although he was no wealthier than Baca, his mansion (built in the 1880s) reveals a very different lifestyle. The railroad enabled him to fill his ornate Second Empire–style Victorian (with mansard roof and elaborate wrought ironwork) with fine furnishings and fabrics brought from New York and imported from Europe. The adjacent **Santa Fe Trail Museum** is dedicated to the effect of the trail on the community. Inside are exhibits covering the heydays of Trinidad as a commercial and cultural center, up through the 1920s. Finish up with a stop at the **Historic Gardens**, a fine example of Southwestern vegetable and herb gardens, as tended by the pioneers, with native plants and heirloom, century-old grapevines. ✉ *300 E. Main St.* ☎ *719/846–7217* ⊕ *www.trinidadco. com or www.coloradohistory.org* 🎟 *$5* ⊙ *May–Sept., daily 10–4.*

The **A. R. Mitchell Memorial Museum and Gallery** celebrates the life and work of the famous Western illustrator, whose distinctive oils, charcoal drawings, and watercolors graced the pages of pulp magazines and ranch romances. The museum also has his personal collection of other masters of the genre, such as Larry Heller and Harvey Dunn, as well as a re-creation of his atelier. The community holds Mitchell in great esteem: he was responsible for saving the Baca and Bloom houses from demolition, and he spearheaded numerous campaigns to restore the downtown area. For a further glimpse into Trinidad history, visit the **Aultman Collection of Photography.** On display are photos by the Aultman family dating back to 1889 which offer a unique visual record of Trinidad. ✉ *150 E. Main St.* ☎ *719/846–4224* 🎟 *Free* ⊙ *Mid-Apr.–Sept., Tues.–Sun. 10–4.*

On the other side of the Purgatoire River, the **Louden-Henritze Archaeology Museum** takes viewers back millions of years to examine the true origins of the region, including early geologic formations, plant and marine-animal fossils, and prehistoric artifacts. ✉ *Trinidad State Junior College* ☎ *719/846–5508* ⊕ *www.tsjc.cccoes.edu* 🎟 *Free* ⊙ *Jan.–Nov., weekdays 10–4.*

☙ The **Trinidad Children's Museum** is in the delightful Old Firehouse Number 1, and it displays fire-fighting memorabilia, such as a 1936 American LaFrance fire truck (children love clanging the loud bell) and the city's original fire alarm system. Upstairs is a fine re-creation of a Victorian schoolroom. ⊠ *314 N. Commercial St.* ☎ *719/846–8220* 🖳 *Free* ◷ *Apr.–Sept., weekdays 1–4.*

Sports & the Outdoors

There is hiking, fishing, horseback riding, and camping in the Purgatoire River valley at the **Trinidad Lake State Recreation Area** (☎ 719/846–6951), 3 mi west of Trinidad on Route 12.

Where to Stay & Eat

$–$$$ ✕ **Black Jack's Saloon and Steak House.** Step inside this 1890s building, where you can toss your peanut shells on the floor from your perch at the full-service antique bar. Between the bar and the leafy-salad kind of bar is an open grill where the most succulent steaks on the Santa Fe Trail are prepared. Those avoiding red meat can go for salmon or swordfish. ⊠ *225 W. Main St.* ☎ *719/846–9501* ▤ *AE, MC, V* ◷ *Closed Mon. No lunch.*

¢–$ ✕ **Main Street Bakery & Café.** In a century-old building decorated with sunny interior murals, this homey café serves fresh-baked breads and desserts, a famous potpie, and Reuben sandwiches. The Oriental chicken salad is a thing of beauty, and ample enough for a full meal. Try the Branding Iron sandwich (roast beef and melted Brie on focaccia), or the Michiganer, turkey breast salad mixed with dried cherries. This spot is usually crowded at breakfast and lunch. Don't want a full meal? Drop in for a divine cinnamon roll and a cup of strong coffee. ⊠ *121 W. Main St.* ☎ *719/846–8779* ▤ *AE, MC, V* ◷ *No dinner.*

★ ¢–$ ✕ **Nana and Nano's Pasta House.** This tiny eatery is saturated with the aroma of garlic and tomato sauce. Pastas are consistently excellent, with standards such as homemade ravioli, gnocchi Bolognese, and rigatoni with luscious meatballs among the standouts. If you don't have time for a sit-down lunch, stop at the deli counter for smashing heros and gourmet sandwiches or takeouts of imported cheeses and olives. Fran Monteleone is your amiable host; it's her secret sauce that will drive you wild. ⊠ *418 E. Main St.* ☎ *719/846–2696* ▤ *AE, DC, MC, V* ◷ *Closed Sun. and Mon.*

$–$$ 🏨 **Tarabino Inn.** This turn-of-the-20th-century Victorian B&B in the Corazon de Trinidad National Historic District is the former abode of the Tarabino brothers, the proprietors of Trinidad's first department store. The rooms are frilly, immaculate, and comfortable, with a dose of modern convenience. ⊠ *310 E. 2nd St., 81082* ☎ *719/846–2115 or 866/846–8808* ⊕ *www.tarabinoinn.com* 🛏 *4 rooms, 2 with shared bath* ♿ *In-room data ports, refrigerators, in-room VCRs, cable TV* ▤ *AE, D, MC, V* ⑩ *BP.*

$ 🏨 **Best Western Country Club Inn.** To apply the term "country club" is exaggerating this lodging's amenities. Rooms are clean and comfortable and are decorated in warm earth tones. ⊠ *Exit 13A off I–25, 900 W. Adams St., 81082* ☎ *719/846–2215* 🖷 *719/846–2480* ⊕ *www.bestwestern.com* 🛏 *55 rooms* ♿ *Restaurant, pool, gym, hot tub, bar, laundry facilities* ▤ *AE, D, DC, MC, V.*

Nightlife

The Other Place (⊠ 466 W. Main St. ☎ 719/846–9012) hires DJs and top local rock bands on weekends to play its intimate classy space.

Cuchara Valley

③⓪ *55 mi from Trinidad (to town of Cuchara) via Rte. 12 northwest.*

From Trinidad, Route 12—the scenic **Highway of Legends**—curls north through the Cuchara Valley. As it starts its climb, you'll pass a series of company towns built to house coal miners. **Cokedale** is nestled in Reilly

Canyon. The entire town is a National Historic Landmark District, and it is the most significant example of a turn-of-the-20th-century coal/coke camp in Colorado. As you drive through the area note the telltale streaks of black in the sandstone and granite bluffs fronting the Purgatoire River and its tributaries, the unsightly slag heaps, and the spooky abandoned mining camps dotting the hillsides. The impressive **Stonewall Gap,** a monumental gate of rock, roughly marks the end of the mining district.

★ As you approach Cuchara Pass, several switchbacks snake through rolling grasslands and dance in and out of spruce stands whose clearings afford views of Monument Lake. You can camp, fish, and hike throughout this tranquil part of the **San Isabel National Forest,** which in spring and summer is emblazoned with a color wheel of wildflowers. Four corkscrewing miles later, you'll reach a dirt road that leads to the twin sapphires of **Bear and Blue lakes** and the resort town of **Cuchara.** Nestled in a spoon valley ("cuchara" means spoon), the area became popular as a turn-of-the-20th-century camping getaway for Texans and Oklahomans because of its cool temperatures and stunning scenery. The quaint Western town consists of one main street lined with boardwalks and shops, bars, and restaurants, mostly open in summer only.

In the Cuchara Valley you'll begin to see fantastic rock formations with equally fanciful names, such as Profile Rock, Devil's Staircase, and Giant's Spoon. With a little imagination you can devise your own legends about the names' origins. There are more than 400 of these upthrusts, which radiate like the spokes of a wheel from the valley's dominating landmark, the **Spanish Peaks.** In Spanish they are known as *Dos Hermanos,* or "Two Brothers"; in Ute, their name *Huajatolla* means "breasts of the world." The haunting formations are considered to be a unique geologic phenomenon for their sheer abundance and variety of rock types.

The Highway of Legends passes through the charming, laid-back resort town of **La Veta** before reaching its junction with Interstate 25 at Walsenburg, another city built on coal, and the largest town between Pueblo and Trinidad. Colorado Springs is 90 mi north on Interstate 25.

Where to Stay & Eat

$–$$$ ✕**Pat McMahon Fine Art & Café.** A combination gallery and restaurant, this new structure in historic downtown La Veta has quickly emerged as the top eatery in the valley. Lunches are basic but tasty Mexican combos, and dinners range from oysters Rockefeller to steaks, fresh seafood, and rack of lamb. ⊠ *105 W. Ryus Ave.* ☎ *719/742–6133* ▤ *MC, V* ⊘ *Closed Mon. and Tues. No lunch Sun.*

$ ▥ **La Veta Inn.** There are antiques in the guest rooms of this historic inn, but the hotel is a basic one. Eight rooms have kitchenettes. The shady courtyard is a selling point, with a fireplace and regular musical entertainment. ⊠ *103 W. Ryus Ave., Box 129 81055* ☎ *719/742–3700, 888/806–4875 for reservations* ▤ *719/742–3105* ⊕ *www.lavetainn. com* ⇨ *20 rooms* ⟐ *Restaurant, in-room data ports, some kitchenettes, cable TV, massage, bar* ▤ *AE, MC, V.*

Sports & the Outdoors

GOLF The Tom Weiskopf-designed **Grandote Peaks Golf Club** (☎ 719/742–3391 or 800/457–9986) is a classic 18-hole mountain course that has been lauded by *Golf Digest.*

HIKING The **San Isabel National Forest** (⊠ 3170 E. Main St., Cañon City, 81212 ☎ 719/269–8500) has a myriad of hiking trails, not to mention campgrounds, fishing streams, and mountain biking terrain. In winter, it's a cross-country skiing destination.

SOUTH CENTRAL COLORADO A TO Z

To research prices, get advice from other travelers, and book travel arrangements, visit www.fodors.com.

AIR TRAVEL

CARRIERS The only commercial service in the region is by Great Lakes Airlines, in and out of Pueblo Memorial Airport. Most area residents drive to Colorado Springs to fly.

🛪 Airlines & Contacts **Great Lakes Airlines** ☎ 719/948-9462 or 800/554-5111 ⊕ www.greatlakesav.com.

AIRPORTS

The area is served by Pueblo Memorial Airport, which receives about three flights a day from United Express, which operates through Great Lakes Airlines. City Cab will pick up from the airport.

🛪 **Pueblo Memorial Airport** ☎ 719/948-3355 ⊕ www.pueblomemorialairport.org.

TRANSFERS 🛪 **City Cab** ☎ 719/543-2525.

BUS TRAVEL

Greyhound Lines serves most of the major towns. Pueblo Transit serves Pueblo and outlying areas. The Trinidad Trolley (summer only) stops at parks and historical sites, departing from the parking lot next to City Hall.

🛪 **Greyhound Lines** ☎ 800/231-2222. **Pueblo Transit** ☎ 719/542-8763.

CAR RENTAL

The highest concentration of car rental agencies is in Pueblo, with a pair of rental counters at the airport. Most cities in south central Colorado lack car rental service.

🛪 **Avis** ☎ 719/948-9665 ⊕ www.avis.com. **Hertz** ☎ 719/948-3345 ⊕ www.hertz.com.

CAR TRAVEL

South central Colorado has mellow weather conditions and good roads. However, there is the occasional snowstorm and there are numerous twisty mountain roads. Gas is readily available in nearly every town.

Pueblo is on Interstate 25. Florissant and Buena Vista are reached via U.S. 24 off Interstate 25; Cañon City and the Royal Gorge via U.S. 50. Salida can be reached via Highway 291 from either U.S. 24 or U.S. 50. Palmer Lake and Larkspur are accessible via Interstate 25 and Highway 105.

🛪 **Colorado Department of Transportation Road Condition Hotline** ☎ 303/639-1111 or 877/315-7623.

EMERGENCIES

🛪 Ambulance or Police **Emergencies** ☎ 911.

🛪 24-Hour Medical Care **Cañon City: St. Thomas More Hospital** ✉ 1338 Phay Ave., Cañon City ☎ 719/269-2000. **La Junta: Arkansas Valley Regional Medical Center** ✉ 1100 Carson Ave., La Junta ☎ 719/384-5412. **Pueblo: Parkview Episcopal Medical Center** ✉ 400 W. 16th St., Pueblo ☎ 719/584-4400. **Salida: Heart of the Rockies Regional Medical Center** ✉ 448 E. 1st St., Salida ☎ 719/539-6661. **Trinidad: Mt. San Rafael Hospital** ✉ 410 Benedicta St., Trinidad ☎ 719/846-9213.

WHERE TO STAY

The rental of condominiums, homes, and cabins is handled by Collegiate Peaks Vacation Rentals in the Buena Vista area, and by Cuchara Vacation Rentals in the Cuchara Valley.

🛪 **Collegiate Peaks Vacation Rentals** ☎ 719/395-2459 or 800/548-1876 ⊕ www.collegiatepeaksvacationhomes.com. **Cuchara Vacation Rentals** ☎ 719/742-3340 ⊕ www.coloradodirectory.com/cucharavacation.

CAMPING The entire area is known for camping. The U.S. Forest Service operates many developed campgrounds, and there are numerous backcountry opportunities as well.

📁 **Forest Service Office for the San Isabel National Forest** ✉ 3170 E. Main St., Cañon City, 81212 ☎ 719/269-8500.

MEDIA

NEWSPAPERS &
MAGAZINES The *Pueblo Chieftain* is south central Colorado's most prominent daily newspaper.

TELEVISION &
RADIO Though local TV is limited to Pueblo, most cities and towns in the area have FM music stations, and most radios can pick up 850 AM (news from Denver) at night.

SPORTS & THE OUTDOORS

HIKING &
CLIMBING The mountains here are serious hiking and climbing destinations. Guide services are a necessity for neophyte climbers.

📁 **Forest Service Office for the San Isabel National Forest** ✉ 3170 E. Main St., Cañon City 81212 ☎ 719/269-8500.

JEEP TOURS Fun Time Jeep Tours has locations in Salida, Buena Vista, and Poncha Springs, and takes customers on four-wheel-drive trips to old mines, ghost towns, and mountain vistas.

📁 Tour Operators **Fun Time Jeep Tours** ✉ U.S. 50, Salida ☎ 719/539-2962 or 888/539-2962.

WHITEWATER
RAFTING With over 100 outfitters working from Salida, Buena Vista, and Cañon City, south central Colorado is one or the top places in the country to go rafting. Arkansas River Tours, Buffalo Joe River Trips, and Echo Canyon River Expeditions are but a few of the reliable rafting outfitters that line U.S. 50 between Cañon City and the Royal Gorge.

📁 River Outfitters **Arkansas River Tours** ✉ Cotopaxi ☎ 800/321-4352. **Buffalo Joe River Trips** ✉ Royal Gorge ☎ 719/395-8757 or 800/356-7984. **Colorado River Outfitters Association** (CROA) ✉ c/o Johnson Communications, 730 Burbank St., Broomfield, CO 80020 ☎ 303/280-2554 ⊕ www.croa.org. **Echo Canyon River Expeditions** ✉ Cañon City ☎ 719/275-3154 or 800/748-2953.

TRAIN TRAVEL

Amtrak stops in Trinidad and La Junta, but the region is otherwise devoid of passenger rail travel.

📁 **Amtrak** ☎ 800/872-7245 ⊕ www.amtrak.com.

VISITOR INFORMATION

📁 **Buena Vista Chamber of Commerce** ✉ 343 Hwy. 24, Buena Vista 81211 ☎ 719/395-6612 ⊕ www.buenavistacolorado.org. **Cañon City Chamber of Commerce** ✉ 403 Royal Gorge Blvd., Cañon City 81212 ☎ 719/275-2331 ⊕ www.canoncitychamber.com. **Heart of the Rockies Chamber of Commerce** ✉ 406 W. Hwy. 50, Salida 81201 ☎ 719/539-2068 or 877/772-5432 ⊕ www.salidachamber.org. **Huerfano County Chamber of Commerce** ✉ 400 Main St., Walsenburg 81089 ☎ 719/738-1065. **La Junta Chamber of Commerce** ✉ 110 Santa Fe Ave., La Junta 81050 ☎ 719/384-7411. **La Veta/Cuchara Chamber of Commerce** ✉ Box 32, La Veta 81055 ☎ 719/742-3676. **Lamar Chamber of Commerce** ✉ 109A E. Beech St., Lamar 81052 ☎ 719/336-4379. **Pueblo Chamber of Commerce and Convention & Visitors Bureau** ✉ 302 N. Santa Fe Ave., Pueblo 81003 ☎ 719/542-1704 or 800/233-3446 ⊕ www.pueblochamber.org. **Trinidad/Las Animas Chamber of Commerce** ✉ 309 Nevada St., Trinidad 81082 ☎ 719/846-9285 ⊕ www.trinidadco.com.

NORTHWEST COLORADO

6

Revised &
Updated by
Lori Cumpston

EONS OF EROSION HAVE SCULPTED the northwest's largely barren terrain, making it difficult to imagine the region as a primeval rain forest. Yet millions of years ago much of Colorado was submerged under a roiling sea. That period left a vivid legacy in three equally precious resources: vast oil reserves, abundant uranium deposits, and one of the world's largest collections of dinosaur remains. Throughout the area the evidence of these buried treasures is made obvious by unsightly uranium tailings, abandoned oil derricks, and the huge mounds of dirt left from unearthing valuable fossils. Some of the important paleontological finds made here have radically changed the fossil record and the way we look at our reptilian ancestors. These discoveries even fueled the imagination of *Jurassic Park* author Michael Crichton: the book's ferocious predator, velociraptor, was first uncovered here.

Grand Junction, the largest city between Denver and Salt Lake City, makes the ideal hub for exploring the region, which includes the starkly beautiful rock formations of the Colorado National Monument; the important petroglyphs of Canyon Pintado; the forest and lakes of Grand Mesa, the world's largest flattop mountain; and the orchards and vineyards of Palisade and Delta to the south and east. Most of the sights are less than a two-hour drive from Grand Junction, from which you can make the loop from Delta to Cedaredge and Grand Mesa to Palisade easily in a day. If you want to break up the trip, stop in the lovely town of Cedaredge overnight. The loop in the opposite direction—including Rifle, Meeker, Craig, Dinosaur National Monument, and Rangely—is quite a bit longer, but there is decent lodging in any of the stops along the way, with the exception of Dinosaur National Monument (unless you're prepared to camp).

Even this less-visited corner of the state has plenty of cultural opportunities for those willing to seek them out. Dotting the area are art galleries, antiques shops, and many quaint eateries with alfresco seating. People are friendly and offer plenty of tourist tips just for the asking. As for quirky festivals, you might have a hard time choosing between the Olathe Sweet Corn Festival, Country Jam, or the Mike the Headless Chicken Festival. The laid back lifestyle here is the perfect example to follow. Chill out and explore the region at your own pace, whether it's learning about its wine industry, taking in a foreign film at the historic Avalon Theater, or tapping your toe to an impromptu jam session at the local coffeehouse.

Exploring Northwestern Colorado

So many choices, so little time. A little planning goes a long way when deciding what attractions to visit in this region. Adventures might range from a bone-jarring mountain bike ride on Kokopelli's Trail—a 142-mi route through remote desert sandstone and shale canyon from Grand Junction to Moab—to a heart-pounding raft trip down the Green River, where Major John Wesley Powell took his epic exploration of this continent's last uncharted wilderness in 1869. Colorado National Monument and Dinosaur National Monument offer endless opportunities for hiking. For the less adventurous, a visit to the wine country makes for a relaxing afternoon, or try your hand at excavating prehistoric bones from a dinosaur quarry. Rich in more recent history as well, the area is home to the Museum of Western Colorado and Escalante Canyon, named after Spanish missionary explorer Francisco Silvestre Velez de Escalante, who with father Francisco Atanasio Dominguez led an expedition through the area in 1776.

About the Restaurants

The region's dining scene is diverse yet affordable. A few restaurants serve more elegant fare, but for the most part, restaurants are casual and friendly. Among the newest chain offerings: Olive Garden, Johnny Carino's, and Chili's. Old favorites include Outback Steakhouse and the Rockslide Brewery. Many of the smaller towns have kid-friendly burger joints that serve up decent hamburgers, french fries, crispy onion rings, and thick, frosty shakes. The area has a nice selection of fast food restaurants, mom-and-pop eateries, brew pubs, sports bars, and restaurants serving everything from Mexican to Chinese cuisines.

About the Hotels

The region is growing and that means there are more lodging choices than ever. In Grand Junction, Horizon Drive has the largest concentration of hotels and motels, conveniently located near Walker Field Airport and within walking distance of a handful of restaurants. For the budget conscious, there are many clean, no-frills motels as well as some of the well known chains, including Super 8 Motel and Comfort Inn. Moderately priced hotels include La Quinta, Holiday Inn, Best Western, and Adam's Mark. History buffs might enjoy a stay at a dude ranch or the famed Meeker Hotel, once frequented by Teddy Roosevelt. For those wanting with all the comforts of home, the area has a nice selection of bed-and-breakfasts, including one that has a llama herd. Be sure to ask for off-season lodging rates, which could save you a bundle.

WHAT IT COSTS				
$$$$	**$$$**	**$$**	**$**	**¢**
RESTAURANTS over $25	$19–$25	$13–$18	$8–$12	under $8
HOTELS over $200	$151–$200	$111–$150	$70–$110	under $70

Restaurant prices are for a main course at dinner, excluding sales tax of 7.75%. Hotel prices are for two people in a standard double room in high season, excluding service charges and 7.75% tax.

Timing

The region is privy to four distinct seasons. The heaviest concentration of tourists is in the summer, when school is out and families hit the road for a little together time. The weather is near perfect with temperatures in the 80's and 90's, although the mercury has been known to top triple digits on occasion. You might have a hard time finding a hotel room during late May and late June due to the National Junior College World Series (baseball) and Country Jam music festival, both in Grand Junction. Popular camping spots can also fill up fast, especially on holiday weekends.

In fall, you'll be treated to an explosion of colors in rich hues of yellow, orange, and red. Days are warm but the crisp, cool nights offer a hint that Old Man Winter is getting restless. There is still time to enjoy activities like fishing, hiking, and backpacking before the snow flies. Grand Mesa is a winter favorite among locals who are looking for a quick fix for cabin fever. Powder hounds can't wait to strap on their newly waxed skis and hit the slopes at Powderhorn Ski Resort. Many area lodges rent snowshoes and cross-country skis. Guided snowmobile tours are also available.

WESTERN SLOPE (SOUTHERN LOOP)

The southern loop of the Western Slope is comprised of Grand Junction, Colorado National Monument, Delta, Cedaredge, Grand Mesa, and Palisade. Probably more popular than the loop to the north, the south-

Numbers in the text correspond to numbers in the margin and on the North-west Colorado map.

6

If you have 3 days

Using 🚗 **Grand Junction** ❶ as your base camp, start your day with a visit to the **Colorado National Monument** ❷. Allow yourself at least three hours to hike, bike, or drive through the monument. You can play golf, raft, or go for a relaxing horseback ride in the afternoon. On day two, drive the southern loop to **Delta** ❸, stopping at Escalante Canyon along the way. After lunch, visit Ft. Uncompahgre and the Delta County Museum, or drive north to **Cedaredge** ❹ and tour Pioneer Town and browse the galleries at the Apple Shed. Continue driving north to 🚗 **Grand Mesa** ❺ and spend the night in a lodge, or camp under the stars. On day three, enjoy a morning of fishing or hiking on one of the many lakes or trails. Finish the day with a tour of the wineries in **Palisade** ❻.

If you have 5 days

Follow the three-day itinerary, and on day four start the northern loop of your trip with a drive to 🚗 **Rifle** ❼. You can spend the day climbing in Rifle Mountain Park or biking the trails around the Roan Cliffs. Other options include touring the Rifle Fish Hatchery or viewing the triple flume cascading down moss-covered cliffs in Rifle Falls State Park. Drive north to **Meeker** ❽ for lunch, tour the White River Museum, and if you have time, drive the Flattops Scenic Byway before stopping in 🚗 **Craig** ❾ for the night. On day five, visit the Museum of Northwest Colorado, then drive to **Dinosaur National Monument** ❿. You can visit the Dinosaur Quarry and spend the rest of the day exploring the park, or take a white-water raft ride, which is highly recommended.

If you have 7 days

For the first five days follow the itinerary above. On day six, drive to 🚗 **Rangely** ⓫, where you can view rock art in the Canyon Pintado National Historic District. After lunch, grab your bike and head for the Raven Rims, or sink a worm or two in Kenney Reservoir while watching the sun set over the water. On day seven, visit the farmers' market in Town Square to gather some fresh eats for a leisurely picnic and take in the sights over Douglas Pass on your drive back to Grand Junction.

---

ern loop offers tremendous diversity. You can white-water raft down the Colorado River and enjoy a winetasting at a highly regarded vineyard on the same day (preferably in that order). You can also play golf at a world-class resort just minutes from downtown Grand Junction; view wild horses in the rugged canyons and plateaus of the Bookcliffs; fish in one of 300 lakes on Grand Mesa; and climb the gnarled, knobby monoliths of Colorado National Monument.

Grand Junction

❶ *255 mi from Denver via I–70 west.*

Grand Junction is where the mountains meet the desert. No matter which direction you look, there is an adventure waiting to happen. The city, with a population of approximately 42,000, is nestled between the picturesque Grand Mesa to the south and the towering Bookcliffs to the north. Surprisingly sophisticated, with a small town flair, this city is the ultimate base camp for a vacation. Whether you're into art galleries, boutiques, hiking, horseback riding, rafting, mountain biking, or winery tours, a new activity awaits you every day.

Grand Junction's cultural sophistication is readily apparent at the Art on the Corner exhibit, which showcases leading regional sculptors whose latest works are installed on the Main Street Mall. Each year the community selects and purchases its favorites for permanent display. Art on the Corner is organized by the **The Art Center,** which rotates its fine permanent collection of Native American tapestries and Western contemporary art, including the only complete series of lithographs by noted printmaker Paul Pletka. The fantastically carved doors—done by a WPA artist in the 1930s—alone are worth the visit. Take time to view the elegant historic homes along North 7th Street afterward. ⊠ *1803 N. 7th St.* ☎ *970/243–7337* ⊕ *www.gjartcenter. org* 🖃 *$2* ☉ *Tues.–Sat. 9–4.*

The **Museum of Western Colorado** relates the history of the area since the 1880s, with a time line, a firearms display, and a Southwest pottery collection. The area's rich mining heritage is perfectly captured in the uranium mine that educates with interactive sound and exhibit stations. The museum also runs the Cross Orchards Living History Farm and the Dinosaur Journey Museum, and oversees paleontological excavations. ⊠ *462 Ute Ave.* ☎ *970/242–0971* ⊕ *www.wcmuseum. org* 🖃 *$5.50* ☉ *May–Sept., Mon.–Sat. 9–5, Sun. noon–4; Oct.–Apr., Tues.–Sat. 10–3.*

The **Cross Orchards Living History Farm** re-creates a historic agricultural community of the early 20th century on its 24½-acre site, listed on the National Register of Historic Places. A workers' bunkhouse, blacksmith shop, country store, and an extensive collection of vintage farming and road-building equipment are among the exhibits. Tours lasting 1½–2 hours are available upon request. ⊠ *3073 F Rd.* ☎ *970/434–9814* ⊕ *www.wcmuseum.org* 🖃 *$4* ☉ *Apr.–Oct., Tues.–Sat. 9–4.*

Fodor'sChoice ★ Ten miles west of Grand Junction, the newly designated **Colorado Canyons National Conservation Area** is home to the second largest concentration of natural arches in the country. Spires, windows, and giant alcoves make up the other curious geological features in the spectacular red rock canyons, some of which are nearly 1,000 feet deep. Spring runoff and summer thunderstorms create glistening waterfalls and plunge pools. Be on the watch for deer, mountain lion, desert bighorn sheep, and golden and bald eagles. You can go hiking, horseback riding, mountain biking, backpacking, and camping. Be prepared for biting gnats from late May to late July. Contact the Bureau of Land Management for a map before venturing out. ⊠ *2815 H Rd.* ☎ *970/244–3000* ⊕ *www.co.blm.gov/ colocanyons/index.htm* 🖃 *Free* ☉ *Year-round.*

Sports & the Outdoors

GOLF ★ The 18-hole championship course at **The Golf Club at Redlands Mesa** (⊠ 2325 W. Ridges Blvd. ☎ 970/263–9270) is set at an elevation of 4,600 feet in the shadows of the Colorado National Monument, just minutes from downtown.

HORSEBACK RIDING **Rim Rock Deer Park** (⊠ 927 17 Rd., Fruita ☎ 970/858–9555), offers everything from one-hour horseback rides in Colorado National Monument to overnight pack rides.

6

Festivals From the wacky to the traditional, the northwestern region of Colorado is home to some of the best festivals in the West. One favorite is the Olathe Sweet Corn Festival held each August. Fruita, at the base of the Colorado National Monument, has Mike the Headless Chicken Days, complete with the Chicken Dance and the Run Like A Headless Chicken 5K Race. There's also the Palisade Peach Festival, Colorado Mountain Winefest, and Cedaredge Apple Fest. Small, homegrown festivals are a great way to experience the sights and sounds of the local culture.

Wine Tours One of Colorado's best-kept secrets is its wineries. Whether you tour the wineries by limousine or shuttle van, its a great way to see how your favorite wine goes from vineyard to glass. You will learn about the grape growing process and what varieties of grapes grow best in Western Colorado's mild climate. Depending on the time of the year, you may also see the grape harvesting and crushing process. Of course the best part of the tour is sampling the wines. Make your experience even more enjoyable with a self-guided bike tour through the vineyards at sunset.

MOUNTAIN BIKING **Kokopelli's Trail** links Grand Junction with the famed Slickrock Trail outside Moab, Utah. The 142-mi stretch winds through high desert and the Colorado River valley before climbing the La Sal Mountains. Those interested in bike tours should contact the **Colorado Plateau Mountain Bike Trail Association** (☎ 970/249–8055). **Over The Edge Sports** (✉ 202 E. Aspen Ave., Fruita ☎ 970/858–7220) offers mountain-biking lessons and half- or full-day customized bike tours.

RAFTING ★ **Adventure Bound River Expeditions** (✉ 2392 H Rd. ☎ 970/245–5428 or 800/423–4668), runs trips on the Colorado, Green, and Yampa rivers (the latter through the canyons of Dinosaur National Monument).

Where to Stay & Eat

$$ ✕ **The Winery.** This is *the* place for the big night out and special occasions. It's very pretty, awash in stained glass, wood beams, exposed brick, and hanging plants. The menu isn't terribly adventuresome, but the kitchen does turn out fresh fish specials and top-notch steak, chicken, prime rib, and shrimp in simple, flavorful sauces. ✉ 642 Main St. ☎ 970/242–4100 ▭ AE, D, DC, MC, V ☉ No lunch.

★ $–$$ ✕ **Dolce Vita.** Hailing from Verona, Massimiliano Perucchini is a fourth-generation chef who graces Main Street both with his northern Italian cuisine and an outdoor patio. His wonderful specialties include Portobello mushrooms marinated in chianti and served on polenta with red onions and pancetta; veal picatta; and chicken with mushrooms, capers, and artichoke hearts. It's a tough call between the homemade cannoli and tiramisu—you may need to try both. ✉ 336 Main St. ☎ 970/242–8482 ▭ AE, D, DC, MC, V ☉ Closed Sun.

$–$$ ✕ **G. B. Gladstone's.** This hangout has its own style of turn-of-the-20th-century decor: stained-glass windows, faux-Victorian gas lamps, and antique skis and kayaks mounted on the walls. It's particularly lively on Friday night, but whatever the day, you can enjoy the freshest seafood, pasta, and steaks in town. Favorites include the prime rib; grilled salmon;

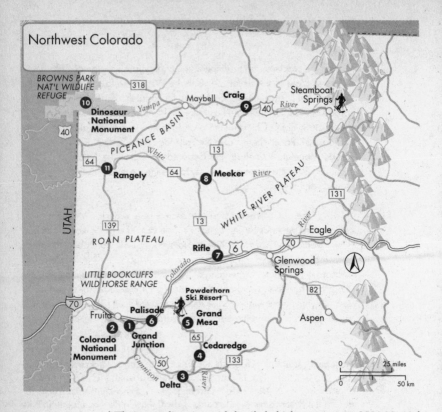

and Thai pesto linguine with broiled chicken strips. ⊠ *2531 N. 12th St.* ☎ *970/241–6000* ☰ *AE, D, MC, V.*

★ $ ✕ **Crystal Cafe & Bake Shop.** Locals flock to this European-style café for its apple pancakes, scrumptious banana-nut French toast, and wonderful array of omelets. The lunch menu has a Greek influence, and popular orders are the grilled veggie pita with homemade feta mayonnaise and Oriental chicken salad. There are also many delicious items for the carb-conscious dieter. ⊠ *314 Main St.* ☎ *970/242–8843* ☰ *MC, V* ⊘ *Closed Sun. No dinner Mon.–Wed.*

$$ 🏨 **Adam's Mark Grand Junction.** By far the premier property in the area, the Adams Mark pampers guests at affordable rates, although some of the units could use renovation. Rooms are large and have welcome extras, such as a phone *and* TV in the bathroom. The bar and nightclub are longtime local favorites. Be sure to ask about the spring getaway and golf packages. ⊠ *743 Horizon Dr., 81506* ☎ *970/241–8888* 🖷 *970/242–7266* ⊕ *www.adamsmark.com* ➥ *273 rooms* ⚭ *2 restaurants, 3 tennis courts, pool, gym, hot tub, bar, nightclub, recreation room, airport shuttle* ☰ *AE, D, DC, MC, V.*

★ $$ 🏨 **Hawthorne Suites L. T. D. Hotel.** With a sofa and two oversize chairs, the plush suites here offer plenty of room to sit back and relax. The many amenities include microwaves, refrigerators, and coffeemakers, and then there's the complimentary full breakfast. Business travelers appreciate the Internet access and those suites with full kitchens. The hotel is in the heart of downtown and within walking distance of restaurants and boutiques. ⊠ *225 Main St., 81501* ☎ *970/242–2525* 🖷 *970/242–0295* ➥ *70 suites* ⚭ *Some kitchens, indoor pool, gym, hot tub, Internet, business services* ☰ *AE, D, DC, MC, V* ⧖| *BP.*

THE MEEKER MASSACRE

IT BEGAN AS A *culture clash, with Nathan C. Meeker, an Indian agent for the U.S. government, on one side and the White River Band of the Ute Indians* on the other. The mining boom was in full swing in the White River valley in 1878, and tension was rising between the Indians and the white prospectors and settlers. Meeker, a former agricultural editor for the New York Tribune, set out to "civilize" the Ute and turn them into farmers. The Ute weren't about to adopt white customs; they considered farming to be woman's work. The horse was their most prized possession, and Ute men preferred to spend their time perfecting their horsemanship.

Meeker became increasingly frustrated with the Ute's defiance and threatened to take their land if they did not cooperate. In a test of wills, he ordered one of his men to plow up a pasture where the Ute

kept their treasured horses, in order to turn it into farmland. On September 29, 1879, the Ute attacked the Indian agency, killing all 11 of the agency employees, including Meeker. They took five white women and children captive and looted and torched the agency. Those held captive were released 23 days later after negotiations between Ute chief Ouray and his wife, Chipeta, and former Indian agent General Charles Adams.

The U.S. Army set up a military camp on the White River to keep peace after the massacre. Negotiations began immediately for a new Ute agreement that would open the Ute reservation to settlers. In 1881, the Ute Indians of western Colorado were forced onto a reservation in northeastern Utah.

$$ **La Quinta Inn & Suites.** Fantastic views of the Colorado National Monument, Grand Mesa, and the Bookcliffs is what you get at this Southwestern-style hotel. Off Interstate 70, the hotel is minutes from Walker Field Airport and downtown and you can walk to the restaurants along Horizon Drive. A heated pool and hot tub are ringed by a lush courtyard with trees, flowers, and a gazebo. The rooms are comfortable, decorated in muted shades of olive green, tan, and coral. Some have refrigerators and microwaves. The third floor is designated for smoking. Kids stay free and there is no fee for pets up to 20 pounds. ✉ *2761 Crossroads Blvd., 81506* ☎ *970/241–2929* 🖷 *970/241–2999* ⊕ *www.lq.com* ⮑ *103 rooms, 5 suites* ⟁ *Pool, gym, hot tub, laundry facilities, business services, meeting rooms, airport shuttle* ▤ *AE, D, DC, MC, V* ⦿ *CP.*

$ **Budget Host.** The owner continually refurbishes this property (you can occasionally catch him scrubbing the floors), whose gray-and-white exterior seems more country inn than motor lodge. Care is also lavished on the smart, fresh rooms, which have an early-American look with Stanley cherry furniture, burgundy carpets, and floral spreads. ✉ *721 Horizon Dr., 81506* ☎ *970/243–6050 or 800/888–5736* 🖷 *970/243–0310* ⮑ *55 rooms* ⟁ *Pool* ▤ *AE, D, DC, MC, V.*

$ **Grand Vista Hotel.** Management does its utmost to create a warm, inviting ambience, and it succeeds, with plush high-back chairs in the welcoming lobby and a private-club look in the main restaurant, Oliver's. Old-fashioned charm and dark mountain colors characterize the rooms. Guests have health-club privileges at the Crossroads Fitness Center. ✉ *2790 Crossroads Blvd., 81506* ☎ *970/241–8411* 🖷 *970/241–1077* ⊕ *www.grandvistahotel.com* ⮑ *158 rooms* ⟁ *Restaurant, patisserie, indoor pool, hot tub, bar, nightclub, meeting room, airport shuttle* ▤ *AE, D, DC, MC, V.*

Nightlife & the Arts

NIGHTLIFE   The **Blue Moon** (✉ 120 N. 7th St. ☎ 970/242–4506) is a favorite neighborhood bar; a "Cheers"-like atmosphere encourages patrons to nurse their favorite brew while catching up with colleagues or friends. **Players Sports Bar** (✉ 743 Horizon Dr. ☎ 970/241–8888 Ext. 121) serves up beverages, appetizers, and light snacks. Occasionally entertainers perform outside on the beer garden stage. A popular watering hole, **G. B. Gladstone's** (✉ 2531 N. 12th St. ☎ 970/241–6000) has a great outdoor patio. The **Rockslide Brewery** (✉ 401 Main St. ☎ 970/245–2111) has won awards for its ales, porters, and stouts. The patio is open during summer.

THE ARTS   **Country Jam** (✉ Country Jam USA Ranch, Mack ☎ 800/530–3020), held every June, draws the biggest names in country music, such as Faith Hill and Charlie Daniels. The 65-piece **Grand Junction Symphony** (☎ 970/243–6787) is highly regarded and performs in venues throughout the city.

Shopping

The best place in the area for Tony Lama boots and Minnetonka moccasins is **Champion Boots and Saddlery** (✉ 545 Main St. ☎ 970/242–2465), in business since 1936. The sweetest deal in town, **Enstrom's** (✉ 200 S. 7th St. ☎ 970/242–1655) is known for its scrumptious candy and world-renowned toffee. One word describes the Main Street boutique **Girlfriends** (✉ 316 Main St. ☎ 970/242–3234): fun. The chintz couch, overstuffed chairs, and the coffee area tucked into a back corner encourage friends to hang out here. If you must shop, the light and airy store offers a line of comfy clothes and one-of-a-kind gifts (check out the novelty birdhouses).

The cute but upscale boutique **Heirlooms for Hospice** (✉ 635 Main St. ☎ 970/254–8556) offers great second-hand designer clothing and shabby-chic furniture. **Working Artists Studio and Gallery** (✉ 520 Main St. ☎ 970/256–9952) carries prints, pottery, stained glass, and unique gifts.

Colorado National Monument

❷ *23 mi from Grand Junction via Rte. 340 west.*

Big, bold, and brilliant are three words that best describe this vast tract of land that was declared a national monument in 1911 at the urging of an eccentric visionary named John Otto. A good way to explore the monument is by trail. There are more than a dozen short and backcountry trails that range in distance from ¼ mi to 8½ mi. The short **Canyon Rim Trail** follows the cliff edge above Wedding Canyon and has fantastic views. Scheduled programs, such as guided walks and campfire talks, are posted at the Visitor Center. Rock climbing is also popular here, as are horseback riding, cross-country skiing, biking, and camping. Cold Shivers Point is just one of the many dramatic overlooks along **Rim Rock Drive**, a 23-mi scenic route with breathtaking views. Be sure to check out Dinosaur Journey if you are entering the monument from the west entrance.

★ ☯   A worthwhile attraction, **Dinosaur Journey**, is just off Interstate 70 opposite the western entrance to the monument. The popular facility was created by the Dinamation International Society, the folks who fabricate robotic dinos. In addition to the amazing lifelike replicas (including a hatching egg), there are more than 20 interactive displays. Children can stand in an earthquake simulator, dig up "fossils" in a mock quarry, or make dino prints in dirt (along with reptile and bird tracks for comparison). Kids get a special passport that's stamped as they visit each dinosaur exhibit, and they have a chance to watch local volunteers at work cleaning and preparing fossils for study. Don't miss the 18-foot high cast of the Brachiosaurus front leg discovered at Riggs Hill in 1900 by researches from the Field Museum of Natural History. ⊠ *550 Jurassic Ct., Fruita* ☎ *970/858–7282 or 888/488–3466* ⊕ *www. dinosaurjourney.com* ☑ *$7* ⊘ *Daily 9–5.*

> **off the beaten path**
>
> ★ **RATTLESNAKE CANYON –** West of the Colorado National Monument, the 7-mi hike into this canyon is well worth it. The intrepid will be rewarded with thrilling natural arches and spires. The canyon, tucked inside Colorado Canyons National Conservation Area, is home to nine arches, making it the second largest concentration of natural arches in the country. The canyon can be reached in summer from the upper end of Rim Rock Drive with four-wheel-drive vehicles. ⊠ *West of Colorado National Monument on King's View Rd.* ☎ *970/244–3000* ⊕ *www.co.blm. gov/gjra/rattlesnakearches.htm* ☑ *Free* ⊘ *Apr.–Nov.*

Sports & the Outdoors

HIKING Of the many trails at Colorado National Monument, one of the more interesting is Serpents Trail, often called the "Crookedest Road in the World" because of its more than 50 switchbacks. Before starting out, pick up a map at the **Visitor Center** (☎ 970/858–3617).

ROCK CLIMBING The starkly beautiful sandstone and shale formations of Colorado National Monument are a rock climber's paradise. Independence Monument is a favorite climb. Experienced desert-rock guide Kris Hjelle owns and operates **Desert Crags & Cracks** (⊠ Box 2803 ☎ 970/245–8513 or 970/256–9284), specializing in guiding and instruction on the desert rocks of western Colorado and eastern Utah.

Where to Stay & Eat

$–$$ ✕ **Fiesta Guadalajara Restaurant.** This authentic Mexican restaurant is family friendly and serves up good food. Try the chili rellenos, chimichangas, or the super nachos. The appetizer combo plate is a meal itself, and to feed an army, order Fiesta Fajitas. Ask about dinner and lunch specials. ⊠ *103 Hwy. 6 and 50, Fruita* ☎ *970/858–1228* ▭ *AE, D, MC, V.*

$–$$ ▣ **Comfort Inn.** Some rooms in this Southwestern-style budget motel have views of the Colorado National Monument. Nearby attractions include a trading post, restaurants, and the monument Welcome Center. Maps of hiking and biking trails are available at the front desk. Business suites have a separate living area, pull-out sleeper sofa, coffee makers, microwaves, and refrigerators. Kids 18 and under stay free. ⊠ *400 Jurassic Ave., Fruita 81521* ☎ *970/858–1333* 🖶 *970/858–1108* ⊕ *www. comfortinn.com* ⇘ *53 rooms, 13 suites* ⚭ *Cable TV, indoor pool, hot tub, laundry facilities, business services* ▭ *AE, D, DC, MC, V* ⏍ *CP.*

$ ▣ **Super 8 Motel.** Beauty on a budget is what you'll find at this motel nestled at the base of the Colorado National Monument. Aside from great views, you have convenient access to Interstate 70 and several hiking and biking trails. Children under 13 stay free. ⊠ *399 Jurassic Ave., Fruita 81521* ☎ *970/858–0808* 🖶 *970/858–3548* ⊕ *www.super8.com* ⇘ *58 rooms, 2 suites* ⚭ *Cable TV, indoor pool, hot tub, laundry facilities, some pets allowed* ▭ *AE, D, DC, MC, V* ⏍ *CP.*

CAMPING △ **Saddlehorn Campground.** Between the juniper trees and piñon pines
¢ of the Colorado National Monument, this campground is first come, first serve. It's relatively uncrowded except during the holidays. The vegetation doesn't provide a lot of shade and wood fires are not allowed. The campground is within walking distance of the Visitor Center,

CloseUp

THE LEGACY OF MIKE THE HEADLESS CHICKEN

MIKE THE HEADLESS CHICKEN was a freak bound for fame. It all started with a run-in with a Fruita farmer who had bad aim, or so the tale goes. The year was 1945. Mike, a young Wyandotte rooster, was minding his own business in the barnyard when farmer Lloyd Olsen snatched him from the chicken coop. It seems Clara, the farmer's wife, wanted chicken for dinner that night. Mike was put on death row. Well, faster than you can say pinfeathers, farmer Olsen stretched Mike's neck across the chopping block and whacked off his head. Apparently undaunted by the ordeal, Mike promptly got up, dusted off his feathers and went about his daily business pecking for food, fluffing his feathers and crowing, except Mike's crow was now reduced to a gurgle. Scientists surmised that Mike's brain stem was largely untouched, leaving his reflex actions intact. A blood clot prevented him from bleeding to death. The headless chicken dubbed "Miracle Mike" toured the freak-show circuit, where the morbidly curious could sneak a peek at his nogginless nub for a quarter. Mike's incredible story of survival (he lived for 18 months without a head!) soon hit the pages of two national magazines, Time and Life. The headless wonder, who was fed with an eyedropper, eventually met his demise in an Arizona motel room, where he choked to death. His legacy lives on in Fruita, where the tiny town throws a gigantic party every May to celebrate Mike's life. Even in death, Mike is still making headlines.

---

where you will find the schedule of summertime ranger programs that take place at the amphitheater. ✉ *Colorado National Monument* ☎ *970/858–3617* 🖷 *970/858–0372* ♿ *Flush toilets, portable toilets, drinking water, grills, picnic tables* ⛺ *80 sites* 🅿 *$10* 🚫 *No credit cards* ⊘ *Year-round.*

Delta

❸ *46 mi from Grand Junction via Rte. 50 south.*

Delta is known as the city of murals. Seven murals, most of them lining Main Street, were painted by local artists in the late 1980s and celebrate various aspects of life in the area, from wildlife in "Delta County Ark" and ranching in "High Country Roundup" to agriculture in "A Tribute to Agriculture" and "Labels of Delta County." Highlights of the area include Escalante Canyon, where you can view Native American rock art and homesteader cabins, and the Council Tree Pow Wow and Cultural Festival, held in September.

Learn about the town's rich history with a visit to **Ft. Uncompahgre**, where docents in period attire guide visitors through a 1826 fur-trading post. ✉ *Confluence Park* ☎ *970/874–8349* 🅿 *$5* ⊘ *Mar.–Oct., daily 10–4.*

One of the more interesting artifacts at the **Delta County Museum** is a collection of guns used in a failed bank-robbery attempt in Delta on September 7, 1893. That day, the notorious McCarty Gang rode into town to rob the Farmers & Merchants Bank. The robbery went bad from the start, when one of the robbers shot and killed the cashier. The gunfire alerted a hardware-store clerk, who grabbed his Sharps rifle and killed two of the robbers during their getaway. ✉ *251 Meeker St.* ☎ *970/874–8721* ⊕ *www.westerncolorado.org/museums* 🎫 *$2* ⊙ *May–Sept., Tues.–Sat. 10–4; Oct.–Apr., Wed. and Sat. 10–4.*

off the beaten path

ESCALANTE CANYON – Named after Spanish missionary explorer Francisco Silvestre Velez de Escalante, who with father Francisco Atanasio Dominguez led an expedition through the area in 1776, Escalante Canyon shelters homesteader cabins (including the 1911 Walker Cabin), Native American rock art, and hiking trails. One of the pioneer homes was built by Captain H. A. Smith. His stone cabin, built into the side of a boulder, has a hollowed-out slab for a bed and a smaller niche carved out of the stone wall to hold a bedside pistol. Signs are visible from the main highway, and the sites are well marked. You can hike the several miles on the dirt road off the main highway or drive right up to the site. ✉ *10 mi north of Delta on U.S. 50* ☎ *970/874–8616* 🎫 *Free* ⊙ *Year-round.*

Where to Stay & Eat

$–$$ ✕ **Delta Fireside Inn.** A Sunday dinner spot, this restaurant serves up the usual selection of chicken, steaks, and seafood. Specialties include prime rib and *jaeger schnitzel* (breaded veal in a hearty brown mushroom sauce). The inn has a lounge as well. ✉ *820 Hwy. 92* ☎ *970/874–4413* 🖃 *AE, D, MC, V* ⊙ *No lunch.*

$ ✕ **Sun Wah Chinese Restaurant.** This casual restaurant is more about food than atmosphere. Locals come for the all-you-can-eat lunch and dinner buffets. Popular menu items include sweet and sour chicken, cashew chicken, and broccoli beef. ✉ *142 Eaton* ☎ *970/874–4884* 🖃 *AE, DC, MC, V* ⊙ *Closed Sun.*

$–$$ 🏨 **Best Western Sundance.** Centrally located within walking distance of downtown, this chain motel has up-to-date rooms, a full service restaurant and lounge, a heated seasonal pool, and a spa and fitness center. ✉ *903 Main St., 81416* ☎ *970/874–9781 or 800/626–1994* 🖨 *970/874–5440* ⊕ *www.bestwestern.com* 🛏 *41 rooms* ⚘ *Restaurant, room service, in-room data ports, cable TV, pool, hot tub, gym, spa, laundry facilities, business services, pets allowed* 🖃 *AE, D, DC, MC, V* 🍴 *BP.*

$–$$ 🏨 **Comfort Inn.** This chain motel is on the north end of Delta, alongside the Gunnison River. It's within walking distance of several stores and fast food joints as well as the downtown area and Confluence Park. There's a complimentary Continental breakfast. ✉ *180 Gunnison River Dr., 81416* ☎ *970/874–1000* 🖨 *970/874–4154* ⊕ *www.comfortinn. com* 🛏 *47 rooms, 4 suites* ⚘ *In-room data ports, some microwaves, some refrigerators, cable TV with video games, some in-room VCRs* 🖃 *AE, D, DC, MC, V* 🍴 *CP.*

CAMPING ⛺ **Riverwood Inn and RV Park.** The motel has 14 rooms with in-room ¢ data ports and cable TV; some have views of the Gunnison River. The RV park has separate laundry and shower facilities and is cable-ready. A 3-acre island space is available for tent sites if you want to camp. Reservations are recommended. ✉ *677 Hwy. 50, 81416* ☎ *970/874–5787* ⊕ *www.riverwoodn.com* ⚘ *Flush toilets, full hook-ups, drinking water, laundry facilities, showers, fire grates, fire pits, grills, picnic tables, electricity, public telephone* 🛏 *28 full hook-ups, 14 rooms* 🎫 *Full hook-ups $21.50* 🖃 *D, DC, MC, V.*

Nightlife & the Arts

NIGHTLIFE A blast from the past, the **Tru-Vu Drive-in Theater** (✉ 1001 Hwy. 92 ☎ 970/874–9556) is a designated historic landmark and one of only 500 remaining drive-in movie theaters in the United States.

THE ARTS   Native Americans gather at the **Council Tree Pow Wow and Cultural Festival** (✉ Confluence Park ☎ 970/874–1718) to share their heritage and culture through dance, music, and song during the last week in September.

Shopping

The **Finishing Touch Gallery** (✉ 347 Main St. ☎ 970/874–8305) is a great place to find original arts and crafts as well as collectibles and Native American jewelry.

Cedaredge

❹ *15 mi from Delta via Rte. 65 north.*

Cedaredge is called the gateway to the Grand Mesa, the world's largest flat-topped mountain. An elevation of 6,100 feet makes for a mild climate that is perfect for ranching, as well as for growing apples, peaches, and cherries. The town is charming with its abundance of galleries, gift shops, antiques stores, and wineries. Attractions include Pioneer Town, a historic village and museum of the American West, and the Grand Mesa Scenic Byway. For the outdoorsman, there's hunting, camping, fishing, and great mountain biking trails. Grand Mesa has over 300 lakes.

The town site was originally the headquarters of a cattle spread, the Bar-I Ranch. **Pioneer Town,** a cluster of 23 authentic buildings that re-create turn-of-the-20th-century life, includes a country chapel, the Lizard Head Saloon, original silos from the Bar-I Ranch, and a working blacksmith shop. ✉ *Rte. 65* ☎ *970/856–7554* 🖾 *$3* ☉ *Memorial Day–Labor Day, Mon.–Sat. 10–4, Sun. 1–4.*

Where to Stay & Eat

¢–$$ ✕ **Berardi's at Deer Creek Village.** After a day of fun, reward your appetite with a delicious array of Italian and European-influenced cuisine. This casual restaurant has a dining room overlooking a golf course, and patio dining too. Steaks, seafood, and pasta dishes (especially seafood pasta) are the mainstay. Reservations are essential on weekends. ✉ *500 S.E. Jay Ave.* ☎ *970/856–7782* ▤ *D, DC, MC, V.*

¢   ✕ **Highway 65 Burgers.** The good old-fashioned hamburgers here are cooked just the way you like them; all meat is fresh, and the burgers are hand-pressed. Favorites include the bacon cheeseburger and hickory cheeseburger, topped off with a thick, frosty malt. There's also sandwiches, chicken, some Mexican food, and ice cream. ✉ *1260 S. Grand Mesa Dr.* ☎ *970/856–4465* ▤ *No credit cards.*

★ $–$$ 🏠 **Cedars' Edge Llamas B & B.** The pretty cedar house and guest cottage offer four neatly appointed rooms. Choose between breakfast in your room, in the breakfast room, or on your private deck or balcony, which affords astonishing 100-mi views of Grand Mesa. The innkeepers, Ray and Gail Record, also raise llamas for sale. ✉ *2169 Hwy. 65, 81413* ☎ *970/856–6836* 🖷 *970/856–6846* ⊕ *www.llamabandb.com* ➪ 4 *rooms* △ *Some refrigerators; no room phones, no room TVs, no smoking* ▤ *AE, MC, V* ⏍ *BP.*

$–$$ 🏠 **Howard Johnson Express Inn.** This economy motel along the Grand Mesa Scenic Byway has the only pool in town and is just a few minutes south of downtown. The Continental breakfast is free, and rooms have coffeemakers and hairdryers. ✉ *530 S. Grand Mesa Dr., 81413* ☎ *970/856–7824* 🖷 *970/856–7826* ⊕ *www.hojo.com* ➪ 31 *rooms* △ *Cable TV, indoor pool, hot tub, laundry facilities* ▤ *AE, D, DC, MC, V* ⏍ *CP.*

CAMPING   △ **Aspen Trails.** At the foot of Grand Mesa outside the city limits, this 23-acre full-service campground gives you both panoramic views and proximity to town. The one-room camper cabins have electricity, but no running water or indoor bathrooms. The gift and souvenir shop has an old-fashioned soda fountain that serves ice cream and deli sandwiches. Propane is available and pets are allowed. ⊠ *1997 Hwy. 65, 81413* ☎ *970/856–6321* ⊕ *www.coloradodirectory.com/aspentrailscamp* ⚲ *Full hook-ups, dump station, drinking water, showers, grills, electricity, public telephone, general store* ⇝ *22 full hook-ups, 20 tent sites, 2 camper cabins* ☒ *Full hook-ups $21, tent sites $15, cabins $36* ▤ *MC, V* ⊙ *Closed Wed. in winter.*

Shopping

Once an apple packing shed, **The Apple Shed** (⊠ 250 S. Grand Mesa Dr. ☎970/856–7007) has been restored and remodeled into a series of unique gift shops and arts and crafts galleries.

en route · The **Grand Mesa Scenic Byway** (☎ 970/856–3100), is 63 mi long and winds its way along Highway 65 through meadows sprinkled with wildflowers, shimmering aspen groves, aromatic pine forests and endless lakes. Grand Mesa is often referred to as an "Island in the Sky" because of its abundance of lakes and reservoirs coupled with the high altitude. Scenic overlooks (Land-O-Lakes is a standout), rest areas, and picnic areas are clearly marked. There are two visitor centers on the Byway, which starts in Cedaredge and ends at Interstate 70 near Palisade.

Grand Mesa

⑤ *15 mi from Cedardege, 32 mi from Palisade via Rte. 65 north and west.*

The world's largest flattop mountain towers 10,000 feet above the surrounding terrain and sprawls an astounding 50 square mi. It's a mecca for the outdoor enthusiast who craves the simple life: fresh air, biting fish, spectacular sunsets, a roaring campfire under the stars, and a little elbow room to take it all in. The landscape is filled with more than 300 sparkling lakes—a fisherman's paradise in summer. The mesa, as it is referred to by locals, offers excellent hiking (Crag Crest Trail is a good choice) and camping (try Island Lake Campground) opportunities. There are also a handful of lodges that rent modern cabins. Powderhorn Ski Resort averages 250 inches of snowfall. Lift tickets are reasonably priced and the skiing is surprisingly good. You can also cross-country ski, snowshoe, snowmobile, or ice fish.

Sports & the Outdoors

FISHING The lakes and reservoirs provide some of the best angling opportunities in Colorado for rainbow, cutthroat, and brook trout. Contact the **Grand Mesa National Forest** (⊠ 2250 Hwy. 50, Delta ☎ 970/874–6600) for information.

HIKING The Crag Crest Trail, a 10.3-mi loop with sheer drops and magnificent views, and the less strenuous Land O' Lakes Trail are two popular choices for hikers. Contact the **Grand Mesa National Forest** (⊠ 2250 Hwy. 50, Delta ☎ 970/874–6600) for more information.

SKIING **Powderhorn Ski Resort** has 20 trails, 4 lifts, 510 acres, and a 1,650 vertical drop. The slopes intriguingly follow the fall line of the mesa, carving out natural bowls. Those bowls on the western side are steeper than they first appear. ⊠ *Rte. 65, Mesa* ☎970/268–5700 ⊕*www.powderhorn. com* ☒ *Lift ticket $38* ⊙ *Dec.–mid Apr., daily 9–4.*

Where to Stay & Eat

$–$$ ✕▨ **Mesa Lakes Resort.** Amid towering pines and wildflower meadows, this rough-cut log lodge overlooks Beaver Reservoir in the Grand Mesa National Forest. The interior is adorned with the heads of trophy animals, farming and horse memorabilia, and local artwork. The cabins have heat, some have full kitchens, and some have bathrooms and fireplaces. The restaurant ($) serves up everything from fresh baked cinnamon rolls to country-fried steak and spaghetti. Try the Black Russian, a hamburger served on rye with Swiss cheese and grilled onions. The on-site store sells picnic supplies and fishing licenses. Guided horseback rides and snowmobile tours are available. ✉ *251 Hwy. 65, 81643* ☎ *970/268–5467* 🖷 *970/268–5467* ⊕ *www.coloradocampgrounds. com* ⌨ *16 cabins* ⟳ *Restaurant, some kitchens, boating; no a/c, no room phones, no room TVs* ▤ *D, MC, V.*

$–$$ ✕▨ **Spruce Lodge Resort.** An abundance of windows offers an excep-
Fodor's Choice tionally pretty view of Ward Lake and the surrounding spruce trees. The
★ decor inside the lodge, built in 1956, changes with the season. The restaurant ($–$$) serves three meals a day and the menu is diverse, with burgers, sandwiches, Mexican cuisine, seafood, steaks, and pastas. The modern cabins are heated and have kitchenettes, microwaves, coffee makers, and hairdryers. French doors open onto a deck with a table, chairs, and an umbrella, as well as an outside grill with picnic table and fire pit. ✉ *Hwy. 65, 20 mi north of Cedaredge* ☎ *970/856–6240 or 800/ 850–7221* 🖷 *970/856–6241* ⊕ *www.sprucelodgeonline.com* ⌨ *10 cabins* ⟳ *Restaurant, bar, kitchenettes; no a/c, no room phones, no TV in some rooms* ▤ *AE, D, DC, MC, V.*

CAMPING ⚠ **Vega State Park.** The park has a high mountain lake that sits in a glo-
¢ rious alpine meadow on the west edge of Grand Mesa. You can camp at four campgrounds: Early Settlers, Pioneer (tents only), Aspen Grove, and Oak Point. The latter two do not have hook-ups. Cabins have heat, electricity, water, central vault toilet, small refrigerators, and microwaves, but no room phones or TVs. The area is popular for boating, waterskiing, and fishing. Weekends and holidays are crowded, so reservations are suggested. The visitor center, a quarter mile south of the dam, has exhibits depicting area history, wildlife, and recreation. ✉ *Rte. 330, 12 mi east of Collbran* ☎ *970/487–3407 or 800/678–2267* 🖷 *970/487–3404* ⊕ *www.coloradoparks.org* ⟳ *Flush toilets, pit toilets, partial hook-ups (electric and water), dump station, drinking water, laundry facilities, showers, grills, picnic tables, public telephone* ⌨ *32 partial hook-ups, 61 without hook-ups, 10 tent sites, 5 cabins* ▨ *Partial hook-ups $16, without hook-ups $12, tent sites $12, cabins $60* ▤ *No credit cards.*

Palisade

❻ *12 mi west of Grand Junction via I–70.*

Palisade is Colorado's version of Napa Valley, with the highest concentration of wineries in the state. Resting between Grand Mesa and a backdrop of peach orchards, the town oozes charm, right down to its stately Victorian homes, tree-lined streets, and homespun festivals. This tiny hamlet serves as a good jumping off point for outdoor activities.

Fodor's Choice **Winery Tours** are a fun way to sneak a peek behind the scenes and learn
★ about the intricate art of winemaking, from vine to bottle. The scheduled tours begin in the air-conditioned comfort of a 14-passenger van operated by American Spirit Shuttle. The tours visit at least four wineries and last approximately four hours. Wine lovers get to sample a variety of Colorado wines in the tasting rooms. For a self-guided tour, visit the Web site www.visitgrandjunction.com and print out its maps and

directions to the wineries. If you're taking the self-guided route, call to reserve tours that take you beyond the tasting room and into the wine-making process. ✉ *204 4th St., Clifton* ☎ *970/523–7662 or 888/226–5031* ⊕ *www.americanspiritshuttle.com* 🖃 *$25* ⊙ *May–Oct., Wed and Sat. 1–5.*

off the beaten path

★ **LITTLE BOOKCLIFFS WILD HORSE RANGE** – The true spirit of the Wild West can be found at this horse range, just one of three in the United States. set aside for wild horses. It encompasses 30,261 acres of rugged canyons and plateaus in the Bookcliffs northwest of Palisade. Eighty to 120 wild horses roam the sagebrush-covered hills. Most are believed to be descendants of horses that escaped from owners in the late 1800s or early 1900s. Most years, new foals can be spotted with their mothers in the spring and early summer on the hillsides just off the main trails. The best season for riding, hiking, or biking the trails is May to September. In summer you might glimpse wild horses in Indian Park or North Soda, but it's a matter of luck. Local favorites for riding include the Coal Canyon Trail and Main Canyon Trail, where the herd often goes in winter. Be sure to bring plenty of water. Vehicles are permitted on designated trails. Beware of frequent summer thunderstorms that can result in flash flood conditions that make roads slick and impassable. ✉ *2815 H Rd., approximately 8 mi northeast of Grand Junction* ☎ *970/244–3000* ⊕ *www.co.blm.gov/gjra/lbc* 🖃 *Free* ⊙ *Daily dawn–dusk.*

Where to Stay & Eat

¢ ✕ **Palisade Cafe.** Changing artwork decorates this light and airy café with a nice selection of breakfast and lunch items, including soups, salads, burgers, French dip, Reuben sandwiches, and vegetarian dishes. Breads used are from the Slice O' Life Bakery. Local beer and wine is served. ✉ *113 W. 3rd St.* ☎ *970/464–0657* ▤ *D, DC, MC, V* ⊙ *No dinner.*

¢ ✕ **Slice O' Life Bakery.** Two of the zaniest bakers in Colorado, Tim and
Fodor'sChoice Mary Lincoln, run this local haunt, a down-home-style bakery known
★ around the region for its melt-in-your-mouth pastries, sweet rolls, Jamocha brownies, muffins, and fruitcakes. Aromatic goodies are baked with whole grains and fresh local fruits. Cold sandwiches, cookies, pies, and many varieties of fresh-baked bread are also available. ✉ *105 W. 3rd St.* ☎ *970/464–0577* ▤ *No credit cards* ⊙ *Closed Sun. and Mon. No dinner.*

$–$$ 🏠 **The Garden House Bed & Breakfast.** This comfortable B&B with coun-try charm and a touch of elegance resides in a small fruit orchard, where benches and a hammock invite you to relax outdoors. Decorated in French country decor, the trilevel home has a spacious feeling with gorgeous oak floors, bay windows, and high beamed ceilings. Guest rooms have private baths and designer linens. Morning beverage tray, after-noon snacks, and evening turndown service are available. Business amenities include fax, copier, and portable phone. ✉ *3587 G Rd., 81526* ☎ *970/464–4686 or 800/305–4686* ⊕ *www.colorado-bnb.com/gardnhse* ⇄ *2 rooms, 2 suites* ⚭ *Lounge, business services; no room phones, no room TVs, no kids under 12, no smoking* ▤ *D, MC, V* ⥁*BP.*

$–$$ 🏠 **The Orchard House Bed & Breakfast.** Kick off your shoes and unwind after a long day of sightseeing at this farmhouse painted in fresh shades of white and gray. A large porch spanning two sides of the house beck-ons you to sit a spell and enjoy two local landmarks: Grand Mesa and the Bookcliffs. Rooms, some with private baths, are named after the res-ident pets. Conrad's Room, or the upstairs honeymoon suite, is deco-rated with brass and country oak graced with navy blue calicos with a touch of Battenburg lace. Cameo's Room has cherry furnishings and

woodland scenes decorating the walls. Bringing your own pet is negotiable. ⊠ *3573 E½ Rd., 81526* ☎ *970/464–0529* 🖷 *970/464–0681*
⊕ *www.theorchardhouse.com* 🍽 *4 rooms, 2 with bath* ♨ *Lounge; no
a/c, no room TVs, no smoking* ⊟ *AE, D, MC, V* ⊙❘ *BP.*

Nightlife

From April to October **Grande River Vineyards** (⊠ 787 Elberta Ave.
☎970/464–5867) hosts a concert series featuring classical, country, blues,
and rock music. The natural landscape contributes to the good acoustics, not to mention the spectacular sunsets. Concert-goers lounge in lawn
chairs, enjoying picnics and dancing barefoot on the grass.

Shopping

Harold and Nola Voorhees (⊠ 3702 G 7/10 Rd. ☎ 970/464–7220) sell
a range of dried fruits, including cherries, pears, apricots, and peaches.

WESTERN SLOPE (NORTHERN LOOP)

The northern loop of the Western Slope is comprised of the towns Rifle,
Meeker, Craig, Dinosaur National Monument, and Rangely. The northern loop is the least well-known section of the state, but it offers some
of the best options for thrill-seekers who want more bang for their vacation buck. You can explore the bike trails along the Roan Cliffs;
white-water raft on the Green River through Ladore Canyon; learn about
Native American petroglyphs at Canyon Pintado; view the largest privately owned collection of cowboy artifacts in the world; and watch
wildlife at Browns Park Wildlife Refuge.

Rifle

❼ *58 mi from Grand Junction via 1–70 east.*

This unassuming community is home to some of the best biking and climbing in the region. In fact, Rifle is generating a serious buzz among
mountain bikers for its series of high-quality trails along the Roan
Cliffs, not to mention its world-class technical climbing at Rifle Mountain Park north of town. And here's a trivia tidbit: Rifle is the only town
in the United States with that name. It seems fitting since gun racks out-
number ski racks on cars.

At 6,000 feet in elevation and 1,305 acres (350 of which are water), **Rifle
Gap State Park** can keep any outdoor enthusiast busy. Even ice climbers
head here to clamber up the frozen waterfalls and ice caves. As you gaze
at the massive rock window of Rifle Gap, try to imagine a huge, orange
nylon curtain billowing between the steep walls. Famed installation
artist Christo did; two of his efforts were foiled due to wind, save for
one amazing day when his *Valley Curtain* piece was gloriously unfolded
for a brief few hours. ⊠ *Rte. 325* ☎ *970/625–1607* ⊕ *www.parks.state.
co.us/rifle_gap* 💲 *$5* ⊙ *Year-round.*

The huge schools of trout at the **Rifle Fish Hatchery** include an intriguing iridescent blue hybrid. The facility raises rainbow and cutthroat trout
for the Colorado Division of Wildlife. Visitors are welcome to view troughs
of fish in different stages of life. ⊠ *Rte. 325, 14 mi north of Rifle*
☎ *970/625–1865* 💲 *Free* ⊙ *Daily 7–4:30.*

Sports & the Outdoors

MOUNTAIN
BIKING
★
The biking around Rifle is gaining momentum among aficionados for the
variety of trails around the Roan Cliffs, through shale, sagebrush, and piñon,
punctuated by panoramic views. Call the **Rifle Chamber of Commerce**
(⊠ 200 Lions Park Circle ☎ 970/625–2085) for maps and details.

ROCK CLIMBING The rock faces and ice caves of Rifle Mountain Park are a magnet for rock and ice climbers, depending on the season. There are about 200 ★ routes to climb, many with exhilarating views. **Natural Progression Rock Guides** (⊠ 289 32 1/2 Rd., Grand Junction ☎ 970/434–8213) is a highly recommended company.

Where to Stay & Eat

$$–$$$$ ✕ **Tortilleria La Rocca II.** This authentic Mexican restaurant and bar with its own *carniceria* (butcher shop) is decked out with the traditional serapes and sombreros and cooks up simple but tasty fare. Menu items range from tacos to tostados, as well as chili rellenos, burritos, tamales, and some seafood. Try the taco salad, *carne asada* (slices of skirt steak cooked over charcoal), or enchiladas. ⊠ *119 W. 3rd St.* ☎ *970/625–4777* ⊟ *MC, V.*

$–$$ ✕ **Rifle Fireside Inn.** This dining spot has an enormous stone fireplace as its centerpiece, as well as a full bar. The owner is Italian, and along with Continental standards, such as prime rib au jus, he offers tasty homemade ravioli and chicken Alfredo. Other menu items include trout, lobster tail, pork chops, burgers, and salads. The inn serves breakfast, lunch, dinner, and a Sunday brunch. ⊠ *1214 Access Rd.* ☎ *970/625–0754* ⊟ *AE, D, MC, V.*

$ 🛏 **Red River Inn.** A snacker's delight, this simple motel just south of Interstate 70 serves complimentary donuts in the morning and hot beverages throughout the day in the lobby, and there's a McDonald's across the street. ⊠ *718 Taughenbaugh Blvd., 81650* ☎ *970/625–3050 or 800/733–3152* 🖶 *970/625–0848* ⊕ *www.redriverinnmotel.com* ⇋ *65 rooms* ⌂ *Restaurant, in-room data ports, some kitchenettes, some microwaves, some refrigerators, cable TV, some pets allowed* ⊟ *AE, D, MC, V.*

$ 🛏 **Rusty Cannon Motel.** This basic motel has the only pool in town and is next to McDonald's, south of Interstate 70. ⊠ *701 Taughenbaugh Blvd., 81650* ☎ *970/625–4004 or 800/341–8000* 🖶 *970/625–3604* ⇋ *88 rooms* ⌂ *In-room data ports, some refrigerators, cable TV, pool, sauna, laundry facilities, some pets allowed (fee)* ⊟ *AE, D, MC, V.*

CAMPING 🏕 **Rifle Falls State Park.** The 60-foot triple-flume Rifle Falls is the cen-★ ¢ terpiece of this state park. Water cascades down moss-covered cliffs, concealing caves that can be explored. The sea of emerald trees is a great place to camp, picnic, or hike along the limestone cliffs. A park pass is required in addition to camping fees. Reservations are recommended. ⊠ *Rte. 325* ☎ *970/625–1607* 🖶 *970/625–4327* ⊕ *www.parks.state.co.us* ⌂ *Pit toilets, partial hook-ups (electric and water), drinking water, fire grates, fire pits, picnic tables, ranger station, playground, swimming (creek)* ⇋ *13 partial hook-ups, 7 tent sites* ▨ *Partial hook-ups $18, tent sites $14* ⊟ *MC, V.*

Shopping

You can find unique items and collectibles such as Coca-Cola bears at **Karylette's Kollectibles** (⊠ 102 East Ave. ☎ 970/625–4694), a cute country store that also sells the work of local artists.

Meeker

8 *43 mi from Rifle via Rte. 13 north.*

Once an outpost of the U.S. Army, Meeker is primarily known as an outdoor playground and is a favorite spot for hunting, fishing, and snowmobiling. Interesting historical buildings include the Meeker Hotel on Main Street, where Teddy Roosevelt stayed.

You can watch professional sheepdogs in action at the annual **Meeker Classic Sheepdog Trials**, a prestigious five-day international competition and one of the town's biggest draws. Sheepdogs and their handlers perform sheep-herding maneuvers on a closed course while competing for a $10,000 purse. The event takes place the weekend after Labor Day. ☎970/878–5510 or 970/878–5483 ⊕ *www.meekersheepdog.com* ✉ *$10.*

Read articles about the "real" facts behind the Meeker Massacre of 1879 and the 1896 Meeker Bank Robbery at the **White River Museum.** It's housed in a long building that served as a barracks for U.S. Army officers. Inside are exhibits such as a collection of guns dating to the Civil War and the plow used by Nathan Meeker to dig up the Ute's pony racetrack. Other items include Chief Colorow's peace pipe, a pair of moccasins made by a Ute woman for a pioneer boy, a bear-hide coat that belonged to a stagecoach driver, and a large Victorian mourning wreath made of human hair. ✉ *565 Park St.* ☎ *970/878–9982* ⊕ *www.meekercolorado. com/museum.htm* ✉ *Free* ⊙ *May–Oct., weekdays 9–5; Nov.–Apr., weekdays 11–3.*

> **off the beaten path**
>
> **FLATTOPS SCENIC BYWAY –** This gravel road east of Meeker stretches 82 mi to Yampa, through an area shaped by molten lava flows and glaciers that gouged tiny jewel-like lakes in the folds of the mountains. The drive is beautiful but desolate, so don't forget to fill up your gas tank in Meeker, Buford, or Yampa before departing. Also, the road can get muddy and dangerously slick when it rains. ☎ *970/638–4516 Yampa Ranger District.*

Sports & the Outdoors

FISHING   The White River Valley is home to some of the best fishing holes in Colorado, including Meeker Town Park, Sleepy Cat Access, and Trappers Lake. Some of the best fishing is on private land, so you need to ask permission and you might have to pay. Your best bet—if you don't want to go it alone—is to hire a guide familiar with the area, such as **JML Outfitters** (✉ 300 Country Rd. 75 ☎ 970/878–4749), who has been in the outfitting business for three generations.

SNOWMOBILING   One of Meeker's best-kept secrets is the fantastic snowmobiling through pristine powder in the backcountry, which some say rivals Yellowstone—without the crowds. Trail maps for self-guided rides are available through the Chamber of Commerce or the U.S. Forest Service, or from **Welder Outfitting Services** (☎ 970/878–9869), which guides snowmobiling in the White River National Forest and Flattops Wilderness.

Where to Stay & Eat

⟳ **$–$$**   ✕ **Market Street Bar and Grill.** Dine in the days of yesteryear with country furnishings, hardwood floors, antiques, and paintings of the area. This country-style restaurant serves steaks, baked trout, delicious homemade fruit pies, and freshly baked bread. There's a kids' menu and full bar, too. ✉ *173 1st St.* ☎ *970/878–3193* ▭ *AE, D, MC, V.*

$–$$ ✕▣ **Meeker Hotel and Cafe.** At this Old West–style restaurant ($–$$$) in a building dating back to the early 20th century, you can peruse vintage photographs and on the menu, lively stories of Meeker's past. Try the homemade soup, chicken-fried steak, and mashed potatoes with cream gravy. Reservations are not accepted. The hotel, listed on the National Register of Historic Places, has a blend of modern and antique furnishings that are more eclectic than Western. The lobby is lined with framed broadsheet biographies of famous figures—such as Teddy Roosevelt—who stayed here, along with a painting of the Meeker Massacre. The bargain-price bunk wing has rooms with shared baths. ✉ *560 Main St., 81641* ☎ *970/878–5062 or 970/878–5255* 🖷 *970/878–3412* ⊕ *www. themeekerhotel.com* ↪ *24 rooms* ⟳ *Restaurant, café, cable TV, bar; no room phones, no smoking* ▭ *AE, D, MC, V.*

★ **$-$$** ✕⌂ **Sleepy Cat Lodge and Restaurant.** Owned by the same family since 1964, this huge lodge with an exposed beam ceiling is filled with beveled glass and the requisite trophies and bearskins mounted on the walls. Soup and salad bar accompany the filling dinners of ribs, huge cuts of steak, teriyaki chicken, and pan-fried trout. Rustic, modern cabins are heated and have full kitchens and showers; some have fireplaces. Motel units have small refrigerators and coffeemakers. There's a TV-viewing area in the lodge. ⊠ *County Rd. 8, Meeker 81641, 17 mi east of Meeker* ☎ *970/ 878–4413* 🖷 *970/878–4618* ⊕ *www.sleepycatguestranch.com* 🛏 *14 cabins, 6 motel rooms* ⟰ *Restaurant, some kitchens, lobby lounge; no room phones, no room TVs* ▭ *D, MC, V* ⊙ *Call for restaurant hrs.*

CAMPING   ⚠**Rimrock Campground.** Below the signature rock cliffs of the White River
¢   Valley, this campground consists of RV sites, tent grounds, and heated cabins. The campground is 3 mi west of downtown and caters to re-tirees and hunters, but families are welcome, too. Spaces are hard to get during the Meeker Classic Sheepdog Trials in mid-September and dur-ing hunting season. Campfires are not allowed. ⊠ *73179 Hwy. 64, 81641* ☎ *970/878–4486* ⊕ *www.rimrockcamp.com/index.htm* ⟰ *Flush toilets, full hook-ups, drinking water, laundry facilities, showers, picnic tables, electricity, public telephone* 🛏 *30 full hook-ups, 6 tent sites, 9 cabins* 🖼 *Full hook-ups $22, tent sites $10, cabins $40* ▭ *MC, V.*

Shopping

Featuring original watercolor paintings and limited edition prints by Col-orado artist John T. Myers, **Fawn Creek Gallery** (⊠ 574 Main St. ☎ 970/ 878–0955) also sells Fremont and Ute rock-art replicas and duck carv-ings made from 100-year-old cedar fence posts. An old-fashioned mer-cantile building with original display cases, tin ceilings, and wood floors, **Wendll's Wondrous Things** (⊠ 594 Main St. ☎ 970/878–3688) sells an eclectic mix of clothing, housewares, body-care products, greeting cards, Brighton jewelry, and Native American turquoise and sterling silver from Arizona. Be sure to check out the local pottery and artwork. There's also a bookstore, bistro, and soda fountain.

Craig

❾ *48 mi from Meeker via Rte. 13 north.*

Craig is home to Colorado's largest coal-processing plant, the Col-orado-Ute Power Station. It's also home to some of the best big-game hunting and fishing in the area. Guided trips to some of the hottest fish-ing spots are available, as are horseback pack trips into the wilderness. Depending on the season, you might spot bighorn sheep, antelope, or nesting waterfowl, including the Great Basin Canada goose.

One of Craig's most prized historical possessions, the **Marcia Car** in City Park was the private Pullman car of Colorado magnate David Moffat, who at one time was full or partial owner of more than 100 gold and silver mines. Moffat was also instrumental in bringing railroad trans-portation to northwest Colorado. He used his private car to inspect con-struction work on the Moffat Railroad line. Named after his only child, the car has been restored and makes for an interesting tour. ⊠ *U.S. 40* ☎ *970/824–5689* 🖼 *Free* ⊙ *Memorial Day–Labor Day, weekdays 8–5.*

The **Museum of Northwest Colorado** elegantly displays an eclectic collec-tion of everything from arrowheads to a fire truck. The upstairs of this restored county courthouse holds the largest privately owned collection of working cowboy artifacts in the world. Bill Mackin, one of the lead-ing traders in cowboy collectibles, has spent a lifetime gathering guns, bits, saddles, bootjacks, holsters, and spurs of all descriptions. ⊠ *590*

Yampa Ave. ☎ 970/824–6360 ⊕ *www.museumnwco.org* ✉ *Free (donations accepted)* ⊙ *Mon.–Sat. 9–5.*

Sports & the Outdoors

FISHING   Around Craig and Meeker, the Yampa and Green rivers, Trappers Lake, Lake Avery, and Elkhead Reservoir are known for pike and trout. Contact the **Sportman's Center** (✉ 360 E. Victory Way ☎ 970/824–3046) for information. Get the scoop on hot fishing spots from **Craig Sports** (✉ 124 W. Victory Way ☎ 970/824–4044) while loading up on tackle and other supplies.

GOLF   **Yampa Valley Golf Course** (✉ 2179 Hwy. 394 ☎ 970/824–3673), by the Yampa River, is an 18-hole course dotted with copses of willow and cottonwood. In winter, tracks are groomed for cross-country skiing.

Where to Stay & Eat

$–$$ ✕ **Bad To The Bone BBQ & Grill.** Kids get a kick out of throwing their peanut shells on the floor at this no-frills barbecue joint. Fresh-cut steaks, prime rib, Cajun dishes, and homemade side dishes are some of the other draws. There's a large deck outside. ✉ *572 Breeze St.* ☎ *970/ 824–8588* 🖃 *D, MC, V.*

$–$$ ✕ **Golden Cavvy.** A cavvy is the pick of a team of horses, and this restaurant is certainly the favorite in town, for the price. Its coffeeshop atmosphere is enlivened by mirrors, hanging plants, faux-antique chandeliers, and the incredible masonry of the 1900s fireplace of the Baker Hotel (which burned down on this spot). Hearty breakfasts, homemade pies and ice cream, burgers, pork chops, and anything deep-fried (try the mesquite-fried chicken) are your best bets. ✉ *538 Yampa Ave.* ☎ *970/824–6038* 🖃 *MC, V.*

$–$$ 🏨 **Holiday Inn.** The amenities of Craig's largest hotel include a recreational center with a pool, whirlpool, and exercise and game rooms, all inside a lush atrium. Rooms done in teal and floral fabrics have electronic key access, irons and ironing boards, and coffeemakers. All rooms and suites are also equipped with workstations that have telephones, Internet access, in-room data ports, and voice mail. ✉ *300 Rte. 13 S, 81625* ☎ *970/824–4000* 🖷 *970/824–3950* ⊕ *www.basshotels.com* ⇨ *152 rooms, 19 suites* ⚭ *Restaurant, in-room data ports, indoor pool, gym, hot tub, bar, nightclub, recreation room* 🖃 *AE, D, DC, MC, V.*

CAMPING   ⚠ **Freeman Reservoir Campground.** It's first-come, first-serve at this
¢   primitive campground on a 17-acre plot inside Routt National Forest. The campground has nice views of the lake and lots of trees, not to mention peace and quiet. You can fish, hike, ride horses, and view wildlife. No motorized boats are allowed on the lake. ✉ *30 mi from Craig off Hwy. 11* ☎ *970/824–5689* ⚭ *Pit toilets, drinking water, fire pit, picnic tables* ⇨ *17 sites* 🏷 *$10* 🖃 *No credit cards* ⊙ *June–Nov.*

---

en route   Outside Craig, U.S. 40 gradually shifts into hillier sagebrush country. This desolate stretch of highway winds through tiny towns every 15 mi or so, including Maybell, Elk Springs, Massadona, Blue Mountain—some are not even on the map. At Maybell, the road forks. If you follow Route 318 northwest for 53 mi you'll reach the **Browns Park Wildlife Refuge** (✉ 1318 Rte. 318 ☎ 970/365–3613), with lacy waterfalls and canyons carved by the Green River and straddled by a swinging bridge. The area was a notorious hideout for the likes of Butch Cassidy and the Sundance Kid, Tom Horn, and John Bennett. This is an unspoiled, almost primitive place, ideal for watching antelope and bighorn sheep, as well as nesting waterfowl such as mallards, redheads, teal, and the Great Basin Canada goose. You might also see elk, pronghorn, and various songbirds. The marshes are closed for nesting season between March and July 31. The route here is complicated, so call for directions. The refuge has two primitive and free campgrounds equipped with pit toilets. Beware: there is no drinking water, firewood, or trash removal.

Dinosaur National Monument

➓ *90 mi from Craig via U.S. 40 west.*

Fodor'sChoice
★ Straddling the Colorado/Utah border, this monument is not a park you just happen upon; you have to seek it out. The Dinosaur Quarry in Utah, 7 mi north of Jensen, is the only place in the park where you can see dinosaur bones and is a must for any dinosaur enthusiast. The Colorado side offers some of the best hiking in the West, along the Harpers Corner and Echo Park Drive routes, and the ominous-sounding Canyon of Lodore (where the Green River rapids buffet rafts). The drive is only accessible in summer—even then, four-wheel drive is preferable—and some of the most breathtaking overlooks are well off the beaten path. A $10 entrance fee, which is good for seven days, is charged only in the Dinosaur Quarry area.

★ ☾ Earl Douglass discovered the **Dinosaur Quarry** as he hunted fossils for the Carnegie Museum in 1909. The quarry is known around the world for containing one of the highest concentrations of fossilized dinosaur bones from the Jurassic period. Today, bones are still visible in the ground inside the buildings covering the deposit. Exhibits detail the world the dinosaurs lived in 150 million years ago and there's a paleontology laboratory where you can watch technicians working on fossils through a window. From Memorial day through Labor Day, a shuttle bus carries visitors from the lower parking lot to the quarry. ⌂ *7 mi north of Jensen, Utah, on Rte. 139* ☏ *435/781–7700* ⊕ *www.nps.gov/dino* ⌸ *$10 per car* ☼ *Daily 8–7.*

off the beaten path
TOUR OF THE TILTED ROCKS – This 11-mi self-guided car tour begins at the Dinosaur Quarry. The drive, which takes one to two hours, reaches prehistoric petroglyph sites, a nature trail, and the historic Josie Morris cabin. Stop at Split Mountain Campground and watch the white-water rafters launch. The last 2 mi of the tour are on gravel, but this portion is well maintained. ⌂ *Dinosaur National Monument* ☏ *435/781–7700* ⊕ *http://www.nps.gov/dino* ⌸ *$10 (park admission)* ☼ *Year-round.*

Sports & the Outdoors

HIKING The park's many self-guided nature walks, include the Desert Voices Nature Trail near the quarry. The trail begins in the Split Mountain area, across from the boat ramp. The 1½ mi loop is moderate in difficulty and features a series of trail signs produced for kids by kids. Prior to departing, stop at the **Visitor Center** (⌂ 4545 E. Hwy. 40 ☏ 970/374–3000) for a map.

RAFTING One of the best ways to experience the rugged beauty of the park is on
★ a white-water raft trip. **Adventure Bound River Expeditions** (⌂ 2392 H Rd. ☏ 970/241–5633 or 800/423–4668) offers two- to five-day white-water raft excursions on the Colorado, Yampa, and Green Rivers.

Where to Stay & Eat

☾ $ ✗ **B & B Family Restaurant.** Capitalizing on its location, this restaurant has a dinosaur emblazoned on the side of the building and serves breakfast, lunch, and dinner. The decor is simple: one wall is papered with potato sacks and another is adorned with cheesy wildlife art; there are also surprisingly beautiful remnants of an old bar with intricate carving and mirrors. The cute menu lists Brontoburgers, Stegosaurus rib-eyes, and Plateosaurus rib-eyes. ⊠ *Ceratosaurus St. and U.S. 40, Dinosaur* ☎ 970/374–2744 ⊟ *MC, V.*

$ ✕ **Miner's Cafe.** Best known for its Mexican dishes, this small café also has some American dishes on the menu. It's open for breakfast, lunch, and dinner and has a kids' menu. ⊠ *420 E. Brontosaurus Blvd., Dinosaur* ☎ 970/374–2020 ⊟ *AE, D, MC, V* ♥ *Closed Sun.*

$ ⊡ **Hi Vu Motel.** This low-priced family motel is in downtown Dinosaur and has a picnic barbecue area. ⊠ *122 E. Brontosaurus Blvd., Dinosaur 81610* ☎970/374–2267 *or* 800/374–5332 🖶970/374–2249 ➬8 *rooms* ♣ *Cable TV, pets allowed; no room phones* ⊟ *AE, MC, V.*

CAMPING ⚠ **Green River Campground.** Five miles from the Dinosaur Quarry Visitor Center on the Utah side, this campground has plenty of shady cottonwoods and is first-come, first-serve. The visitor center offers kids' programs and ranger talks on paleontology at the campfire circle. ⊠ *Cub Creek Rd., 5 mi east of Dinosaur Quarry, 81610* ☎ 970/374–3000 *or* 435/781–7720 ⊕ *www.nps.gov/dino* ♣ *Flush toilets, drinking water, fire grates, picnic tables, public phone* ➬ *88 sites* ⊠ *$12* ⊟ *AE, D, MC, V.*

Rangely

⓫ *20 mi southeast of Dinosaur National Monument, 96 mi from Grand Junction via Rte. 139 south and 1–70 east.*

The center of one of the last areas in the state to be explored by European settlers, Rangely was dubbed an "isolated empire" by early pioneers. You can search out the petroglyphs left by Native American civilizations or just stroll the farmer's market in Town Square. If you enjoy backroad mountain biking, the Raven Rims have an abundance of trails. A good starting point is at the corrals in Chase Draw. You may even spot elk, mule deer, coyotes, and other wildlife as you spin your wheels through the multihued sandstone rims and mesas north of town.

One of Rangely's most compelling sights is the superb Fremont petroglyphs—carved between 600 and 1300—in Douglas Creek Canyon, south

★ of town along Route 139. This stretch is known as the **Canyon Pintado National Historic District** and the examples of rock art are among the best preserved in the West; half the fun is clambering up the rocks to find them. A brochure listing the sights is available at the Rangely Chamber of Commerce. ⊠ *209 E. Main St.* ☎ *970/675–5290* ⊕ *www.co.blm. gov* ⊠ *Free* ♥ *Daily.*

Sports & the Outdoors

FISHING Just below Taylor Draw Dam, **Kenney Reservoir** draws anglers in search of black crappie, channel catfish, and rainbow trout. The best fishing is right below the dam. You'll need a Colorado fishing license (available in town). If you hook one of Colorado's endangered pikeminnow, you'll have to throw it back. You can also go camping, boating, waterskiing, wildlife–watching, and picnicking. Locals come to the reservoir to watch the the sun's last rays color the bluffs behind the lake. Visit the **Chamber of Commerce** (⊠ 209 E. Main St. ☎ 970/675–8476) for a fishing license. ⊠ *5 mi east of Rangely on Hwy. 64* ☎ *970/675– 5290* ⊕ *www.rangely.com/kenney.html* ⊠ *Free* ♥ *Closed Nov.–Mar.*

For a pre-recorded fishing report, call the **Colorado Division of Wildlife** (⊠ 711 Independent, Grand Junction ☎ 303/291–7534), from mid-April to Labor Day.

MOUNTAIN
BIKING
The best mountain biking trails north of town are in the Raven Rims, named in honor of the abundant population of the large, noisy birds that live in the area. Contact the **Town of Rangely** (⊠ 209 E. Main St. ☎ 970/675–8476), for trail information. **Rangely Chamber of Commerce** (⊠ 209 E. Main St. ☎ 970/675–5290) is another good source of information.

Where to Stay & Eat

$ ✕ **Cowboy Corral.** One of the oldest restaurants in town, this laid-back eatery with a kids' menu serves up burgers, sandwiches, pork chops, steaks, and some Mexican food. The super burrito, buckaroo burger, and chicken-fried steak are popular. Separate dining areas with tables and booths are designated for smoking and non-smoking patrons. ⊠ *202 W. Main St.* ☎ *970/675–8986* ▤ *AE, D, MC, V.*

$ ✕ **Los Tres Potrillos.** This casual Mexican restaurant has the usual selection of burritos and tacos and the only patio in town. Try the fajitas, enchiladas, and carne asada. Mexican pottery, serapes, and sombreros in green, orange and black make up the colorful backdrop. ⊠ *302 W. Main St.* ☎ *970/675–8870* ▤ *AE, D, MC, V* ⊙ *Closed Sun.*

$ ▥ **Four Queens Motel.** A room at this motel in the heart of Rangely comes with a queen- or king-size bed, a table, and two chairs. Amenities include refrigerators and coffeemakers. A microwave and coin laundry are available in the common area. Guests also have access to the Rangely Recreation Center, which is equipped with a pool, sauna, hot tub, weight room, gym, pool tables, and outdoor basketball court. ⊠ *206 E. Main St., 81648* ☎ *970/675–5035* ▤ *970/675–5037* ⮑ *32 rooms* ⚬ *Refrigerators, cable TV, laundry facilities, business services* ▤ *AE, D, DC, MC, V.*

CAMPING
¢
△ **Buck 'n' Bull RV Park & Campground.** This campground is one of the area's newer ones. Shade trees and proximity to Kenney Reservoir and Canyon Pintado are also definite pluses. You can fish, watch wildlife, and play golf at Cedar Ridges Golf Course. Ask about the golf package. ⊠ *2811 E. Main St., 81648* ☎ *970/675–8335 or 866/675–8335* ⚬ *Flush toilets, full hook-ups, partial hook-ups (electric and water), dump station, drinking water, showers, picnic tables, electricity* ⮑ *10 full hookups, 4 partial hook-ups, 10 tent sites* ▤ *Full hook-ups $18, partial hook-ups $16, tent sites $10* ▤ *MC, V* ⊙ *Apr.–mid-Nov.*

Shopping

Fresh produce, baked goods, and live entertainment can be found at the **Main Street Farmers' Market** (⊠ Town Square ☎ 970/675–5290), held Saturday from 8:30 to 12:30. One of the more popular items is the elk jerky.

A woodburning stove graces the front of charming **Sweetbriar** (⊠ 781 W. Hwy. 64 ☎ 970/675–5353), a little store that sells a variety of gifts and home decor. It carries everything from candles to clocks and angels to dragons. Hot-sellers include touch lamps and Denver Broncos hats and other collectibles.

NORTHWEST COLORADO A TO Z

To research prices, get advice from other travelers, and book travel arrangements, visit www.fodors.com.

AIR TRAVEL

CARRIERS ▰ **America West** ☎ 800/235–9292 ⊕ www.americawest.com. **Skywest/Delta Connection** ☎ 800/453–9417 ⊕ www.skywest.com. **United Express** ☎ 800/241–6522 ⊕ www.ual.com.

AIRPORTS

Walker Field Airport (GJT), the only major airport in the region, is served by America West Express, Sky West, and United Express. A Touch With Class has regular limo service into Grand Junction and outlying communities. Sunshine Taxi serves Grand Junction.

🛪 **Walker Field Airport** ✉ Grand Junction ☎ 970/244-9100.

TRANSFERS 🚕 Taxis **A Touch With Class** ☎ 970/245-5466. **Sunshine Taxi** ☎ 970/245-8294.

BIKE TRAVEL

Several routes through Grand Junction are well suited to bicycle use. The city also has designated bike lanes in some areas. You can bike along the Colorado Riverfront Trails, a network that winds along the Colorado River, stretching from the Redlands Parkway to Palisade. Many of the towns in this region are far apart and are serviced by narrow two-lane highways with little or no shoulder.

BUS TRAVEL

Greyhound Bus Lines serves most of the major towns in the region. Bus service is provided into Grand Junction from Denver, Durango, Los Angeles, Las Vegas, and Salt Lake City.

🚌 **Greyhound Bus Service** ☎ 800/231-2222 ⊕ www.greyhound.com.

CAR RENTAL

The region is served by most of the national rental-car agencies. Avis and Hertz are located in the Walker Field Airport terminal. Enterprise is in downtown Grand Junction, with free pick-up. Depending on where you're traveling, you might want a four-wheel drive

🚗 **Avis** ☎ 800/331-1212 ⊕ www.avis.com. **Enterprise** ☎ 800/325-8007 ⊕ www.enterprise.com. **Hertz** ☎ 800/654-3131 ⊕ www.hertz.com.

CAR TRAVEL

Interstate 70 (U.S. 6) is the major thoroughfare, accessing Grand Junction, Rifle, and Grand Mesa (via Route 65, which runs to Delta). Meeker is reached from Rifle via Route 13 and Rangely and Dinosaur via Route 64. U.S. 40 east from Utah is the best way to reach Dinosaur National Monument and Craig.

Most gas stations in the smaller towns are open until 10 PM during the summer, and even some automated credit-card pumps shut down at that hour. Grand Junction has gas stations that are open 24 hours.

Most roads are paved and in fairly good condition. Summer is peak road construction season, so expect some delays. Be prepared for winter driving conditions at all times.

🚓 **Colorado State Patrol** ☎ 970/249-4392 ⊕ www.csp.state.co.us. **Road Report** ☎ 877/315-7623 ⊕ www.cotrip.org. **AAA Colorado** ☎ 970/245-2236 ⊕ www.aaa.com.

EMERGENCIES

🚑 Ambulance or Police **Emergencies** ☎ 911.

🏥 24-Hour Medical Care **Craig Memorial Hospital** ✉ 785 Russell Ave., Craig ☎ 970/824-9411. **Delta County Memorial Hospital** ✉ 100 Stafford La., Delta ☎ 970/874-7681. **Pioneers Hospital** ✉ 345 Cleveland St., Meeker ☎ 970/878-5047. **St. Mary's Hospital** ✉ 2635 N. 7th St., Grand Junction ☎ 970/244-2273.

WHERE TO STAY

CAMPING   Camping in the region ranges from rugged back-country camping to developed campsites that generally have electrical hook-ups and visitor center services with flush toilets and showers. Grand Mesa has exceptional camping, and for the most part, remains largely undiscovered except by the locals.

🅵 **Colorado Campground and Lodge Owners Association** ☎ 970/247-5406 ⊕ www.campcolorado.com.

MEDIA

NEWSPAPERS & MAGAZINES
The region's largest daily newspaper is the *Grand Junction Daily Sentinel,* which has a circulation of approximately 30,000. Smaller towns—including Cedaredge, Palisade, and Meeker—have community newspapers.

TELEVISION & RADIO
Grand Junction has three main television stations: KJCT-TV Channel 8, an ABC affiliate; KREX-TV Channel 5, a CBS affiliate; and KKCO-TV Channel 11, an NBC affiliate. There are a handful of AM radio stations and more than a dozen FM stations that serve area listeners, including Colorado Public Radio KPRN 89.5, Magic 93.1 (top 40), 95 Rock (classic rock), Moose Country 100.7 (country), and MIX 104.3 (adult contemporary).

SPORTS & THE OUTDOORS

FISHING
There is an incredible variety of fishing options in and around the region (Grand Mesa alone has more than 300 lakes). For licensing information, contact the Colorado Division of Wildlife. Additional information is available from the U.S. Fish and Wildlife Service.

🅵 **Colorado Division of Wildlife** ✉ 711 Independent, Grand Junction 81505 ☎ 970/255-6100 ⊕ www.wildlife.state.co.us. **U.S. Fish and Wildlife Service** ✉ 764 Horizon Dr., South Annex A, Grand Junction 81506 ☎ 970/243-2778 ⊕ www.mountain-prairie.fws.gov.

HIKING
Whether you're looking for a short hike or an all-day excursion, you'll find lots of hiking trails throughout the national parks and forests that make up the region. For trail maps, contact the Bureau of Land Management or U.S. Forest Service.

🅵 **Bureau of Land Management** ✉ 2815 H Rd., Grand Junction 81506 ☎ 970/244-3000 ⊕ www.co.blm.gov/recweb. **Grand Mesa National Forest** ✉ 2250 Hwy. 50, Delta 81416 ☎ 970/874-6600.

MOUNTAIN BIKING
Mountain biking trails are available for people of all abilities throughout the region. For trail maps covering western Colorado and parts of Utah, send $2 to Colorado Plateau Mountain Bike Trail Association. Much useful information is posted on its Web site.

🅵 **Colorado Plateau Mountain Bike Trail Association** ✉ Box 4602, Grand Junction 81502 ☎ 970/249-8055 ⊕ www.copmoba.com. **Bureau of Land Management** ✉ 2815 H Rd., Grand Junction 81506 ☎ 970/244-3000 ⊕ www.co.blm.gov/recweb.

TOURS

American Spirit Shuttle offers scheduled and customized tours of Colorado National Monument, Grand Mesa, and area wineries. Dinosaur Journey leads one- and three-day paleontological treks that include work in a dinosaur quarry. Eagle Tree Tours runs tours of Colorado National Monument and the Grand Junction area, including some with four-wheel-drive vehicles, hiking, or biking. Jurassic Tours leads winery tours and specializes in little known or hard to reach locations, including Unaweep Canyon, Canyon Pintado, and Colorado National Monument.

🅵 **Tour Operators American Spirit Shuttle** ✉ 204 4th St., Clifton ☎ 888/226-5031 ⊕ www.americanspiritshuttle.com. **Dinosaur Journey** ✉ 550 Jurassic Ct., Fruita ☎ 970/858-7282 ⊕ www.dinosaurjourney.org. **Eagle Tree Tours** ✉ 538 Teller, Grand Junction ☎ 970/241-4792. **Jurassic Tours** ✉ Box 626, Fruita ☎ 970/256-0884 ⊕ www.jurassictours.com.

TRAIN TRAVEL

Amtrak provides daily service to the east and west coasts through downtown Grand Junction.

🚆 Train Information **Amtrak** ☎ 800/872-7245 ⊕ www.amtrak.com.

VISITOR INFORMATION

🚆 **Battlement Mesa Chamber of Commerce** ✆ Box 93, Parachute 81635 ☎ 970/285-7934. **Cedaredge Chamber of Commerce** ✆ Box 278, Cedaredge 81413 ☎ 970/856-6961 🖷 970/856-7292 ⊕ www.cedaredgecolorado.com. **Delta Chamber of Commerce and Visitors Center** ✉ 301 Main St., Delta 81416 ☎ 970/874-8616 or 800/436-3041 🖷 970/874-8618 ⊕ www.deltacolorado.org. **Greater Craig Chamber of Commerce** ✉ 360 E. Victory Way, Craig 81625 ☎ 970/824-5689 🖷 970/824-0231 ⊕ www.colorado-go-west.com. **Grand Junction Area Chamber of Commerce** ✉ 360 Grand Ave., Grand Junction 81501 ☎ 970/242-3214 or 800/352-5286 🖷 970/242-3694 ⊕ gjchamber.org. **Meeker Chamber of Commerce** ✆ Box 869, Meeker 81641 ☎ 970/878-5510 🖷 970/878-0271 ⊕ www.meekerchamber.com. **Nucla/Naturita Area Chamber of Commerce** ✉ 230 W. Main St., Naturita 81422 ☎ 970/865-2350 🖷 970/865-2100. **Palisade Chamber of Commerce** ✉ 319 Main St., Palisade 81526 ☎ 970/464-7458 🖷 970/464-4757 ⊕ www.palisadecoc.com. **Plateau Valley Chamber of Commerce** ✉ 103 Main St., Collbran 81624 ☎ 970/487-3833 ⊕ www.coloradodirectory.com/plateauvalleycc. **Rangely Chamber of Commerce** ✉ 209 E. Main St., Rangely 81648 ☎ 970/675-5290 🖷 970/675-8471 ⊕ www.rangely.com. **Rifle Area Chamber of Commerce** ✉ 200 Lions Park Circle, Rifle 81650 ☎ 970/625-2085 🖷 970/625-4757 ⊕ www.riflechamber.com.

INDEX

FODOR'S KEY TO THE GUIDES

America's guidebook leader publishes guides for every kind of traveler.
Check out our many series and find your perfect match.

FODOR'S GOLD GUIDES

America's favorite travel-guide series offers the most detailed insider reviews of hotels, restaurants, and attractions in all price ranges, plus great background information, smart tips, and useful maps.

COMPASS AMERICAN GUIDES

Stunning guides from top local writers and photographers, with gorgeous photos, literary excerpts, and colorful anecdotes. A must-have for culture mavens, history buffs, and new residents.

FODOR'S CITYPACKS

Concise city coverage in a guide plus a foldout map. The right choice for urban travelers who want everything under one cover.

FODOR'S EXPLORING GUIDES

Hundreds of color photos bring your destination to life. Lively stories lend insight into the culture, history, and people.

FODOR'S TRAVEL HISTORIC AMERICA

For travelers who want to experience history firsthand, this series gives in-depth coverage of historic sights, plus nearby restaurants and hotels. Themes include the Thirteen Colonies, the Old West, and the Lewis and Clark Trail.

FODOR'S POCKET GUIDES

For travelers who need only the essentials. The best of Fodor's in pocket-size packages for just $9.95.

FODOR'S FLASHMAPS

Every resident's map guide, with dozens of easy-to-follow maps of public transit, restaurants, shopping, museums, and more.

FODOR'S CITYGUIDES

Sourcebooks for living in the city: thousands of in-the-know listings for restaurants, shops, sports, nightlife, and other city resources.

FODOR'S AROUND THE CITY WITH KIDS

Up to 68 great ideas for family days, recommended by resident parents. Perfect for exploring in your own backyard or on the road.

FODOR'S HOW TO GUIDES

Get tips from the pros on planning the perfect trip. Learn how to pack, fly hassle-free, plan a honeymoon or cruise, stay healthy on the road, and travel with your baby.

FODOR'S LANGUAGES FOR TRAVELERS

Practice the local language before you hit the road. Available in phrase books, cassette sets, and CD sets.

KAREN BROWN'S GUIDES

Engaging guides—many with easy-to-follow inn-to-inn itineraries—to the most charming inns and B&Bs in the U.S.A. and Europe.

BAEDEKER'S GUIDES

Comprehensive guides, trusted since 1829, packed with A–Z reviews and star ratings.

OTHER GREAT TITLES FROM FODOR'S

Baseball Vacations, The Complete Guide to the National Parks, Family Vacations, Golf Digest's Places to Play, Great American Drives of the East, Great American Drives of the West, Great American Vacations, Healthy Escapes, National Parks of the West, Skiing USA.

At bookstores everywhere.

www.fodors.com/books